THE CONDUCT OF THE DUTCH

DOUGLAS COOMBS

THE CONDUCT

OF THE

DUTCH

BRITISH OPINION

AND THE

DUTCH ALLIANCE

DURING THE

WAR

OF THE

SPANISH SUCCESSION

THE HAGUE AND ACHIMOTA MCMLVIII
PUBLISHED BY MARTINUS NIJHOFF FOR
THE UNIVERSITY COLLEGE OF
GHANA PUBLICATIONS BOARD

PRINTED IN THE NETHERLANDS

ACKNOWLEDGEMENTS

This book is based upon a thesis approved for the degree of Doctor of Philosophy in the University of London in 1953, following a course of study under the supervision of Professor G. J. Renier. It is chiefly to Professor Renier that any merit that this work may possess is attributable, though I am well aware that the inimitable wit and wisdom that he expended upon my guidance are but ill requited here. I am also deeply grateful to Professor Renier's distinguished predecessor in the Chair of Dutch History and Institutions, Professor P. Geyl, for his warm interest and encouragement and great practical assistance. I owe a special debt to the guidance that I received from Dr. Ragnhild Hatton, who with characteristic generosity undertook the onerous and tedious task of reading and criticising the original thesis in draft form. I should like to thank Dr. A. J. Veenendaal, Mr. B. van 't Hoff, Mr. Fernand Renier and Mr. Richard Burkett for advice, encouragement and assistance in various forms. I must also point out how much this study owes to the devoted bibliographic labours of the late Professor W. T. Morgan.

I am grateful to the University College of Ghana, and particularly to the Publications Board and its Secretary (Professor L. J. Lewis), for a generous grant in aid of publication.

For the typing of two separate versions of this work, for all sorts of secretarial chores, for constant encouragement and protection from distraction, and for a great deal besides, I have to thank my wife.

CONTENTS

NOTE ON DATING AND ABBREVIATIONS

Unless otherwise stated, events within the British Isles are dated in old style (O.S.), and those elsewhere in new style (N.S.). A similar principle has been adopted in referring to documents; thus in the notes, explicit indication of the style used in dates of letters, etc., is only normally given when the place of origin is not stated or apparent.

The meaning of abbreviations used in the notes is explained in the Bibliography.

INTRODUCTION

I

The story of the attitude of Englishmen to the Dutch in the later seventeenth century – a story of the complex interplay of engrained hostility and growing consciousness of common interest – has already been told in some detail.[1] With the death of the Stadtholder-King, however, the subject seems to have lost its attraction for the historian. Much has been written of the workings of the Anglo-Dutch alliance in the years that followed, but little has been done to relate the development of 'official' attitudes and policies to the fluctuations and preconceptions of public opinion. Perhaps the very intimacy of the two countries for most of queen Anne's reign has made enquiries as to what one thought of the other seem of little moment.[2] Such a view would be plausible enough: conflict is certainly more spectacular and often more revealing than unity.[3] It is nonetheless obvious that the subjection of an alliance to the stresses of war may both reveal the underlying attitudes of the partners to each other and also invest their day-to-day reactions to each other's behaviour with a heightened significance. This is a truism which the present study is designed to illustrate.

The ultimate object of this work is, through an examination of what

---

[1] See below, Ch. II, pp. 16-17 and notes.

[2] Something like this might be inferred when a notable study of England and the Dutch wars is concluded by a quotation deprecating the old hostility from a work published in 1701: C. H. Wilson, *Profit and Power* (London, 1957), pp. 157–8.

[3] There is perhaps another and more fortuitous reason why no study of the British attitude to the Dutch at this time has been forthcoming. Similar studies for the seventeenth century have been inspired not only by the rivalry of the two nations (and, later, by the advent of a 'Dutch King'), but also, and very largely, by the great influence exercised by the Dutch in this century on almost every aspect of English life: see G. N. Clark, 'Dutch Influences in British History', *De Nieuwe Gids* (October 1923); J. F. Bense, *Anglo-Dutch Relations ...* (The Hague, 1924); T. de Vries, *Holland's Influence on English Language and Literature* (Chicago, 1916); W. Cunningham, *Alien Immigrants to England* (London, 1897); C. H. Wilson, *Holland and Britain* (London, (1946)). By the end of the century this source of inspiration is fast disappearing, as the tide of influence begins to turn. It is, incidentally, arguable that this process is in some way connected with the decline of hostility. Certainly the period when the Dutch were most emulated is roughly coincidental with the period when they were most disliked.

was being said and written of the Dutch in public and private during the War of the Spanish Succession, to discover what effect popular feeling had upon official attitudes and policies, and, on the other hand, how much the politicians attempted, and how well they succeeded, in the shaping and control of such feeling. It will be shown that the subjects of queen Anne adopted a common standpoint from which to view the Dutch, a standpoint comparable for its near-universality (though for nothing else) to the hostility of bygone days, and that the judgments and attitudes formed from this standpoint played their part, first in preserving, and then in wrecking, the alliance of the Maritime Powers. It will also become apparent that, even if the darkest days of mutual animosity were past, anti-Dutch feeling could still be fostered and played upon with success for political purposes. The last years of the war seem, in this respect, a sort of epilogue to the classic period of Anglo-Dutch rivalry. Indeed, the anti-Dutch propaganda campaign before and during the third Dutch war looks in retrospect like an amateurish rehearsal for its triumphant successor of 1711–12.

This is not a study of Anglo-Dutch relations as such, though of course it has been necessary to say something of the basic and quasi-permanent assumptions of the English concerning the United Provinces and their inhabitants.[1] Nor is it the story of the Alliance, a subject which is certainly crying out for re-assessment from the English side.[2] One final warning to the reader: in a study of this nature, precise conclusions are not to be looked for. As Professor Laprade has so wisely written, 'for most of the questions that matter in a history of public opinion there are no certain answers'.[3]

2

In seventeenth-century Europe popular opinion came to play an increasingly important part in public affairs. The support and sympathy of the governed – at least of that portion of them that could be said to be politically conscious, and even, on occasion, of the illiterate mob – was coming to be widely recognised as a desirable or even necessary instrument of government and of opposition. We may see this demonstrated in the Dutch Republic by the pains that were taken

---

[1] See below, Ch. I, *passim.*
[2] See my article 'The Augmentation of 1709: A Study in the Workings of the Anglo-Dutch Alliance', *E.H.R.*, lxxii (1957), p. 642,
[3] W. T. Laprade, *Public Opinion and Politics in Eighteenth-Century England* (New York, 1936), p. 27.

by its rulers during the Anglo-Dutch wars to keep their people informed of their country's cause and the issues at stake. Even Louis XIV, in the latter years of his reign, was not above sounding and even appealing to the opinion of his subjects.[1] But in no country did 'public opinion' count for more than in England. 'Ce n'est pas ici comme en Angleterre', wrote Madame in 1712, since 'il n'est pas permis à personne si ce n'est aux ministres de parler des affaires de l'état'.[2] A year later Bolingbroke made the same comparison, pointing out ruefully to Prior 'that in our country, it is not enough to do well, and to be able to reply, before impartial judges, to reasonable questions: we must be ready to answer the most absurd queries, that malice can invent, or ignorance put'.[3] For all its imperfections and abuses, the system of government by annual meetings of Parliament meant that the views of the electors, at least, might play a real part in the government of the country. Even those who had no vote might exercise some influence, particularly in London, where there were various means, behind all of which loomed the threat of physical force, of bringing pressure to bear on governments.

The best evidence of the power of public opinion in English politics is the pains taken by the politicians to mould and control it. Swift, with his unique experience in this field, explained the matter thus:

A particular person may, with more safety, despise the opinion of the vulgar, because it does a wise man no real harm or good, *but the administration a great deal*; and whatever side has the sole management of the pen, will soon find hands enough to write down their enemies as low as they please ...

The influencing of opinion, in fact, had now become one of the essential tasks of ministers and their opponents alike; and, since the publication of parliamentary debates was forbidden, the only method open to them was the patronage of writers or subsidising of publications.[4] We know a good deal less about the mechanics of these operations than some literary historians like to assume, but two things at least are clear: first, that side by side with the literary patronage of Halifax and Dorset, and closely connected with it, grew up more avowedly propagandist ties between writers and patrons, and, secondly, that (in Professor Laprade's words) 'from the beginning, English newspapers

---

[1] C.-G. Picavet, *La Diplomatie Française au Temps de Louis XIV* (Paris, 1930), pp. 320–1.
[2] *Ibid.*, p. 317.
[3] Bolingbroke to Prior, 1 Sept. 1713, Windsor Castle, *B.L.* iv, p. 253.
[4] *C. W.* 175, pp. 124–5 (my italics); A. Beljame, *Men of Letters and the English Public in the Eighteenth Century* (London, 1948), p. 212; L. Hanson, *Government and the Press, 1695–1763* (Oxford, 1936), pp. 2–3.

were primarily intended to mould opinion'.[1] The press was remarkably free, but there were now incentives more powerful than fear of the pillory to influence pamphleteers and journalists. Indeed, in 1703 the *Observator* could deny the need for reimposing legal restraints on publishing on the grounds that the ministry could never be injured by criticism,

since they have a number of dependants, ready upon all occasions to write in justification of their measures, nay to gild over the worst of their actions, and give a fair colour to their most pernicious designs.[2]

As a guide to public opinion the ephemeral publications of queen Anne's reign are therefore irremediably corrupt. Yet, *faute de mieux*, they are indispensable to the student of opinion, for without them the materials at his disposal would be impossibly limited. The better his knowledge of the aims and views of the politicians, the greater will be his faculty for distinguishing between what reflects opinion, and what is intended to shape it; but this, of course, will never be infallible, and a clear-cut distinction is rarely possible.[3]

It is nonetheless arguable that a little too much has been made of the influence of politicians on the press in the reign of queen Anne. It has often been assumed that the preponderant role of political topics in the writings of the period, resulting in the decline of so-called non-partisan journalism, was due mainly, if not solely, to the great power of political patronage and subsidies; and this has been duly lamented by the literary historians.[4] It is broadly true, as Hervey noted, that 'all the good writing' of the reign 'was confined to political topics, either of civil, military, or ecclesiastical government',[5] but it would be surprising had it been otherwise in a nation divided against itself on two great political questions – the Succession, and the role of the Church in relation to the State. The issues arising from the conduct of the war and of the peace intensified this preoccupation with political affairs. Given this background, even those works produced at the

[1] W. T. Laprade, 'The Power of the English Press in the Eighteenth Century', *South Atlantic Quarterly*, xxvii (1928), p. 427.

[2] Cited in Hanson, *op.cit.*, p. 9.

[3] There are also considerable pitfalls of a more strictly bibliographic nature to imperil the historian's use of ephemeral literature. For an authoritative sketch of these see Professor Mark Thomson's contribution to S. Pargellis and D. Medley, *Bibliography of British History, 1714–1789* (Oxford, 1951), p. 11.

[4] *e.g.* D. H. Stevens, *Party Politics and English Journalism, 1702–1742* (Wisconsin, 1916). Apart from exemplifying the view that literature was 'perverted' by the politicians this book is of interest mainly for its unwitting demonstration of how little is known with any certainty of their relations with the press.

[5] Cited in Hanson, *op.cit.*, p. 92.

direct instigation of the politicians are not necessarily to be written off as so much hack-work. But the main justification for the use of ephemeral literature for the history of opinion must remain that without it such history could not be written. There is no substitute, so that the following assertion, made on the title page of a volume of the *Somers Tracts*, is no less than the regrettable truth:

The Bent and Genius of the Age is best known in a free Country by the Pamphlets and Papers that come daily out, as the Sense of Parties, and sometimes the Voice of the Nation. [1]

[3] *Somers Tracts*, 2nd collection (1750), iii, title-page.

CHAPTER I

THE BACKGROUND

I

The story that is to be presented is, on the surface at least, one of constant change. The slightest alteration in affairs at home or abroad was liable to be reflected in an alteration of the attitude of Englishmen towards their Dutch ally. That such changes were of no trivial nature can be seen in the example of the celebrated writer on commercial matters, Charles Davenant. Davenant's attitude towards the Dutch during the course of the war was transformed from hostility to friendship, and then back once more to a thinly disguised hostility. For all his time-serving, these fluctuations in Davenant's opinion of the Dutch were but a reflection, albeit an exaggerated one, of those experienced by very many of his fellow-countrymen.

If the English attitude towards the Dutch was so liable to drastic alteration its expression was none the less inevitably coloured by certain prejudices, preconceptions and assumptions which were as permanent as the attitude itself was ever-changing. It would seem wise, before examining the dynamics of this constantly developing attitude, to essay a static picture of the more important beliefs which thus affected the guise in which it appeared.

Few of these beliefs, of course, were peculiar to the England of queen Anne. They were much the same as those held by Englishmen for many years past, and, indeed, many of them had long since been more or less codified – above all by Sir William Temple and Sir Josiah Child.[1] Nor were they markedly different, especially as regards the character and habits of the inhabitants, from the beliefs concerning the Dutch nation that were prevalent at this time in other countries – in France,

---

[1] C. H. Wilson, *Holland and Britain* (London, (1946)), pp. 22–3. Useful surveys of the British attitude towards the Dutch during the seventeenth century may be found in essays by two Dutch scholars: Fruin's 'De Nederlanders der Seventiende Eeuw, door Engelschen Geschetst' (*Verspreide Geschriften* (The Hague, 1901), pt. iv), and N. B. Tenhaeff's 'Pamfletten uit de 17e Eeuw' (*Verspreide Geschriften* (Groningen-Batavia, 1949), pt. i).

for example.[1] It is dubious whether the Englishman's mental picture of his Dutch neighbour had that uniquely English quality attributed to it by the Dutch scholar who found that 'all the qualities which the Englishman's philosophy of life made him despise, he called Dutch', and again that 'the Englishman saw in us .... all the traits he hated to see in himself'.[2] Nor should one conclude, from the special hostility of the English to the Dutch nation during the seventeenth century, that the Dutch were singled out from amongst all other foreigners for peculiar contempt. The traditional distrust (to use the mildest term) of foreigners operated fairly impartially, and we may be sure that the Englishman's image of a Frenchman, say, or an Irishman, was no more flattering to its subject than that of a Dutchman.

2

First and foremost there was the belief that the Dutch were the richest people in the world, since, as one traveller asserted,

The Trade of the *Hollanders* is so far extended, that it may be said to have no other bounds, than those which the Almighty set to the World at the Creation.[3]

The great wealth that the Dutch gained by trade was a byword in England, as indeed it had been throughout much of the seventeenth century. Until late in that century it had been closely linked with the doctrine, sedulously propagated at the time of Charles II 's Dutch wars, that the trading interests of Britain and the Dutch Republic were mutually antagonistic. In 1695, for example, a speech which touched on this subject was prepared for a debate in the Commons (though, in true Ciceronian style, it remained undelivered). This fiery oration warned Englishmen of the great danger in which they stood of becoming 'a Colony to the *Dutch*', 'our Enemies in Trade, though planted among us'.[4]

The cry that the Dutch were 'our Enemies in Trade' was still heard in the reign of queen Anne, but it no longer had the power to stir popular feeling as once it had done. This was not merely because commercial jealousy of the Dutch tended to be overcome by consciousness of common political interest; it also reflected a growing realisation

[1] R. Murris, *La Hollande et les Hollandais au XVIIe et au XVIIIe Siècles vus par les Français* (Paris, 1925), *passim*.
[2] Cited in W. J. B. Pienaar, *English Influences in Dutch Literature and Justus van Effen as Intermediary* (Cambridge, 1929), pp. 18–19.
[3] *C.W.*132, p. 51. See also pp. 12, 27 and 120.
[4] *C.W.* 147.

that Dutch prosperity was not necessarily indicative of English
economic decay. In matters of commerce, in fact, the Dutch were no
longer greatly feared. Nevertheless, it was universally recognized that
there was much that England could still learn from them. It was still
widely believed that the Dutch had discovered the infallible technique
of commercial success, the close imitation of which was necessary for
any nation aspiring to this end. Thus, though the allegedly unsurpassed
wealth of the Dutch excited enthusiastic admiration amongst some and
outspoken envy amongst others, nearly all writers on trade matters,
whatever their political allegiance, agreed in advocating the emulation
of Dutch methods and regulations as a means of improving the wealth
of Britain. Even the most unbending Tories, much as they disliked the
Dutch for the republicanism of their constitution, the unconcealed
Erastianism of their Church, and the memory of their late Stadtholder
and those who had followed him to England, could not but wonder at

their prudent Administration, the Greatness of their Trade, their wonderful
Parsimony, the Willingness of their People to undergo all kind of Taxes, and
their Justice in allotting them as well as collecting them.[1]

Writers who held no brief for any other aspect of Dutch life or government were loud in their praises of Dutch commercial methods, urging
English imitation of their great use of credit, their relatively lenient
debt laws and their government's concern for the welfare of trade. One
out of many of such authors was Sir Francis Brewster, whose *New
Essays on Trade* was published in October or November 1702. Brewster
was no unqualified admirer of the Dutch; his book contains references
to their shortcomings both as allies and also in their political institutions, and to the dangers resulting from the great number of 'foreign'
holdings in British funds. The burden of his work, however, is the
desirability of the systematic encouragement by the government of
trade and manufacture, and many of his pages are devoted to showing
that they arranged these matters better in the Dutch Republic. Their
encouragement of fishing, their frugality, their strict limitation of the
salaries paid to public officials, their industry, their eschewing of
foreign luxuries, their admission of *necessary* imports without duty,
their eagerness to increase their population, and their practice of laying
by stores in times of plenty; all this and more won his praise. Their
naval management, too, he found far superior to that of Britain.[2]

Whiggish writers went even further in their praises. They held up

---

[1] *Examiner*, i, 14, 2 Nov. 1710.
[2] *C.W.* 15, pp. 6–8, 34, 40–4, 51–6, 59, 71–2.

the Dutch as models of frugality and industry, urged that, like them, England should employ none but merchants and traders in government posts which were related to commerce, and hinted that the Dutch government, in which, they alleged, there was 'the greatest Equality of any perhaps on Earth', was 'the most adapted for the General Gain of the People'.[1] One of the several eulogies of this sort occurred in Peter Paxton's *Discourse Concerning the Nature, Advantage, and Improvement of Trade*, published in 1704. This illustrated many of the maxims that it laid down by reference to the Dutch. Paxton did not deny that the Dutch were still serious rivals to England in certain commercial fields; yet he went on to give example after example of ways in which she should do well to imitate them. It was industry, he declared, not the hoarding of silver, that brought profit in trade; the Dutch, he pointed out,

who are a parsimonious and industrious people, put no restraint upon their Subjects in Trade, Silver being carried abroad as well as other Goods, and yet continue the richest nation in *Europe*.

It was our misfortune, he continued, that the great inequalities in our state made it impossible for us to induce people to consume only those goods that could be cheaply produced,

whereas in those Governments that do not permit such mighty Inequalitys amongst them, there is not the same Temptation to Luxury and Vanity.

Of no people was this more true than the Dutch, the highest of whom lived with parsimony and frugality. Thus, though they were rich they lived cheaply, and were thus able to sell cheaply:

The *Dutch* .... submit to the Use of such things as Necessaries of Life as are in their *Nature cheap*, in that they are *plentifully and easily produced*.

This admirable characteristic, he added,

does not proceed from any Natural Advantages *that People* have beyond their Neighbours, but that they are perfectly *indebted to the Narrowness of their Country, and Nature of their Constitution*.

The former was conducive to the concentration of population, which in turn was highly favourable for manufactures, and made industriousness essential. The latter was praiseworthy in that it permitted no great differences in the qualities and conditions of the inhabitants; no hereditary honours or accumulation of large estates were tolerated; the upper classes lived simply; the laws were 'contrived for common advantage' because they were made in common, and were thoroughly

---

[1] *C.W.* 165, p. xiii.

executed because there was no division between the legislative and
executive powers; and there was freedom for the exercise of religion
and the entry of foreigners. 'For these reasons', Paxton declared, 'the
Dutch may flourish in trade, and abound in Wealth, beyond any of the
neighbouring Nations'; and he went on to advocate changes in English
laws on the Dutch model. His treatise is of interest if only because it
shows clearly why a 'Whiggish' admiration for the constitution of the
merchant Republic was so marked a characteristic of those subjects
of queen Anne whose livelihood was dependent upon trade and
commerce.[1]

One of the main complaints of writers on commercial matters was,
as it had long been, the neglect by Britain of her 'Golden Mine', the
fisheries off the coast of Scotland. The Dutch were much involved in
this matter since they it was, according to such writers, who profited
by this neglect; it was, indeed, frequently suggested that their virtually
unchallenged enjoyment of the 'British Fishery' was the major cause
of the startling rise to wealth and power of their Republic. The many
pamphlets written on this subject throughout the reign of queen Anne
set out to appeal to British envy of the wealth which the Republic
gained from what were properly, it was alleged, Britain's own resources.
Often they disclaimed any intention of driving the Dutch completely
out of the fisheries, but they always favoured the imitation of their
industry and their methods and prophesied the vast wealth which
would accrue to Britain as a result. This, for example, was one of the
main arguments of a pamphlet published in 1702 advocating the union
of England and Scotland and dedicated to the Commissioners newly
appointed for this purpose. In the past, this stated, the Dutch had done
their best to prevent such a Union for fear of thereby losing 'their
Fishing on the Coast of *Scotland*', and with reason, for not only did
this fishing employ a vast number of workers in the Republic and bring
it great wealth but it also served as a 'great nursery of Seamen':

The Dominion of the Seas consists in the multitude of Shipping: Shipping is not
of use without Seamen; and Seamen are not bred without Nurseries, neither is
there any such Nurseries in the world as Fisheries; witness the *Hollanders*, who
for extent of Land, and number of Inhabitants are far inferior to *England*, and
yet where the *English* have one seaman, they have three, and all those mostly
bred by their Fishings on the Coast of *Scotland*, where they Yearly fish with
upwards of three thousand Busses, and every Buss yearly breeding eight Seamen; so that their three thousand Busses, if they have occasion, do yearly breed
them twenty four Thousand Seamen.[2]

[1] *C.W.* 138, pp. 16, 36–9, 47, 68–70.
[2] *C.W.* 11, pp. 6–8, 15–16.

This advocacy of the wholesale development of the fishing industry, which was often presented in conjunction with long disquisitions concerning Britain's sovereignty of the seas, was not confined to the adherents of any one political creed. In October 1702 the Whig *Observator* deplored the fact that this industry had been allowed to fall into the hands of foreigners, but added:

We have not lost that Right, nor have Foreigners a Legal Possession of our Fishery, which is altogether *Neglected* and *Despised* by us; and we cannot be angry with Foreigners for taking up what we fling away.[1]

3

Thus there was broad agreement between Englishmen of all political complexions on the desirability of emulating the Dutch in matters of commerce, and particularly in their exploitation of the Scottish fisheries. The subject of the constitution of the United Provinces, on the other hand, was one on which opinion was deeply divided. Though they might urge imitation of Dutch commercial practice, there were no other Dutch institutions that Tories could bring themselves to approve. Their nostrils were offended by the odour of republicanism, and worse still to them seemed 'Dutch divinity'. By this term they sought to convey their abhorrence both of the Calvinistic religion of the Dutch and also, curiously enough, of the materialistic irreligion which was for them so notorious a feature of Dutch life. To Whigs, however, perhaps the most attractive aspect of Dutch government was the subordination of Church to State and to reasons of state. How admirable, they exclaimed, that the clergy should be subject to the control of the civil authorities; how praiseworthy, and how good for trade, that there should be freedom of profession for all religions. They were loud in their praise of the Republic as the home of 'toleration' and, though the Tories sometimes challenged this assertion in order to gain a point in argument, it is clear that the Dutch were believed by most Englishmen to allow 'freedom' in matters of religion. Dutch civil government also won the aversion of Tories and the praise of Whigs, but in this case the latter were somewhat less uncritical – perhaps because, though they would have welcomed the introduction of the Dutch system of Church-state relations into England, their enthusiasm for republicanism was more academic than real. It was realised that the Dutch government was by no means of that 'popular' kind for

[1] *Observator*, i, 48, 7 Oct. 1702.

which some Whigs had a sentimental regard, but rather of an oligarchical nature. 'The people', explained the Whig philosopher Shaftesbury,

are not perfectly represented; but thro' the ease and secure of the Governmt, a few or a select number have the Administration of Affairs.[1]

It is, in fact, possible to make a fairly clear distinction between a 'Tory' and a 'Whig' attitude towards the constitution and government of the Dutch Republic. Even Professor Walcott, who has subjected the old-fashioned dichotomy of party to some searching criticism, admits the existence of 'Whig' and 'Tory' positions on certain issues.[2] Nowhere can these be found more clearly than in the realm of foreign affairs, above all where the Dutch are concerned. Here admiration for, or aversion from, Dutch government tended to colour a man's whole view of the Republic and its people. Shaftesbury explained this, though in highly partisan terms, in a letter to a Dutch friend:

There is no need I should tell you that in all our nation the only lovers of Holland are the lovers of liberty, called Whigs. The contrary party (the Tories) are inveterate, and I remember a saying of one of the best and wisest of our latter patriots, who used often to give it for a rule, 'that if you would discover a concealed Tory, Jacobite, or Papist, speak but of the Dutch, and you will find him out by his passionate railing'.[3]

The extremes to which these divergent attitudes could go are well illustrated by Shaftesbury himself and by Jonathan Swift, whose views of the Dutch have lately been investigated by an American scholar.[4] For Shaftesbury, always on the alert for the inroads of absolutism in Church and state in England, nothing could be more admirable than a country where these dangers had been so successfully avoided, namely 'that wise Commonwealth of Holland, the parent and nursing mother of Liberty'.[5] Moreover, its preservation of its 'perfect' liberty was the best means of preserving and enhancing our own.[6] Envious of Dutch freedom in religion,[7] and unconcerned by their commercial prosperity,[8] Shaftesbury was yet, by his own account, not typical of the Whig attitude in one respect. Most Whigs, he declared, favoured 'the Tory interest on your side' – that is, the Orangists – and

[1] Shaftesbury to Furly, 13 Jan. 1708/9 (O.S.), *Forster*, pp. 250–3.
[2] R. Walcott, *English Politics in the Early 18th Century* (Oxford, 1956), p. 156 and *passim*.
[3] Shaftesbury to van Twedde, 17 Jan. 1705/6, St. Giles', *Rand*, pp. 347–52.
[4] J. Kent Clark, 'Swift and the Dutch', *Hunt. Lib. Quart.*, xvii (1953–4). What follows on Swift is derived from this study.
[5] Shaftesbury to Jean le Clerc, 8 Feb. 1704/5, St. Giles', *Rand*, pp. 328–34.
[6] Shaftesbury to van Twedde, *loc.cit.*
[7] Shaftesbury to Basnage, 21 Jan. 1706/7, St. Giles', *Rand*, pp. 372–7.
[8] Shaftesbury to 'Teresias', 29 Nov. 1706, St. Giles', *Ibid.*, pp. 366–9.

were averse from 'the Commonwealth Party', owing to their veneration for the late Stadtholder-King. Shaftesbury yielded to none in his admiration for king William – 'the very founder of liberty, our good lawgiver, and establisher of our state' – but it was otherwise with William as Prince of Orange. For Shaftesbury, though not, he explained, for his less informed fellow-Whigs, 'Stadtholder, Governor, or Captain General' could be equated with 'any other form of tyranny'.[1]

If Shaftesbury's pro-Regent outlook was unusual even for a Whig, Swift's antipathy to the whole theory and practice of Dutch government marked the extreme of Tory opinion. I am not concerned here with Swift's reaction to Dutch opposition to the Tory peace, which deepened this antipathy but certainly did not create it. Swift had begun his career as a friend and admirer of the Dutch, but as his views on Church-state relations crystallised so his respect for the Republic diminished. He came to believe that 'toleration' should be strictly limited to the exercise of religion, with not a grain of political power allowed to dissenters. Any further concession, he believed, would lead to the deterioration of religion and thus of public morality. 'To have admitted that religious freedom, in Locke's sense, was a positive good would have been to give up his whole argument on the proper relationship between church and state . . . . Thus he was obliged to explain away the Dutch example'. So he argued that this example was irrelevant for England because of the wide differences in climate, culture and historical background; nor would it be wise to emulate a people whose basically commercial economy made them inferior to England with her essentially agrarian one. In any case they were not so 'free' in matters of religion as their admirers supposed. They had their national church, and state employments were reserved for its members. Above all their constitution was not stable, their vaunted internal tranquillity being due solely to external pressures. Remove the threat of invasion and its glaring defects would become apparent. Dutch government, in fact, was 'the worst constituted Government in the World to last'.

4

Such questions were for those who took pleasure in considering the problems of government, but many subjects of queen Anne with little knowledge of such matters had none the less a firm picture in their minds of the people of the United Provinces. This was a picture which,

---

[1] Shaftesbury to van Twedde, *loc.cit.*

in its essentials, varied little with differences of political allegiance. The distinction between Whig and Tory views of the Dutch 'national character' was more of phrase than of meaning. As an explanation of Dutch prosperity the Whig might point to the 'frugality' and 'parsimony' of the inhabitants, where the Tory would speak of their 'avarice' and 'greed'. In business, according to the Whigs, the Dutch were commendably 'sharp', with an eye to the main chance; to the Tories they seemed dishonest and faithless. To the Tory the Dutch appeared dull, heavy, flat, insensible – perhaps even clownish and downright stupid. The Whig might deny all this; but was it really so very different from admitting that 'the *Dutch* abound much more in Wisdom than Wit and Fancy, and are little vers'd in these more refin'd Passions'?[1] Joseph Addison, at one time the self-styled 'Whig-Examiner', seems to have been struck by this aspect of the Dutch character. We find him describing the Dutch as 'more famous for their industry than for wit and humour'; again, 'they are a trading people, and in their very minds mechanics. They express their wit in manufacture as we do in manuscript'.[2] There was little dispute that the Dutch language would 'scarce allow 'em to be Orators, and much less Poets', and that neither the universities nor learning in general were

very considerable . . . . in a Country where Profit is much more in Request than Honour, not being so much incouraged as Trade, which seems here to be arrived to a Pitch unknown to all the World besides . . . .[3]

As an English scholar remarked,

the Dutch learning is generally at a low Ebb, & they certainly take the wrong Method in heaping notes upon notes. [4]

They were thought, too, to be thorough, unmartial, patient, law-abiding and given to drink. Coldness was a quality often attributed to them, above all to their women. 'The women generally are sleepy enuf', lamented one gay traveller, 'and keep a good distance, especially from strangers . . . . .'.[5] When Englishmen contemplated the diet of fish, vegetables, bread and dairy produce on which, so it was said, these Dutch 'butter-boxes' lived, all political differences were forgotten as Whig and Tory alike were overcome by a mixture of amazement and distaste; amazement that any people could do what the Dutch had

---

[1] *C.W.* 165, p. 38.
[2] P. Smithers, *Life of Joseph Addison* (Oxford, 1954), p. 68; *Tatler*, 129, 2–4 Feb. 1709/10.
[3] *C.W.* 165, pp. 47–8.
[4] J. Bennett to T. Hearne, 24 Sept. 1709 (O.S.), *Hearne*, ii, p. 268, n.
[5] R. Kenyon to Mrs. Kenyon, May (1702?), *H.M.C. XIV pt. iv*, pp. 428–9.

done on this 'barbarous' diet and distaste at the mere thought of a
meal which did not consist principally of meat.

These, then, were the most fundamental of the popular beliefs
current in queen Anne's England concerning the virtues and vices of the
Dutch, both as to their persons and as to their institutions. The development of the British attitude towards the Dutch alliance would be
governed by more immediate, if more transient, influences; but these
basic assumptions and preconceptions would go far to determine the
terms in which this development was expressed.

CHAPTER II

A NEW REIGN AND A NEW WAR
<1702>

I

In 1674 the Parliament of England forced its king to withdraw from the war that he was fighting, in alliance with Louis XIV of France, against the Dutch Republic. Thus there came to an end the series of naval and colonial conflicts with the Dutch in which the commercial rivalry of the two nations had culminated.

Desire for friendship with the Dutch played little part in bringing about the revulsion of feeling in England against the third Anglo-Dutch war. Indeed, this arose from dissatisfaction with the domestic rather than with the foreign aspects of the king's policies. In the last analysis, however, these two were inseparable: mounting fear of Popery and arbitrary government at home did not sort well with connivance at the crushing of a free Protestant nation by the arch-exponent of Catholic despotism. Perhaps, after all, the gravest and most immediate challenge to English interests and independence came not from the merchant fleets of the Dutch but from the armies and 'pensions' of *le roi soleil*. Gradually this conviction grew, and with it came, inevitably, a certain decrease in the intensity of anti-Dutch feeling. In this sense, the years between the Treaty of Breda and the Treaty of Westminster were a real turning-point in Anglo-Dutch relations. They marked the end of half a century during which hostility to the Dutch, born of commercial jealousy, had to all intents and purposes become part of the English character.[1] Anglo-Dutch relations could now revert to their more usual state, in which, to use Professor Renier's terms, 'The political-strategic factor, which made for collaboration, ... overshadowed the economic factor, which made for divergence ....'.[2]

---

[1] C. H. Wilson, *Profit and Power* (London, 1957), pp. 143–4; G. B. Hertz, *English Public Opinion after the Restoration* (London, 1902), Ch. I.

[2] G. J. Renier, *Great Britain and the Establishment of the Kingdom of the Netherlands, 1813–15* (London, 1930), p. 10. There were, of course, economic factors which themselves facilitated the lessening of hostility: see C. H. Wilson, *Profit and Power*, pp. 154–5; Ph. de

The events of 1688 themselves illustrated the change that had occurred; they would have been unthinkable twenty or thirty years earlier if only on account of the nationality of William III. Yet the advent of a Dutch king was not followed by any further movement of opinion in favour of the Dutch – quite the contrary, in fact. It is true that England joined the Republic in her struggle against Louis XIV but many Englishmen came to regard this war as a needless and wanton expenditure of English wealth and life in the interests of the Dutch. English dislike of foreigners and 'foreign' rule; the personal unpopularity of William and his foreign 'favourites'; the familiar tendency for a sense of obligation to breed resentment rather than gratitude; the apparent loss of England's erstwhile prosperity: all this fostered the belief that the war was being fought solely to enrich and aggrandize the Republic, and brought about a certain revival of the always latent hostility to the Dutch.[1]

In the last years of William III – the years of peace – hatred of foreigners in general and of the Dutch in particular reached a height which it had never attained even in the blackest years of the war. When the Commons defied the king by revoking Crown grants of Irish lands to foreign 'favourites' and disbanding the partly Dutch standing army their success was assured; as van Alphen says, 'scarcely any difference of opinion about their actions against the foreigners was to be expected from the people of England'.[2]

The gentlemen of England felt little concern when, on the long-awaited death of the heirless Charles II of Spain, Louis XIV abandoned his agreements with William III for the peaceful partition of the coveted Spanish empire, in favour of the defunct monarch's will, under which the entire Spanish monarchy passed to Philip of Anjou, Louis' grandson. So indifferent were they to the dangers consequent upon a Franco-Spanish dynastic union that William III was forced to acknowledge Anjou as Philip V, rightful king of Spain. Not even Louis XIV's seizure of the Dutch Barrier fortresses in the Spanish Netherlands could wholly rouse them out of their indifference; but when the French king's subsequent actions made it clear that he planned to stifle English trade with Spain and the Spanish Netherlands, and above all, when at the deathbed of James II he pledged himself to recognise his

Vries, 'L'Animosité Anglo-Hollandaise au XVIIe Siècle', *Annales* (*Économies-Sociétés-Civilisations*), 1950, p. 47.

[1] *Van Alphen, passim.* See also A. Browning, *ed., English Historical Documents, 1660–1714* (London, 1953), pp. 24, 26.

[2] *Van Alphen*, pp. 247 sqq., 277.

son as king of England, tempers began to rise. However much many of them might secretly long for 'James III' as king – if only he would change his religion! – Englishmen had no intention of accepting him at the point of a French musket.

Thus even the Tories, for all their dislike of the king's policies, began to prepare for war. William, however, wanted something more than such slow, grudging and, as he saw it, unreliable support for his plans of a Grand Alliance to curb once and for all the exorbitant power of France. He knew that he could look to the Whigs for enthusiastic backing for a war in defence of trade and the Protestant Succession. The Whigs, indeed, were anxious that the war should be fought not merely on the basis of safeguarding these interests, securing the Dutch Barrier, and compensating the Emperor for the disappointment of his pretentions to the Spanish Empire; they were eager, as their pamphleteers emphasised, to extend these aims of the Grand Alliance to include the driving of Anjou from the throne of Spain. William was aware that such a plan was not yet acceptable to opinion in either Britain or the Republic, but he made clear his wish for increased Whig representation in the Commons when he dissolved Parliament in November 1701. For this the Tories never forgave him. Young Henry St. John, writing to the veteran Sir William Trumbull, now retired from public life, asserted that this was yet another example of the control of English affairs by the Dutch. King William's countrymen, he explained, were 'resolved not to enter into a war but upon the foot of the last, and in short to push us foremost as a blind to cover them', and were consequently determined to have their tools, the Whigs, in power in England.[1]

Such sentiments as these were not prompted merely by annoyance that the king had seen fit to try to obtain a more Whiggish Parliament. They were an expression of the very real and widespread suspicion that, under 'Dutch' rule, Britain had become no more than a tool for the execution of 'Dutch' policies in the interests of the Republic. This did not, it is true, prevent the Commons from agreeing, in William's last parliament, to the implementation of his Grand Alliance policy. Most Englishmen were by now convinced of the necessity of war, and those who were not, or who considered that it should be waged on lines different from those planned by the king, chose for the time being not to press their objections.

Of all this Marlborough, now William's chief lieutenant in England,

[1] St. John to Trumbull, 12 Nov. 1701 (O.S.), *H. M. C. Downshire I pt. ii*, pp. 810–11.

was well aware. He felt obliged to warn the Dutch Grand Pensionary Heinsius that, although the Commons was certain to approve the proposed English contribution to the allied armies, yet this matter might be the occasion of 'some angry speeches'. He feared, too, that the expression by Dutch gazettes and newsletters of a preference for Whigs rather than Tories might be enough to alienate the latter from the policy of the Grand Alliance.

The unanimity of the Commons in agreeing the furnish the quota of troops stipulated by the Treaty of Grand Alliance was presented by Marlborough to Heinsius as evidence 'that the Gentlemen of England are intierly in the interest of Holland'.[1] This assertion may be seen as part of Marlborough's 'management' of the anxious Dutch. The gentlemen of England in fact saw a very clear distinction between the interests of 'Holland' and England, and it was entirely their concern for the latter which led them to support the war policy of William III. Of the powerful group of High Tories, many wanted a war in which they would have as little to do with the Dutch or Dutch interests as was humanly possible, and some were even opposed to the war altogether. For the moment the High Tories kept themselves within bounds; only after the death of the king did they give full vent to their feelings. Meanwhile they contented themselves with keeping up their sidelong and virulent attacks on 'foreign' rule.

It is true that the views and policies of the Whigs gave considerably more evidence than those of the Tories of a penchant for 'the interest of Holland'; but the Whig gains in the general election of December 1701 owed little to this fact. The growing popularity of the Whigs has been well explained by Lecky. 'The strong national jealousy', he writes,

of foreign rulers, and foreign policies, and foreign interference, which was usually the strength of the Tory party, was as vehement as ever, though it had for the moment been enlisted on the side of the Whigs. It was no attachment to the Dutch sovereign, no desire to alter the disposition of power on the Continent in the general interests of Europe that animated the electors, but solely resentment at French interference; and few English sovereigns have ever sunk to the tomb less regretted by the mass of the English nation than William III.

To this shrewd analysis of the state of feeling at the end of William's reign Lecky adds the comment that

With such sentiments prevailing in the nation, it is not surprising that the accession of Anne should have been followed by a violent reflux of Tory feeling.[2]

---

[1] Marlborough to Heinsius, 9 and 20 Jan. 1701/2, (London), *van 't Hoff*, pp. 6–7.
[2] *Lecky*, pp. 30–1.

It was, indeed, with relief and even joy that the news of William's end was received, and in the months that followed there were many indications that the war against France had not dispelled feelings of rivalry, of enmity even, towards the Dutch; but Lecky's words are not an accurate guide to the development of English opinion towards the Dutch during the first year of the reign of queen Anne.

With the accession of an 'entirely English' queen the High Tories became extremely vocal in expressing their distaste for all things foreign – not least, for all things Dutch. Their exuberance was, in part, justified, for, in her conception of the part which the Church and the sovereign should play in afrairs of state, in her refusal to accept to the full the principles which the Whigs had attempted to deduce from the 'Glorious Revolution', the queen was one of them. There was, however, one vital point on which she differed from them: the war against France. The High Tories had as little liking for the war policy of William III as they had for his person. Not all of them admitted that England should go to war with France again, and those who did were strongly opposed to the strategy of a continental land-war as envisaged by the late king. To Albemarle, mourning the death of his master and friend and apprehensive of the fate of the Alliance that he had created, they appeared 'fort contraires au bien public et surtout des ennemis de nostre république'.[1] The queen, on the other hand, encouraged and supported by the Marlboroughs, had little hesitation in maintaining unbroken the war policies of her unlamented brother-in-law. This difference between the queen and those of her subjects to whom she belonged by belief, by inclination and by temperament was one of the most important factors in English politics in the early years of the war. What gave it special importance was the fact that, on this issue, the majority of her politically effective subjects stood behind the queen. Only when both sovereign and subjects were weary of a war which they no longer considered either necessary or desirable would the breach be healed; then and only then would the High Tories regain the promised land of power and patronage.

The queen and most of her people were for carrying on the war policies of William III; but there was not yet, except perhaps among Whig politicians and a few merchants with an eye to advantages to be won in the Spanish Indies, anything that can be called enthusiasm for war. The imminent conflict with France was regarded as a necessary evil, a prospect to be accepted but scarcely welcomed. Acceptance

---

[1] Albemarle to Heinsius (extract), April 1702, *von Noorden*, i, p. 193.

there assuredly was – the magnitude of the Tory victory at the polls in the summer of 1702 would have been unlikely had Tory candidates rejected the principles of the Grand Alliance – but it was not until after Blenheim that any real enthusiasm for the war appeared amongst the people of England. Had there been in 1702 (or, for that matter, in 1703) that almost feverish greed for victory which existed in 1705 English opinion would have given much shorter shrift to the alleged obstruction of Marlborough by Dutch deputies and generals than it actually did; there would, in fact, have been a revulsion of feeling in Britain similar to that which actually occurred in 1705.

There is one other important point which Lecky tends to obscure. Though it is true that William's death was followed by a 'reflux of Tory feeling', it should be remembered that this event actually made it easier for Tories and Whigs alike to adopt a more friendly attitude towards the Dutch. It had been William's misfortune to be disliked and distrusted by both Whig and Tory, and it was natural that, during his lifetime, some at least of their feelings towards him should have been transferred to his native country. After his death the case was altered, except, of course, for the vocal and influential minority of High Tories, for whom an inveterate hostility to the Dutch was almost an article of faith. More moderate men could now adopt a more friendly tone towards the Republic without in the least forswearing their disapproval of the Dutch king and his favourites. The Whigs, already pro-Dutch by inclination and by policy, were ready, now that the king's cold and unlikeable personality was no longer with them, to glorify his memory. This quasi-sanctification of William by the Whigs no doubt had its roots in quite genuine feelings of gratitude, and even in a certain posthumous affection, but it was also a useful political weapon. By its means they were able at the same time to defend themselves against charges of republicanism, and to turn the tables on the Tories by reminding those self-righteous defenders of the royal prerogative of their own 'ungrateful' and even 'anti-monarchical' conduct.

2

There were few tears shed in England when, on 8 March 1701/2, death claimed her king, and few indeed were those who shared the distress of that pious Scot, Captain Blackader, that 'our dear Deliverer is taken from us'.[1] A fortnight later one lady wrote:

[1] *Blackader*, p. 174.

I am asuereid of one thing, that noe King can bee less lamentid then this has bin, evin by thos that was his greitest admeirers in his life tiem. I due not mean thos that has lost ther plasis & other profit consarnes; the very day hee dieid, ther was severall expressions of Joy publickly spok in the streets- of having one of ther own nation to rain over them; and that now thay shoud not have ther money carried bee you (beyond?) say (sea?) to in rich other nasions, bot it would be spent Amonx them, and tradin wod be beter.[1]

The most outspoken 'expressions of Joy' came, naturally enough, from the Jacobites and the near-Jacobite High Tories. Loud and long they sang the praises of Sorrel, the horse whose stumble had caused William's fatal fall. Much was made of the contrast between the black days which had at last ended and the golden age that was dawning, an age that would revive the glories of Elizabethan England. The Whigs, as self-appointed guardians of the 'Glorious Revolution', felt obliged to produce rejoinders to all this, and at the same time Bishop Burnet, in his *Compleat History* of William III, sketched out the almost hagiographic picture of that king which was soon to be incorporated in the Whig creed.[2]

Apart from those of the Whigs, expressions of regret at the news of William's death were perfunctory and conventional, and even in these were sometimes evident untimely intimations of rivalry with the Dutch. The queen herself, in a celebrated passage in her speech to both Houses of Parliament on March 11th, hinted broadly at the pleasure which most Englishmen felt at the end of 'foreign' rule. 'It shall be my constant endeavour', she declared,

to make you the best return for that duty and affection which you have expressed to me, by a careful and diligent administration, for the good of all my subjects: And as I know my own heart to be entirely English, I can very sincerely assure you, that there is not any thing you can expect or desire from me, which I shall not be ready to do, for the happiness and prosperity of England ....

The words 'entirely English' were seized on eagerly, above all by the

---

[1] Mrs. E. Adams to Sir J. Verney, 21 March 1701/2 (O.S.) *Verney Letters*, i, pp. 106-7. Amongst those who stood to lose 'ther plasis & other profit consarnes' there were certainly some Dutchmen. The exiled Earl of Ailesbury was able to rejoice that England was now being purged 'of the Dutch locusts and plunderers' (C. Bruce, *Life and Loyalties of Thomas Bruce* (London, 1951), p. 236). But just how far this 'purge' went it is difficult to estimate. Anne lost no time in removing the hated Portland from his place as Ranger of Windsor Park, and from the Privy Council, but it does not seem that there was any wholesale removal of royal servants of Dutch origin; even Albemarle retained his command of the first troop of the Horse Guards. The lists of royal servants printed in Chamberlayne's *Angliae Notitiae* during Anne's reign reveal many names with a 'Dutch' ring, particularly in the more menial positions. These Dutchmen, one of the legacies of William III, had no doubt proved themselves indispensable.

[2] *C.W.* 17. For a detailed account of the publications inspired by the king's death (many of which are to be found collected together in *C.W.* 145, ii) see *van Alphen*, pp. 307 *sqq*.

High Tories. As the historian Stanhope notes, they 'touched precisely the right chords of popular feeling', and they formed the principal emblem of the many medals struck to commemorate the queen's coronation.[1]

The addresses which poured in from all parts of the country congratulating the queen on her accession left no doubt of the favour with which was viewed an 'entirely English' sovereign. It was nevertheless of great importance to the queen and her advisers that the new and exclusively English reign should enjoy the goodwill of the Dutch Republic; otherwise the Grand Alliance, which they were determined to maintain, would fall apart. On March 9th addresses were voted by both Houses stressing their determination to maintain the alliances contracted by William III, and a day later the queen wrote to the States-General to assure them that

we shall always look upon the interests of England and those of your State, as inseparable, and united by such ties as cannot be broke without the utmost prejudice of both nations.[2]

The first reports of the reaction of the Dutch to the news of the king's death were highly encouraging. It was said that they were redoubling their efforts to take the field, and Henry St. John was confident that the imminent arrival of Marlborough at The Hague would soon 'settle the minds of people' there. 'God be thanked', wrote another member of parliament, 'the Dutch seem resolved to joyne heartily with us against the French'. From The Hague itself the English envoy Alexander Stanhope reported that the Dutch seemed 'as Steady and resolute as is possible to pursue the measures resolved on before according to his late Matie's Plann', and also determined to shelve the question of appointing another Stadtholder in order to avoid the disputes this would infallibly cause. On March 28th (N.S.), the day on which Marlborough arrived at The Hague, not only Stanhope, but also Dayrolle, his secretary, and Warre, an under-Secretary of State at that time at the Dutch capital, were confident of the firmness and vigour with which the Dutch were determined to carry out William's plans, 'so that', as Warre put it,

there is no doubt to be made, but that the Union between England and Holland

---

[1] *Votes of the House of Commons, in the Parliament begun ... Dec. 30, 1701*, pp. 125–6; Stanhope, P. H., 5th Earl, *The History of England ... 1701–1713* (London, 1870), p. 40; A. Strickland, *Lives of the Queens of England* (London, 1848), xii, p. 67.

[2] *Cobbett*, vi, cols. 3–4; Anne to States-General, 10 March 1701/2, St. James, *Post Man*, 946, 24 March 1701/2; Marlborough to Heinsius, 8 and 13 March 1701/2 (O.S.), *van 't Hoff*, pp. 10–11.

will continue as firme as ever being cimented by a common interest and the joint inclinations of both Nations for the publick Good.[1]

Marlborough was speedily convinced of the truth of these observations. and his confidence was justified by the firm answer of the States to a haughty memorial delivered to them in the name of Louis XIV by the French agent Barre. This answer, thought Stanhope, if printed in English, would have an even better effect in England than had had the previous resolution of the States for adhering to the Alliance.[2] At home, the Whigs were loud in their praises of this 'pertinent and becoming' reply. Characterising it as a testimony both of the States' 'candid Intentions to support the Confederacy' and of the wisdom of their councils, they celebrated 'the growing Union between *England* and *Holland*'.[3]

3

The accession of Anne, a High Church queen, had made the High Tories second only in influence in affairs of state to the Marlboroughs and Godolphin, her friends and advisers. They demanded that a clean sweep be made of all that remained from the bad old days of William III. In insisting that Whigs and Whiggery be rooted out of the government of England they could be sure of widespread support. Expostulations about 'Whiggish' financial administration, in particular, always sounded sweet in the ears of English gentlemen, for, as one of them pointed out in a letter to Robert Harley concerning the land tax,

upon the foot you now are, you certainly ruin those that have only land to depend on, to enrich Dutch, Jews, French, and other foreigners, scoundrel stock-jobbers and tally-jobbers, who have been sucking our vitals for many years.[4]

The High Tory offensive was by no means limited to this topic. In a series of pamphlets published soon after the accession of Anne they demanded not merely that Whiggish policies at home should be abandoned, but they also attacked that other hateful Whiggish legacy

---

[1] St. John to Trumbull, (16 March) 1701/2 (O.S.), *H. M. C. Downshire I pt. ii*, pp. 811–12; Stanhope to Stepney, 27 March 1702, Hague, Add. Ms. 7068; *ibid.*, Warre to (Stepney), 28 March 1702, Hague; Dayrolle to Ellis, 28 March 1702, Hague, Add. Ms. 28910; Stanhope to (Vernon), (28 March 1702), (Hague), S. P. Holl. 224; T. Johnson to R. Norris, 17 March 1701/2, London, *Norris Papers*, pp. 79–82.

[2] Marlborough to Godolphin, 4 April 1702, Hague, *H. M. C. IX pt. ii*, p. 464; Stanhope to Vernon, 11 April 1702, Hague, S. P. Holl. 224.

[3] *Observator*, i, 2, 8 April 1702; *Post Man*, 1067, 29 Dec. 1702; *Annals*, i, pp. 13–14.

[4] ? to (Harley), 10 March 1701/2, London, *H. M. C. Portland VIII*, p. 96.

of William III, the Grand Alliance against Louis XIV. The most
sensational of these pamphlets was *The History of the Last Parliament*,
by James Drake, which appeared about the time of the king's death,
and the preface of which was subsequently condemned by the Lords.
In defending the record of the late Parliament Drake was able to
asperse the policies of William, and he paid particular attention to the
criticisms that had been made of that Parliament for being hesitant
to enter another war. Had we declared war after the Dutch had recognised Anjou, he pointed out,

we had by so doing made ourselves Principals, who need only to be seconds; and
had brought ourselves under a Necessity of demanding that Succour from them,
which now they have been forc'd to beg from us.

Had we declared war first, he went, on they would certainly have
reaped every possible advantage from this; perhaps they might even
have left us in the lurch, in which case we would have been rightly
reproached 'for putting the Probity of our Friends to so severe a Test
as to try whether they would Sell us, or not ....'. Even had they
chosen our side, they would have placed a very heavy obligation –
perhaps a debt – upon us, for

let us suppose 'em as affectionate to us, and our King, as the most zealous
Advocates for 'em can alledge, we know 'em to be upon all occasions very watchful, and discerning of their own interests, a People that let slip no advantages,
and know how to set a sufficient value upon their favours, and part not with
them so easily, as some of their Neighbours; that pride themselves more in
Gallantry, and false Notions of Honour, which ought to have less share in National Transactions, than usually they have. Allowing 'em in this case to act with
their usual Prudence and Sagacity, when both sides shall be forc'd to court 'em,
and we in Manifest Danger of Ruin, unless we prevail; can we imagine that they
would neglect to make the best of so fair a Market for the Succours they should
afford? For tho' it be equally, or more their Interest than ours, that the Power of
France should receive a Check, yet were we engaged past receding with Honour,
or Safety, and they yet to make their Election of Peace, or War, we must oblige
'em by some favourable Conditions to determine on our side, and at the least be
content to take our Measures and share of that War from their Appointment; all
which by a seasonable Hesitation we have avoided ....[1]

Drake only attacked William's war policy by implication, though what
he had to say of the Dutch both at home and in England was far from
complimentary. Other writers were bolder, encouraged no doubt by
the fact that 'Dutch William' was safely in his grave. One writer
argued that the English quota should be paid in money, not men – the
'blue water' policy of Chatham was already known to the High Tories –
and asked whether

[1] *C.W.* 63, pp. 7–14, 60 *sqq.*

England ought to contribute as much to the support of the Confederacy, as the *Dutch*, whose Countreys are contiguous to the Enemies Territories, and therefore in more Danger .... ?

A poem entitled *The Miseries of England, From the Growing Power of her Domestick Enemies* was franker still, and in a few lines it summed up the High Tory attitude to the war. We should wait, it declared, 'with due Patience and Discretion', till 'our Rich Neighbours' craved our aid

> On the same Terms they lately gave us theirs;
> We were the Suff'rers, they Advantage made,
> And little less than all the Charge we paid,
> Besides a liberal Present for their useless Aid ....
> *England* be wise, and make thy self amends,
> Return the costly favours of thy Friends,
> Let now thy Justice to thy self be seen,
> And be as kind as they to us have been;
> Neither be aw'd, or yet by flatt'ries drawn,
> Tho' our Foes Threaten, and our Neighbours fawn,
> To call a distant Evil on our Heads,
> And take upon our selves what Holland dreads;
> But make the Charge e'er we the War begin,
> Just equal to the Danger we are in;
> And if assist our Friends with further Aid
> To be allow'd and that Expence repaid;
> For why should we that have least cause to fear,
> Defend a Neighbour whom the Danger's near,
> And we endure the Toil, and pay the Cost,
> When they, without our Help, must needs be lost'.[1]

Such sentiments did not go unchallenged. Drake's suggestion that the Dutch might have 'sold' us if we had been the first to declare war was described in one 'answer' as a 'wild and wicked notion', and it was argued that the 'depressing of *Holland* and exalting of *France*' by the Tories clearly showed their Jacobite intentions. Another pamphlet asserted that the maintenance of 'the Ballance of Europe' was vital for our safety, and that

by uniting with *Holland*, we do follow our true interest, which hath ever been successful to this Nation, which is to be still Masters at Sea, and by Embracing

[1] *C.W.* 170, p. 2; *C.W.* 130, pp. 11, 15–17.

the Emperor's Interest, we may hope for a considerable Portion in the Spoils of the *Spanish Indies*.[1]

The fate of the Grand Alliance, however, was to be decided not in the press but in the council-chamber. On May 2nd, at a Council held to frame the declaration of war, the High Tory leaders Rochester and Nottingham made their final attempt to secure the participation of their country in the war as an 'auxiliary' rather than as a 'principal', with the emphasis on the war at sea rather than by land. In reply, Marlborough, Godolphin and others declared, in words that they would have cause to remember in the next few years,

that the Dutch were a cautions people, and, if they had the direction of the war, on that side, they would probably content themselves, with taking some towns on the frontiers, and so secure themselves a barrier against France, but would not easily be brought to venture a battle, and consequently we must expect a lingring war; whereas, if our general commanded in chief in Flanders, and we furnish'd them with such forces as would render them abundantly superior to the enemy, they might be brought to consent to hazard a general battle, and a good peace obtained in little time.[2]

These arguments won the day, and their victory was made apparent to the world by the simultaneous declaration of war on France by the queen and the States-General on May 4th (O.S.). For the moment, however, domestic rather than foreign battlefields were uppermost in the minds of English politicians, for, with the speedy dissolution of William's last parliament, a general election was imminent. Most of the pamphlets already referred to were no doubt designed as election propaganda. Indeed, whether they dealt with William's war policy or not, an outstanding characteristic of Tory pamphlets at this election was their suggestion that the Whigs' aim was and would be to give the Dutch complete control of English affairs. Of all the writers who made this point, none aroused more interest than Davenant with his *Tom Double Return'd out of the Country*. This work, which won the condemnation of the Lords, included the suggestion not only that the Whigs had poisoned the minds of the Dutch against the English Tories, but also that the large Dutch holding in English funds operated to the advantage of the Whigs, since it helped to engage the Dutch in their measures.[3]

In the election held in July the Tories won a handsome victory. After the election, as before it, most of them declared that their only

---

[1] *C.W.* 167, pp. 10, 19; *C.W.* 34, pp. 8–9, 16–17.
[2] Stanhope, *op.cit.*, p. 40; *C.W.* 114, pp. 548–9.
[3] *C.W.* 33, pp. 41 *sqq.*

goal was to humble France, sustain the Dutch and restore credit by good financial administration. There was a general belief in the sincerity of these professions, reported L'Hermitage, the Dutch agent in London; as Shaftesbury wrote to his friend Furly, a merchant at Rotterdam,

the people now have an opinion that these men and this very Ministry will serve their turn, and carry on things abroad for their honour, and pursue the warr vigorously. They have been the party that have of late years acted the patriot, and they have now purged themselves by the solemnest of oaths, the abjuration, and by their professing their zeal for a warr and against France. Now that they are, say they, in good hands, even youabroad are willing to think well of our Ministry.[1]

Shaftesbury was a great lover of Holland, a man who, though he had not known him personally in the days of his greatness, made a point of making much of Portland after his disgrace. He was also a shrewd observer. The new ministry was indeed anxious that it should be well thought of by the Dutch and that such good opinion should be made known in England. Speaker Harley, who worked closely with the new Lord Treasurer, Godolphin, acted personally and through agents to counter the 'lyes and storys' spread by the Whigs in the Republic, and to convince the Dutch of 'the just hopes they may have from the ensuing Parliament'. From The Hague on November 10th (N.S.) Winchilsea, *en route* for Hanover on a complimentary mission, reported to the Secretary of State Nottingham that the temper of the new parliament at its opening had proved very welcome to the Dutch, though, he added, there was some resentment of a slur cast upon William III in the address of the Commons on the queen's speech. In fact the words in question, claiming that the queen and her ministers had 'signally retrieved the antient honour and glory of the *English* nation', had 'occasioned a warm debate' in the Commons. Those who defended them urged that in William's reign 'things had been conducted by strangers, and trusted to them; and that a vast treasure had been spent in unprofitable campaigns in *Flanders*'. 'The Partition treaty', says Tindal, 'and every thing else, with which his reign could be loaded, was brought into the account', and the retention of the word 'retrieved' (rather than 'maintained') was carried by a majority of a hundred votes, 'all who had any favour at Court, or hoped for any, voting for it'.[2]

---

[1] L'Hermitage to States-General (transcript), 7/18 Aug. 1702, London, Add. Ms. 17677 YY; Shaftesbury to Furly, 10 Aug. 1702 (O.S.), *Forster*, pp. 179–82.

[2] (Harley) to (Godolphin), 9 Aug. 1702 (O.S.), Add. Ms. 28055; Winchilsea to (Nottingham),

There were other events in this session of Parliament which can have given little pleasure in the Republic. True, both the queen, in announcing her intention of making Marlborough a Duke, and the Commons, in refusing to make him the financial grant that she had proposed, praised him for settling an 'entire confidence' between England and the Republic – the Commons added that he had

therein vindicated the gentlemen of England, who had, by the vile practices of designing men, been traduced, and industriously represented as false to your majesty's allies, because they were true to the interest of their country –

but there were other developments which cast considerable doubt upon the existence of such confidence. Above all, the Tories made determined attacks upon the favourites of William III. The most far-reaching of these was an attempt to resume all the late king's grants – a blow obviously aimed at Portland and Albemarle, which came to nothing only because the Whigs ingeniously countered it by suggesting that a provision for the resumption of all James II's grants should be 'tacked' to it. Nor was it only in Parliament that such a measure was urged, for there appeared a pamphlet entitled *The Exorbitant Grants of William III Examin'd and Question'd*, the evidently Jacobite author of which asserted that 'nothing ever appear'd to the Contrary; but that the *Dutch* and *French* (*i.e.* Huguenots) came over (in 1688) for no other Intent but to enslave the People, and trample upon the Rights and Liberties of *Englishmen*'. By the queen's accession, he continued,

God has been pleased to free us from a Foreign Yoke, and to restore the Blood of our Kings to rule over us, and to pour such Blessings upon her Majesty's Arms in the first Ten Months of her Reign, with little Expence and render'd more to retrieve the Honour of *England*, than ever *William* the 3d. did at the Expence of about 70 Millions Sterling throughout his whole Reign, which makes a vast Difference 'twixt being Govern'd by an *English* Born Princess, and a Foreigner. .

William's favourites, especially Albemarle, were also vilified by the new Whig periodical, the *Observator*. Its author, John Tutchin, wrote often and at length of the desirability of a 'nearer Union betwixt *Holland* and *England*', and of the inseparability of their interests, but he was not yet ready to glorify the memory of William III.[1]

The most controversial measure proposed during this Parliamentary session was an Occasional Conformity Bill, designed to prevent the

10 Nov. 1702, Hague, Add. Ms. 29588; *C.W.* 182, p. 574; I. S. Leadam, *Political History of England*, ix (London, 1909), pp. 25–6.

[1] *Cobbett*, vi, cols. 57–8; *London Gazette*, 3867, 3 Dec. 1702; *C.W.* 9, pp. 23 *sqq.*; *Observator*, i, 68, 71–2, 74, 79, 84–6, 26 and 30 Dec. 1702, 6 and 23 Jan., 10, 13 and 17 Feb. 1702/3.

evasion by Protestant Dissenters of the provisions of the Test Acts by means of occasional and exceptional reception of the communion in an Anglican church. This was a measure dear to the hearts of many Tories, whose views were thus expressed by the pamphleteer Baron:

Since our *Nation* is become an *Amsterdam* of *Religions*, 'tis requisite we should have so much of the *Amsterdam Government*, as not to let the *Tolerated* be our Governours.

The eagerness of the Tory Commons to make this bill law was eventually thwarted by the obstruction of the predominantly Whig House of Lords. The latter suggested that the passing of the Bill might give 'great Disgust and Offence to our Allies abroad', and exhorted the Commons instead to follow the Dutch example, reminding them that

The Book that goes under the Name of Mr. De Wit shows, that the Dutch reckon that the Woollen Manufactures can never have a Settlement among us as with them, because they who must work them, cannot have so entire a Liberty of Conscience here as there.[1]

4

On his visit to The Hague in March, Marlborough observed that the Dutch leaders were 'shie of speaking of a Generallissim', for fear that this might give rise to quarrels between rival claimants to the command of the allied armies. He thought that they would 'be necessitated to make a resolution very quickly', but three weeks later no appointment had been made, and Stanhope reported that 'our Armies want a head extreamly'. The queen was anxious that her husband, Prince George of Denmark, should obtain the coveted position, but Stanhope found the States not much inclined

to make either our Prince George or any body else Capt. Genll., being rediculously jealous of loseing again the liberty they thinke they have lately recovered.

The precipitate retreat of Tilly from Xanten on April 26th, however, caused some consternation at The Hague, and on May 2nd Warre, still at the Dutch capital, wrote that

it is commonly discoursed, that there is want of conduct among the Generall officers, and that it is absolutely necessary to make a Captain Generall.

<hr>

[1] *C.W.* 13, p. 29; *C.W.* 27, iii, pp. 293–326. Another action of the Commons in this session that was scarcely designed to delight the Dutch was the address to the queen of January 20th asking her 'to concert measures for furnishing her forces in Holland and Flanders, as far as possible, with the manufactures, corn and other products of England'. That this was no mere partisan request was shown by the *Observator's* celebration of the queen's acquiescence to it (*Luttrell*, v, pp. 259–60, 21 Jan. 1702/3; *Observator*, i, 82, 3 Feb. 1702/3).

When it was argued at the Privy Council of May 2nd (O.S.) that it was desirable to have a British general in command in Flanders no appointment had in fact been made. It was not until the beginning of July (N.S.) that Dayrolle was able to report that the Dutch had handed over supreme command of their armies to Marlborough, a decision which, he added, seemed to satisfy most people, 'si ce n'est quelques parans et amis des Généraux Hollandais'.[1]

On taking up his command Marlborough had much to do to quiet Dutch apprehensions concerning the safety of Nijmegen, which Boufflers, shortly before, had only just failed to take by surprise. This preoccupation made the Dutch reluctant to sanction his plan of crossing the Meuse and threatening Brabant. He was far from pleased to be thus thwarted by their 'extravagant fears'. One of the Dutch field-deputies, Geldermalsen, saw clearly that 'Mylord Marlborough ne peut que être vivement triste de se voir à la tête d'une armée supérieur et lié à la porte d'une ville', and was, with some reason, apprehensive of the effect all this might have on opinion in England, where, he feared, 'ils ne seront pas contents des faiblesses de notre gouvernement'. At last Marlborough carried his point, and on July 25th he marched off in the direction of Brabant. [2] As he had calculated, Boufflers had no choice but to follow him, and by August 1st the two armies were in positions that seemed to favour an attack by the Allies. The Dutch field-deputies at first agreed to sanction an attack, but withdrew their approval at the eleventh hour, in the morning of August 2nd. On the following day they again refused to allow an attack. Thus Marlborough suffered the first of many setbacks at the hands of these civilian representatives of the States-General. He was beginning to learn by painful experience that the limitations upon his authority as commander were not merely formal.

[1] Marlborough to Godolphin, 4 April 1702, Hague, *H.M.C. IX pt ii*, p. 464; Stanhope to Stepney, 25 April 1702, Hague, Add. Ms. 7068; Warre to Ellis, 2 May 1702, Hague, Add. Ms. 28911; *ibid.*, Dayrolle to Ellis, 2 May and 4 July 1702, Hague. Until recently it has been assumed that Marlborough was formally appointed commander-in-chief of the armies of the States-General. In his edition of the Heinsius-Marlborough correspondence Mr. van 't Hoff has challenged this assumption and has given good reasons for believing that Marlborough enjoyed this position only in so far as the Dutch forces were united with English troops under his command, and not otherwise. It is certainly much easier to account for Marlborough's difficulties with the Dutch generals, especially in 1703, if this conclusion is accepted (*van 't Hoff*, pp. xii-xiii).

[2] Geldermalsen to Heinsius (extract), 9 July 1702 (N.S.), *von Noorden*, i, p. 260; Marlborough to Goldolphin, 13 July 1702, Duckenburg, *Coxe*, i, pp. 89–90; Marlborough to Nottingham, 13 July 1702, Over-Asselen, *Murray*, i, p. 8; Marlborough to Heinsius, 13 July 1702, Duckenburg, *van 't Hoff*, p. 18; Cardonnel to Ellis, 17 July 1702, Over-Asselen, Add.Ms. 28918; Marlborough to Heinsius, 20 July 1702, Over-Asselen, *van 't Hoff*, pp. 19–20.

No official report of this first difference between Marlborough and the deputies was ever made public, but it was soon rumoured in England that, as Nottingham's correspondent in Rotterdam put it, the Dutch had been too 'timorous and Dubious' to fight. Harley expressed his regret at the news, at the same time remarking that

when I consider the temper & ye maximes of those with whom he (Marlborough) is to act I do admire he hath been able to bring them to do what they have done.

L'Hermitage reported to his masters that there seemed to be a widespread belief throughout the country that the deputies had prevented a battle. Marlborough himself had no doubt that the deputies' actions had robbed him of victory. Though he made no official complaint, he confided to his wife in a letter of August 3rd that

these last three or four days have been very uneasy, I having been obliged to take more pains than I am well able to endure . . . . I was in hopes the day before yesterday I might have done her (the Queen) some service.[1]

For all his chagrin, Marlborough knew that more harm than good would be done by complaining. Thus, when he wrote to Godolphin on August 21st of the States' extreme negligence in failing to send sufficient supplies to the detachment besieging Venlo, he added a warning that all this was

fit only to be known by the Queen and the Prince; for a friendship with these people is absolutely necessary for the common cause and her Majesty's service, and I am in hope that the prudence of the Pensioner this winter may order matters so that their parties may unite, and then there can be no doubt but everything will go better.

Any hopes that Marlborough may have had of an immediate improvement were soon shattered, for on August 23rd and 24th he was again prevented from attacking the French forces, first by the recalcitrance of the Dutch general Obdam, and then once more by the adverse opinion of the deputies. Once again he concealed his annoyance in his report to the States-General, attributing his failure to attack to the fact that the enemy had been able to place themselves behind marshy ground; but it was an open secret that in his view (as his secretary Cardonnel wrote to the Secretary at War Blathwayt)

if we had engaged on Wednesday in the afternoon as his Excellency had given positive orders to do, we could not, in all probability, have failed of a glorious victory, for what the letter mentions of the *marais* and the disadvantage of the

[1] Marlborough to Sarah, 3 Aug. 1702 (N.S.), *Churchill*, ii, pp. 134–5; (J.Hill) to Nottingham, 11 Aug. 1702, Rotterdam, Add. Ms. 29588; Harley to (Godolphin), 2 Aug. 1702, Brampton, *Thibaudeau*, v, pp. 77–8; (L'Hermitage) to States-General (transcript), 4/15 Aug. 1702, London, Add. Ms. 17677 YY.

ground, is rather to cover the omission in not advancing so soon as they were ordered than any thing else.

Marlborough explained to Godolphin that, despite his very 'ill humour', he 'thought it much for her Majesty's service to take no notice' of the fact that he had been robbed of 'a very easy victory'; 'but', he added,

my Lord Rivers, and almost all the general officers of the right, were with me when I sent the orders, so that notwithstanding the care I had taken to hinder it, they do talk ....[1]

The 'talk' in the army speedily reached The Hague, where Stanhope feared that the latest disappointments, together with those that had occurred at the beginning of August, would not 'sound well when our Parliamt. meets', and from there it travelled to London. The story, as Sir Charles Hedges, Nottingham's colleague as Secretary of State, heard it, was that

The Earl of Marlborough pushes the French from one camp to another, and if some others in the army had been as ready as his Lordship to have taken advantages the French army had been in all likelihood entirely defeated more than once.

One lady, on hearing the news, was prompted to reflect on

the miss we have of King William who had command of all, and need not ask live to fight when he saw fit. So tis concluded the Duch will only defend us from being hort, but doe us noe good; which is the common polycys of Princis to lett non grow great ....

'The Dutch', added this well-informed correspondent, 'ever loved to beseeg towns, rather than fight in the fild'.[2]

Thanks at least in part to Marlborough's self-restraint, the news of the latest disappointment to his plans caused no very serious reaction at home, but his trials had not yet ended. He found the negligence of the Dutch in supplying necessaries for the siege of Venlo almost incredible, and he was hard put to it to bring them even to continue this siege when they learned that Boufflers was making a diversion in Flanders. 'Never were people so apt to be frighten'd upon the least occasion as we are', commented Cardonnel, who echoed the words of his master in remarking that

---

[1] Marlborough to Godolphin, 21 Aug. 1702, Everbeeck, *Churchill*, ii, p. 142; Marlborough to States-General, 26 Aug. 1702, Helchteren, *Murray*, i, pp. 24–5; *ibid.*, i, p. 26, Cardonnel to Blathwayt, 27 Aug. 1702, Helchteren; Marlborough to Goldophin, 27 Aug. 1702, Helchteren, *Coxe*, i, p. 94.

[2] Stanhope to Stepney, 29 Aug. 1702, Hague, Add. Ms. 7068; Hedges to Rooke, 21 Aug. 1702, Whitehall, *C. S. P. Dom. Anne*, i, p. 217; Lady Gardiner to Sir J. Verney, 21 and 25 Aug. 1702 (O.S.), *Verney Letters*, i, pp. 111–12 (the first of these letters is dated 21 July in error).

it is not to be imagined the backwardness and sloth of these people, even for that which is for their own good.[1]

Godolphin, soon to face a new and untried Parliament, did not welcome these reports; ' the very Governmt. of Holland', he complained to Nottingham,

is so slow and unhinged, as I may call it, that unless they are made sensible of that this Winter, nothing can goe onn there next year, as it ought to doe.

He learnt, too, that the High Tories were making the most of popular dissatisfaction, and that there were

reflections spread abroad, of nothing being done this campaigne when the ally's have so great a superiority, which they make use of to shew the warre is carryed on in a very wrong method.[2]

Venlo surrendered on September 23rd, the garrison being alarmed by preparations by the besiegers which were in fact nothing more harmful than a *feu de joie* to celebrate the fall of Landau. By this, wrote a British officer to a correspondent at home,

you may judge what probability there was of success when we might have engaged with a superiority of number on our side; no stone walls, nor any impediment but a morass in Mr. Dopt's (Obdam's?) noddle.

The fall of Venlo was followed by the successful sieges of Roermond and Liège, in the course of which Cardonnel found much to complain of in the conduct of Coehoorn, the 'Dutch Vauban', and Marlborough himself grew increasingly critical of the eagerness of the Dutch generals, under Athlone, to put a speedy end to the campaign.[3]

On October 20th, three days before the fall of Liège, the British envoy to Hanover wrote as follows from Amsterdam:

The Earl of Marlborough has made a glorious campaigne in spite of both French and Dutch, the later of which oppos'd it more (I thinke) then the former.

The Jacobite Earl of Ailesbury, who loathed most things Dutch, thought that Marlborough had done wonders to achieve amicable coöperation in the field between English and Dutch units, 'for the

[1] Marlborough to Heinsius, 14 and 21 Aug. 1702, Everbeeck, *van 't Hoff*, pp. 23–5; Marlborough to Godolphin, 31 Aug. 1702, Asch, *Coxe*, i (1st. edn.), p. 136; Marlborough to Heinsius, 4 and (5?) Sept. 1702, Asch, *van 't Hoff*, pp. 27–9; Cardonnel to Tucker, 4 Sept. 1702, Asch, Add. Ms. 28918; *ibid.*, Cardonnel to Ellis, 11 Sept. 1702, Asch; Marlborough to Godolphin, 14 Sept. 1702, Sutendal, *Churchill*, ii, pp. 145–6.
[2] Godolphin to (Nottingham), 6 Sept. 1702, Bath, Add. Ms. 29588; Craggs to Godolphin, 10 Sept. 1702, London, *Thibaudeau*, i, p. 254.
[3] R. Pope to T. Coke, 25 Sept. 1702, Sutendal, *H. M. C. XII pt. iii*, p. 16; Marlborough to Godolphin, 28 Sept. 1702, Sutendal, *Coxe*, i (1st edn.), pp. 139–40; Cardonnel to?, 2 Oct. 1702, Sutendal, S. P. Mil. 2; Marlborough to Heinsius, 14 Oct. 1702, Camp before Liège, *van 't Hoff*, p. 35; Geldermalsen to Heinsius (extract), 14 Oct. 1702, *von Noorden*, i, pp. 264–5.

English hated the Dutch mortally ...'. For Englishmen at home, however, the successes of September and October seem to have obliterated any memory of the earlier disappointments; in published summaries of the campaign the latter were hardly mentioned. In the Republic, certainly, there were no misgivings. The Judge-Advocate Henry Watkins, in his usual racy style, reported on December 12th the way in which the end of the campaign was being celebrated at The Hague;

Every man and Woman in the Hague that has Two suits of Cloths is looking out the worst for tomorrows fireworks, and the best for the Princess of Nassaus Ball the next night in the House in the Wood. Rejoycing here is a new thing and the expence very extraordinary. If frequent occasions occurr the accustomed frugality must be practiced, or we shall be undone by Conquest.[1]

5

The war at sea occupied a special place in the hearts of all Englishmen, and from the very beginning of the war the ever increasing backwardness of the Dutch in the sphere of naval warfare was a plentiful source of irritation for many English gentlemen. At the outset there was friction over the methods which the Dutch used to man their ships. The English government complained

that English seamen were enticed from the Merchants Ships, into the States Service, and that the Masters were forced immediately to pay them their Wages,

and Stanhope was instructed to do his utmost to have this practice forbidden. At the same time there was another and more serious complaint; it was reported that the Dutch admiralties were claiming to extend their 'embargo' (that is, the taking a fifth man out of any merchant ship for their own navy) to British ships calling at Dutch ports.[2] The same sort of difficulties about differences in national usage arose when the two countries began to discuss the terms on which a 'cartel' for the exchange of prisoners made at sea could be made with France. The ministry found the Dutch reluctant to agree 'not to exchange prisoners taken at sea but in concert with us', and suspected that they were engaged in making a separate agreement with France.[3]

[1] (Cressett) to Ellis, 20 Oct. 1702, Amsterdam, Add. Ms. 28912; ibid., Watkins to Ellis, 12 Dec. 1702, Hague; Bruce, op.cit., p. 237.
[2] (Ellis?) to Stanhope (draft), 19 June 1702, Whitehall, Add. Ms. 28911; Hedges to Stanhope (copy), 23 June 1702, Whitehall, F. E. B. Holl. 69; Stanhope to Hedges, 7 July 1702, Hague, S. P. Holl. 224; Board of Trade to Hedges, 1 July 1702, Whitehall, C. S. P. Dom. Anne, i, p. 149.
[3] Stanhope to Hedges, 21 Nov. 1702 and 5 Jan. 1703, Hague, S. P. Holl. 224; ? to ?, 2 Feb. 1703, Amsterdam, S. P. Holl. 574.

While such differences as these exercised the Admiralty, Sir David Mitchell went in July 1702 as their representative to The Hague to concert the details of the campaign at sea. In this, as in all his subsequent visits, he found the Dutch admiralties exasperatingly backward in complying with the plans which he put before them. By the middle of August he was pleading with the ministry to allow him to return home, since he could see no prospect of ever obtaining from the Admiralties an answer, favourable or otherwise, to his propositions. After promising that they would provide thirty ships of the line for the joint battle fleets of the two powers, he complained, they had sent only twenty, and had thus greatly prejudiced the chances of intercepting Châteaurenault and the Spanish treasure fleet on its return from the Indies. This deficiency, he thought, was largely due to their exaggerated fears that the French admiral Pointis and his fleet might slip out of Dunkirk, and the excessive number of warships that they were consequently keeping before that port. He could, moreover, obtain no answer to the proposals he had made for the implementation of Godolphin's cherished scheme of a joint naval and military expedition to the Spanish Indies.[1]

Mitchell soon had added matter for complaint, for at the beginning of September the Dutch drew off those of their ships that had been guarding Dunkirk without taking any action to strengthen the squadron under Shovell which was to intercept Châteaurenault. As for the expedition to the West Indies, the Dutch at last agreed to provide a contingent of men and ships, but they stipulated that their expenses should be reimbursed by the Emperor. Godolphin had expected the Dutch to participate in the expedition,

both from a desire of having their share of the booty, & a jealousy of our getting any new Acquisition in those parts without them;

but he was far from pleased at the condition which they had attached to their agreement. As he saw it, to charge the Emperor with the expenses of the expedition would prejudice the right of Britain, as stated in the Treaty of Grand Alliance, to take whatever she conquered in the Spanish Indies, and thus the main incentive to such a venture would disappear. This right was never put to the test, for, owing to the half-hearted and dilatory preparations of the Dutch, the expedition

---

[1] Mitchell to Nottingham, 22 and 29 Aug. 1702, Hague, S. P. Holl. 225; Marlborough to Heinsius, 31 Aug. 1702, Asch, *van 't Hoff*, pp. 26–7; Hedges to Rooke (abstract), 21 Aug. 1702, Whitehall, *C. S. P. Dom. Anne*, i, p. 217.

never sailed.[1] It was well known in London in January 1703 that the real reason for the abandonment of the expedition was that the States had no desire to help Britain acquire colonies at Spain's expense, and considered that the men and ships involved could be employed more usefully elsewhere – to bring Portugal over to the side of the Allies, for example. L'Hermitage reported that many Englishmen agreed with this latter view, but the ministry told the Dutch in plain terms that it seemed to the queen

bien fâcheux que des accidents ayent empêché que la jonction des escadres, qui avoit ésté si bien concertée et de si bonne heure l'année passée, n'ait pu se faire plustot pour une expédition dans l'Amérique, que l'on croyoit pouvoir estre d'un plus grand avantage pour toute l'alliance ....

As Morgan has remarked,

From this time forward Anglo-Dutch recrimination, rather than co-operation, prevailed with reference to the South Sea.[2]

Meanwhile another experiment in Anglo-Dutch coöperation had met with a belated and perhaps undeserved success. A joint expedition under Ormonde and Rooke failed miserably in its primary object – the capture of Cadiz – and when the news of the failure reached The Hague it was accompanied by a letter from the Dutch admiral Almonde putting the sole blame for this fiasco on the British admirals. It was indeed common knowledge that 'there was no good understanding between our Admiral and the Dutch, nor their land officers and ours'. In the Republic Almonde's allegations were completely accepted, and Winchilsea reported that

loud exclamations, Clamours, & ill mannered reflections are made by people of all degrees (of Character not excepted), on our late miscarriage of Cadiz, and no less then a sacrifice must be made they say, to attone for the bad success of that Expedition .... and a Parliament business at least they hope to make it; perhaps not so much to have the truth enquired into, as to hinder past Enormitys of their friends from being brought to account, by the long time may be spent of this session in this affair.[3]

[1] Burchett to Warre, 12 Sept. 1702, Admiralty Office, Add. Ms. 29588; *ibid.*, (Godolphin) to Nottingham, 15 Sept. 1702, Bath; H. Elliot, *The Life of Sidney, Earl of Godolphin* (London, 1888), pp. 237–9; *C.W.* 114, p. 572.

[2] Heinsius to Marlborough, 12 Jan. 1703, Hague, *van 't Hoff*, p. 45; L'Hermitage to States-General (transcript), 15/26 Jan. 1702/3, London, Add. Ms. 17677 WWW; *ibid.*, Hedges to (Dutch ambassadors?) (transcript), 18 Jan. 1702/3, Whitehall; P. J. Welch, *The Maritime Powers and the Evolution of the War Aims of the Grand Alliance* (unpublished M. A. thesis, London, 1940), pp. 84–5; W. T. Morgan, 'The South Sea Company and the Canadian Expedition', *Hispanic American Historical Review*, viii (1928), 2, p. 151; W. T. Morgan, 'The Origins of the South Sea Company', *Political Science Quarterly*, xliv (1929), p. 21.

[3] E. Harding to G. and T. Finch, 2 Oct. 1702, Faro, *C. S. P. Dom. Anne*, ii, pp. 299–303; Dayrolle to (Ellis), 24 Oct. 1702, Hague, Add. Ms. 28912; (Winchilsea) to (Nottingham), 24 Oct.1702, Hague, Add. Ms.29588; J.S. Corbett, *England in the Mediterranean ... 1603–1713*,

Hedges, replying to Winchilsea, regretted that he had not more information concerning the disappointment at Cadiz 'for confuting the Rude discourses of the People in Holland concerning that matter', but he added, in words that speak volumes about the Tory view of the Dutch scheme of government, that

the longer your Lordship stays in that Country, and the more you are acquainted with the manners of the People the less you will wonder at their free way of expressing themselves upon all Politick occurrences.

Meanwhile the High Tories made what capital they could of the news of the failure of a plan that had originally been conceived by William III, and the *Observator*, itself sometimes critical of the late king, sprang for once to the defence of his memory, asking

Did he not Unite us to the *Dutch* in Bonds of Friendship and Interest, little Inferiour to that of a National-Union . . . . ? [1]

To the disgust of both Winchilsea and Stanhope, the news that the Spanish treasure fleet had eluded the patrolling English squadron and got safely into Vigo harbour was received with unconcealed delight by the merchants of Amsterdam, many of whom had a considerable financial interest in its cargo. This pleasure was short-lived, however, for the report quickly followed of the destruction of that fleet and the partial capture of its cargo by Ormonde's Anglo-Dutch force in Vigo Bay on October 23rd (N.S.). In his report of this triumph to the States-General Ormonde paid high tribute to the Dutch troops under his command, and at home, where some unfavourable reports had been circulating of the conduct of those troops at the taking of Port St. Mary, near Cadiz, a ballad composed to celebrate the action gave laudatory, if incidental, mention to the 'stout Hogen Mogen'.[2]

The success at Vigo gave added force to the High Tory argument that the proper way to conduct the war was by means of naval warfare and sea-borne expeditions. At the beginning of 1703 appeared a pamphlet, written by John Dennis, which was devoted to the exposition of this theme. Dennis presented a detailed plan for the conduct of an intensive war at sea, and considered various objections to the desira-

ii (London, 1904), p. 214; J. W. Fortescue, *A History of the British Army*, i (London, 1899), p. 407; *C.W.* 114, pp. 565, 567.

[1] Hedges to Winchilsea (copy), 23 Oct. 1702, Whitehall, F. E. B. Misc. 204; *Observator*, i, 58, 11 Nov. 1702.

[2] *Post Boy*, 1148, 22 Sept. 1702; (Winchilsea) to (Nottingham), 24 Oct. 1702, Hague, Add. Ms. 29588; Stanhope to Stepney, 7 Nov. 1702, Hague, Add. Ms. 7068; Ormonde to States-General (transcript), 19 Nov. 1702, London, Add. Ms. 17677 YY; 'Sailors Account of the Action at Vigo', in *Firth*.

bility of this, one of which was that 'the *Dutch* would not comply with it'. To this he replied that it as much concerned the Dutch to put an end to the war in the shortest possible time as it did us, and he added:

If this Expedient is sufficient for the ruining of the *French* Commerce, and the securing our own, why then the *Dutch* would act most unreasonably, if at a time when we so chearfully contribute, beyond what we are obliged to by antient Treaties, to their support and Assistance by Land, where their Danger is so much greater, and so much nearer than ours, they should refuse to contribute their part to our common Support at Sea, where our Concern is equal.[1]

In the early months of 1703 it seemed that the States would not need pressing to make a considerable effort at sea in the coming 'season'. From Amsterdam Nottingham's correspondent, the Reverend Dr. Cockburn, sent highly encouraging reports of that city's activities in fitting out its ships, and added that for the 'joint secret expedition' to the Mediterranean, too, they were 'working to fit out all yt can go to sea in this City'.[2] The high expectations which were entertained in London of the Dutch contribution to the sea war were, however, doomed to disappointment, and it would no doubt have been better for the temper of the English ministers if Cockburn's delusive reports had never been made.

6

The theme of Anglo-Dutch trade rivalry in the West Indies was one which was constantly being brought to the attention of the ministry throughout the war. The Dutch island of Curaçao, above all, was a peculiarly painful thorn in the flesh of the British West Indian colonies. There were long-standing complaints of illegal trade between Curaçao and the American colonies, and even directly between those colonies and the Republic itself. Both these trades were in contempt of the Navigation Acts, involved Britain in a loss of customs duty, and were highly prejudicial to the prosperity of the West Indian colonies. To prevent the direct trade between the American plantations and the Republic it was suggested at the beginning of July by the Commissioners of Trade that English consuls at Dutch ports should be empowered to search any ships that called there from the plantations; 'but', they added, with considerable understatement, 'we see that this would be very hard to carry out'.[3]

[1] *C.W.* 59, pp. 22–3.
[2] Cockburn to (Nottingham), 9 March and 10 April 1703, Hague, Add. Ms. 29588.
[3] Journal of Council of Trade, 19 May 1702, Whitehall, *C. S. P. Col.*, *1702*, pp. 328–9; Board of Trade to Hedges, 1 July 1702, Whitehall, *C. S. P. Dom. Anne*, i, p. 149.

The war made the existence of Curaçao yet more unwelcome to the West Indian planters and merchants, already concerned at the reported development of the Dutch sugar plantations in the East Indies. To the government at home they pointed out that if the commanders of naval squadrons were to continue to exercise their right of 'pressing' men their commerce would be much reduced:

.... this point absolutely ruins the whole bysyness of privateers settling here and will make them all run to Currisaw, by which the Dutch will reap the benefit from the English.

More serious still was the complaint, voiced by the governor of Jamaica, that trade between Curaçao and the Spanish Indies continued. His words show that the merchants of Jamaica were moved more by feelings of envy of their more fortunate Dutch competitors than by righteous indignation:

The Dutch from Curacao are, I understand, as busy in their Trade with the Spaniards as if there were no war, tho' it has been declared there for near a month's time. That Island is under the jurisdiction of their West India Company, and I suppose the Directors at Amsterdam give particular directions to their Governor there to be sure they must supply the Spaniard with both ammunition and provision, and I am afraid our Northern Plantations will send most of theirs thither, for if they carry on that trade, our people will meet with a better price there then at this Island, which will by that means be disfurnished. And it has been represented to me as a grievance by some of our merchants that the Dutch were suffered to trade and our hands tyed up, and truly we are no more able to live without a trade with the Spaniard then they.[1]

The receipt of this complaint prompted the Commissioners of Trade to recommend that Stanhope be instructed to press for this trade to end; but the suggestion of the Jamaica merchants that they, too, should have permission to trade with the Spaniard was not welcomed at home. On the contrary, a proclamation was issued in February formally prohibiting all trade and commerce between 'H.M.Plantations' and the French and Spaniards. As a recent writer has remarked, 'the Jamaicans, we may be sure, paid little attention to this prohibition except to protest against it'. The first protest, however, came not from Jamaica but, apparently, from merchants at home. Though approving the prohibition as far as the French were concerned, they urged that to stop all trade between the plantations and the Spaniards would be highly prejudicial to England,

for it will debar us from vending our native commodities to them for pieces of eight or other valuable goods, and this trade tho' in time of war may be and is

[1] (Selwyn) to ?, 19 June 1702, C. S. P. Col., 1702, p. 402; ibid., pp. 460-3, Beckford to Board of Trade, 10 July 1702, Jamaica; Luttrell, v, p. 196, 21 July 1702.

carryed on with the Spaniards in a private manner, besides that if such a prohibition be strictly kept to, it will throw part of the Spanish Trade into the hands of the Dutch, who have several plantations lying so near the Spanish Coast that altho' they may have a formal direction from the States General to the same effect, yet will they monopolize that trade undiscerned by us, without regard to the direction of the States General on whom 'tis well known they have little dependance when the interest of Trade prevails, in parts as remote as the West Indies.[1]

7

As Sir George Clark has said, 'almost from the first day when the English entered the war, they were occupied with their jealousy of the Dutch' on account of the open trade that continued between the Republic and France. Sir George has shown the very different postulates upon which Dutch and English based their respective attitudes to this question. The English believed that suspension of trade was an effective weapon of war, and that their 'balance of trade' with France was in any case adverse; the Dutch had a tradition of 'business as usual' in any circumstances, and of trading wherever they could regardless of any restrictive theory.[2] Whatever its academic justification, however, the peculiar intransigence of English hostility to Dutch trade with the enemy sprang to a very large extent from plain envy of the riches which the Dutch were believed to be gaining thereby. It was only in the period of intense enthusiasm for the war after Blenheim that this envy was overcome by a feeling for the solidarity of the alliance, and then, significantly enough, it began to be said and believed that their trade with the enemy was not, after all, really profitable to the Dutch.

On May 21st, 1703, both Houses of Parliament addressed the queen asking her to press the States-General to agree to a total prohibition of correspondence and commerce with France and Spain. According to Warre, who had been sounding opinion in Amsterdam, there seemed to be a good prospect that this proposal would meet with success. Amsterdam was against a free trade with France, he reported, if only because Rotterdam was for it; and, in any case, Dutch merchants who had a large stock of French merchandise on their hands would press for a prohibition of trade so as to send prices up. Stanhope, too, was of opinion that most of the provinces were for a prohibition. These

---

[1] Board of Trade to Nottingham, 2 Dec. 1702, Whitehall, *C. S. P. Col.*, *1702–3*, p. 5; *ibid.*, p. 272, 'Reasons against prohibiting trade and commerce with Spain in the West Indies', (rec'd) 18 March 1702/3; R. Bourne, *Queen Anne's Navy in the West Indies* (New Haven, 1939), p. 162.

[2] G. N. Clark, 'War Trade and Trade War, 1701–13', *Ec. H. R.*, i (1927–8), p. 269.

sanguine expectations were by no means shared by Marlborough. On June 9th he presented a memorial on this subject to the States-General, but from the first he felt little hope that anything would come of it.[1]

The States of Holland began to deliberate the question of prohibiting trade and correspondence on June 15th, and both Stanhope and Dayrolle believed that they could observe a disposition amongst them to comply with Marlborough's memorial. At home, too, the *Post Boy* announced that there was 'some likelihood' of Dutch compliance. On June 23rd, however, Stanhope sent home the first of a long series of despatches which took a far gloomier view of the prospects of success. They way in which the rumour that England was planning to reopen a 'passage of letters' between Dover and Calais had been welcomed in the Republic as a pretext for continuing their own correspondence with the enemy had convinced him that, even if the Dutch prohibited trade, they would never prevent commerce by letters.[2] As he foresaw, the States of Holland resolved, at the beginning of July, to prohibit trade with the enemy, but came to no resolution on the question of correspondence.

The question of the stoppage of correspondence was, in English eyes, a vital one. According to the contemporary annalist Boyer, the apparently indispensable assistance rendered by Dutch merchants to the French Court in paying their armies in Italy and, later, in subsidising the Elector of Bavaria, was 'the chief reason' for English insistence that the States-General should prohibit correspondence with the enemy. Therefore both Marlborough, by letter, and Stanhope, in person, continued to importune the Grand Pensionary Heinsius in this matter. Marlborough declared that Dutch failure to comply with the queen's request

will have a very ill effect in the winter .... for I find the pepel of England will presse that matter farther then I am afraid you apprehend they will.

In London, Hedges used another line of argument with the Dutch ambassadors who had come over to concert the details of the fighting alliance of Britain and the Republic, telling them that

[1] Warre to Ellis, 23 May 1702, Amsterdam, Add. Ms. 28911; Warre to Nottingham, 23 May 1702, Amsterdam, S. P. Holl. 224; *ibid.*, Stanhope to Hedges, 6 June 1702, Hague; Marlborough to States-General, 9 June 1702, Hague, *C.W.* 113, ii, p. 140; Cardonnel to (Stepney), 9 June 1702, Hague, Add. Ms. 7063; *C.W.* 114, p. 550; F. W. Wyon, *A History of Great Britain during the Reign of Queen Anne* (London, 1876), i, p. 83.

[2] Dayrolle to (Ellis), 16 June 1702, Hague, Add. Ms. 28911; Stanhope to (Stepney), 16 and 30 June 1702, Hague, Add. Ms. 7068; *Post Boy*, 1105, 9 June 1702; Stanhope to Hedges, 23 June 1702, Hague, S. P. Holl. 224.

passage of letters can signify nothing, nor be of any use unless in order to trade, designed to be clandestinely carried on ....

While Stanhope waited for the States of Holland to take this matter into consideration, he became more and more convinced that, whatever official decisions were taken, the Dutch would ignore them; 'the Dutch will trade in despight of all prohibitions', he wrote, their government not being 'masters of the People in that perticular'.[1]

The mood of the States of Holland when it met on September 13th convinced Stanhope that little would be done in the matter of correspondence, and a week later he had the melancholy pleasure of reporting that this prophecy had been proved correct. The States had merely confirmed their previous resolution to prohibit trade and the remittance of money by bills of exchange, which, as Stanhope represented to Heinsius, was quite 'insignificant .... so long as letters are suffered to pass'. It was, moreover, far from certain that the rest of the provinces would agree even to this prohibition, the opposition of Zeeland to it being particularly violent; and, indeed, as the weeks went by no progress was made in obtaining this consent. On October 24th Winchilsea wrote to Nottingham that

the Whole City of Amsterdam .... declare very openly against prohibiting Commerce with France, and do not scruple to own they will never be brought to it, on several specious counts, but the Truth is very well known, which is the profit they make by bills of exchange from France, and I am informed by a very intelligent person & knowing in the affairs of that Country, the armys of F(rance) have been furnished all this Summer that way & could not otherwise been supplyed. I must add on this subject they do not spare laughing at us for stopping the Packquet Boat on our side .... [2]

When, on December 6th (N.S.), the Austrian envoy at The Hague protested to the States-General about the payment of French troops from Amsterdam, Stanhope commented that

All that he and we and the Government here to back us can do will never be able to hinder their merchants from trading how and wherever they shall think it for their advantage.

There seemed, he thought, no reason 'why the Emperour should not indulge the same liberty to his towns that desire it', since nothing would ever be done 'in good earnest' by the Dutch to prohibit trade

[1] Marlborough to (Nottingham), 9 July 1702, Over-Asselen, S. P. Mil. 2; Stanhope to Hedges, 11 July, 11 Aug., 5 and 12 Sept. 1702, Hague, S. P. Holl. 224; Marlborough to Heinsius, 18 July 1702, Over-Asselen, *van 't Hoff*, pp. 18–19; *ibid.*, p. 22, same to same, 2 Aug. 1702, Petit Brughel; *ibid.*, p. 23, same to same, 8 Aug. 1702, Peer; Stanhope to Stepney, 12 Sept. 1702, Hague, Add. Ms. 7068; *Annals*, i, p. 172.

[2] Stanhope to Hedges, 15 and 22 Sept. 1702, Hague, S. P. Holl. 224; (Winchilsea) to (Nottingham), 24 Oct. 1702, Hague, Add. Ms. 29588.

with the enemy. A call on the Pensionary on January 1st, 1703, during which he discovered that three provinces had still not consented to agree to the resolution that Holland had taken, confirmed him in his belief that

whatever the Provinces or States Generall may resolve they will never be able to hinder their people from trading where there is any hopes of gaine.

All he could do was to continue his representations; on January 6th, for example, he presented a memorial complaining that Dutch Ministers

do not joyn with her Matie's in the severall Courts where they are imployed, in pressing the prohibition of commerce with france and Spaine, but seem rather for a neutrality in that point . . . .

This memorial, he thought, like that of the Austrian envoy complaining that French agents were buying or hiring Dutch ships, was 'like to be as well executed as the rest that are or shall be made to restrain their commerce'.[1]

The House of Commons which met in November 1702 was not one likely to view with complacency the little progress that had been made in this affair since Marlborough had presented his original memorial. If commercial rivalry was no longer a ruling passion it was still far from dead, and the Tories least of all could be expected to acquiesce in the retention by the Republic of advantages from which England had voluntarily cut herself off; we need not talk, with Wyon, of 'the pressure of the mercantile influence' in order to explain their attitude. Marlborough, indeed, assured the Dutch ambassadors in London that the whole nation was so intent upon the prohibition as to be deaf to all argument. The chance of the Commons came on January 4th, when the queen, after many appeals from the States, finally recommended to the House a Dutch request, originally made on November 27th (N.S.), for an augmentation of the army in the Low Countries. This request had the wholehearted support of Marlborough, who, on December 4th (N.S.), had assured Heinsius that

if wee can't be much stronger this next campagne, then wee were in this last, the great endeavors now used in France must make it a very fatall campagne to the Allyes.[2]

---

[1] Stanhope to Hedges, 8 Dec. 1702, 2, 5 and 9 Jan. 1703, Hague, S. P. Holl. 224; Stanhope to Stepney, 29 Dec. 1702, Hague, Add. Ms. 7068; Stanhope to States-General, 6 Jan. 1703, (N.S.), *C.W.* 113, ii, p. 308.

[2] Marlborough to Heinsius, 4 Dec. 1702, Briel, *van 't Hoff*, pp. 38–9; Stanhope to States-General, 5 Dec. 1702 (N.S.), *C.W.* 113, ii, pp. 284–5; *ibid.*, ii, pp. 285–6, Hedges to Dutch ambassadors, 3 Dec. 1702, Whitehall; Report of Dutch ambasadors, 9 Jan. 1703 (N.S.), *von Noorden*, i, pp. 298–303; Wyon, *op.cit.*, i, p. 147.

The House's reply expressed 'the greatest Regard' for the 'interest
and preservation' of the States, but insisted, as Marlborough had
foreseen, that England should not be charged with the pay of any
additional troops until the Dutch agreed to

an immediate stop of all posts, and of all letters, bills, and all other correspondence with France and Spain . . . .

In a long debate the Whigs did their best to prevent this stipulation
being madei ;n their view it arose from ill-feeling towards the Dutch
or even from something worse. Burnet summed up their feelings:

The manner in which it was managed shewed a very ill disposition towards the
Dutch; and in the debate they were treated very indecently . . . . some seemed to
hope, that the opposition which would be raised on this head might force a peace,
at which many among us were driving so indecently, that they took little care
to conceal it.[1]

The Whigs tried once more to remove the offending condition when,
on January 7th, the reply to the queen's message was finally approved.
A motion to this effect was rejected by only 193 votes to 122, as
compared to the majority of almost two to one when the proposed
reply had been framed three days earlier. There had evidently been
some second thoughts among the more moderate Tories; as L'Hermitage remarked on the following day

quelques uns qui avoient eu mardy le plus d'empressement à y faire mettre la
clause, n'estoient pas hier de cet avis.[2]

The ministry hastened to make the most of the Commons' vote.
Marlborough, who seems to have been confident that the Dutch would
now comply, presented the demand to Heinsius as a warning that

the whole bent of the nation is soe possest of the necessity of forbidding all
commerce with France and Spain, that I tremble when I think of the consequences that may happen, if this should occation any coldness betwine England
and Holland.

Hedges did not wait for the opinion of the Lords (who, on January
9th, fell in with the views of the Commons) in order to point out to
Stanhope

how ill the consequence will be if the States should not heartily and Thankfully
Close with this Proposition since all England is convinced of the necessity of it
and that it is as much their Concern as Ours if they do not regard the Particular

---

[1] Marlborough to Heinsius, 30 Dec. 1702 (O.S.), *van 't Hoff*, p. 44; L'Hermitage to States-
General (transcript), 5/16. Jan. 1702/3, London, Add. Ms. 17677 WWW; *Cobbett*, vi, cols. 96–
7; Clark, 'War Trade and Trade War', p. 271; *C.W.* 18, v, pp. 48–9.

[2] *Luttrell*, v, p. 255, 7 Jan. 1702/3; L'Hermitage to States-General (transcript), 8/19 Jan.
1702/3, London, Add. Ms. 17677 WWW.

Advantages of Private men and the filthy lucre of a Pernicious Trade more than the safety of their own Country and their reducing France to Honble terms of Peace.[1]

It was on January 22nd (N.S.) that the news of the Commons' decision arrived at The Hague, where, according to Stanhope, it occasioned 'a great ferment'. ''Tis probable they may comply', he added, 'but how honestly their Merchants will execute is another question'. Dayrolle reported that the general opinion was that Amsterdam would give in to the new demand, but ten days later Stanhope, who had formally communicated the British terms to the States-General on January 27th, found that it was, in fact, only the violent opposition of Amsterdam that was preventing the speedy acquiescence of all the Provinces. He hoped that 'the necessity of their affairs' would bring them over, though there was, he reported,

an idle discourse in town here, as if Amsterdam would rather charge themselves with the ten thousand men, than consent to the stoppage of letters.

'Their gain by that commerce', he commented, 'must be thought very considerable, or such a thought would never have come into people's heads'. The States of Holland took up this matter once more in the first week of February, and on the 9th of that month Dayrolle reported that all the other provinces (except Utrecht, which had already agreed to the queen's stipulation) were waiting to follow Holland's lead, but that the attitude of Amsterdam made a satisfactory resolution from Holland unlikely. Three days later he was somewhat more hopeful, though Amsterdam was much divided on the question and influenced by the rumour that the English were planning to rob her of her trade.[2]

In England, according to L'Hermitage, confidence persisted that the Dutch would comply with the queen's demand. This confidence owed nothing to the reports to Nottingham and Hedges of Cockburn, minister to the Anglican community at Amsterdam. As late as April 10th (N.S.) he wrote

That of breaking off Commerce and Correspondence can't go down, all grin and fret at it.

Even if commerce were to be prohibited, he added, there were

---

[1] Marlborough to Dopff, 5 Jan. 1702/3, St James', *Murray*, i, p. 66; Marlborough to Heinsius, 5 Jan. 1702/3, *van 't Hoff*, p. 46; Hedges to Stanhope (copy), 8 Jan. 1702/3, Whitehall, F. E. B. Holl. 69; L'Hermitage to States-General (transcript), 12/23 Jan. 1702/3, London, Add. Ms. 17677 WWW.

[2] Stanhope to Stepney, 23 Jan. 1703, Hague, Add. Ms. 7069; Dayrolle to (Ellis), 23 Jan., 9 and 12 Feb. 1703, Hague, Add. Ms. 28913; Stanhope to State-General, 27 Jan. 1703, *C.W.* 113, ii, pp. 310–11; Stanhope to Hedges, 2 Feb. 1703, Hague, S. P. Holl. 224.

ways and means Concerted to Elude it, by employing Danish and Swedish Vessels and ye like which I beleive will be wink'd at in favour of ye Merchts. Could you send out a Sufficient number of ships to scour ye seas, to watch and examine ye ships which go to & come from France, 'twill be of more use to stop Commerce and straiten France than all prohibitions.

There were some grounds for Cockburn's suspicions, for the ministry had already been informed that it was a common practice of Swedish and Danish ships coming from France to arrange to be 'captured' by Dutch privateers and thus have their cargo sold openly as 'prize'. None the less, for all his gloomy predictions, Cockburn was quite mistaken in asserting that the Dutch would not impose a prohibition of trade and correspondence. Their reluctance to do so was outweighed by their desire for the projected augmentation, and at the beginning of April a convention was made between the queen, the Emperor and the States-General naming June 1st as the day on which would begin a prohibition for one year of all trade and correspondence with the enemy, except in all products of Spanish possessions outside Europe and in articles needed for Dutch manufacture.[1]

Cockburn was taken aback by the news that the agreement had been reached, but he continued to send home pessimistic forecasts of its outcome. 'In my judgment 'twill turn to nothing', he wrote on May 1st, since the Dutch would claim that their performance of its terms was conditional on their execution by all the Imperial territories, above all Hamburg. Ten days later he reported that the news of French successes on the upper Rhine had so alarmed Dutch merchants that they were now most unlikely to submit to any prohibition whatsoever. He emphasised, too, that the prohibition had been agreed to 'only to please ye English', since the Dutch were still unconvinced that their trading with the enemy was any prejudice to the common cause.[2]

Once more contrary to Cockburn's expectations the States-General issued, towards the end of May, decrees putting into execution the agreement made with the queen and Emperor. Stanhope, however, writing to Stepney on May 22nd, displayed an undiminished scepticism as to

[1] T. Johnson to R. Norris, 14 Jan. 1702/3, London, *Norris Papers*, pp. 121–2; ? to ?, 2 Feb. 1703, Amsterdam, S. P. Holl. 574; Burchett to Warre, 30 Jan. 1702/3, Admiralty Office, *C. S. P. Dom. Anne*, i, p. 563; L'Hermitage to States-General (transcript), 5/16 Feb. 1702/3, London, Add. Ms.. 17677 WWW; Cockburn to (Hedges?), 10 April 1703 (N.S.), S.P. Holl. 225; (Cockburn) to (Nottingham), 10 April 1703 (N.S.), Add. Ms. 29588; 'The substance of a conference ... at St. James's 5 Apr. 1703', Lansdowne Ms. 849; Clark, 'War Trade and Trade War', pp. 271–2.
[2] Cockburn to (Nottingham), 17 April, 1, 11 and 15 May 1703, Amsterdam, Add. Ms. 29588.

the ability of the States to enforce the performance of its decrees. 'To tell you my thoughts plainly', he wrote,

I fear it will be very scurvily executed and a thousand tricks found out to elude it, but that is nothing to you or me; if it satisfy the Parliam:t all will be well.

Whether or not the one-year prohibition which came into force in the Dutch Republic, as planned, on June 1st, was likely to satisfy the Parliament, the lugubrious Dr. Cockburn felt little joy at its beginning. He felt even less in the days that followed, for, as he wrote to Hedges on June 15th,

The Interruption of Trade which was never here before is so grievous and so hard upon particulars, yt I'm confident t'will incline all to end ye warre as soon as possible, & perhaps to accept of any peace. If ye warre continue long in these terms, t'will bring ym very low, and they yt are low are apt to be tempted.[1]

If, as Burnet believed, some Tories had insisted on Dutch acceptance of the prohibition of trade and correspondence with the enemy in the hope of breaking up the alliance, it began to seem as if their desires might be gratified – unless a change in British opinion made possible an alteration in the 'terms' of the war.

---

[1] Stanhope to Stepney, 22 May 1703, Hague, Add. Ms. 7069; Cockburn to (Hedges?), 15 June 1703 (N.S.), S.P. Holl. 225.

CHAPTER III

THE HIGH TORY MENACE
⟨1703–4⟩

I

William III had done much to foster a measure of unity among the
various Tory groups, in that while he lived all Tories could join in
opposition, open or tacit, to him, his policies and his favourites. After
his death, however, the fundamental divisions between High Tories
and 'moderates' became more and more apparent. Above all there was
the conflict within the ministry between the advocates of a continental
land-war and the champions of a 'blue-water' strategy, a conflict
which was inevitably reflected in a difference of attitudes towards the
Dutch alliance. If the High Tories had had their way, the Dutch, to
them the traditional rivals, if not enemies, of England, would have
been allies in name only. In war their aim was freedom from continental
entanglements, and of all entanglements they welcomed least those
that bound them to the antimonarchical, Erastian and upstart
Republic. In this they were worlds removed from the 'moderates',
above all from Marlborough, who was convinced that the keystone
of the Grand Alliance was Anglo-Dutch solidarity, and that this could
be achieved and maintained only by the closest coöperation and
mutual confidence. This conviction, in turn, had a marked effect on
the attitude of the 'moderate' Tories towards domestic affairs. For
them the overriding test of any measure was now whether it would aid
or harm the prosecution of the war. They favoured in principle the
Bill for the suppression of Occasional Conformity, but they began to
turn against the measure when they saw that its passage would lead
to schism at home and distrust abroad. Similarly, they believed that
England still had many bones to pick with the Dutch Republic, but
were convinced that such matters should be allowed to sleep until the
war was won. The High Tories, on the other hand, less convinced of
the necessity of the war and, in any case, caring nothing for the effects
of their actions on their allies, possessed few such inhibitions.

In the first two years of Anne's reign the High Tories were well represented in her ministry, and what is remarkable is how little, rather than how much, they were able to do in this time to put their views into practice. The reason for this was, of course, that the queen, though by nature a High Tory in almost every other way, subscribed to the 'moderate' views on the war and the Dutch alliance. Most of her High Tory ministers recognised this and made some attempt to adapt themselves to it for fear of losing the royal favour; only the queen's uncle, Rochester, was from the outset openly defiant of the supremacy of the two apostles of the 'moderate' Tory war policy, Marlborough and Godolphin, with the result that in February 1703 he was forced to quit the ministry.

In 1702 and 1703, then, the war policy of William III and Marlborough was in the ascendant. The successes of 1702 were not sufficient, however, to awaken any real enthusiasm for the war in England, and the disasters, disappointments and vexations of 1703, as we shall now see, threatened to turn public opinion, if not completely against the war, then at least in favour of the attenuated strategy advocated from within the ministry by Nottingham. The misfortunes of 1703, and especially those imputed to the negligence or backwardness of the Dutch, emboldened Nottingham and his followers to come out more openly in favour of a different method of waging the war. Marlborough was in a thoroughly awkward position. He, too, was far from satisfied with the conduct of the Dutch, but he was at least convinced that they were making the greatest effort that their resources would allow, and he was not the man to change his basic beliefs about the conduct of the war merely because he had been disobliged by some Dutch generals. He had, then, together with Godolphin, to withstand the increasing pressure which the High Tories were placing upon him to make a drastic alteration in the conduct of the war. This was no easy task since, with a House of Commons as then constituted, the Treasurer and the General were in no position, without some striking success in vindication of their policy, to bid defiance to the 'High Fliers'. The queen, it was true, was still behind them, but they could not be sure how far she would go in support of their policies. She could not be altogether unheedful of public opinion if it spoke clearly and unmistakably; she had, after all, no desire to go the way of her grandfather or, for that matter, of her father. Thus, throughout 1703 and 1704, the most important question in English politics was whether events would win the support of their fellow-countrymen – hitherto given somewhat apathetically to the 'moderate' war policy – for the

High Tories and their extra-European strategy. By April 1704 the cleavage within the ministry could no longer be ignored, and the queen was forced to make a choice between her servants; but the resulting removal of Nottingham and his followers from the Cabinet did not solve the problems of Marlborough and Godolphin. The High Tories, without the responsibility of office, were now free to hound the ministers, and could look forward to the next session of Parliament with high hopes of at last achieving that power in the state which they had expected to receive in 1702.

2

In the spring of 1703 the English envoy Stanhope found that affairs in the Dutch Republic wore an aspect that did not augur well for the success of the war against France. 'The disorders .... in these Provinces between the Royalists and Republicans about chooseing and deposing their Magistrates', he reported, were increasing daily, and in Zeeland had even resulted in insurrection. 'It seems', he added, 'as if it was onely the present warr that keeps them together from cutting one anothers throats'; but how long they would stay in 'the present warr' was itself dubious. The Swedish minister at The Hague was said to have made peace overtures on behalf of France, and Stanhope feared that if his reported offers were genuine, they 'might be a dangerous temptation to the Rabble of this Government, who begin to be impatient under their present pressures'. The government was in any case in a chaotic state, he declared, and in the army things were no better; the generals were incapable of taking a 'fixed and Steddy' resolution, and what they did one day they undid the next.[1]

Stanhope's views on the state of the Republic at the outset of the campaign of 1703 were fully shared by Marlborough, who was concerned not only about the difficulties in which this might involve him but also about the use that would be made of any such difficulties by his High Tory colleagues at home. If any shortcomings of the Dutch, he wrote to his wife on June 10th,

should produce a coldness between England and Holland, France would then gain their point .... we should not only lose our liberty, but our religion also must be forced....

[1] Stanhope to Hedges, 16 March and 27 April 1703, Hague, S.P. Holl. 224; Stanhope to Stepney, 24 and 27 April 1703, Hague, Add. Ms. 7069.

This, he declared, was precisely what Rochester and his friends were hoping to achieve:

.... if they can once be strong enough to declare which way the war shall be managed, they may ruin England and Holland at their pleasure, and I am afraid may do it in such a manner as may not at first be unpopular; so that the people may be undone before they can see it.[1]

Such fears were to continue to possess Marlborough throughout the campaign, and to grow as he learnt from home of the use that the High Tories were making of the conduct of the Dutch.

What was particularly exercising Marlborough at the beginning of June was Dutch backwardness in a sphere in which the High Tories were especially sensitive to any mismanagement, naval warfare. His apprehensions were justified, for the unfortunate story of the Mediterranean fleet in 1703 aroused feeling in England and indignation in the breasts of Nottingham and his friends. The intention of Britain and the Dutch was to send a joint fleet to the Mediterranean in the hope of taking Naples for the Emperor, but from mid-April onwards it became apparent that the Dutch ships would not be ready at the desired time. While Stanhope prodded at The Hague and Stepney grumbled from Vienna, impatience grew at home at the continued failure of the twelve Dutch men-of-war to arrive.[2] At the beginning of June Marlborough received a letter from Nottingham on this subject by which he was convinced that there would 'be an ill use made this winter of the Dutch ships coming so late'.[3]

On June 15th Stanhope presented a memorial on this subject to the States-General which did not mince matters. The English ships, he pointed out, had now been waiting at Spithead more than six weeks for the Dutch squadron to arrive, and this despite the fact that at no time had the winds been unfavourable for their passage. It appears that the squadron had already sailed for its rendezvous with the English when this memorial was presented, but it was in any case now too late for the joint fleet under Shovell to do much more than 'show the flag' along the coast of Italy and prevent the French Toulon fleet from sailing. In Amsterdam Dr. Cockburn was told that the reason for the

---

[1] Marlborough to Sarah, 10 June 1703, Hanef, *Coxe*, i, p. 134.

[2] Stanhope to Hedges, 27 April 1703, Hague, S.P. Holl. 224; Marlborough to Heinsius, 10 May 1703, Camp before Bonn, *van 't Hoff*, pp. 66–7; Stepney to Shrewsbury, 12 May 1703, Vienna, *H. M. C. Buccleuch II pt. ii*, pp. 654–6; Marlborough to Heinsius, 21 May 1703, Maestricht, *van 't Hoff*, p. 69; L'Hermitage to States-General (transcript), 14/25 May 1703, London, Add. Ms. 17677 WWW (dated in error '14/25 Mars').

[3] Marlborough to Heinsius, 2 and 5 June 1703, Thys, *van 't Hoff*, pp. 72–3; Marlborough to Godolphin, 11 June 1703 (N.S.), *Coxe*, i (1st edn.), p. 201.

long delay had been the difficulty of manning the ships, but in his opinion there might be other and perhaps deeper causes. These he explained in a letter to Nottingham of June 26th:

How ye States Counsels & measures appear to you I know not, but I have observ'd ym this year a little heavy, & without yt vigour which ye present war seems to require, whether it be because ye Members of ye States are not well united among ymselves, or not so skilfull in management being formerly only Tooles to act as ye Stath——r directed, or a little diffident of ye English, or afraid to forward their designs as may be not so much for their own Interest tho they are not willing to have yt suspected, or yet their funds are failing, or afraid to drain ym, not having now ye Spaniard to reckon with as before, whom they us'd to charge with ye Expences of flanders tho t'was for their own defence, neither expecting secret or Extraordinary assistance as lately. Which of these or whether something of each may occasion a Retardment, I leave to your Lordship's better judgement.[1]

The recriminations of the English ministry at the delay of the Dutch in sending their squadron lasted long after those ships had sailed. Hedges continued to send vehement protests to Stanhope at the way in which, in Stanhope's own words,

They have most shamefully failed us in their quota of Shipping this Summer which was to be 40 of Line and 12 ffrigates, of which 36 great Shipps to joyne with ours; whereof they have only sent us 18, nor have they above 24 more in condition, 12 whereof are gone Northward to meet their East India men, and the other 12 before Zeeland Dunkirk and Ostend.

Not content with Stanhope's representations, the ministry instructed Richard Hill, the new envoy to Savoy, to inform the Dutch leaders, while he was at The Hague,

how prejudicial it has been to us, and even to the States themselves, as well as to the common cause, that they have not sent us their quota of ships, or that the ships sent have not come in due time for the performance of those services which have hitherto been resolved on . . . .

While such reproaches poured from the ministry, however, the Whig *Observator* lavished praise on four Dutch warships, which, though heavily outnumbered, had fought Pointis' squadron to the finish in order to save a Dutch fishing fleet. Tutchin drew some pointed comparisons between this and the recent conduct of English sea-captains. 'The *Dutch* Sea Commanders', he declared,

are strange Creatures, they lye always in the way to have their Bones broken: I could advise 'em to some People who would soon Learn 'em how to save their Ships and teach 'em how to sleep in a whole Skin. [2]

[1] Cockburn to (Hedges?), 15 June 1703 (N.S.), S. P. Holl. 225; Stanhope to (Fagel) (transcript), 16 June 1703, Hague, Add. Ms. 17677 WWW; Cockburn to (Nottingham), 26 June 1703 (N.S.), Add. Ms. 29588; Corbett, *op.cit.*, ii, p. 233.
[2] *Observator*, ii, 24 and 25, 30 June and 3 July 1703; Stanhope to Stepney, 17 July 1703,

A hitch in the negotiations with Savoy made Hill's stay at The Hague unexpectedly long, and during it he was entrusted with the preliminary negotiations with the Dutch Admiralties of the naval quotas for 1704. At first he was highly doubtful of the usefulness of such negotiations, but by September 11th he was of opinion that

the great losses which they have suffered this year from these (Dunkirk) pirates, and the rage which the people here are in against them, and against their own Admiralties for it, will dispose them to come into any good measures for the future.

Cockburn confirmed that the news of the burning of the Greenland fishing fleet by the French had raised 'a grumbling in all against ye management of sea affairs', and added that it was commonly said that the Admiralties were 'penny wise but pound fool'. Nottingham, however, was not to be mollified with assurances of good behaviour for the future; in the instructions that he sent to Hill on October 19th can be detected considerable bitterness and perhaps a determination to demonstrate the unworkability of Marlborough's war policy:

You know that what we shall be able to set out will depend very much upon the condition in which Sir Cloudesley Shovel and Graydon's squadrons shall be at their return; and if we should not be able to fit out so many as our proportion of the whole, that shall be needful, amounts to, the States, instead of objecting any deficiency on our part after their own failure this year, should rather exceed their proportion, if it be necessary for their defence, since we have no army to defend us, and they have all ours in their service.

Small wonder that, receiving such letters, Hill should have written to Marlborough to warn him that the Dutch deficiences in 1703 at sea would 'give occasion to somebody or other to make a noise in the winter'.[1]

3

Hill's main task during his protracted stay at The Hague did not concern the war at sea. It was to join with Stanhope in reaching agreement with the Dutch leaders about the terms on which the Grand Alliance might be enlarged by the addition of Portugal and Savoy. There was no difference of principle here between English and Dutch;

Hague, Add. Ms. 7069; Hedges to Stanhope (copy), 6 July 1703, Whitehall, F. E. B. Holl. 69; Instructions for Hill, 26 July 1703, Windsor, *Hill Corres.*, i, p. 3.

[1] Hill to Marlborough, 5 Sept. 1703, Hague, *Hill Corres.*, i, pp. 255-6; Cockburn to (Nottingham), 7 Sept. 1703 (N.S.), Add. Ms. 29589; Hill to Nottingham, 7 and 11 Sept. 1703, Hague, *Hill Corres.*, i, pp. 256-8, 262-4; *ibid.*, i, pp. 44-7, Nottingham to Hill, 19 Oct. 1703, Whitehall.

the only real disagreements were as to method. The Dutch leaders did not shrink in the least from the broadening of the aims of the Alliance which such additional engagements would inevitably involve, but they were determined not to commit the Republic to provide more additional money and men than its resources would allow.[1] That this was the basis of their attitude to these negotiations was evident to Hill and Stanhope, but others outside the Republic tended to read a deeper meaning into their hesitations and bargainings; and once more we find Nottingham apparently doing his utmost to fan the flames of dissension between England and the Dutch.

While John and Paul Methuen negotiated in Lisbon to bring Portugal into the Grand Alliance, the Dutch Ambassador Schonenberg also treated for an alliance between his country and the Portuguese. At the beginning of May Stanhope learned that there were only two obstacles to agreement between Portugal and the Dutch; an old claim of the Dutch West Indies Company and the demand of the Portuguese for freedom for their priests to exercise their religion in Cochin. With that complete conviction of the utter materialism of the Dutch so typical of Englishmen of his time, Stanhope remarked that

the first being a matter of interest, it will be hard to make the Dutch recede from, but I do not take them to be so straight laced in Religion as to break off on account of the second.

It was not until June that details arrived of the draft Treaty of Alliance concluded on May 16th at Lisbon between the queen, the king of Portugal, the Emperor and the States-General. By this the Allies agreed to recognise the Archduke Charles of Austria as king of Spain, and to send to the aid of Portugal 12,000 troops, of which Nottingham, who would gladly have seen the main theatre of war removed from Flanders to the Iberian peninsula, lost no time in pressing the Dutch to provide their share.[2]

From the outset difficulties arose about the performance of the still unratified Treaty. Marlborough foresaw that the Dutch would not take kindly to the suggestion that the English quota of troops should be taken from the queen's army in Flanders, and Stanhope privately

[1] This point is well made in Welch, *op.cit.*, pp. 122-3; and see also I. F. Burton, 'The Supply of Infantry for the War in the Peninsula, 1703-1707', *Bulletin of the Institute of Historical Research*, xxviii (1955), p. 40. The view that the Dutch 'naturally hated' the commitment to obtain the entire Spanish monarchy for the Habsburgs still has its adherents, notably Dr. Maurice Ashley, who has recently reasserted it (M. Ashley, *Marlborough* (London, 1939), p. 46, and *England in the Seventeenth Century* (London, 1952), p. 197).

[2] Stanhope to Stepney, 1 and 8 May 1703, Hague, Add. Ms. 7069; Marlborough to Nottingham, 14 June 1703, Hanef, *Murray*, i, pp. 117-8.

sympathised with the Dutch dislike of this proposal. Even Marlborough however, did not guess how unacceptable to the Dutch would be the English assumption that they would provide half of the quota due from the Emperor. In answer to Stanhope's memorial of June 16th urging them to a speedy fulfilment of their obligations they made it clear that they had no intention of joining with England in performing the Emperor's duties for him. They told him that their resources would no longer allow them to go on making augmentations and additional expenses on a basis of equality with the queen; this Stanhope believed, but he was not confident that it would meet with a favourable reception at home. Marlborough was quite sure that it would not; his alarm at the use that the High Tories might make of this latest development can be seen in his letter to Stanhope of June 23rd, in which he declared how 'concerned and surprised' he was at the news, and

how ill it will be relished in England, especially at this juncture, when everybody is so much out of humour at the great disappointment we have long laboured under for want of their Mediterranean squadron, and while it concerns us all so very much that they should not be actually providing their quota. . . . [1]

Marlborough did not misjudge the reception which his colleagues at home would accord to the news. Hedges sent strong protests through both Vrijbergen, the Dutch envoy in London, and Stanhope; to the latter he indicated what the results of Dutch obstinacy in this matter might be:

It is not to be doubted but upon Second thoughts they will consider what very ill consequences such a Proposall may produce, and especially when the Parliament meets, for it will infallibly putt them upon making very strict inquiries, and particularly how the States have complyed with their Quota of the Land Forces as well as those of the Sea.

The Dutch leaders, Stanhope found, were 'perplexed' by this reply, but nothing that he could say would convince them that the queen was 'throughly resolved' not to take upon herself the sole responsibility for providing the Emperor's quota. Though representatives of the Admiralties met to discuss what would be necessary for the expedition which was to take the Archduke Charles to Portugal, Stanhope reported that the English reply had brought all preparations to a standstill, nor, he wrote on July 17th, had a single province yet ratified the Treaty. He confided in Stepney his sympathy with their attitude

[1] Stanhope to Cardonnel (copy), 16 June 1703, Hague, Stowe Ms. 244; Stanhope to (Fagel) (transcript), 16 June 1703, Hague, Add. Ms. 17677 WWW; Stanhope to Stepney, 19 June 1703, Hague, Add. Ms. 7069; Marlborough to Stanhope, 23 June 1703, Hanef, *Murray*, i, p. 123; Marlborough to Heinsius, 25 June 1703, Hanef, *van 't Hoff*, p. 77.

to what was being asked of them; ''t is certain they are very poor', he wrote, 'and lye under great difficulties to find money'.[1]

Stanhope discovered that the Dutch ambassador in Lisbon had in fact entered into no agreement to supply half the Emperor's quota, as he was alleged to have done, but he found himself unable to convince his superiors of this. Their determination not to give way in their demand was expressed in the instructions given to Hill on July 26th (O.S.). On his arrival at The Hague Hill found that not only was there no prospect of the Dutch submitting, but also that they were now determined that all future augmentations should be on the basis of the Queen's two-thirds to their third. The ratification of the Treaty by the States-General, reported by Stanhope on August 28th, brought the solution of this problem no nearer. All his endeavours, Stanhope warned Hedges, were doomed to failure, since they grew 'daily more obstinatly resolved', and Hill found that all he could get from the Dutch leaders was 'ultra posse non est obligatio'. 'I must add, my Lord', he wrote to Godolphin on August 28th,

that they have almost convinced me of their inability to do much more than they now do. I must also observe a great change in their ways of doing business here: when the Stadtholder had convinced the Pensioner a thing was done. The Pensioner takes nothing now upon himself, and there is great difficulty to convince seven Provinces, who are obliged to the King of France for all the union that is left in these countries .... [2]

To such pessimistic reports Hedges replied in terms that revealed once more the preoccupation of the ministry with the coming session of Parliament. 'I do not find', he wrote to Hill on August 19th,

any disposition here to send you any new orders for the Pensioner, neither can I hope yt greater advances should be made on this side, since I am afraid it will do neither ye States nor us any service, when wee meet at Westminster next Winter.

These apprehensions were fully shared by Marlborough who expressed them four days later in a letter to Heinsius:

It gives mee great trouble to see the business of Portugal goe as itt does, for I forsee that some who doe not wish well, will be able to make an ill use of itt, I mean in England.

[1] Hedges to Stanhope (copy), 15 June 1703, Whitehall, F. E. B. Holl. 71; Hedges to (Vrijbergen) (transcript), 18 June 1703, Whitehall, Add. Ms. 17677 WWW; Dayrolle to (Ellis), 29 June 1703, Hague, Add. Ms. 28914; Stanhope to Marlborough (copy), ? June 1703, Hague, Stowe Ms. 244; Stanhope to Stepney, 3 and 17 July, Hague, Add. Ms. 7069.
[2] Instructions for Hill, 26 July 1703, Windsor, *Hill Corres.*, i, p. 3; Stanhope to Stepney, 14 Aug. 1703, Hague, Add. Ms. 7069; Hill to Nottingham, 24 Aug. 1703, Hague, *Hill Corres.*, i, pp. 241-4; *ibid.*, i, pp. 247-8, Hill to Godolphin, 28 Aug. 1703, Hague; Stanhope to Blathwayt, 28 Aug. 1703, Hague, Add. Ms. 41683; Stanhope to Hedges, 28 Aug. 1703, Hague, S. P. Holl. 224.

The ministers, moreover, were ill pleased with the insistence of the Dutch that should provide no more ships for the Portugal expedition than they were obliged to by the usual proportion of five English ships to three Dutch. 'It is wonderful', wrote Nottingham to Hill on August 20th (O.S.) at Godolphin's prompting, 'that they can insist upon the proportion of 5 to 3 from Portugal, and forget the Mediterranean squadron'.[1]

None the less, Hill's representations of the powerlessness of the Dutch to do more were beginning to have their effect on most of the ministers. On August 31st, for example, he reported that they would 'take it unkindly if they are pressed much farther'; to embroil ourselves with the Dutch on this question, he added, would be particularly unfortunate, since they were now

wonderfully satisfied with our Queen, and with her administration, and a little industry will not put them out of conceit with her ministry.

Four days later he assured Nottingham that lack of funds was the reason for the States' continuing backwardness in naval matters, and that, far from being able to make up part of the Emperor's quota, they had not even 'the funds ready for the execution of their own third'. He was confident, however, that they would provide this 'very honestly, though not so soon as you could wish', and added that

When the affairs are once engaged in Portugal, either good or bad success there may oblige the States to more vigorous resolutions. I think at present they are not so sanguine upon this expedition as our people in England are; either because their genius and temper are less lively and less fond of new and bold designs; or because they are less accustomed to carry on a war at that distance and pay their troops by bills of exchange, or because they are fearful of weakening themselves at home whilst so powerful an enemy is at their frontiers; or because they do not look upon this Portugal enterprise as their own design, being drawn into it, as they say sometimes, in a great measure, out of complaisance to the Queen.

Hill's warning words against pressing the Dutch too far went home. Marlborough had long sympathised with Dutch opposition to Nottingham's plan to draw men for Portugal from the armies in the Low Countries, and Godolphin began to be anxious for the fate in the Republic of the project for including Savoy in the Alliance if the current dissension continued. Hedges was ordered, at the beginning of September (O.S.), to instruct Hill 'not to make them uneasy, since it can

---

[1] Godolphin to (Nottingham), 3 Aug. 1703, Windsor, Add. Ms. 29589; Hedges to Hill (copy), 19 Aug. 1703, Bath, F. E. B. Misc. 204; Nottingham to Hill, 20 Aug. 1703, Whitehall, *Hill Corres.*, i, pp. 16–17; Marlborough to Heinsius, 3 Sept. 1703, Val Notre Dame, *van 't Hoff*, pp. 89–90.

have no good effect', and from a letter that he wrote to Nottingham on September 4th it seems probable that he no longer saw eye to eye with his patron and fellow-Secretary on the desirability of insisting further. 'I will not pretend', he wrote,

to answer your Ldps reasonings concerning ye Emperors quota for Portugall, but I am perswaded ye dutch either cannot or will not advance any part of it, & of ye two evills, I think ye least is rather to charge ye nation with it, then to have ye loss of ye Treaty imputed to us.[1]

Stanhope, too, pointed out to his masters that the Republic was suffering from a lack of 'both money and credit, beyond what you can imagine in England'. It was to this, he emphasised, that was largely due the backwardness of the States' naval preparations for the Portugal expedition, though he did not know to what to ascribe the reluctance of many army officers to take part in it. He did not fail to observe the gradual change of heart of his own government, and as early as September 6th (N.S.), he wrote to Stepney that

rather than loose the Treaty, I have some reasons to believe the Queen will take it all upon herself, and deduct it another year from the Succours she sends into this country, which will be very reasonable, since experience shows they will suffer no disadvantage to be made of the great superiority we have this year over ye Ennemy.

Stanhope was not mistaken; on September 23rd he was able to tell Heinsius of the Queen's resolution to pay for the whole of the Emperor's quota. Two days later he wrote to Stepney of the great difference that this message had already made to the diligence with which the Dutch were preparing for the expedition. A few days before he had been told that they would not be ready until the end of October, but now he was assured that all preparations would be completed by the middle of that month. There was no doubt, he declared, that 'want of money' had been 'the reall cause' of their backwardness, but on September 28th he was able to inform Stepney that

they have given out money sufficient to their Admiralties, who have set all hands at worke, and where there is money, a great deal of buisness is done in a short time in Holland.[2]

Stepney, meanwhile, was becoming more and more irritated at the

[1] Marlborough to Heinsius, 29 May 1703, 'Vhoign', *van 't Hoff*, pp. 71–2; Marlborough to Hill, 30 Aug. 1703, Val Notre Dame, *Murray*, i, pp. 170–1; Hill to Hedges, 31 Aug. 1703, Hague, *Hill Corres.*, i, pp. 249–51; *ibid.*, i, pp. 251–4, Hill to Nottingham, 4 Sept. 1703, Hague; Godolphin to (Nottingham), 25 Aug. 1703, Bath, Add. Ms. 29589; *ibid.*, Hedges to Nottingham, 2 and 4 Sept. 1703, Bath.
[2] Stanhope to Stepney, 6, 21, 25 and 28 Sept. 1703, Hague, Add. Ms. 7069; Stanhope to Hedges, 14 and 21 Sept. 1703, Hague, S. P. Holl. 226.

reluctance of the Dutch to participate in the negotiation then on foot
for an alliance with the Duke of Savoy. Stepney appreciated that the
States were 'already upon the full stretch', but neither he nor Hedges
could understand why they refused to instruct their ambassador in
Vienna to give some sign of their 'readiness to contribute towards
bringing the treaty to a good conclusion'. The Dutch – 'a people',
commented Hill, 'who will expect a pennyworth for their penny' –
objected that they could not undertake obligations until they knew
what they were, but Stepney chose to regard this as a pretence to
conceal their real reluctance to come into a treaty at all. In a letter
written on October 5th Stanhope confirmed Stepney in this suspicion:

I judged the same as you do, from the Pentionary's discourse about that Treaty,
that the People are by no means ready for such a new expence, haveing enough
on their hands to comply with Portugall notwithstanding all the Queen has
generously done to ease them . . . .

Four days later, however, Stanhope had had second thoughts on this
matter; he wrote to Stepney that he was too pessimistic about the
prospects of Dutch coöperation, and reminding him that

they have a vast number of persons to manage before they can obtain a Resolution in a matter of this moment, and therefore are to be let alone to bring it
about their owne way . . . . if they could be sure here of fair dealing there, the
difficulties here, I fancy, will be easily, and in a short time, overcome.

Stanhope knew the Dutch and their government better than Stepney:
the measures which they took to support Savoy after she had publicly
deserted Louis XIV justified his confidence and convinced Stepney
that they desired to 'purchase the alliance at any reasonable rate'.[1]
The growth of Stanhope's confidence about Dutch participation in
the Savoy treaty was, however, accompanied by the rapid loss of his
newly-acquired faith that the preparations for the Portugal expedition
would be speeded up. His letter of October 5th told Stepney of his
fears that the Dutch would

not only be forced to make the King of Spaine stay longer than is fitting for the
twelve Shipps they have promised, but faile at last as to two or three of them,
they cannot help it here, the Government is all to peeces, and must be new
moulded before they can be usefull either to themselves or their friends.

The events of the next fortnight confirmed Stanhope in these opinions.
On October 9th he heard the welcome news that instead of twelve
ships the States now intended to send twenty-four. Even the discovery

[1] Hill to Nottingham, 11 Sept. 1703, Hague, *Hill Corres.*, i, pp. 262-4; Stepney to Shrewsbury, 29 Sept. 1703, Vienna, *H. M. C. Buccleuch II pt. ii*, pp. 678-9; Stanhope to Stepney,
5, 9 and 12 Oct. 1703, Hague, Add. Ms. 7069; Welch, *op.cit.*, pp. 137-40.

that in practice this would mean that eighteen would be sent, and that the new 'King of Spain''s voyage might be delayed a further month on their account, did not prevent Stanhope feeling some pleasure at this development. A week later, however, he was told that this augmentation would not, after all, be made. He ascribed such fluctuations of policy to the illness which for some time past had kept Heinsius from the conduct of public affairs. 'His long absence already', he wrote to Stepney on October 16th,

has been a great retardment to all buisness, especially our Portugall preparations for there is no man of despatch among them besides himselfe, nor can I believe a word the rest tell me who vary every two days, and nothing is to be relyed on, either as to number of Shipps, or time when they will be ready . . . .

By the end of October Heinsius had returned to his duties, but Hill found that even he would not 'take anything upon himself now'. 'It is not', he added somewhat sadly, 'just the same Pensioner we had here six years ago'.[1]

On November 2nd Archduke Charles of Austria, now titular King of Spain, arrived at The Hague, and Hill was ashamed to find, after all his 'solicitations and reproaches', that the Dutch seemed readier than the English for the expedition that was to take the new King to Portugal. England as yet had sent only four frigates to carry the King and his court across the Channel. Two months later, however, King Charles was still in the Republic, and on December 28th one of Ormonde's correspondents put the blame for this firmly on the Dutch:

The contrary winds have long detained the King of Spain in this country, which is wholly to be attributed to the ill conduct of the Admiralty here, for when he first came the wind was very fair and continued so above a fortnight after Sir George Rooke arrived, and all the English preparation in readiness, but those of the Dutch were in no forwardness, which occasioned the delay . . . .

He was in England for Christmas, however, and early in 1704 the expedition at last set out for Lisbon.[2]

4

For Marlborough and Godolphin the shortcomings of the Dutch in the war at sea and the Portugal expedition brought not only annoyance but uneasiness lest the High Tories might find resulting dissatisfaction

[1] Stanhope to Stepney, 5 and 16 Oct. 1703, Hague, Add. Ms. 7069; Stanhope to Hedges, 9 and 16 Oct. 1703, Hague, S.P. Holl. 226; Hill to Nottingham, 3 Nov. 1703, Hague, *Hill Corres.*, i, pp. 277–8.

[2] Hill to Nottingham, 2 Nov. 1703, Hague, *Hill Corres.*, i, pp. 276–7; F. Hamilton to Ormonde, 28 Dec. 1703, Breda, *H. M. C. Ormonde n.s. VIII*, pp. 50–2.

at home a powerful support for their cherished aim of changing the 'method' of the war. This mixture of indignation and fear is again evident in their reaction to the conduct of the Dutch in the campaign in the Low Countries in 1703. Their fear was apparently well founded, for the way in which the Dutch time after time thwarted Marlborough's plans seemed to be a powerful argument in favour of the High Tory policies.

From the outset of the campaign of 1703 Marlborough found occasion for 'spleen'. It was with reluctance that he gave way to the insistence of the Dutch that it should be opened with the siege of Bonn, and it was with a great deal of annoyance that he found on April 19th that their preparations were so backward that the Dutch general Coehoorn now advocated postponing the attempt until the end of the year. Marlborough found this suggestion 'scandalous', and the siege went forward until the fall of the city on May 15th. After this success Marlborough set out for Maestricht, the recent defence of which against Villeroi by the new Dutch commander Ouwerkerk did not go unpraised in England. Marlborough was now ready to put into execution his 'great design' for the capture of Ostend and Antwerp. For this scheme to be successful the coöperation of Coehoorn was essential, but that general succeeded in persuading the States-General to allow him to force the French lines in Flanders rather than participate in the capture of Ostend. 'It is no wonder', Marlborough bitterly commented,

that Cohorn is for forcing the French lines, for as he is governor of West Flanders he has the tenths of all the contributions.[1]

From June 9th onwards Marlborough importuned the States for permission to attack the French covering Antwerp, but without success. As the days went by Cardonnel remarked on the inactivity of the Dutch armies, and when the news came that they had joined forces he commented that this would not 'much forward the business', since Coehoorn would scarcely agree with either Obdam or Slangenberg, 'especially the latter, whose temper, 'tis generally said, is insuperable'. On June 22nd Marlborough appealed to Heinsius for permission to attack. If this were not given, he declared, it would be best to stand

---

[1] Marlborough to Heinsius, 18 April 1703, Maestricht, *van 't Hoff*, p. 59; Marlborough to Godolphin, 20 April 1703, Cologne, *Churchill*, ii, p. 211; *ibid.*, ii, p. 212, Marlborough to Sarah, 20 April 1703, Cologne; Marlborough to Heinsius, 27 April 1703, Camp before Bonn, *van 't Hoff*, pp. 63–4; Marlborough to (Godolphin), 31 May 1703, Thys, *Coxe*, i, pp. 119–20; Marlborough to Heinsius, 8 June 1703, Thys, *van 't Hoff*, pp. 73–4; *Annals*, ii, p. 120.

on the defensive in the Low Countries and send the rest of the army into Germany; and he ended with assurances that

If I had been born att Amsterdam, I could not be more desirous for the prosperity of Holland then I am, being truly convinced that when you are unfortunate, England must be undone.

His appeal was in vain and the reply which he received from Heinsius prompted him to reflect that

the faction are so great in Holland that the pensionary dares not take anything upon himself, so that I fear at last things will go wrong for want of a government.

To Godolphin he confided, on July 2nd, that 'the lucre of having a little contribution from the Pais de Waes has spoiled the whole thing', adding that

the French are very cautious, and the Dutch will venture nothing; so that, unless it happens by chance, I think there will be no battle.

Before this letter was sent off, however, he learnt that the army under Obdam had been surprised by the French at Eeckeren. 'Since I have sealed my letter', he told Godolphin,

we have a report come from Breda that Opdam is beaten. I pray God it be not so, for he is very capable of having it happen to him.[1]

The report of a total defeat at Eeckeren came from the lips of Obdam himself, who had left the fight imagining all to be lost. After his departure, however, Slangenburg had rallied the Dutch and fought his way through the enveloping French to safety. When this became known the Dutch hailed the batttle as a victory, though the first reports of it, according to Cockburn, had aroused 'general dissatisfaction' not only with their own generals but with Marlborough too. In England Eeckeren was regarded, if not as a victory, at least as a battle in which the honours were equal. Every one was amazed, reported L'Hermitage, that the surprised and outnumbered Dutch should have come off so well. The annalist Jones enlarged on the 'incredible Bravery' of the Dutch, and the *Observator* hailed the action as an unqualified success, though it noted the 'retirement' of Obdam, 'which the People at *London*', it commented, 'say is a Modish way of expressing a Man's running away'. This last point was made, too, in a satirical *Catalogue of Books* which appeared in the following year, and included among its items

---

[1] Cardonnel to Ellis, 11 and 25 June 1703, Hanef, Add. Ms. 28918; Marlborough to Heinsius, 22 June 1703, Hanef, *van 't Hoff*, pp. 76–7; Marlborough to Godolphin, 2 July 1703, Moll and Baden, *Coxe*, i, pp. 122–3; *ibid.*, i, p. 126, Marlborough to ?, n.d.

The whole art of Warr, of Encamping, Retreating and Running away, & written originally in Dutch by Baron Opdam .... & dedicated to ye Duke of Malb: 2 Vol: follio.[1]

Marlborough did not share the pleasure of his allies nor the complacency of his countrymen. Not only was he being accused, above all by Slangenburg himself, of allowing Obdam to fall into a trap against which he had in fact warned him, but the action at Eeckeren had been a setback to his 'design', the success of which he considered as of the utmost importance. This setback was all the more galling to him since he well knew how desirable for the very maintenance of the Alliance was a convincing victory in the Low Countries. Without it, he feared, the Dutch would never be brought to 'venture some thing' to retrieve the rapidly worsening military situation in Germany, and only by its means could the mouths of the High Tory critics be stopped. He knew that these latter were becoming daily more vocal, and was convinced, as he wrote to his son-in-law Sunderland on July 8th, that the purpose of their 'angry' exclamations that 'the manner of making the warr must be changed' was to 'mortifie me, & frighten Holland to a peace ...'. When the news of the Dutch losses at Eeckeren reached Vienna, Stepney concluded that they would make it easier to 'frighten Holland to a peace'; he feared that the Dutch would not 'hold out many such trials'.[2]

Marlborough even apprehended that the Whigs might, as a political manoeuvre, join with the High Tories in demanding 'that the war must not be offensive in this country', in which case, he feared, the Dutch would not 'think themselves very safe in our friendship'. Such a result, he told his Duchess, would be England's ruin, since there were

a thousand reasons for preserving our friendship with the Dutch; for as we save them, so they must preserve us from the arbitrary power of the Pretender, and the Earl of Middleton, which must be entirely governed by France. May God preserve me and my dearest love from seeing this come to pass! But if we should quarrel with the Dutch I fear it might happen.[3]

The persistence of Marlborough extorted from the States-General, after Eeckeren, permission to attack the French lines before Antwerp.

[1] Cockburn to (Nottingham), 3 July 1703 (N.S.), Add. Ms. 29589; Cockburn to (Hedges?), 3 and 6 July 1703 (N.S.), S. P. Holl. 225; L'Hermitage to States-General (transcript), 29 June/10 July 1703, London, Add. Ms. 17677 WWW; *Observator*, ii, 25, 3 July 1703; *Jones, 1703*, p. 334; *C.W.* 22.

[2] Marlborough to Godolphin, 5 July 1703, Thielen, *Churchill*, ii, p. 231; Marlborough to Sunderland (copy), 8 July 1703, Vorselaer, Add. Ms. 34518; Stepney to Shrewsbury, 14 and 21 July 1703, Vienna, *H. M. C. Buccleuch II pt. ii*, pp. 664–7.

[3] Marlborough to Sarah, n.d., *Coxe*, i, p. 136. For the threat of Whig defection from the 'land-war' policy see also *von Noorden*, i, pp. 353–4.

After some delay, caused, according to Cardonnel, by the extremely 'dilatory proceedings' of the Dutch, Marlborough was ready to attack by July 23rd, but once more he was thwarted by their objections and hesitations. His quartermaster-general Cadogan was infuriated by this new setback; 'our miscarriages this campagne', he wrote to Raby, the envoy at Berlin,

have been so grose and so repeated that an account of them would be as tedious to your lordship, as the suffering of them has been uneasie to us.

Marlborough himself expostulated with Heinsius by letter. No success, he pointed out, but rather 'some great misfortune' would result from the independence of Coehoorn's army, and the opportunities allowed to 'the quarels and animositys of privatt pepel' to 'make a delay'. All this, he added,

gives mee soe much trouble, that I know not if I shall be able to outlive this campagne, but I am sure I have not coridge to make another . . . . I own to you that I have the spleen to a very great degree.

In England little seems to have been known about this latest disappointment except that the French had thwarted an attack by retiring; there even seems to have been a rumour, which the *Observator* referred to with overt disapproval, that 'Master *Swangenburgh*, the *Dutch* General, that knock'd so many *French* Fellows Brains out 't other Day' had been more eager for the attack than Marlborough.[1]

Marlborough now yielded to the inevitable, abandoned his design and marched off to the Meuse to besiege Huy, leaving Coehoorn, still intent on procuring 'contributions', in West Flanders. He agreed with Godolphin that this was 'as the French expression is, a pis aller', but explained that, 'as Cohorn has managed his business for these last six weeks, we had nothing else to do'. To Stepney he explained that his move was 'owing to M. de Cohorn's stubbornness and the dissensions among those generals', and Stepney's disappointment at this change of plan must have been typical of that of many Englishmen. 'Our Dutch Deputies and Generals', he commented,

have made nothing on't; our armies are marching towards the Meuse, for Huy and Limbourg, which is but mean game, after the hopes they had raised in us.

He was writing to the Duke of Shrewsbury, William's Whig minister, whose ill health had led him to take up residence in Italy. Shrewsbury

[1] Cardonnel to Ellis, 16 July 1703, Vorselaer, Add. Ms. 28918; Marlborough to Heinsius, 21 July 1703, Vorselaer, *van 't Hoff*, pp. 82–3; *ibid.*, p. 84, same to same, 24 July 1703, Calmpthout; Cadogan to (Raby), 27 July 1703, Calmpthout, Add. Ms. 22196; *Observator*, ii, 31, 24 July 1703.

cannot have been much surprised at the news, for his reaction to the preparations of the Dutch for attacking the lines before Antwerp had been to suspect that 'the mountain will bring forth a mouse'.[1]

The trenches before Huy were opened on August 17th, and Marlborough began to plan what would follow the fall of that fortress. He himself was strongly for resuming his plan of attacking the lines, but he foresaw considerable difficulties from all those who 'think they have a right of being consulted before anything is positively resolved'. At The Hague, Hill shared these hopes and fears; all the provinces except Holland, he reported, were 'miserably divided into partys', but all the Dutch generals were 'as if they had been bit by a mad dog'. Marlborough's apprehensions were only too well founded; at a Council of War held on August 24th, the day before the surrender of Huy, the Dutch generals argued against his plan and in favour of the siege of Limbourg. Marlborough referred the difference of opinion to the States, but in his letter he warned them that

il y a de l'apparence qu'on serait de mauvaise humeur chez nous cet hiver, si la campagne se passait sans faire quelque chose de considérable avec une telle superiorité.

In a private letter to Heinsius he expressed himself yet more clearly:

I can't forbear telling you that all the disafected pepel in England will take ocasion to make use of the arguments given by your Generals, to convince our Parlaiment men, that the warr ought to be made in other places and not in this country.[2]

Although on this occasion the Deputies were behind the Duke, 'the cautious spiritt of this Republick', as Stanhope called it, won the day, and the States decided in favour of their generals, men, according to Hill, 'as would make any other man as mad as themselves', and described by Cadogan as 'equally incapable of shame as reason'. On August 30th the Deputies conferred once more with their generals, but Cardonnel believed them to be too 'timerous' to 'determine anything till they have writ to The Hague & hear again from thence'. 'In the mean time', he added,

---

[1] Marlborough to Godolphin, 6 Aug. 1703, Houthalen, *Coxe*, i, pp. 127–8; Marlborough to Stepney, 11 Aug. 1703, Borchloen, *Murray*, i, pp. 157–8; Shrewsbury to Hill, 16 Aug. 1703, Rome, *Hill Corres.*, ii, pp. 742–3; Stepney to Shrewsbury, 18 Aug. 1703, Vienna, *H. M. C. Buccleuch II pt. ii*, pp. 670–1.

[2] Marlborough to Sarah, 23 Aug. 1703, Val Notre Dame, *Churchill*, ii, p. 247; Marlborough to States-General, 26 Aug. 1703, Val Notre Dame, *Murray*, i, pp. 166–8; Marlborough to Heinsius, 26 Aug. 1703, Val Notre Dame, *van 't Hoff*, pp. 88–9; Hill to (Nottingham?), 26 Aug. 1703, Hague, S.P. Holl. 224.

the opportunity may be lost. These proceedings put my Lord Duke very much
out of humor as foreseeing we are like to do little more this Campagne.[1]

This was no exaggeration of Marlborough's feelings. In letters to
Godolphin and Heinsius he complained bitterly of the conduct of the
Dutch generals. 'If I might *have millions* given mee', he told the
Pensionary,

to serve another yeare and be obliged to doe nothing but by the *unanimous
consent* of the Generals, I would much sooner dye; for besides that nothing can
be a secritt, all disiplin after the maner wee live must be lost ....

He wrote too of the ill effect that 'unreasonable opposition' had had
on his health, and declared his intention of having nothing to do with
the command of Dutch troops for the future except under very
different conditions. His greatest wish, he told Godolphin, was to leave
'an Army that is to do no more but eat forage', though he emphasised
his desire for Anglo-Dutch solidarity. In an official letter to the
States-General he declared publicly that an opportunity had been
lost, and expressed his apprehension lest some mischief might come
of it.[2]

Marlborough's views were fully shared by English soldiers with the
army and diplomats at The Hague. Hill reported that Marlborough was
'in great esteem and veneration with every body in spite of their own
Generals', but that one of the major weaknesses of the Republic was
'the want of a due subordination in their Generals, and their incom-
patibility one with another'. Another observer at The Hague remarked
that the States were 'so dilitary in any bold undertaking, yt their
consent never comes till it is too late', and Cockburn attempted to
explain why, in his view, they were for 'shunning a battle'. 'Some
ascribe it', he wrote,

to weakness of spirit, others to prudence because ye consequences are uncertain.
The temper of the Dutch is to be slow, & ye present policy is judg'd to be rather
to protract ye war than to make a speedy end to it. They would rather weary
france than Irritate (?) him, and if the war was soon ended, they would be too
ready to split asunder within. Parties and factions are only kept quiet now because of ye common danger of ye war. They who have been in ye Government

[1] Cadogan to (Raby), 27 Aug. 1703, Camp before Huy, Add. Ms. 22196; Stanhope to
Blathwayt, 28 Aug. 1703, Hague, Add. Ms. 41683; Hill to Godolphin, 28 Aug. 1703, Hague,
Hill Corres, i, pp. 247–8; Cardonnel to Ellis (p.s.), 30 Aug. 1703, Val Notre Dame, Add. Ms.
28918.

[2] Marlborough to Godolphin, 30 Aug. 1703, Val Notre Dame, *Churchill*, ii, p. 247; Marlborough to Heinsius, 3 Sept. 1703, Val Notre Dame, *van 't Hoff*, pp. 88–90; Marlborough to
States-General, 6 Sept. 1703, St. Trond, *Murray*, i, p. 173; Marlborough to Godolphin, 6 Sept.
1703, St. Trond, *Churchill*, ii, p. 248. On October 17th Marlborough submitted to Heinsius
detailed proposals designed to remedy the 'peu de discipline dans l'armée' (Marlborough to
Heinsius, 17 Oct. 1703, Düsseldorf, *van 't Hoff*, pp. 96–7).

would stay in it, till opposite partys be either quashed or brought to terms which may give ym security.

Cadogan, too, deplored the inglorious end to the campaign. On September 20th he wrote to Raby that in eight or ten days Limbourg would be taken, and that Marlborough was for trying something more, but that

the obstinacy of some and the want of resolution of others being as invincible as they think the French, nothing more will be thought of then winter quarters.

This prophecy was correct, but a letter written to Godolphin by Marlborough on October 11th shows that by this time, although he was still talking of retiring, the Duke's bitterness had gone; in its place was a heightened anxiety as to the use that might be made at home of the way the campaign was ending:

What I am going to say now does not proceed from my being at the head of the Army, for I hope this is my last year of serving; but I beg of you for the good of England to consider what measures ought to be taken; for, if it be true that an offensive war must not be made in this country, I have but too much reason to apprehend that the consequences of that would be that the Dutch would not think themselves safe. I think they have been much to blame in not venturing something this summer; but that must not let me forget that when they are ruined, we are undone.[1]

5

'The anger of the English army spread to the home front', writes Trevelyan, and in these words he states an assumption that has often been made by historians who have considered the campaign of 1703 in the Low Countries. It is an assumption with little evidence to support it. Certainly Marlborough, and Godolphin too, feared that the conduct of the Dutch would give, as Godolphin put it, 'but too just a handle for clamour against our great expense of carrying on this war in their country'. Certainly, too, Nottingham was considerably emboldened by the course of events. In a letter to Hill of October 19th he described Heinsius' opinion

that a vast army is necessary in Flanders .... and that our great effort must still be there

as 'useless and ruinous'. There is, nevertheless, nothing to point to the existence of much popular indignation. There is no record of its

---

[1] Hill to Hedges, 31 Aug. 1703, Hague, *Hill Corres*, i, pp. 249–51; Chetwynd to Ellis, 7 Sept. 1703, Hague, Add. Ms. 28914; Cockburn to (Nottingham), 11 Sept. 1703 (N.S.), Add. Ms. 29589; Cadogan to (Raby), 20 Sept. 1703, St. Trond, Add. Ms. 22196; Marlborough to Godolphin, 11 Oct. 1703, Alderbeesten, *Churchill*, ii, p. 249.

expression during the session of Parliament of 1703–4. MostEnglishmen probably did not themselves feel strongly enough about the war to be enraged by the fact that, as the Earl of Chesterfield put it,

it has long been a maxim amongst them (the Dutch) not to exasperate their enemies by bloody battles in hopes of conquest, but rather to secure what they have, and expect an advantageous peace.[1]

The danger to the Alliance in 1703 arose not so much from any great revulsion of feeling against the Dutch as from the growth of public apathy towards the indecisive continental war. Such apathy would offer little opposition to the schemes of the High Tories.

Perhaps, too, the ministry's critics were less adept in pointing the moral of the year's happenings than Marlborough had feared. Indeed, it was apparently shortly before the opening of the second session of Anne's first Parliament that the 'blue-water' camp lost a most valuable adherent. Sir Charles Hedges, Nottingham's protegé and fellow-Secretary, underwent a change of heart. Only a short time earlier Marlborough had regarded him as the prospective leader of the group in the Commons which he expected to challenge his policies in the coming session. If Hedges and his friends succeeded, he had declared, England would be undone. At the beginning of November, however, Hedges wrote to Stepney in terms which showed that he was no longer in sympathy with Nottingham's views. 'Wee must', he asserted,

make the best use Wee can of the Dutch, and if they do not move so fast as Wee could wish Wee must consider that Wee cannot move long without them.

It is indeed strange to find the High Tory Secretary rebuking the Whig envoy for his impatience with the Dutch.[2]

Perhaps the defection of Hedges spiked the guns of the High Tories, or perhaps, by once more fixing the attention of Parliament on the issue of Occasional Conformity, they actually forestalled any detailed examination of the conduct of the Dutch. At all events, the long apprehended attack in the Commons on the 'Dutch' war policies of Marlborough did not materialise, though in many other matters the High Tories were embarrassingly and persistently vocal. There was instead remarkable unanimity in voting, on November 17th, subsidies

---

[1] Godolphin to Harley, 26 Sept. 1703, Bath, *H. M. C. XV pt iv*, pp. 68–9; Chesterfield to T. Coke, 4 Oct. 1703, Bretby, *H. M. C. XII pt. iii*, p. 26; Nottingham to Hill, 19 Oct. 1703, Whitehall, *Hill Corres.*, i, pp. 44–7; *Trevelyan*, i, p. 316; F. Taylor, *The Wars of Marlborough, 1702–9* (Oxford, 1921), i, p. 141.

[2] Marlborough to Sarah, n.d., *Coxe*, i, p. 136; Hedges to Stepney (copy), 5 Nov. 1703, Whitehall, F. E. B. Misc. 204. *Cf.* Hedges to (J. Methuen) (copy), 3 Dec. 1703, Whitehall, F. E. B. Port. 108.

for carrying on the war on the lines already established for another
year. There was, of course, some opposition to this. One member,
attacking the alliances with Savoy and Portugal, represented England
as already ruined by her allies, and another declared that it was
useless to conclude alliances with the Dutch, since they made no
attempt to fulfil their terms. In reply, however, the Dutch were
praised, and it was said that it was both for the interest and for the
honour of Britain to support them in the war, and that to fail to do so
would be to court our own ruin. The speedy voting of supplies by the
Commons was announced to the Dutch leaders by Marlborough in
letters in which he emphasised his own pleasure that 'the designs of
some few ill affected pepel are quite disapointed', and that

il paraît généralement toute la disposition qu'on peut souhaiter pour maintenir
et cultiver la bonne union et amitié si nécessaire entre nous et l'État pour notre
intérêt commun.[1]

On November 26th the Commons decided to renew the augmentation
of troops agreed to at the beginning of the year on the same conditions
as those on which it had originally been granted; in other words,
provided that the States continued their prohibition of commerce and
correspondence with the enemy. They were informed by the queen on
December 30th that she considered this so necessary that she was
ordering her minister at The Hague to insist upon it with the States-
General. Stanhope, however, who had already sounded Heinsius and
others on this question, feared that it would 'not pass their Provinces
with that ease you seem to imagine in England'.

Ever since the prohibition had been imposed British observers in
the Republic had noted the eagerness of the Dutch to reopen trade
relations with France. There had even been reports that attempts
were being made to establish underhand channels of commerce, but
above all the growing dissatisfaction of the Dutch merchants was
remarked upon. 'Ye prohibition of Commerce', wrote Cockburn in
August, 'is daylie more and more complained of. It causes divers who
were judged topping Merchts to play Bankrupt. The Country cannot
bear it long'. Hill, too, reported that

this Province of Holland, which is the only one now in order, is a good deal
aggrieved by the prohibition of trade and correspondence, and take it very
unkindly that we did force them into it,

[1] L'Hermitage to States-General (transcript), 19/30 Nov. 1703, London, Add. Ms. 17677
WWW; Marlborough to Heinsius, 26 Nov. 1703 (O.S.), *van 't Hoff*, p. 98; Marlborough to
Buys, 7 Dec. 1703, St. James', *Murray*, i, p. 216; *ibid.*, i, pp. 221-3, Marlborough to Witsen,
21 Dec. 1703, St. James'.

and, again, that

the additional 10.000 men, which the Queen entertained here this last summer, did not give these people so much satisfaction, as the condition which the House of Commons tacked to it did give them vexation; and I am apt to believe, that they will think, and perhaps do think, of openeing their commerce and correspondencies again the 1st of June next, whatever it should cost them.[1]

Even before the prohibition had come into effect the ministry had been warned that the Dutch would evade it by means of collusion between neutral merchant ships and Dutch privateers. It was therefore with some satisfaction that Stanhope noted that the activities of the Zeeland privateers, after the imposition of the prohibition, were much resented by the neutral powers. He reported that 'those Pyrates' the Zeeland privateers took prisoner all ships, 'friends, neutrals and Ennemies' coming from France or Spain, and immediately declared what they had taken to be 'good prize'. The 'insolence' of the Zeelanders he reported, was 'insupportable', and the States-General could not bring Zeeland to give any satisfaction to the many complaints made against their privateers, especially by Denmark. They valued 'no more any order of ye States General', wrote Stanhope, 'than of ye Divan of Algeir', and he was delighted when, in the following year, the King of Denmark seized an East-Indiaman from Zeeland in reprisal for their depredations. When he was instructed to press the claims of English merchants against Zeeland privateers he advocated the imitation of what 'ye King of Denmark has show'd us', 'at which', he added, 'I am assured ye Province of Holland and particularly the merchants of Amsterdam are not at all offended'. The annalist Jones pointed out a few years later that the Zeelanders had

frequently given not only trouble to the States in respect to their Allies, but sometimes even to their own Provinces;

though he added that in this matter the States-General had 'given Her Majesty all the smooth Returns and Satisfaction they were capable of . . . . '.[2]

[1] Hedges to Stanhope (copy), 22 June 1703, Whitehall, F. E. B. Holl. 69; Cockburn to (Nottingham), 14 Aug. 1703 (N.S.), Add. Ms. 29589; Hill to Godolphin, 28 Aug. 1703, Hague, *Hill Corres.*, i, pp. 247–8; *ibid.*, i, pp. 262–4, Hill to Nottingham, 11 Sept. 1703, Hague; L'Hermitage to States-General (transcript), 26 Nov./7 Dec. 1703, London, Add. Ms. 17677 WWW; Stanhope to Hedges, 18 Dec. 1703, Hague, S. P. Holl. 226; *Cobbett*, vi, cols. 171–2.
[2] Stanhope to Hedges, 7 Aug. 1703, Hague, S. P. Holl. 224; Dayrolle to (Ellis), 25 Sept. 1703, Hague, Add. Ms. 28914; Stanhope to Hedges, 1 Jan. and 12 Feb. 1704, Hague, S. P. Holl. 226; Stanhope to Harley, 12 Aug. 1704, Hague, S. P. Holl. 227; *ibid.*, Stanhope to Hedges, 4 Nov. 1704, Hague; G. N. Clark, 'Neutral Commerce in the War of the Spanish Succession and the Treaty of Utrecht', *British Year Book of International Law*, 1928, pp. 74–6; *Jones, 1707*, pp. 20–1.

If the Dutch were not much in the minds of Parliament during this session, they were often present in those of the Board of Trade, as the Lords were reminded on December 21st when Weymouth presented the Commissioners' report.

Ever since the prohibition of trade in February 1703 between the British plantations and the Spanish Indies, complaints had been pouring in from the former that the Dutch at Curaçao still enjoyed a virtually free trade with the Spaniards. Not only did this appear grossly inequitable, but it was pointed out that merchants in the American colonies, rather than not trading with the Spaniards at all, were now carrying on an illegal trade through Curaçao, to the great gain of that island.[1] The Jamaicans revenged themselves by taking captive Dutch vessels which they found to be trading with Spanish possessions, but at the same time both they and the Pennsylvanians suggested that their Governors be allowed to connive at trading with the Spaniards. This, declared Sir Gilbert Heathcote,

is done by the Hollanders from Curasoa, and we have as good an appetite for gold and silver as they have, and much better conveniencys from Jamaica to gratifye it.

The position was summed up by the Commissioners in their report. The British plantations, this declared, had strictly observed the prohibition of trade with the Spaniards, but

the Dutch, with a different regard to their interest, do contrive by all ways and means to engage the Spaniards in those parts to a commerce with them, and, for the better ingratiating themselves with that people, have called in their privateers and enjoy a free and open trade with the Spaniards there far greater than ever, which gives very great discouragement to her Majesty's subjects, and occasions their carrying the several commodities of the plantations (contrary to the Acts of Trade) to the Dutch, to be vended by them to the Spaniard or carried to Europe, for which her Majesty's subjects receive in exchange from the Dutch commodities of the growth of Europe . . . .

To prevent this last abuse the Commissioners recommended that the laws should be more strictly enforced by Customs officers; and they added the following somewhat vague advice:

And whereas it has been found by long experience that the irritating the Spaniards by private attempts upon the land in America has only tended to the loss of a considerable trade without any real advantage to her Majesty's subjects and

---

[1] Quary to Board of Trade, 25 July and 14 Aug. 1703, Philadelphia, *C. S. P. Col., 1702-3*, pp. 572 and 645-6; *ibid.*, pp. 748-51, Bennett to Board of Trade, 19 Oct. 1703, Bermuda; *ibid.*, pp. 779-80, Board of Trade to Nottingham, 29 Oct. 1703, Whitehall; Nottingham to Godolphin, 15 Nov. 1703, Whitehall, *C. S. P. Dom. Anne*, ii, p. 200; Bourne, *op.cit.*, pp. 162-3; C. Nettels, 'England and the Spanish-American Trade, 1680-1715', *Journal of Modern History*, iii (1931), 1, pp. 19-20.

is the present cause of turning that trade into the hands of our neighbours, we further humbly offered that such measures might be taken herein, as to her Majesty's great wisdom should seem meet, so that her Majesty's subjects be not excluded from an equal advantage of trade with others in those parts.[1]

The Commissioners of Customs were loath to accept the suggestion that their officials had been failing in their duty, but in February 1704 the appeal to the queen's 'great wisdom' bore fruit. In that month, following the receipt of a memorial from the States-General advocating such a step, Nottingham sent circular letters to the Governors of the plantations informing them that the queen had decided to allow trade with the Spanish Indies except in stores of war, ammunition, 'and such commodities as are prohibited by law to be carryed from H. M. Plantations directly to any foreign country'. The Governors were also instructed that,

the Dutch having promised to injoyn their privateers in these parts not to disturb H. M. subjects in this trade, you must in like manner require all the privateers under your jurisdiction not to molest any of the Dutch in their trade to and from the Spanish Dominions except only in case of their carrying stores and ammunition of war.

Appropriate instructions were sent to the Captains of privateers in May.

By thus yielding to the importunities of the colonists the ministry had abandoned the principle of a universal prohibition of trade with the enemy and had thus made their own position in insisting that the Dutch continue this prohibition in Europe less unassailable. Even this concession, however, far-reaching though its implications were, did not put an end to the complaints of the West Indian colonists about the activities of the Dutch at Curaçao. In December 1704, for example, the Governor of Jamaica pointed out that

Severall ships from England and Ireland take out their clearings for Jamaica and some other of H.M. Colonies in the West Indies and go directly to Curasao .... with the English manufactory, by which means they draw the Trade from the English to the Dutch.[2]

[1] Heathcote to (Board of Trade?), 28 Aug. 1703, C. S. P. Col., 1702-3, pp. 660-1; ibid., pp. 714 and 842, Handasyd to Board of Trade, 6 Oct. and 27 Nov. 1703, Jamaica; 'Report from the Commissioners of Trade and Plantations', 21 Dec. 1703, H. of L. Mss., v, p. 324.
[2] Commissioners of Customs to Godolphin (abstract), 30 Dec. 1703 (O.S.), Cal. Tr. Papers, 1702-7, p. 219; Lowndes to Popple, 8 Jan. 1703/4, Treasury Chambers, C. S. P. Col., 1704-5, p. 5; ibid., p. 69, memorial from Vrijbergen, 13 Feb. 1703/4, London; ibid., pp. 49-50, Popple to Warre, 18 Feb. 1703/4, Whitehall; ibid., pp. 113-4, Instructions to Privateers, 4 May 1704, St. James'; 'Report from the Council of Trade and Plantations', 30 Nov. 1704, H. of L. Mss., vi, pp. 89-91; Handasyd to Hedges, 17 Dec. 1704, (Jamaica), C. S. P. Col., 1704-5, pp. 339-41.

6

The ease with which Parliament had voted supplies for the coming campaign should not blind us to the threat to the policies of Marlborough and Godolphin that existed at the beginning of 1704. 'The ministry of Godolphin', says Taylor,

came into existence 'to reduce the exorbitant power of France'. By the outcome of its foreign policy it must stand or fall. Judged by the results of two years of war and taxation, it appeared to be falling.[1]

Certainly another year of frustration and disappointment abroad could hardly fail to lose the ministry its control of Parliament. Disappointed Whigs would join with hostile High Tories to make government impossible.

It was thus essential for the ministry's survival that a victory should vindicate the policy that it had inherited from William III; but this policy depended for its success upon Anglo-Dutch coöperation, and there was little sign at the beginning of 1704 that this was likely to be any greater in the coming campaign than it had been in the preceding one. On January 1st Cockburn reported that the damage caused in the Republic by the same 'great storm' which had swept southern England was being "industriously concealed', 'yt ye people may not be discouraged, who are already very much cast down with their heavy taxes and want of trade'. A fortnight later he wrote that many Dutchmen were being imposed upon by rumours to the effect that England had entered the war only so as to ruin them. 'I pray God', he added,

disappoint those designs & endeavours to disturb ye Queens reign in Britain & to prevent a breach and misunderstanding betwixt England & this State which would certainly endanger ye protestant Interest.[2]

When Marlborough and his secretary Cardonnel arrived back at The Hague in mid-January they, too, found affairs in a most unpromising state. 'The complaints', wrote Cardonnel to Ellis on February 12th,

are generall for want of Money & Trade, and the Divisions and Parties encreasing every day, when the utmost united efforts should be exerted to keep the Government from sinking.

Marlborough, too, found evidence of a 'great want of money', and to this he attributed the extreme backwardness of Dutch preparations for the campaign in the Low Countries. Neither in the question of

---

[1] Taylor, op.cit., i, p. 152.
[2] Cockburn to (Nottingham), 1 and 15 Jan. 1704, Hague, Add. Ms. 29589.

increasing his powers, nor in that of his proposal to invade France by
way of the Moselle, could he obtain from the States a definite reply.
Cadogan was disgusted by the attitude of 'these Herring-sellers', and
Cardonnel commented that

these people are so stupid and are so little sensible of the danger at their doors,
that one would believe by the little regard they have to their own safety, they
were predestinated for ruin.[1]

Marlborough arrived home once more in the middle of February
(O.S.), but the news of the unpromising attitude of the Dutch had
preceded him. Before the end of January several large bets had been
made that within two years the Republic would have made a separate
peace with France, although L'Hermitage alleged that the real object
of those who placed these bets was not to make money but to 'jetter
de la deffiance, afin d'alliener les esprits'. However, in one of the first
issues of his new periodical, the *Review*, Daniel Defoe spoke out
strongly in praise of the Dutch as allies. Thanks to their 'exact Management', he declared, the confederates were in a better 'posture' in
Flanders than anywhere else.[2]

Marlborough's true design was not to invade France; the Moselle
project was, on this occasion, being used merely to cover his plan of
marching to the Danube to counter the French threat to the heart of
the Empire. This was a plan which, apart from all other considerations,
it was evidently necessary to conceal in a Republic where complete
secrecy in affairs of state was virtually impossible. When he arrived
back at The Hague on April 21st, it seemed that the States would be
unwilling even to swallow his bait of a march to the Moselle. 'Matters
are very little mended since we left this place', Cardonnel reported,
and Marlborough wrote to his Duchess:

I find great unwillingness here to part with any troops, which gives me a great
deal of trouble; for I wish this country so well that I should take pleasure in
seeing them do everything that is for their good, but they are, as well as we, so
eaten up by faction that I am afraid they will run great risk of being undone.[3]

While 'faction' at home came to a head in a 'cabinet crisis' precipitated
by Nottingham, which ended in the removal of him and his followers

[1] Marlborough to Hedges, 1 Feb. 1704, Hague, *Murray*, i, pp. 226–7; Marlborough to
Godolphin, 8 Feb. 1704, Hague, *Coxe*, i (1st edn.), pp. 226–7; Cardonnel to Ellis, 12 and 19
Feb. 1704, Hague, Add. Ms. 28918; Cadogan to (Raby), 17 Feb. 1704, Hague, Add. Ms. 22196.
[2] L'Hermitage to States-General (transcript), 28 Jan./8 Feb. 1703/4, London, Add. Ms.
17677 WWW; *Review*, i, 4, 11 March 1703/4.
[3] Cardonnel to Ellis, 22 April 1704, Hague, Add. Mss. 28918; Marlborough to Godolphin,
25 April 1704, Hague, *Churchill*, ii, p. 306; *ibid.*, ii, p. 307, Marlborough to Sarah, 25 April
1704, Hague.

from the ministry, Marlborough made it clear to the States that, if necessary, he and the troops in the queen's pay would march alone to the rescue of the Emperor. On May 2nd he was ready to leave in three days time, and to his wife he wrote;

I shall not continue in this country long, for I intend to go higher up into Germany, which I am forced as yet to keep here a secret, for fear these people would be apprehensive of letting their troops go so far.

Faced with this stubbornness the States gave way; as Stanhope remarked, they 'knew not how to hinder it'. Stanhope found, however, that 'great murmuring' arose against the Moselle project; 'most of the States, and ye generality of the people' were 'not very well satisfied'. 'Ye design he goes on', he reported,

is much against the grain of this people here, who never think themselves safe at home without a superiority of 40,000 men, and never dare think of hazarding anything to make an acquisition upon their Ennemies.

Marlborough himself was well aware that not only were the High Tories now determined to revenge themselves upon him but also that

if we have not success, I shall be found fault with, by those in this country that will think themselves exposed for want of troops I shall have in Germany ....[1]

On May 19th Marlborough's army set out on its great march, ostensibly for Coblentz. It would be strange if Marlborough had not welcomed his new freedom from the limitations to his authority that he had endured in the Low Countries, and if this had not been an inducement for him to execute this project. As Raby wrote to Hill in Berlin,

I don't question but we shall have a good account of him, now he is free from the clog of the Dutch generals and deputies.

Much, however, still depended upon the Dutch if the great venture was to succeed. Soon after setting out, Marlborough heard from Ouwerkerk, now commanding the armies in Flanders, that Villeroi seemed to be moving as if to threaten the army marching towards Coblentz. He therefore wrote to the States urging them to augment his forces in view of this development, and was highly gratified to learn that Ouwerkerk and the other Dutch generals in Flanders had already sent a similar request to the States, and that the latter had 'a ready disposition .... to do anything that shall be thought necessary'. Important as this readiness was, however, it was not as vital to the

---

[1] Marlborough to Sarah, 2 May 1704, Hague, *Churchill*, ii, p. 308; Stanhope to Stepney, 2 and 6 May 1704, Hague, Add. Ms. 7069; Stanhope to Hedges, 2 and 6 May 1704, Hague, S. P. Holl. 226.

success of the allied plans as what Trevelyan has called the 'magnanimous' manner in which the Dutch at last received the news that they had been deceived, and that Marlborough's real objective was the Danube.[1]

The acquiescence of the States in Marlborough's request for 'noe orders .... that will put mee out of a condition of reducing the Elector (of Bavaria), was not ill-advised. The resulting victory at Blenheim more than revived the drooping fortunes of the Grand Alliance, and of the Godolphin ministry too. While the hopes of France were being cut short on the Danube, however, the allied armies in Flanders were engaged in a far from memorable campaign. In the two months of June and July they penetrated the French lines no less than three times, but, although superior in number to the armies opposing them, retired on each occasion. At The Hague Stanhope grew more and more impatient as the news of these lost opportunities arrived. The conduct of the Dutch generals he characterised as 'unpardonable' and 'too gross to be endured'. 'We have a brave army', he complained,

and very desirous of action, superiour to the Enemy above 15000 men, yet by the little good understanding among their Generalls, nothing at all has yet been done more than eating up forage, nor is there any appearance of their doing better hereafter, at least for this Campagne.

By their first withdrawal Marlborough considered that the Dutch had 'lost a very great opportunity' – not least of making his own task easier. The new Secretary of State, Harley, also criticised them on these grounds; 'if you had acted to purpose', he wrote to Stanhope on July 25th,

while you had a superiority they (the French) could not have spared so many men to have gone for the Danube.

Even the news of Blenheim, and Marlborough's praise for the conduct on that field of the officers and men in the pay of the States, could not blind Stanhope to the misdeeds of the Dutch commanders in Flanders. When he wrote to Marlborough of the universal joy which this news had caused among the Dutch, he could not forbear to add: 'It were happy your example could influence a little here on the Maes'. On August 22nd he told Stepney that

Our Army here thinke enough is done on the Danube, and that nothing is expected from them, wherein they are in the right but certainly the States their

---

[1] Raby to Hill, 17 May 1704, Berlin, *Hill Corres.*, i, pp. 101–3; Stanhope to Hedges, 23 May 1704, Hague, S. P. Holl. 226; Marlborough to Sarah, 27 May 1704, Braubach, *Churchill*, ii, pp. 330–31; *Trevelyan*, i, p. 346.

Masters are in the rong, for if when they saw the incapacity of their Generalls they had put others in their places, the warr might have been ended this Campagne.

To Hill, too, although he commended the speed with which the States had given orders to make up the losses among their troops on the Danube, he wrote in a similar vein: 'had they behaved themselves like our friends on the Danube', he declared, 'this year had ended the war'.[1]

At home, however, the rejoicing for Marlborough's victory swept away the memory of the disappointments in Flanders. Few Englishmen could detach themselves so much from the excitement of the moment as to spare time to reflect, like Harley, that

it is very much to be lamented that the States Army is not under that Conduct as to improve the ferment this Glorious Success has rais'd.

The most marked characteristic, indeed, of the celebration of Blenheim in England was perhaps the way in which the part played in that victory by foreigners – apart from Eugene – was completely forgotten. It was not enough for Englishmen that their general had won a 'famous victory'; they wished, perhaps needed, to believe that it had been as 'entirely English' as their queen's heart. This desire is evident in most of the many undistinguished pieces of verse inspired by the event. In John Dennis' *Britannia Triumphans*, for example, the Dutch are mentioned once, and then only parenthetically as the 'cautious' recipients of the territory already won in Flanders. The silence concerning the role of non-British troops at Blenheim, who made up almost five-sixths of the allied armies, was broken only by the voice of Defoe, who drew attention to this aspect of the congratulatory address sent from Oxford to the queen:

> '.... A Day and Conduct so well known,
> Entirely *En—sh* and our own!
> That neither *German, Dutch* nor *Dane*,
> Aided with Councils, or with Men,
> Nor drew a Sword, nor fir'd a Gun,
> But only look'd and loo'd us on!' [2]

[1] Stanhope to Stepney, 10 June, 11, 18 and 25 July, 22 and 29 Aug. 1704, Hague, Add. Ms. 7069; Marlborough to Harley, 15 June 1704, Ebersbach, *Coxe*, i, p. 165; Marlborough to Heinsius, 19 June 1704, Gross Süssen, *van 't Hoff*, pp. 111–12; Harley to Stanhope (copy), 25 July 1704, Whitehall, F. E. B. Holl. 72; Marlborough to States-General (translation), 17 Aug. 1704, Steinheim, *C. W.* 115, i, p. 406; Stanhope to Marlborough (copy), 19 Aug. 1704, Hague, Stowe Ms. 245; Stanhope to Hill, 9 Sept. 1704, Hague, *Hill Corres.*, i, pp. 154–5.

[2] Harley to Stanhope (copy), 22 Aug. 1704, Whitehall, F. E. B. Holl. 72; *Supplement to Advice from the Scandal Club*, 2, Oct. 1704; *C.W.* 58, p. 24.

7

It was not only in the activities of their army in Flanders that Stanhope found the Dutch conduct of the war in 1704 unsatisfactory. There was also the question of their attitude towards the two new allies, Portugal and Savoy. The first fruits of the Portugal alliance were, indeed, far from encouraging. Nothing was accomplished in the field because of a bitter quarrel between the English and Dutch commanders, Schomberg and Fagel. Schomberg's animosity towards the latter arose from the fact that the King of Portugal had chosen to place them both on an equal footing. It was the contention of England that her general should have supreme control over the English and Dutch forces in Portugal, if not over the Portuguese, and the speedy replacement of the impossible Schomberg by Galway did not in any way involve abandonment of the claim.[1]

While this quarrel went on Stanhope was pressing the States to comply with the queen's request for an augmentation of the forces already sent to Portugal. From the outset he had little hope of getting much satisfaction from the States, who, he complained, were 'intolerably slow' in such matters. Harley wrote to Marlborough urging him to write to the States on this subject himself, 'for I fear', he explained

if they should be backward, it would have very ill effects next winter with us here, and give a handle to angry men to do mischief . . . .

The unfortunate Stanhope found himself pressed to bring his 'very hard task' to a successful conclusion by both Harley and Marlborough, but he could still obtain nothing but 'dry and discouraging answers' from Heinsius. As the weeks went by he made no real progress in this matter; at the beginning of October he felt that there were 'some hopes', but on October 21st he admitted in a letter to Stepney that agreement was as far off as ever. 'They tell me', he added,

they shall be caution for a million of Cruzados to be lent suddenly to that King, which being a considerable Service to the common cause in these parts, they thinke ought reasonably to excuse them for any other aditionall charge at present.[2]

---

[1] Wyon, *op.cit.*, i, p. 287; Fortescue, *op.cit.*, i, p. 447; T. Somerville, *History of Great Britain during the Reign of Queen Anne* (London, 1798), p. 67.

[2] Stanhope to Harley, 4 July 1704, Hague, S. P. Holl. 226; Harley to Marlborough, 11 July 1704 (O.S.), *H. M. C. XV pt. iv*, p. 100; Stanhope to Marlborough (copy), 1 Aug. 1704, Hague, Stowe Ms. 245; Marlborough to Stanhope, 11 Sept. 1704, Langencandel, *Murray*, i, pp. 460–1; Stanhope to Harley, 25 Sept. and 3 Oct. 1704, Hague, S.P. Holl. 227; Stanhope to Stepney, 21 Oct. 1704, Hague, Add. Ms. 7069.

To Stanhope this story no doubt seemed similar to those he had heard earlier in the year to excuse the slow and incomplete payment of the States' subsidy to Savoy. Like Marlborough, he believed that this was due 'to nothing but their great want of money'. 'The truth is', he wrote to Hedges on May 16th, 'their want of Money at present is so great, that they will say any thing to gaine a little time'. The delays of the Dutch in paying these subsidies were a sore trial for Hill, now at Turin. 'Her Majty pays fairly', he wrote to Godolphin,

& his R.H. ventures bravely his person, his estates, & his crown : but they both want ye just assistance of their allies.[1]

8

At sea, as on land, the year 1704 gave matter for rejoicing; but to the ministry it also gave cause for complaint against the Republic. The news of the capture of Gibraltar on August 3rd had scarcely arrived in England when it became known that six Dutch warships had been recalled from the joint fleet under Rooke which was now guarding the newly-acquired fortress. Harley took this to heart; 'all here', he wrote to Stanhope on August 15th,

who wish well to ye Common cause and good Understanding between England and Holland cannot but be sensibly affected with this unseasonable recalling Six of their ships from Sr George Rooke, in a time wn it is possible there may be a General Engagement.

Marlborough, too, feared the effect that the Dutch action might have on opinion at home. 'If any misfortune should happen to Sir George Rooke', he warned Stanhope, 'the whole blame will be laid at their door, and there will not be those wanting at home to blow the coals, which may prove of very ill consequence'. Fortunately for Anglo-Dutch goodwill the 'General Engagement' which did take place at Malaga was a victory for the Allies, at least in so far as it saved Gibraltar. At The Hague Stanhope delivered his reproaches and the Dutch leaders seemed ashamed, but at home Englishmen had no desire to contemplate what might have been. The importance of Rooke's achievement was undoubtedly magnified by his fellow High Tories for party purposes, but it seems in any case to have been celebrated as a victory by most Englishmen. One printed 'letter from Gibraltar' which proclaimed

---

[1] Marlborough to Hedges, 1 Feb. 1704, Hague, *Murray*, i, pp.226-7; Stanhope to Hill (copy), 25 March 1704, Hague, Stowe Ms. 245; Stanhope to Hedges, 16 May 1704, Hague, S.P. Holl. 226; Hill to Godolphin, 3 June 1704, Turin, Add. Ms. 28056.

it as such was almost certainly not the work of the High Tories, for it paid this tribute to the Dutch sailors:

The *Dutch*, on their Parts, fought like *Devils*, and were continually pelting the *French;* They were, for the most part, less Ships than those they Engag'd, yet they gave the Enemy their Belly full, and made them glad to Sheer away 1

With the capture of Gibraltar arose the problem of the provision of a garrison. Though the town was held in the name of Charles III of Spain, it was impossible to expect that king in title only to provide forces to guard it. The view of the English ministry from the capture of Gibraltar until 1711 was that the Dutch should share with England in the expense of defending the place, and the lack of interest which the States showed in this was a constant, if minor, cause of annoyance. From the beginning they made it clear that they had no great enthusiasm for the task, and an under-Secretary of State was prompted by their reluctance to make any provision to write these interesting lines:

Merchants (as they are) will still have a greater regard to their private-personal interest than to the general-public good; and I wish that principle of theirs does not, one time or other, put us here out of humour; they cannot forbear being too thrifty, and endeavouring to persuade us that their security ought to be more our concern than their own, and, consequently, oblige us to take upon us as much of the expense of the war as they please.

By October 21st Stanhope had not obtained a satisfactory answer on this matter, and was able to confirm how well founded were Marlborough's fears that

the States will not easily be brought at present to bear any share in the expense.2

9

The Commons had made it clear, during the session of Parliament in the winter of 1703–4, that they expected the Dutch to renew the prohibition of commerce and correspondence with the enemy which was due to end on June 1st, 1704 (N.S.). In accordance with their wishes the ministry set about pressing the Dutch leaders to take such a step; and it saw nothing incongruous in simultaneously agreeing to

1 Harley to Stanhope (copy), 15 Aug. 1704, Whitehall, F. E. B. Holl. 72; Marlborough to Stanhope, 11 Sept. 1704, Langencandel, *Murray*, i, pp. 460–1; Stanhope to Harley, 3 Oct. 1704, Hague, S.P. Holl. 227; *Annals*, iii, appendix, pp. 68–71.
2 Tucker to Hill, 3 Oct. 1704, Windsor, *Hill Corres.*, i, pp. 162–3; Stanhope to Stepney, 21 Oct. 1704, Hague, Add. Ms. 7069; Marlborough to Hedges, 3 Nov. 1704, Berencastel, *Murray*, i, p. 526.

allow the West Indian and American colonies to resume their trade with the Spanish Indies. The Dutch, however, were evasive in their replies and patently reluctant to continue this unprecedented restriction. Stanhope's memorials had no result, and on June 3rd he wrote to Hedges that, despite all his efforts, he could obtain no definite statement of the States' intentions. All that Heinsius would tell him was that the States-General had taken no resolution in the matter, and that any person who opened up trade or correspondence with France or Flanders would therefore do it at his peril. 'I have never', Stanhope declared, 'known them so misterious with me, in any thing I have had to do with them as in this'; but he went on to conjecture at a solution of the 'mistery', 'which is', he wrote,

that they did not think fit to deliberate on this point in the States General, and therefore in that respect the Pensionary said true they had done nothing, but by his leave, as Pensionary of Holland, he went a little too farr, for the States of Holland, after several debates, at last came to a resolution not to renew the prohibition, but let it fall, and consequently leave all things in the state they were before that prohibition and as they were from the time of the First Declaration of warr till they were restrained by that prohibition. By these means the Trade will be almost open and posts pass as freely as ever, but whereas this is done only by the States of Holland, and the States General have not seemed to concern themselves in the matter, they think they have the échapatoire to excuse themselves to England, if they should find this proceeding much resented there, by saying it was not their act, but only that of a particular Province.

This too was the opinion of Dayrolle, who though that the States-General were waiting to observe the English reaction to this move before taking any resolution.[1]

The reaction of Harley, now the responsible minister, was both immediate and forthright, and showed plainly that the ministry was above all concerned at the effect that the reopening of Dutch trade with France might have on the outcome of the coming session of Parliament. He instructed Stanhope to lay 'very plainly' before Heinsius

the great mischief this may produce, and ye handle it will give to ill intentioned persons to create a misunderstanding next Winter. The time of doing it gives a worse aspect, for if ye Prohibition were continued till Our Parliament meet, it may be more likely to have them in a good temper, whereas this will put them out of humour, and give them such a ferment as may render them capable of ill impressions, and the States, perhaps, may see, too late, the ill effects of this Conduct.

[1] Hedges to (Vrijbergen) (transcript), 22 Feb. 1703/4, Whitehall, Add. Ms. 17677 WWW; Stanhope to Hedges, 3 June 1704, Hague, S.P. Holl. 226; Stanhope to Stepney, 3 June 1704, Hague, Add. Ms. 7069; Dayrolle to (Ellis), 6 June 1704, Hague, Add. Ms. 28916; Clark, 'War Trade and Trade War', pp. 272-3.

Marlborough, too, warned Heinsius that

you are doing all you can for the distroing your friends in England and all those that wish well to the common cause.

There was another dangerous aspect to this question, since the re-opening of trade with France by the Dutch would mean that Dutch ships trading thither would become fair prize for British warships and privateers. There had already been some friction between the English and Dutch governments about the capture and condemnation as prize of two Dutch ships which were alleged to have been trading with France, and it was easy to foresee that there would soon be much more. 'Ye more I think of ye consequences of it', lamented Harley, 'ye more fatal they appear'.

Both in conference with Heinsius and in a memorial Stanhope put Harley's warnings plainly before the Dutch, but he found Heinsius 'as dry in his answers' as ever. The Pensionary claimed that, at the queen's request, the Republic had prohibited trade and correspondence for a year, but had found that 'it did their Ennemies little or no hurt at all and themselves a great deal'. He pointed out, too, that the Scottish Parliament had also decided to reopen trade with France, an argument which Stanhope found it very difficult to counter. After this interview with Heinsius on June 19th, Stanhope had little hope that his representations would achieve anything. 'If anything can change their mindes', he confided to Stepney,

it will be the difficulties made in both ffrance and fflanders to receive any of their commodities; some shipps haveing already been refused admittance, and no answer come to the Letters of three or four Posts.[1]

Harley's anxious indignation was not appeased, for he continued to talk of the 'ferment' in England and the 'very harsh Construction' that would be put on the States' conduct; but Stanhope's daily solicitations had no effect. The States of Holland took the question into consideration once more, but only, he surmised, so as to 'find out ye most plausible reasons they can to satisfy Her Majesty'. He was convinced that the States-General, too, were determined not to renew the prohibition; and though he expressed the hope that their reasons might 'be satisfactory to her Majestie and the House of Commons',

[1] Harley to Stanhope (copies), 30 May and 2 June 1704, Whitehall, F. E. B. Holl. 72; Marlborough to Heinsius, 19 June 1704, Gross Süssen, van 't Hoff, pp. 111–12; Stanhope to Stepney, 20 June and 11 July 1704, Hague, Add. Ms. 7069; Stanhope to (Harley), 20 June 1704, Hague, S. P. Holl. 226; ibid., Stanhope to States-General (copy), 21 June 1704, Hague. For details of a payment to the commander of a privateer 'for his concern in the capture of two Dutch ships' see Cal. Tr. Bks., 1704–5, p. 256, 31 May 1704.

he obviously expected the worst. At the beginning of September it again seemed that, as he had long hoped, the continued refusal of France and Flanders to receive Dutch goods in exchange for their own might succeed where his appeals had failed. If the Dutch were to renew their prohibition on this account, he commented, 'we shall be the less beholden to them, since 'tis our Ennemies that forced it upon them'; and Marlborough, covering the siege of Landau at Langencandel, agreed that 'they had certainly much better have done it with a good grace at the beginning'. On September 30th, however, Stanhope had to report that the States of Holland had separated without taking any action in this matter, and three days later he declared confidently in a letter to Harley that 'nothing will be done to your satisfaction'.[1]

With the reopening of Parliament imminent, the ministry had failed to bring their Dutch allies to acquiesce in the strongly expressed will of the Commons. Already the ministry's survival appeared to be threatened by the certain renewal of the conflicts between Lords and Commons over the Occasional Conformity Bill and the case of Ashby and White, and now the High Tories had been presented with a weapon which it seemed that they might use to secure the adoption of their own war policies or, failing that, to break the Alliance. If the Commons were in a mood to be roused by the prospect of ungrateful and avaricious Republicans flouting the queen's wishes then, as the ministers well knew, the High Tories could and would do all this. The temper of the Commons, in this matter, perhaps above all others, would show whether the ministry and its policies, and even the Grand Alliance itself, were to survive.

---

[1] Harley to Stanhope (copy), 13 June 1704, Whitehall, F. E. B. Holl. 72; Stanhope to Harley, 15 July 1704, Hague, S.P. Holl. 226; Stanhope to Stepney, 18 July 1704, Hague, Add. Ms. 7069; Stanhope to Marlborough (copy), 1 Aug. 1704, Hague, Stowe Ms. 245; Stanhope to Harley, 5 and 30 Sept., 3 Oct. 1704, Hague, S.P. Holl. 227; Marlborough to Stanhope, 11 Sept. 1704, Langencandel, *Murray*, i, pp. 460-1.

CHAPTER IV

THE ALLIANCE HOLDS FIRM
⟨1704–5⟩

I

Throughout 1704, both before and after Blenheim, the ministers of Queen Anne made gloomy forecasts of the temper of the Parliament which they would have to meet when winter came. They knew that their ousted High Tory colleagues would be out for revenge, and they greatly feared the consequences of their manoeuvres. They do not seem to have been fully aware of the transformation of the British attitude to the war that Blenheim had brought about. England had tasted blood, and was eager for more; the old apathy had vanished almost overnight. The 'safe', profitable and limited strategy advocated by the High Tories no longer had much attraction; it seemed prosaic and uninspired now that the exaltation of victory in a great battle had been experienced.

When opinion swung thus in favour of Marlborough's policies the English attitude to the Dutch was inevitably affected. They were no longer looked on as, at best, unfortunately indispensable allies in an unfortunately inevitable war, but as partners in the eager pursuit of victory and glory. In this sense it is true that, as enthusiasm for the war grew, so English esteem for the Dutch grew with it; but as we shall see demonstrated to the full in 1705, this process had as corollary that now, if the partnership of the Dutch should prove unsatisfactory, feeling in England would turn against them with a violence as yet unknown in Anne's reign. When this happened the Alliance was saved only by the overriding determination of England to maintain it, and a consequent basic goodwill towards the Dutch. What was remarkable at this time, in fact, was not the so often emphasised revulsion of feeling against the Dutch but rather the failure of the enemies of the ministry to turn it to any account. Historians of this period have devoted much space to describing the indignant reaction of Englishmen to Dutch conduct in the field, but have omitted to indicate, let alone to explain, the extraordinary and complete lack of success of the determined High Tory attempt to make political capital of this. It is high time for it to be realised that it is in this that lies the true importance of the year 1705 in the history of the Anglo-Dutch alliance, and not in that wave of national anger of which we have had so many vivid and even exaggerated descriptions.

2

Not until Parliament met could the ministry know for certain the effect that Blenheim had had on its countrymen. Meanwhile, as the ministers anxiously waited, the High Tories did all they could to ensure that the mood of the coming session would be favourable to their policies. They took their stand above all on the issue of Occasional Conformity, and a significant number of slighting references to the Dutch began to appear in their violent tirades against the schemes of Whigs and Dissenters. To these, one pamphlet declared, the Dutch were 'Brethren', who, it was alleged,

denied all the Christianity they had, out of pure stark staring Conscience to gain a Trade, and what they did at *Amboyna* was but little more than what our good natur'd *Low Flyers* did here and in *Scotland* 1641 till 1660, and what they have endeavoured ever since....

A poem entitled *Faction Display'd* depicted a gathering of Whigs lamenting William III's death, but cheered by the declaration of 'Clodio' (Wharton) that

> We may on his unfinish'd Scheme proceed.
> We may 'gainst Pow'r repos'd in One inveigh,
> And call all Monarchy Tyrannick Sway.
> We may the Praises of the *Dutch* advance,
> Rail at the Arbitrary Rule of *France* ....

A new periodical, called the *Rehearsal*, was started by the nonjuror Charles Leslie to combat the Whig *Observator* and the 'ministerial' *Review*. This, too, lumped together Whigs, Dissenters and Dutch. It suggested, for example, that the Great Fire of London had been started by the Whigs, at the behest of the Dutch.[1]

The High Tory writers did not have the field to themselves. The Godolphin ministry was beginning to take a more active interest in the use of the press, and it was, apparently, at its instigation that Charles

---

1 *Rehearsal*, 5 and 6, 2 and 9 Sept. 1704; *C.W.* 140, p. 4; *C.W.* 166, p. 9.

Davenant, hitherto an advocate of High Tory policies, had produced his lengthy *Essays upon Peace at Home and War Abroad* at the end of 1703. In this work, which attracted much attention, the views of the 'moderates' achieved full expression for the first time. It emphasised above all the need for union at home if the country were to play as effective a part as possible in the war abroad, and advocated that to this end all controversial measures – above all the Occasional Conformity Bill – should be shelved until the war was won. In support of this it pointed, in addressing itself to the queen, to a fact 'of Infinite Importance at this Juncture', namely that

your Conduct at Home has brought the *States General,* not by the Influence of Power, but of Love, to join with *England* in stricter Bands of Friendship, to come in with their whole Weight, and to embrace with more Warmth than ever, the Common Cause of *Europe.*

At the same time it defended Marlborough from criticisms of his conduct of the campaigns in the Low Countries in 1702 and 1703. Those who voiced these, it declared, had never considered 'the difficulties a General lies under who Commands Confederate Troops, and who must act in concert with others'.

One of the main purposes of the *Review*, which first appeared in the spring of 1704, was to keep before the eyes of politically conscious Englishmen the doctrines enunciated by Davenant in his *Essays*. Defoe preached the necessity of national unity both because such sentiments were congenial to him and because the unfortunate consequences of the publication of *The Shortest Way with the Dissenters* had made him dependent for his livelihood, if not for his freedom, upon the goodwill of Harley and Godolphin. In an early issue he made clear his attitude towards the Dutch alliance by deploring suggestions which had appeared in some news-sheets to the effect that the Dutch were treating underhand with France both for peace and for the re-opening of trade. These, he declared, were malicious rumours deliberately spread by France to divide the Republic and England. 'If ever we pretend to Match the French Power', he declared, 'no use must be made, or heed given to such stories on both sides, as tend to divide the Confederacy'. He refused to retract a word of this when it became known, at the beginning of June, that the Dutch in fact had not renewed the prohibition of trade and correspondence with the enemy. It was quite untrue, he pointed out, that the Dutch had made a treaty of commerce and correspondence with France; all that had happened was that the time for the Prohibition of Correspondence by Letters which was agreed to by the States being expir'd, and it being plain to them, that the end, which was the preventing of Intelligence, is not obtain'd, they do not think fit to renew it again.[1]

The ministry had now come out openly against the Occasional Conformity Bill, and, as the appointed time for the meeting of Parliament approached, the supporters and opponents of the Bill fell upon each other with redoubled violence. Here, for example, is the way in which a pamphlet written against the Bill criticised an author who had urged its merits:

His falling in so insolent a manner on our chief *Allies*, the *Dutch*, as Enemies and Incendiaries, as *formerly burning our City*, and *still Stirring up ill Blood, fomenting* and *managing Factions among us; as Intermeddling with our Government, and by Bribery, interposing in the Calling and Dissolving our Parliaments*, is insufferable, and what I am sure he can produce no proof of. But yet if it should chance to be believed, as 'tis likely enough it may among some People . . . . it may have a very fatal Effect, and such a one no doubt, as was designed by it.[2]

The ministry could indeed be certain that their opponents in Parliament would do everything they could to embarrass them on this issue; but they were just as apprehensive of the outcome of a possible High Tory attack in a field in which the Dutch were much more directly concerned – trade and correspondence with the enemy. The High Tories, who, while in office, had made some attempt to restrain their feelings towards 'our good Friends the Dutch', if only because they knew the queen to be behind Marlborough's policies, were throwing restraint to the winds now that they had been ejected from the ministry. The ministers had every reason to fear that they would not hesitate to use the question of prohibition of trade to asperse the Dutch and thereby to stir up a ferment against the 'moderates'' whole conception of the conduct of the war. Even Defoe's lofty rebukes in the *Review* betrayed a certain anxiety, and as soon as it was known in England that the prohibition had not been renewed Godolphin confided in Harley that 'the opening of the Trade in Holland' was 'like to prove a very uneasy matter'. This anxiety was not dispelled by the joyful news from the Danube. The *Observator* was up in arms at the suggestion in Dyer's written news-letter of October 21st that the Dutch 'had not performed the Articles of their Alliance with England', which suggestion it declared was 'spread about the Country to Create Animosities, and to support the Spirits of the Enemies of England'. On the eve of the

---

[1] *C.W.* 29, dedication and p. 411; *Review*, i, 20 and 27, 13 May and 6 June, 1704.
[2] *C.W.* 134, p. 28.

opening of Parliament L'Hermitage reported that 'les bien intention-nées qui tâchent de s'oposer à tous les mauvais prétextes' were very worried about the possible consequences in England of the news that Louis XIV had just consented to allow the resumption of normal trading relations with the Dutch. The Godolphin ministry prepared to face the Parliament uncertain whether that body would agree with the suggestion, included in a popular list of maxims about the European powers, that 'England and Holland pays for all', or whether it would follow the High Tories in taking the view that England paid for all, but Holland took all.[1]

The speech with which the queen opened the third session of her first Parliament showed that the ministry, for all its uneasiness, had no intention of compromising with the High Tory views on the conduct of the war. It called upon the Commons for

such Supplies .... as may be requisite for carrying on the next year's service both by sea and land, and for punctually performing our treaties with all our allies; the rather, for that some of them have just pretensions depending ever since the last war.

The ready response of the lower House to this appeal showed how great had been the effect of Blenheim on the English attitude to the war and to the Dutch alliance. The High Tories, as was expected, proposed that the augmentation in the Low Countries should be renewed only on condition that all commerce and correspondence between the Republic and the enemy be suspended. The House, which only a year earlier had given whole-hearted support to a similar motion, threw out the proposal and voted the augmentation without attaching any condition. Instead it sent a message to the Board of Trade asking for its opinions as to the best means of restraining commerce with France.

The question of Dutch trade with France had only been shelved, not dismissed, and it was to be raised again before the session ended. Nonetheless Stanhope, who had had no opportunity of judging at first-hand the state of opinion in England after Blenheim, was as-tonished that this obstacle to the voting of supplies had been brushed aside so easily. He was full or praise for Harley's 'manadgement' in this matter, and promised to do his best to 'prevent ye accepting or negotiating of any Bills by which ye french forces are payd', adding,

---

[1] (Godolphin) to (Harley), 25 (May?) (1704) (O.S.), Duke of Portland Mss.: Lord Godol-phin; R. Palmer to R. Verney, 12 June 1704 (O.S.), *Verney Letters*, i, pp. 98–9; L'Hermitage to States-General (transcript), 27 Oct./7 Nov, 1704, London, Add. Ms. 17677 ZZ; *Observator*, iii, 68, 9 Dec. 1704.

however, that 'in matters of money and negotiating Bills, I know them too well to undertake anything for them'.[1]

The ease with which supplies had been voted despite the High Tory attempt to call attention to Dutch trade with the enemy had shown that Blenheim had won the strong support of all but the most extreme Tories for the ministry's war policies. The position of Godolphin and his colleagues was still far from enviable, however; from the High Tories they could expect little but opposition, and the 'moderates' alone were not numerous enough to guarantee them control of either House. More and more the fate of their policies was in the hands of the 'Junto' Whigs, and these were not likely to give their favours without expecting payment. Their claims to a greater share in the government grew more and more insistent, but Godolphin was prevented from giving them any substantial satisfaction by the well-known dislike of the Queen for both their persons and their persuasions. It was even rumoured that the Junto, dissatisfied with the treatment it was receiving from the ministry, might join with the High Tories to bring it down. Both the new parliamentary situation, arising from the removal of the High Tories from the ministry, and the fact that the Whigs were pre-eminently the exponents of that enthusiasm for the war that was now sweeping the country, made the government to some extent dependent on Whig support even before the 1705 election.

This was well illustrated in the critical struggle over the Occasional Conformity Bill which occurred in this session of Parliament. When the High Tories proposed to 'tack' this bill to a money bill – a procedure that would have made amendment by the Lords impossible – Whigs and 'moderates' joined to defeat this attempt; but when the High Tories, now termed 'tackers' by their opponents, introduced the bill itself, few 'moderates' could find it in their hearts to vote against it, and it was once more left to the Whig Lords to throw out a measure that would have been so disruptive of national unity. In the debate on the 'Tack', on November 28th – as in the paper warfare about Occasional Conformity that had preceded the session – mention was made of the Dutch. In introducing the 'tacking' motion Bromley asserted

that the employing persons of a different religion from that established by law

---

[1] L'Hermitage to States-General (transcript), 14/25 Nov. 1704, London, Add. Ms. 17677 ZZ; Stanhope to Harley, 25 Nov. 1704, Hague, S.P. Holl. 227; Stanhope to Stepney, 28 Nov. 1704, Hague, Add. Ms. 7069; Board of Trade to Commons (copy), 21 Nov. 1704, Whitehall, C.O. 389/18; *Cobbett*, vi, cols. 355-6.

had never been practised by any wise government, and was not allowed even in Holland.

For Bromley to quote the example of the Dutch republic was akin to the devil citing scripture, but a pamphlet that was published in reply to his speech had an answer to this damnable iteration:

There is scarce a town in Holland (whatever some have affirmed to the contrary) where the Remonstrants, as well as the Calvinists, have not sometimes been in their public Offices. Some of the Generals of the Army, and Governors even of their Frontier Towns, are at this very time *Roman* Catholics. They do not only employ all Christians without Distinction, but even Jews . . . . [1]

This was a debate which was to be revived when the election of 1705 drew near.

In December the Whig Lords considered that the time was ripe for pressing Godolphin and Marlborough for that increased representation in the ministry that they regarded as their due. They accordingly launched an attack on the Admiralty, a branch of the administration whose conduct aroused widespread dissatisfaction throughout the war and which was largely a preserve of the High Tories. Thus began the Whig pressure to which the Treasurer and the General were to be subjected almost unceasingly for the next six years.

The attack on the Admiralty was little more than a political manoeuvre, but while it lasted it threatened to bring to the surface some of the less happy aspects of Anglo-Dutch naval coöperation. As Dayrolle had reported in March, the Admiralties of Zeeland and Friesland had provided only a very small part of their due contribution of ships since the beginning of the war; and when Sir David Mitchell arrived once more at The Hague at the end of November to make arrangements for the next year, Stanhope found that

there is little appearance yet, they will come up near to what we demand either as to Shipps or land men on Board . . . .

Marlborough, too, when he reached The Hague in the middle of December, found Mitchell dissatisfied and despondent.[2]

On December 6th (O.S.) the Whig Lords launched their offensive. They asked, among other things, that

the agreement between sir David Mitchel and the states general, relating to their quota of men of war, be laid before them.

Nothing of importance seems to have come of this request, but before

---

[1] *Cobbett*, vi, cols. 359–60; *C.W.* 2, p. 82.

[2] Dayrolle to Ellis, 18 March 1704, Hague, Add. Ms. 28914; Stanhope to Stepney, 28 Nov. 1704, Hague, Add. Ms. 7069; Marlborough to Hedges, 12 Dec. 1704, Hague, *Murray*, i, p. 553; *ibid.*, i, p. 556, Marlborough to Harley, 16 Dec. 1704, Hague.

this Harley had already instituted some enquiries of his own into Dutch fulfilment of their naval quotas. 'Many very honest gentlemen', he declared,

are very uneasy possessed with a notion that we perform our parts, and the States suffer the Common Cause to Languish and our Efforts to be fruitless for want of Supplying their proportions last Year at Sea.

Stanhope, carrying out Harley's instructions, found it difficult to obtain the necessary information, 'since', he explained,

I can not trust to the accounts of any Dutchman from whom no sincerity is to be expected in a matter of this nature where, if they speak truth, they must necessarily condemn themselves . . . .

From Mitchell, however, he was able to obtain evidence that the complaints of which Harley had written were 'but too justly grounded'. The Dutch had broken up the Dunkirk squadron by refusing to send their ships north of Goeree, sent ships to northern waters and counted them as part of their quota in defiance of British objections, provided no ships for the Channel, and withdrawn 'six of their eighteen in the Mediterranean when we stood most in want of them'. All this, Stanhope reported, they did not disown, but merely declared 'that they were able to do no more'. In private, he continued, 'they alledge also the same inability as to next summer'. Stanhope's findings seem to have gone no further than Harley, and it was perhaps fortunate that they were never presented to Parliament. As for Mitchell, not until February 8th was his mission completed, and then 'pas du tout à notre satisfaction', as Dayrolle wrote, since the Dutch would promise no more than they had performed in 1704.[1]

Though the Whig Lords pressed their enquiry into the management of the war at sea they stood beside the ministers when, also on December 6th, the High Tories in the Lords launched yet another assault. On this occasion, a debate on 'the state of the nation', they attacked the ministry, and above all Godolphin, for having advised the queen to give her assent to the Scottish Act of Security, whereby the Scottish Parliament had stipulated that the next successor to the Throne of Scotland should not be the same person as the English successor, unless England had previously satisfied Scotland both as to her conditions of government and of trade. Only the support of the Whig Lords saved Godolphin from censure; though the Whig Peter-

[1] *Luttrell*, v, p. 495, 7 Dec. 1704; Harley to Stanhope (copy), 7 Dec. 1704, Whitehall, F. E. B. Holl. 72; Stanhope to Harley, 19 and 30 Dec. 1704, Hague, S.P. Holl. 227; Drummond to Ellis, 30 Dec. 1704 and 20 Jan. 1705, Amsterdam, Add. Ms. 28916; Dayrolle to Stepney, 10 Feb. 1705, Hague, Add. Ms. 37155.

borough, ever unpredictable, made some remarks that might almost have been written by a High Tory propagandist. The ex-Secretary of State Vernon commented that Peterborough

carried his discourse farther than there seemed to be any occasion for, towards an apologizing for the ministry, who he thought were to be pitied in having such a load upon them, as to be contesting at the same time, with the folly of Portugal, the obstinacy of the Emperor, the Selfishness of the Dutch, and the madness of Scotland, all superadded to the power of France.

In this debate, too, Lord Haversham, a recent convert from Whiggery to High Toryism, lamented, as he was often to do in subsequent years, the export of coin and bullion from England, above all to the Republic. Godolphin retorted that this was an inevitable consequence of a European war; the only way to prevent it, he added, 'was by clapping up a peace with France'.[1]

It was evident that the Godolphin ministry, whose war policies now had the whole-hearted and enthusiastic backing of most of their politically conscious fellow-countrymen, had no intention of 'clapping up a peace with France'. Moreover, they were not much concerned in December 1704 about the possibility that their Dutch ally might take such a step. There had already been some vague rumours of French emissaries at The Hague, but they had not been taken very seriously, and on December 19th (N.S.) Stanhope was able to send a report which was reassuring in this respect, if not in others. 'I do not as yet', he wrote,

see the least reason to suspect the States have any thoughts of making a separate peace, but for an unactive warr, 'tis what they most certainly design. They can not, or will not enter into ye account that a little extraordinary expence now, may probably save them ten times as much hereafter. I believe their wills are very good, but can not indure to part with more money or sooner than they think is absolutely necessary for the present.[2]

This calm confidence in the intention of the Dutch to stand by Britain, however parsimoniously, should be noted well. It was soon to vanish from British official circles, never to reappear.

3

In the first months of 1705 Nottingham's successor Harley became increasingly impatient with the unsatisfactory attitude adopted by

---

[1] Vernon to Shrewsbury, 8 Dec. 1704 (O.S.), Somerville, op.cit., pp. 618–9; Cobbett, vi, cols. 369–71.

[2] Stanhope to Harley 19 Dec. 1704, Hague, S.P. Holl. 227.

the Dutch leaders in matters of mutual interest. Mitchell's negotiations at The Hague, Dutch delay in ratifying the treaty recently made by Marlborough at Berlin, and renewed rumours of clandestine Franco-Dutch negotiations; none of these improved the Secretary's temper, but the sorest point in all his dealings with the Dutch at this time was undoubtedly the continuing dispute about commerce and correspondence with the enemy.

The Commons had not allowed this matter to delay the voting of supplies, but had referred it to the Board of Trade. On November 21st the Board made its report. It advocated the introduction of a Bill imposing strict and severe penalties against those subjects of the queen found trading with France, but this proposal was made in such a manner as to cast some doubt upon the advisability of such a measure 'whilst there is or may be an open Trade carryed on between some of her Majesty's allies and France'. In making its recommendation the Board was no doubt influenced by the report that it had received from one Galdie, concerning the credit which some French bankers had in Holland. The only way to prevent this from being of injury to the allied cause, this report suggested, was for correspondence between Holland and France to be once more prohibited.[1]

Desirable as such a proposition might seem to the English ministers, reports from The Hague left them in no doubt of the very different Dutch views on the subject. Dayrolle was despondent about the chances of reaching any understanding on this question, and made it clear that

ils ne sont principalement occupés que de l'établissement d'un commerce libre avec l'Ennemi, tandis qu'en Angleterre on prend toutes les mesures nécessaires non seulement pour l'empêcher, mais pour rompre aussi toute correspondence avec lui.

In fact the ministry had already shown, both in its instructions to the colonial governors and privateers of the previous year, and in those issued on January 2nd 1704/5, concerning neutral ships trading between Spain and England, that it was willing to waive a strict prohibition of trade where predominantly British interests were concerned. When the Lords came to debate the annual report of the Board of Trade, however, it became clear that Parliament was not yet in a mood to extend such favours to the Dutch. Nottingham's proposal, made on January 19th, that steps should be taken to prevent the importation of French goods from Holland (in fact already prohibited

---

[1] Galdie to Board of Trade (copy), (rec'd) 20 Nov. 1704 (O.S.), C.O. 388/9; Board of Trade to Commons (copy), 21 Nov. 1704, Whitehall, C.O. 389/18.

by the Navigation Acts) met with a significantly warm welcome, even though Halifax, Godolphin and others denied his allegations that the Dutch were conducting this traffic at one hundred per cent. profit, and that there would soon be no coin left in England if a stop were not put to it. On the other hand, in an Act which was subsequently passed formally introducing penalties for British subjects found trading with France it was specifically stated that trade might be carried on with what were somewhat disingenuously called 'the Dominions of Charles the Third King of Spain'. The Dutch envoy Vrijbergen was not slow to point out that the allowing of such latitude was scarcely consistent with the ministry's disapproval of Dutch trade with France.[1]

Vrijbergen's arguments were far from acceptable to Harley. Not only was the Secretary personally exasperated by the Dutch attitude, but he was fearful that the continuing popular feeling on the subject might have parliamentary repercussions. Stanhope, however, was unwilling to communicate Harley's veiled threats of 'reprisals' to the Dutch government, fearing, as he wrote on February 10th (N.S.) that

they have reserves on their side also, for we see every day prints published, though own by no body, with proposals of peace by a new Treaty of Partition ...

The spectre of a separate Dutch peace with France had been raised, and would not be exorcised until the 1709 Barrier Treaty bound the Provinces fast to the Whig Junto. Previous rumours to this effect had gained little credit amongst the English ministers, but now it began to seem that there might be some cause for concern. Heinsius had communicated a French 'proposition' to Marlborough, there were renewed reports that there were French emissaries at The Hague, and Dayrolle thought it significant that three deputies had urged the conclusion of a peace at the last meeting of the States of Holland.[2]

Despite such portents, Harley would not be appeased on the question of trade with the enemy. He seemed to take a memorial from Vrijbergen concerning Dutch ships seized while trading to France

---

[1] L'Hermitage to States-General (transcript), 23 Jan./3 Feb. 1704/5, London, Add. Ms. 17677 AAA; Portland to Heinsius (extract), Jan. 1704/5, *von Noorden*, ii, p. 282; Dayrolle to Stepney, 10 Feb. 1705, Hague, Add. Ms. 37155; J. Cooke to Popple, 9 April 1706, Doctors' Commons, *C.S.P. Col.*, *1706–8*, p. 105; *Annals*, iv, pp. 6–7. For the Act in question (Anne 3 & 4, c. XIII) see *Statutes at Large*, iv, p. 183. It was approved by the Lords on March 3rd (*L.J.*, xvii, p. 687), and is described by Sir George Clark as the highwater mark of the wartime prohibition of trade ('War Trade and Trade War', p. 276).

[2] Marlborough to Heinsius, 9 Jan. 1704/5 (O.S.), *van 't Hoff*, p. 160; Harley to Stanhope (copy), 23 Jan. 1704/5, Whitehall, F. E. B. Holl. 72; Dayrolle to Stepney, 3 Feb. 1705, Hague, Add. Ms. 37155; Stanhope to Harley, 10 Feb. 1705, Hague, S. P. Holl. 228.

as a personal affront, and his letters continued to contain forebodings of some dire but unspecified reprisals. But Stanhope's warnings soon had their effect on him; at first he grudgingly admitted, after a letter full of complaints, that

after all, it is an Enemy hath sown these jealousies; and every good man must do his part to preserve a good Understanding between the two Nations . . . . ,

but soon he was more seriously concerned:

I heartily wish that our good friends the States would have been pleased to have taken any other method than what they have, we are studying all we can heer to preserve their reputation with our country, and they suffer ill-intentioned persons to embitter the spirits of their People against us: I wish the root do not lye deeper and that the malignity you mention in your last be not owing to the Artifices of the French who would make them engage rashly in an insecure peace.

Their fears that 'this people would have flown out into some desperate extremes' – in other words, their determination to put the solidarity of the alliance before all other issues – were leading Harley and the ministry to adopt a more conciliatory attitude. The queen was persuaded by Marlborough to issue the Order in Council of March 15th which released the Dutch ships that had been seized and allowed them unobstructed passage to France for the future provided that they carried neither goods belonging to the enemy nor contraband. Negotiations were set on foot to arrive at a satisfactory definition of contraband, and on March 31st (N.S.) Stanhope was able to report that the whole matter was very near a composure. Official restraint was allowing public indignation to cool, despite all the High Tory efforts, which were soon to be renewed, to keep the controversy alive.[1]

This whole episode is not only an illustration of the value placed on the Dutch Alliance by the English at this time, but a striking refutation of the view that commercial jealousy dominated our attitude towards the Dutch. It should be noted, however, that in this instance the ministry was anticipating, rather than following, the trend of public opinion. Most Englishmen in the spring of 1705 must have found the Order in Council just as 'extraordinary' as did Lediard more than thirty years later, and it is significant that the queen waited until after the prorogation of Parliament before issuing it. Harley's fears betrayed his knowledge that the bulk of M.P.'s did not believe Godolphin's assurances that Dutch trade with France did England no harm; and

---

[1] Harley to Stanhope (copies), 6 and 16 Feb. 1704/5, Whitehall, F. E. B. Holl. 72; Stanhope to Harley, 24 Feb. and 31 March 1705, Hague, S.P. Holl. 228; Marlborough to Heinsius, 7 and 9 March 1704/5 (O.S.), *van 't Hoff*, pp. 169–70; *Annals*, iv, pp. 6–7; *C.W.* 113, iii, p. 687; *von Noorden*, ii, pp. 283–4.

the ministry thought it wise to justify its action by pointing out that the queen had already taken measures formally to open a trade with Spain.[1]

The Order in Council, necessitated though it had been by fear of Dutch peace moves, was also a reflection of the changing official attitude to trading with the enemy. A new viewpoint was to gain wide currency before the year ended, and it had already been well expressed in some articles in Defoe's *Review*. It was, quite simply, that 'We ought to Trade with every Nation we can Bubble', and that we had no right to blame the Dutch for making use of this excellent maxim. From this Defoe went on to condemn those who said,

Let us make them stop the Trade, or send over no more Forces to help them; a Parcel of *Dutch* Sons of W——s, and the like,

and those who bemoaned the export of bullion to Holland, as if it were possible to carry on a war without money. That such views could, and did, gain the upper hand, first in official and then in wider circles, is all the more remarkable if we consider that 'the year 1705 marked the lowest stage of the depression of commerce, during Queen Anne's wars'.[2]

4

No sooner had the New Year opened than the High Tory Tackers, smarting from their parliamentary rebuff over Occasional Conformity and indignant at the 'desertion' of their queen from the High Church cause, launched a number of fierce attacks in pamphlet form upon the ministry and its policies. It was not only baffled rage, however, that urged the High-Fliers on, but an eager anticipation of the parliamentary dissolution and general election necessitated by the provisions of the Triennial Act of 1694.

In this campaign, one of the most bitterly contested of the eighteenth century, the High Tories' chief plank was their unchanging battle-cry of 'The Church in Danger'; but one of the first blows they struck in the contest, four months before the dissolution, took a significantly

---

[1] *C.W.* 114, p. 631. 'You will allow mee on this occasion to inform you that we do not propose to ourselves much trade with Spain, but the trew intention of getting this bille for the opening of the trade with Spain was only to enable Her Majesty to release your Shipes and to give such orders as that they may not for the futor have any farther trouble' (Marlborough to Heinsius, 7 March 1704/5 (O.S.), *van 't Hoff*, p. 169).

[2] *Review*, i, 83, 88 and 94, 19 Dec. 1704, 6 and 27 Jan. 1704/5; Clark, 'War Trade and Trade War', p. 279.

different form. This was a pamphlet entitled *Great Britain's Union, and the security of the Hanover succession Consider'd* .... L'Hermitage, reporting its appearance to his masters on January 16th, wrote that it was conjectured to be the work of the erstwhile Whig Lord Haversham. Of its two main points, one was the many advantages that would accrue from the residence in England of the heir-presumptive. This proposal was known to be most distasteful to the queen, and was pressed by the Tackers throughout the year in the vain hope of embarrassing the ministry's relations either with Anne or with the Electoral House. The pamphlet's other main topic was better calculated to cause mischief. Pointing out the dangers to England from the Scottish Act of Security, the author demonstrated how essential was a better understanding between the two countries; and what better way to achieve this than by letting the impoverished Scots into English trade, and, more specifically, by establishing a 'Joint-Stock' of both kingdoms for fishing?

The implications of the author's argument must have been obvious to his readers, familiar as they were with the details of the century-long dispute over Dutch exploitation of the 'Scottish fisheries'. The author was none the less determined to leave not the least doubt as to his meaning, and so he went on:

.... let us a little consider what great advantages the *Dutch* have over us with respect to our *Trade*, our *Quotas*, and our *Coin*, either from our ignorance, or their Influence and Designs upon us.

The next six pages were devoted to just such an examination. English trade, he found, was greatly prejudiced by Dutch enjoyment of liberty of commerce with France whilst this was prohibited to England; not only were the Dutch establishing a flourishing trade with France but they were reaping handsome dividends from the French goods that they exported to England. They were coveting what parts of England's East Indian trade they had not already engrossed, and there was ample reason to expect them to secure separate commercial advantages by a secret agreement with France. Meanwhile, he continued, the money we were pouring into Europe enriched the Dutch and impoverished us, and would be far better employed in

maintaining our Dominion of the Seas, and making ourselves Masters of the principal Places of Strength and Importance in *America* .... which by our League with the House of *Austria* we may keep.

Manpower for such projects would not be wanting if we let the Scots join with us, 'which', he added, would so unite both Nations in one and the same Interest that I can attribute it to Nothing but the *Power* of a *Foreign Interest* (this being the thing of all others the *Dutch* most dread) such a project has not been attempted . . . .

Why, he asked, could we obtain no official statement on Dutch fulfilment of their naval quotas, though we heard they were to provide only one ship in four in 1705? Why should *we* send agents to *them* to arrange such matters? And was it not a fact that they melted down the silver coin we sent them to stop it coming home again?

I have been the larger on this Head to convince you how much it is our interest to strengthen ourselves as far as possible by bringing in the *Scotch Nation to a Union with us in the Fishing Trade*; for want of which, the advantages the *Dutch* make by that Trade are too many here to be enumerated.

The importance of this pamphlet lies not so much in the arguments presented – mostly the old anti-Dutch trading slogans revived under a new pretext – as in the timing of its appearance. The High Tories, baffled in their attack on the Dissenters, and estranged from the queen, were throwing all restraint aside in a renewal of open attacks upon the Dutch; an activity not only thoroughly congenial to them but also designed to catch votes in the coming elections. For the moment, however, these attacks were on a limited front; they played only a minor part in election propaganda, and it was not until after the Tackers' failure at the polls and the opportunity for criticism provided by Dutch conduct in the field that the offensive became a general one. L'Hermitage was sufficiently impressed by this pamphlet to send a detailed account of it to his masters, but he was confident that its arguments would find little support, since people knew

qu'on distingue principalement les Jacobites, en ce qu'ils tâchent de jeter les semences de division entre l'Angleterre et leurs Hautes Puissances, dans la persuasion que rien ne sera plus nuisible aux interêts du Prince de Galles, que la bonne intelligence entre les deux nations . . . . ;

probably a fair summary of the state of feeling at that moment.[1]

The anonymous author of this pamphlet had deliberately chosen as one of his major topics the ancient bone of contention of fishing rights, with its background of a century's envy and ill-will. That this and other questions relating to British 'sovereignty' of the seas were still live issues was further demonstrated by the publication in the same year of Alexander Justice's *A general Treatise of the Dominion and Laws of the Sea* . . . . ., a work of antiquarian learning rather than of polemics. This book included almost 200 pages of legal, historical and

[1] L'Hermitage to States-General (transcript), 16/27 Jan. 1704/5, London, Add. Ms. 17677 AAA; *C.W.* 85, pp. 10–15.

mythological argument designed to show that the absolute sovereignty of the 'British Seas' was vested in the Crown. Here the long story of Dutch violations of British sovereignty was related in all its detail. Justice firmly disclaimed any intention of creating bad blood against Holland, and there is no reason to doubt his sincerity in proclaiming his high esteem for the Dutch both as allies and as fellow-Protestants; at the same time he made it clear that, as one who had studied the subject deeply, he had no doubt that what had happened once might happen again, and

> that 'tis not only convenient, but necessary (*Tractare Amicum tanquam Inimicum futurum*) to be so discreet and cautious in raising the Fortunes of our Friends, as not to put it in their Power to be Dangerous in case they should turn Enemies; which I hope they shall be no more.[1]

On March 12th, as her last resource in breaking the deadlock between Lords and Commons in the case of Ashby v. White, the queen prorogued Parliament, and three weeks later, on April 4th, dissolved it. The election fight was on, and, for the ministry as for the public, all other issues paled into insignificance. In the bitter pamphlet war that characterised this election, the Dutch were not altogether forgotten; the Tackers no longer scrupled to make use of and play upon whatever anti-Dutch feeling might exist. In a satirical poem attacking Occasional Conformity the Devil was described as *'that Hogen Potentate'* and gold was said to be 'the great idol of the D—h'. In his *Historical Account of Comprehension* .... William Baron showed how the Dutch had restrained the intolerant spirit of Calvinism only by the adoption of a thorough-going Erastianism, it being implied that this step was only too easy for such an irreligious people. On the other side, the opponents of the Occasional Conformity Bill pointed to the Republic's toleration in religious matters as the source of its power and prosperity.[2]

No great importance can be attached to all this: these were propagandists anxious to make out a case, though the attention that they paid to Church-State relations in the United Provinces is somewhat striking. More important, perhaps, is the fact that it was thought fit to publish, on April 30th, a pamphlet which Defoe had written for the 1702 elections but which had not then appeared. This made great play with the Tories' opposition to William III, their rejoicing at his death and their avowed aversion to the Dutch. The implicit moral of all

---

[1] *C.W.* 111, pp. 171–87.

[2] *Churchill*, iii, p. 23; *C.W.* 141, pp. 2–3; *C.W.* 12, pp. 41, 67 *sqq.*; *C.W.* 16, pp. 3–4. One Tacker pamphleteer went so far as to deny that Dutch Catholics were ever 'put into any Employment, or trusted with any Power' (*Reviewer Review'd*, 1).

this was what L'Hermitage had thought was firmly planted in people's minds, namely that true patriotism and enmity towards the Dutch were incompatible. Not that Defoe's writings at this time give evidence of untempered adulation of the Republic; on the contrary, his fantastic satire *The Consolidator*, published on March 26th, criticised both English and Dutch – particularly the latter – for gross inconsistency and lack of principle in their various dealings with Philip V and Charles III. In particular he accused the Dutch of unworthy motives in – allegedly – taking the lead both in recognizing the former and in setting up the latter. Though it would be misleading to describe this long and entertaining work as anti-Dutch, its attitude towards the Republic was certainly more critical than that of the two-volumed *History of the Republic of Holland*, also published in 1705. The body of this work was taken direct from such writers as Grotius and Neuville (with, incidentally, no mention of the Amboyna 'massacre' and its repercussions) but the preface seems to have been specially written and gives a good indication, even if in exaggerated terms, of the genuine wonder that Englishmen still felt at the sudden rise to greatness of their neighbours:

To see a Powerful Republick spring from Necessity and Despair, and infeeble a Monarchy that threaten'd all *Europe*, to view the various steps, the concurring Circumstances, and the surprizing Events of their Counsels, must needs be equally Diverting and Instructive. The shining Instances of all Military and Peaceful Vertues that are here met with, are such as are scarce to be match'd in the Records of Time: the Steddiness of the People, the Solidity and Firmness of their Counsels, and their unwearied Diligence in struggling for Liberty, not only to themselves, but to their Neighbours, will be a lasting example for Posterity to imitate .... [1]

The outcome of the elections of 1705 was decided less by any question of policy than by the at least partial withdrawal of the queen's favour from the High Tories.[2] The striking Whig gains in this election were none the less due in part to the new enthusiasm in England for the war. This enthusiasm had served the ministry well, for it had thwarted the attacks of the High Tories; but the election, by increasing the dependence of Godolphin and his colleagues upon the Whigs, had sown the seed of future difficulties.

---

[1] *C.W.* 36, *passim*: *C.W.* 40, *passim*; *C.W.* 102, preface.
[2] On this and all other aspects of the 1705 election see E. Cunnington, *General Election of 1705* (unpublished M.A. thesis, London, 1938).

5

The increased power of the Whigs in Parliament was to be of fateful importance in determining British policy in the war and, in consequence, the course of Anglo-Dutch relations. Parliament would not meet until the autumn, however, and in the meantime English eyes turned once more to foreign fields. In Portugal they were to see little of any consequence, and for this the ministry held the Dutch largely to blame. Early in April Stanhope reported not only that the Dutch would try to evade any responsibility for the upkeep of Gibraltar (still besieged by land) but also that they were showing great remissness in sending ships and subsidies to Portugal. Even before the end of 1704 the new British commander Galway had begun to send home disquieting accounts of the conduct of the Dutch commander Fagel. By May, 1705, Galway was complaining that

> Mr. Fagell est toujours oposé à tout ce que je propose, ainsy je vous dois répèter que je ne puis estre utile au service icy, quelque peine que je me donne, au contraire je ne puis plus demeurer icy . . . .

Five days later John Methuen reported in similar vein on the activities of the Dutch ambassador Schonenberg:

> Monsr. Schonenbergh on all occasions opposes whatever I mention at any time relating to ye cooperating with our fleet with all ye violence & greater than you can imagine.

These letters set the tone for an endless series of complaints throughout the summer. Galway accused Fagel of deliberate obstruction and inveterate jealousy, and insisted that he and Schonenberg were in league with a faction at the Portuguese court to ruin Methuen and himself.[1]

These were serious accusations, and might have aroused considerable feeling at home had they been widely known. Not the least disquieting aspect of the situation, so far as the ministry was concerned, was that the veteran Huguenot general Galway was to some extent the protegé of the Junto. Godolphin, spurred on by Galway's repeated requests for recall, decided to act. Sunderland, who, as a sop to the Whigs,

---

[1] Marlborough to Heinsius, 26 Dec. 1704, St. Albans, *van 't Hoff*, p. 157; Stanhope to Stepney, 3 April 1705, Hague, Add. Mss. 7069; Stanhope to Harley, 7 April 1705, Hague, S.P. Holl. 228; Galway to (Godolphin), 28 May 1705, Notre Dame du Carrion, *Thibaudeau*, v, p. 333; Marlborough to Heinsius, 29 May 1705 (N.S.), *van 't Hoff*, p. 174; Galway to (Godolphin), 30 May 1705, Angela, *Thibaudeau*, v, pp. 333–4; Methuen to (Godolphin), 2 and 7 June, 1705, Lisbon, Add. Ms. 28056; Galway to (Godolphin), 5 July 1705, Lisbon, *Thibaudeau*, v, pp. 334–5; Galway to (Godolphin), 13 July 1705, Lisbon, *Coxe*, i, p. 330.

had been chosen to carry the queen's congratulations to the new Emperor, Joseph, was instructed to seek satisfaction in this matter at The Hague while on his way to Vienna. Both Godolphin and Somers wrote to Portland asking him to assist this mission while Marlborough importuned Heinsius to the same effect. Sunderland was to press the States-General to do their part to

remove all Obstructions which happen from Our and their Ministers not agreeing in the proper methods for promoting the Common Cause.

Above all, he was to demand supreme command of a united allied and Portuguese army for Galway, especially since

the expenses the States are at for that Service is so much less a proportion to what is done by us.

If the States shal deny a thing which hath so many arguments for it, & no good one against it,

remarked Harley,

many persons will have too much ground to suspect that they have different views in this affair from al honest people in England.[1]

On his arrival at The Hague, Sunderland found Heinsius anxious to help, but the general outlook far from encouraging. It was explained to him that the forms of the Dutch government made such a concession very difficult to obtain. Meeting with no success, he went on his way, leaving the negotiations in the hands of Stanhope, who, like Marlborough, felt no optimism as to the result. The 'difficulties raised' by the Dutch and their 'unaccountable perseverence' swelled the indignation that Harley felt at the news of the fiasco on the Dyle. Not until the end of August was there any progress made, and then relief came in the unexpected guise of a request from Fagel for permission to return to Holland. Whig and Tory alike expressed undisguised pleasure at this development, and it inspired Harley, even in the midst of the controversy that the conduct of the Dutch deputies and generals in Flanders was arousing, to enlarge on 'that firme union between England and the States-General, which is so absolutely necessary for our mutual safety'. Such congratulations were somewhat premature, for Fagel, with his preparations for returning to Holland already made, was called upon to take charge of the siege of Badajoz after

[1] Marlborough to Heinsius, 21 June 1705, Biebrich, *van 't Hoff*, pp. 185–6; Instructions for Sunderland (copy), 17 June 1705, Windsor, F. E. B. Misc. 203; Somers to (Portland), 21 June 1705, London, Add. Ms. 34515; Marlborough to Heinsius, 1 July 1705, Maestricht, *van 't Hoff*, pp. 189–90; Sunderland to (Godolphin), 24 June 1705, London, Add. Ms. 28056; Marlborough to Heinsius, 12 July 1705, Lens les Beguines, *van 't Hoff*, pp. 191–3; Harley to Sunderland (copy), 3 July 1705, Whitehall, F. E. B. Emp. 39; *von Noorden*, ii, p. 203.

the serious injury sustained by Galway on October 11 had put him *hors de combat*. His conduct of this melancholy finale to a fruitless campaign gave added point to English complaints, and soon afterwards he left Portugal for good, but protests from Methuen about 'the Conduct of the States or of their Ministers' continued to arrive at Whitehall.[1]

6

The passions aroused by the Portugal dispute had remained firmly locked within official breasts,[2] but it was otherwise with those evoked by the conduct of the Dutch in Flanders. From the very outset the attitude of the Dutch generals had been, in English eyes, unpromising. When Marlborough conferred with them at The Hague to concert arrangements for the campaign he thought that the number of troops that they demanded for service in the Low Countries while he confronted Villars on the Moselle was exorbitant, especially since 'at the same time they do not as much as pretend to act otherwise than on the defensive'. Three weeks later he was on the Moselle, having obtained 'most things I wished for', but Cardonnel voiced the Duke's growing conviction that the armies under Ouwerkerk were set on a purely defensive campaign. Indeed, their conduct in the field where, so St. John alleged, they were 'frightened out of their wits' by Villeroy, aroused in both military and ministerial circles not only criticism but also apprehensions lest they might 'be tempted to receive Propositions of Peace', as Marlborough put it. Marlborough's despatches clearly show that fear lest the Dutch might make a separate peace unless he was there both to aid and watch them was an important motive for his march back to Flanders from the Moselle. Godolphin's reaction to this plan (announced in Marlborough's despatch of June 16th) echoed the Duke's feelings:

Lord Marlborough being so near them in Holland will not only be a bridle upon

---

[1] Sunderland to Godolphin, 29 June 1705, Hague, Add. Ms. 28056; Harley to Sunderland (copy), 10 July 1705 (O.S.), F. E. B. Emp. 39; Harley to Stanhope (copies), 24 July, 3 and 28 Aug., 4 Sept. 1705, Whitehall, F. E. B. Holl. 72; Marlborough to Harley, 10 Aug. 1705, Meldert, *Murray*, ii, p. 214; *ibid.*, ii, p. 258, same to same, 7 Sept. 1705, Tirlemont; Sunderland to (Godolphin), 9 Sept. 1705, Vienna, Add. Ms. 28056; *Luttrell*, v, pp. 559–60, 6 Sept. 1705; Methuen to (Godolphin), 13 Oct. and 2 Nov. 1705, Lisbon, Add. Ms. 28056.

[2] Thus *Jones* has much to say of this campaign in Portugal, but gives no hint of the Galway-Fagel dispute. In 1708, however, there appeared in London a translation from the Dutch of Fagel's account of the campaign (*C.W.* 77). Its publication was presumably an attempt on the part of Peterborough or his friends to discredit Galway.

their negotiations, but taking away their fears it will also take away their power of proceeding upon them.[1]

When they joined the Dutch Marlborough and his entourage were not pleased with what they found. Cardonnel, though full of praise for the Dutch rank and file, was sure that the generals had not the least intention of fighting; Stanhope received the same impression at The Hague. In the event, the Dutch were 'drawn in insensibly', as Cardonnel had foreseen, to the forcing of the lines of Brabant, on July 18th (N.S.). Even in this hour of personal triumph, Marlborough, anxious as ever not to arouse anti-Dutch feeling in England, urged Godolphin not to emphasise the relative smallness of the part played by 'Monsieur Overkirk's army'. He could not, however, prevent the subsequent refusal of the Dutch generals to march their tired infantry on to Louvain from causing impatience among some of the British generals. Orkney, for one, saw 'no forwardness in any of these men'. The Dutch, he wrote,

are so untoward in everything, and my Lord so pestered with them, that it is a wonder he doth not leave the army.

Captain Blackader, without singling out the Dutch for criticism, recorded in his diary that

We are all fretting and uneasy about this mismanagement and blunder, that we have not improven our victory as we ought to have done . . . .

The army was in no mood to have the resolutions of its victorious general thwarted, no matter by whom, and its indignation at the continuation of this process in the next month was soon to be communicated to politicians and private men at home.[2]

For the moment, however, Defoe could rejoice at Marlborough's exploit by twitting the Tackers with the news that the general whom they now hated as a renegade had gained another victory. Rather

---

[1] Marlborough to Godolphin, 24 April 1705, Hague, *Coxe*, i, p. 266; *ibid.*, i, p. 267, Marlborough to Sarah, 4 May 1705 (N.S.); Cardonnel to Ellis, 15 May 1705, Juliers, Add. Ms. 28918; St. John to T. Coke, 28 May 1705, Whitehall, *H. M. C. XII pt. iii*, p. 61; Marlborough to Eugene, 11 June 1705 (N.S.), *Coxe*, i, p. 280; (Godolphin) to (Harley), 3 June 1705 (O.S.), *H.M.C. Bath I*, pp. 69–70; Marlborough to Godolphin, 16 June 1705 (N.S.), *Coxe*, i, p. 282; *ibid* i, pp. 281–2, Marlborough to Sarah, 16 June 1705, Elst; *ibid.*, i, p. 285, same to same, 18 June 1705, Treves; Marlborough to Bradford, 21 June 1705, Biebrich, *Murray*, ii, p. 122; (Godolphin) to (Harley), 21 June 1705, Windsor, *H. M. C. Bath I*, p. 70. See also Marlborough's despatches to Wratislaw, Hedges and Harley in *Murray*, ii, pp. 85–112.

[2] Cardonnel to Stepney, 6 and 16 July 1705, Lens les Beguines, Add. Ms. 7063; Stanhope to Stepney, 9 July 1705, Hague, Add. Ms. 7069; Marlborough to Heinsius, 16 July 1705, Lens les Beguines, *van 't Hoff*, p. 193; Marlborough to Godolphin, 18 July 1705, Tirlemont, *Coxe*, i, p. 295; Orkney to (Hamilton?), 20 July 1705, Vlierbeck, *E.H.R.*, xix, pp. 311–14; *Blackader*, p. 250.

than this, he mocked, they would have preferred to see the Dutch gain the day single-handed

so we could have pretended to rejoyce as livelily as formerly we used to Counterfeit Sorrow for them, when they were beaten.

For the moment, too, Marlborough could reflect with pleasure that his success had banished from Dutch minds all thoughts of a separate peace, the fear of which continued to alarm the ministry until it received news of the action. His pleasure was short-lived, for soon his private letters were full of complaints about Dutch reluctance to resume the offensive. 'It is very mortifying to find much more obstruction from friends than from enemies', he told Godolphin, his closest friend, though, as usual, his language to Harley, his colleague only, was more restrained:

I cannot forbear telling you, that I meet with greater Difficultys from Our Friends to move forward, than I could have expected.[1]

On July 30th (N.S.) the Dutch generals, with Slangenburg as spokesman, forced Marlborough to call a halt in mid-career to the attempt that was at last being made to force the passage of the Dyle. The letters of the warlike chaplain, Francis Hare, mirror the feelings of Marlborough's entourage. He suggested to his correspondents at home that the action of the generals was deliberately taken to revenge themselves on Marlborough for having duped them about the attack on the lines; he inveighed particularly against the 'impertinence' of Slangenburg; and he expressed the deepest pessimism about the outcome of a campaign in which unlimited powers of obstruction seemed to reside in 'an ally that will hazard nothing'. Blackader found that the action on the Dyle was 'variously talked of; commended and censured according to men's various humours'. His own view, he told his wife, was that 'by the blessing of God, we could have beat them if we had gone over'; and he added that

it is commonly believed here, that both at the lines and now, it is the States and their Generals, that hinder us to fight, and to improve our advantages as we might. So that if you have a value for my safety and preservation, you should go and thank the States for it.

Marlborough's reaction to the fiasco on the Dyle was to send his

[1] Marlborough to Sarah, 20 July 1705, nr. Louvain, *Coxe*, i, p. 296; Hedges to Methuen (copy), 10 July 1705, Whitehall, F. E. B. Port. 108; Marlborough to Anne, 23 July 1705, nr. Louvain, *Coxe*, i, p. 296; Marlborough to Heinsius, 27 July 1705, Vlierbeck, *van 't Hoff*, pp. 196–7; Marlborough to Harley, 27 July 1705, Vlierbeck, *Murray*, ii, p. 190; Marlborough to Godolphin, 29 July 1705, Vlierbeck, *Coxe*, i, pp. 303–4; *Review*, ii, 60, 21 July 1705; Harley to Marlborough, 28 July 1705 (O.S.), *Coxe*, i, pp. 297–8.

subordinate, the Dutch lieutenant-general Hompesch, to The Hague with a message for the States-General, in which he appealed for greater discretionary powers. Without these, as he pointed out in a letter to Heinsius, it would be 'impossible to attempt anything considerable with success or advantage'. To Heinsius he hinted of the dangers of constant councils of war and of 'private animosity'; in the private correspondence that was seen by Godolphin alone he spoke his mind more freely. Not only did he declare the impossibility of working with Slangenburg, but he clearly implied that there had been some leakage of information about the late attack from a council of war to the enemy.[1]

On the 23rd July/3rd August a day was appointed by the queen for rendering thanks to God for Marlborough's recent success; but on the same day the Holland letters containing news of the attempt on the Dyle reached London, and feelings of gratitude for divine blessings were mingled with those of another kind. 'Plusieurs officiers Anglois ont icy écrit à leurs amis', reported L'Hermitage,

pour leur marquer le chagrin où ils estoient de ce qu'on n'avoit passé le Dyle, et leurs lettres ont fait beaucoup de bruit et ont donné lieu à divers discours, que chacun fait suivant ses diverses vues.

The annalist Jones tells us that, as was to be expected, 'the Male-contents in *England* failed not to improve the Occasion, (as they usually do) to rail against the *Dutch* ...'. Thus Harley, himself indignant that we had had 'a victory ravished out of D: of Marl-borough's hands by the caution of Our Ally', was at the same time concerned by the way in which these reports had 'sour'd the people heer against those who they apprehend have hindred D. Marlborough from fighting'. On August 7th (N.S.) Stanhope was able to send the news that Hompesch had that day returned to the army with in-structions from the States-General that Marlborough and Ouwerkerk alone, 'with ye approbation of the Three Deputys of the States', should make all resolutions. Stanhope found comfort in this concession, but the view in which Marlborough himself heartily concurred was expressed three days later by General Ingoldsby, who wrote that nothing could be done unless Marlborough had power to command the allied troops as he commanded the queen's.[2]

---

[1] Marlborough to Heinsius, 30 July and 2 Aug. 1705, Meldert, *van 't Hoff*, pp. 198–9; Hare to G. Naylor, 30 July and 3 Aug. 1705, Meldert, *H. M. C. XIV pt. ix*, pp. 202–4; Marlborough to Godolphin, 3 Aug. 1705, Meldert, *Coxe*, i, p. 305; Hare to ?, 3 Aug. 1705, Meldert, *Thibau-deau*, ii, p. 238; Blackader to Mrs. Blackader, 23 July 1705 (O.S.), Camp nr. Tirlemont, *Blackader*, pp. 258–60.

[2] L'Hermitage to States-General (transcript), 24 July/4 Aug. 1705, London, Add. Ms.

The situation was full of menace to the alliance of the Maritime Powers: at home the English people were 'sour'd'; the ministry, in addition, was once more resentfully apprehensive lest the Dutch should make a Partition Treaty with France, and annoyed at the manner in which the contraband negotiations were dragging on;[1] while many in the army were mortified and angry. Only a spark was needed to detonate an explosion that might endanger the Grand Alliance, an explosion of English opinion against the Dutch. That spark was more than amply provided by the refusal of the Dutch deputies to sanction the attack proposed by Marlborough at Overyssche on August 18th (N.S.), and the explosion duly occurred.

Marlborough's feelings at this new and humiliating frustration, which he had barely been able to restrain in the heat of the moment, were, unprecedentedly, allowed to appear, though in a most moderated form, in his official correspondence. The reason for his moderation was, as he told his Duchess, lest he should, by angering the Dutch, give 'the French an advantage'; the ministry at home, or at least one of its servants, also obeyed this motive in removing from Cardonnel's account of the day's happenings all mention of the Dutch refusal to fight before publishing it in the *Gazette*. In his private letters the Duke gave vent to his mortification, and his belief that Slangenburg, whose opinions the deputies had followed, had single-handed deprived the alliance of the opportunity, albeit one which might have cost many lives, of dictating a peace to the French King. His letter to the States-General in which he reported his difference of opinion with the deputies went through the hands of Stanhope, and the first reaction of this staunch Whig and friend of the Dutch to the news was one that boded ill for its reception by the Tory squires at home. 'If your people were sour'd before against those who hindered the Duke from fighting last time at the Dyle', he wrote to Harley,

this will raise their spleen much higher, as it has mine to such a degree, that I dare not venture to speak a word about it, for fear of letting slip something that may not become me, for I am quite lost, when I come to consider what may be the consequences of it, and how much this confirms the suspicions we had before, making them now pas't all doubt –

17677 AAA; Harley to Raby (copy), 27 July 1705, Whitehall, F. E. B. Prussia 51; Stanhope to Harley, 7 Aug. 1705, Hague, S. P. Holl. 228; Ingoldsby to Ormonde, 10 Aug. 1705, Meldert, *H. M. C. Ormonde n.s. VIII*, p. 174; Harley to Stanhope (copy), 31 July 1705, Whitehall, F. E. B. Holl. 72; Marlborough to Godolphin, 13 Aug. 1705, Meldert, *Coxe*, i, pp. 305–6; *Jones, 1705*, p. 260.

[1] Stanhope to Harley, 18 Aug. 1705, Hague, S. P. Holl. 228; St. John to Marlborough, 18 Aug. 1705, Whitehall, *Coxe*, i, p. 304.

suspicions, that is, of Dutch longings for immediate peace.[1] While Marlborough wrote to correspondents of his 'uneasiness' and disappointment, Stanhope added fuel to the fire by having Marlborough's letter to the States published at The Hague. All the world could now read his famous postcript:

J'ai le coeur si plein, que je ne saurois m'empêcher de représenter, dans cette occasion, à Vos Hautes Puissances que je me trouve ici avec beaucoup moins d'Autorité que quand J'avois l'honneur de commander leurs Troupes, l'Année passée en Allemagne.

With the publication of this letter there could no longer be any pretence that all was well with the command of the allied army; and the fury of the Dutch with their own generals and deputies, which Stanhope somewhat complacently reported, gave some slight indication of what the reactions of the English were likely to be.[2]

Stanhope's labours were not in fact necessary to fill the gaps in the *London Gazette*'s account of the incident, for there was a whole army of correspondents in the field. Not all of them, indeed, joined with the fiery and reverend Dr. Hare in his view that 'it is true the camp was very strong, and it would have cost a great many men, but it was very well worth it, and could not easily have miscarried'; one Captain Richard Pope, for example, gave the arguments for and against the attack, saying that he would 'not be impertinent enough to give my opinion, where such great doctors differ'; but angry, puzzled gentlemen at home were readier to be told who was in the wrong than to be asked to decide the question for themselves. It was enough for them to learn (in Blackader's words) that

You may thank your friends the Hollanders again, for it is said generally, that we owe it most to them, our sleeping in a sound skin on this occasion.[3]

[1] Marlborough to Sarah, 19 Aug. 1705 (N.S.), *Coxe*, i, p. 312; *ibid.*, i, pp. 312 and 314, Marlborough to Godolphin, 19 and 24 Aug. 1705 (N.S.); Marlborough to Heinsius, 19 Aug. 1705 (N.S.), *van 't Hoff*, p. 203; *ibid.*, pp. 203–4, Marlborough to Slingelandt, 19 and 21 Aug. 1705 (N.S.); Marlborough to Wratislaw, 20 Aug. 1705, Basse Wavre, *Murray*, ii, pp. 225–6; ? to (Trumbull), 20 Aug. 1705, Wavre, *H. M. C. Downshire I pt. ii*, pp. 841–2; Stanhope to Harley, 21 Aug. 1705, Hague, S. P. Holl. 228.

[2] Marlborough to States-General, 19 Aug. 1705, Basse Wavre, *C.W.* 113, iii, pp. 478–9; Marlborough to Hill, 21 Aug. 1705, Basse Wavre, *Hill Corres.*, i, pp. 216–17; Marlborough to Eugene, 23 Aug. 1705, Corbais, *Murray*, ii, p. 230; Marlborough to Shrewsbury, 24 Aug. 1705, Corbais, *H. M. C. Buccleuch II pt. ii*, p. 710; Marlborough to (Portland?), 24 Aug. 1705, Corbais, *H. M. C. XIV pt. iv*, p. 230; Marlborough to Sarah, 24 Aug. 1705, Corbais, *Coxe*, i, p. 264; Marlborough to Heinsius, 24 Aug. 1705, Corbais, *van 't Hoff*, p. 205; Stanhope to Harley, 25 Aug. 1705, Hague, S. P. Holl. 228; Marlborough to St. John, 31 Aug. 1705, Tirlemont, *Murray*, ii, p. 248.

[3] Blackader to Mrs. Blackader, 9 Aug. 1705 (O.S.), Wavre, *Blackader*, pp. 261–3; Hare to F. Godolphin, 24 Aug. 1705, Corbais, *Thibaudeau*, ii, pp. 238–9; R. Pope to T. Coke, 26 Aug. 1705, Ramey, *H. M. C. XII pt. iii*, p. 62; Hare to G. Naylor, 27 Aug. 1705, Ramey, *H. M. C. XIV pt. ix*, pp. 206–8; *ibid.*, pp. 204–6, same to same, 30 Aug. 1705, Basse Wavre.

It was not until eleven days after the deputies and 'that beast Slangenberg' had thwarted Marlborough's plans that the first news of the
event reached England. On its arrival, Stanhope's prediction was
verified – 'spleen' was the order of the day. In Flanders, Marlborough's
annoyance, never given much rein, had now been replaced by a firm
resolve never to serve with Slangenburg again, nor, indeed, ever again
to command in the Low Countries unless with greatly increased powers.
Meanwhile, he told Heinsius, he had taken the resolution for the rest
of the campaign 'of not exposing my own honour nor the publick good
by making any scheme', though he would execute any the Dutch
deputies and generals might agree on. But his suspicion that 'those
that are for peace' would welcome nothing better made him more
reluctant than ever to appeal to the Dutch people against their
generals, and thus redouble the bitterness of the faction struggles
within the Republic; and even in the heart of such a man as Cardonnel,
the 'uproare', the feuds, and the publication of vindications and
counter-vindications no longer elicited partisan enthusiasm but only
a weary 'I wish to God we were out of the feild'.[1] In England, however, the news was fresh, and it was not surprising that there, where
Blenheim had created an insatiable appetite for victory and where the
passage of the lines had excited high hopes it 'gave occasion to much
talk', to use the laconic phrase in which the obviously embarrassed
L'Hermitage reported to his masters the outburst of hurt English
pride. 'A long swell rolled across England', writes Churchill.

Marlborough knew that in fastening a reproach upon the Dutch he would find a
ready response. The Whigs, the advocates of vigorous war, were bound to
support it. The Tories marched up eager for a quarrel with those Continental
obstructionists and shirkers for whom English citizens had sacrificed too much
already. The Queen shared these sentiments with spontaneous warmth, and the
Cabinet responded. Harley, as Secretary of State and Speaker, gave full vent to
the national mood.

As a description of the state of opinion in the country immediately
upon receipt of the news of Overyssche this passage could hardly be
bettered, but it gives no hint of the more interesting and less foreseeable
developments that were shortly to take place.[2]

[1] Marlborough to Heinsius, 27 Aug. 1705, Ramey, *van 't Hoff*, pp. 206–7; Marlborough to
Godolphin, 27 Aug. 1705, Ramey, *Coxe*, i, p. 315; *ibid.*, i, p. 318, same to same, 31 Aug. 1705
(N.S.); *ibid.*, i, p. 318, Marlborough to Sarah, 31 Aug. 1705, Tirlemont; Cardonnel to (Stepney),
31 Aug. 1705, Tirlemont, Add. Ms. 7063. One at least of Marlborough's entourage seems to
have relaxed his self-control once the campaign was ended, for at the beginning of December
(N.S.) Brigadier Palmes was reported to have challenged Slangenburg to a duel (Dayrolle to
Stepney, 4 Dec. 1705, Hague, Add. Ms. 37155).

[2] L'Hermitage to States-General (transcript), 21 Aug./1 Sept. 1705, London, Add. Ms.
17677 AAA; Taylor, *op.cit.*, i, p. 334; *Churchill*, ii, p. 593.

Harley's reaction was immediate. On the very day that the news arrived he proposed to a meeting of the Cabinet that an emissary should be despatched to The Hague to remonstrate with the Dutch and to demand a more absolute command for Marlborough, and he sent an express to Marlborough himself for his views on this proposal. To Stanhope he expressed himself thus:

This cursed disappointment in Brabant puts me out of al Temper, and the consequences of it may be so fatal that I dare scarce trust myself to think upon it any further than to endeavour to obviate the mischiefs it may bring ... ;

but this self-imposed restraint did not prevent some bitter reflections on his part on the integrity of the Dutch generals. Godolphin lost no time in telling Vrijbergen that if the States did not give full authority to Marlborough Britain would withdraw her forces from Flanders. Indeed, now that Marlborough himself had lost patience, no Englishman, from Lord Treasurer to hack-poet, felt the need to restrain the expression of his pent-up disgust with Dutch deputies and generals. It was even being said in London that as soon as the war with France was over Britain would make her reckoning with the States. An extreme Tory like the non-juror Hearne did not allow his rooted distrust of Marlborough to deter him from joining in the chorus of condemnation of the Dutch, while for the moment the Whigs too indulged in the joys of righteous indignation. Sunderland, detached from the Junto at Vienna, thought it 'impossible to speak' of the Overyssche incident '& keep within bounds', and the *Observator* blamed the deputies for preventing 'another *Hockstedt* bout', remarking also that 'if these *Deputies* are capable of *Direction*, they are capable of *Command*, and fitter for *Generals* ....'. Even so, this Whig periodical's tone was remarkably unhysterical, and when Somers wrote to Portland about the situation there was a change of emphasis in the Whig attitude that was significant. It was no longer mainly a question of reproaches; Somers' fear was that the Tackers would make use of the controversy in order to make a speedy peace favourable to France. Already, he warned Portland, they were, ironically enough, using 'great industry .. to persuade us that a great party in Holland are earnest for a peace, even among the States'.[1]

This last allegation, so assiduously spread by the High Fliers, was certainly lent some colour by the reception of French proposals by

[1] Harley to Marlborough, 18 Aug. 1705 (O.S.), Coxe i, pp. 315–16; *Hearne*, i, p. 31, 20 Aug. 1705; Harley to Stanhope (copy), 21 Aug. 1705, Whitehall, F. E. B. Holl. 72; Sunderland to (Godolphin), 5 Sept. 1705, Vienna, Add. Ms. 28056; Somers to (Portland) (copy), 28 Aug. 1705 (O.S.), Add. Ms. 34515; *Observator*, iv, 43, 29 Aug. 1705; *von Noorden*, ii, pp. 288–9.

Heinsius, though on August 15th (N.S.) he communicated them to Marlborough, who in turn sent them to Godolphin on September 2nd with an assurance that Heinsius was 'entirely in the interest of England'. It was quite otherwise, though, he thought, with Welland and Buys, who were 'at the head of the faction'. In these circumstances Harley's suggestion that a mission should be sent to The Hague placed Marlborough in a peculiar difficulty. On the one hand, indignant Englishmen, both inside and outside the ministry, demanded satisfaction; on the other, Marlborough, however much his personal feelings might lead him to sympathize with this, had no desire to force Heinsius and his friends into the arms of those Dutchmen who inclined towards a 'bad' peace. The Republic, as he saw it, was the hinge of the Grand Alliance; and he used all his influence to make sure that his countrymen saw it too.[1]

For the moment, the pressure of public opinion in favour of some sort of retaliation or remonstrance was extremely strong. In ministerial circles it expressed itself in Harley's proposal; but in the coffee-houses and taverns it adopted a less restrained form. Jones relates that 'the Tongues of our domestick Malecontents were more loose than ever against the *Dutch* ...'.[2] The extreme manifestation of such feeling was a long poem entitled *The D— Deputies. A Satyr*. No other publication of this time reached such heights of vituperation, it is true, but that this work was ever published indicates the state of feeling in the country, for it is as abusive as anything published against the Dutch in the bitter years after 1710. It seems significant that there is no record of any official proceedings against those responsible for it. In this one poem are contained all the traditional anti-Dutch war-cries, all expressed in the most unrestrained form. Amboyna, hypocrisy in religion, the rule of self-interest, their barbaric diet and way of life; each of these topics, and many more, has its several place in this onslaught on 'those sons of *Mud*, the D——, who worship *Mammon*'. One quotation must suffice to convey the flavour of this work:

---

[1] 'It is impossible for me to express the trouble the last disappointment has given. However, I must be careful not to speak all the truth for fear of offending the Dutch, which would give a great advantage to the common enemy': Marlborough to Sarah, 2 Sept. 1705, Tirlemont, *Coxe*, i, p. 319; *ibid.*, i, pp. 325–6, Marlborough to Godolphin, 2 Sept. 1705, Tirlemont; Marlborough to Hedges, 7 Sept. 1705, Tirlemont, *Murray*, ii, pp. 258–9.

[2] *Jones, 1705*, p. 297.

Instructed Deputies now Interpose
As Enemies to us, Friends to Our Foes.
With dull Disputes ward off the fatal Blow,
And in one Hour a whole *Campaign* undo.
How could I curse the B——r B——s for't,
And sink em, as their Fathers were, at *Dort*.
Degenerate Race! Sprung out of *Mire* and *Slime*,
And like a *Mushroom* ripen'd in small Time.
They are destructive Vermine, that will spread
O'er all the Earth, like the most pois'nous weed.[1]

Well might Stanhope wish for Marlborough's presence in England 'to prevent the mischievous consequences of our differences with these people'. Marlborough was not idle, however, in such prevention; as soon as he received Harley's suggestion that 'some person of distinction' be sent out, he wrote asking him to delay this move, since

at this juncture, while they are in such a ferment on this very occasion, as you must know from all hands, and that there are such divisions reigning amongst them, I can no ways think it for the Public good, or her Majtys Service, as believing it might rather give an advantage to the ffrench and those who wish them well, or at least are over forward for a Peace, of which I must own there are to many even amongst the States themselves, then effect what end you propose...

Six days later, however, Harley was instructing Stanhope to discover the Dutch reaction to his plan, and it was common knowledge that such a mission was contemplated and that certain 'persons of distinction' were being considered.[2]

Meanwhile Marlborough's equanimity was once more showing signs of wear. His communication to the States-General on the taking of Léau had what was, for him, an almost peevish tone, which was probably due to the annoyance he felt with them for not having answered his celebrated letter on the Overyssche incident.[3] When he learnt of the omission from the *Gazette* he protested with what

---

[1] *C.W.* 66, pp. 5–6.

[2] Stanhope to Stepney, 1 Sept. 1705, Hague, Add. Ms. 7069; Marlborough to (Harley), 2 Sept. 1705, Tirlemont, *Murray*, ii, p. 249; *Luttrell*, v, p. 585, 25 Aug. 1705; Harley to Stanhope (copy), 28 Aug. 1705, Whitehall, F. E. B. Holl. 72; L'Hermitage to States-General (transcript), 28 Aug./8 Sept. 1705, London, Add. Ms. 17677 AAA; Marchioness of Granby to Duke of Rutland, 28 Aug. 1705 (O.S.), *H. M. C. XII pt. v*, p. 183; *Hearne*, i, pp. 40–2, 2, 7 and 8 Sept. 1705.

[3] After expressing his pleasure at being able to congratulate the States on the fall of Léau, Marlborough added: 'J'aurais été ravi de l'avoir pu faire sur quelque chose de plus d'importance ...': Marlborough to States-General, 5 Sept. 1705, Tirlemont, *Murray*, ii, p. 255. See also Marlborough to Heinsius, 31 Aug. and 5 Sept. 1705 (N.S.), *van 't Hoff*, pp. 207–9; Marlborough to (Portland?), 7 Sept. 1705, Tirlemont, *H. M. C. XV pt. iv*, pp. 242–3.

Godolphin thought uncommon warmth. This letter, and others of the same period, show that Marlborough was convinced that the 'common people' of the Republic were fully behind him, and that only his restraint had prevented them from making things most uncomfortable for the Dutch Government. At the same time he was anxious that the indignation that they had already expressed should induce their government to give him more authority in the field; hence his approval of Stanhope's action in publishing his letter, and his anger at the *Gazette's* amendment, which made it appear that he had nothing to complain of.[1]

By the end of August arrangements for the projected mission were complete. The Lord President, Pembroke, had been chosen, and had received his instructions. These were, for the most part, drawn up with remarkable moderation. Pembroke was to use the greatest care not to precipitate the Republic into the arms of France, though, in addition to seeking a cure for late ills, he was to declare as tactfully as possible that there could be no peace until Charles III had Spain and the Indies. The only passage of these instructions that has a note of menace is probably an expression of the ministry's genuine apprehension as to the temper of the approaching session of Parliament:

You will plainly represent to them that it will be very uneasy to our subjects to give them supplies another year, for a war which is to be carried on after this manner.

L'Hermitage was convinced that the tone of the mission would be conciliatory, and Harley hoped that Pembroke's 'gentleness ... will render him very acceptable to the Dutch'.[2]

The preparations for this mission coincided with substantial moves on the part of the States to appease feelings in England, moves which eventually gave Marlborough, in practice if not on paper, the increased authority he demanded. Stanhope, for one, had no doubt that the alarm caused by the rumours of the mission had caused these concessions; Lamberty, writing thirty years later, attributed them rather to the moderation with which the English Government had acted.[3]

---

[1] Marlborough to Stanhope, 5 Sept. 1705, Tirlemont, *Murray*, ii, p. 255; Marlborough to Godolphin, 9 Sept. 1705, Tirlemont, *Coxe*, i, p. 320; (Godolphin) to (Harley), 5 Sept. 1705, Winchester, *H. M. C. Bath I*, p. 75. Similarly, Marlborough seems to have believed that it was the Dutch people who were restraining the 'peace party' from encouraging French overtures (Marlborough to Godolphin, 27 Aug. 1705, Ramey, *Coxe*, i, p. 325).
[2] Instructions for Pembroke, (c. 30 Aug. 1705) (O.S.), *H. M. C. XV pt. iv*, pp. 237–8; L'Hermitage to States-General (transcript), 31 Aug./11 Sept. 1705, London, Add. Ms. 17677 AAA; Harley to Stepney (copy), 31 Aug. 1705, Whitehall, F. E. B. Emp. 39.
[3] Cardonnel to Stepney, 14 Sept. 1705, Tirlemont, Add. Ms. 7063; Marlborough to Godol-

In a sense, both were right. Moderation is certainly apparent when it is realised that it was not until Sept. 10th/21st that Marlborough had the interview with Buys at Turnhout which was the prelude to the States' concessions, but that it was five days *before* this that Godolphin informed Harley that, in view of Marlborough's letters on the subject, the mission would be postponed. On the other hand, rumours that Pembroke's journey was imminent circulated freely long after the ministry had secretly decided not to send him, and served to keep the Dutch in an acquiescent mood. As the news of Dutch concessions reached England, the postponement was indefinitely prolonged, but the project remained a topic of public speculation for some time to come.[1]

Feeling was beginning to grow less intense, especially in Whig circles, where it was now thought that 'the best thing one can do is nott to look back'; and Marlborough, even before the States' concessions, was using the invaluable Portland as a medium for assuring the Dutch leaders of his 'utmost endeavours ... for the continuation of the good correspondence between the two nations ...'. In September, according to Jones, 'the noise against the *Dutch* and their Deputies about the miscarried Design upon the *Ische* began to be pretty well over ...'.[2] A pamphlet published at some date between September 1st and October 27th indicated, however, that what L'Hermitage disparagingly referred to as 'l'opinion populaire' was not entirely appeased. Entitled *The D—— Politicks Examin'd ...*, this was a lengthy and detailed consideration of the Overyssche incident, which, beginning on a moderate note, (for the author 'would not Incur the Imputation of being an Enemy to the *Dutch*') worked up to a sustained flow of abuse of the deputies, who were accused of treachery and

phin, 14 Sept. 1705, Tirlemont, *Coxe*, i, pp. 322–3; Stanhope to Harley, 15 Sept. 1705, Hague, S. P. Holl. 228; Stanhope to Stepney, 15 and 22 Sept. 1705, Hague, Add. Ms. 7069; *C. W.* 113, iii, p. 494.

[1] L'Hermitage to States-General (transcript), 4/15 Sept. 1705, London, Add. Ms. 17677 AAA; (Godolphin) to (Harley), 5 Sept. 1705, Winchester, *H. M. C. Bath I*, p. 75; Harley to Newcastle, 6 Sept. 1705 (O.S.), *H. M. C. Bath I*, p. 75; Harley to Newcastle, 6 Sept. 1705 (O.S.), *H. M. C. XIII pt. ii*, p. 190; *Luttrell*, v, p. 589, 6 Sept. 1705; *Hearne*, i, pp. 43–4, 9 and 13 Sept. 1705; Marlborough to Harley, 22 Sept. 1705, Aerschot, *Murray*, ii, pp. 270–1; Marlborough to Godolphin, 24 Sept. 1705, Aerschot, *Coxe*, i, pp. 323–4; Marlborough to Sarah, 24 Sept. 1705, Aerschot, *P. C. D. M.*, i, pp. 12–14; Marlborough to Heinsius, 29 Sept. 1705, Herentals, *van 't Hoff*, pp. 215–6; *Annals*, iv, p. 90. Portland as well as Marlborough seems to have been active in representing to Godolphin the dangers of the projected mission (*Coxe*, i, p. 316). C. T. Atkinson is entirely mistaken in suggesting that Pembroke actually went to The Hague (*Marlborough and the Rise of the British Army* (New York, 1921), p. 273).

[2] Marlborough to (Portland?), 17 Sept. 1705, Tirlemont, *H. M. C. XV pt. iv*, p. 247; Somers to Newcastle, 8 Sept. 1705, Belbar, *H. M. C. XIII pt. ii*, pp. 190–1; Sunderland to Sarah, 19 Sept. 1705, Vienna, *P. C. D. M.*, i, pp. 10–12; *Jones, 1705*, p. 343.

cowardice. Did we deserve, this writer asked, after we had made ourselves principals in a struggle in which they would have thought themselves fortunate to have had us as auxiliaries,

to have not only our General insulted, and controul'd by their *Ch—se m——s* and *S—p–b——s*, but the Common Cause endamag'd, and the Expence we enter'd into for their Sakes, prolong'd by an Unnecessary Protraction of the War, meerly to continue the Private Advantages they receiv'd from our Remittances, &c.?

None the less, this pamphlet was well documented and well argued, and hardly to be compared with the inflammatory *Dutch Deputies*; its burden was not the irremediable sinfulness of all Dutchmen, but the need to 'free our councils from the Clog of D——s'. Boyer, in the volume of his *Annals* published in the spring of 1706, made much of the fact that this work was 'publickly sold, and escaped uncensur'd', but we learn from Lamberty that it was to all intents and purposes suppressed. The authorities did not, apparently, think it advisable, with popular feeling as it was, to proceed against those responsible; but on receipt of a protest from the Dutch envoy they took measures to prevent its being sold, while Vrijbergen set himself to buy up all existing copies.[1]

Abroad, the States continued their efforts to appease Marlborough, and at home confidence in the solidarity of the alliance began to return. Optimistic bets that the war would soon end victoriously were again made, and the news sheets began to stigmatise the rumours that the Dutch were angling for peace as French propaganda. The anxiety that the ministry felt throughout the winter at the continued presence of French emissaries at The Hague was not communicated to the public, and vigorous steps were taken to repudiate the declaration of Poussin, French minister at Copenhagen, that a treaty of peace was on foot in Holland. On the other hand, the queen's speech at the opening of the new Parliament on October 27th gave two very broad hints to the Dutch: in the first place, the declaration that there could be 'no peace without Spain' was, as Leadam puts it, 'directed to determine the hesitation of the Dutch' over proposals which had been brought to The Hague by Rouillé, and, secondly, a later passage was plainly a demand that there should be no more Overyssches:

.... I make no doubt but measures will soon be so concerted, as that, if we be not wanting to ourselves, we shall see the next campaign begin offensively on all sides against our enemies, in a most vigorous manner.[2]

---

[1] *C.W.* 69, p. 48; *Annals*, iv, p. 91; *C.W.* 113, iii, p. 493; Wyon, *op.cit.*, i, p. 341.
[2] Watkins to (Stepney), 21 Sept. 1705, Aerschot, Add. Ms. 7077; Marlborough to Godol-

It now began to appear, however, that English military opinion was not entirely unanimous in placing all the blame for the disappointing results of the Flanders campaign on the Dutch. British officers now had more leisure to write home, and many of them may have sent appraisals of the campaign not unlike the celebrated letter of Major Cranstoun which came to the notice of Harley's intelligence system. The major, for whose ability Marlborough himself expressed high regard, came to the considered conclusion that

Faults there have been and miscarriages, and those great too, but where to lodge them is hard to tell, and we hope you will not look too narrowly into them since it cannot probably do any good.

On the question of Overyssche, Boyer wrote a few months later:

I must confess, that having had an Opportunity to discourse several Officers of that Army, I found them much divided in their Opinions: Tho' still the greater Number, and particularly the Horse-Officers, were for the Attack.[1]

7

Although feeling about the Overyssche incident might seem to be losing some of its intensity, the campaign of 1705 had given the High Tories an opportunity for pressing home an assault upon the ministry and its policies which they were not likely to ignore. In the Lords, on November 15th, Haversham inaugurated the double attack already foreshadowed at the beginning of the year. In a forthright speech that straightway appeared in print he attacked the Allies – this time with reference to the 1705 campaign – and demanded the invitation of the heir-presumptive. He paid particular attention, not only to allied 'misconduct' in the field, but also to the immense wealth, which, he alleged, the Dutch were accumulating from the war, and he dwelt upon their concern for the 'Ballance of Trade', which, he said, England might do well to emulate – a veiled suggestion that England should throw up the European war and seek her advantage in the Indies. All the leading High Tory peers spoke in favour of Haversham's motion to invite the Princess Sophia to England, one remarking that

phin, 24 Sept. 1705, Aerschot, *Coxe*, i, pp. 323–4; L'Hermitage to States-General (transcripts), 14/25 and 18/29 Sept. 1705, London, Add. Ms. 17677 AAA; Stanhope to Harley, 24 Oct. and 15 Dec. 1705, Hague, S. P. Holl. 228; J. Vernon to Harley, 27 Oct. 1705, Copenhagen, *H. M. C. Portland IX*, pp. 202–3; Stanhope to Stepney, 27 Oct. 1705, Hague, Add. Ms. 7069; Marlborough to Godolphin, 1 Nov. 1705, Frankfort, *Coxe*, i, p. 326; *Annals*, iv, pp. 95–6; Leadam, *op.cit.*, p. 69; *Cobbett*, vi, cols. 451–2; *C.W.* 113, iii, p. 707; Wyon, *op.cit.* i, p. 399.

[1] (J. Cranstoun) to (R. Cunningham), 1 Oct. 1705, Herentals, *H. M. C. XV pt. iv*, pp. 250–5; *Annals*, iv, p. 88 (*cf. C.W.* 18, v, pp. 207–8). For some indication of the feelings of the Dutch generals see *von Noorden*, ii, pp. 168–73.

when the Republic had made its treaty with France there would be no way open for her to come! In reply it was said that the true way to safeguard the succession was to humble France, and to achieve this it was necessary to bind England and the Dutch still closer, not to attempt to break up the alliance, which was what the High Tories, with their attacks on the Dutch, were aiming to do. As Somers explained five months later to the future George II, the strongest objection that the Whigs had to the proposal to invite his grandmother to England was the manner in which it had been made, and in particular the implication

that we could not go on no farther with the Dutch (wch. was in effect to say we must make Peace) .... [1]

The motion was defeated, but Haversham returned to the attack a week later with a representation of the 'miserable state' of England and a proposal, supported by Rochester, that her Majesty should be asked for an

account to be laid before this House of the occasions of our disappointments after our march to the Moselle and at Overisch and in not prosecuting the success on forcing the enemy's lines.

The arguments of his opponents were similar to those used a week before; it was said that 'our commerce with our allies was wholly in the crown', and hence

the entering into that matter was not at all proper for the House, unless it was intended to run into rash and indiscreet censures, on design to provoke the Allies, and by that means to weaken, if not to break the alliance.

On this occasion, not only was Haversham's proposal defeated by 53 votes out of 73, but Wharton thereupon moved to address the queen to preserve good relations with the Allies, especially the States, and this was carried.

On the same day in the Commons there was an attempt made to tack Dutch agreement to cease trading with France to a renewal of the 1703 augmentation. The High Tories, rebuffed on the issue of Dutch conduct in the field, were now hoping to use the feelings aroused by that conduct to launch yet another attack at this weak spot in the ministry's armour. Unfortunately for them, the debate showed that there had been a change of feeling on this issue both inside and outside the ministry during the course of the year. Whig speakers denied, as

[1] L'Hermitage to States-General (transcript), 20 Nov./1 Dec. 1705, London, Add. Ms. 17677 AAA; Somers to Electoral Prince of Hanover, 12 April (1706), London, Stowe Ms. 241; *C.W.* 181, pp. 12–17; *Trevelyan*, ii, pp. 89–94.

Godolphin had done in January, that the Dutch reaped any great advantage from their trade with France; they alleged that the trade England had opened up with Spain was infinitely more profitable. The proposal was defeated by over 60 votes; well might L'Hermitage congratulate his masters on an excellent day's work in both Houses.[1]

On the issue of Dutch trade with France, people were beginning to reconcile themselves to what Stanhope told Harley, as the latter sent more and more bitter complaints to The Hague about delays and evasions in the 'Contraband' negotiations:

I do not really believe it to proceed from any root of bitterness against us, or that there is any thing more in it, than a settled maxim among their people, never to debarr themselves of any branch of Trade whatever, which, whether they get by it or no, they are always pleased, when they have it in their power to use it, or let it alone, and murmuring against their Governors whenever they find themselves restrained.

This process of reconciliation was evident during those very negotiations, in the course of which the English Admiralty gradually abandoned many of the objections which it still made to Dutch trade with France after the Order in Council. Considerable light is thrown upon the motives behind this acceptance of the *fait accompli* of Franco-Dutch trade by a memorial addressed to Godolphin by Charles Davenant a few days after the Commons' debate. Davenant, now Inspector-General of the exports and imports, came to the conclusion that the French trade was probably doing considerable economic harm to the Dutch, a fact which placed the English in something of a dilemma: on the one hand it seemed that they should press for its prohibition, to prevent the French from gaining; on the other, if they did not, 'the Rivals of our trade' would 'be humbled'. He resolved this dilemma in favour of continuing the 'toleration' by introducing two other considerations: first, the considerable amount of English manufactures which the Dutch, as a result of their trade with France, were able to smuggle into France and Flanders, and the consequent gain to England; secondly, the fact that any English attempt to force them to end the French trade would be so seriously resented by the mass of Dutchmen as to put an impossible strain on Anglo-Dutch relations.[2]

For the ministry November 22nd marked the end of a crisis; a week

[1] L'Hermitage to States-General (transcripts), 23 Nov./4 Dec. and 27 Nov./8 Dec. 1705, London, Add. Ms. 17677 AAA; *H. of L. Mss.*, vi, pp. 300–1; *Cobbett*, vi, cols. 475–6; *Annals*, iv, p. 199; *von Noorden*, ii, p. 291.

[2] Stanhope to Harley, 28 July 1705, Hague, S. P. Holl. 228. For the memorial and its history see my article, 'Dr. Davenant and the Debate on Franco-Dutch Trade, *Ec. H. R.*, 2nd. ser., x (1957), pp. 94–103.

later L'Hermitage was able to rejoice in the prompt concurrence of the Commons in Wharton's motion to address the queen in these words:

.... being justly alarmed by the many artifices which the emissaries of France have put in practice this last year, in order to raise jealousies and create misunderstandings, amongst the Allies engaged in this necessary war, for the support of the liberties of Europe .... [we] do most humbly beseech your majesty to use all possible endeavours to preserve a good correspondence amongst all the confederates, and, in a most particular manner, to maintain and cultivate a strict friendship with the States-general of the United Provinces ....

The Whigs had followed the lead of the Junto; the 'queen's Men' had let themselves be guided by Marlborough; and, as a result, L'Hermitage could report that

la pluralité des voix dans l'une et la autre chambre songe principalement à cimenter l'union et particulièrement avec Vos Hautes Puissances.[1]

The High Tories had but one card left to play, namely an appeal to the country by means of the press. Here, too, their opponents' hand proved too strong for them, and it became increasingly apparent that feeling about Dutch conduct in the field no longer possessed the vigour and one-sidedness which they would have liked to see, and with which subsequent writers have endowed it. Haversham's speech was widely read, but not, according to L'Hermitage, 'fort applaudie par de bons gens'. In reply Defoe printed a series of 'Reflections' in his *Review* in which he poured the most withering scorn upon the machinations of the Tackers. He mocked at their suggestions that the Dutch would make a separate peace as 'an old Threadbare Project', and drew particular attention to Peterborough's 'Encomiums of the *Dutch*'. He roundly accused Haversham of trying to break up the alliance, and rejoiced (as, too, did Tutchin in the *Observator*) at the address of both Houses, and particularly at the honour done to the Dutch,

to Testifie how much they Esteem their Friendship in this Confederacy, and how resolv'd they are to Maintain it,

by beseeching the queen to cultivate a strict friendship with the States-General. The best that Haversham could manage in reply was a *Vindication* which was a rather tedious repetition of his previous allegations, with a few fresh details apparently culled from The *D——h Politicks Examin'd*, and some gloomy reflections on the way in which we were pouring our bullion and specie into Holland. This interchange came to an end early in 1706 with an unanswerable *Reply* from Defoe. Were we to hold an entire nation guilty of the misdeeds of individuals,

---

[1] L'Hermitage to States-General (transcript), 30 Nov./11 Dec. 1705, London, Add. Ms. 17677 AAA; *Cobbett*, vi, col. 476.

he pointed out, we should first accept responsibility for the misconduct of our own people – at Cadiz, for example. The Dutch appeared to have given full satisfaction to Marlborough, and, in any case, we had no right to upbraid the Dutch with being over-cautious; if we had as much to lose by a single misfortune in Flanders as they, we should be no more venturesome.

.... Remote from home, where, if defeated, they can have time to turn round, collect their forces, and defend themselves; None are forwarder for Action than the *Dutch*; at their own Door they are wary, and infinite reasons justify them in it; they were always so, we confederated with them under such circumstances, and ought to expect it; to say they held our Hands from Finishing the War, is as uncertain, as to say, That taking *Saar Louis* would open a way to *France* is Un-Geographical ....[1]

The most striking refutation of Haversham's charges occurred in a pamphlet entitled *A Letter to the Author of the Memorial of the State of England*, published in the first few days of 1706. This aroused extraordinary interest at the time, and certainly merits close attention in any study of opinion. It professed to undertake to 'answer' John Toland's *Memorial of the State of England* (probably published in the summer of 1705). It agreed with Toland that moderation and toleration were both necessary and desirable, but denied that any credit was due to the ministry in this respect; it was the Whigs alone that were responsible for their establishment and preservation. Having thus acknowledged his allegiance, the author launched a series of thinly veiled attacks on the leading ministers, and on Marlborough in particular. His criticism of the Duke was directed mainly at the conduct of the campaign in Flanders, and Slangenburg himself could hardly have done better; indeed, the Dutch general's apologia was quoted in detail and his actions praised. The author attributed Marlborough's dissatisfaction with the Dutch to his 'exorbitant desire of command', and accused him of hoping to make a good bargain for himself with France

by selling them a Peace to the inconceivable loss and detriment of his own Country and the Confederates.

Having been thwarted in this design by the steadfastness of the Dutch, it was probable that his next move would be 'to take such measures as may continue the War as long as possible'.

The appearance of this pamphlet caused no little stir, which was considerably increased when it became known, a few days later, that

[1] *Review*, ii, 114, 116–8, 27 Nov., 1, 4 and 6 Dec. 1705; *Observator*, iv, 72, 8 Dec. 1705; *C.W.* 180, pp. 6–8; *C.W.* 53, pp. 25–6.

its author was the well-known rector of Sutton, William Stephens, a strong Whig of quasi-republican leanings, and that he was prepared to defend his work. (In the event he escaped the pillory by the narrowest of margins and wrote a full recantation). The High Tories were overjoyed at this fine opportunity of attacking their Whig enemies, who, in turn, lost no time in disavowing completely the unfortunate Stephens, their contention being that his pamphlet was merely a 'High-Church' device for blackening the Whigs.[1]

It was nonetheless undeniable that a Whig had written a spirited defence of the Dutch deputies and generals; and it seems fair to say that, in so doing, Stephens was expressing, though in a highly exaggerated form, feelings that were common to many Whigs at this time. We have already seen the change in tone of the Whig leaders and the way in which Defoe, still a Whig unless it suited Harley's purpose that he should not be, had answered Haversham. Boyer, too, when he considered the 1705 campaign in the spring of 1706, showed the same tendency. Of the failure to follow up the crossing of the lines he wrote that it was 'certainly an Over-sight, which History knows not where to charge', and he gave not the slightest indication that the failure of the Dyle crossing had had any connection with Dutch recalcitrance. In presenting the arguments for and against an attack at Overyssche he showed an almost complete lack of partiality. Another Whig annalist, Jones, did not hesitate to assert that the 'slight Attempt' at the Dyle had been 'much Misrepresented', and warned his readers not to be 'Impos'd upon'.

As early as the first week of September the third Earl of Shaftesbury, as strong a friend of the Dutch as he was a Whig, had also given evidence of a viewpoint not far removed from that of Stephens. Normally a supporter, with reservations, of Marlborough and Godolphin, he was temporarily consumed by the suspicion that they were making use of differences with the Dutch in order to make a 'treacherous peace'.

Wee are in great jealousyes (he wrote) of a peace carrying on; and that the am-

---

[1] *C.W.* 172, pp. 17–25. The extraordinary interest aroused by this pamphlet is mirrored in the pages of Hearne's journal, in the columns of the *Rehearsal*, the *Review*, and the *Observator*, and in at least two 'answers' that Stephens' remarks provoked. One of these praised Marlborough's decision to return from the Moselle in the following terms: ' ... who was it fit the Duke should Expose? The *Germans* who had exposed him, and who were not in a Condition for want of Supplys to Act; or, the *Dutch* who had done their Part Honourably, parted with their Army from Home, to joyn in concerted Measures with the Confederates, had March'd 160 Miles, and fac'd the Enemy, before the other were in Condition to appear' (*C.W.* 156, pp. 24–7).

bitiouse designs of some great men push them to raise disturbance between England and Holland for any pretence, the better to colour the ill terms they have made for us.

'Tis really the buisness of some people at Court to raise all the ill apprehensions they can of the allyance and to magnify the advantages of France; when at the same time I am satisfyed we are offered any terms from France which is much lower than we imagine. But Courtiers have their misteryes, and this is now a very great one, that our Court should be willing affaires abroad should look ill. But curse be on those who now do all they can to blow the coals between England and Holland, and make this misunderstanding to be a ground of giving such terms to France as may keep Europe still in terrours, and England under the pretended necessity of a standing force! God give us eyes to see through those misteryes of iniquityes! [1]

It is not without interest that Stephens was reported to have defended himself by attempting to inculpate Shaftesbury, with whom he was acquainted. This gave great annoyance to Shaftesbury, who by the beginning of 1706 was convinced that he (and, by implication, others) had misjudged Marlborough and Godolphin. Writing to a Dutch correspondent at this time he could assert that neither 'our Ministry or nation' was interested in a separate peace. But if the Treasurer and the General were no longer the villains of the piece it did not follow that the Dutch had been in the wrong. 'The misunderstanding between us last summer' had in fact been due to unfounded 'jealousies' on both sides, which in turn had arisen from nothing more than 'the private piques between great men'.[2]

It might be argued that the Whigs' attitude was influenced by a desire to remind the ministry that they were a political force and not merely hangers-on, or even to warn it that it was playing with fire in resisting the Junto's demand for representation in the cabinet. But there was more than mere calculation behind their reluctance to see the Dutch aspersed. Just as the High Tories' desire to make political capital out of any alleged misdeeds of the Dutch was increased by their genuine aversion to all things Dutch, so the ties between the Whigs and the Republic – sentimental memories of William III, grateful memories of the Revolution, republican tendencies (almost wholly academic) and religious sympathies – tended to bring them to its defence.

---

[1] Shaftesbury to Furly, 4 and 11 Sept. 1705, Chelsea, *Forster*, pp. 216–19; *Annals*, iv, pp. 77–88; *Jones, 1705*, p. 255.

[2] Shaftesbury to van Twedde, 17 Jan. 1705/6, St. Giles', *Rand*, pp. 347–52; *ibid.*, pp. 354–5, Shaftesbury to Stephens, 17 July 1706, Chelsea; *ibid.*, pp. 383–5, Shaftesbury to R. Molesworth, 13 Dec. 1707, St. Giles'.

8

The alliance had held firm despite the disappointments of the campaign in the Low Countries, but the devotion to the solidarity of the Grand Alliance that had characterised British opinion, both public and official, in this crisis, could not reasonably be expected to survive many more trials of such a nature. Hence, whatever the optimism of coffee-house gamblers might lead them to wager, the ministry was annoyed and alarmed as the year drew to a close by the inaction of its Protestant allies in preparing for the campaign of 1706. Already they had fallen down in their payments to Savoy, and their ships had been withdrawn from the combined fleet at a critical moment. There was therefore little surprise that they were 'tedious and scrupulous' in arranging a loan for the Emperor's Italian forces, and it was only with great difficulty that Marlborough succeeded in persuading the States to take upon themselves the third part of the cost of sending a reinforcement of ten thousand men to Eugene.[1] There was little hope that the Dutch would not once more find a way to avoid their naval obligations; and, although Mitchell delivered a strongly-worded memorial to the States-General pointing out their shortcomings in these matters, he had accomplished nothing by the end of the year. Nor was there much prospect that, when an agreement was made, the Dutch would supply any more ships than in 1705. Just before his departure for England Marlborough was able to overcome Dutch recalcitrance concerning an augmentation for Portugal and the provision of funds for the war in Catalonia, but even he had little hope of persuading the States to agree to another augmentation for the Low Countries. He was well aware that, as an observer at The Hague put it, 'they are indeed much wasted by the war, and their affairs are in great disorder'.[2]

Particular annoyance was felt by the ministers at the 'supine indifference' of the Dutch to the troubles in northern Europe. The ministry strongly resented the States' 'froideur' towards disturbances

[1] Harley to Newcastle, 14 Sept. 1705 (O.S.), *H. M. C. XIII pt. ii*, p. 186; Hill to Godolphin, 21 Oct. 1705, Turin, *Hill Corres.*, ii, pp. 650-1; Harley to Sunderland (copy), 19 Oct. 1705, Whitehall, F. E. B. Emp. 39; Marlborough to Godolphin, 25 Dec. 1705, and 4 Jan. 1706, Hague, *Coxe*, i, p. 369; Marlborough to Harley, 1 Jan. 1706, Hague, *Murray*, ii, pp. 372-3.

[2] *Cowper*, p. 5, 21 Oct. 1705; Marlborough to Harley, 14 Nov. 1705, Vienna, *Murray*, ii, pp. 323-4; Dalrymple to Mar, 17 Nov. 1705, Hague, *H. M. C. Mar & Kellie*, p. 239; Mitchell to States-General (copy), 3 Dec. 1705, Hague, S.P. Holl. 225; Stanhope to Harley, 8 and 15 Dec. 1705, Hague, S. P. Holl. 228; Marlborough to Godolphin, 15 Dec. 1705, Hague, *Coxe*, i, p. 368; *ibid.*, i, p. 370.

at Danzig and their nonchalant attitude to the dispute about the Bishopric of Eutin.[1] The only bright spot in this otherwise gloomy picture of the Dutch war effort, as seen by the English ministers, was provided by the conduct of the Dutch at the siege and capture of Barcelona, as reported by Peterborough and Shovell. At the outset of the Anglo-Dutch expedition which accomplished this feat of arms Peterborough had sent home complaints of the 'unequall supply' of ships from the Dutch; but in his letter to the queen of October 13th, upon the capture of the Catalan capital, the Earl, never noted for bestowing undeserved praise upon others, wrote:

I must not omit to let your Majesty know, how happy we have been in a perfect Agreement with the Officers of the States General, of Sea and Land; Nothing has been desir'd from the Dutch Admirals, or offer'd to the Dutch Generals, which has not been complied with, even beyond what could be hop'd, or reasonably desir'd.

Shovell, too,

complained to the Admiralty that his ships were reduced to thirty rounds of shot a gun, and he drew comparisons with the Dutch, who were much better supplied and were able to provide far more than their proper share for the siege.[2]

Heartening as this news from Spain might be, it could not dispel the growing anxiety in official circles about the apparent readiness of the Dutch to put an end to the war. Godolphin expressed this feeling well when he wrote: 'One can't depend but Holland will be treating upon every Accident that happens'. For his part, the best assurance that Marlborough could give the Treasurer in mid-December was that 'they are very much devid'd, but I hope the greatest part is for the Carrying on of the Warr'. By the end of the year he felt certain that the States would venture another campaign, but he added that 'as they pretend to want everything, it will not be with that vigour it ought'.[3]

Such anxiety must have been confined almost entirely to the ministers and those who enjoyed their confidence, but even here it was

[1] Harley to Robinson (copy), 17 Aug. 1705, Whitehall, F. E. B. Sweden 154; Stanhope to Harley, 5 Jan. 1706, Hague, S. P. Holl. 228; Harley to Stanhope (copy), 28 Dec. 1705, Whitehall, F. E. B. Holl. 72.

[2] Peterborough to Godolphin, 30 May 1705 (N.S.?), Add. Ms. 28056; Peterborough to Anne, 13 Oct. 1705, Barcelona, *Annals*, iv, appendix, p. 19; J. H. Owen, *The War at Sea Under Queen Anne, 1702–1708* (Cambridge, 1938), pp. 151–2. Peterbrough's words may be compared with the historian Stanhope's assertion that the Dutch officers at Barcelona were 'but sluggish in the field' (Stanhope, P. H., 5th Earl, *The History of the War of the Succession in Spain* (London, 1833), p. 158).

[3] (Godolphin) to (Harley), 'Wednesday near 11 at night' (Dec. 1705?), Duke of Portland Mss.: Lord Godolphin; (Marlborough) to (Godolphin), 18 Dec. 1705, Hague, Add. Ms. 28056; Marlborough to Godolphin, 22 and 25 Dec. 1705, Hague, *Coxe*, i, p. 369.

by no means universal. In this respect it is interesting to compare two contrasting impressions of the Dutch reactions to the queen's speech at the opening of Parliament. Secretary Harley heard

that the ill-intentioned in those parts gave a very wrong turn to the part of the queen's speech which relates to the monarchy of Spain, as if that was to eternise the war,

and this elicited from him some decidedly peevish comments about their 'rotten, whimsical barrier'. The Whig Sunderland, on the other hand, found on his return to The Hague from his mission to Vienna that both the speech and the recent parliamentary defeats of the High-fliers

have put a new life into all those that wish well in this country, and have as much damped all the others, who were very high before.

Both men were, at this time, eager for the vigorous prosecution of the war until France was humbled and Charles III established on the Spanish throne; both allowed these considerations to dictate their fundamental attitude towards the Dutch. The comparison of their views on the Dutch reaction to the queen's speech shows how much divergence could exist within this broad area of agreement. The clue to this difference is a simple one. Both men would have liked to see what Sunderland thought he saw, but, as often happens, each saw what he *expected* to see. The Whig possessed a degree of confidence in the Dutch ally which was unknown to the Tory.[1]

Little of these matters which were vexing Godolphin and his colleagues can have been known in circles outside the ministry; but there was widespread speculation in the closing days of the year as to the real purpose for which Buys was coming to London. On December 25th (N.S.) Marlborough, in a letter to Godolphin, prophesied that the States would soon find a pretext for sending one of its members to the Queen, the 'true business' of the embassy being 'to represent to her majesty their sad condition'. Eleven days later L'Hermitage learnt of the projected mission and also of its overt object – to assure the queen of the States-General's desire for the best possible relations. Three days after this he assured his masters that, though there were some who connected this forthcoming visit with rumoured peace negotiations, all 'well-intentioned' people were content to accept it at its face value, and as such it was very welcome to them.[2]

---

[1] Harley to Marlborough, 4 Dec. 1705 (O.S.), *Coxe*, i, p. 383; *ibid.*, i, p. 377, Sunderland to Sarah, 22 Dec. 1705, Hague.
[2] Marlborough to Godolphin, 25 Dec. 1705, Hague, *Coxe*, i, p. 369; L'Hermitage to States-

L'Hermitage's excessive and perhaps calculated optimism about the state of English opinion respecting the Dutch makes him a not always reliable guide, particularly in the later years of the Godolphin ministry. We do not need his assurances, however, to perceive that the strains and stresses of the year 1705 had shown that a considerable proportion of the politically active people of England was, for whatever reason, 'well-intentioned' towards the Dutch. The High Tories, after initial failure in their agitation about Dutch trade with France, had been given an almost miraculous second chance to achieve their ends. They had been able to play upon a grievance which, rightly or wrongly, most Englishmen, eager for another Blenheim, felt sincerely and felt deeply, and yet, with this great advantage, they had failed to shake either the ministry or the alliance.[1]

The reasons for this failure have already been indicated; they were many and varied. The restraint of Marlborough, who played a difficult part with consummate skill; the management of Godolphin and Harley; the policy, perhaps, of the Junto; the sympathies, certainly, of the Whigs: all played their part. In the last analysis, however, it is difficult to believe that the 'Rochester faction' could have suffered such a singular defeat had there not existed in England a considerable stock of goodwill, engendered by the reaction to Blenheim and not yet used up, towards the Dutch. A contemporary observer did not fail to grasp this point. 'Observe', he adjured his readers,

that the ill consequences of this Action [*i.e.* Overyssche] that some were afraid of were happily prevented, by the Wisdom of those, who were sensible, that Unity and Concord were the only Cement of the Grand Alliance, tho' the Emissaries of *France* were big with Hopes of some Misunderstandings, and fomented the same with all imaginable industry.[2]

General (transcripts), 25 Dec. 1705/5 Jan. 1706 and 28 Dec. 1705/8 Jan. 1706, London, Add. Ms. 17677 BBB.
 [1] *Churchill*, ii, pp. 593-4, esp. the quotation from Gallas' despatch of August 4th. The depth of the High Tory failure was shown when, early in 1706, one of their pamphleteers, William Pittis, published his *Two Campaigns in one Panegyrical Essay upon his Grace the Duke of Marlborough's Successes in the Years of 1704 and 1705*. This contained not a single derogatory remark concerning the role of the Dutch in the 1705 campaign.
 [2] *Jones, 1705*, p. 298.

CHAPTER V

THE PROBLEM OF PEACE
‹1706›

I

In 1705 the Anglo-Dutch alliance was menaced by differences over the conduct of the war; in the following year it was threatened even more seriously by the problem eternally besetting all fighting alliances of sovereign states – disagreement over a peace. Writers on these matters have tended to lay too much emphasis on the ill-will felt in England towards the Dutch as a result of military disappointments in 1705. Conversely, it may be argued that there has been too little said of the annoyance felt in English ministerial circles as the events of the *annus mirabilis* of 1706 revealed the wide divergence between the Dutch idea of a 'good' peace and their own.

The anxiety that the ministry had felt in the autumn and early winter of 1705 lest the Dutch should encourage French overtures for peace were as nothing compared to the anguish that it had to endure in the latter half of 1706; its patience with, and goodwill towards its ally suffered accordingly. If most Dutchmen realised that the disappointments of 1705 gave no sure foundation for obtaining their own cherished aims of an extensive, secure barrier and substantial trading advantages, the situation as they saw it after the brilliant successes of 1706 wore a very different aspect. Not only was France ready to promise all they wanted, but the presence of Allied armies in Flanders and Brabant, and, for a time, in Madrid, seemed an ample guarantee that her king would make good his offers. Such an attitude was anything but compatible with the growing conviction in English official quarters that the entire Spanish monarchy not only should but could be obtained for Charles III.

All this had a curious effect upon the official attitude in England towards the Dutch ally. From 1705, until new factors were introduced with the change of ministry in 1710, it was in the years of victory that this was most bitterly, outspokenly and lastingly hostile; and the more brilliant the victory, even if it was won largely by the valour and skill of Dutch troops, the more hostile did it become. This was simply due to the fact that while each victory seemed to many Dutchmen to place them in a satisfactory position for negotiating a good peace, the more and more Whig-dominated government in London would be content only with terms which in effect involved either the conquest of France or the indefinite prolongation of the war. Thus the official or unofficial peace negotiations that followed each successful campaign plunged the English ministers into an agony of apprehension, impatience, and resentment; and of no year is this more true than of 1706.

Thus in the years of relative military failure, even though this was always ascribed to Dutch misconduct, Godolphin and his colleagues were better able to master their annoyance with their war-weary ally, however great it may have been. Allied failure in the field meant that the French would be less likely to give the Republic the sort of peace it wanted, and consequently that the secret 'pourparlers' and negotiations of those recalcitrant Dutchmen would give far less cause for alarm to a government which was itself united on one point only – the continuation of the war.

2

Although Marlborough had completed most of the preliminary arrangements for the next campaign with the Dutch before he returned home, the conferences at The Hague for the settlement of naval quotas dragged on well into the New Year. It was not until the middle of January that Mitchell, who had been there since November 20th, could obtain any definite reply from the States, although Stanhope felt certain that they were already fully resolved on the size of their contribution on Mitchell's arrival. Mitchell protested strongly against the States' declared intention of continuing the arrangement whereby an entirely Dutch squadron guarded the North Sea and an entirely English one the Channel, but his plain speaking about the ineffectiveness of the previous year's North Sea squadron seems to have had as little effect as did the representations made on the same subject to Buys during his much talked of, but uneventful, visit to London. The fact that the Dutch were 'deficient in their Quota as to the sea' was presented by Dr. Charles Davenant to his son Henry as evidence that 'none of the Confederates Act their Parts to the utmost stretch but ourselves'.[1]

[1] Mitchell to States-General (transcripts), 28 Nov. and 3 Dec. 1705, Hague, Add. Ms. 17677

Nor was this all that the ministry found to displease them in the news from The Hague. They learnt from Stanhope of the continuing dilatoriness of the States concerning the dispute over the civil administration of the Bishopric of Eutin (Lubeck), where the rival claims of the Administrator of Holstein-Gottorp and Prince Charles of Denmark might, it was feared, lead to a renewal of war between Sweden and Denmark. This, in turn, might perhaps result in the entry of Charles XII into the War of the Spanish Succession as an ally of Louis XIV, and would at the very least rob the Allies of the invaluable Danish mercenaries. While such fears haunted the English government Stanhope found that all his proposals for joint mediation were answered by an inexplicable indolence. Harley apprehended 'a fatal rupture in those parts' as a result, but in fact the States approved in principle the proposal put forward through Stanhope 'that the Administrator be restor'd to ye civil possession .... until that affair be decided in such way as shall be agreed on by both partys'. Further difficulties arose, however, when the mediating allies found that the disappointed claimant, Prince Charles, would accept this solution only in return for a substantial monetary compensation, which they would have to provide. The delay of the Dutch in agreeing to this gave new matter for complaint to the English ministers, as did their 'parsimony' in calculating their contribution, which, indeed, amounted to only one-third of that made by the English.[1]

Stanhope, already weakened by the illness which was soon to make him incapable of conducting affairs, did not contemplate the situation within the Republic in the spring of 1706 with any satisfaction. The insistence of several provinces that Slangenburg should be given a command; the way in which the populace of Rotterdam encouraged the desertion of newly-arrived British recruits; above all, the activities at The Hague of the Marquis d'Alègre: all this gave cause for uneasiness. D'Alègre, a French prisoner-of-war on parole, had been commissioned by Louis XIV to make overtures of peace to the Dutch, and his delay in returning to England after the expiry of his leave

AAA; Same to same (transcript), 13 Jan. 1706, Hague, Add. Ms. 17677 BBB; Same to same (copy), 18 Jan, 1706, Hague, S.P. Holl. 225; Stanhope to Harley, 18 Jan. 1706, Hague, S. P. Holl. 228; (Godolphin) to (Harley) (2 letters), n.d., Duke of Portland Mss.: Lord Godolphin; C. Davenant to H. Davenant, 15 March 1705/6 (O.S.), Add. Ms. 4291.

[1] Stanhope to Harley, 28 Jan. and 2 Feb. 1706, Hague, S.P. Holl. 228; Stanhope to Stepney, 29 Jan. 1706, Hague, Add. Ms. 7069; Harley to Robinson, 5 Feb. 1705/6, Whitehall, Thibaudeau, v, p. 78; Harley to Vernon (copy), 28 May 1706, Whitehall, F. E. B. Denmark 4; Marlborough to Harley, 22 July 1706, Helchin, Murray, iii, p. 11; ibid., iii, pp. 166–7, same to same, 11 Oct. 1706, Grametz; C.W. 113, iv, p. 227.

caused considerable disquiet there.[1] Not until his arrival at the end of March (O.S.) were these fears set at rest, for with him came the news that the Dutch had refused to listen to peace proposals until the campaign was at an end; but three weeks after this Harley wrote to Buys (now newly returned to Holland) in terms that betrayed his continuing apprehension lest their growing internal dissensions should dispose the Dutch to strike a bargain with France.[2]

The news from the Iberian peninsula at this time served only to heighten such suspicions. Godolphin, who had already heard that the States were once more reluctant to bear their share of the cost of maintaining Gibraltar, began in April to receive discouraging reports from the peninsula itself. In Lisbon Galway told Methuen that 'if the King of France sent Mr. Schon.[enberg] here for his service he could not better serve him than he does now', and the ailing old ambassador, in reporting this, urged that complaints should be made at The Hague about the Dutch minister's 'malitious & indeed villainous' proceedings. A month later Peterborough sent from Barcelona observations on the 'strange remisness of the Dutch' in providing neither provisions nor recruits for the troops in their pay.[3]

There is, of course, in any study of international relations a tendency to emphasise disagreement and dissension, and to ignore the less easily detected areas of agreement. Tension is much more spectacular than *détente*, and infinitely more vocal. It is as well to remember, then, that the irritation with its Dutch ally which the ministry felt at this moment as a result of the pinpricks to which it was subjected was as nothing compared to that aroused by the military disappointments of the previous year. The feeling which they aroused outside official circles was smaller still. Of the matters which were giving the ministry cause for concern, only the activities of d'Alègre seem to have attracted any public attention. Only among American and West Indian planters, increasingly apprehensive of competition from Dutch tobacco grown

[1] Stanhope to Stepney, 12 Feb. and 9 April 1706, Hague, Add. Ms. 7069; Marlborough to Heinsius, 8, 12 and 15 Feb. 1705/6, London, *van 't Hoff*, pp. 224–6; 'Un officier anglais' to Stanhope, 19 March 1706, Rotterdam, *Vreede*, pp. 14–15. See also Marlborough's letters in *Murray*, ii, pp. 403–27.

[2] L'Hermitage to States-General (transcript), 29 March/9 April 1706, London, Add. Ms. 17677 BBB; R. Bridges to Trumbull, 30 March 1706 (O.S.), *H. M. C. Downshire I pt. ii*, pp. 843–4; Harley to Buys (copy), 19 April 1706, Whitehall, F. E. B. Holl. 73. See also the 'note to Mr. Secretary Harley', n.d., *Murray*, ii, p. 485.

[3] (Godolphin) to (Harley), Feb. 1705/6, *H. M. C. Bath I*, p. 80; J. Methuen to (Godolphin), 19 and 26 April 1706, Lisbon, Add. Ms. 28056; *ibid.*, (Peterborough) to (Godolphin), 26 May 1706, Barcelona. After Methuen's death (13 June), Marlborough was anxious to have Schonenberg recalled (Marlborough to Halifax, 14 Aug. 1706, Helchin, *Murray*, iii, p. 83).

in Holland and sugar from the East Indies, were there any audible murmurings against the Dutch at this time.[1]

3

Marlborough's first and overriding task on his arrival at The Hague was to obtain permission to take his English troops to Italy to assist the hard-pressed Eugene. At first he found the Dutch leaders accommodating, though they would do nothing without the consent of Amsterdam and were 'positive that they dare not consent to the letting their countrymen go'; but their alarm on receiving the news of Villars' victory on the Rhine at the beginning of May put paid to these plans. Marlborough's chagrin was considerable when he realised that he was doomed to spend another campaign in the company of Dutch deputies, and it was not diminished when he found that the Dutch armies were not yet ready to take the field. 'God knows I go with a heavy heart', he wrote to Godolphin, 'for I have no prospect of doing any thing considerable', and at home Defoe explained to his readers that 'no great Enterprize' was to be expected in Flanders, adding, however, that we could not blame the Dutch for insisting on keeping their troops there.[2]

The victory won at Ramillies on May 23rd (N.S.), and the subsequent fall of Flanders and Brabant into allied hands, were therefore as unexpected in England as they were welcome. The Whig writers, in particular, were not slow to note that 'Poor Master *Overkirk* and his *Dutchmen* bore the brunt of the Battel, and Behaved themselves with a deal of Bravery', and thus to turn the tables on the Tory libels on the previous campaign. These were those very troops, Defoe pointed out, 'of whom we used to say a thousand Reproachful Things, and reckon them as nothing . . .', and Tutchin exulted that 'Nothing goes down at the *Taverns* but the Duke of *Marlborough*, and my Lord *Overkirk*'. Not altogether in keeping with this spirit was a poem

[1] Quary to Board of Trade, 2 April 1706, Plymouth, *C. S. P. Col.*, 1706–8, pp. 98–9; *ibid.*, p. 105, Sir. J. Cooke to Popple, 9 April 1706, Doctors' Commons; *ibid.*, pp. 107 and 212, Board of Trade to Hedges, 11 April and 30 Aug. 1706, Whitehall; *ibid.*, pp. 121–2, Virginia Merchants to Board of Trade, 26 April 1706; *ibid.*, pp. 161–2, B. Granville to Board of Trade, 23 June 1706, Barbados.

[2] Marlborough to Godolphin, 19 April 1706, Hague, *Coxe*, i, p. 402; *ibid.*, i, p. 405, same to same, 15 May 1706 (N.S.); Cardonnel to Stepney, 7 May 1706, Hague, Add. Ms. 7063; *Review*, iii, 58, 14 May 1706.

addressed to Marlborough which, while rejoicing in his success, pointed out the indebtedness of the Dutch to 'our Queens'.[1]

Godolphin's reaction to the news of Ramillies was not one of unmixed rejoicing. With considerable foresight he predicted that this setback, together with their misfortunes in Spain, would induce the French to give *'carte blanche* to Holland' in order to detach the Dutch from the Alliance, and he besought Marlborough to 'have a watchful eye upon this danger'. At this time the Lord Treasurer's fears seemed exaggerated. Both Stanhope and Hare were sure that the Dutch were in such good humour that 'there is nothing now they will not let the Duke do'. When Marlborough himself visited The Hague to prevail upon the States to release some of their troops for a descent on the French coast he declared that he had 'all the reason imaginable to be satisfied with the expressions these people have made'. He thought that the success would 'stop the mouths' of those who inclined to an insecure peace, and that by the end of the campaign France would be too weak to be able to quibble about giving 'reasonable terms' to *all* the allies. He evidently hoped that a speedy peace would resolve the problem posed by the very different ideas of the States-General and the Court of Vienna as to what should be done with the newly conquered Spanish Netherlands for the remainder of the war. On the one side the Austrians demanded that effective and not merely nominal control should be vested straightway in Charles III; on the other, the Dutch flatly and very reasonably refused to countenance this until such time as a Barrier to their satisfaction was settled and secured. They were all the more obstinate in this matter because of the wide divergence, long since evident but not till now of much practical importance, between their own interpretation and that favoured by the Austrians of the Fifth Article of the Grand Alliance, by which the Allies pledged themselves to recover the Spanish Netherlands 'with the intention that they should serve as a dyke, rampart and barrier to separate and keep off France from the United Provinces'.[2]

For England, Marlborough declared on June 10th (a day after his arrival at The Hague) that the queen claimed nothing for herself in

[1] *Observator*, v, 19 and 21, 22 and 29 May 1706; *Review*, iii, 62 and 90, 23 May and 27 July 1706; *To his Grace the Duke of Marlborough on his late Success in Flanders, 1706* (in *C.W.* 145, iv, pp. 77–8).

[2] Godolphin to Marlborough, 17 May 1706 (O.S.), *Coxe*, i, p. 419; Hare to G. Naylor, 3 June 1706, Merlebeck, *H.M.C. XIV pt. ix*, p. 211; Marlborough to Sunderland, 3 June 1706, Merlebeck, *Murray*, ii, p. 552; Marlborough to Sarah, 10 June 1706, Hague, *Coxe*, i, p. 432; Stanhope to Harley, 11 June 1706, Hague, S.P. Holl. 228; Marlborough to Goldophin, 24 June 1706, Rousselaer, *Coxe*, i, p. 431; *Trevelyan*, ii, p. 146.

the Spanish Netherlands. He knew, as Geikie points out, that 'the Dutch had not forgotten that in the negotiations that took place at The Hague with d'Avaux preparatory to the formation of the Grand Alliance and the declaration of war, England had stipulated for the right to place garrisons' in Ostend and Nieuport. For this reason he assured Godolphin, who was pressing him for an attack on Dunkirk, not only in order to end the menace of the French privateers but also with a view to the advantages which might accrue to England from its possession, that 'it is much more for Her Majesty's service and England, not to be master of any towns in this country since it would create a jealousy both at home and abroad'. The Dutch leaders were well satisfied with his declaration.

The situation was nevertheless more dangerous than even Godolphin had realised. It was not only that France was ready to go to great lengths to tempt the Dutch to desert the alliance, and that the Dutch themselves, already weary of the war, were still more eager for peace now that the cherished Barrier was within their grasp; it was also that the least reluctance on the part of England to allow the Republic what it considered its due share of immediate control of the Spanish Netherlands might well drive it into the arms of France. This was a real dilemma for the English ministry, trying as it was by every possible means to persuade the House of Habsburg to exert itself more in the common cause, and accounts for much of its exasperation with the Dutch in the latter half of 1706. It seems, in this connection, somewhat unnecessary to emphasise, as does Dr. Veenendaal in his important work on the Anglo-Dutch condominium, England's fear of Dutch expansionist aims and jealousy of Dutch commercial advancement. Such feelings did indeed exist, but the overriding preoccupation of the Godolphin ministry with the successful maintenance of the Grand Alliance is sufficient to explain its equivocal attitude to the problem of the Southern Netherlands.[1]

4

There can be little doubt that when, in the evening of June 27th, Marlborough received the famous patent from the Emperor offering him the Governorship of the Spanish Netherlands, he convinced himself that his acceptance of this position would be to the advantage

[1] Marlborough to Godolphin, 21 June 1706, Rousselaer, *Coxe*, i, pp. 430–1; *Geikie*, pp. 9–13; *Churchill*, iii, p. 156; *Veenendaal*, pp. xiv–xv; Stanhope, *History of England* ..., p. 224.

not only of John Churchill but also of the whole Grand Alliance. He no doubt felt that the situation in Flanders and Brabant was badly in need of clarification (he had already heard that the inhabitants of Antwerp were dismayed by rumours that they were to be annexed by the Dutch), and that the Emperor's offer, which probably did not come as a complete surprise to him, provided a solution which would avoid the dissensions inseparable from joint administration. It was probably the worst miscalculation he ever made.

Geikie asserts (and in this he has been followed by more recent writers) that Marlborough 'did not anticipate that any difficulties would be raised' by the Dutch. In fact Marlborough's correspondence reveals that from the first he was somewhat dubious of the Dutch reaction to his proposed elevation. He repeatedly begged Heinsius for his opinion, at the same time giving him such fulsome assurances as that

your thoughts is what shall govern me; for I do asure you, if they would give me this country for my life, I would not take itt, if it were not liked by the States.

Unsupported by other evidence, these phrases might seem to be dictated merely by politeness rather than by any real suspicion that the proposal might not be acceptable to the Dutch. But in fact they *are* supported by a letter of June 28th from the Duke to Godolphin, in which he wrote: 'I must take care that they [the Dutch] take no jealousy, whatever the Queen's resolution may be'. In the light of these words it can be seen that Marlborough's letters to Heinsius in fact reveal genuine uneasiness about the Dutch response.[1]

On July 1st Marlborough's worst fears about Dutch jealousy were confirmed by the warnings of the Dutch treasurer-General Hop, whom he consulted. He may have been resentful, but he cannot have been surprised. Far from complaining to Godolphin about Hop's attitude, he protested that if he should find that Heinsius expressed the same uneasiness about his appointment he would refuse it,

for the advantage and honour I might have by this commission is very insignificant, in comparison of the fatal consequences that might be, if it should cause a jealousy between the two nations.

The sentiments that he expressed to Heinsius were almost identical.[2]

[1] Cadogan to Marlborough, 5 June 1706, Borgh, *Vreede*, pp. 34–5; Marlborough to Heinsius, 28 June and 1 July 1706, Rousselaer, *van 't Hoff*, pp. 239–40, 242; Marlborough to Godolphin, 28 June 1706 (N.S.), *Coxe*, i, pp. 437–8; *Geikie*, pp. 15–17; Ashley, *Marlborough*, p. 78.

[2] Marlborough to Godolphin, 1 July 1706, Rousselaer, *Coxe*, i, p. 439; Marlborough to Heinsius, 3 July 1706, Rousselaer, *van 't Hoff*, pp. 242–3; *ibid.*, p. 244, same to same, 6 July 1706, Harlebeck.

By July 6th Marlborough had received confirmation of Hop's warnings from the Pensionary, and he wrote to Godolphin to let him know of his determination to decline the offer. Dr. Veenendaal conjectures that this decision was influenced by the knowledge that acceptance might well have brought the 'peace party' to the fore in the Republic and thus have led to Marlborough's dismissal by the States-General from the post of deputy Captain-General.[1] Perhaps so, though if the rejection of the offer is to be characterised as a piece of sordid calculation, one trembles to think what Dr. Veenendaal would have had to say of its acceptance! Indeed, the essence of Marlborough's predicament was that, whatever decision he took, he was henceforth bound to be the object of Dutch distrust, both in his own day and long after.

In his letter to Godolphin of July 6th Marlborough expressed misgivings about what the Dutch might do in the Spanish Netherlands: 'It is certain', he wrote,

if they follow their own inclinations, they will make such demands upon this country, as will very much dissatisfy the house of Austria, and be thought unreasonable by all the Allies, of which the French would be sure to make their advantage.

Three days later he was presented by Hop with a copy of a resolution of the States-General of June 19th which seemed to provide the amplest possible justification for his fears. By this resolution the States took upon themselves exclusively (though in consultation with the queen) the *de facto* government of the Spanish Netherlands.

There can be no doubt that Marlborough was shocked by this revelation. He felt that he had been tricked, betrayed, and humiliated. To Heinsius he pointed out that formal assurances of protection had already been given to the 'liberated' provinces in the queen's name, and that it was consequently impossible for her to relinquish all authority there; and in his correspondence with Godolphin there began to appear a tone which he had never before used when speaking of the Dutch. He begged his colleague to 'find some way of not letting them play the fool', declaring that

such is their temper, that when they have misfortunes they are desirous of peace upon any terms, and when we are blessed by God with success, they are for turning it to their own advantage, without any consideration how it may be liked by their friends and allies.

---

[1] *Veenendaal*, p. 36. How far this suggestion is consonant with Mr. van 't Hoff's conclusions about Marlborough's command of the Dutch armies (see above, p. 31n.) is a point which seems to require further study.

For the first time, too, he expressed his resentment of the attitude the Dutch leaders had taken towards his appointment as Governor, a resentment that deepened as he realised that every criticism that he made of their plans for governing the Spanish Netherlands was thought by the States to proceed from his wrath in being thus thwarted. At the same time he assured Godolphin that the 'peace party' in the Republic was far too strong, and far too ready to take advantage of any difference with the queen, for him to have acted in any other way with regard to the Emperor's patent. It was to this party's machinations that he attributed Dutch dilatoriness in preparing for the siege of Menin; but, for all his bitterness, he had not yet lost his confidence in the goodwill of the mass of the Dutch people:

.... at the same time that I say this to you, the greatest part of the people are very honest, and wish well to the common cause; but those that are of the contrary faction are most active and diligent.[1]

On July 19th Marlborough wrote to Godolphin to let him know that in an interview two days earlier Hop had agreed to abandon the resolution of June 19th and to set up a Condominium in the Spanish Netherlands. Meanwhile, annoyance at the conduct of the Dutch had been rapidly growing amongst the English leaders. When he first heard from Marlborough of the arrival of the Emperor's patent, Godolphin hastened to discover the reactions of the queen, who 'liked it very well', and – significant choice! – of Somers and Sunderland, who 'seemed to think there was no reason for the Dutch not to like it as well as we do ...'. He was utterly amazed on learning that the Dutch did not look with favour upon the appointment, and both he and Anne assumed that the machinations of the 'French party' were at the bottom of 'all this folly and perverseness'.

There is, on the other hand, little evidence to be found of any knowledge of these happenings outside official circles. Boyer, in his survey of the year's events, makes no mention of them, and even thirty years later the extent of Lediard's information was that

It is said, upon this Occasion, that the Government of the *Spanish Netherlands* was propos'd to the Duke of *Marlborough*; But he generously refusing the Offer, it was settled, by his Grace and the Deputies of the States *General* ....

Of this matter, as of others which made the ministry annoyed with its Dutch ally in 1706, the mass of Englishmen remained in profound

[1] Marlborough to Godolphin, 6 July 1706, Harlebeck, *Coxe*, i, p. 440; Marlborough to Heinsius, 10 July 1706, Harlebeck (2 letters), *van 't Hoff*, pp. 245–7; Marlborough to Godolphin, 12 and 14 July 1706, Helchin, *Coxe*, i, pp. 442 and 482; Same to same, 14 July 1706, Harlebeck, *Churchill*, iii, pp. 165–6.

ignorance – perhaps a negative indication of the ministry's concern lest public opinion should turn against the Republic.[1]

5

From the first there was friction in the conduct of the Condominium in the Spanish Netherlands. The behaviour of Hop at Brussels, complained Marlborough, 'disobliged' many of the most prominent citizens, and the Duke assured Heinsius

that we are doing our utmost to make the people of quality and all others wish the return of the French.

The English ministry consequently decided, at Marlborough's prompting, to send George Stepney, then envoy at Vienna, to Brussels with the avowed aim of moderating the conduct of the deputies who represented the States-General there. He would also represent the queen at The Hague, whence the ailing Stanhope was about to be recalled at his own request. Marlborough warned his colleagues that the Dutch would not be pleased with this appointment, 'they being so foolish as to affect everything that may make these people think they have the absolute government of them'.

It has been suggested by Dr. Veenendaal that Marlborough and his government used the conduct of Hop (which he does not attempt to palliate) simply as a pretext (*een voorwendsel*) to increase English authority in the Condominium, and that the appointment of Stepney was thus merely another illustration of England's jealousy of Dutch influence in the Spanish Netherlands. That such jealousy existed is undeniable – it was to be displayed in the latter stages of the 1706 Barrier negotiations – but that it was the most important consideration behind Stepney's transfer is highly improbable. It was the duty of Marlborough, both as soldier and as statesman, to keep Flanders and Brabant loyal to Charles III, and it is indisputable that the behaviour of Hop ('by farr ye worst of the Gang', according to Cardonnel) had given ground for legitimate doubts of the ability of a predominantly Dutch administration to do this. There seems little need to search for concealed motives in order to account for Stepney's appointment.[2]

[1] Godolphin to Marlborough, 24 June 1706, Windsor, *Coxe*, i, p. 438; *ibid.*, i, pp. 440–1, same to same, 4 July 1706 (O.S.); Anne to Sarah, 4 July 1706 (O.S.), *H.M.C. VIII pt. i*, p. 51; Marlborough to Godolphin, 19 July 1706, Helchin, *Coxe*, i, p. 444; *C.W.* 115, ii, p. 77.
[2] Marlborough to Godolphin, 15 Aug. 1706, Helchin, *Murray*, iii, p. 84; Marlborough to

While these political manoeuvres were taking place, the campaign went on; Marlborough the soldier did not allow the preoccupations of Marlborough the diplomat to hinder him in his task of wresting the strong places of Flanders and Brabant from the French grasp. Immediately after Ramillies he was able to assure Heinsius 'that we are so blessed, that we are of one mind in this army', but he could not rejoice in this happy condition for long. He found much to complain of in the conduct of the Dutch army in the sieges of Ostend and Menin, and he attributed its slowness to an eagerness for peace. On the other hand, Raby (accompanying the King of Prussia on a visit to the army) thought it due rather to Dutch parsimony, while General Ingoldsby saw it as an indication that 'the Dutch Generals, when once so, are very cautious of their actions and careful of their persons'.[1]

The fall of Menin on August 25th was followed by an attack in force on Dendermonde, which fell after a week's siege, though not before the Dutch deputies had once more roused the ire of Marlborough's entourage by their 'fear and a Foolish good husbandry to save a little powder'. 'The undertaking of anything more considerable' being prevented by the condition of the Dutch magazines, the Duke next laid siege to Ath, which in turn fell on October 2nd. Meanwhile, after a prolonged and vain wait for the arrival of the Dutch contingent for the expedition that was to make a descent on the French coast, Godolphin had decided to divert this enterprise to the coast of Spain. He now feared – as it happened, mistakenly – that when the States learnt that the new destination was to be Seville and Cadiz they would show even less enthusiasm for the venture than they had hitherto displayed.[2]

Continuing success in the field was not accompanied by any decrease of the mutual distrust with which English and Dutch regarded each

---

Heinsius, (16 Aug. 1706) (N.S.), *van 't Hoff*, pp. 257–8; Marlborough to (Harley), 7 Sept. 1706 (N.S.), *H.M.C. Bath I*, p. 95; Marlborough to Godolphin, 9 Sept. 1706 (N.S.), *Coxe*, i, pp. 454–5; Cardonnel to Stepney, 11 Sept. 1706, Velaine, Add. Ms. 7063; *Veenendaal*, pp. 59–60.

[2] Marlborough to Heinsius, 24 May 1706 (N.S.), *van 't Hoff*, p. 234; *ibid.*, pp. 238–9, 242, same to same, 24 June and 1 July 1706, Rousselaer; Raby to (Stepney), 22 July 1706, Camp at Helchin, *Wentworth Papers*, p. 18; Halifax to (Godolphin), 2 Aug. 1706, Helchin, Add. Ms. 28055; Marlborough to (Harley), 5 Aug. 1706 (N.S.), *H.M.C. Bath I*, p. 86; Ingoldsby to Ormonde, 19 Aug. 1706, Helchin, *H.M.C. Ormonde n.s. VIII*, p. 251.

[3] Marlborough to Sir Strafford Fairborn, 14 July 1706, Helchin, *Murray*, ii, p. 696; *ibid.*, ii, pp. 700–1, Marlborough to Harley, 15 July 1706, Helchin; *ibid.*, iii, p. 5, Marlborough to Fairborn, 18 July 1706, Helchin; St. John to Harley, 27 July 1706, Portsmouth, *H.M.C. Bath I*, p. 85; (Godolphin) to (Harley), n.d., Windsor, Duke of Portland Mss.: Lord Godolphin; Godolphin to (Rivers), 18 Aug. 1706, Windsor, *H.M.C. Bath I*, pp. 89–90; (Hare) to (Godolphin), 9 Sept. 1706, Velaine, Add. Ms. 28056; Hare to G. Naylor, 9 Sept. 1706, Velaine, *H.M.C. XIV pt. ix*, pp. 214–5; Dalrymple to Mar, 9 Sept. 1706, Alost, *H.M.C. Mar & Kellie*, p. 276; Godolphin to Heinsius, 17 Sept. 1706, Windsor, *Vreede*, pp. 144–5; *Annals*, v, p. 311.

other's conduct in the affairs of the Condominium. On the English side, suspicions of Dutch intentions and 'pretensions' in the Spanish Netherlands were greatly increased when it became known that the French had offered the Republic the virtual sovereignty of those territories in return for a peace on the basis of a partition of the Spanish Monarchy.[1] However, much as the English ministry might resent 'the folly of affecting the sovereignty' of the Spanish Netherlands which (in its view) had afflicted the Dutch leaders, it was anxious not to incline them to a favourable reception of the French offers by withstanding this 'folly' too vigorously. For this reason Godolphin agreed to the Pensionary's request that Stepney should not take up his duties at Brussels until he had conferred with a representative of the States-General at The Hague. Marlborough considered that it was quite unreasonable of the Dutch thus to delay the new envoy, 'for', he declared,

'tis certain as they have hitherto managed it, nothing but the Queen's authority, and good offices, can keep these people [viz. of the Spanish Netherlands] in any tolerable measures of the Dutch.

The Duke was especially critical of Dutch views on financial administration under the Condominium. The offer of the Governorship of the Spanish Netherlands, however, had made it impossible for Marlborough any longer to appear as an impartial critic of Dutch designs, and by the end of the year his position in this respect had been still further weakened.[2]

6

In the latter half of July the inevitable result of victory, which Godolphin had dreaded ever since Ramillies, duly occurred; peace offers from France arrived at The Hague. These came through two main channels, first to Marlborough and the Dutch from the Elector of Bavaria and his representatives, and secondly, from the Dutchman Hennequin, acting on behalf of the French War Minister Chamillart, to the Dutch alone. It was these latter proposals which were to be of most consequence. Although they communicated them to Marlborough (who promised strict secrecy) the Dutch leaders were sorely tempted

[1] See below, p. 140–1.
[2] Marlborough to Slingelandt, 10 Oct. 1706, Grametz, *Murray*, iii, pp. 165–6; Marlborough to Heinsius, 12 Oct. 1706, Grametz, *van 't Hoff*, p. 276; (Godolphin) to (Harley), 3 Oct. 1706, Newmarket, *H.M.C. Bath I*, pp. 106–7; Marlborough to Harley, 21 Oct. 1706, Cambron, *Murray*, iii, pp. 183–4; Marlborough to (Stepney), 6 Dec. 1706, St. James', Add. Ms. 7058.

by the suggestion that the Spanish monarchy should be partitioned, and the Spanish Netherlands disposed of as they saw fit. Such a basis for negotiation was quite unacceptable to a government whose queen had recently and resolutely declared that the entire Spanish monarchy should be won for Charles III.

Marlborough, though carefully avoiding the precise statement of his own views on the matter, made this clear when on August 21st and 28th he replied to Heinsius' importunities, but he confided to Godolphin that he had little hope that the Republic would continue the war. Well-informed as ever, he knew that 'it is publicly said at The Hague that France is reduced to what it ought to be, and that if the war should be carried further, it would serve only to make England greater than it ought to be'. No doubt, too, he was beginning to realise that, in addition to this national jealousy, the suspicions that his toying with the Emperor's patent had aroused made it impossible even for those Dutch statesmen most in sympathy with the English attitude any longer to place complete faith in him. Geikie has shown that Marlborough was indeed, owing to his reluctance to abandon all hope of one day obtaining the coveted governorship, being forced to play a double game with the Dutch and Austrians in the matter of the government of the Spanish Netherlands.[1]

Godolphin's reaction to the French proposals was unfavourable in the extreme. The middle of a campaign was no time for negotiation, he declared, and to Buys' persuasions he replied with a demand that was to be of fatal consequence to the alliance in the years ahead. He insisted that before any negotiation with France could be begun the allies should first agree among themselves their basic and unalterable demands, of which they would then give each other mutual guarantees in a treaty of 'preliminaries'. This stipulation, which would obviously frustrate the desire of many Dutchmen to partition the Spanish monarchy, could not, he told Marlborough in his letter of September 2nd (O.S.), be refused by the Dutch unless they were

absolutely resolved to throw off the mask, declare themselves open friends to France, and not under any obligations to keep farther measures with the Queen.

He warned Marlborough against showing any 'complaisance', for, he said, the more we gave way to them the more 'assuming' would they become.[2]

---

[1] Marlborough to Heinsius, 19 July, 21 and 28 Aug. 1706, Helchin, *van 't Hoff*, pp. 248–9, 259, 262–3; *ibid.*, p. 251, Heinsius to Marlborough, 27 July 1706, Hague; Marlborough to Godolphin, 23 and 30 Aug. 1706, Helchin, *Coxe*, i, pp. 481–2; *Geikie*, p. 23.

[2] *Geikie*, pp. 62–3; Godolphin to Marlborough, 2 Sept. 1706, Windsor, *Coxe*, i, pp. 481–2.

Marlborough considered Godolphin's demand right and reasonable, but he had no great hope of persuading the Dutch of this. As day after day went by in that anxious September he found more and more signs of an inveterate 'jealousy' amongst them. In this term he included their annoyance at the attitude adopted by both Austria and England towards the election of the Bishop of Münster;[1] their jealousy of the increasingly apparent predominant position of England in the Alliance; and their dislike and distrust of the English and Imperial attitude towards the government of the Spanish Netherlands. The result of all this, he thought, was that they were inclined to put more faith in French assurances of immediate and substantial advantages in the Spanish Netherlands than in English goodwill towards their Barrier claims in some future joint negotiation. The news of the allied retreat from Madrid only strengthened this inclination.[2]

When the news that Eugene had relieved Turin (on September 7th) and broken the French power in Italy arrived in England, Lord Keeper Cowper thought that this encouragement would prevail with the Dutch to 'bear up longer'; but Marlborough still found an ominous 'backwardness' in the field, and doubted his ability to persuade them 'to carry on the war one year longer with vigour'. Harley, too, suspected that, in making strong representations to the Emperor concerning his breaking off negotiations with his rebellious Hungarian subjects, the States were attempting to make the maintenance of the Alliance

The proposal for a 'preliminary' treaty had, in fact, already been made by Heinsius to Halifax on July 2nd, but the English envoy had refused to countenance it (Geikie, pp. 41–2).

[1] 'It is fortunately unnecessary in this connection to do more than refer to the long wrangle between the States who supported the Bishop of Paderborn and the Emperor who supported the Bishop of Osnabruch for the See of Munster. The chief importance of the dispute for our present purposes, is that it brought the English to the side of the States against the Emperor' (Geikie, p. 31, n.). This attempt to dispose of this topic in a few words is understandable but, regrettably, unsatisfactory. From the time the candidates were first nominated (in June 1706) the queen and her government gave their support to the Emperor's choice, and only finally withdrew this in November as a result of Dutch immovability and Austrian high-handedness. It is not easy to see why the ministry risked driving the Republic into the arms of France during these crucial months by opposing its wishes in a matter in which England had no direct interest. Its policy seems to have been determined partly by respect for the Emperor's wishes in a question affecting Imperial territory, partly by Osnabrück's alleged ability to provide 'a good body of troops' for the common cause, but mostly by Marlborough's personal relations with the Emperor, from whom he still hoped one day to receive the great position that the Dutch had forced him to refuse. For a detailed study of the Dutch attitude to the election see H. O. Lang, Die Vereinigten Niederlande und die Fürstbischofs- und Coadjutor-wahlen in Münster im 18-Jahrhundert (Münster, 1933), pp. 7–97. The Anglo-Dutch dispute is related in some detail but with characteristic lack of insight into English motives in G. van den Haute, Les Relations Anglo-Hollandaises au début du XVIIIe Siècle, d'après la Correspondance d'Alexandre Stanhope, 1700–6 (Louvain, 1932).

[2] Marlborough to (Harley), 20 Sept. 1706 (N.S.), H.M.C. Bath I, pp. 98–9; Marlborough to Godolphin, 20, 23 and 26 Sept. 1706, Grametz, Coxe, i, pp. 483–5.

impossible. Godolphin could scarcely believe that the Dutch people would follow their leaders into a peace, and he adjured Marlborough to use all possible means to make them understand that 'the queen will not be compelled in the matter'.[1]

The activities of d'Alègre at The Hague earlier in the year had given the English ministers a bad scare, and it is therefore not surprising that they decided to ensure that, whatever France might tempt her with, the Republic would at least stand by, and, if necessary, defend, the Protestant Succession. It was to assist in obtaining a guarantee to this effect that the Junto leader Halifax joined Marlborough at The Hague after the latter's arrival there on April 25th (N.S.). The first formal step in these negotiations does not seem to have been taken until May 8th, when Marlborough, about to leave for the army, sent a memorial to the States-General proposing the conclusion of a Succession treaty. In a sense this move represented an attempt by Godolphin and the Whigs to convince the House of Hanover that their rejection of Haversham's motion for inviting the Princess Sophia to England did not involve any weakening of their adherence to the Protestant Succession.[2] The proposal had been foreshadowed in a pamphlet published in February which, for reasons entirely unconnected with that suggestion, had been subsequently condemned by both Houses of Parliament as a seditious libel.[3]

While Marlborough was in the field Halifax and Stanhope negotiated with the Dutch leaders at The Hague for a treaty to guarantee the English Succession. At first the Dutch objected to the inclusion of a clause which made the prior recognition of Anne by France the *sine qua non* of any peace negotiation; after seemingly giving way on this, they insisted that a clause should be inserted whereby the queen should engage herself to assist in procuring their Barrier. To Halifax such a demand was far from objectionable, and his comments upon it in a letter to Somers reveal the typically Whig policy which led straight to the Barrier Treaty of 1709:

[1] Harley to Stepney (copy), 27 Aug. 1706, Whitehall, F.E.B. Emp. 39; Marlborough to Sarah, 26 Sept. 1706 (N.S.), *Coxe*, i, p. 460; *ibid.*, i, pp. 455–6, Marlborough to Godolphin, 27 Sept. 1706, Grametz; *ibid.*, i, p. 484, Godolphin to Marlborough, 18 Sept. 1706, Windsor; Cowper to Newcastle, 18 Sept. 1706, London, *H.M.C. XIII pt. ii*, p. 197.

[2] Marlborough to States-General (transcript), 8 May 1706, Hague, Add. Ms. 17677 BBB; *Geikie*, pp. 3–4. What follows is no more than a bare outline of the ensuing negotiations, since I have no wish to duplicate Geikie's definitive study.

[3] *C.W.* 88. In this was included a letter written from Hanover on 12 Jan. 1706 to the Earl of Stamford by Sir Rowland Gwynne. It was this which contained the suggestion of a guarantee of the succession and which was condemned by Parliament on 12 March (*Cobbett*, vi, cols. 519–32).

In my opinion, they should word this as strong, and as particularly as they pleased; for I think it is our interest that their barrier should be as good as we can get for them; and if they insist upon it too much, it will be the greater tie upon them, not to make peace, till it is procured for them. Perhaps this alone is better than all the rest; for if they are thus drawn in, at their own desire, to oblige themselves not to run too fast into a peace, it were the most desirable part of the treaty.

As Halifax travelled to Marlborough's camp to consult him about the new Dutch demand the Duke himself sent a full-blooded protest to Portland about the difficulties being made at The Hague over this treaty. Three days later, however, on July 24th, Halifax wrote to Portland assuring him that he had found 'the Duke of M——— as forward to gain a Barrier for the Dutch as they can desire', and two days after this Marlborough expressed his confidence that 'the queen will make no difficulty of warranting the barrier for the States, if they will not be unreasonable'.[1]

Both Marlborough and Halifax seem to have felt at this time that the Dutch should demand as much as was compatible with avoidance of offending the other Allies, and the ministers at home were also, so Halifax informed Portland, 'of our sentiments about the Barrier ...'. This last was not strictly true, for, although the ministry approved the principle of a reciprocal treaty, Godolphin interpreted the Dutch preoccupation with their Barrier as a sure sign that 'they think of joining their interest to that of France, whenever a peace comes; and for that very reason the longer we can keep it off the better'. A few days in Marlborough's camp served to convince Halifax too that there was an 'evil spirit' amongst the Dutch, as could be seen in the late dispute over the government of the Spanish Netherlands, and Somers, whom we find acting as unofficial adviser to the ministry throughout these negotiations, warned him against putting too much power into the hands of the Republic while this spirit was abroad.[2]

When Halifax returned to The Hague he found the States strangely backward in continuing the negotiations, and Marlborough wrote to Heinsius to warn him that this 'coldness' towards the Succession Treaty

[1] Marlborough to Heinsius, 15 July 1706, Helchin, *van 't Hoff*, pp. 247–8; Halifax to Somers, July 1706, *Hardwicke S.P.*, ii, pp. 468–9; Halifax to Harley, 16 July 1706, Hague, Somerville, *op.cit.*, pp. 614–5; Marlborough to Portland, 21 July 1706, Helchin, *Murray*, iii, pp. 10–11; Halifax to (Portland) (transcript), 24 July (1706) (N.S.), Add. Ms. 34515; Marlborough to Godolphin, 26 July 1706 (N.S.), *Coxe*, i, p. 482.

[2] Halifax to Somers, 26 July (1706), Helchin, *Hardwicke S.P.*, ii, pp. 469–70; *ibid.*, ii, pp. 470–1, Somers to Halifax, n.d.; Godolphin to Marlborough, 19 July 1706 (O.S.), *Coxe*, i, p. 482 (wrongly headed 'Marlborough to Godolphin' by Coxe); Halifax to Portland (transcript), 2 Aug. 1706, Helchin, Add. Ms. 34515; Marlborough to Heinsius, 3 Aug. 1706, Helchin, *van 't Hoff*, pp. 253–4.

might do 'much hurt' in England. The cause of this 'coldness' was, in fact, the attempt of the French to seduce the Dutch from the alliance by the promise of unlimited advantages in the Spanish Netherlands. This offer had a profound effect on the Dutch attitude to the proposed treaty; not unnaturally the Dutch leaders were encouraged to raise the terms on which they were prepared to guarantee the English Succession. On August 18th the States presented their proposals to Halifax, who, not understanding perfectly Heinsius' verbal translation into French of the Dutch resolution, thought them agreeable to Marlborough's wishes, and hurried home to England with them. When he fully understood their tenor, however, the Whig statesman, who only a month before had hoped that the States would word their demands as strongly as possible, was completely taken aback. These proposals, which omitted the preliminary recognition of the queen and bound England to support almost unlimited Dutch claims in the Spanish Netherlands, were, he thought, so excessive that the Dutch must have put them forward only so as to be better able to bargain. He was convinced that Heinsius, at least, took this view, but he also suspected that 'de certaines gens en Hollande' were using the Barrier negotiations in order to delay the signing of the Succession Treaty until they knew the outcome of the English ministry's attempt to bring about a Union with Scotland.[1]

With Halifax's return to London the negotiations for a Treaty of Succession and Barrier reached a standstill. The ministry, unanimous in thinking the Dutch demands excessive – 'by that proposal the Dutch have desired the whole Spanish Netherlands', protested Halifax a little later in a letter to Portland – were fearful of communicating this opinion to Dutch leaders who were still toying with French proposals which offered them even more than they had demanded of the English, with whom, indeed, they now showed little interest in negotiating. Emboldened by the news of victory in Italy, however, Halifax let the States know that their project was considered unacceptable, and insisted that particularised demands be substituted for the vague and virtually unrestricted commitments that the Dutch were asking the English to enter into on their behalf.[2]

---

[1] Marlborough to Heinsius, 10 Aug. 1706, Helchin, *van 't Hoff*, pp. 255–6; (Halifax) to (Elector of Hanover) (copy), 23 Aug. 1706 (O.S.), Stowe Ms. 222; *Geikie*, p. 49.

[2] Marlborough to Heinsius, 11 Sept. 1706, Velaine, *van 't Hoff*, p. 266; *ibid.*, pp. 268–9, same to same, 23 Sept. 1706, Grametz; Halifax to (Elector of Hanover) (copy), 20 Sept. 1706 (O.S.), Stowe Ms. 222; Halifax to Portland (extract), 24 Sept. 1706 (O.S.), *von Noorden*, ii, p. 350; Halifax to Heinsius, 8 Oct. 1706 (O.S.), *Vreede*, pp. 165–70; *Geikie*, pp. 53–5.

7

On September 21st Godolphin received Buys' reply to his letter suggesting a treaty of 'Preliminaries', a reply which showed how different was the conception of a 'good' peace of the Lord Treasurer of England from that of the Pensionary of Amsterdam. Buys favoured the definition of preliminaries but wanted them incorporated in the Treaty of Succession and Barrier; for the rest, he advocated the cession of Naples and Sicily to Philip V and enlarged on the ruinous state of the Republic's finances. Godolphin considered this letter as further proof, if any were needed, of the 'insuperable eagerness' of the Dutch for a peace, and Marlborough's letters to him and to Harley confirmed this impression. The beginning of October (N.S.), however, found Marlborough slightly less gloomy about the chances of continuing the war. Though still 'very sensible of the ill-humours that reign in Holland' he asked Godolphin and Harley to write to Heinsius and Buys urging them to carry on the struggle. They would be very troublesome, he knew, but the hope, which he had never wholly abandoned, that the Dutch people would not allow them to conclude a separate peace seems to have been growing stronger. It would also assist matters, he thought, if he were provided with a project for a 'preliminary' treaty to set before them, and also if he had the queen's permission to speak his mind plainly on all their present differences – a fairly plain indication that he considered the crisis was past.[1]

None the less, he was well aware that two new dangers had arisen to menace the continuation of the alliance. The first was that, as the consummation of the Union with Scotland grew more and more likely, so the jealousy of English power and influence which he had already noted in the Republic would increase. The second arose from the embarrassments in which Godolphin was becoming involved at home. The admission of Sunderland into the Cabinet, which the Whigs were demanding as the price of their continued support, was meeting with stubborn resistance from the queen, secretly encouraged by Harley. Unless he could persuade the queen to give way Godolphin could choose only between resignation and a loss of parliamentary control occasioned by the withdrawal of Whig support. The confusion resulting from either event would be such, declared Marlborough, that it would

[1] (Godolphin) to (Harley), 21 Sept. (1706), Windsor, Duke of Portland Mss.: Lord Godolphin; Marlborough to Godolphin, 4 and 11 Oct. 1706, Grametz, *Coxe*, ipp. 488–9; Marlborough to Harley, 11 Oct. 1706, Grametz, *Murray*, iii, pp. 166–7; Marlborough to Godolphin, 14 Oct. 1706, Cambron, *Coxe*, i, p. 489.

certainly lead to the Dutch making their peace with France, which, he ruefully told his Duchess, 'will gratify many of the Tory party ...'.

Whatever his difficulties at home, however, Godolphin continued to take a firm line in his letters to Heinsius and Buys. He rejected out of hand their argument that the finances of the Republic were in a worse state than those of England; insisted that to give Naples and Sicily to Philip V would be to make the French 'entire masters of the Mediterranean'; mentioned the need for alterations to the Dutch Barrier project; and refused to agree that a Barrier treaty could be a satisfactory substitute for a treaty of general preliminaries acceptable by all the allies. The root of all the present difficulties, he confided to Marlborough, lay in the 'greediness' of Holland, a sentiment in which his friend concurred; he was beginning to feel, however, as Marlborough now did, that public opinion in the Republic would make it very difficult for the States to make peace in defiance of England.[1]

An examination of the state of feeling about these events outside official quarters in England provides little positive evidence of any kind from which to form a conclusion. Leadam talks of a 'general irritation' with the Dutch, but this seems to be merely a guess based on the false surmise that Englishmen as a whole knew as much of the course of events as did the Cabinet. They certainly did not, and it is highly probable that the lack of indication of any feeling on this subject is due to the fact that public opinion was neither alarmed nor even much interested by the rumours that were arriving from The Hague. Identical rumours had accompanied the end of almost every previous campaign, but nothing had come of them. The only contemporary pamphlet that I have found which dealt with the Dutch reaction to the French proposals was itself a translation of one originally published in Holland, and evidently the work of a pro-English author.[2]

There can, nevertheless, be little doubt that Godolphin accurately reflected the mood of the great majority of politically conscious Englishmen in his refusal to countenance the Dutch desire to negotiate on the French terms.[3] Only the High Tories must be excepted, who, as

---

[1] Marlborough to Sarah, 1 Oct. 1706 (N.S.), *P.C.D.M.*, i, pp. 48–9; Marlborough to (Harley) 7 Oct. 1706 (N.S.), *H.M.C. Bath I*, p. 105; Marlborough to Sarah, n.d., *Coxe*, ii, p. 5; *ibid.*, ii, pp. 6–7, Marlborough to Godolphin, 12 Oct. 1706, Grametz; (Godolphin) to (Harley), 3 Oct. 1706, Newmarket, *H.M.C. Bath I*, pp. 106–7; Godolphin to Marlborough, 4 Oct. 1706, Windsor, *Coxe*, i, pp. 485–8; *ibid.*, i, pp. 489–90, same to same, 10 Oct. 1706, Newmarket; *ibid.*, i, p. 491, Marlborough to Godolphin, 21 Oct. 1706, Cambron.

[2] Leadam, *op.cit.* p. 84; *C.W.* 120.

[3] See L'Hermitage's report of 4 October, in which he emphasises the strength of feeling in England against any negotiation unless the surrender of Dunkirk by France and several,

Marlborough said, would be pleased to see the war end no matter how this was achieved. One of their most powerful reasons for desiring this was their hope that with the end of the war the Whigs, from the first the war-party, would lose their following and influence. It is equally true, of course, that the fear of losing their rapidly increasing power after a peace played a large part in deciding the attitude of the Whigs. Dutch eagerness for peace put Sunderland out of humour; and even such an arch-Batavophil as Shaftesbury felt called upon to reproach his Dutch friends when he realised that the choice lay between humouring the Dutch and continuing the war. Shaftesbury, however, had special contacts both with the ministry and Holland, and thus knew more than most of what was really going on. A good indication of the blissful ignorance of the Whig rank and file is given by the *Observator* of October 5th, in which Tutchin wrote that by far the greatest of Marlborough's services to 'the *Common Cause* and the Interest of *England*' was

his cultivating a Good and Sincere Correspondence betwixt *England* and Holland, putting it out of the Power of our Enemies to create a Misunderstanding betwixt us, which Rivets the Interest of both, the Consequence of which is the Support of the *Confederacy*.[1]

Had the harassed old Lord Treasurer, seeking refuge at Newmarket from affairs of state, cared to deny himself the pleasures of the racecourse for long enough to read these words, they might well have afforded him some bitter amusement.

It was none the less becoming apparent to Marlborough, and to a lesser degree to Godolphin, that any real danger of the Dutch insisting upon peace was, for the moment, past. The arrival at The Hague of Helvétius (a naturalised Frenchman of Dutch origin, who had been employed by Louis XIV to insinuate offers of peace to the Dutch in the autumn of 1705), and the communication of fresh overtures to Marlborough and the Dutch field deputies by the Elector of Bavaria on October 21st, undoubtedly caused Marlborough and Godolphin renewed alarm, yet these events did not plunge them back into that deep pessimism which had engulfed them only a few weeks before. Godolphin still felt that, in the last resort, a direct appeal to the Dutch people would thwart the designs of their rulers; while Marlborough, though suspicious that the Elector's overtures had been encouraged by some

other articles 'par raport à la nation Angloise' are agreed upon as 'preliminaries' (L'Hermitage to States-General (transcript), 4/15 Oct. 1706, London, Add. Ms. 17677 BBB).

[1] Shaftesbury to Furly, 11 Oct. 1706, Hampstead, *Forster*, pp. 224-8; *Observator*, v, 58, 5 Oct. 1706.

in Holland in order to embarrass him, was chiefly concerned lest they should make the Dutch 'less zealous in their preparations for the next campaign'. The events of the autumn had convinced him, however, that, deplore it as he might, his continued presence in the Low Countries throughout each campaign was absolutely essential.[1]

The two main points for concern which the ministry now perceived in the conduct of their ally were, first, the 'immoderate' way in which they were pressing their 'pretensions' in the Spanish Netherlands, and the consequent deterioration of Austro-Dutch relations; and, secondly (another aspect of the same 'unreasonableness'), their obstinate insistence on the unaltered maintenance of their project for the Barrier clause of the Succession Treaty. In both these matters the English leaders had to walk warily, or so they thought, lest a too uncompromising attitude on their part might give a new advantage to the Dutch 'peace party'.

It was the 'folly of affecting the sovereignty' of the Spanish Netherlands, to which the French offers had incited them, which made both the conduct of the Dutch there and their attitude to the Barrier provisions of the Succession Treaty so unreasonable, thought Godolphin. It was high time that both this Treaty and that defining the 'preliminaries' were concluded, declared Harley; but, though Halifax was confident of success, Marlborough, pausing at Brussels on October 29th on his way to The Hague, feared that the whole winter would not be long enough to conclude the Succession Treaty, for the Dutch leaders were

all so very extravagant concerning their barrier, that I despair of doing any good till .... they see that they have it not in their power to dispose of the Low Countries at their will and pleasure, in which the French flatter them.[2]

Three days after his arrival at The Hague on November 9th Marlborough was able to submit to his government a project drawn up by the Dutch leaders for a treaty of 'preliminaries' on the basis of 'no peace without Spain'. This was subsequently approved by the queen and ministry, though Godolphin feared that, unless a time limit were placed

---

[1] Dayrolle to Harley, 15 Oct. 1706, Hague, S.P. Holl. 229; Marlborough to Sarah, 18 Oct. 1706, Cambron, *Coxe*, ii, pp. 15–16; Marlborough to Heinsius, 23 Oct. 1706, Cambron, *van 't Hoff*, p. 279; Godolphin to Marlborough, 13 Oct. 1706, St. James', *Coxe*, i, p. 490; *ibid.*, i, pp. 491–2, Marlborough to Godolphin, 24 Oct. 1706, Cambron; Marlborough to Harley, 25 Oct. 1706, Cambron, *Murray*, iii, p. 191.

[2] Godolphin to Marlborough, 13 Oct. 1706, St. James', *Coxe*, i, p. 490; (Harley) to (Godolphin), 15 Oct. 1706, Brampton, *H.M.C. Bath I*, pp. 109–11; Halifax to Robethon (copy), 18 Oct. 1706, Stowe Ms. 241; Marlborough to Godolphin, 29 Oct. 1706, Brussels, *Coxe*, i, p. 492.

on French acceptance of these terms, the court of Versailles would deliberately protract their consideration of them so as to 'encourage their friends in Holland'.[1] The next task that awaited Marlborough, Stepney, the Imperial minister Sinzendorf and the Dutch leaders was a consideration of the Elector of Bavaria's suggestion for an open conference. Godolphin had already been delighted to learn that Buys and his friends were unlikely to be able to extract much advantage from this proposal, to which Marlborough was instructed on October 21st (O.S.) to make, if possible, a reply in concert with the States-General.[2]

Marlborough and Stepney soon gained the impression that Dutch continuation of the war was now certain. Further reassurance came when, on November 20th, the Deputies of the States-General communicated the Elector's suggestion to the ministers of the Allies and proclaimed the determination of the Republic to stand by her allies' demands. It was for Louis XIV to make the next move; his attempts to entice the Dutch away from the Alliance had failed. Englishmen outside the ministry, who knew little or nothing of the suspense of those anxious weeks in September and October, could delight in the 'firmness' of their Dutch ally. The Lords, in their address on the queen's speech at the opening of Parliament on December 3rd (O.S.), gave voice to the 'universal pleasure and satisfaction', as too did the Commons, though indirectly and in less glowing terms.[3]

8

The Lords, too, like Tutchin in the *Observator*, expressed anxiety that such a Barrier might be procured for 'the States-General (in whose security we must always think the interest of England is engaged) as may be to their just satisfaction'. The ministry might well have retorted that there seemed to be little danger of the Dutch neglecting

[1] Marlborough to Hedges, 12 Nov. 1706, Hague, *Murray*, iii, pp. 214–15; Godolphin to Marlborough, 'Oct. 22' 1706, *Coxe*, i, pp. 494–5. If the dating of these events adopted by Geikie (working from documents in the Rijksarchief)'is correct, the true date of this second letter must be 9/20 November. The Treaty was never ratified by the States-General, and consequently had no force (*Geikie*, pp. 71–2).

[2] Hedges to Marlborough, 21 Oct. 1706, Whitehall, *Coxe*, i, pp. 493–4; (Godolphin) to (Harley), 23 Oct. 1706 (O.S.), *H.M.C. Bath I*, pp. 114–15.

[3] Marlborough to Godolphin, 16 Nov. 1706, Hague, *Coxe*, i, p. 497; L'Hermitage to States-General (transcript), 19/30 Nov. 1706, London, Add. Ms. 17677 BBB: (Stepney) to Raby (copy), 3 Dec. 1706, Hague, Add. Ms. 7075; *Luttrell*, vi, p. 111, 26 Nov. 1706; *Observator*, v, 73, 27 Nov. 1706; Shaftesbury to Furly, 2 Dec. 1706, St. Giles', *Forster*, pp. 228–31; *C.W.* 113, v, pp. 306–11; *Cobbett*, vi, cols. 544–5.

their own interests in this matter. On October 21st (O.S.) Godolphin informed Marlborough that he still thought the Dutch Barrier demands too general, and on the following day Halifax, who had not returned to Holland, outlined the attitude of the ministry in a letter to Stepney. He feared that, when the Dutch could be prevailed upon to particularise their proposals, they might well demand some places that would serve rather as a Barrier against the Spanish Netherlands than against France:

Dendermond can serve them to no other purpose but to influence the Trade, and Ostend is the Entrance of all our Traffique, And if Menin, Ipres &c. be given them in that Quarter, I think their frontier will be sufficiently cover'd on that side, tho' Ostend were left open to admit our Trade at all times, or our Succours in case of Need.[1]

From these few words we can learn much of the English attitude towards the Dutch Barrier. In the summer, it had not been mere impetuousness that had made Halifax willing that the States should make their Barrier demands as strong as possible. His Whiggish outlook on foreign affairs involved a tendency automatically to support the claims of the Republic against those of the Austrians; he shared the prevailing anxiety in Whig circles about the Protestant Succession, and was consequently eager that nothing should stand in the way of the conclusion of the Succession Treaty; and the growing conviction amongst the Whigs that their political survival depended upon the continuation of the war was an additional reason for him to desire the best possible relations with the Dutch. Since that time, however, several factors had combined to cool his ardour. The increasing likelihood of a Scottish Union had, in Whig eyes, diminished the immediacy of the danger to the Protestant Succession, and, more important still, the nature of the Dutch Barrier project and the anxiety of the Dutch to make a 'bad' peace had made even the most fervent Whig wonder just how much security there was for England and English trade in Dutch possession of virtual sovereignty in the Spanish Netherlands. For all their pro-Dutch inclinations, the Whigs could not bring themselves to make the future of English trade in the Spanish Netherlands dependent upon the goodwill of the States-General. They might not believe that control of those territories would give the Republic the hegemony of Europe, but they were chary of allowing such power over English interests to a nation whose anxiety

---

[1] Godolphin to Marlborough, 21 Oct. 1706 (O.S.), *Coxe*, i, p. 493; Halifax to (Stepney) (copy), 22 Oct. 1706, London, Add. Ms. 7077; *Observator*, v, 74, 30 Nov. 1706; *Cobbett*, vi, cols. 544–5.

for peace seemed to them a sign of marked pro-French tendencies, and in whose eagerness to defend the Protestant Succession they had considerably less faith than at the beginning of the year.

It is worthy of note that in 1706 not only the ministry but also the Junto (not represented in the government until Sunderland replaced Hedges on December 3rd) were not so desperate for the continuation of the war that they were prepared to sacrifice what were generally thought of as vital national interests. Once it seemed to Halifax and his friends that those interests were in danger, they sprang to their defence as resolutely as any Tory; a fact which inspired Harley, now playing a double game both at home and abroad, to 'confide' in Vrijbergen that their criticisms of the Dutch Barrier claims were prompted by a desire 'to pay court to the English nation' [1]. At this time and later – until 1709, in fact – the attitude of the ministry – Whig and Tory alike – to the Dutch Barrier claims was governed first and foremost by the determination to guard essential English interests in the Spanish Netherlands.

From the moment of his arrival at The Hague Marlborough realised that the aspirations that the French offers of complete control of the Spanish Netherlands had engendered amongst the Dutch were not yet dead, though he saw a good prospect, as he wrote to Hedges on November 12th, that the States might at last 'be brought to a particular declaration'. Such a declaration was, indeed, made soon afterwards, but it was almost diametrically opposed to the views of Austria, and the complete failure of the attempt to reach an Austro-Dutch agreement was acknowledged when Sinzendorf left for Vienna on November 25th. Marlborough, who had adopted throughout a temporizing and non-committal attitude towards the rival claims, had set out the day before for London, and Stepney was left to attempt to reach a bilateral agreement with the Dutch.

It cannot have escaped the English ministers that the irreconcilable Habsburg opposition to the Dutch proposals had greatly improved England's bargaining position. The Emperor's attitude, in fact, was bound to make the Dutch more anxious for an English guarantee of their Barrier and less likely to make peace with France until such a guarantee was obtained. Hence, from the English point of view, there was now a good deal to be said for prolonging the Barrier negotiations

---

[1] Vrijbergen to Heinsius (extract), 17 Dec. 1706, *von Noorden*, ii, p. 560. *Cf.* Harley's letter to Godolphin of 15 October (*H.M.C. Bath I*, pp. 109–11), which contains a hint of disapproval of Halifax's steadfast opposition to the Dutch Barrier project.

as long as possible. The Dutch, as Halifax had foreseen, had placed Ostend and Dendermonde among their demands, and it was against their inclusion that English objections, prompted by fears both for their trade with the Spanish Netherlands and for their security, were centred. Stepney, instructed by Marlborough not to give way on these claims, found Heinsius 'Firm as a Rock' in maintaining them, and on December 10th he wrote to the Duke that it might be as well to concede them since the Pensionary now seemed to be more moderate in his financial demands. Marlborough would not hear of this, though he declared emphatically to Heinsius his heartfelt desire to see the Treaty completed, and Halifax, while protesting that nobody could have better wishes for the 'Security or Advantage' of the Republic than he, wrote that

should the Queen's Ministers put those places into the hands of the Dutch, they could not satisfy people here, that they had not put all the Trade of Flanders under their directions, and the distinction of *Ius Praesidii et Fortalitii*, will never be understood upon the Exchange.[1]

He also expressed the hope that the Lords' address of December 4th [2] would have a good effect in Holland, but Stepney had to report to Marlborough on December 21st that, on the contrary, there had been a considerable recrudescence of 'Nationall Jealousy' amongst the Dutch owing to the news of the arrival of a patent from Charles III constituting Marlborough as Governor of the Spanish Netherlands. On December 28th Stepney told Sunderland that he thought that the addresses of both Houses could not fail but have a good effect, but meanwhile he made no progress with his negotiations, and saw little prospect of any. On January 4th he informed Marlborough that the confirmation of the report of Charles III's patent had caused a 'very great clamour', and that Heinsius insisted that Marlborough again decline the offer. Cardonnel, who, a week before, had assured Stepney that if 'every body in England were as well acquainted as we are with ye humour & management of those people ... we should not hold long together', was completely beside himself over this latest development. 'Nothing in the world', he wrote to Stepney on December 27th (O.S.),

---

[1] Marlborough to Hedges, 12 Nov. 1706, Hague, *Murray*, iii, pp. 214–15; (Stepney) to Marlborough (copies), 30 Nov., 7 and 10 Dec. 1706, Hague, Add. Ms. 7064; *ibid.*, (Stepney) to Halifax (copy), 7 Dec. 1706, Hague; Halifax to (Stepney) (copy), 6 Dec. 1706 (O.S.), Add. Ms. 7077; Marlborough to (Stepney), 6 Dec. 1706, St. James', *Murray*, iii, pp. 244–6; Marlborough to Heinsius, 13 Dec. 1706, London, *van 't Hoff*, p. 285; *ibid.*, pp. 288–9, same to same, 24 Dec. 1706, St. James'; *Geikie*, pp. 75–8; *von Noorden*, ii, pp. 429–35.

[2] See above, p. 150.

could make me desirous his Grace should take ye Government upon him but the
obstinacy & ingratitude of the Dutch, who I take for the most part of them, to
be the mere scum of the earth.[1]

The day before Stepney sent his warning letter Marlborough had once
more bowed to the storm and intimated to the court of Charles III that

the unreasonable jealousies in Holland will not permit me to exert that authority
with which H.M. is pleased to invest me till the business of the Barrier is settled,
wherein I find no less difficulty.

Four days later, on December 27th (O.S.), he sent to Stepney and,
in a less emphatic form, to Heinsius and Slingelandt, complaints of
the 'ungrateful returns' that he had received. The Duke was still
obsessed by the lure of this dazzling prize, and the refusal of the
Dutch to countenance his acceptance of it, coupled with their eagerness
for peace, had, it was now quite evident, soured him in a way which
the most contrary actions of their field deputies and generals had
never been able to bring about.[2]

This episode could not be expected to facilitate the Barrier negotiations, and the same was true of the growing divergence between
English and Dutch views on financial administration under the
Condominium. These negotiations, in fact, petered out in the early
months of 1707, as can be seen from the correspondence that passed
between Stepney and Harley at this time. The Secretary declared
that he could not understand how Ostend could serve as a Barrier
except against England, and assured Stepney that no Englishman
could approve of such unreasonable demands, which would, if widely
known, cause much jealousy and ill-feeling. Stepney, who could not
make the slightest headway, soon became convinced that further
discussion could lead only to dispute and might even be dangerous
to the alliance; and we may take leave of this dying negotiation with
a summary of the situation which he sent to Harley on January 18th
(N.S.). He had argued, he said

that Dendermonde was only a Barriere agst ye Spanish Netherlands & to
influence the Inland-Trade by the Dutch being masters of ye Schelde on one

---

[1] (Stepney) to Marlborough (copy), 21 Dec. 1706, Hague, Add. Ms. 7064; Same to same
(copy), 24 Dec. 1706, Hague, Add. Ms. 7075; Cardonnel to (Stepney), 14 and 27 Dec. 1706,
Whitehall, Add. Ms. 7063; Stepney to Sunderland (draft), 28 Dec. 1706, Hague, Add. Ms.
21551; (Stepney) to Harley (copy), 28 Dec. 1706, Hague, Add. Ms. 7059; Stepney to Marlborough, 4 Jan. 1707, Hague, *Coxe*, i, pp. 447–8.

[2] Marlborough to J. Stanhope, 23 Dec. 1706, St. James', *Murray*, iii, pp. 256–8; *ibid.*, iii,
p. 270, Marlborough to Stepney, 27 Dec. 1706, St. James'; *ibid.*, iii, p. 271, Marlborough to
Slingelandt, 27 Dec. 1706, St. James'; Marlborough to Heinsius, 27 Dec. 1706, London, *van
't Hoff*, p. 289.

side as they already are on ye other; & That Ostende is properly a Barriere agst England, and ought to be left open to admitt our Trade at all times & our Succours in time of need. But there is no disputing with them, or at least no hope of bringing them over . . . .

His use of words identical to those employed by Halifax in his letter of October 22nd (O.S.) indicates the fundamental and unchanging nature of the stand taken by the English government.[1]

9

In his letter to Stepney of December 24th Harley had declared that it must be ill-founded jealousy of English trade that made the Dutch so obstinate in the matter of Ostend and Dendermonde; and, lapsing into the vague platitudes which came so easily to his pen, he continued:

the world is wide enough for us both to Trade, the conjunction of our Naval strength is our mutual interest, and inseparable friendship with a Union of Counsels is what only can make both Nations secure and formidable.

Fine-sounding words, no doubt reflecting the quite genuine lessening of commercial rivalry which we have seen, for example, in the course of the trade and correspondence dispute; but scarcely to be taken at their face-value where direct Dutch competition with English trade and manufacture was concerned. The reception accorded to Dutch proposals for the reduction of the high duties on the importation of their linens into England was a good illustration of this. Benjamin Furly, an English merchant resident in Rotterdam, took it upon himself to urge this reduction upon English political leaders, though as early as October 11th (O.S.) Shaftesbury had warned him how improbable it was that the Whigs and Court party combined, well-disposed as they were to the proposal, could

recover such a past game as to alter the funds established by taking off dutyes, in a case where the other party will stickle to the utmost, with that very intent to embroyl us with Holland, and so putt a base and unhappy end to a gloriouse and successfull warr.

Nothing daunted, Furly represented the case for reducing these impositions to the influential Duke of Shrewsbury, newly returned to England from Italy, arguing that unless something were done soon the States would place heavy retaliatory duties on English goods.

[1] Harley to Stepney (copies), 24 and 31 Dec. 1706, and 3 and 14 Jan. 1706/7, Whitehall, F.E.B. Holl. 73; Stepney to Harley, 18 and 21 Jan. 1707, Hague, S.P. Holl. 230. For Halifax's letter see above, p. 151.

Shrewsbury thought the proposal, though reasonable, impracticable, for

we have too many in this nation, [who] though very unjustly, cry out on the Dutch that they having [sic] trade with France, the advantage of returns [and] great part of our money spent in their country . . . .

A memorial on this matter was presented by Vrijbergen and considered by the Board of Trade, but on March 14th, 1706/7 Harley had to inform Dayrolle that, though the Ministry was doing all it could to further the Dutch request, 'we labor very much up hill, for even the Merchants that trade to Holland, are not very fond of Mr. Vryberge's proposal'. From the complaints that continued to arrive from Holland later in the year, it is apparent that the ministry's efforts, which we may suspect were not as energetic as Harley would have had the States believe, did not receive the necessary parliamentary sanction.[1]

IO

It will by now be apparent that, although it is of crucial importance in the development of the attitude of English political leaders towards the Dutch, 1706 is a year of little interest in considering the wider field of 'public opinion'. The conduct of the Dutch had exasperated Godolphin as never before, the bitterness of disappointment and the acuteness of anxiety had made Marlborough's attitude more and more equivocal, and even the Whig leaders had resented Dutch views both on peace and on their Barrier; but it has already been seen that there is some negative evidence to show that those outside the highest circles knew little of these matters.

Ignorance was not the only reason for their unconcern; their minds were fully occupied with the question of Union with Scotland, which had at last lost its academic quality and become an increasingly imminent possibility. Even here, however, we find that the Dutch were not entirely forgotten. Towards the end of 1706 there came to the ears of members of both the English and Scottish governments stories that influential people in the Republic, jealous and apprehensive of the results of a Union, were sending letters and even large sums of

[1] Shaftesbury to Furly, 11 Oct. 1706, Hampstead, *Forster*, pp. 224–8; Furly to (Shrewsbury), 25 Dec. 1706, Rotterdam, *H.M.C. Buccleuch II pt. ii*, pp. 711–17; Harley to Stepney (copy), 24 Dec. 1706, Whitehall, F.E.B. Holl. 73; Shrewsbury to Furly, 27 Dec. 1706, Heathrop, *H.M.C. Buccleuch II pt. ii*, pp. 717–18; Shaftesbury to Somers, Jan. 1706/7, St. Giles', *Rand*, pp. 371–2; Harley to Dayrolle (copy), 14 March 1706/7, Whitehall, F.E.B. Holl. 73; Harley to Godolphin (abstract), 20 Sept. 1707 (O.S.), *Cal. Tr. Papers, 1702–7*, pp. 535–6; *ibid.*, p. 546, Commissioners of Customs to Godolphin (abstract), 7 Nov. 1707 (O.S.).

money into Scotland to dissuade the Scots from consenting to such an arrangement. Similar reports of arms and money being sent to Scottish 'malcontents' from the Republic had been investigated in 1703, but neither Stanhope nor Cockburn had been able to discover any real foundation for them. On December 27th (O.S.) Harley wrote to Stepney asking him to investigate these rumours, and the reply that the latter sent home eleven days later was similar to that made by Cockburn more than three years before. Nobody in Holland was himself carrying on such intrigues, Stepney thought, though French money might have been sent from Amsterdam for that purpose; on the other hand, it was certain that there would always be 'a Nationall jealousy founded on a prospect of Trade', and Dutch apprehensions lest the Scottish fishery should flourish as a result of Union were such that, although Stepney thought the stories unlikely, he would not describe them as impossible. As one of Princess Sophia's English correspondents wrote of the Union a fortnight later: 'The Dutch ... are not for it, because it is against their Interest ...'.

Meanwhile, in Scotland, pamphlets were being published to prove that a 'Coalition' with the Dutch would be a far less objectionable method of gaining the advantages proposed from an 'Incorporate Union' with England. The ubiquitous Defoe, now in Edinburgh as the secret agent of the English ministry, set himself to explode such notions in a pamphlet published in the Scottish capital early in 1707. After asserting that trade between Scotland and the Republic was greatly to the advantage of the latter, and that it was most doubtful whether, in any case, the Dutch would be willing to 'coalite', he dealt with examples of Dutch 'kindness' to Scotland that had been quoted. Was it kindness on their part or on ours, he asked (he had assumed the role of a Scottish patriot), that made them rich at the expense of our fishery, or that allowed them to own most of the ships in our harbours? [1]

On May 1, 1707, the Union of Scotland and 'our Potent Neighbour' (as the 'True Born Englishman' described his own country!) was at last accomplished, and Stepney's investigations became as superfluous as was now the journalist's continued presence in Edinburgh.

[1] G. Clarke to Nottingham, 9 Jan. 1702/3 (O.S.), *C.S.P. Dom. Anne*, i, p. 490; Cockburn to (Nottingham), 3 Aug. 1703 (N.S.), Add. Ms. 29589; Hedges to Stanhope (copy), 13 Aug. 1703, Whitehall, F.E.B. Holl. 69; Stanhope to Hedges, 21 Sept. 1703, Hague, S.P. Holl. 226; Mar to Sunderland, 10 Dec. 1706, Edinburgh, *H.M.C. Mar & Kellie*, pp. 353–4; Harley to Stepney (copy), 27 Dec. 1706, Whitehall, F.E.B. Holl. 73; Stepney to Harley, 18 Jan. 1707, Hague, S.P. Holl. 230; Hutton to (Electress of Hanover), 24 Jan. 1706/7, Whitehall, Stowe Ms. 223; *C.W.* 35, pp. 22–6, 34–5.

CHAPTER VI

OFFICIAL ANXIETY AND PUBLIC APATHY
⟨1707–8⟩

I

In the year 1706 the attitudes of the English governmental leaders towards their Dutch ally had been crystallised by disillusionment. The patent reluctance of the Dutch to continue the war with vigour had engendered feelings which were to remain virtually unchanged for the next two years. Godolphin, possessed by unremitting apprehension and distrust, now took towards the Republic a 'firm' line tinged with more than a little desperation; Marlborough, though more calm, was no more confident of the reliability of the recalcitrant ally, and was, in addition, doomed by his own ambition both to suspect and to be suspected. The goodwill of the Whigs, who in this period improved their position both in the ministry and in parliament, was now limited by the unspoken provisos that the Dutch should neither end the war nor press their claim to Ostend.

The year 1707 was one of almost unmitigated disaster for the allied cause, and with its many setbacks and disappointments enthusiasm for the war amongst the majority of politically active Englishmen disappeared irrevocably. It is strange that the consequent growth of war-weariness in England should have eventually resulted in increasing hostility towards the Dutch, themselves for the most part only too anxious to put an end to the conflict, but this was precisely what occurred.

This was not merely because Dutch war-weariness expressed itself in caution in the field lest by 'venturing' they should lose their already substantial gains, while in many quarters in England the same feelings took the form of a desire for an 'all-out' allied effort which would, so it was thought, bring France speedily to her knees. More important still was the growing conviction amongst those not in the secrets of the ministry that a prolonged, indecisive struggle, while ruinous to England, was just what was desired by the States, whom every year of war, it was thought, made more and more prosperous.

This belief was compounded of jealousy of the alleged prosperity of the Republic and annoyance at its alleged defects as a fighting ally. It was fostered, but not created, by out-of-office Tories, to whom the failures of 1707 gave the chance that the successes of 1706 had denied them. They were able to make capital, above all, of the shock felt in England at the smashing defeat administered to the Allies at Almanza. They could contrast the allegedly puny efforts that the ministry and the Dutch were making in Spain with the vast expenditure of men and money that was being made in the Low Countries, and all to win a few more towns for the Dutch. If the war was really to put Charles III on the Spanish throne, they asked, why did we not concentrate our efforts there and in the Spanish Indies? Why, in any case, did we neglect the war by sea in favour of this endless and profitless struggle to enrich the Dutch? Such words made a strong appeal to that commercial jealousy of the Dutch which was beginning to stir more strongly in English breasts now that the spell of Blenheim had been broken.

The spread of these ideas was gradual; indeed, they did not achieve complete and open expression until 1710–11. None the less, the growing weariness with the war in the years 1707–8 led to the resurrection of Tory opposition from its erstwhile impotence. One of the outstanding phenomena of these years was a ministry more and more committed to the prolongation of the war leading a people whose goodwill towards their chief ally was becoming less and less.

2

With the arrival of the New Year the affairs of Northern Europe were once more weighing heavily upon the English ministry. Not only had the formal renunciation of his claims to the Bishopric of Eutin not yet been obtained from Prince Charles of Denmark, but an additional problem was raised by the request of Charles XII of Sweden that England and the States should recognise Stanislas, whom he had placed on the throne of Poland after deposing Augustus of Saxony. The situation was complicated by the extremely strained relations between the Protestant warrior-king and the Jesuit-controlled Emperor.

The English ministry was not slow to observe, however, that the deciding factor in Dutch policy in this matter was a desire not 'to disoblige the Czar', the inveterate enemy of Charles XII, and thus imperil Dutch trade to Russia, by recognising Stanislas. Stepney thought that this consideration might 'have some weight' in England, too, but Godolphin, anxious to appease the Swedish King, was annoyed by the inaction of the Dutch, whom he suspected of secretly encouraging Czar Peter to continue the war in Poland. By March Harley began to think that some more sinister motive – probably, though he did not say so, a desire to divide the alliance and so end the war – lay behind the extraordinary 'backwardness' of the States both in this matter and that of Eutin, where they were finding fault with the renunciation to which Charles of Denmark was being asked to subscribe. He had even heard, on good authority, that insinuations had been made to Charles XII that it was England that was holding back the States from compliance in these matters. A memorial on the subject of the 'agnition' of Stanislas, presented by Vrijbergen near the end of March, left him convinced that, if the States did anything at all in this affair, it would be with a bad grace.[1]

Marlborough's persuasions at The Hague, where he arrived on April 16th (N.S.), made the Dutch 'more easy' about Eutin, but had no real effect on their attitude towards Stanislas. At first the Duke thought them 'more pliant' in this matter, but when he decided to pay a flying visit to Charles XII at Altranstadt it was only with difficulty that he obtained the States' leave, and the opposition of Amsterdam made it impossible for him to get any powers to treat on the 'agnition' question while he was there. Before leaving for Altranstadt, on April 20th, he wrote to Godolphin that Dutch views on this question were still dominated by the 'fear of disobliging the Czar'.

On his return to The Hague after his memorable interview with the 'Gothick hero' Marlborough found the States willing to agree to a form of renunciation for Charles of Denmark. All that now remained before this tedious affair could drag itself to a close was for the States to agree to their proportion of Prince Charles' compensatory 'pension'; and, as Harley foresaw, the 'dilatory forms' of their government gave a pretext for delays, the real purpose of which, he suspected, was to 'hinder their payment of what they had promis'd'.[2]

---

[1] Stepney to Harley, 10 Dec. 1706, Hague, S.P. Holl. 230; Marlborough to Heinsius (p.s.), 24 Jan. 1706/7, London, van 't Hoff, p. 298; (Godolphin) to (Harley), 20 Feb. 1706/7 (O.S.), H.M.C. Bath I, p. 162; Harley to Stepney (copies), 11 and 18 March 1706/7, Whitehall, F.E.B. Holl. 73; Dayrolle to Harley, 5 April 1707, Hague, S.P. Holl. 229; Harley to Robinson (copies), 25 and 28 March 1707, Whitehall, F.E.B. Sweden 154; C.W. 113, iv, p. 445.

[2] Marlborough to Harley, 19 April 1707, Hague, Murray, iii, pp. 344–5; Stepney to Harley, 19 April 1707, Hague, S.P. Holl. 230; Marlborough to Godolphin, 20 April 1707, Hague, Coxe, ii, pp. 43–4; (Stepney) to Lewis, 20 April 1707, Hague, S.P. Holl. 230: Marlborough to Pulteney, 10 May 1707, Hague, Murray, iii, pp. 359–60; Harley to Pulteney (copies), 6 May

On the other hand, no progress at all could be made in the question of joint recognition of Stanislas. We do not hear many more complaints from England of the Dutch attitude in this matter, however, for the ministry had had second thoughts about the advisability of this step and was glad to use the intractability of the Republic as an excuse for its own inactivity. This change in English policy seems to have been due to the knowledge of Charles XII's plans for a Russian campaign that Marlborough had obtained at Altranstadt. The English ministry now desired to await the outcome of this venture before committing itself to recognize Stanislas. The Dutch had had their way, and in November 1708 we find Dayrolle ascribing the Czar's action in facilitating Dutch trade with Archangel to his gratitude for the States' refusal to comply with England in this affair.[1]

3

The beginning of almost every year of the war had brought forth a heavy crop of English complaints concerning Dutch 'backwardness' in preparing for a vigorous campaign. To this rule 1707 was something of an exception. On the vital question of Dutch willingness to fight a vigorous campaign in the Spanish Netherlands before listening to further peace overtures, the reports of English observers were, for once, all favourable. The air was full of rumours of the activities of unofficial emissaries, both French and Dutch, but Dayrolle, Manchester (on his way to Venice) and Cadogan, now married to a Dutchwoman but as suspicious as ever of Dutch policies, were unanimous in finding 'all things in a good disposition' at The Hague. Cadogan even considered that Marlborough might well be able to conclude the Barrier negotiation on his arrival, so 'intent' were the States to settle it and so high did the Duke's credit now stand.[2]

Elsewhere, however, opinions on these subjects were more diverse. As early as January 1st the *Observator* praised the Dutch for the forwardness of their preparations, and over four months later described them as 'our best ally' in defending them against the hoary accusation,

and 24 June 1707, Whitehall, F.E.B. Denmark 4; Marlborough to Harley, 27 June 1707, Meldert, *Murray*, iii, pp. 445-6.
[1] Harley to Robinson (copy), 8 July 1707, Whitehall, F.E.B. Sweden 154; Marlborough to Heinsius, 25 Aug. 1707, Soignies, *van 't Hoff*, pp. 338-9; Dayrolle to Boyle, 20 Nov. 1708, Hague, S.P. Holl. 231.
[2] Manchester to Sunderland, 29 March 1707, Hague, *Cole*, p. 436; Dayrolle to Harley, 1 April 1707, Hague, S.P. Holl. 229; Cadogan to (Raby), 5 April 1707, Hague, Add. Ms. 22196.

resurrected by Leslie in his pamphlet *The Wolf Stript*, of having instigated the Great Fire of London. Sunderland, the new Secretary of State, welcomed Manchester's report, though he thought that if it were true that the new French offers had not satisfied even Welland 'they must be very scandalous ones indeed'. Cardonnel, on the other hand, found himself, in mid-January, 'more and more dissatisfied with the humour' of the Dutch, and wanted to be 'well ridd' of them; and Shrewsbury, who, less than four months before, had noted 'how much the Duke of Marlborough is beloved by the people' of Amsterdam, wrote on March 26th (O.S.) that the Dutch would 'not be prevailed on to continue the war much longer'. In Berlin, too, Raby was somewhat dubious about Cadogan's assurances. The 'wrong measures' that the Dutch had taken all the winter, he wrote to the Quartermaster-General, and particularly their insistence on the inadmissible demand of Ostend and Dendermonde, made him fear the power of the pro-French party in the Republic. His sentiments were much like those that Louis XIV's foreign minister Torcy had expressed on April 7th, two days earlier: 'The allies grow weary of the war, they will quarrel in their anxiety to secure good terms for themselves'.[1]

The situation as Marlborough saw it when he arrived at The Hague was one neither for rejoicing nor yet for despair. He was afraid that Buys spoke for 'a great many more in Holland' in continuing to advocate a partition of the Spanish monarchy, but he was confident of 'making this campaign'. While the Duke was *en route* for Altranstadt, however, the allied armies in Spain suffered the disastrous defeat of Almanza. When the news of this setback arrived on May 10th, two days after his return to The Hague, Marlborough was alarmed by its effect on the Dutch people and leaders. His alarm grew on discovering, after his arrival at Brussels on May 13th, that 'their aversion to the present government, and the disorders it lies under' made the news welcome to many of the Spanish Netherlanders. Above all, he feared that the States would now give their field-deputies 'orders to act here with more caution than the urgency of affairs requires'; and on May 30th he had to inform Godolphin that the deputies had, in fact, received orders to avoid an engagement, but that he was doing his

---

[1] Shrewsbury's Journal, 15 Dec. 1706, *H.M.C. Buccleuch II pt. ii*, p. 796; *Observator*, v, 83, 1 Jan. 1706/7; Cardonnel to Watkins, 17 Jan. 1706/7, Whitehall, *Thibaudeau*, 2nd ser., ii, p. 66; Sunderland to Manchester, 25 March 1707, Whitehall, *Cole*, p. 437; (Shrewsbury) to Vernon, 26 March 1707, Heathrop, Add. Ms. 40776; Torcy to Petkum (translation), 7 April 1707 (N.S.), *H.M.C. XIV pt. ix*, p. 320; (Raby) to Cadogan (draft), 9 April 1707, Berlin, Add. Ms. 22196; *Observator*, vi, 14, 19 April 1707.

best to keep this news from the army, 'since that must have an ill effect', the Dutch troops being as eager to engage as any others. Nor was this all: most of the Spanish Netherlanders, he was now convinced, would welcome the return of the French, 'which is occasioned by the unreasonable behaviour of the Dutch' – no doubt a reference to the attempts of the Dutch deputies at Brussels to reform the financial administration in Flanders.[1]

Thus ensued a long period of enforced inaction in the Low Countries. Though the letters of his generals reveal that he, as well as they, was mortified by the conduct of the Dutch, Marlborough retained his self-command throughout, and behaved with great circumspection. He knew that, for all their caution, 'our friends in Holland are desirous of good success', and he could understand, even if he could not sympathise with, the Dutch reasoning thus expressed by Raby (playing the Devil's advocate for once!):

. . . . there is this to be said for the Hogen Mogens that if you beat the French they retire behind their strong towns, wch. will cost you the summer to take, but if they should have the good luck they had in Spain, all flanders and Brabant is lost at a stroke for you . . . .

By the end of June his hopes that he might soon persuade the Dutch to 'venture' were reviving, but he assured Sunderland that he would not risk an engagement 'unless the probability were on our side',

---

[1] Marlborough to (Harley), 16 April 1707, Hague, *H.M.C. Bath I*, p. 168; Marlborough to Godolphin, 20 April 1707, Hague, *Coxe*, ii, pp. 43–4; Same to same, 10 May 1707, Hague, *Murray*, iii, p. 357; *ibid.*, iii, pp. 360–1, Marlborough to Wratislaw, 10 May 1707, Hague; Marlborough to Godolphin, 15 May 1707, Brussels, *Coxe*, ii, pp. 66–7; *ibid.*, ii, pp. 69–70, same to same, (30 May 1707), Beaulieu; Marlborough to (Harley), 2 June 1707 (N.S.), *H.M.C. Bath I*, pp. 172–3; Marlborough to Sarah, 13 June 1707, Meldert, *Coxe*, ii, p. 72; *Veenendaal*, chapters IX and XI, *passim*. The Dutch historian Slothouwer (*De Staatsman Sicco van Goslinga* (The Hague, 1885), pp. 27–8) accuses Marlborough of playing a double game, since at the same time that he was complaining to Godolphin of Dutch inaction in the field he was writing to Heinsius of his own unwillingness to give battle. Slothouwer is not alone in thinking that the Duke's resentment of the Dutch attitude in the matter of the Governorship of the Spanish Netherlands had 'decided him to show them that he would not produce rabbits out of a hat, when his military tricks were so ill requited' (Ashley, *Marlborough*, p. 84); but there is no evidence to support the Dutch writer's imputation of downright duplicity. The letter to Heinsius that he quotes (of 30 May) assures the Pensionary that Marlborough is 'not for venturing *unless we have the advantage on our side*' (my italics), but also presses the need to 'act with some vigor' (*van 't Hoff*, pp. 311–12). In his letter of the same date to Godolphin, also quoted by Slothouwer, the Duke explains that his cautious military tactics are designed to convince the Pensionary of the truth of his assurances, in the hope that he will be allowed to 'venture' 'if an advantage should offer itself' (*Coxe*, ii, pp. 69–70). Here is no duplicity, but merely Marlborough's apparently reluctant acceptance of the necessity of not venturing except with an advantage. The fact that this reluctance is less marked in his letter to Heinsius is an example of quite legitimate 'management' of the indispensable but alarming Dutch ally. To characterise this as duplicity is to show a suspicion of Marlborough's motives worthy of Goslinga himself!

since any setback would greatly encourage the already very strong inclinations for peace among the Dutch.[1]

On July 4th, the Duke was of opinion that the Dutch wanted to avoid action until some news arrived of the Toulon expedition, to which so many allied hopes were pinned. Three days later, however, his hopes had faded; the expedition he now considered a pretext for inaction, 'since it is the daily discourse in this army, as well as in Holland, why should they venture, since they have already in their hands what will be a sufficient security to them?' His suspicions were increased by the States' desire to make one more effort to persuade the Emperor to end his war with the Hungarian rebels. This proposal was suspected by Marlborough, Harley, and even Stepney, whose attitude in this matter had much angered the Viennese court in the past, of being made with the design 'of throwing more blame upon the Impll. Court, & then makeing a desperate ill use of it by precipitating a Peace next winter'. On July 18th, in a letter to Godolphin, Marlborough enlarged upon the hopelessness of the situation. If Louis XIV were to repeat the Hennequin proposals now, he asserted, the Dutch would grasp at them, and

it is as certain that the Dutch will never more this war venture any thing that may be decisive, being of opinion that they have already enough in their possession for this security, and that France will assist them in disposing of this possession as they shall think best for their security.

In these circumstances the Duke was much alarmed when, a fortnight later, reports reached him that Louis' go-between Helvétius was once more in the Republic.[2]

Godolphin's reaction to Marlborough's forebodings was most interesting. Although he himself had urged less than two months before that England and Holland should if necessary make peace separately

[1] Lumley to Hanmer, 16 June and 7 July 1707, Meldert, *Hanmer Corres.*, pp. 105–6 and 112–13; Cadogan to (Raby), 16 June, 7 and 24 July 1707, Meldert, Add. Ms. 22196; Marlborough to Godolphin, 23 June 1707, Meldert, *Coxe*, ii, pp. 88–9; (Raby) to Cadogan (draft), 25 June 1707, Berlin, Add. Ms. 22196; Marlborough to Sunderland, 27 June 1707, Meldert, *Coxe*, ii, p. 102; Marlborough to Harley, 27 June 1707 (N.S.), *H.M.C. XV pt. iv*, p. 420; Cadogan to Brydges, 27 June 1707, Camp at Meldert, G. Davies, 'The Seamy Side of Marlborough's War', *Hunt. Lib. Quart.*, xv (1951–2), pp. 36–7. In the last-named article Mr. Davies shows that Cadogan's annoyance with the Dutch was at least partly due to their inaction having spoiled one of his shady financial transactions (pp. 23–4).

[2] Marlborough to Godolphin, 4 July 1707, Meldert, *Coxe*, ii, p. 105; Harley to Stepney (copy), 27 June 1707, Whitehall, F.E.B. Holl. 73; Marlborough to Sunderland, 7 July 1707, Meldert, *Coxe*, ii, pp. 105–6; *ibid.*, ii, pp. 109–10, Marlborough to Godolphin, 18 July 1707 (N.S.); Stepney to Harley, 18 July 1707, Brussels, S.P. Holl. 230; Marlborough to Heinsius, (31 July 1707, Meldert), *van 't Hoff*, pp. 331–2; *ibid.*, pp. 334–5, same to same, 8 Aug. 1707, Meldert.

from the Emperor, he now thought that the queen should warn the States 'that they must expect the last resentment' from her if they took any step towards peace without her 'participation and consent'. English public opinion would never tolerate such conduct:

Parliament nor England will not lie down and die, because the Dutch find their account in peace, but rather inclined to think .... that they may yet get the better of both France and Holland together ....

Seconded by Halifax and Somers, he proposed that the Grand Alliance be put on a broader basis, 'and that the foundation of the whole should be, never to admit the inclinations of the States to peace', except in accordance with the preliminaries.

Marlborough found these 'reasonings' to be 'very right' but feared that the only reason known to the Dutch was that of self-interest. They would never be brought to subscribe to the 'preliminaries', and now that the news had come that Eugene and the Duke of Savoy had entered Provence the best course would be to await the success or failure of that expedition: 'if that should not succeed, you will find no hearts left in Holland', but success might bring 'happy days' – advice curiously inconsistent with his earlier suggestion that this was merely a pretext for Dutch inaction.[1] It would be most inadvisable, he told the Lord Treasurer, for Parliament to play any part in settling the management of the next campaign, as Godolphin had also suggested; the resulting inquiry into previous campaigns would play right into the hands of the High Tories. In all this advice Godolphin concurred, and he expressed pleasure at the resolution on the States which gave Marlborough sufficient freedom of action to begin, on August 10th (N.S.), a fruitless attempt to bring Vendôme to battle. None the less, he regarded his plan as postponed only, for 'England has entirely swallowed the advantages hoped for against France this summer', he wrote, and if these failed to materialise,

The parliament will certainly enter into the reasons and causes of this proceeding, and will not probably be very well satisfied, unless they find there has been some better expostulation upon it with the States, and some better regulations made. And if this should have been wholly neglected, or but too long delayed, it would certainly give the greatest handle imaginable against the war.[2]

[1] Godolphin to Marlborough, 17 May 1707 (O.S.), Coxe, ii, pp. 83–4; ibid., ii, pp. 115–17, same to same, 13 July 1707, Windsor; (Marlborough) to (Harley), 25 July 1707 (N.S.), S.P. Mil. 2; Marlborough to Godolphin, 27 July, 1 and 10 Aug. 1707, Meldert, Coxe, ii, pp. 113–15, 117–18 and 120–1 (the last of these is wrongly dated 4 Aug. by Coxe); ibid., ii, p. 117, Godolphin to Marlborough, 17 and 21 July 1707 (O.S.); ibid., ii, p. 154, Marlborough to Sunderland, 7 Aug. 1707, Meldert; ibid., ii, pp. 134–5, Marlborough to Godolphin, 25 Aug. 1707, Soignies.
[2] Godolphin to Marlborough, 25 July and 4 Aug. 1707, Windsor, Coxe, ii, pp. 119–20, 126; ibid., ii, pp. 125–6, Marlborough to Godolphin, 8 Aug. 1707, Meldert; ibid., ii, p. 122, same to

No better testimony could be found of the growth of war-weariness and annoyance with the Dutch in England in the summer of 1707.

4

While Marlborough was in the field Stepney dealt with the affairs of the Condominium. One of his tasks was to procure from the Council of State at Brussels a resolution, similar to that taken by the States in early June, to forbid the negotiation of French 'billets de monnaie', or the export of gold or silver to enemy lands. This Dutch resolution, taken as a result of Marlborough's complaints that the French army was paid from Holland and the Spanish Netherlands, and formulated by the French refugee banker Huguetan, had given considerable pleasure to the English, even though Godolphin considered that 'a stop of the posts for three months' was what was really needed, and Stepney thought the Dutch too rigorous in their subsequent demands on the Council of State.[1] An English colonel in Marlborough's army wrote home that 'this we reckon almost as good as another battle if they keep their word'; and great was the annoyance of the ministry in the following year when it was learnt that the French armies in Flanders were once more receiving 'great remittances' from Amsterdam. Stepney found less to welcome in a Dutch project to use 'the Posts & Duties of Entrée and Sortie in the [Spanish] Nlds' as a fund for a loan to Charles III. After scrutinising the terms of this project he began to suspect that the Dutch intended to use it to 'form some pretension to Ostende'[2].

The onset of the illness that drove Stepney home to die left Marlborough directly in charge of these matters at the end of August, and he soon found himself at odds with the Pensionary with regard to the patent given to Quiros, governor of Limburg, by Charles III, to receive oaths of fidelity from the inhabitants of the Spanish Netherlands.

same, 22 Aug. 1707, Genappe (Coxe's date for this letter is 11 Aug., but this is presumably O.S., since Marlborough did not arrive at Genappe until 14 Aug. N.S.).

[1] Marlborough to Heinsius, 15 May 1707, Brussels, *van 't Hoff*, p. 310; Godolphin to Marlborough, 22 May 1707 (O.S.), *P.C.D.M.*, ii, pp. 242–4; Dayrolle to Harley, 3 June 1707, Hague, S.P. Holl. 229; Marlborough to Buys, 20 June 1707, Meldert, *Murray*, iii, p. 427; Stepney to Harley, 25 July 1707, Brussels, S.P. Holl. 230; *C.W.* 113, iv, p. 603; *Veenendaal*, pp. 141–4.

[2] Col. Windham to A. Windham, 8 Aug. 1707, Meldert, *H.M.C. XII pt. ix*, p. 198; Stepney to Cardonnel, 10 and 13 Aug. 1707 (N.S.), S.P. Mil. 2; Boyle to Dayrolle (copy), 4 Aug. 1708, Whitehall, F.E.B. Holl. 74; Marlborough to Godolphin, 23 Aug. 1708, Amougies, *Coxe*, ii, p. 304; Dayrolle to Boyle, 24 Aug. 1708 (N.S.), S.P. Holl. 231; Marlborough to Godolphin, 24 Dec. 1708 (N.S.), *Coxe*, ii, pp. 343–4; Same to same, 7 Jan. 1709, Brussels, *Churchill*, iv, pp. 47–8.

To Godolphin it seemed that the refusal of the Dutch to allow Quiros to exercise his commission could be explained only by a pretension to sovereignty on their part – unless they were deliberately seeking for 'a handle to be cross'. Marlborough was of the same mind. Heinsius seized the chance of this dispute to raise the question of the unfinished Barrier Treaty. In May Godolphin had been apprehensive lest the 'peace-party' should succeed in making the Dutch 'uneasy, without any ground', about their Barrier, but to these latest overtures he replied that England would never give in over Ostend, though, 'that being granted', she might then agree 'in the other desires' provided they agreed to augment their forces and pursue the war with vigour in 1708. On this basis Marlborough considered that the affair was 'impossible to be settled', and, moreover, that any attempt to settle it would 'occasion very great uneasiness between England and Holland'. His policy, therefore, continued to be one of procrastination.[1]

5

The news of the failure of the Toulon expedition, which reached The Hague about the beginning of September, set the seal upon a thoroughly black year for the allies. Its arrival in London elicited from Godolphin a response which must have been just as deep but not nearly as short-lived in many of his fellow-countrymen. He felt that in the campaign that was dragging to its close all the allies had been tried and found hopelessly wanting. The best course for the future, he thought, would be for Britain to concentrate her efforts in Spain and on the French coasts, since a defensive war was, in any case, the best that could be expected in Italy, Germany, or the Netherlands.

Marlborough, convinced as he now was that the French would court battle in the Low Countries in 1708, could not agree with Godolphin; on the contrary, he pressed the need for an Anglo-Dutch augmentation there. He agreed emphatically with Sunderland that Almanza had given the Dutch 'peace-party' a great chance, though for his part the Secretary added: ' … I am confident that people [the Dutch] will be of the side of England in this, whenever they are spoken plainly to, notwithstanding Buys and his friends who I take to be the Harley of Holland'. The Duke also agreed with his son-in-law that it was all

---

[1] (Godolphin) to Harley, (May 1707), *H.M.C. XV pt. iv*, p. 415; Heinsius to Marlborough, 20 Aug. 1707, Hague, *van 't Hoff*, pp. 336–7; *ibid.*, pp. 338–9, Marlborough to Heinsius, 25 Aug. 1707, Soignies; Marlborough to Godolphin, 8 and 12 Sept. 1707, Helchin, *Coxe*, ii, pp. 145–6, 147–8; *ibid.*, ii, pp. 152–3, Godolphin to Marlborough, 9 Sept. 1707, Windsor.

the more necessary for England 'to show a spirit upon this occasion', but Godolphin was despondent about the likelihood of the coming parliament voting any supplies for the next campaign until it saw what the other allies were doing, let alone of its taking the lead in an augmentation of forces. That apprehensions about the temper of the first Union Parliament were not confined to official circles is shown by some graphic lines in a letter that Sir Hans Sloane received from a friend in the country:

Wee are much concern'd here for our disappointments abroad & for deadness of trade & Want of Money at home, wee shall go belly deep I am afraid if wee do not ly fast next session.[1]

At the end of September (N.S.) Marlborough looked forward to his approaching journey to The Hague with little enthusiasm. Even if the Dutch had the will to make an augmentation he doubted whether they would have the power, and he suspected that their thoughts ran rather upon a partition of the Spanish Monarchy. The futile campaign had made him 'quite weary', and his temper cannot have been improved by the new-found belligerency of the field-deputies, which Cadogan related thus:

.... it being now impossible to come att the Enemy .... our Deputys are now grown Lyons and talk of nothing but attaquing them.

Well might Petkum, envoy from the Duke of Holstein-Gottorp, write to Torcy from The Hague that 'the affairs of the Allies remind me of a house on fire'.

His flying visit to The Hague on October 6th and 7th did nothing to mitigate the Duke's gloom. On the contrary, he was now confident that, far from augmenting their troops, the Dutch would act in the Low Countries in 1708 not otherwise than as in 1707. A rumour that the Tories were to revive the 'invitation' project was having a very bad effect at The Hague, and the news that had leaked out that England was demanding a commercial treaty from Charles III had prompted the Pensionary to renew his representations about Ostend. Godolphin, meanwhile, was receiving by 'almost every post' letters from Buys urging the conclusion of peace, to which he gave the adamant reply that

---

[1] Sunderland to Marlborough, 30 Aug. 1707, Althorp, *Coxe*, ii, p. 156; Marlborough to (Harley), 12 and 22 Sept. 1707 (N.S.), *H.M.C. Bath I*, pp. 179, 181; G. Copley to Sloane, 3 Sept. 1707, Sprotbrough, Add. Ms. 4041; Marlborough to Godolphin, 19 Sept. 1707, Helchin, *Coxe*, ii, p. 144; *ibid.*, ii, pp. 156–7, Marlborough to Sunderland, 19 Sept. 1707, Helchin; *ibid.*, ii, pp. 152–3, 161–2, Godolphin to Marlborough, 9 and 12 Sept. 1707, Windsor; *ibid.*, ii, p. 144 (description of letters from Godolphin to Marlborough).

if they will proceed to settle their state of war they may have such terms as will satisfy and secure their allies.[1]

When, almost a month later, Marlborough returned to The Hague after journeying to Düsseldorf and Frankfort, he found that matters had grown worse. There was now even less likelihood of a Dutch augmentation and even more of a Dutch peace. There was nothing he could do at The Hague, for the Dutch would continue the war only if, as Dayrolle put it, they saw 'England earnest upon the matter'; and it was partly with this in mind that Marlborough yielded to the importunities of Godolphin and hurried home.

Marlborough's fears about the Dutch were perhaps exaggerated. Cadogan, whose recent appointment to the late Stepney's posts necessitated his remaining at The Hague, soon realised that the fact that Holland was 'perfectly well disposed' was bound to conquer the 'aversion' of most of the other provinces to carrying on the war.[2] The Duke's apprehension that in Parliament there might be some developments unpalatable to the Allies was not, however, altogether unfounded; the session of the first Parliament of Great Britain gave many indications that the disappointments and disasters of 1707 had reawakened feelings of rivalry towards the Dutch.

6

As Sloane's correspondent had put it, there was much concern in the country 'for our disappointments abroad & for deadness of trade and want of Money at home'. We have already seen, in Godolphin himself, a hint of the widespread reaction to the 'disappointments abroad'; and we find Defoe complaining at the beginning of October that

It is a common Question among some of our People – Ay, ay, you are always getting this Town and that Town from the French: the Emperor gets, the King of *Spain* gets, the *Dutch* get, but what does *England* get, what additions to *Britain* by all your Victories?

On November 12th, the *Observator*, in considering the work before the

[1] Cadogan to (Raby), 22 Sept. 1707, Helchin, Add. Ms. 22196; Petkum to Torcy (translation), 29 Sept. 1707 (N.S.), *H.M.C. XIV pt. ix*, pp. 321–2; Marlborough to Harley, 29 Sept. 1707, Helchin, *H.M.C. Bath I*, p. 183; Marlborough to Godolphin, 3 Oct. 1707, Helchin, *Coxe*, ii, p. 164; *ibid.*, ii, p. 165, same to same, 7 Oct. 1707, Hague; *ibid.*, ii, pp. 168–9, same to same, 13 Oct. 1707, Westrem; *ibid.*, ii, pp. 173–4, Godolphin to Marlborough, 9 Oct. 1707, Newmarket.

[2] Marlborough to Sarah, 8 Nov. 1707, Hague, *Coxe*, ii, p. 175; Marlborough to Electress of Hanover, 9 Nov. 1707, Hague, Stowe Ms. 223; Dayrolle to Manchester (abstract), 15 Nov. 1707, Hague, *H.M.C. VIII pt. ii*, p. 92; Marlborough to J. Stanhope, 15 Nov. 1707, Hague, *Murray*, iii, pp. 644–5; Cadogan to (Raby), 18 Nov. 1707, Hague, Add. Ms. 22196.

new Parliament, voiced in moderate terms the prevailing mood:

....the State of the War Abroad, with Respect to the Part our Allies bear in it, and also what Advantages any of 'em may reap by it, to the Detriment of our present or future Trade and Security, is fit to be enquir'd into.[1]

Anxiety about the 'deadness of trade' had been increasing throughout the year, and to a considerable extent it took the form of jealousy of the Dutch. One of Stepney's first tasks was to send a series of memorials to the States-General concerning the activities of Zeeland privateers which ignored the liberty of commerce with Spain set up by the queen, and he was soon convinced that his Dutch colleagues in the Anglo-Dutch 'Conference' at Brussels 'would gladly see our Pacquet boats taken & our Trade intercepted to that port' (Ostend). There were complaints from the gunsmiths that '*Dutch*-made Pieces' were bought for the English forces, and the Virginia tobacco merchants continued their lament over the 'northern markets' stolen from them by cheap Dutch tobacco. As early as March Shrewsbury noted that 'there is a notion that we are such Rivals in Trade that the next warr will be with them', and in September one of Hearne's correspondents gave full voice to a sentiment which would have found some echo, however small, in the hearts of most of his fellow-countrymen:

But what can you exspect from Dutchmen, who have no regard to conscience, and honesty, and equitable dealing, if they stand in the way of their gaine ....

It was at this time that a pamphlet was published to show that the riches of the Dutch were in no way due to the merits of their trading principles, which were intrinsically bad, but merely to neglect of their own commerce by the English. Its tone was not friendly:

Considering their Treasure, I can't blame their Fears, being so near at hand to the *French*, and all that staggers my belief in the vastness of their Riches, is the smallness of their quota of Men of War, and their Forces in Flanders, which by this account should be so much more than ours ....[2]

The apparent opportunity offered by the Union for putting right a century of 'neglect' gave the question of the British fishery a special interest. There was widespread confidence that the combination of Scottish labour and English capital could win for Britain a substantial

[1] *Review*, iv, 101, 4 Oct. 1707; *Observator*, vi, 73, 12 Nov. 1707. See also above, pp. 167–8.

[2] Stepney to States-General (transcripts), 5 Nov. and 10 Dec. 1706, Hague, Add. Ms. 17677 BBB; Same to same (transcript), 16 Jan. 1707, Hague, Add. Ms. 17677 CCC; Stepney to Sunderland, 31 March 1707, Brussels, S.P. Holl. 230; (Shrewsbury) to (Vernon), 22 March 1706/7, Heathrop, Add. Ms. 40776; *Observator*, vi, 6, 23 March 1706/7; *Journal of C. of T., 1704–8/9*, pp. 372 and 389, 6 and 17 June 1707; T. Smith to Hearne, 20 Sept. 1707 (O.S.), *Hearne*, ii, p. 47n.; *C.W.* 113, iv, p. 659; *C.W.* 10, p. 80.

share in the 'rich Golden Mine' which was assumed to be the source of Dutch prosperity. Writers on this subject often disclaimed any malice towards the Dutch; they should not be annoyed, it was said, if we wished to imitate them. This argument was not usually concluded as frankly as by the Earl of Cromarty, who hoped that by 'worming ourselves' into the fishery we should

fell two doggs with one stone, at once sett up Roam and cause Carthage to fall by fairly takeing of its base on which it did rise, and yet without hindering them from the claim of their greatest man and greatest lawier, viz: mare liberum. For tho' they fish with us they can never equall us; if English purses, Scots hands and provisiones and Brittains strength joine cordially and prudently .... [1]

When, on November 12, the Junto joined with the 'Tackers' to launch an attack on the ministry in the Lords, it is significant that they chose the 'decay of trade', coupled with naval mismanagement, as subject for complaint. They were aware that the strength of popular feeling on those matters made them good levers with which 'to squeeze places for themselves and their friends out of a Prime Minister, whose general policy they cordially approved'. The subsequent debate on the state of the nation, on November 19th, gave Haversham his chance to dilate on these subjects: 'Your Ships have been taken by your Enemies, as the *Dutch* take your Herrings by Shoals upon your own Coasts ...', he declared.

That this simile touched on a point about which there were strong feelings in England was shown by the attention paid to it by Defoe in his *Modest Vindication of the Present Ministry* ...., as well as to a slighting reference made by the same speaker to Dutch trading with France. As far as the latter was concerned, wrote Defoe, the Republic, as a sovereign power, was entitled to take what measures it pleased; as for the former complaint,

our Herrings it's true, are taken on our Coasts, by a People more Industrious than ourselves; and tho' 'tis beyond all Contradiction that some Acknowledgment ought to be made for that allowance, a fitter opportunity might be taken for it.

Warming to his subject he went on to sneer at the little success Haversham and his friends had had in working up feeling against the Dutch in the winter of 1705; but other publications which appeared

---

[1] Sir R. Gwynne to Electress of Hanover, 2 April 1707, Hamburg, Stowe Ms. 223; Cromarty to Mar, 10 July 1707, Ethie, *H.M.C. Mar & Kellie*, pp. 402–3 ('Carthage' is an allusion to Shaftesbury's 'Delenda est Carthago'; the 'greatest lawier' is, of course, Grotius); L'Hermitage to States-General (transcript), 11/22 July 1707, London, Add. Ms. 17677 CCC; *C.W.* 110, pp. 35–48, 89.

in the next few months showed that there was no lack of support for Haversham's more recent remarks.[1]

Even in the protracted inquiry by the Lords into the affairs of the Admiralty, and the public discussion that went on around it, the Dutch were by no means forgotten. When the *Observator* started, in October, to prepare the ground for the Whig onslaught on Admiral George Churchill, it praised Dutch management in naval affairs loud and long, and held it up as a model for imitation, particularly in so far as government encouragement of privateers was concerned. As the enquiry got under way, however, its tone began to change. Advocating greater concentration on naval and less on military warfare it explained why William III had neglected the naval war:

He was a native of another Country, whose Interest, especially in Naval-Affairs, makes them naturally jealous of the Increase of our Naval Glory, or Shipping . . .

This was no reason, it continued, why we should neglect these things now, especially since the Dutch had secured themselves such a good frontier. This argument was expanded in a pamphlet published at about the same time. Now that we had procured the Dutch a good Barrier, this said, we should think of doing something for ourselves

with relation to our Trade lest it take another Channel, and so we who have done more than any of the Allies, should also come to suffer more than any of them by this long and expensive war.

This is the more reasonable, because our Allies, the *Dutch* are very careful of their Trade, and maintain an advantageous Commerce with the *French*, notwithstanding the War; and likewise with the *Spanish West Indies* by way of *Curassao*; so that they have brought home double the Plate from thence since the War, that they did in time of Peace, whereas we have brought home far less.[2]

The commissioners of Trade themselves condemned the impressment of seamen at Jamaica by the Royal Navy as tending to make English merchants send their goods to the Spanish West Indies *via* Curacao. There was no law to forbid this, they admitted, but it was 'of great prejudice to the trade of her Majesty's plantations'.

In this connection it may be of interest that Defoe, persisting in his self-appointed task of convincing English manufacturers and merchants that it was better to outdo the Dutch in skill and industry than to revile them, now found it necessary to assure his readers that

---

[1] *Observator*, vii, 7, 10 March 1707/8; *Scots Observator*, 3, 20 March 1707/8; *C.W.* 181, p. 28; *C.W.* 46, pp. 2–3; *C.W.* 4; Taylor, *op.cit.*, ii, p. 67.

[2] *Observator*, vi, 62, 64, 74–5, 78, 81–2, 84 and 86, 4 and 11 Oct., 15, 19 and 29 Nov., 10, 13, 20 and 27 Dec. 1707; *C.W.* 109, pp. 24–5.

there was no danger of England losing her American colonies to the Republic.[1]

7

On December 19th, the 'alliance' between the Junto and Tackers ended as suddenly as it had begun, though the Whig Lords did not relent in their subsequent hounding of the Admiralty. In the debate on Spain that day in committee in the Lords not only did the Whigs not support the High Tories, but they pushed through an address in terms most unpalatable to them. There was, indeed, no purpose in further prolonging their 'rebellion'; they had made their point, and could now leave the unfortunate Godolphin to ponder for a while the necessity of choosing between them and 'trickster' Harley. So equivocal by now was Harley's conduct, and so convinced was Godolphin of the necessity of vigorous support for Marlborough's war policy, support which Harley's followers seemed increasingly unwilling to give,[2] that in fact the Treasurer had no choice at all.

This fact was emphasized by the debate of December 19th, in which Rochester, supported by Nottingham, proposed that 20,000 men be sent to Spain from Flanders, where a purely defensive war should be fought. This proposal elicited from Marlborough the warning that any advantage gained by the French in the Low Countries as a result of such a move might well 'force the Dutch to a separate peace'. The Whigs gave no encouragement to the proposal, which came to nothing. In its place Somers successfully moved an address to the queen, which, in its final form, became the celebrated declaration that no peace could be safe and honourable if 'Spain, the West Indies, or any part of the Spanish Monarchy' were suffered to continue in the power of the House of Bourbon. Marlborough and Godolphin resisted an article desiring the queen to press her allies to use their utmost endeavours, 'declaring that they were well assured the Emperor and the Dutch would not exert themselves more'. In fact, this article as finally agreed referred solely to the Emperor, in accordance with views expressed by Somers, though 'Ld Rochester, Ld Nottingham, Etc., were for including the Dutch in this Question'. This whole debate was a final proof, if proof were needed, that no 'measures' of any kind could be taken with the

[1] *H. of L. Mss.*, vii, pp. 265–6, 28 Nov. 1707; *Review*, iv, 138 and 160, 30 Dec. 1707 and 19 Feb. 1707/8.

[2] For an authoritative survey of the political situation in the winter of 1707–8 see G. Davies, 'The Fall of Harley in 1708', *E.H.R.*, lxvi (1951), pp. 246–54.

High Tories (as Harley seemed to wish) if the Grand Alliance was to be kept together.

On January 15th, 1708, in a letter praising the ministry and rejoicing at the maintenance of 'good correspondence between Brittain and Holland ... notwithstanding our late pullbacks', Shaftesbury wrote as follows:

the Ministry, and in particular that noble Duke [Marlborough] has been severly question'd by the malignant party, and inveigh'd against for being too much Dutchmen. Thank Heaven that our Ministry cannot by their worst enemys be reproached for being Frenchmen; and for that other reproach, I hope they will ever hold it honourable. I am sure it is one of the main reasons that makes me so much their friend.

There is some irony in the fact that ministers who had just accepted a resolution that was likely to make their relations with the war-weary Republic more difficult should have been praised in such terms by so sincere a friend to the Dutch. However, the overriding consideration with both ministry and the Whigs was probably, as Taylor suggests, to convince the Dutch once and for ever

that England would never permit them to retire from the contest merely because a potential barrier had been acquired for Holland.[1]

Though the importunities of the Junto and the intrigues of Harley made life more and more difficult for the ministry at home, English observers in the Low Countries derived considerable satisfaction from the attitude of the Dutch leaders. Dayrolle and Cadogan both thought them inclined to support the demand for 'the Spanish monarchy entire', and found little cause for alarm in the rumoured comings and goings of French emissaries; though the latter, it is true, was concerned by the 'general dissatisfaction' with the 'oppression' of the Dutch that he found at Brussels. Moreover, although it was quite clear, as Marlborough told Heinsius in a letter of December 5th (O.S.), that Parliament would do nothing about an augmentation unless the Dutch took the lead, Godolphin's gloomy prognostications about the readiness of this body to provide for the 1708 campaign had proved incorrect. Cadogan was thus able to report on December 19th (N.S.) that the 'unanimity and Dispatch' in these matters at Westminster was having a 'wonderful effect .... in Holland'. Above all, it had encouraged the Dutch leaders to take vigorous steps to put an end to 'the Troubles

---

[1] Addison to Manchester, 23 Dec.1707 (O.S.), *Addison's Letters*, pp. 84–6; Sir J. Perceval to Dr. Perceval, 27 Dec. 1707, London, *H.M.C. Egmont II*, pp. 219–21; Shaftesbury to Furly, 15 Jan. 1707/8, St. Giles', *Forster*, pp. 240–50; *Annals*, vi, pp. 297–303; Taylor, *op.cit.*, ii, p. 72.

and Disorders in the Province of Gueldre'. Torcy's hopes that the resolution of the Dutch would be adversely affected by the news of 'Lord Faversham's (*sic*) complaint .... that the Dutch are admitted too freely to the herring fishery off the coast' were dashed by a discouraging report from Petkum.[1]

In January, as it became known that French emissaries were offering the Dutch commercial advantages in return for peace, the optimism of Dayrolle and Cadogan became more restrained. The first now reported that the Provinces were in so bad a way that, if Louis XIV were once more to offer 'to remove the Duke of Anjou to Italy', they would probably insist upon negotiating with him; and the latter replied to Raby's sceptical inquiries as to the steadfastness of the Dutch to the Alliance that

their present situation is, they are afraid to make Peace on the Terms France proffers, and they are afraid to make war in the vigorous manner England proposes.[2]

Soon, however, Cadogan had no time to speculate on such matters. The reports that started to arrive in mid-February that an expeditionary force was assembling at Dunkirk kept him fully occupied. At first it seemed doubtful whether the French intended to invade Britain or Zeeland. A few weeks previously Harley had been making indignant inquiries about Zeeland's naval effort, but now Cadogan was able to report that this province 'intended to furnish their Quota of Ships, which they have not done the whole war'. The Republic, in general, he and Dayrolle assured the ministry, was working 'with all imaginable diligence' to fit out men of war in answer to the French challenge, and their preparations did not slacken when it became evident that the purpose of the expedition was to carry the Pretender and a French army to Scotland.[3]

In England, meanwhile, the affairs of the ministry had reached their

[1] Cadogan to (Raby), 5, 8 and 29 Dec. 1707, Brussels, Add. Ms. 22196; Marlborough to Heinsius, 5 Dec. 1707, St. James', *van 't Hoff*, pp. 356-7; Torcy to Petkum (translation), 18 Dec. 1707 (N.S.), *H.M.C. XIV pt. ix*, p. 325; Cadogan to Harley, 19 Dec. 1707, Brussels, S.P. Flanders 57; Dayrolle to (Harley), 20 Dec. 1707, Hague, S.P. Holl. 229; Dayrolle to Manchester, 24 Dec. 1707, Hague, *Cole*, p. 507; Petkum to Torcy (translation), 29 Dec. 1707 (N.S.), *H.M.C. XIV pt. ix*, pp. 325-6.

[2] Dayrolle to Harley, 3 and 10 Jan. 1708, Hague, S.P. Holl. 231; (Raby) to Cadogan (draft), 10 Jan. 1708, Berlin, Add. Ms. 22196; *ibid.*, (Raby) to Robinson (draft), 11 Jan. 1708, Berlin; *ibid.*, Cadogan to (Raby), 19 Jan. 1708, Brussels; C. T. Atkinson, *Cambridge Modern History*, v, Ch. xiv (Cambridge, 1908), p. 420.

[3] Harley to Dayrolle (copy), 30 Dec. 1707, Whitehall, F.E.B. Holl. 74; Cadogan to (Harley), 12 Jan. 1708, Brussels, S.P. Flanders 57; Cadogan to (Raby), 26 Feb. 1708, Brussels, Add. Ms. 22196; Dayrolle to Harley, 2 March 1708, Hague, S.P. Holl. 231; Dayrolle to Boyle, 9 March 1708, Hague, *H. of L. Mss.*, viii, p. 103.

crisis. The suspicion thrown on Harley by the Greg affair had enabled Marlborough, Godolphin and the Junto to thwart the queen's attempt to put him in Godolphin's place, and he had had no alternative but to resign, which he did on February 11th. It was therefore Boyle, the new Secretary of State, whose duty it was to inform Dayrolle of the queen's pleasure 'with the Zeal the States show and the great Preparations they are making'. Soon he was able to communicate not only the queen's feelings of gratitude and indebtedness, but also the praise of both Houses of Parliament (in their joint address of March 5th) for 'the Zeal the States-General have shown upon this occasion', and the queen's reply thereto:

I am also very well pleased with the Justice which you have done the States-General, in taking notice of their timely care for our safety, and their readiness to give us all possible assistance.

The subsequent 'disappointment' of the expedition gave 'great satisfaction' to the Dutch, according to Dayrolle, and Cadogan's report that it had 'disposed them to consent to every thing that shall be proposed for acting with Vigour the next Campagne' gave no less satisfaction to Sunderland.[1]

By the end of May Sunderland had cause for even deeper satisfaction, namely that the General Election had resulted in 'the most Wig Parliament ... since the revolution', a result in which the recent attempt by the Pretender must have played a very large, if not an overwhelming part.[2] The Dutch had not passed entirely without mention in the 'literature' of the election; in two pamphlets written in support of the ministry we can detect anxiety lest opponents might make capital from the cooler public attitude towards the Republic. Defoe, in his *Advice to the Electors of Great Britain*, advised the rejection of any candidates 'that have been for withdrawing Part of our Forces from *Flanders*, which could tend only to make *Holland* accept a peace upon any terms'; and a pamphlet published somewhat earlier recalled 'the malicious reproach' made by the Tories to William III 'that he prolong'd the War to enrich the *Dutch*'[3].

[1] Boyle to Dayrolle (copies), 24 Feb. and 5 March 1707/8, Whitehall, F.E.B. Holl. 74; Boyle to Meadows (copy), 5 March 1707/8, Whitehall, F.E.B. Emp. 39; *Observator*, vii, 7, 10 March 1707/8; Dayrolle to Boyle, 3 April 1708, Hague, S.P. Holl. 231; Cadogan to (Boyle), 3 April 1708, Hague, S.P. Flanders 57; Sunderland to Sarah, 6 April 1708, Whitehall, *Coxe*, ii, p. 216; *H. of L. Mss.*, viii, pp. 32–3; *Cobbett*, vi, cols. 725–7.

[2] Sunderland to Newcastle, 27 May 1708, Whitehall, *Trevelyan*, ii, pp. 349–50. This result in fact fulfilled Addison's pre-election hope that 'the Late intended Invasion may have a good influence on Elections and recommend such as are Entirely in the Revolution principles' (Addison to Manchester, 9 April 1708, Cockpit, *Addison's Letters*, pp. 107–8).

[3] *C.W.* 37, p. 4; *C.W.* 83, p. 2.

8

On April 14th (N.S.), four days after his arrival at The Hague to discuss the forthcoming campaign with Eugene, Marlborough received a visit from the Burgomasters of Amsterdam, which, together with 'all that I can observe on this side', gave him 'very mallincolly reflections'. Not only did they press the conclusion of the Barrier Treaty, but they represented 'the impossibility of their being able to continue the Warr longer than this Campagne'. Godolphin's views on the Barrier question were now that England would be 'easy' provided that Ostend remained in the hands of Charles III and – a new proviso – Dunkirk were demolished. What alarmed Marlborough, however, was the other representation that had been made to him, and his alarm increased when, immediately on his return from Hanover on May 3rd, he received another visit. This time the Burgomasters went so far as to ask that the queen should join the States in proposing peace negotiations to France in July if Louis XIV had not himself made overtures by that time. In addition they proposed an 'expedient' to end the deadlock over Ostend, namely, that half its garrison might be Spaniards.

The eagerness for peace of 'the most zealous part of the Dutch' alarmed the Duke 'very much', and he ascribed it, as he informed the queen, not to any fears of France, but to 'what passed in England last winter' and 'the continual intelligences they have of your Majesty's being resolved to change hands and parties'; intelligences which, he assured his Duchess, were spread in Holland by Harley and his friends 'for the inducing of these people to a peace [to] which God knows they are but too much inclined'. For the next two months his fears that 'one way or other the Dutch will have peace' and that this would be their last campaign were undiminished.[1]

When Marlborough learnt that Ghent had thrown its gates open to the French on July 5th he was not far from despair. 'The States have used this country so ill,' he wrote to Godolphin on July 9th,

that I in no ways doubt but all the towns in this country will play us the same trick as Ghent has done, whenever they have it in their power.

In his view it was the 'arrogant and arbitrary proceedings' of the

---

[1] (Marlborough) to (Godolphin), 20 April 1708, Hague, Add. Ms. 28056; Godolphin to Marlborough, 16 April 1708 (O.S.), *Coxe*, ii, p. 214; *ibid.*, ii, pp. 215–16, Marlborough to Godolphin, 3 May 1708, Hague; Marlborough to Sarah, 6 May 1708, Hague, *P.C.D.M.*, i, pp. 114–17; Marlborough to Anne, 9 May 1708, Ghent, *Coxe*, ii, pp. 220–1; *ibid.*, ii, p. 239, Marlborough to Godolphin, 28 May 1708, St. Renelle; *ibid.*, ii, pp. 244–6, same to same, 18 June and 2 July 1708, Terbank.

Dutch (to borrow a phrase used earlier in the year by Cardonnel) that caused the defection of Ghent and later Bruges from the cause of Charles III. In his study of the Anglo-Dutch Condominium Dr. Veenendaal has clearly shown the fallacy of this view. His detailed rebuttal of the charge that the Dutch were solely or even primarily responsible for these events provides a much-needed and wholesome corrective to the muddled and biassed notions of every English writer on these matters. It is none the less true that in his confidential correspondence Marlborough expressed the conviction that the guilt belonged to the Dutch, and to the Dutch alone. Dr. Veenendaal is hardly able to ignore this fact; he suggests, therefore, that it was Marlborough's deliberate policy to throw undeserved blame upon the hapless Republic. He tells us that Marlborough was prepared to do this because he was the representative of a nation which was violently jealous of Dutch influence in the Spanish Netherlands. To support this assertion he brings forward a single piece of evidence: a letter written by Marlborough to Heinsius on August 8th which includes the words: 'As we have lost the hearts of all the people of this country ...'. The use of 'we' in this context, he suggests, shows that Marlborough was in fact aware of British responsibility for the loss of Ghent and Bruges.

This argument seems singularly wide of the mark. Even the most cursory comparison of the letters written by Marlborough to the Dutch leaders with those that he wrote to his colleagues, above all to Godolphin, will reveal the very considerable tact and circumspection that he was accustomed to use in discussing the shortcomings of the Republic with the former. For the rest, we may well feel, with Dr. Veenendaal, that it is fantastic that the defection of Ghent, which had been occupied by British troops, should have been ascribed to Dutch misgovernment; the fact remains, however, that this was the opinion amongst Englishmen at that time. For example, Boyer, no enemy of the Republic, wrote in 1709 that the disaffection in Ghent, Bruges, and Antwerp arose because the citizens were 'impatient of the *Dutch* Government'. It is unnecessary to endow Marlborough with Machiavellian attributes in order to explain this unpalatable fact. A much more likely explanation is that their undoubted jealousy of Dutch influence in the Spanish Netherlands (not to mention a very human inability to believe that they were themselves in the wrong) made Englishmen generally, from Marlborough downwards, eager to assume without any misgivings that these misfortunes were the fault of the Dutch.[1]

[1] Cardonnel to Cadogan, 27 Feb. 1707/8, Whitehall, *Veenendaal*, p. 157; Marlborough to

Two days after Marlborough had written to Godolphin the bitter words to which Dr. Veenendaal rightly takes exception, the allied armies fought and won the battle of Oudenarde. At home the celebration of this remarkable feat of arms seems to have been on a significantly subdued scale. Even Shaftesbury's rejoicing at the 'glorious news' was somewhat marred by his concern at the hostility to Marlborough now apparent in some quarters in the Republic. It is true that it was probably at this time that a ballad appeared 'in praise of our Three Fam'd Generals', in which the aged Ouwerkerk was for the first and last time accorded the esteem usually reserved for Marlborough and Eugene:

> To *Auverquerque* exalt your Glasses,
> And just to his Valour let us be,
> Who tho' not youngest of the three,
> For brave exploits there's few surpasses.

This handsome tribute was not, however, of English origin! [1]

Any hopes that Marlborough may have had that the victory would change the attitude of Buys and the burgomasters of Amsterdam to the war were speedily disappointed. Godolphin expressed no surprise on discovering that their inclinations remained the same,

taking it always for granted that they will endeavour to make use equally of good success, and of ill success towards their aim, which is peace; and on the other side, we must continue our endeavours as zealously, to keep them on as long as we can, in the expectation of farther advantages by doing so.

As July turned August Marlborough began once more to apprehend that 'as long as we can' would be no longer than to the end of the campaign, for he was convinced that the States-General would follow any lead given by Amsterdam. He considered his fears confirmed by the unwillingness of the field-deputies to countenance a thrust into France (though here they had Eugene on their side), and when he learnt that French troops were ravaging the Isle of Cadsand he was anxious about the use that the 'peace-party' might make of the alarm that this would cause. He feared that the States might once

Godolphin, 9 July 1708, Herfelingen, *Coxe*, ii, pp. 252–3; *Veenendaal*, Ch. xii, *passim*, esp. pp. 196–202; A. J. Veenendaal, 'The Opening Phase of Marlborough's Campaign of 1708 in the Netherlands', *History*, Feb. and June 1950.

[1] Shaftesbury to Furly, 22 July 1708, Chelsea, *Rand*, pp. 387–8; *C.W.* 142, pp. 1–3 ('Translated from the French by Mr. Durfey'). Jones, in his annals for 1708, gives a laudatory account of Ouwerkerk's life which goes so far as to credit him (unjustly) with 'a great share in the Glory of forcing the Enemies' Lines' in 1705 (*Jones, 1708*, pp. 420–4).

more send orders to their deputies that would hamstring him, but he hoped that Dutch fears would be overcome by 'their eagerness' for the 'contributions' that he would be able to exact by sending detachments into Picardy. At the same time he had reports from The Hague 'that these people are resolved to have peace on any conditions'. 'This may prove fatal', he commented, 'but if they are determined, we shall find it very difficult to hinder it . . . . .'. The best he hoped for from Heinsius, on August 20th, was that he would give no encouragement to Buys and the 'peace-party' until the siege of Lille had been decided one way or the other. Meanwhile he found cause for concern in the continuing disaffection of the Spanish Netherlands, which he attributed to the 'insolence' of the Dutch.[1]

In one essential, at least, the pattern of 1706 was repeating itself in 1708: victory in the Low Countries led to dissension between England and the Dutch as to the practicability of an immediate peace. The similarity was considerably heightened when, at the beginning of September, Marlborough received from Charles III a renewed offer of the Governorship of the Spanish Netherlands. He communicated it only to the queen, Godolphin, and his Duchess, for, as he told the latter, 'if this were known before the peace, it would do hurt in Holland'. In December, however, the news became known at The Hague, where Marlborough's subsequent repetition of his renunciation was considered merely part of his 'prudent dissimulation', as Charles III himself had called it.[2]

8

Meanwhile the resistance of Lille confounded all the early sanguine hopes of its besiegers. A day before the battle at Wynendael, which alone made possible the continuation of the siege, Marlborough heard that the Elector of Bavaria was returning from Germany with a great detachment, 'which', he added, 'will give them no little alarm in Holland'; and a few days after that engagement Petkum consoled

[1] Marlborough to Godolphin, 26 and 30 July, 3 and 6 Aug. 1708 (N.S.), *Coxe*, ii, pp. 272–3, 274–8; Marlborough to Halifax, 26 July 1708, Wervik, *Murray*, iv, p. 129; Lumley to Hanmer, 2 Aug. 1708 (N.S.), *Hanmer Corres.*, pp. 115–16; Godolphin to Marlborough, 23 July 1708, Windsor, *Coxe*, ii, pp. 269–70; *ibid.*, ii, pp. 284–6, Marlborough to Sarah, 6 Aug. 1708 (N.S.); Same to same, 13 Aug. 1708, Helchin, *Churchill*, iii, p. 486; Marlborough to Godolphin, 20 Aug. 1708, Helchin, *Coxe*, ii, pp. 303–4.

[2] Marlborough to Godolphin, (7 Sept. 1708) (N.S.), *Coxe*, ii, p. 316; Marlborough to Sarah, 7 Sept. 1708 (N.S.), *P.C.D.M.*, i, pp. 144–5; Pesters to Heinsius, 18 Dec. 1708 (N.S.), *Veenendaal*, p. 239.

Torcy with the thought that there would be 'many complaints' in the next British Parliament, 'the nation being much discontented at the loss of Bruges & Ghent'. Six weeks later this prediction was confirmed by St. John, who had not found a seat in the May election; in the celebrated letter to Harley in which he wrote 'For God's sake let us be once out of Spain!' he also reported that 'they are in great uneasiness about the close of the campaign in Flanders; the fault is to be laid on the Dutch'.[1]

The resistance of the French at Lille, the citadel of which was still holding out when St. John wrote these lines, had indeed done much to extinguish any revival of enthusiasm for the war in the Low Countries that had been produced by Oudenarde. In England the tendency that resulted was to 'lay the fault on the Dutch'; in the army it was rather to press once more for an augmentation. Without this, wrote Stair on October 24th (N.S.), the French would do their utmost to retake Oudenarde next campaign before the allies could be in the field; but on the other hand the mere fact of the States' proposing it to the queen 'would break the heart of the French'. The great question was whether Marlborough could persuade them to 'give in to it'. Three days later Harley indicated to Harcourt how *he* would view any such proposal:

Our military prowess and conduct is now famous, and the Dutch will rely upon it, and as for our economy it is very good, as long as money flowed and stocks would run, who but we – we sucked till the blood came, and no regard to what was to come after; now everything is run out of breath, the mines are worked out, we have a necessity created of a long war, and that is now to be made an argument for most extravagant burdens this next year.

Ever sensitive to public opinion, Marlborough's erstwhile supporter was making himself the spokesman of the growing popular dislike of the ministry's policy towards the war and towards the allies.

Marlborough, who seems to have shaken off his despair of getting the Dutch to continue the war, fully agreed with Stair that an augmentation would be 'the only way of bringing France to a speedy and good peace'; the States' agreement to this would have an especially great effect on the French, he thought, and the concurrence of the field deputies in these views gave him hopes that he might be able to persuade them to comply. At home, too, the proposal now seemed

---

[1] Marlborough to Godolphin, 27 Sept. 1708 (N.S.), *Coxe*, ii, p. 320; Petkum to Torcy (translation), 4 Oct. 1708 (N.S.), *H.M.C. XIV pt. ix*, p. 331; (St. John) to (Harley), 6 Nov. 1708 (O.S.), *H.M.C. Bath I*, pp. 193–4.

likely of success. The death of the Prince of Denmark on October 28th (O.S.) had broken Anne's resistance to the admission of Wharton and Somers to the Cabinet, and the Junto, now temporarily satisfied in their demands, would back such a project to the hilt. On November 12th Godolphin wrote to Marlborough that the proposal was to be made in the queen's speech at the opening of Parliament; and the resulting address which the Lords made to the queen on November 18th, desiring 'the most pressing instances with your allies, to show a suitable vigour', augured well for its success.[1]

His anxiety for an augmentation did not, however, prevent Marlborough from putting out peace 'feelers' in an exchange of letters with his nephew and opponent Berwick. In what Legrelle calls 'L'unique lettre qui ait vraiment une signification marquée', dated October 30th, Marlborough expressed the opinion that if the French commander Burgundy were to send propositions to himself, Eugene and the field-deputies, 'cela ferait un tel effet en Hollande que, certainement, la paix s'ensuivrait'. The purpose of this extraordinary remark has long been a matter of dispute. Marlborough's detractors suggest that he was offering to sell the interests of the Grand Alliance for French gold, while Churchill and his disciple Ashley credit him with the laudable aim of trying 'to prevent any separate negotiations which might cut the ground from under the British Government's feet'. The latter surmise seems a plausible one at first sight, for Marlborough must have been well aware that, as Dayrolle reported seven days later, politicians and private persons at The Hague were once more in correspondence with the French about peace. According to Churchill, then, this interchange of letters was prompted by Marlborough's fear 'that the Dutch were about to quit the Alliance'. There is, however, no other evidence that *at this time* Marlborough considered Dutch defection as imminent.

What is quite clear is that, whatever his ultimate aim, Marlborough was angling for information about what the French were prepared to offer as the price of peace. Legrelle's view is that this was in fact his only aim, and thus that his remark to Berwick about Dutch eagerness for peace was meant merely to induce Louis XIV to show

---

[1] Stair to Mar, 24 Oct. 1708, Rousselaer, *Stair Annals*, i, pp. 239-40; Marlborough to Heinsius, 25 Oct. and 6 Nov. 1708 (N.S.), *van 't Hoff*, pp. 406-8; Harley to Harcourt, 16 Oct. 1708 (O.S.), *H.M.C. Bath I*, pp. 192-3; Marlborough to Godolphin, 16 Nov. 1708 (N.S.), *Coxe*, ii, pp. 329-30; *ibid.*, ii, p. 330, Godolphin to Marlborough, 12 Nov. 1708 (O.S.); *Cobbett*, vi, col. 754. On the augmentation see my article, 'The Augmentation of 1709: A Study in the Workings of the Anglo-Dutch Alliance', *E.H.R.*, lxxii (1957).

his hand. The acceptance of Legrelle's thesis seems to involve an assumption about the Duke's attitude towards the Dutch very different from that adopted by Churchill. If in fact he was using the known inclination of the Dutch towards peace to induce the French to declare themselves, then his assurances to Berwick about the effect of French proposals upon the Dutch were almost certainly disingenuous; it was precisely because he now felt some confidence, however limited, in the 'firmness' of the Dutch that he ventured to give his enemies such deceptive encouragement. In any case, Churchill's ideas as to Marlborough's ultimate purpose do not stand up to close examination. If the Duke really feared that the Dutch were about to quit the alliance, and was therefore anxious to forestall separate Franco-Dutch negotiations, why should he go out of his way to convince the French of the ease with which the Dutch might be seduced from the Alliance? On the other hand, the surmise that Marlborough was trying to sell the Allies to Louis XIV is based on a view of his character that Churchill's work has made it difficult to accept. It seems, then, that the most likely explanation of this curious interlude is that offered by Legrelle: that the whole episode was, on Marlborough's part, little more than a polite game designed solely to elicit information, and that the emphasis placed by Marlborough on the Dutch desire for peace was merely a move in the game. It may even be that the deliberate solicitation of French peace offers by such means indicated a new-found confidence that the Dutch would stand firmly by the queen in any negotiation.[1]

The city of Lille surrendered on October 22nd, but the citadel held out, and the French were still masters of Ghent and Bruges. While besieging Lille Marlborough tried to blockade these two towns, and he was not pleased to discover that despite this 'they have every thing that they want from Holande'. 'If the States will not punish those that break their laws,' he wrote to Heinsius on October 4th, 'wee take a great deall of pains to little purpose'. A month later Dayrolle was able to report that the States-General had renewed their prohibition of this traffic on penalty of death, but he added his own opinion that

---

[1] Marlborough to Berwick, 30 Oct. 1708 (N.S.), A. Legrelle, *Une négociation Inconnue entre Berwick et Marlborough, 1708–9* (Ghent, 1893), pp. 21–2; Dayrolle to Boyle, 6 Nov. 1708, Hague, S.P. Holl. 231; *Churchill*, iv, pp. 23 *sqq.*; Ashley, *Marlborough*, p. 103; Legrelle, *op.cit., passim.* That Marlborough had other subsidiary motives in this affair cannot be doubted. Certainly he had an eye to any possible pecuniary advantage that he might derive by ensuring that the conduct of the peace lay in his hands, and in this sense he was indeed attempting to forestall the Dutch.

the 'mercenary desire of profit' of the Rotterdam and Zeeland merchants would find ways to get round this.[1]

The long campaign, in the event, came to a triumphant end, though Marlborough complained bitterly of the difficulties placed in his way by the Dutch generals after the death of the trusted Ouwerkerk on October 18th. A great march by Marlborough's army saved Brussels from the Elector of Bavaria on November 28th, on December 9th Boufflers at last surrendered the citadel of Lille, and Ghent and Bruges succumbed to siege on January 2nd. Manchester, returning from his mission to Venice, found 'great joy' at the relief of Brussels at The Hague, where there was now a disposition to continue the war and to augment the Dutch forces. Eight days after relieving Brussels, Marlborough painted the other side of the picture in a letter to Godolphin. 'Had not God favoured our passage of the Scheldt', he wrote, Brussels and Antwerp would have been in great danger, 'for not only the towns, but the people of this country hate the Dutch'. At home, however, the Whig *Observator* praised the work of the Dutch Deputies at Brussels in inspiring both inhabitants and troops to resist Max Emmanuel.[2]

9

On December 3rd Marlborough wrote to Godolphin about the proposed augmentation. His letter gives an interesting indication both of his newly recovered hopes that the Republic would continue the war, and of his apprehension that Englishmen were growing dissatisfied with the Dutch contribution to the struggle:

I cannot end this letter without assuring you that I know the difficulties of Holland to be so great, that I hope every honest man in England will be contented with their furnishing only one-third in the augmentation; for it is most certain that they now subsist only by credit, and that the ill-affected in that country have no hopes left but that England will insist upon their giving one half.

Some even clearer indications of the increasing impatience of Englishmen with their ally had been given a year earlier when Joseph Addison, himself a member of the ministry, had published his *Present State of the War and the Necessity of an Augmentation, Consider'd.*

[1] Marlborough to Heinsius, 4 Oct. 1706 (N.S.), *van 't Hoff*, p. 403; Dayrolle to Boyle, 9 Nov. 1708, Hague, S.P. Holl. 231.
[2] Marlborough to Heinsius, 6 and 16 Nov. 1708, Rousselaer, *van 't Hoff*, pp. 407–9; Manchester to Boyle, 30 Nov. 1708, Hague, *H.M.C. VIII pt. ii*, p. 102; Marlborough to Godolphin, 6 Dec. 1708 (N.S.), *Coxe*, ii, pp. 339–40; *Observator*, vii, 83, 1 Dec. 1708.

This was a detailed argument in favour of an augmentation, but its main interest here is in the 'Popular Objections' that it set out to combat. The greatest of these, which Addison admitted 'fell in' very much 'with the Prejudices and little Passions of the Multitude', was that *England* contributes much more than any other of the Allies, and that therefore, it is not reasonable she shou'd make any addition to her present Efforts'. In fact, however, he continued, all Britain's allies furnished as much as she did proportionately to their strength and resources. Some, he added, would object British poverty and point to Dutch prosperity; and he went on to counter this objection in a passage which combined some very common English opinions on the Dutch way of life with some almost exclusively Whig views on the effect of the war in the Republic:

Holland indeed flourishes above the rest in Wealth and Plenty; But if we consider the infinite Industry and Penuriousness of that People, the Coarseness of their Food and Raiment, their little Indulgences of Pleasure and Excess, it is no wonder that notwithstanding they furnish as great Taxes as their Neighbours they make a better figure under them. In a Commonwealth there are not so many overgrown Estates as in Monarchies, the Wealth of the Country is so equally distributed, that most of the Community are at their Ease, though few are plac'd in Extraordinary Points of Splendour and Magnificence. But notwithstanding these Circumstances may very much contribute to the seeming Prosperity of the *United Provinces*, we know they are indebted many Millions more than their whole Republic is worth, and if we consider the variety of Taxes and Impositions they groan under at a time when their private Dissensions run high, and some of the wealthiest parts of the Government refuse to bear their share in the Publick Expence, we shall not think the Condition of that People so much to be envied as some amongst us would willingly represent it.

Addison's advocacy was not in vain. On December 15th (O.S.) the Commons voted an augmentation of 10,000 men in Flanders. There was no direct opposition, though one venturesome member declared, according to L'Hermitage,

qu'il seroit bon de différer, jusqu'à ce qu'on scût ce que Vos Hautes Puissances voudraient faire à proportion, et qu'on ne devoit pas si promtement se déterminer, et qu'il sembloit qu'on avoit en veue de soulager la Hollande, au préjudice de la Grande Bretagne ....

Before the end of the year the news arrived that the States had resolved to augment their own forces by 6,000 men. Writing to Dayrolle on December 28th (O.S.) Sunderland expressed his delight at this development and his confidence of the 'good effect' it would have in England. This too was the view stated by L'Hermitage in the report he sent to The Hague three days later. He described at length the intense pleasure that all 'well-intentioned' people had derived from the States' resolution, and the great gratitude and goodwill towards the Dutch which they were expressing. To L'Hermitage, always inclined to accept the Whigs as the spokesmen for public opinion, the outlook for the Anglo-Dutch alliance in 1709 seemed promising; but already the Junto were taking measures which would go far to ensure the eventual break-up of that alliance. [1]

[1] Marlborough to Godolphin, 3 Dec. 1708 (N.S.), *Coxe*, ii, pp. 338–9; L'Hermitage to States-General (transcripts), 17/28 Dec. 1707 and 31 Dec. 1707/11 Jan. 1708, London, Add. Ms. 17677 DDD; Sunderland to Dayrolle (copy), 28 Dec. 1708, Whitehall, F.E.B. Holl. 74; Addison to H. Newton, 31 Dec. 1708 (O.S.), *Addison's Letters*, pp. 123–5; *C.W.* 1, pp. 35–42.

CHAPTER VII

THE FATEFUL BARGAIN

⟨1709⟩

I

The greatest political asset of the Junto Whigs throughout Anne's reign had been their enthusiasm for the war. To this, at least in part, they owed their gains in the election of 1705 and the parliamentary power that had enabled them to extort ministerial places from a hostile queen. By 1709 they were at last within sight of complete domination of the ministry. The queen was forced to accept Orford as a minister, while Marlborough was unceremoniously deprived of his supreme control in dealings with the allies. Parliament proved to be a faithful executor of the Junto's wishes, at least in so far as foreign policy was concerned.[1] There were, it is true, some unfortunate incidents, as when 'there was an advantage taken a Saturday when the house was thin' to ask why the money raised by means of 'contributions' was presented to the Dutch for their siege expenses; but this was passed off with the declaration that 'the inquiring into that matter might raise jealousy in our best Ally, the Dutch'. The best measure of the Whiggishness of this Parliament is that the Junto was able to push through an act for naturalizing foreign Protestants, a measure peculiarly abhorrent to all shades of Tory, and the desirability of which was advocated by reference to the example of 'the wise and politick' Dutch.[2]

---

[1] Professor Walcott has punctured the legend of Junto gains in the English elections of 1708 (Walcott, op.cit., p. 150), but it is clear enough that the Junto leaders had good reason to be contented with the demeanour of the Commons in the two ensuing sessions.

[2] P. Wentworth to (Raby), 25 Jan. 1708/9, London, Add. Ms. 34143; Review, v, 144, 26 Feb. 1708/9; L'Hermitage to States-General (transcript), 5/16 March 1708/9, London, Add. Ms. 17677 DDD; Leadam, op.cit., p. 167. It was not long before the strong popular feeling against this measure was clearly manifested. The Bishop of Worcester felt constrained to issue a public protest against these 'murmurings', in which the example of the Dutch was once more quoted in support of the Act (Annals, viii, appendix, pp. 43–9), while Defoe lamented this notorious 'Contempt ot Foreigners' of which England had already given only too much evidence. As a 'letter' which he printed in the Review pointed out, 'The humour of the English work-People is at this time so averse to Foreigners, that some of them have declared (as I am inform'd) that if they come to work among them, they will be occasion of their Deaths ...' (Review, vi, 45 and 56, 16 July and 11 Aug. 1709). The volume of protests against the Act continued to increase until its repeal in 1712.

In fact, however, the Whigs' great asset was rapidly becoming a potential liability, and a very dangerous one too. While 'all their thoughts were concentrated on the one object of keeping the coalition firmly cemented together', the thoughts of Englishmen as a whole were centred less and less on the 'honour' and 'glory', and more and more on the many hardships, that resulted from such a policy.

The gradual growth of war-weariness in England had already brought with it a less friendly attitude towards the Dutch. In 1709 this link was strengthened by two new factors, one of immediate importance, the other of almost incalculable significance for the English attitude towards the Dutch in the years to come. The first was the breakdown of the negotiations for peace, which some at least of the English leaders deliberately attributed to the intractableness of the Dutch, an attribution only too readily accepted in England. The second was the Barrier Treaty, which in effect bound the Dutch to the policy of *guerre à outrance* at the very moment when English opinion had irrevocably hardened against it.

All this does not appear clearly in any casual survey of the year 1709. Even a careful study yields no more than a broad hint that these developments in public opinion were under way; and this is found almost exclusively in private correspondence, and very little in pamphlets and periodicals. Only in questions which involved commercial rivalry – as, for example, in the disputes about the future conduct of the African trade or the exportation of English corn – was there much public criticism of the Dutch. The ministry's opponents, it seems fair to assume, were not yet sure enough of public feeling against the prolongation of the war and the conduct of the allies to make much use of these themes, their untimely exploitation of which in earlier years had been a major cause of their misfortunes. Only after the election of 1710 had given them confidence would they no longer hesitate to give voice to their feelings on these matters, feelings which were evidently not of overnight growth. In a sense, public opinion in 1709 about the war and the Alliance, as, to a far smaller extent, in 1708, had 'gone underground'. The Junto were speaking for almost no one but themselves, while the Tories, wary of being once more branded as 'Frenchmen', preferred to use other devices to make capital from popular discontent. For the understanding of public opinion towards the Dutch in 1709 it is not only permissible, but also essential, to read history backwards.[1]

[1] The views put forward here owe much to Miss M. A. Ransome's unpublished M.A. (London) thesis, *The General Election of 1710* (1938), Introduction and Ch. I, section iii.

2

On December 10th (O.S.) 1708 Godolphin wrote to Marlborough as follows:

Somers and I seem entirely to agree that the chief motive at this time with the States for pushing the War, is because no other way appears of coming at peace in such a manner as will be pleasing in any degree to England, but that in the bottom the States have the same kindness for peace and perhaps more than ever; and considering that the King of France may in all probability incline to leave that matter very much in the disposition of the States, that there may be no room for nor pretence for mistaking the opinion of England, we have resolved some heads relating to this business.

By the next post he sent these 'heads' of proposals, which were based on an uncompromising application of the principle of the 'Spanish Monarchy Entire'. In reply Marlborough pressed for more explicit explanations concerning the Dutch Barrier, to which Godolphin answered that, with the exception of Ostend, the Dutch might be made easy in all other 'particulars relating to that matter which themselves could reasonably desire'. Thus was declared the policy towards the Dutch of the ministry which the Junto now bade fair to dominate: a policy of buying Dutch adherence to the prolongation of the war at the cost of concessions to the Republic's Barrier demands.

It was already widely known in London that 'some new insinuations of peace' had been made at The Hague. On January 16th (N.S.) Marlborough, who was at The Hague obeying his instructions to press the States to make their augmentation equal to the queen's, was officially notified of new French proposals based on the idea of partitioning the Spanish monarchy. He was apprehensive that the States, whom he thought unreasonably confident that the French would not venture another campaign, might well prefer a partition treaty to a continuation of the war. He told the Emperor that, exhausted as they were, the Dutch certainly hoped that the next campaign would be the last.[1] Meanwhile, Godolphin's letter concerning the Barrier had not arrived, and Marlborough was able to counter Dutch importunities on this head with the plea that he had no instructions. Already apparently sensing the disposition of the Junto, he urged Godolphin that this question and that of peace should be transacted in England,

---

[1] Godolphin to Marlborough, 10 Dec. 1708 (O.S.), *Geikie*, pp. 100–101; T. Butler to Trumbull, 28 Dec. 1708 (O.S.), *H.M.C. Downshire I pt. ii*, p. 867; Marlborough to Boyle, 16 Jan. 1709, Hague, *Murray*, iv, p. 398; Marlborough to Godolphin, 17 Jan. 1709 (N.S.), *P.C.D.M.*, ii, pp. 298–9; Marlborough to Joseph, 19 Jan. 1709, Hague, *Murray*, iv, pp. 401–3. See also *Geikie*, p. 101, and *Coxe*, ii, p. 387, for descriptions of other letters.

'that the dispute that may arise may not fall singly upon me'. Back in Brussels at the beginning of February, he noted with pleasure that, though perhaps they were designed to 'incline the Dutch to hearken to peace', the movements of considerable numbers of French troops on the frontier were in fact making the States 'omit no endeavours to augment their Forces'.[1]

In reply to the French offers communicated to them by Marlborough, Godolphin and Somers took their stand on the principle first laid down in 1706, that no steps should be taken towards a peace until 'preliminaries' were settled between England and the States. In addition, the Treasurer warned the General, he and Somers were concerned about the States' 'uneasiness', as reported by Portland, at Marlborough's reluctance to discuss the Barrier. Portland's hint that Buys might be sent over to make representations on that matter was making them particularly anxious. For his part Godolphin considered that, if only the Dutch would not be obstinate about Ostend and would agree to the razing of Dunkirk,

there remains no more to bring this affair to a fair and friendly conclusion, but to agree that both nations should stand upon the same foot, as to their trade with the two countries, which they did before the war . . . .

'And, perhaps,' he added meaningly, 'this may be a useful preliminary to be settled on that side; but Buys coming would hurt everything'. Behind these words we can sense the apprehensions of the Junto lest the, to them, unreasonable delays on Marlborough's part in setting on foot negotiations for a Barrier Treaty might give Buys and Harley an opportunity to renew their acquaintance. Marlborough expressed his agreement on the question of 'preliminaries' in a letter to Godolphin of February 17th, but he added a warning that 'the inclinations for peace at the Hague are greater than is believed in England'.

Five days later, however, back at The Hague, he found that the reception so far accorded to the French proposals was not such as to prevent his being 'assured of making the next campaign', while Cadogan wrote to Raby that

tho' I believe this Republick heartily tired of the war, yet I am persuaded they will hearken to no other Peace than the entire restitution of the Spanish monarchy . . . .[2]

---

[1] Marlborough to Godolphin, 23 Jan. 1709, Hague, *P.C.D.M.*, ii, pp. 296–7; *ibid.*, ii, pp. 303–5, same to same, 4 Feb. 1709, Brussels; Same to same, 7 and 13 Feb. 1709, Brussels, *Coxe*, ii, pp. 388–9; Marlborough to Boyle, 7 and 10 Feb. 1709, Brussels, *Murray*, iv, pp. 429–30, 433–4.

[2] Godolphin to Marlborough, 27 Jan. 1708/9 (O.S.), *Geikie*, pp. 101–2; Same to same, 4

On March 8th Marlborough sailed for home, having successfully withstood pressure both from his colleagues and from the Dutch to begin in earnest new negotiations for a Treaty of Succession and Barrier. He was, however, fighting a losing battle, for the Junto, with its newly acquired ministerial strength, was soon to precipitate the final and decisive phase of these discussions. To their tenderness for safeguarding the Protestant Succession the Whigs now added a determination to bind the Republic once and for all to the principle of 'No peace without Spain', and to this end they were prepared to go to lengths never before envisaged by the Godolphin ministry. In this they parted company with Marlborough. On several counts the Duke found himself unable to subscribe to their views. In the first place, he was convinced that Louis XIV was no longer in any position to persuade Philip V to abandon Spain, and hence was privately sceptical of the practicability of 'No peace without Spain' – though not, it should be added, of the eventual conquest of the 'Spanish monarchy entire'. Moreover, he considered that the concessions that the Dutch would demand as a reward for abandoning their claim to Ostend would be so unacceptable to the Emperor and the King of Prussia as to endanger the very existence of the Alliance. He was also convinced that the terms which the Dutch would ask would prove equally unacceptable to his war-weary countrymen. Finally he felt sure, or so he declared, that such a treaty would in no way bind the Republic to the Alliance; on the contrary, once it had been signed the Dutch would use it as a counter for bargaining in a separate peace negotiation with the French. It is clear that, although in the last weeks of 1708 his fears that the Republic would insist on peace had somewhat abated, Marlborough still joined with his colleagues in thinking that there was a very real danger of the Dutch seceding from the Alliance. Unlike the Junto, on the other hand, he considered that agreement to a Barrier Treaty to the liking of the Dutch was too dangerous a price to pay for their adherence, which, in any case, it was most unlikely to obtain.

Marlborough arrived in London to find that Parliament was taking a hand in these affairs. On March 2nd (O.S.) both Houses presented a joint and unanimous address to the queen declaring that no peace could be considered honourable without the restitution of the entire

---

Feb. 1708/9 (O.S.), *P.C.D.M.*, ii, pp. 306–7; *ibid.*, ii, pp. 307–8, Marlborough to Godolphin, 17 Feb. 1709, Brussels; *ibid.*, ii, pp. 311–13, same to same, 22 Feb. 1709, Hague; Marlborough to Wratislaw, 22 Feb. 1709, Hague, *Murray*, iv, pp. 454–5; Cadogan to (Raby), 22 Feb. 1709, Hague, Add. Ms. 22196.

Spanish monarchy, the recognition of the Protestant Succession by Louis XIV, the removal of the Pretender from France, the destruction of Dunkirk harbour, and Barriers for Savoy and for the Dutch. The speech in which, on February 28th, Halifax proposed this address was full of praise of the United Provinces, and it was his intention, as he wrote to the Elector of Hanover, that this move should lead to a renewal in earnest of the Barrier negotiation. The Junto, in fact, by now fully aware of Marlborough's reluctance to begin a negotiation to which he could see no good end, had decided to force his hand. On February 26th Sunderland had not hesitated, in an interview with Vrijbergen, to criticise his father-in-law's attitude. He had further declared:

I am of opinion it would be better for both the nations to arrange and conclude a reciprocal treaty with regard to the Barrier and Succession, and the condition of a future peace between England and the States, than if our generals lay encamped upon the plains of Paris.

None the less the ministry would still not hear of the inclusion of Ostend in the Barrier.[1]

3

The news that the French emissary Rouillé had passed through Brussels on March 9th (N.S.) on his way to Antwerp arrived in London three days after the presentation of the joint address. Rouillé's mission was to open negotiations for peace on the assumption that Naples and Sicily might be granted to Philip V, and the States-General had granted him a passport and appointed Buys and van der Dussen to confer with him. The ministry learnt of this development by a letter from Cadogan, but the public manner in which the French King had deliberately chosen to proceed, and which, according to Dayrolle, was causing the States-General some embarrassment, meant that the story simultaneously became public property.

The reaction of the ministry to the news was undoubtedly one of alarm. Marlborough declared, somewhat disingenuously, that Heinsius had deceived him, but the event made the Junto all the more determined to forestall the French by pressing forward with the Barrier Treaty; Marlborough was therefore given full powers to negotiate

---

[1] Vrijbergen to Heinsius, 26 Feb. 1708/9 (O.S.), *Geikie*, p. 104; L'Hermitage to States-General (transcript), 1/12 March 1708/9, London, Add. Ms. 17677 DDD; Halifax to (Elector of Hanover), 4 March 1708/9 (O.S.), Stowe Ms. 223.

both this and an agreement on preliminaries, and prepared to return to The Hague. Meanwhile he wrote to Heinsius urging him to take the control of the negotiations with Rouillé into his own hands, since he was unable to believe that Buys and van der Dussen 'have talked with that vigor that our affaires requiers'. So desperate were the French for peace, he declared, that 'if they be told honestly and plainly what we will have, they will consent to itt', and he assured the Pensionary that

I find the Queen and all that serve Her of the opinion of the Parlaiment, that the intier monarque of Spain, and that of Dunkerk, must be part of the prelimenaries.

At the same time Cadogan was ordered to leave Brussels, where he was finding the company of the Dutch deputy van den Bergh less and less endurable, in order to be able to keep an eye on Rouillé's proceedings at The Hague.[1]

Opinion outside the ministry is, as usual, more difficult to assess. L'Hermitage reported that the first reaction of many people was that for the States to have given Rouillé their passport showed clearly that they had already come to an understanding with Louis XIV about preliminaries, and this can probably be accepted, for it was precisely the opinion of the not untypical Raby when the news reached Berlin. On March 14th (O.S.) Portland, working hard to pave the way for the Barrier Treaty, warned Heinsius that 'the jealousies on account of these pourparlers in Holland increase in England and will soon be growing to unkind distrust'; and a week later L'Hermitage had to admit that everyone was most anxious to know what was happening at The Hague, though as usual he sugared the pill with some fulsome assurances of general confidence in the continuing 'firmness' of the States-General. When Marlborough left London to return to The Hague the veteran Tory Trumbull's correspondent Thomas Butler summed up the talk in Tory circles in his usual confused way. The peace would not be ready for Parliament, it was thought, until the end of the campaign. Marlborough would probably desert the Whigs, that 'party adapted to the Dutch Government' who 'were interested at home for to support the war to the last', now that the Dutch were

---

[1] Cadogan to (Raby), 12 March 1709, Brussels, Add. Ms. 22196; Dayrolle to (Boyle), 15 March 1709, Hague, S.P. Holl. 232; L'Hermitage to States-General (transcript), 8/19 March 1708/9, London, Add. Ms. 17677 DDD; Marlborough to Heinsius, 8, 12 and 15 March 1708/9, London, *van 't Hoff*, pp. 429, 431; Marlborough to Wratislaw, 11 and 15 March 1708/9, St. James', *Murray*, iv, pp. 471, 473; *ibid.*, iv, p. 473, Marlborough to Sinzendorf, 15 March 1708/9, St. James'; *ibid.*, iv, p. 474, Marlborough to Eugene, 24 March 1708/9, St. James'.

so wise as to know when they were well, having resolved to leave off play now they were great winners.[1]

The Tories were now hinting, too, that the eagerness of the Dutch for peace would make the restitution of the entire Spanish monarchy impracticable. Insinuations to this effect appeared in the *Monthly Mercury* and in the *Post Man*, and gave rise to indignant protests. Though only six months before, in his *Review*, Defoe had approved of a peace which would leave Naples, Sicily and other Spanish territories to Philip V, he now ranged himself with the advocates of the 'Spanish Monarchy entire'. The *Daily Courant* vigorously denied that the Dutch could have any different thoughts in the matter. 'Their usual Wisdom and Foresight', it declared, would not allow them to grant the French such an accession of power in the Mediterranean, and it added, in a passage which gives an interesting hint of another reaction to the news of Rouillé's mission:

I give no Manner of Heed to the Suggestions of some Persons, that the Dutch may perhaps be induc'd by Jealousy (however causeless) of Aversion in us to their Commonwealth, to be the more easy and favourable to the French in making of Peace, that they may oblige them in Requital to be their Friends against us at any unhappy Conjecture.

Perhaps the most useful evidence of public opinion about the 1709 peace negotiations is to be found in Charles Gildon's *The Golden Spy*, published at this time or a little later. This work is largely a collection of *contes scabreux*, including that of the unfortunate experience of one 'Monsieur Vander Vermin' in Madame de Montpensier's bed, a Rabelaisian story in which the familiar English preconceptions about Dutch boorishness appear in an unusual guise. In his last section, 'Of Peace and War', however, the author leaves his anecdotes, and relates a conversation in a coffee-house. The first speaker asks why if France is as low as we are told, we do not march our armies into her and reduce her instead of wrangling about peace. The second replies that the weakness of France has been exaggerated, and that perhaps this is just as well, in view of the dangers of Austrian power; what is needed, he declares, is a partition treaty, and all the more so since

tho' the *Dutch* are our Good Confederates and Allies at present, yet I do not think it good Policy to have them entirely secure on the *Terra Firma*, for should they

---

[1] L'Hermitage to States-General (transcripts), 8/19 March and 22 March/2 April 1708/9, London, Add. Ms. 17677 DDD; Portland to Heinsius (translation), 14 March 1708/9 (O.S.), *Churchill*, iv, p. 56; (Raby) to Cadogan (drafts), 28 March and 9 April 1709, Berlin, Add. Ms. 22196; T. Butler to Trumbull, 25 March 1709 (O.S.), *H.M.C. Downshire I pt. ii*, pp. 871–2.

be so, I know not what Designs they may form against *Great Britain*, that is their rival in Trade.

An 'old Whig' then protests that this is 'little less than Treason, at least against the Interest of all the High Allies, as well as our Nation', and advocates the policy of the 'Spanish Monarchy Entire'. Finally 'a jolly sort of Man' – whose sentiments are obviously designed to appeal to the reader – confounds them all by declaring that what people want is peace, 'And which way soever you compass it, 'tis not a Half Penny Matter'! [1]

On April 9th (N.S.) Marlborough arrived at The Hague to relieve Cadogan, who was still confident that

they have their Bromleys and their Hanmers here as well as we have in England, but the Greater number of those which govern are in the True Interests of their Country, and beleive with us no Peace can be secure or lasting without obtaining the whole monarchy of Spain . . . .

This, too, was the impression that Cardonnel gained, but Marlborough knew that the situation was not so simple. He realised that even the large 'peace-party' was not satisfied with Rouillé's proposals, and he was confident that 'the most solid part of the Government' wanted only a 'good' peace. What Heinsius told him, however, confirmed his belief that there was universal weariness with the war in the Republic, and he expressed the fear 'that if ffrance gives a satisfactory answer as to their Barier, we shall find great difficulty in putting a stop to this unseasonable Negociation . . .'. He continued to assure the Courts of Vienna and Barcelona that, though many of them had a great desire for peace, the Dutch would stand by their allies, but in the letters that he wrote to his colleagues on April 16th he was somewhat less sanguine. Not only had Buys visited him to urge the abandonment of the 'Spanish Monarchy Entire' demand, but Heinsius, who, he was sure, had every desire to coöperate with Britain, had told him in strict confidence 'that their Circumstances are such they shall be necessitated to take such a peace as they can gett, for they are not able to go on with the Warr'.

He felt sure, too, that there would be 'a great deal of trouble and difficulty' concerning the Barrier. The claims which the States were preparing at his request would be extravagant, he feared, and he realised that he himself was compromised by the fact that he had not yet formally refused the renewed offer of the Governorship of the

---

[1] *Review*, v, 73 and 153, 14 Sept. 1708 and 19 March 1708/9; *Daily Courant*, 2322, 4 April 1709; *C.W.* 84, pp. 278 *sqq.*

Southern Netherlands which had been made on February 9th; although, as Geikie has shown, he had in fact abandoned all hope of this post. His apprehensions were amply confirmed when, on April 18th, he received an outline of the States' demands, which, he wrote to Godolphin, 'encloses what might be thought a great kingdom'. They were, if anything, more sweeping than those which had proved unacceptable in 1706 – and they included Ostend and Dendermonde! [1]

At home the ministry had for some time been growing restless at the Dutch attitude both to the Rouillé mission and to the question of preliminaries. The States seemed to be 'more cool and negligent in taking care of their friends' than of themselves, and Godolphin wrote to Marlborough insisting that he put an end to this situation by revealing his complete instructions concerning preliminaries. This he did on April 23rd, and at the same interview Heinsius informed him in return that Rouillé had made new proposals. Marlborough felt an absolute confidence in the integrity of the Pensionary, and in the sincerity of the assurances he gave that no step towards peace would be taken without the participation of the allies, yet, as he wrote to Boyle,

upon the whole matter by what I hear from others, and the observations I make among the people of the Government I perceive a thorough inclination for the Peace, and that it will be difficult to bring them to break off these negotiations.

Under these circumstances, as he explained apologetically in a letter to Charles III's minister Moles, he could scarcely refuse to discuss the Dutch Barrier claims, but, determined as he was not to conclude a treaty inimical to the interests of Britain or of the Alliance as a whole, he sailed once more for England on April 29th for consultation. The reception of the Barrier claims had, meanwhile, revived in Godolphin all that bitterness towards the Dutch that had never been far from the surface since the anxious days of 1706. The proposals, he complained, showed 'very little consideration for King Charles, any more than for the Queen', and he added:

I hope they will think fit to have a little more regard to both, before the conclu-

---

[1] Cardonnel to Tilson, 10 April 1709, Hague, S.P. Mil. 4; Cadogan to (Raby), 12 April 1709, Hague, Add. Ms. 22196; Marlborough to Duke of Savoy, 12 April 1709, Hague, *Murray*, iv, pp. 474–5; *ibid.*, iv, pp. 475–7, 479–80, Marlborough to Boyle, 12 and 16 April 1709, Hague; Marlborough to Godolphin, 12 and 16 April 1709, Hague, *Churchill*, iv, pp. 57–8; Marlborough to Moles, 16 April 1709, Hague, *Murray*, iv, pp. 478–9; *ibid.*, iv, pp. 477–8, Marlborough to Charles III, 16 April 1709, Hague; *ibid.*, iv, pp. 480–1, Marlborough to Wratislaw, 17 April 1709, Hague; Marlborough to Godolphin, 19 April 1709 (N.S.), *Coxe*, ii, p. 398; *Geikie*, appendix i. For the Dutch barrier proposals see *Geikie*, pp. 117–18.

sion of this affair; and one can't help admiring the great modesty of the States, in asking all these terms for themselves, when, at the same time, they make a difficulty to have the single town of Dunkirk demolished, at the instance of the Queen.

Of Dutch 'impatience' for a peace he remarked: 'I wish it may not prove a determined resolution of gratifying their enemies, and gaining advantages for themselves, at the expense of their allies'.[1]

Owing to the public manner in which Louis had opened these negotiations for peace, English people outside the ministry knew much more about them than any previous ones, and their interest in them was commensurately greater. In the last days of April the prevailing impression seems to have been that there was no longer much chance of the Dutch 'peace party' getting its way. Defoe extolled the Dutch for the 'manifest Proof' that they had given of 'their Fidelity to the grand Alliance', and rejoiced at the mortifications that Rouillé and his master were having to endure. The common hope, reported L'Hermitage, was that the war would continue for another campaign, and this, wrote one of Trumbull's correspondents, was what Marlborough had prevailed upon the Dutch to consent to. Burnet, too, thought they were 'in a very good disposition to adhere to their allies'. On the other hand, there were enough suggestions made that the Dutch were ready to make peace on the terms already offered for Vrijbergen to complain to the ministry about them. Peter Wentworth summed up the talk on the subject thus:

Some of the Dutch wish him [Rouillé] to stay but the majority is resolved to have the demands of all the Allies sattisfied. It has been talk't as if the French had offer'd the Dutch such advantageous termes that they had a great inclination to leave us & the Emperor in the lurch but now' tis said they are resolved to [press?] on vigorously with the war. So that the Officers reckon themselves sure of another Campaigne. But they are still in some pain whilst Rouillé stays at ye Hague.[2]

Meanwhile the ministry was forming a Counter-Project to the Dutch Barrier proposals, in which 'every one ... of the important provisions of the Project ... was radically altered'. This Counter-Project, to-

[1] Godolphin to Marlborough, 4 April 1709 (O.S.), *Geikie*, p. 115; Boyle to Marlborough, 12 April 1709 (O.S.), Somerville, *op.cit.*, p. 633; Godolphin to Marlborough, 12 April 1709 (O.S.), *Coxe*, ii, pp. 398–9; Marlborough to Boyle, 23 April 1709, Hague, S.P. Holl. 233; Cardonnel to Tilson, 23 April 1709, Hague, S.P. Mil. 4; Marlborough to Godolphin, 24 April 1709, Hague, *Churchill*, iv, pp. 64–5; Marlborough to Moles, 24 April 1709, Hague, *Murray*, iv, pp. 488–9.

[2] *Review*, vi, 8 and 10, 21 and 26 April 1709; P. Wentworth to (Raby), 22 April 1709, London, Add. Ms. 34143; L'Hermitage to States-General (transcript), 26 April/7 May 1709, London, Add. Ms. 17677 DDD; R. Bridges to Trumbull, 27 April (1709), London, *H.M.C. Downshire I pt. ii*, p. 874; *Luttrell*, vi, p. 434, 28 April 1709; *Foxcroft*, p. 421.

gether with a repetition of Marlborough's former instructions concerning the preliminaries and a proposal for renewing the Grand
Alliance before a general peace, was included in the instructions given
to the Duke and his newly-appointed colleague, Townshend, on May
2nd (O.S.).[1]

4

Four days after the Duke's departure for England the French Foreign
Secretary Torcy arrived at The Hague in a last attempt to obtain the
peace that his country so desperately desired. English observers in
the Republic were very much alarmed, but the subsequent resolution
adopted by the States-General that they would take no steps in the
matter except in conference with Marlborough and Eugene gave
considerable satisfaction both to the ministry and to Dayrolle, whose
task it was to report these developments. Though it was still being
said in London that peace was 'unavoidable, by the great inclination
the Dutch showed thereunto', Dayrolle was now confident that 'tout
se fera de concert', and even that 'leur Barrière ne nous embarassera
pas'. Cadogan, too, was 'persuaded that France will agree to everything
we shall demand, as long as we continue friends and united amongst
one another, which the States give new and strong assurances of';
though he could not resist adding: 'you know they are the only power
in the whole alliance that can possibly be suspected'.[2]

A day after his return to The Hague with Townshend on May 18th
Marlborough was able to send important confirmation to London of
the States' 'firmness', despite Torcy's entreaties. He had overcome
the Pensionary's objections to the English proposals for preliminaries.
To his Duchess he wrote that 'Every thing goes so well here, that there
is no doubt ot its ending in a good peace'. These 'acceptable accounts
of the Steadiness of the Dutch, & the disappointments of the ffrench
intrigues there' (as Robinson wrote from Hamburg) had a very good
effect in London, according to L'Hermitage, though Peter Wentworth
reported a rumour that 'for fear they should be tempted' we were
taking steps 'to get as good as we can for ourselves'. On May 28th a

    [1] Instructions for Marlborough and Townshend, 2 May 1709, St. James', S.P. Holl. 233;
Geikie, p. 123.
    [2] Dayrolle to Boyle, 7 May 1709, Hague, S.P. Holl. 232; Cadogan to Brydges, 12 May 1709
(N.S.), *Hunt. Lib. Quart.*, xv (1951–2), p. 30; Sir T. Cave to (Lord Fermanagh?), 3 May 1709,
London, *Verney Letters*, i, p. 269; Berard to Duke of Leeds, 14 May 1709, Utrecht, *Thibau-
deau*, iii, p. 130; Boyle to Dayrolle (copy), 6 May 1709, Whitehall, F.E.B. Holl. 74; Dayrolle
to Raby, 17 May 1709, Hague, Add. Ms. 31131.

statement of preliminaries, signed by the representatives of Austria, Great Britain, and the Republic, was presented to Torcy, who referred it to Versailles. On all sides the assent of Louis XIV was confidently expected; 'it is not to be expressed the joy these people have', reported Marlborough, 'not doubting that the peace is sure'. Despite all Marlborough's very real fears and misgivings, the Dutch leaders had chosen to act in concert with the Whigs. They knew, as Professor Geyl has pointed out, that any peace which they might obtain without the willing coöperation of their British ally would deprive them of the advantages for their overseas trade, above all in Spanish America, on which they had built so many hopes. They saw little profit in receiving the Spanish Netherlands at the hands of the French by means of a separate peace if at the same time they were excluded from trading with Southern Europe and Spanish America by the sea-power of an inevitably alienated Britain. Surely, they reasoned, it would be better to throw in their lot with the British ministry, which, by joining the Whig Townshend to the intractable Marlborough, had at last shown itself in earnest to make substantial concessions to their Barrier claims.[1]

On June 7th (N.S.) Rouillé announced that this master refused to accept Article XXXVII of the preliminaries. The States-General thereupon took what Hare called the 'noble resolution' of adhering to the preliminaries and conducting the war with all possible vigour. Marlborough was well pleased with their firmness, though he anticipated a 'good deal of ill humours' from the 'peace party' if the French too were resolute. Townshend could not praise Heinsius' 'zeal and Steadiness' too highly, and his secretary Horatio Walpole considered the people of Amsterdam so exasperated that, if the French persevered in their refusal, they would,

be willing to use them, as their hosts use strangers when they object against ye reckoning, & ask for particulars, double ye bill, & force them to pay it.

Dayrolle's observations in Rotterdam and The Hague made him believe that 'the late proceedings of the French have done more good than if there had been no negotiation, the people being animated at it everywhere'.[2]

---

[1] *Coxe*, ii, pp. 401–2 (description of Marlborough's letters of 19 May); Dayrolle to Raby, 21 May 1709, Hague, Add. Ms. 31131; Robinson to Raby, 24 May 1709, Hamburg, Add. Ms. 22198; L'Hermitage to States-General (transcript), 13/24 May 1709, London, Add. Ms. 17677 DDD; P. Wentworth to (Raby), 13 May 1709, London, Add. Ms. 34143; Marlborough to Godolphin, 31 May 1709, Hague, *P.C.D.M.*, ii, pp. 322–3; *Kernproblemen*, pp. 201–12.
[2] Hare to G. Naylor, 7 June 1709, Hague, *H.M.C. XIV pt. ix*, pp. 223–4; Marlborough to

In England, too, indignation at the 'duplicity' of the French was the general reaction in ministerial circles, and this was mingled with admiration of the firm stand taken by the Dutch. The indignation resulted above all from the disappointment of the sanguine hopes that had arisen when it was learned that the preliminaries had been agreed. On May 28th (O.S.), for example, the Whig Shaftesbury had written to his Rotterdam correspondent Furly that the war was as good as over: 'All our eyes are on your affaires at the Hague, and we expect to hear more no of camps'. Godolphin, however, had never expected the French to agree, though he was as ready as Boyle and all the ministry to praise the 'firmness of Holland'.[1]

Marlborough, meanwhile, was beginning to have second thoughts about Article XXXVII, which virtually called upon Louis XIV to drive his grandson from Spain. In two letters to Godolphin he hinted that the preliminaries contained enough securities for French good conduct without this article, and that Spain could be conquered speedily once there was a truce with France. But the two friends, already drifting away from each other on the Barrier question, were equally out of sympathy in this matter, for Godolphin had already written to explain the impossibility of this before he received Marlborough's letters. Little, in any case, could be hoped for from the Emperor, he declared, and as for the Dutch:

I leave you to judge by all the rest of their proceedings what share they would take of the charge of that war after they were once easy and their frontier secure to them.

The really extraordinary part of Marlborough's behaviour at this time, as Geikie has pointed out, is that he deliberately attempted to suggest that it was the intractableness of Heinsius and the other Dutch leaders that had made the preliminaries so uncompromising and had thus prevented agreement. Evidently he realised that, when the transient mood of indignation with Louis XIV was past, public opinion would begin to search for the true authors of the prolongation of the war. Already it was being said in London, so L'Hermitage reported, that the breaking off of negotiations was

Godolphin, 7 and 8 June 1709, Hague, *P.C.D.M.*, ii, pp. 324–6; Townshend to (Boyle), 11 June 1709, Hague, S.P. Holl. 233; *ibid.*, H. Walpole to Tilson, 11 June 1709, Hague; Dayrolle to Boyle, 11 June 1709, Hague, S.P. Holl. 232.

1 Shaftesbury to Furly, 28 May 1709, Chelsea, *Forster*, pp. 254–5; Godolphin to Marlborough, 31 May 1709 (O.S.), *Geikie*, p. 129; L'Hermitage to States-General (transcript), 3/14 June 1709, London, Add. Ms. 17677 DDD; Boyle to Townshend,3 June 1709, Whitehall, *B.D.I. France*, pp. 15–16; Lady R. Russell to Lady Granby, 4 June 1709 (O.S.), *H.M.C. XII pt. v*, p. 189; Boyle to Townshend (copy), 7 June 1709, Whitehall, F.E.B. Holl. 75.

Un tour du Duc de Marlborough qui n'a pensé en exzigeant de si rudes condit-tions, que d'obliger la France à les refuser à fin d'avoir un prétexte de continuer la guerre, et qu'il a sceu si bien ménager les esprits en Hollande que c'est luy qui a entraîné les Hautes Puissances à le seconder.

Now he was doing his best, in conversation with Albemarle, in corre-spondence even with his intimate friend Godolphin, to dissimulate all responsibility.[1]

Immediately after the French rejection of the preliminaries Towns-hend was instructed to urge the States to resolve that this agreement would be no longer binding on the Allies if it were not accepted by Louis XIV before a specified date. When the ministry learnt, however, that such a proposal might 'hazard a division among the Provinces' they agreed to let it drop. Thus was set the tone of the future relation-ship between the Godolphin ministry and the Republic; from now on the Cabinet would take the primrose path of concessions in order to preserve Dutch 'Unanimity' in prosecuting the war. Unfortunately for them, opinion in England was beginning to examine the preliminaries more critically; a somewhat cryptic letter from Butler to Trumbull shows not only an awareness of the unreasonableness of breaking off negotiations on the question of Article XXXVII but also a conviction that the entire preliminary agreement was the result of a sinister plot between the ministry and the Dutch, who had 'borrowed our Crown and Government for their wars abroad'.

On the question of Article XXXVII, however, the ministry was adamant, turning as deaf an ear to the hints of Heinsius as they had to those of Marlborough. Meanwhile the Duke's 'whispering campaign' about the responsibility for the breakdown of the negotiations was beginning to bear fruit. The same Colonel Cranstoun whom we saw criticising Marlborough's conduct in 1705 wrote home from the field that

It is certain the Imperial Ministers and Prince Eugene were not for breaking upon that point [Art. XXXVII] and however the Duke of Marlborough went into the opinion of the Pensionary and those who were for standing to all we demanded, yet it is not believed to have been his real judgment, but on the contrary that he was for passing from that article.[2]

[1] Albemarle to Heinsius, 11 June 1709, Brussels, *Geikie*, p. 132; Marlborough to Godolphin, 13 June 1709, Ghent, *P.C.D.M.*, ii, p. 331; Same to same, 16 June 1709, Ghent, *Coxe*, ii, pp. 409–10; Godolphin to Marlborough, 6 June 1709 (O.S.), *Geikie*, p. 130; L'Hermitage to Fagel, 21 June 1709 (N.S.), W. Reese, *Das Ringen um Frieden und Sicherheit in den Entschiedungs-jahren des spanischen Erbfolgekrieges, 1708 bis 1709* (Munich, 1933), p. 273.
[2] Boyle to Townshend (copies), 10 June and 12 July 1709, Whitehall, F.E.B. Holl. 75; T. Butler to Trumbull, 20 June 1709 (O.S.), *H.M.C. Downshire I pt. ii*, p. 878; (Cranstoun) to R. Cunningham, 5 Aug. 1709, Willemean, *H.M.C. XV pt. iv*, pp. 496–9.

It was not only his attempts to load the Republic with the blame for the breakdown of the peace negotiations which were diminishing what remained of mutual trust and goodwill between Marlborough and the Dutch leaders. The affairs of the Condominium, too, were once more giving rise to considerable differences. In particular, a complicated dispute between the Duke of Arensberg and his mother the Dowager-Duchess was a fruitful source of friction. When Marlborough learned of the steps which, contrary to his advice, the Dutch deputy van den Bergh had taken in favour of the Duke his feelings, as expressed in his letters to Heinsius, were comparable to those that Hop's conduct had aroused in him three years before. 'The behaviour of M. de Vandenberg is such that it is impossible for me to be silent', he complained, and he went on to suggest that the Deputy was 'so very weak' that he was 'intierly governed' by the less amenable members of the Council of State. On this occasion, however, his protests were unavailing, and he continued to complain to the Pensionary of the 'faction and disorder' for which van den Bergh was responsible. 'In a very little time,' he warned Heinsius,

the weak government of M. de Vandenberg will cause the same effect as that of the Duke d'Albe, tho' the caracters of the men are very different.[1]

5

The Barrier negotiations, which Townshend had reopened at The Hague, began but slowly. The first obstacle was the reluctance of the Dutch to admit a clause concerning the restitution of the entire Spanish monarchy. Marlborough pointed out that the omission of this provision would be harmful to Charles III, 'nor', he added, 'do I believe the Parliament would approve of such a condescension', but the ministry, alarmed at the tone of Heinsius' reply to a letter from Torcy, and assured by Townshend that

nothing will contribute more towards making ye people of this country unanimous, & firm to the interest of ye Allys .... than .... to remove the difficultys about ye Barriere ....,

proposed an 'expedient' for this point on July 15th (O.S.).[2]

[1] Marlborough to van den Bergh, 20 June 1709, Lille, *Murray*, iv, p. 511; *ibid.*, iv, pp. 515–16, Laws to Marlborough, 22 June 1709, Brussels; Marlborough to Heinsius, 23 and 24 June 1709, Loos, *van 't Hoff*, pp. 440–1; *ibid.*, pp. 455 and 471, same to same, 15 Aug. and 22 Oct. 1709 (N.S.); *Veenendaal*, ch. xiv, *passim*.
[2] Boyle to Townshend, 5 July 1709 (O.S.), *C.J.*, xvii, p. 77; Marlborough to Godolphin, 18 July 1709 (N.S.), *P.C.D.M.*, ii, pp. 349–50; Townshend to Boyle, 23 July 1709, Hague, S.P. Holl. 233; Boyle to Townshend, 15 July 1709, Whitehall, Somerville, *op.cit.*, pp. 630–4.

The Junto's policy towards the Dutch was becoming more and more distasteful to Marlborough. Believing as he did that the inclinations of the Dutch were now such that they would grasp at any opportunity to come at a peace, even if this involved the partition of the Spanish monarchy, he insisted that the omission of this vital clause would provide them with just the opportunity they were seeking. Such an attitude was not necessarily inconsistent with his deprecation of Article XXXVII. This he condemned because it made it impossible for the Allies first to conclude a truce with France and then undertake the conquest of Spain; he did not contest the desirability of the *eventual* conquest of the whole Spanish monarchy. Thus, though he disliked his colleagues' insistence on 'No Peace without Spain', he could perfectly consistently take his stand on the principle of the 'Spanish Monarchy Entire'. Townshend, too, was alarmed by the strong disposition towards a speedy peace which he saw everywhere. This was manifested in a reluctance to demand cautionary towns in Spain as an 'expedient' for Article XXXVII, and in the fact that the Dutch leaders themselves did not dare to be as firm as they would have wished in the continuing interchanges with France about such an 'expedient'. Even Horatio Walpole, who was so good a Whig as to want the Dutch to be 'High and Mighty' in the Spanish Netherlands so long as our trade to Flanders was 'no ways prejudiced', recognised that only 'constant success' could 'keep this people in heart'.[1]

The reaction of Townshend and the Junto to this situation was very different from that of Marlborough. We can see it plainly in Townshend's own words (in a letter of August 2nd (N.S.)):

.... since there is no hopes of obtaining that ye Article relating to ye restitution of ye whole Spanish Monarchy should be joyned to this treaty, I am apprehensive that should we continue to insist upon this point, we may force this people to think of getting their Barrier, from another hand. I must therefore be of opinion that it is for her Majestys service that ye most expeditious means should be taken to remove ye difficulty, especially since something wch relates to a peace is in agitation.

As a result of his representations Boyle sent him, on August 2nd (O.S.), a notification that the queen was willing to omit everything from the treaty not relating to the Barrier and the Succession; though he added

1 Marlborough to Godolphin, 25 and 30 July 1709 (N.S.), *P.C.D.M.*, ii, pp. 351–4; H. Walpole to Tilson, 30 July and 6 Aug. 1709, Hague, S.P. Holl. 233; *ibid.*, Townshend to Boyle, 2 and 9 Aug. 1709, Hague; Marlborough to (Townshend), 5 Aug. 1709 (N.S.), Add. Ms. 41178; Marlborough to Godolphin, 6 Aug. 1709, Orchies, *P.C.D.M.*, ii, pp. 356–7; Marlborough to Sunderland (transcript), 12 Aug. 1709, Orchies, Add. Ms. 34518; Marlborough to (Townshend), 13 Aug. 1709, Orchies, Add. Ms. 41178; Marlborough to Godolphin, 16 Aug. 1709 (N.S.), *Coxe*, ii, p. 413.

the not very effective proviso that Townshend should first report what effect this concession was likely to have on Dutch determination to press on with the war and stand by the preliminaries.

It seems clear that this enquiry, which elicited from Townshend a a glowing picture of the loyalty to England that would result from the concession, was inserted by Godolphin in order to delay a final decision. The Treasurer's position at this time is not easy to define. He did not yet go all the way with the Junto, for he wrote to Marlborough that he was apprehensive that he would be obliged to accede to 'the positive resolution of the Whigs to gratify the Dutch'. On the other hand, his belief that Harley intended to 'force the Queen into peace, by refusing necessaries for war, and by agreeing with Holland in every thing that relates to peace ....' made him more anxious to appease both the Junto and the Dutch, and also to re-open negotiations on the basis of the preliminaries, than was the Duke. Marlborough's arguments about the Spanish Monarchy entire clause, he wrote on August 11th, were 'unanswerable' and the queen shared this opinion, but he was uncertain how much longer he could stand out against the Junto.[1]

Godolphin, in fact, was in process of changing his mind, but Marl- borough's uncompromising attitude was unalterable. When he learnt on August 19th (N.S.) that the ministry had taken the decision which would make possible the omission of both the entire monarchy and the Dunkirk clauses from the Treaty, he made his position clear in a num- ber of important letters. In addition to repeating his earlier warnings as to the consequences of this omission, he now gave Godolphin the more general assurance 'that whenever England shall comply with the States as to their barrier now desired, they will think it more their interest to be well with France than England'. 'As soon as they have obtained their desire in the barrier', he wrote to Sarah, 'they can have no other thought or interests but that of making the peace as soon as possible'. He expressed sympathy with Godolphin's desire for fresh peace negoti- ations, but told him that England would have been able to enter these with much more prospect of advantage if the instructions of August 2nd had never been sent to Townshend. Under these circumstances,

    [1] Townshend to Boyle, 2 and 20 Aug. 1709, Hague, S.P. Holl. 233; Godolphin to Marl- borough, 26 July 1709, St. James', *P.C.D.M.*, ii, pp. 358–62; Boyle to Townshend (copy), 2 Aug. 1709, Whitehall, F.E.B. Holl. 75; Godolphin to Marlborough (abstract), 2 Aug. 1709 (O.S.), *Coxe*, ii, p. 413; Same to same, 4 Aug. 1709 (O.S.), *P.C.D.M.*, ii, pp. 355–6; *ibid.*, ii, pp. 363–5, same to same, 11 Aug. 1709, Windsor. In this last letter Godolphin, referring to the Barrier Treaty, writes: '... it is with a good deal of difficulty that I have been able to give it any delay'.

therefore, he asked to be relieved of the necessity of signing a treaty now assuming a form so abhorrent to him.[1]

Godolphin was considerably embarrassed by the necessity in which he found himself of declaring for either Marlborough or Townshend. He now felt, he told the former, that there was ' a good deal to be said for both these opinions'. For a time he clung to the hope that the speedy renewal of peace negotiations would make a declaration unnecessary. Such a renewal seemed all the more desirable to him since he was sure that the States could not, in any case, be prevented from having dealings with France; and he now expressed agreement with Marlborough's plan of obtaining a truce with France and then conquering Spain. Three days after he had written in this vein to Marlborough, however, he informed Sunderland of his decision to send full powers to Townshend to complete the Treaty as agreed, declaring 'that it would not be productive of those fatal consequences which the Duke apprehended'.

As Geikie has pointed out, it was not weakness that had brought the Treasurer round to Townshend's way of thinking. It may have been partly exasperation with the attitude of Charles III to the cession of Minorca, and, also, perhaps, a grateful reaction to the news that the States had resolved to stand by the preliminaries and to insist on cautionary towns in Spain as well as in Flanders as an 'expedient' for Article XXXVII. Above all, however, as Geikie has shown, Godolphin, like the Junto, and unlike Marlborough, hoped that the concessions that England was making in the Barrier negotiations would bind the Republic to her so firmly as to make a formal guarantee of 'the Spanish Monarchy entire' unnecessary. This confidence was fully demonstrated two weeks later when the ministry agreed to drop their proposal (made on August 16th (O.S.)) for a new alliance for the recovery of the entire Spanish monarchy.[2]

The news from Holland, indeed, seemed to warrant such confidence. Though he recognised the impossibility of preventing the Dutch having any dealings with the French 'untill they should give ye allys greater proofs of their sincerity', Townshend was able to report, on August 30th (N.S.), that they had taken the lead in rejecting an al-

[1] (Marlborough) to (Godolphin), (19 Aug. 1709?) (N.S.), Add. Ms. 28056; Same to same, 19 Aug. 1709 (N.S.) and n.d., *Coxe*, ii, pp. 412–13, 415; Marlborough to Sarah, 19 Aug. 1709 (N.S.), *P.C.D.M.*, i, pp. 200–2; *ibid.*, ii, pp. 373–7, Marlborough to Godolphin, 22 and 26 Aug. 1709 (N.S.).

[2] Godolphin to Marlborough, 14 Aug. 1709, Windsor, *P.C.D.M.*, ii, pp. 366–9; Boyle to Townshend (copies), 16 Aug. and 2 Sept. 1709, Whitehall, F.E.B. Holl. 75; *Coxe*, ii, p. 416 (description of letter from Godolphin to Sunderland, 17 Aug. 1709 (O.S.)); *Geikie*, pp. 143–7.

ternative proposed by Torcy to the 'expedient' for Article XXXVII put forward by the Allies. This he attributed to 'a greater Spiritt than was imagined in this people against accepting any project by wch France should obtain a peace, & ye Allys still be left engaged in War with Spain . . . .'.

Marlborough accepted his defeat as gracefully as he could, but he very significantly urged Godolphin to do nothing of himself, 'but to let the Whigs be answerable'. For all their assurances, he warned, the Dutch would never leave off their dealings with the French court, and if the proposal of August 16th were not implemented the greatest part of the burden of the war in Spain would be on the queen.[1]

What really gave the ministry cause for alarm, however, was the news, communicated to them by Townshend, that Heinsius had got wind of the negotiation that was going on for the cession of Minorca to the queen. This negotiation had been conceived, and was being executed, by General James Stanhope, who had captured the island in the name of Charles III on September 30th, 1708. On December 19th he wrote to Sunderland urging that England demand absolute sovereignty over the island. One of the resulting advantages that he had in mind he outlined as follows:

I hope the Dutch will always be our friends; but if they should ever be otherwise, they will never be able to carry on their trade to the Levant without our leave, if we remain masters of this place: and I confess this was one reason why I did not desire any troops of that nation, when I went on with this expedition, that they might have no pretensions to share it with us.

Stanhope was authorised to enter into such negotiations, though at the same time Marlborough warned him that, if the Dutch learned anything of the affair, their jealousy would make matters very difficult. Stanhope was quite undismayed; on March 29th he wrote to Marlborough that

what we demand is so natural that I believe all the world expects we should keep it and will be surprised at our modesty if we desire nothing more, and as for the Dutch they will have very ill grace to oppose us in that matter if they pretend as they doe that we should be assisting to them in obtaining a barrier.

He was soon enraged by the reluctance of the Court of Barcelona to accede to his demands, but on June 15th he was able to report that

---

[1] Townshend to (Boyle), 30 Aug. and 3 Sept. 1709, Hague, S.P. Holl. 233; Marlborough to Godolphin, 3 Sept. 1709 (N.S.), *P.C.D.M.*, ii, pp. 379–80; *ibid.*, i, pp. 211–13, Marlborough to Sarah, 7 Sept. 1709 (N.S.). While bound to support the ministry's policy in public, Marlborough did what he could to undermine it in private, especially as regards the 'expedient' for Article XXXVII by which Louis XIV was required to deliver up three towns in Spain to the Allies. See his letter to Heinsius of 2 Sept. (N.S.), *van 't Hoff*, p. 462.

Charles had made a conditional surrender. He set little store by the objection that he knew would be raised, that the Dutch would seek corresponding advantages in the form of an increased Barrier. In his view the house of Austria had deserved so little from the queen that 'they would be very rightly served if we complied with the demands of the Dutch, how exorbitant soever'. In any case, as he wrote to Sunderland,

no acquisitions of the Dutch on the Continent ought to give us jealousy, since it [sic] would rather diminish than increase their power at sea,

a development for which, he said, there was a precedent in the history of Venice.[1]

None the less, the ministry was highly embarrassed when it received Townshend's letter of August 3rd (N.S.) announcing that Heinsius knew of these negotiations, and even more so when it learnt from his letter of September 6th that the Pensionary had also heard of the secret treaty of commerce with Charles ratified in January 1708. Townshend had denied all knowledge of these matters, but it was impossible for the ministry to adopt this course. Since nothing had been settled about Minorca it was able to give somewhat disingenuous assurances, but it was forced to go further to quiet its ally's apprehensions concerning the secret treaty. Boyle's instructions to Townshend of September 2nd (O.S.) announced its new policy. In order to allay the fears of the Dutch, he wrote,

Her Majesty .... is willing and ready to joyn with them in procuring the like advantages of Trade with Spain and the West Indies for both Nations; provided the Dutch will insist at the next Treaty of Peace, that England and Holland shall be upon the same foot and have equal benefit of Trade in all the Dominions of France....

It was not with a good grace that the Junto was yielding up these advantages, as is indicated by a disgruntled afterthought in the same letter:

It is impossible not to observe that the Assistance the Dutch have afforded the King of Spain in this Warr bears no proportion to the great efforts her Majty has made for the Service of that Prince.

Here, for once, Marlborough saw eye to eye with his colleagues. 'I can't hinder thinking it very partial in the dutch,' he wrote to Townshend, 'to find fault when they are to have so many great towns and the Province of

---

[1] J. Stanhope to Sunderland, 19 Dec. 1708 and 15 June 1709, Barcelona, Stanhope, *War of the Succession in Spain*, appendix, pp. 81–3, 94–5; Marlborough to J. Stanhope, 26 Jan. 1709, Brussels, *Murray*, iv, pp. 408–9; J. Stanhope to Marlborough, 29 March 1709, Port Mahon, B. Williams, *Stanhope* (Oxford), 1932), p. 89; Same to same, 15 June 1709, Barcelona, *Murray*, iv, pp. 562–3; Williams, *op.cit.*, Ch. iii, *passim*.

Geldre'. Even he, however, agreed entirely on this occasion that 'the Conjunctor requiers our doing every thing in our power to please them ....'.[1]

With Boyle's instructions of September 2nd, the final form of the Treaty was established. Though Marlborough's disapproval remained as strong as ever Townshend's eagerness to conclude must have been increased by his observation of the Dutch reaction to the battle of Malplaquet (Sept. 11th (N.S.)). 'If Holland pleases, it is now in our power to have what peace we please', wrote Marlborough from that bloody field; but both Dayrolle and Walpole noted that the news of the terrible Dutch losses was having a most 'dispiriting' effect upon the 'popularity' at The Hague, even though, as Townshend reported, Heinsius and the States-General were 'in very good humour'.[2] The difficulties which he encountered at the beginning of October in persuading the States not to send the unofficial intermediary Petkum back to Paris could not but convince Townshend of the urgent need of countering 'that eagerness to be treating of a peace which is always showing at the Hague' (as Somers called it) by finishing the Treaty. This conviction was more likely to be strengthened than otherwise by Marlborough's gloomy warnings that the French were relying on the Dutch desire for 'any peace'.[3]

[1] Boyle to Townshend (copies), 23 Aug. and 2 Sept. 1709, Whitehall, F.E.B. Holl. 75; Townshend to Boyle, 6 Sept. 1709, Hague, S.P. Holl. 233; Marlborough to (Townshend), 13 Sept. 1709 (N.S.), Add. Ms. 41178; Godolphin to Marlborough (abstract), 13 Sept. 1709 (O.S.), *Geikie*, p. 153.

[2] Marlborough to Godolphin, 11 Sept. 1709 (N.S.), *Coxe*, ii, p. 462; Dayrolle to (Boyle), 16 and 20 Sept. 1709, Hague, S.P. Holl. 232; H. Walpole to (Tilson?), 17 and 20 Sept. 1709, Hague, S.P. Holl. 233; Boyle to Townshend (copy), 9 Sept.1709, Whitehall, F.E.B. Holl. 75; Godolphin to Marlborough, 12 Sept. 1709, Windsor, *P.C.D.M.*, ii, pp. 393–6; *ibid.*, ii, pp. 396–8, Marlborough to Godolphin, 23 Sept. 1709 (N.S.); Marlborough to Sarah, 23 Sept. 1709 (N.S.), *Coxe*,ii, pp. 464–5; Marlborough to Sunderland (transcript), 26 Sept. 1709 (N.S.), Add. Ms. 34518.

[3] Marlborough to (Townshend), 14 Oct. 1709 (N.S.), Add.Ms. 41178; Townshend to (Sunderland), 18 Oct. 1709, Hague, S.P. Holl. 233; Sunderland to Townshend (copy), 14 Oct. 1709, Whitehall, F.E.B. Holl. 75; Somers to Marlborough (transcript), 14 Oct. 1709 (O.S.), Add. Ms. 34518. One reason for the difficulties that the States made about putting an end to Petkum's journeyings, according to Townshend's letter of 18 October, was their 'apprehensions of ye bad consequences that ye troubles of ye North may produce'. Indeed, after the Russian victory at Poltava, there seemed an imminent danger that the rulers of Denmark, Prussia and Hanover 'would simultaneously withdraw their 60,000 men from the various French fronts, to fight out their rival claims in a general scramble for Charles XII's lost inheritance' (*Trevelyan*, iii, p. 75). In this alarming situation the English found their Dutch ally annoyingly backward in using its influence to prevent the outbreak of general hostilities in the North (Pulteney to Townshend, 6 and 10 Aug. 1709, Copenhagen, Add. Ms. 38500; *ibid.*, Pulteney to H. Walpole, 10 Sept. and 2 Nov. 1709, Copenhagen; Boyle to Townshend (copy), 26 Nov. 1709, Whitehall, F.E.B. Holl. 75). Almost two years later, St. John was to lay all the blame for the troubles in the North upon the Dutch and their habit of 'shifting off matters to gain time' (St. John to Whitworth (copies), 8 and 18 May, 1711, Whitehall, F.E.B. Prussia 52).

Meanwhile, the big guns of the Whigs were being brought to bear upon Godolphin to ensure that he would not, at the last moment, withdraw his approval of the Barrier Treaty. A conversation with the Governor of the Bank of England on September 8th convinced him that the Whig financial and commercial interests were fully behind the Junto in their advocacy of the 'Spanish Monarchy entire' and their rejection of a peace, such as that which Marlborough had advocated, which would leave them 'to an after game for the recovery of Spain'. All the more reason, then, to procure a Treaty the concluding of which, as Sunderland put it,

must have a very good effect upon the minds of the people in Holland and keep them steady in not making any hasty step towards different measures from England.

Not that Godolphin ever imagined that the Junto and the Whig merchants spoke for all Englishmen. He knew, as he told Marlborough, that there were many 'malicious people' who would 'rail' if there was no peace, and these he saw no prospect of satisfying. Before the year was out Shrewsbury, who was little given to exaggeration, estimated that these were in fact 'the generality of the nation', and even asserted, in a letter to Harley, that most members of Parliament, 'when discoursed singly in the country', agreed with this longing for peace.[1] A similar impression is given by the correspondence between James Brydges, Paymaster to the Forces Abroad, and his erstwhile colleague Henry St. John. On June 11th Brydges wrote that though things abroad had a very good prospect, nothing but peace would be able to 'make ye Sessions easie' in the coming winter. St. John, writing from the country, replied thus:

Peace is at this time the most desirable publick and private Good. If you will not think yt I putt on to much of the Country Esqr. Ile Venture to tell you, that wee want it more than perhaps any man out of the Country can Imagine. Glorious Successes and the hopes of a last Campaigne are Soveraigne Cordials. They Elevate the few spirits we have left and we are not seen to pine or Languish; but should the Distemper Continue the strings of Life may brack at once . . . .

Brydges found this 'unquestionably' true; 'a war of 20: years', he declared,

must certainly drain ye ready mony & put every one into very difficult circumstances who have not other supports then Land, and I do not see how wee can support it to ye hight it must be another year, should we be put to it . . . . .[2]

[1] Godolphin to Marlborough, 9 Sept. 1709, Windsor, *P.C.D.M.*, ii, pp. 391–3; Sunderland to Townshend (copy), 21 Oct. 1709, Whitehall, F.E.B. Holl. 75; Shrewsbury to (Harley), 3 Nov. 1709, Heathrop, *H.M.C. Bath I*, p. 197.
[2] Brydges to St. John, 11 June and 8 July 1709 (O.S.), *Hunt. Lib. Bull.*, ix (1936), pp. 123–5; *ibid.*, viii (1935), pp. 161–2, St. John to Brydges, 26 June and 26 July 1709, Bucklebury.

On October 29th (N.S.) Townshend was able to send the completed Treaty to London. The Junto, eager as they were to buy Dutch adherence to 'No peace without Spain' and give them a good Barrier, were aghast at the terms to which Townshend had agreed. The Dutch had not only screwed every possible advantage out of the concessions that the ministry had already made, but had induced Townshend to exceed his instructions in the matter of the Barrier fortresses, above all by the inclusion of Dendermonde. The Treaty itself, and the correspondence between Townshend and the ministry that followed its reception in London, have been dealt with so fully by Geikie as to need little detailed description here. Townshend defended himself vigorously against all the Cabinet's complaints, but his final reply to every one was that he was

fully convinced that there was no other way left to keep this people firm to the Common Interest against France but the giving them satisfaction in an affair wch is of such immediate importance to their security.

This argument was conclusive. Fatally eager to avert the danger of 'separate measures' by the Dutch, the ministry submitted. For a little while it held out against approving the separate article that ceded Upper Guelders to the States, in which affair Townshend had been given the futile instructions of supporting the claims of the King of Prussia 'in such a manner as to give no disgust or jealousy to the Dutch'. However, when what Boyle called the 'menacing Insinuations' of the Pensionary on that subject had been communicated to it, it surrendered unconditionally, though with much talk of the gratitude that it expected from the States in return for its complaisance. On December 6th (O.S.) ratification was completed.[1]

6

In concluding the Treaty of Barrier and Succession the Whigs, intent upon prolonging the war until France was broken, had thrown all consideration of public feeling to the winds. Even in the *annus mirabilis* of 1706, as we have seen, they had been aware that English opinion would never stomach Dendermonde in the hands of the Dutch; yet now, in a war-weary country where their power depended almost solely upon an illusory parliamentary majority, they had guaranteed

[1] Boyle to Townshend (copy), 30 Aug. 1709, Windsor, F.E.B. Holl. 75; Same to same (extracts), 1, 8, 15, 18, 26 and 29 Nov., and 9 Dec. 1709 (O.S.), *C.J.*, xvii, pp. 77 *sqq.*; Townshend to (Boyle), 19 and 26 Nov., and 1 Dec. 1709, Hague, S.P. Holl. 233.

to the Dutch not merely Dendermonde but much else that would be almost as distasteful to their fellow-countrymen. Their own initial dismay on receiving the terms that Townshend had agreed was no good omen for the reaction of the gentlemen of England whenever the news became public. For the moment, however, the secret was well kept in England, though Marlborough, probably behind his colleagues' backs, took care that the Austrians were informed, while at the same time disclaiming any hand in the matter.

None the less, the Junto had no reason to be dissatisfied with the dividend reaped from their acquiescence in the Treaty. As Townshend foresaw, the States, urged on by Marlborough, replied to the French overtures made through Petkum at the beginning of December with

a seasonable and vigorous Resolution of carrying on the Warr against France untill the French are obliged to accept of such a Peace as the Allys have required for their Common Security.

This maintenance of that 'firmness' already praised in the Commons' reply to the queen's speech gave much satisfaction to the ministry, which was expressed in a letter from the queen to the States-General. Even Marlborough, still apprehensive as to the effects of the Barrier Treaty, showed his pleasure in a letter written to Townshend on December 13th (O.S.):

I do with all my heart congratulate the just and Vigorous resolution of the States .... we ought to omitt Nothing that may be in our powers for the aug-menting the army if it be possible now that this matter of the Barier is intierly setled to the satisfaction of the States. I hope from henceforward there will never be any thing that can hinder a ferm freindshipe between the two nations.

There was a strict limit to the Duke's satisfaction, however – a limit imposed by doubts as to how long, now that they had the Barrier Treaty in their pockets, the Dutch would maintain this attitude. He confided something of these doubts to Heinsius in a letter written from London on December 12th (O.S.). 'Frankly' and 'as a friend' he told the Pensionary that unless 'Holland were willing and able to continue for three yeares longer the Warr' she was wrong to insist that France should 'do so treacherous a thing as to deliver towns in Spain' as well as in Flanders. Once more he pressed the desirability of tackling Spain separately after a truce with France.[1]

There was no response. The Junto's policy had succeeded, and what

---

[1] Marlborough to Heinsius, 29 Nov. and 12 Dec. 1709, London, *van 't Hoff*, pp. 473, 475–6; Marlborough to (Townshend), 29 Nov. and 13 Dec. 1709, London, Add. Ms. 41178; Boyle to Townshend (copies), 29 Nov. and 13 Dec. 1709, Whitehall, F.E.B. Holl. 75; Anne to States-General (transcript), 23 Dec. 1709, St. James', Add. Ms. 17677 DDD; *Cobbett*, vi, cols. 803–4.

Marlborough had never believed possible had in fact occurred; the Dutch had bound themselves hand and foot to the war policy of the English Whig leaders. The myth in which many Englishmen already believed had actually been translated into fact; the ministry and the Dutch *were* in league to prolong the war, even though, contrary to popular belief, it was the Dutch and not the ministry who were being bribed to do so.

CHAPTER VIII

THE TORY VICTORY
⟨1710⟩

I

It used to be assumed that the fall of the Godolphin ministry was, in Lecky's words, 'beyond question mainly due to the exertions of the clergy'. There were, it was admitted, 'some murmurs ... at the reckless prolongation of a war which produced much distress among the poor; but on the whole they were not very serious, and the approaching downfall of the ministers was mainly due to the alienation of the Queen and to the opposition of the Church'.[1]

In more recent years it has become apparent that popular discontent concerning the conduct and prolongation of the war played a major part in the political crisis of 1710. The change of ministry, of course, was fundamentally due to the alienation of the queen from her existing ministers.[2] Yet even here public feeling was all important. The queen, warned by the failure of her attempt to oust Godolphin at the beginning of 1708, and fearful of the apparent strength of the Junto, would take no such step again until she was quite sure of the support of the mass of her subjects. Here lay Godolphin's real blunder in precipitating the trial of Sacheverell. By so doing he presented the queen and her secret advisers with a perfect test of public feeling towards the ministry, the result of which showed them that they were sure of attaining their ends, provided that they acted with reasonable caution.

What were the springs of this popular feeling against the ministry which gave the queen courage to act, and which confirmed her judgment by making the Tories supreme in the Commons? From 1707 onwards the current of opinion outside ministerial circles was running against both the war and the allies. In 1711 this eventually appeared in the open as a raging torrent; but in 1710, too, it is clearly visible. It is true that, as Miss Ransome has noted, 'the amount of actual

---

[1] *Lecky*, i, pp. 50. 59.

[2] It is difficult to take very seriously Finlater's assertion, reported by Dartmouth, that Godolphin and the queen had a secret understanding, both hoping that a new ministry would be better able to withstand Dutch 'extortions' (*C.W.* 18, vi, p. 144).

election propaganda on the subject of the war was less than that
dealing with the doctrines of Hereditary Right and Non-resistance,
and very considerably less than that produced by the Sacheverell
trial', but, as Sir Charles Petrie points out, the fact that there *was* open
controversy concerning the ministry's war policy is in itself significant.
Miss Ransome makes one surmise to explain the apparent hesitation
on the part of the Tories to make capital of war-weariness and impatience with the allies. 'This was no doubt due', she writes, 'to their
uncertainty as to the extent to which the war was unpopular in the
country. The uncertainty was ended by the election results'.[1] An
additional explanation may be that the Tories were very much afraid
that any public promises of a speedy peace would induce the Dutch
to seek their own advantage in a separate peace with France; a fear
which certainly accounted for much of their double-dealing when in
office.

It is undeniable that religious feeling, respect for the Crown's known
wishes, and the influence of the clergy were important factors in
deciding the outcome of the election. There can be little doubt, however, that popular feeling against the war and the allies was of very
much more influence than the amount of election propaganda devoted
to it would lead one to believe.[2] This view is supported by the reactions
of Godolphin himself to the storm that was gathering around him.
One of his letters to Marlborough displays an awareness that the
Sacheverell affair was being used as a medium for voicing *existing*
discontent with the government and its policies. Others demonstrate
his conviction that, whatever issues the election might be fought on,
Harley, were he victorious, would concentrate his efforts in an attack
on the old ministry's policy towards the allies (and, thus, indirectly
on the allies themselves).[3] It is indeed evident from what followed in
1711 that Harley was far more concerned with procuring peace than
with bolstering up the Established Church. The desire of the Tories
for peace was in fact the open secret of the 1710 election, and we of the
twentieth century, accustomed to elections in which the 'platform'
of the victorious party bears little relation either to the policies that
it genuinely intends to pursue, or to the reasons why it is elected to
office, should find nothing unfamiliar in this situation.

Godolphin's observations of Harley's real intentions were shrewd;

[1] Ransome, *op.cit.*, pp. 28, 33; Sir C. Petrie, *Bolingbroke* (London, 1937), p. 134.
[2] K. Feiling, *A History of the Tory Party* (Oxford, 1924), pp. 437–8; Ashley, *England in the Seventeenth Century*, p. 209.
[3] See below, pp. 220, 228

but he miscalculated when he went on to hope that public opinion
in such an eventuality, would be on the side of the Allies and against
the Tories. He had reckoned without the final disillusionment of the
breakdown of the Geertruidenberg negotiations, which, like the failure
to obtain a peace the year before, was widely ascribed to the obstinacy
of the Dutch; 'as if', wrote a contemporary annalist, 'the old Ministry,
the Pensionary, and his Friends, were averse to Peace, and had a
Design to perpetuate the War for their own Interest ...'. It is commonly supposed that the 1709 Barrier Treaty also turned public opinion
against the Dutch in 1710, but all the evidence is to the contrary.
It was not until August 24th, 1710, that the *Examiner* made the first
public revelation that such a Treaty even existed, and more than a
year was to elapse after this before its actual provisions became
known outside ministerial circles.[1]

2

The reactions of the king of Prussia to the news of the Barrier Treaty,
which Marlborough's calculated indiscretions had made known to
him, were the immediate preoccupation of Boyle, as Northern Secretary,
in the first days of 1710. The king's threats to recall all his troops in
the service of the Allies if his demands were not complied with evoked
a curious response from the Junto. Although they had approved the
Separate Article allotting the Upper Quarter of Guelders to the Republic which was the cause of all this trouble, they regarded the Dutch
as solely responsible for these inconveniences, especially when the
States seemed disinclined to make concessions. In their own eyes, at
least, the Junto had no moral responsibility for the results of an
agreement which had been obtained from them, as they thought, under
duress. There could be no clearer indication of the Whig attitude to
the Townshend Treaty. Now that the Treaty was actually signed
their outlook was much nearer to that of Marlborough, who told
Raby that the Dutch had given Prussia 'too much provocation', and
assured the Prussian Grumbkow that 'il est trop tard à présent de s'y
opposer, ou d'en faire du bruit, mais il ne me paraît pas poutrant que
la chose soit sans remède'. The Duke's hopes were not in vain, for the
king was eventually mollified by far-reaching promises.[2]

---

[1] *Examiner*, i, 4, 24 Aug. 1710; *Jones, 1710*, p. 433; O.B. Miller, *Robert Harley, Earl of
Oxford*, (Oxford, 1925), pp. 22–3.
[2] Boyle to Townshend (copies), 3 Jan., 7 and 14 Feb. 1709/10, Whitehall, F.E.B. Holl. 77;
Marlborough to Raby, 6 Jan. 1709/10, St. James', *Murray*, iv, pp. 674–5; *ibid.*, iv, pp.675–6,

On January 10th (O.S.) the ministers received yet more disquieting news. To their 'great concern' they learnt of Heinsius' consent to *pourparlers*

for settling an Expedient in relation to the 37th Article of the Preliminary Treaty, in case the French King will give authentick assurances of signing all the other Articles.

'It is to be feared', Boyle exclaimed in a letter to Townshend,

that the most solemn Declarations of the States will be but little depended upon for the future, since they are so lyable to change without any visible reason for that alteration.

Three days later, however, on January 13th, Cardonnel's letter to the Judge-Advocate Watkins gave evidence of a very different, and undoubtedly much more typical, reaction to the news, which had, he wrote,

given a general notion about the town of a sudden [peace] and puts us in great expectation of the next letters. I wish they may confirm the good news, for we want it here as much as anywhere else.

One of the 'next letters' to arrive was a report from Townshend that the evident and widespread desire for an immediate peace amongst the Dutch had much 'disheartened' the most 'zealous' people there.[1]

Four days earlier Townshend had sent word of yet another cause of alarm. Through the agency of Petkum, Torcy had sent to the Regents of Amsterdam copies of two letters written by Charles III's minister Moles, one to the Emperor and one to Marlborough, both making bitter complaints of Stanhope's continued importunities concerning the island of Minorca. As soon as Marlborough received the news he wrote to Heinsius and Sinzendorf assuring them that Stanhope had obviously not yet heard of the declaration that Townshend had made on this subject at The Hague, but in his letter to Townshend himself he showed that he was somewhat annoyed by Dutch suspicions:

I shou'd think the Queen's behaviour during the whole course of this Warr, without the least regarde to her own interest, shou'd be sufficient to justifye her Maty from any aspersion of this kind, especially with all those who have their own interest so much att heart.

Marlborough to Grumbkow, 6 Jan. 1709/10, St. James'; Boyle to Dayrolle (copy), 7 Feb. 1709/10, Whitehall, F.E.B. Holl. 74; Cardonnel to Watkins, 7 Feb. 1709/10, Whitehall, *Thibaudeau*, 2nd ser., ii, p. 81; *Geikie*, pp. 169–71.
[1] Boyle to Townshend, 10 Jan. 1709/10, Whitehall, *B.D.I. France*, pp. 17–18; Marlborough to Eugene, 10 Jan. 1709/10, St. James', *Murray*, iv, p. 678; Cardonnel to Watkins, 13 Jan. 1709/10, Whitehall, *Thibaudeau*, 2nd ser., ii, p. 80; Townshend to Boyle, 28 Jan. 1710, Hague, S.P. Holl. 233; A. Legrelle, *La Diplomatie Française et la Succession d'Espagne*, iv (Paris, 1892), pp. 516–17.

Townshend was nevertheless instructed to repeat his assurances.[1]

At this anxious time, when, in addition to their other cares, they had to contend with the more and more open hostility of the queen, the ministers learned that Buys, on whose inauspicious 'forwardness at this juncture' Marlborough had already remarked, had declared for the abandonment of the May preliminaries and an immediate peace. Boyle gave full vent to the indignation of the Junto, and expressed great concern at Townshend's report, in a letter of February 11th (N.S.), that, although the States had decided to stand by the preliminaries, yet the extreme lowness of public credit in every province except Holland was rapidly destroying all zeal for the war. Cardonnel's reactions to these developments have great interest. Himself now a member of the government, a few weeks in England had evidently sufficed to convince him that the disposition of the Junto was no longer that of his fellow-countrymen. In letter after letter to Watkins he reiterated the need for peace. When he heard of Buys' declaration he wrote:

This makes us impatient for the next letters; our Affaires here require a Peace as much as they do on your side; I should be glad to yeild something rather than prolong the warr.[2]

Like L'Hermitage, Cardonnel felt that the States' decision to support the preliminaries was 'generally approv'd of here'; but, when the news came on February 14th that the States had sent passports for French plenipotentiaries to treat on the basis originally agreed to by Heinsius, his feelings were very different from those of the Junto, who gave a most reluctant acquiescence to these proceedings, and instructed Townshend to 'be very watchful while the French Ministers are among you that no Conferences be held but in your presence'. Cardonnel, on the other hand, wrote:

pray God they [French Plenipotentiaries] may never return till we have a good Peace, tho' it should not be to the satisfaction of everybody.

The Junto was genuinely alarmed; although it was impossible for Townshend to attend the conferences if the embarrassing presence of Austrian and Prussian representatives was to be avoided, yet it

[1] Marlborough to Sinzendorf, 20 Jan. 1709/10, Windsor, *Murray*, iv, pp. 679–80; Marlborough to Heinsius, 20 Jan. 1709/10, Windsor, *van 't Hoff*, pp. 480–1; Marlborough to (Townshend), 20 Jan. 1709/10, Windsor, Add. Ms. 41178; Boyle to Townshend (copy), 20 Jan. 1709/10, F.E.B. Holl. 77; *C.W.* 113, vi, p. 8; Williams, *op.cit.*, p. 84.

[2] Marlborough to (Townshend), 20 Jan. 1709/10, Windsor, Add. Ms. 41178; Boyle to Townshend (copies), 31 Jan. and 7 Feb. 1709/10, Whitehall, F.E.B. Holl. 77; Cardonnel to Watkins, 31 Jan. 1709/10, Whitehall, *Thibaudeau*, 2nd ser., ii, p. 81; Townshend to Boyle, 11 Feb. 1710, Hague, S.P. Holl. 233.

held out on this point for a fortnight before giving way, and meanwhile
Parliament submitted an address asking the queen to send Marlborough
back to The Hague immediately. Even the tactful L'Hermitage
hinted to his masters that this address was the result of a certain
dissatisfaction with recent developments, and indeed the Junto
could hardly be expected to be soothed by such reports as that written
by Dayrolle on February 21st (N.S.):

Such, I have observed, is the nature of people here, that upon the least appearance of fair dealing from that part [France] They almost forget they have been
cheated and deceived for these 40 or 50 years, as tis to be feared they will be on
this occasion.[1]

Marlborough was at The Hague by the beginning of March (N.S.).
He realised immediately that, although the allied representatives
Buys and van der Dussen were being 'very just in insisting upon the
entire monarchy' in their meetings with the French at Geertruidenberg,
the inclination of the States and the Dutch as a whole was for 'putting
an end to the war at once, by giving the Duke of Anjou a *partage*'.
Well into April his letters to Godolphin repeat this theme. 'Every man
in this State', he declared, was for giving Sicily to Philip if that would
satisfy France, and most would add Sardinia as well. The plan, once
advocated by Marlborough and now put forward by the Imperialists,
of a separate war with Spain after a peace with France, now made
no appeal to them; what they wanted was a complete and general
peace, which, Marlborough admitted, 'in my opinion is as absolutely
necessary for the Queens service as for these people'. He urged Godolphin that the Parliament should remain in session to consider the
terms that the conference might produce, 'for shou'd it be refus'd or
grant'd without the Knowledge of Parl: I fear it might cause very great
uneasiness'. On the other hand, although he and Townshend reported
on March 25th that 'we perceive here every day a greater uneasiness
under the burthen of the Warr, and a more general inclination to
Peace, by giving some Partage to the Duke d'Anjou', yet he also
observed increasing suspicions of French sincerity among the Dutch
leaders, which gave him reason to hope that the States would enter
vigorously into the impending campaign. By April 11th Dayrolle,
too, was convinced that it was only 'pour satisfaire les foibles de ce

[1] Cardonnel to Watkins, 7, 10 and 14 Feb. 1709/10, Whitehall, *Thibaudeau*, 2nd ser., ii,
pp. 81–2; L'Hermitage to States-General (transcripts), 7/18 and 17/28 Feb. 1709/10, London,
Add. Ms. 17677 DDD; Dayrolle to Boyle, 21 Feb. 1710, Hague, S.P. Holl. 234; Boyle to
Townshend (copies), 14 and 17 Feb. 1709/10, Whitehall, F.E.B. Holl. 77; *ibid.*, Boyle to
Marlborough and Townshend (copy), 28 Feb. 1709/10, Whitehall; *Cobbett*, vi, cols. 893–4.

pays' that the French ministers were being allowed to remain at Geertruidenberg.[1]

To Godolphin this last was welcome. Although he believed that it would be politic to allow the Dutch statesmen to 'please their People' by continuing the negotiations, he was certain that by merely taking the field the allies would 'oblige France to give better terms than they have as yet proposed'. To the plan of a separate peace with France he opposed the argument that he had already used in 1709 when Marlborough himself had advocated this course, namely that in the subsequent war in Spain little could be expected from the Emperor 'or even from the States, who have all along shown themselves much less concerned for the recovery of Spain than we are'. While Godolphin and the Junto thus insisted that the Dutch should honour their side of the Barrier Treaty bargain by trying the fortunes of war once more, a junior member of the government wrote in words which, like those of Cardonnel two months before, were a more accurate reflection of English opinion:

I must observe to you that wee are almost as much desirous of the Peace as the Dutch for without Peace I apprehend wee shall find ourselves very much plunged in our Mony affairs....[2]

3

While Marlborough sent his reports from The Hague the impeachment of Dr. Sacheverell before the House of Lords pursued its course. This reverend gentleman, in a sermon preached at St. Paul's Cathedral on November 5th, 1709, had attacked the doctrines of the Glorious Revolution and vilified the Lord Treasurer (or so, at least, Godolphin thought). For both the Junto and Godolphin his trial was an attempt to impress the queen with their strength and indispensability; and as such it was a disastrous failure. On March 19th (N.S.), nine days after it had begun, Marlborough wrote to Robert Walpole that 'the tumult and disorders it had occasioned make a great noise here, even to the prejudice of the public'. However great the 'noise' at The Hague, it

---

[1] Marlborough to Godolphin, 1, 11, 12 and 19 March, 5 and 13 April 1710, Hague, *Churchill*, iv, pp. 235–9; Marlborough and Townshend to Boyle, 12 and 25 March 1710, Hague, S.P. Holl. 235; Marlborough to King of Prussia, 14 and 24 March 1710, Hague, *Murray*, iv, pp. 695, 701; Marlborough to Godolphin, 18 and 28 March 1710, Hague, *Coxe*, iii, pp. 36–7; Marlborough to Stair, 22 March 1710, Hague, *Murray*, iv, pp. 609–700; Dayrolle to Raby, 11 April 1710, Hague, Add. Ms. 31131.

[2] Godolphin to Marlborough (transcripts), 23 March 1709/10 and 4 April 1710 (O.S.), Add. Ms. 34518; J. Taylor to Watkins, 4 April 1710, Whitehall, Add. Ms. 38852; Godolphin to Sarah, 8 April 1710, Newmarket, *P.C.D.M.*, i, pp. 300–1.

was as nothing to the 'tumult and disorder' in London, where the prosecution of the incautious doctor had finally, as has been well said, burst the 'lowering cloud of discontent'.

A passage from a letter written to Marlborough by Godolphin on March 5th describes the way in which the trial of Sacheverell was being made the pretext for the expression of pent-up dissatisfaction with the ministry:

I certainly wish it had never begun; for it has occasioned a very great ferment, and given opportunity to a great many people to be impertinent, who always had the intention, but wanted the opportunity of showing it.

Among the 'impertinences' themselves we find evidence that the connected dislikes of the war and of the Dutch were not slow to take advantage of an opportunity, so long denied them by fear and uncertainty, for expression. Verses addressed to the queen during the trial advised her to

> . . . . slip no time, the jest is gone too farr,
> Take a good heart and let them see you dare
> Declare yourself ane enemy to such
> As would destroy the Monarchy and Church
> And ruin Britain, to make up the Dutch.

In support of Sacheverell was published *An Auction of State Pictures*, an uncomplimentary gallery of 'Low-Church Faces'. In this a 'portrait' of Portland was seized on as an opportunity to insult both the late Earl (with remarks about his mean extraction and his conduct of the Peace of Ryswick) and his native country; the 'auctioneer' was made to cry:

What do you think of this, put it in at what you will? Will no Body speak; set it by Boy, for I see they don't relish *Dutch* ware.

The author of *A Speech Without Doors* tried to stem the tide; he inquired of Sacheverell whether his advocacy of non-resistance meant that he believed that the king of Spain was still the lawful sovereign of the Dutch, and if it did not seem that 'Almighty God, by his peculiar Providence to this People', had 'justify'd their Conduct' in resisting their rulers. A somewhat later pamphlet sought to show up Sacheverell by contrasting Dutch and French reactions to the trial; and with ill-concealed anxiety advised its readers that he who could 'Spue out Invectives' against 'the late Happy Revolution', and whose talent was 'to Damn the Dutch', was 'one of the *Pretender's* forlorn Hopes'.[1]

[1] Godolphin to Marlborough, 5 March 1709/10 (O.S.), *Coxe* iii, p. 25; Marlborough to R.

The trial reached its end – so unsatisfactory for the ministry – on March 23rd (O.S.), with the imposition of a purely nominal punishment upon Sacheverell; but the ferment continued. The days of the Godolphin ministry were numbered now that the queen was assured of popular support. Meanwhile Marlborough was preparing to take the field. He assured Godolphin that after the campaign had been under way about a month, they would be able to see clearly whether the Dutch – or the French – really intended to go on with the war. Before this critical period was up, however, he had passed the lines of La Bassée, and hoped that this would keep the Dutch firm. At the same time he assured the Austrian Wratislaw that in England as well as the Republic people were beginning to be 'extrêmement las de la guerre'. Although at the beginning of the siege of Douai Cadogan was very pleased with the 'Inclinations of the Deputys of the States att the Army, to furnish and provide everything wanting', yet a month later, on June 2nd, when the siege was still going on, Marlborough warned Godolphin that the Dutch were 'so alarmed by our divisions in England' that in the event of an unsuccessful battle 'they would consent to whatever peace France should insist on'.[1]

Well might the Dutch take alarm at the 'divisions in England', which were now plain for all to see. On April 14th, eight days after her last meeting with the Duchess of Marlborough, queen Anne had taken her first overt step to rid herself of the Junto by appointing Harley's new ally, Shrewsbury, as Lord Chamberlain. The unconsulted Godolphin protested loudly, and part of the letter in which he did so is especially interesting because it revealed what was to be the ministry's first line of defence against the queen's disfavour. The new appointment, wrote the Treasurer, might well oblige the entire ministry to resign,

And I leave your Majesty to judge, what effect this entire change of your Ministers will have among your Allies abroad, and how well this War is like to be carried on, in their Opinion, by those who have all along opposed and obstructed it, and who will like any Peace the better, the more it leaves *France* at Liberty, to take their time of imposing the *Pretender* upon this Country.

These Considerations must certainly make Holland run immediately into a separate peace with France . . . .

Walpole, 19 March 1710, Hague, *Murray*, iv, pp. 696–7; *C.W.* 8, pp. 12–13; *C.W.* 56, pp. 7–8; *C.W.* 5, pp. 23–4, 47; Miller, *op.cit.*, p. 23; *Lockhart Papers*, p. 508.

[1] Marlborough to Godolphin, 13 April 1710, Hague, *Churchill*, iv, p. 238; Same to same, 20 April 1710, Tournai, *P.C.D.M.*, ii, pp. 420–1; Marlborough to Wratislaw, 3 May 1710, Camp before Douai, *Murray*, v, pp. 15–16; Cadogan to (Sunderland), 5 May 1710, Camp before Douai, S.P. Flanders 59; Marlborough to Godolphin, 2 June 1710 (N.S.), *Coxe*, iii, p. 49.

This argument must have seemed to the ministry to pierce the one chink in the queen's armour of hostility, for, for all her aversion from Whiggery, she had never shared the High Tories' distaste for the war. Accordingly it laboured hard to press this point home. Godolphin suggested to Marlborough that he should write to Shrewsbury describing the bad effect that the rumours of Sunderland's impending dismissal and a subsequent dissolution of Parliament were having on the Dutch, and this the Duke accordingly did on June 19th (N.S.). Somers urged Townshend to persuade Heinsius to write a similar letter to the Austrian envoy in London, Gallas. They did not yet fully realise that the queen, like many others of her subjects who did not approve the Tackers' views of the war, was determined to put an end to the seeming Whig policy of prolonging the war in the interest of the Allies, especially the Dutch.[1]

Though they were urged from political motives, the apprehensions of the ministers were in fact largely genuine. 'The impatience of the States to conclude & sign the peace', as Boyle described it, was making them fear that they would get little Dutch support in pressing any 'further demands' (to Newfoundland and Hudson's Bay, for example) over and above those included in the preliminaries. Both Somers and the Lord Steward Devonshire privately expressed such fears to their colleagues, and these receive some confirmation from a letter sent to Harley from the siege of Douai by Orrery, who, though he served under Marlborough, was no friend of his. He hoped that there was 'some prospect of peace' since the size of the French army made the Dutch disinclined to venture a battle for fear of gaining another crippling victory like Malplaquet. None the less, there was some exaggeration employed in the ministry's warnings. Buys and van der Dussen knew the part that their allies expected them to play at Geertruidenberg and they played it well. To so well-informed and so bellicose an observer as Hare they seemed still 'as averse ... as anybody can wish them to be' to anything but a general peace with France *and* Spain.

While the fate of the Godolphin ministry hung in the balance, at Geertruidenberg the couriers from Versailles came and went. On July 22nd (N.S.) Dayrolle reported that the Dutch leaders were now completely disillusioned about the sincerity of the French, even though 'they are very fond here of the name of peace'. One week later

---

[1] Godolphin to Anne, 15 April 1710, Newmarket, *C.W.* 26, pp. 293–4; Godolphin to Marlborough, 29 May 1710 (O.S.), *Coxe*, iii, pp. 78–9; *ibid.*, iii, p. 86, R. Walpole to Marlborough, 6 June 1710, Whitehall; *ibid.*, iii, pp. 81–2, Marlborough to Shrewsbury, 19 June 1710 (N.S.).

the French plenipotentiaries, unable to make the Dutch retreat from the demand that Louis should expel his grandson from Spain, acted on instructions from their court and left Geertruidenberg for Paris. With their departure the negotiations were at an end. The Dutch had duly paid another instalment towards the price of the illusory benefits of the Barrier Treaty.[1]

4

On June 14th (O.S.) Sunderland received his long-awaited dismissal, and the ministry was thrown into confusion. The queen, made wise by the warnings that the Junto themselves had given her, ordered Boyle on June 16th to instruct Townshend to tell Heinsius that this step was not intended to discredit Marlborough, nor did she intend any further changes. Godolphin rashly sought to improve the occasion. Not only did he join with his colleagues in urging Marlborough not to throw up his command, but he suggested to the Duke that the best use that could be made of the queen's actions would be

for Heinsius and the States to return an answer by Vryberg, that they are very much concerned for what has happened to Sunderland, who was known to be so great a friend to them and to the common cause; that they are very glad to hear the Queen has no intention to make any other changes; but if there be the least thought of parting with the Parliament, as is very industriously spread in that country by the friends of France, it will be utterly impossible to hinder these people from running into peace immediately, just as France pleases, leaving England and the Queen to shift for themselves, without any security against the pretensions of the Pretender.

He advised the Duke, moreover, to write once more to Shrewsbury informing him that if Parliament were dissolved the allies would make their peace with France without waiting to try the temper of the new Parliament. He still hoped that this argument would place Harley and his friends, who, as he well knew, had as their prime object the making of an advantageous peace, in something of a dilemma.

As Townshend reported to Boyle on July 18th (N.S.), the 'consternation for feare ye Parliament should be dissolved' was very great at The Hague, and Godolphin's advice was in fact superfluous. As Halifax put it, the States 'took a rise' from the queen's assurances to them 'to

[1] Boyle to Townshend (copy), 30 May 1710, Whitehall, F.E.B. Holl. 77; Somers to Marlborough, 6 June 1710 (O.S.), *Trevelyan*, iii, pp. 326–7; (Orrery) to (Harley), 21 June 1710, Camp near Douai, *H.M.C. XV pt. iv*, pp. 544–5; Devonshire to Newcastle, 11 June 1710 (O.S.), *H.M.C. XIII pt. ii*, pp. 210–11; Hare to G. Naylor, 26 June 1710, Le Brayle, *H.M.C. XIV pt. ix*, pp. 230–1; Dayrolle to Boyle, 22 July 1710, Hague, S.P. Holl. 234; A. Legrelle, *op.cit.*, iv, pp. 572–3.

return thanks to the Queen for communicating that agreeable news, and to desire her Majesty not to dissolve Parliament which had showed so much zeal for her Majesty and the common cause'. When this representation was made by Vrijbergen on June 30th its effect was quite different from what the Treasurer had intended. He had reckoned without the growing hostility to the Dutch which was waiting only for the chance to express itself. This was that chance; though the queen, well advised by Shrewsbury and the self-important Somerset, contented herself with ordering Townshend to reprimand the States 'in the civilest and softest manner' for presuming to meddle with the internal affairs of her kingdom.[1]

It needed little prescience to foretell, like Brydges, that the Dutch Memorial would 'exaspirate to the utmost those whom Her Majesty has hearkened to of late'. Anne's reply to Vrijbergen's message was not made public, but much delight was occasioned by the rumour that she had written thus:

I am surpriz'd, a matter of this kind should come from the *States* .... It is the greatest Insult that ever was offer'd to the Crown of *England*. However, it shall not lessen my Esteem of my Allies, nor alter my Resolution in my own Affairs.

Some writers, like Edward Ward, resorted to the time-honoured trick of pretending that the message was not genuine, but

.... A Whiggish Sham,
Contriv'd on this side Amsterdam ....,

and thus were able to rail against 'the proud *Hogen State*' and 'Whiggish Lies' at one and the same time. To all this '*Traducing* and *insulting* our *best* Friends', as one Whig pamphlet called it, the Whigs had no effective reply, though they could, and did, point out that the queen had already provided precedents for what the Dutch had done in her dealings with her allies. They could, in *Seldom Comes a Better*, a pamphlet which used the allegory of a 'lawsuit' for the war long before the better-known *Law Is A Bottomless Pit*, advance more positive arguments; for example, that 'Partners in the same Cause have a right of offering Advice, for prevention of a Common Ruin', or again, that the Dutch

well knew, that the *expecting Gentlemen* were not their friends formerly; and there can be no reason given, why they who were not *then* their Friends shou'd be so *now*.

---

[1] Boyle to Townshend (copies), 16 June and 4 July 1710, Whitehall, F.E.B. Holl. 77; Godolphin to Marlborough, 16 June 1710 (O.S.), *P.C.D.M.*, ii, pp. 444–6; Marlborough to Godolphin, 5 July 1710 (N.S.), *Coxe*, iii, pp. 94–5; *ibid.*, iii, pp. 99–100, 109, Godolphin to Marlborough, n.d. and 3 July 1710 (O.S.); Townshend to (Boyle), 18 July 1710, Hague, S.P. Holl. 235; Halifax to Newcastle, 8 July 1710 (O.S.), *H.M.C. XIII pt. ii*, pp. 211–12.

.... Their being unacceptable to their Neighbours ought to be a very cogent Motive to them, not to meddle *yet*, if they have any thing in view besides *meer Profit*.

All this reasoning, however, was powerless to stem the flood of feeling unleashed by the fancied insult. More than one Tory author fell on the query propounded by Halifax in his anonymous *Seasonable Queries concerning a New Parliament*. In this pamphlet, opposing the dissolution of Parliament, the Whig leader had asked, *inter alia*,

Whether any thing could be more proper and seasonable than the late Memorial from the States, in which they represented in a most decent and affectionate manner the absolute necessity of continuing the present Parliament?

The reply which the High Churchman Atterbury made to this showed that the High Tories no longer felt any need to pay more than the smallest lip-service to the idea of Anglo-Dutch solidarity:

I have all due Regard for the States of Holland, and their great Wisdom, but do believe, it is plain, that such a Memorial was without any Precedent, and occasion'd thro' the means of *Joab*, and *Vulp*; and by the Inadvertency of some there in Authority, who brought this matter to pass, which upon Maturer Deliberation. such a Wise People had never intermeddled in: For had Her Majesty ever once failed to furnish timely Her *Quota* of Money, Men, and Ships? and does She not generously consent, to enable them the better to continue the War, that they shall Trade with *France*, when Her Subjects wants that Benefit? and what is it to the *Dutch*, I humbly speak it, when Her Majesty dissolves this Parliament or makes Choice of a New Ministry, provided She performs Her Articles of the Grand Alliance, which they have not the least Reason to doubt .... I may modestly add, that if We had taken upon Us to advise the States to make a Statholder, or Change their great Ministers of State, they might have taken it ill to intermeddle in their Affairs; tho' in the Memory of Man, and long before, we had a Seat and Voice amongst them, to their perpetual benefit, and their interest is still, and ever must be inseparable from Ours.

Another Tory plagiarised *The Character of a Trimmer* in asserting that the actions of 'the Faction' showed that

rather than lose their darling Power here, they will basely truckle to a Foreign Power to support them in it, sacrifice the Honour of their Native Country to one which owes all its Greatness and Prosperity to this; and when *England* might ride Admiral at the Head of the Confederates, will be content to have her look like the Kitchen Yatch to the High and Mighty States, rather than submit to the Will and Pleasure of their lawful Mistress; and whether this be a proper Figure for our Nation to make in the Map of Christendom, let any moderate Man judge.

The Memorial was indeed a godsend to the enemies of the ministry. It aroused much popular feeling against both the ministers and the Dutch, it placed a powerful weapon in the hands of Tory propagandists, and, in addition to all this, it undoubtedly strengthened the determination of the queen to rid herself of her masterful 'servants'. As a correspondent explained in a letter to the future George II at the beginning of September, the memorial and the similar letter from the Emperor,

dont l'Origine, et la Source ont esté concerté ici, par la Caballe, et envoyé hors du Royaume, pour y rentrer au sujet de nos Changemens dans le Ministère, ont donné des raisons assez fortes à S. M. d'en être très fâché, et avec beaucoup de justice.[1]

In the anxious weeks that followed Sunderland's dismissal the Whig journalists showed much more spirit than the Junto. They were joined in their vain fight by two pamphleteers who would one day stand as the epitome of eighteenth-century Whiggery in Church and State. In his *Four Letters to a Friend in North Britain* Robert Walpole compared the present clamour for a dissolution to that after the death of Charles II of Spain, and recalled that the coolness of the resulting Parliament towards the Dutch had forced us to recognise Philip V. Benjamin Hoadly – 'limping Ben' – animadverted on the countless 'loyal' addresses that had been sent to the queen since the beginning of the Sacheverell affair. One point he seized on was the use of the word 'Republican' by the addressers as a term of abuse. 'What', he asked,

if this great cry against *Republican* Principles should be design'd only as a Singular Respect to our *Chief Allies*, at this Critical Juncture, and when the strictest Union between them and this Nation is of such Importance? or as the highest Token of Gratitude to that Republick which help'd to save Us, when We were devoted to Destruction .... But seriously, whatever we might judge from our Armies abroad, One would think, in truth, by some late *Addresses* at home, that we were now fighting against the *States of Holland*, and not the *Monarch* of *France*. I need say no more.

Thus the noise of battle rolled throughout the summer of 1710 in the pamphlets, the periodicals, and the news-sheets. The Whigs were well to the fore – indeed, their vociferousness was out of all proportion to their following – but with the impending appearance of the *Examiner* the journalistic balance of power would begin to correspond more closely to the state of feeling in the country.[2]

5

On August 7th Townshend, in the queen's name, publicly praised

---

[1] Brydges to Stair, 3 July 1710 (O.S.), *Hunt. Lib. Quart.*, iii (1939–40), pp. 230–2; *Moderator*, 20, 28 July 1710; Dr. Hutton to Electoral Prince of Hanover (copy), 5 Sept. 1710, London, Stowe Ms. 241; *Annals*, ix, pp. 232–3; *C.W.* 197, cantos xiii and xv; *C.W.* 152, p. 17; *C.W.* 163, pp. 6, 13–14; *C.W.* 131, pp. 144–7; *C.W.* 7, pp. 4–5.

[2] *C.W.* 195, pp. 18–19; *C.W.* 103, pp. 18–19.

the conduct of the Dutch throughout the Geertruidenberg negotiation; but, as Boyer wrote in the following year, 'notwithstanding this publick Declaration .... many Persons in England entertain'd Jealousies, of the Dutch being sole Managers of the late negotiation ....'. Once more the Dutch were blamed for the failure to obtain peace; and now these 'jealousies' were sharpened by the very real suspicion, fostered by his ill-timed request in October 1709 to be made Captain-General for life, that Marlborough was planning, perhaps with Dutch aid, to become a second Cromwell. On August 11th (O.S.) Viscount Weymouth wrote to the poet-diplomat Prior of 'Messieurs de Buyse and Vanderdussen, the now arbiters of peace and war'; and four days before this an anonymous correspondent sent to the one-time under-Secretary of State Ellis a summary of the state of the peace and the war almost as illegible as it is interesting:

No Peace without restitution of the Spanish monarchy to the House of Austria was the voice of the Parliament of England, but that this should be done by the French King singly, seems to be a new turn [?] advanced in the proposition by the Dch. Dpts at St. Gbg under which lyes the fallacy. But when men in influence somewhere head [?] their chief aims on accomodating the Interests of a Party, and men employed otherwise are contented in concert to humour such Party Interests; whilst the Armyes draw their subsistence from a certain Country for the further advantage of their Trade. & consumption of their product; whilst all the Towns that are taken are given to their possession for their reimbursement hereafter before [being] restored; and whilst all the contributions gained from the Enemy ruan only into their Canals in abatement of their present charge, tho' we Country folk have payd taxes cheerfully in order to a lasting peace, yet most of us feare we may be in misericordia if we neglect a favourable opportunity for it, to continue the warr in such unequall terms with our neighbours ....

This letter, despite confused expression and inadequate punctuation, offers an almost unique picture of English feeling, both about the failure to obtain peace and about the conduct of the war, in the summer of 1710. It would be very many years before Englishmen could absolve the Dutch of prime responsibility for prolonging the war in 1710. Almost ninety years later Coxe was seriously to assert that the Godolphin ministry itself had tried 'to lower the demands of the Dutch' at Geertruidenberg.[1]

The shadow of dismissal was now looming over Godolphin himself, but the Treasurer had evolved a plan which he thought might eventually thwart Harley's machinations. It depended for its success upon

[1] Townshend to States-General, 7 Aug. 1710, Hague, C.W. 113, vi, pp. 76–7;? to Ellis, 7 Aug. 1710 (O.S.), Add. Ms. 28916; Weymouth to Prior, 11 Aug. 1710, Longleat, H.M.C. Bath III, p. 439; Annals, ix, pp. 41–2; Coxe: Walpole, i, p. 28.

numerous factors, not the least of which was the devotion of the States
and Emperor to Marlborough, of which at this time the Duke himself
felt confident. When the queen announced her intention of dissolving
Parliament, as Godolphin was certain she would, he, Somers, Wharton,
and Devonshire would retire *en bloc*; but Marlborough, on the other
hand, would stay at his post and improve the occasion by enlarging
on the 'ill consequences of these measures with the allies'. Then, if a
'good' parliament ensued ('of which', Godolphin wrote, 'I have pretty
good hopes') Marlborough would be in a commanding position. The
great thing was for Marlborough to keep the States and the Emperor
true to the Alliance whatever happened in England in the next few
months. Even after his dismissal, on August 8th, Godolphin worked on
Vrijbergen and his fellow envoys to ensure this, and from The Hague
Horatio Walpole sent encouraging reports of the disposition of the
Dutch. 'I believe', he wrote to his brother Robert on August 18th (N.S.),

this people can be kept very steady to the honest interest of England, and to
the common cause, until they see what the commons of Great Britain are like to
doe.

Godolphin's plan was remarkable for two things: amazing optimism,
together with a very shrewd reading of Harley's underlying intentions
and future programme. Godolphin had known Harley too well to find
him inscrutable. He saw clearly that, in any new Parliament, 'the main
point to be considered will be, whether the allies must be supported or
deserted'. The more vigorous and loyal the allies then appeared, he
thought, the more difficult would be the task of those of the latter
opinion, and thus 'the malicious insinuations of Mr. Harley &c.' would
be rendered 'still more absurd and malicious; their main point being',
as he wrote to Marlborough, 'to convince parliament that you never
was in earnest to conclude the war'.[1]

Had Englishmen been able to observe the efforts of the doomed
ministry, at Marlborough's instigation, to induce the States and the
Emperor to increase their efforts in Spain, they might have paid less
heed to these 'malicious insinuations'. Instead, as Harley and his
friends gained office one by one in place of the ousted Whigs, they
read the *Examiner*. This weekly sheet, the first number of which
appeared on August 3rd, was to be of great importance both in the
stating and the shaping of opinion. As Swift was later to explain,

---

[1] Marlborough to Godolphin, 2 Aug. 1710 (N.S.), *Coxe*, iii, pp. 101–2; *ibid.*, iii, pp. 120–1,
125–6, 167, Godolphin to Marlborough, 31 July, 9 and 20 Aug. 1710 (O.S.); H. Walpole to
R. Walpole, 18 Aug. 1710, Hague, *Coxe: Walpole*, ii, 1, pp. 32–4.

Upon the rise of this ministry, the principal persons in power thought it necessary, that some weekly paper should be published, with just reflections upon former proceedings, and defending the present measures of her Majesty.

Possibly financed by Harley, it was certainly directed by St. John, who was able, through its columns, 'to make his private opinions appear to be established Tory doctrines'.

One of the first tasks that the new periodical set itself was the systematic and venomous annihilation of the arguments contained in the so-called *Letter from Monsieur Pettcum to Monsieur Buys*. This pamphlet, the importance of which is amply proved by the space that the *Examiner* thought necessary to devote to it, was the expression *par excellence* of the Whig argument that the intrigues of Harley and his friends were the reason why the French had continued the war, and that this fact by itself justified the Memorial which the Dutch had presented after Sunderland's dismissal. The Memorial itself the *Examiner*, in reply, characterised as one of 'the most indecent steps that ever were taken towards the *Crown of* England, by any of its *Allies*'. In the issue of August 24th there appeared a 'letter' which set out to 'prove', in an ironic vein, that the Memorial was too shameful even for the Dutch to have written. The irony was not sustained throughout – there are some scarcely veiled jibes at Dutch greed, for example – but it is unmistakable in passages such as the following:

Some there are who would divide us, who artfully insinuate, whilst they pretend that there has been deliver'd a *Memorial* .... That there are Ministers who are Partial to the *Dutch*, and care not how *Britain* is burthen'd, so they find their Profit in easing *Holland*.

For the first time for five years, the Tories were daring to make capital out of anti-Dutch feeling; once more such sarcastic appellations as 'our great Friends the *D--ch*' were in use.[1]

Harley, meanwhile, now Chancellor of the Exchequer, was not neglecting to ascertain Dutch reactions to the 'ministerial revolution'. The reports that he received at the beginning of September from Drummond, the Amsterdam merchant who now became his unofficial agent in Holland, and Rivers, *en route* for Hanover, were encouraging. He summed them up later, on October 30th, in his 'Plan of Administration'. Good ministers abroad, he noted, were essential for the successful conduct of foreign affairs, and

---

[1] Marlborough to Boyle, 4 Aug. 1710, Viler Brulin, *Murray*, v, pp. 38–40; Boyle to Townshend (copies), 1 and 18 Aug., 5 Sept. 1710, Whitehall, F.E.B. Holl. 77; *Examiner*, i, 3 and 4, 17 and 24 Aug. 1710; *Moderator*, 28, 25 Aug. 1710; *C.W.* 177, p. 123; *C.W.* 122, pp. 48–9, 52; Hanson, *op.cit.*, pp. 96–7; Stevens, *op.cit.*, pp. 35–6, 71.

The Hague is the centre of business and intelligence, and is first to be taken care of.

The vigour of the Queen's proceedings, hath recovered the respect only due to her Majesty; and those in Holland, who had their eyes elsewhere, begin to turn them to her Majesty. It is necessary that this should be cultivated by an able Minister there.

As Rivers had told him, either Townshend should be won over, 'he being very well liked there', or he should be replaced by another who 'may satisfy them that the late change of our Ministry will not be in any way prejudicial to the common cause'. By far the most important part of Harley's plan, however, concerned the relation between policy towards the Allies and opinion in England:

.... the most popular thing to England, is, to press all the allies to keep exactly to what they have agreed to do in their treaties; the partiality to them has been much complained of, and the pressing, roundly, their exact performance is the likeliest way to obtain peace.[1]

With his characteristic talent for 'management', Harley had hit upon a policy which would hold his ill-assorted followers together. The 'moderates' would join wholeheartedly in pressing the allies 'roundly', in the belief that this would lead to more vigorous prosecution of the war, and a speedy and triumphant peace. The extremists, too, would support this policy in the hope that the non-compliance of the allies with these demands would so anger British opinion that the queen would be able to desert them, a situation in which their well-known chauvinist tendencies would bring them to the fore. It was the policy that Godolphin had foreseen in August; but at the end of October Harley knew what Godolphin had not been able to know, that in executing it he was sure of popular support, provided that he acted with reasonable caution. This was the lesson of the election of October 1710.

6

With the dissolution of Parliament on September 30 (preceded on September 23rd by the resignation of Cowper, the last senior Whig minister remaining in office) the fight for the mastery of the Commons was on. Although 'The Church in Danger!' was still the Tories' main cry, there was none the less more discussion of foreign affairs at this election than at any previous one of the reign. This is doubly significant

---

[1] (Drummond) to (Harley), 2 Sept. 1710, Amsterdam, *H.M.C. XV pt. iv*, pp. 572–3; Dr. W. Stratford to E. Harley, 28 Aug. 1710, Oxford, *H.M.C. Portland VII*, p. 15; Rivers to (Harley), 12 Sept. 1710, Hague, *H.M.C. XV pt. iv*, pp. 580–1; 'Mr. Harley's Plan of Administration', 30 Oct. 1710, *Hardwicke S.P.*, ii, pp. 485–8.

because then, as now, it was unusual for foreign policy to loom large in the minds of English electors. For the most part the line that the Tories took towards the war and the Dutch in their election campaign was a moderate, 'Harleian' one. Gentle reproaches were once more made concerning the Memorial, gentle hints were given that all collusion with the Whigs must cease; and at the same time self-consciously generous assurances were given of the goodwill of the new ministry towards the Republic. The Memorial, though condemned, was ascribed rather to the machinations of the Junto than to a deliberate intention of insulting the queen, and the firmness of the new ministry to the war and to the Allies was proclaimed. The intention of these pamphlets is clear: to win the votes of all 'honest Whigs' and men of no party for a policy which would, it was said, combine the best of both Whig and Tory ideas. In this programme Defoe, who had returned to his old master Harley on the fall of Godolphin, had a special part to play. Known as a Whig, he could usefully, and probably with more sincerity than has sometimes been allowed, repudiate the arguments of the High Tories but at the same time suggest that Harley deserved the trust of all honest men. In *A Supplement to the Faults on Both Sides*, for example, he displayed his untarnished Whiggery by condemning the attitude of the Tories to the king and the Dutch in the previous reign, but at the same time commended Harley as a man above party considerations. It was an ingenious propaganda technique, and for the moment Defoe was probably the most influential writer on the Tory side. His later eclipse by Swift was a reflection of the decline of Harley's moderation in face of the opportunist extremism of St. John.

Even in the autumn of 1710 the voice of St. John could be heard. The *Examiner* was doing its part, advising the electors to choose those

who love their own Countrymen better than any *Foreigner* whatsoever; and would neither be enslav'd by the *French*, nor *bubbled* by any *other Nation* . . . . ;

or, again, ironically declaring that

those are the best *Friends* to their Country, who love a *Dutchman*, a *Palatine*, or even a *Frenchman*, better than a *Britain* . . . .

St. John himself, in his *Letter to the Examiner*, gave an almost unique pre-election indication of the views on the war of the ministerial 'right-wing'. In arguments that were to become highly familiar in the next two years, he vilified the old ministry for their conduct of the war. He attacked them both for prolonging the conflict – a good peace could have been made after Ramillies, he declared – and for making Flanders

the main theatre of war, and all this, he hinted, had been done in collusion with, and for the profit of, the Dutch. He also did not fail, of
course, to devote some indignant comment to the Dutch Memorial.
His arguments were echoed in Davenant's *Sir Thomas Double At Court*,
in which the Whigs were accused of having turned a blind eye to
Dutch failure to fulfil their obligations, particularly at sea, and of
having 'loaded us, to spare them'.[1]

This approach was not typical of Tory propaganda at this time. In a
sense it was a 'feeler', the response to which showed the Tories that, if
they failed to obtain a more vigorous war effort from the allies, they
could be confident of support in proceeding to more drastic measures.
This the Whigs realised, and they pounced upon St. John's pamphlet
in the vain hope that he had gone beyond what the electorate would
stomach. To this end Cowper produced *A Letter to Isaac Bickerstaff*
which contained a careful defence of the Allies from St. John's insinuations, and Addison, too, in the short-lived *Whig-Examiner*, drew attention to 'this Author's Aspersions of the *Dutch* and *Germans*'.

Another line of argument favoured by the Whigs was that a Tory
Parliament would bring in the Pretender, and that the Dutch, though
they were the 'mortal enemies' of the Jacobites, would hasten to make
a separate peace with France, and thus gratify their 'earnest wish for a
Peace', if they saw elected a House of Commons which would 'favour
France in the prosecution of the War . . . .'. All these arguments were
powerless, however, against the popular feeling that was evoked by
such election addresses as the following:

Your Poll is desired for the Four worthy Citizens undernam'd . . . . who are for
Cultivating a good Understanding with our Protestant Neighbours without
Complimenting away our *Commerce*, or inviting them to *intermeddle* in the Affairs of our Government; or to send over the *Scum* of their Countries, to make
ourselves, who already abound in Poor, yet Poorer . . . .

The result of the election was a victory by more than two to one for
those who were 'Firm to our Foreign Alliances, without suffering any
State or Power less Great and Perfect than our own, to Impose new
Laws upon us, or alter the Best and most Happy form of Government on Earth' over those who, according to the same source, were
endeavouring 'to bring in Foreign Models and Schemes of Government
upon us'.[2]

---

[1] *Examiner*, i, 9 and 10, 28 Sept. and 5 Oct. 1710; *C.W.* 98, pp. 36–7; *C.W.* 72, pp. 20–2;
C.W. 118, pp. 3–4; *C.W.* 57, pp. 30–31; *C.W.* 161, pp. 6–10, 15–16; *C.W.* 32, p. 71.

[2] *Whig-Examiner*, 2 and 4, 21 Sept. and 5 Oct. 1710; *Post-Boy*, 2404, 10 Oct. 1710; *C.W.* 28,
pp. 13–15; *C.W.* 61, pp. 13–14, 32; *C.W.* 187, p. 1.

CHAPTER IX

THE DOUBLE GAME OF THE OXFORD MINISTRY
⟨1710–11⟩

I

Ever since the battle of Ramillies there had been a fundamental difference of opinion between the Dutch and English leaders as to the desirability and practicability of peace. Partly, at least, in the interests of their own political survival, the Whigs had insisted on prolonging the war far beyond what the Dutch judged to be either wise or necessary. As the price of Dutch adherence to this policy they had made secret and far-reaching promises to the Republic in the shape of the Treaty of Succession and Barrier. The election of October 1710 radically altered this situation. The Whig domination of the Commons was ended, and at the helm there stood a ministry which had the overwhelming mass of public opinion behind it in its determination to have a speedy and advantageous peace. Just as the Whigs had found their advantage in enthusiasm for the war, so the support which Harley and his followers gained at the polls was largely an expression of acute war-weariness. For the maintenance of that support, as they saw it, peace was now essential.[1]

This end, they realised, could be achieved in one of two ways: by persuading their allies to strike a decisive and crippling blow at France, or by the speedy conclusion of a negotiated peace. In either case it seemed essential, in 1711, to carry the Dutch with them. The first method presupposed a vigorous effort on the part of the Republic, while Dutch refusal to participate in negotiations begun by England might wreck the ministry, especially since the Tories still had to take care not to revive doubts of their loyalty to the Protestant Succession. In any case coöperation with the Dutch was essential in order to ensure that they did not steal a march on England and themselves arrange a peace with France which gave them advantages at our expense – as many Englishmen considered that they had already done at Ryswick.

[1] Feiling, *op.cit.*, pp. 437–8; *Hanmer Corres.*, p. 20.

To each of these methods, however, there was a serious obstacle. The policy of victory by the 'pressing roundly' of the allies, which Harley favoured in October 1710, was dependent for its success upon speed. The longer a concerted and vigorous effort by the whole Grand Alliance was delayed, the greater would English war-weariness become and the more irresistible would be the pressure placed on the ministry to seek peace by other means. This Harley must have realised as he gazed at his own back-benches at the opening of the new Parliament and sensed their rapidly growing impatience with the indecisive progress of the war. Moreover, as St. John was very well aware, there was virtually no hope of any increased exertions from the Imperialists.

In these circumstances, little reliance was ever placed upon the policy of 'pressing roundly', though a vigorous pretence was kept up, largely in order to conceal from fellow-countrymen and allies alike the underhand intrigues that were going on behind the scenes. St. John, as capable of righteous indignation as he was devoid of scruple, was genuinely disgusted by the lukewarm Dutch reaction to the 'pressing' to which he subjected them; but his jealous and hostile attitude towards the Dutch had deeper causes than the traditional Tory dislike of the Dutch and his own annoyance at the alleged disparity of the British and Dutch war efforts. He believed that the Dutch, whose attitude at Geertruidenberg had left them little to hope for from the deeply offended Louis XIV, were now all the more determined to claim every advantage promised them in the fatal Barrier Treaty; but he also knew that this Treaty was the complete and culminating expression of a policy towards the war and the allies of which the people of Britain were thoroughly weary, a policy the public reaction to which was in part responsible for the overwhelming support that he and his colleagues had found at the polls. It was thus the 1709 Barrier Treaty which formed the most serious obstacle to the policy of a negotiated peace. It was not only that the ministry itself was jealous of the advantages promised to the Dutch and eager to whittle them down in order to obtain French consent to the acquisitions that it coveted: Gibraltar, Port Mahon, and, above all, the *Asiento*. There was also the vital objection, as St. John himself warned the Dutch leaders, that English public opinion would find the terms of the still unrevealed Treaty most unpalatable. The English ministry was therefore highly annoyed to find that the Dutch clung desperately to the main provisions of the Treaty, and its annoyance was sensibly increased by the knowledge that this tenacity was being encouraged by the Whigs.

Professor Geyl rightly makes much of the 'perfidy' of the Tory ministers, but it must be admitted that they had no reason to believe that the Dutch leaders would be willing to recede from the main provisions of the Barrier Treaty. They were in a thoroughly difficult position, for there could no longer be any real understanding between Britain and the Republic without an alteration either in the policy of the Dutch leaders or in the mood of the English people. This, of course, is no excuse for the conduct of the ministry, which made no real attempt to establish an *entente* with the Dutch leaders. Trevelyan occasionally leans over backwards in trying to be fair to the Tory ministers, but his judgment in this matter seems characteristically sound. 'The preposterous conduct of the Whig Ministers in 1709-10', he writes, 'had rendered it very difficult for their successors to obtain peace for Europe without bad faith. But the traditional Tory dislike of the Dutch enabled them to make the *volte-face* with peculiar gusto and ruthlessness at the expense of the duped Republic'. There is certainly no reason to believe that St. John and the High Tories would have been willing to countenance the Barrier Treaty even if their countrymen had been in a mood to accept it. As Geyl has written, St. John and his followers 'waren tegen het Townshend-tractaat niet minder dan tegen voortzetting van de oorlog, en de nieuwe koers was tegen de bondgenoten niet minder dan tegen de Whigs gericht. De oude naijver op de Hollandse concurrent vond in de Tory-regering een gretig gehoor'. It is nevertheless important to realise that the ministers were in no position to acquiesce in the terms of the Treaty even had they themselves been willing so to do.[1]

It was in these circumstances that Harley, and, after Guiscard's attempt on Harley's life, St. John, actively pursued the underhand negotiations with France that had begun in the summer of 1710. The obstinacy of the Dutch in the matter of the Barrier Treaty, the downright hostility of the High Tories towards the Republic, the popular demand for a speedy peace, and its own desire for special and exclusive advantages – all made this the ministry's chosen path to peace. In this way the problem of Dutch concurrence was put off. Instead of being allowed to participate in negotiations in which its demands would be voiced from the very beginning and in which the differences between the English and the Dutch would probably have

[1] *Kernproblemen*, pp. 173, 212–16; *Trevelyan*, iii, p. 33.

become public knowledge, the Republic was to be presented with a *fait accompli*, which it would be forced to accept by the fear that Britain and France would otherwise conclude a separate peace. Open conflict between the ministry and the Dutch might alarm moderate men in England and would certainly be seized upon by the Whigs as evidence that the ministers wished to undermine the Protestant Succession. These dangers were considerably lessened by the course that the Tory leaders followed. Once the Republic had consented to a conference, so they calculated, any attempt on its part to recover the ground it had lost in the secret Anglo-French negotiations could be represented to the English people as yet another evidence of its desire to prolong the war – at England's expense, of course.

These well-laid plans were somewhat upset by the premature revelation of the outcome of the Anglo-French negotiations, and, after some anxious weeks, the ministry had finally to resort to drastic measures to prevent English opinion from siding with the disgruntled allies.

2

Harley's 'public' policy towards the allies was set forth in the queen's speech at the opening of Parliament on November 25th, which urged that the war be pressed vigorously, especially in Spain, in order 'to procure a safe and honourable peace for us and all our allies, whose support and interest I have truly at heart'. In the Commons' reply to this, however, there appeared more enthusiasm for cajoling the allies than for their 'support and interest'.[1] It was evident that the election had produced a Commons which Harley would find difficult to satisfy with any policy which did not bring a speedy and advantageous peace.

The result of the election had placed the High Tories in a favourable position; and only another Blenheim could prevent its continual improvement as long as the war lasted. Their reaction to this pleasing situation can be seen in the contemporary press. Before the election they had for the most part thought it better to play down their hostility to the war and to the Dutch, but the size of the Tory victory, and particularly the composition of the House of Commons, encouraged them to appear in their true colours. Joseph Trapp was well to the fore with two pamphlets that reflected upon the designs of the Whigs

[1] *Cobbett*, vi, cols. 928, 930–2.

to impose a 'Dutch Government' upon Britain, and Charles Hornby, in the first part of his *Caveat against the Whiggs*, supported such suggestions by describing the way in which 'these good Neighbours of ours' had encouraged revolution in Charles II's England. The *Examiner*, too, inveighed against 'Republican Politicks'.

The most striking instance of the growing realisation that political capital could once more be made of anti-Dutch feeling is provided by the final section of Charles Davenant's *New Dialogues upon the Present Posture of Affairs* ....., which appeared about the beginning of December. The last 25 pages of this work were devoted to a consideration of the trade between the United Provinces and France, a subject doubtless suggested to Davenant by the French prohibition of commerce with the Dutch on November 19th (N.S.). What is extraordinary about these remarks is that they are obviously based upon the memorial which Davenant had drawn up for Godolphin in 1705, the tone of which was highly sympathetic towards the Dutch, but which was now given a very different tenor by means of judicious alterations, omissions and additions. For example, after his original explanation of why the Dutch were anxious to trade with France, Davenant now saw fit to add that if England was not able to check these inclinations she should herself have followed suit. The implications of this argument in December 1710 were evident; Davenant was urging that Britain should take advantage of the tacit invitation to her merchants that Louis XIV had made in banning trade with the Dutch. What had been the obstacles, he asked, that had prevented Britain from imitating the Dutch in this till now? In answer he declared that

We have a Faction within our own Bowels, ready to sacrifice the Safety, Trade, and Honour of their Native Country, to the Notions they have entertain'd of a Commonwealth: Abundance of Flattery has likewise interven'd; and on these Accounts some have either carelessly, or corruptly, look'd upon several Steps made, conducing to the Weakness of *England* and the Strength of *Holland* .... Besides that of breaking the Prohibition, divers Instances may be given, wherein, as to our Trade, they have not dealt with us in such a Friendly manner, as might have been expected from Good Neighbours, who were engag'd in a Common Cause, and who yearly expended such a Mass of Treasure, in obtaining for them such a strong Barrier; whereof one half would long ago have reduc'd *Spain*, which has been our chief Concern in the immediate War we have upon our Hands.

There can be no doubt that Davenant had undergone a considerable change of heart since his defection from the High Tories in the days of the 'Tack'! He now added to his former contention that the Dutch were ruining themselves by 'luxurious living' the assertion that

They seem to run into that Error which has prov'd the Ruin of all Common-Wealths; that is, they grasp at too large an Extent of Territory, and too much Dominion; and I cannot help thinking, the Constitution of the United Provinces was much safer when the Strong Towns in *Flanders* were in *Spanish* Hands.

Davenant did not stop here; he made it clear to his readers that he was referring to the Dutch gains under the 1709 Barrier Treaty. The provisions of this Treaty had never been disclosed, although its existence must have been common knowledge by this time. Davenant himself proclaimed his ignorance of its terms, but from what he had to say in this context it seems likely that the new ministers had taken him into their confidence. The war, he declared,

has certainly run their Publick into further Debts, but it has not (as I can hear) Impoverish'd their Individuals; and contemplate 'em as a Commonwealth, I cannot but think they are now a richer and much more potent State than they were at the Commencement of the War, *and almost a Match for any Power*. But I shall be able to say more upon this Subject, when I have seen the *Treaty of Guaranty for the Barrier*, and what is thereby stipulated and agreed.[1]

This was strong meat, even if served with the sauce of 'moderation'; and it was perhaps to offset the impression given by declarations of this kind, including some of his own letters to Drummond, that St. John assured that go-between on December 3rd (O.S.) that

the barrier which the States have obtained we are perfectly satisfied with; we look upon Holland as the frontier of Britain, and upon these two nations together as the bulwark of the Protestant interests. Suffer no jealousy of another kind to prevail. [2]

These may have been the sentiments of some of his colleagues, but they certainly were not his own. The Barrier Treaty, however, was to be kept in reserve until it was needed to tip the scales of public opinion against the Dutch; and the ministry was, in any case, not yet ready to risk breaking with the Dutch by repudiating it.

3

From the moment they took office it was essential for Harley and his colleagues to have reliable information of the attitude of the Dutch towards them and their policies. Unwilling to rely upon the reports of Townshend (who, nevertheless, was not immediately recalled, partly,

---

[1] *Examiner*, i, 22, 28 Dec. 1710; *C.W.* 184, pp. i–iii; *C.W.* 185, p. 11; *C.W.* 105, pt. i, p. 11; *C.W.* 30, pp. 222–47. For Davenant's 1705 memorial see above, pp. 119, and my article 'Dr. Davenant and the Debate on Franco-Dutch Trade', *Ec.H.R,*. 2nd ser., x (1957). For evidence of knowledge of the existence of the Barrier Treaty see *Examiner*, i, 4, 24 Aug. 1710.

[2] St. John to Drummond, 3 Dec. 1710, Whitehall, *B.L.*, i, pp. 34–8.

perhaps, lest this might alarm the Dutch) the ministry turned to the Amsterdam merchant Drummond for information. His first reports were encouraging; on January 13, 1711 (N.S.), for example, he wrote that 'the opinion of the leading men of this State in relation to matters in England is in proportion grown as good as our credit in money affairs, and this with daily increase ...'. Two months later he was somewhat concerned at the alarm expressed by the Dutch at the news that Raby was to replace the popular Townshend, but on May 29th, some time after this change, he reported that Heinsius was 'more convinced of the honest and good intentions of the Queen's Friends than ever before'.

This was a point which Defoe was at pains to impress upon his readers in two pamphlets which were in the same 'middle of the road' vein that he had adopted in 1710. Still obviously trying to win Whig support for Harley, he declared in *A Spectator's Address to the Whigs*, published in March, that his master had 'cur'd the Suspicions and Jealousies Artfully spread amongst the Confederates', had 'Satisfied them in the Queen's Measures', and 'disappointed those that expected Separate Treaties and Separate Peace would have followed our Alterations ....'. In his *Eleven Opinions about Mr. H———y*, published about the beginning of June, he went even further, describing the 'exact harmony of measures' which once more existed between the Allies, asserting that nothing was done but by 'mutual concert', and suggesting that '*Mynheer Hyensius's* Character of Mr. H———y' would be a 'Panegyrick'.[1]

The anxiety of the ministers to know the minds of the Dutch leaders was due to their fear of being forestalled in the negotiation of a peace rather than to any hope of genuine Anglo-Dutch coöperation in this sphere. Perhaps Harley would have preferred such coöperation, but to St. John and the High Tories it seemed both undesirable and impossible; and as the war dragged on, the gentlemen of England grew more and more impatient for a speedy peace, and the position of the extremists in the Harley ministry grew stronger. It was necessary for the moment to delude the Dutch leaders into believing that coöperation with the new English ministry might be possible; it was even necessary to dupe the English people into thinking that all was well with the workings of the Anglo-Dutch alliance, for the Whigs would have been quick to seize upon any admission to the contrary

[1] (Drummond) to (Harley), 13 Jan., 10 March and 29 May 1711, Amsterdam, *H.M.C. XV pt. iv*, pp. 651–2, 663, 690–2; *C.W.* 55, p. 10; *C.W.* 42, pp. 78–80.

as evidence of the ministry's pro-French leanings; but the High Tories now took few pains to hide their hostility towards the Dutch.

St. John, characteristically, ascribed the alarm that the Dutch felt at the news of Raby's appointment to the workings of a guilty conscience. They were aware, he asserted, that there were 'some latent resentments' in England at the way they had worked hand in glove with the Whigs to impose upon us and to set themselves above us. In fact, these resentments were very far from being merely 'latent' in High Tory circles and least of all in St. John himself, despite his assurances to Townshend of the queen's desire for 'the best understanding imaginable' with the States. The *Examiner* made sidelong attacks on the part played in English affairs by the Dutch since 1688, and the Memorial presented in 1710 by the unfortunate Vrijbergen was now a favourite theme for the High Tory pamphleteers, one of whom recalled that

> The D——hm-n too must frown and pout,
>   The ill-bred Cur,
>   Did make a stir,
> And dar'd to say, 'twas wrong they shou'd be turn'd out.[1]

In all these attacks the Whigs were made to share the odium with the Dutch, on account of their 'being far more zealous for a *neighbouring Nation* than for *their own*'. As Drummond wrote in July, the Dutch had previously 'entertained a prepossession against the Queen's friends and her Majesty's true interest' owing to 'the malicious informations and insinuations of Vryberge and her Majesty's own ministers'. With the High Tory writers the words 'Republican' and 'Commonwealth' were now favoured terms of abuse, and it was to this predilection that Oldmixon was referring, when, in his *History of Addresses*, published later in the year (probably in October) he made these comments about a 'Republican':

I fancy the Monster has been so much talk'd of, if he could be come at, and fix'd at the *Marlborough's* Head in *Fleetstreet*, a Penny might be made of him; and a Republican, an Antimonarchical just arrived from *Utopia*, wou'd sound as well as an Elephant or a Tiger just landed from *Bengal*: Alive! Alive! In the People would crowd; but I don't believe they'd like him, he'd look so much like a *Dutchman*; and those Butter-boxes have join'd so heartily with us in beating the *French*, that they won't soon be forgiven for't by some Men, who are not

---

[1] St. John to Townshend (copy), 16 Feb. 1710/11, Whitehall, F.E.B. Holl. 79; St. John to Raby, 23 March 1710/11 (O.S.), *B.L.*, i, pp. 124–8; *Examiner*, i, 26, 25 Jan. 1710/11; *C.W.* 23, p. 11.

Antimonarchicals; and who remember the 14000 well arm'd and disciplin'd they lent us to remove Passive-Obedience.

To the Tories, however, this was no laughing matter, and in August an unfortunate ship-master was fined £ 200 at Exeter Assizes for having declared that 'it would never be well with England, till the Government was as 'tis in Holland'.[1]

4

The Dutch did not have to wait long after St. John had replaced Boyle as Secretary of State for the Northern Department to discover what 'pressing roundly' meant. As the weeks went by he built up a whole series of complaints against the Republic, and it soon became evident that he had decided that the matter in which he was to press the Dutch the most roundly was that of naval warfare.

He asked Dayrolle for full details of the extent to which the various Dutch admiralties were fulfilling their quotas, and learnt that their long-standing deficiencies were bound to continue 'as long as this warr'. He explained at length to Townshend

how unkindly the Queen would have just reason to take it of them, and how much it must be resented by ye Nation, if they should continue so absolutely to neglect the sea, which is Our Frontier, whilst we are exhausting ourselves not only to secure their Barrier, but to add to their Dominions.

It was partly to insist that the Dutch fulfilled their quota obligations at sea that Sir James Wishart travelled to The Hague at the end of January, full of determination to deal summarily with 'a very artfull people who may be ready to trifle wt me by delaying tyme'.[2]

From the very first Wishart saw little hope that his remonstrances would have any effect. As the weeks went by he complained bitterly of 'indecent and unmannerly trifling', and 'frivolous excuses and delays'. St. John became more and more indignant as he received these choleric reports. The Dutch must stand by their treaty obligations, he insisted, the more so in view of the absolute necessity for naval command of the Mediterranean now that Charles III was doing so badly in Spain. When he learnt that the States proposed to fit out

---

[1] (Drummond) to (Oxford), 24 July 1711, Amsterdam, *H.M.C. Portland V*, pp. 47-9; *C.W.* 183, p. 16; *C.W.* 137, p. 311; *Political State*, ii, p. 148.

[2] St. John to Dayrolle, 8 Dec. 1710, Whitehall, Add. Ms. 15866; Dayrolle to St. John (copy) 26 Dec. 1710, Hague, F.E.B. Holl. 76; St. John to Townshend (copies), 23 Jan. and 6 Feb. 1710/11, Whitehall, F.E.B. Holl. 79; Wishart to St. John, 26 Feb. 1711, Hague, S.P. Holl., 237.

only thirteen men-of-war for the year 1711 he informed Wishart that the queen did not consider this 'as either kind or equitable' on their part, though he instructed him not to reject their proposals absolutely. On March 27th (N.S.) Wishart obtained their final resolution. So little difference did this display from their earlier decision that Wishart could with difficulty 'containe within the bounds of decency'. This Resolution, declared St. John to both Raby and Vrijbergen, was a 'flat denial of what her Majty has all the right in the world to insist upon', all the more remarkable in view of the fact that she was actually augmenting her troops in Flanders. Marlborough could hold out little hope that the Dutch could be persuaded to do more.[1]

St. John deeply resented the failure of Wishart's mission. Once more, he complained to Raby in a letter of April 10th, our convoys and cruisers for guarding our shipping and our coasts would be insufficient because of the need to make up the gaps left by the Dutch in the fighting squadrons. 'We are so unhappy', he declared,

as to have put ourselves on a foot of doing every thing that we are bid to do, and of having nothing done that we ask, tho' the former be against reason, and without Treaty, and tho' the latter be agreeable to both.

It was not merely the Dutch refusal to fulfil their naval quota that was annoying to St. John. Wishart had another and highly secret task at The Hague: to persuade the Dutch to join in an expedition to the West Indies. This project was very near to St. John's heart, but made little appeal to the Dutch. The idea of any joint expedition in those waters was indeed somewhat chimerical, in view of the very real rivalry of the two nations there, and not very surprisingly Wishart made no progress in this matter. St. John's resentment was not decreased.

At the beginning of May reports reached London that the French were once more preparing to return the Pretender, together with an armed force, to British soil. To Raby St. John sent forthwith an urgent demand that the Dutch should furnish a squadron to help in guarding the Channel, 'att least till this alarm is over'. If they failed

---

[1] Wishart to St. John, 6, 24 and 27 March 1711, Hague, S.P. Holl. 237; St. John to Drummond, 2 March 1710/11, Whitehall, *B.L.*, i, pp. 86–91; St. John to Wishart (copies), 6, 13 and 16 March 1710/11, Whitehall, F.E.B. Holl. 79; St. John to Dayrolle (copy), 13 March 1710/11, Whitehall, F.E.B. Holl. 74; St. John to Marlborough and Townshend (copies), 13 and 16 March 1710/11, Whitehall, F.E.B. Holl. 79; Marlborough to St. John, 31 March 1711, Hague, *Murray*, v, pp. 289–91; Wishart to States-General (transcript), 2 April 1711, Hague, Add. Ms. 17677 EEE; St. John to Raby (copy), 23 March 1710/11, Whitehall, F.E.B. Holl. 79; St. John to (Vrijbergen) (transcript), 30 March 1711 (O.S.), Add. Ms. 17677 YYY.

in this, he wrote, 'ye Queen must look on herself as being ill treated & such proceedings will teach her to be more backwards in encreasing her Force abroad'. By May 22nd the French expedition had not materialised, but neither had the required Dutch assistance. 'If the danger had been really as imminent as some people would have made us believe it was', commented St. John, 'we should have had little help from ye Guarantees of our Succession'. Raby's continued representations and remonstrances were fruitless. By June 12th St. John realised that it was now unlikely that the attempt would be made, but he was not slow to draw a moral, in a letter to Orrery, from the failure of the Dutch to supply one ship to join the English Channel fleet. 'We have had an opportunity', he wrote,

of seeing what excellent guarantees of our succession the Dutch are likely to prove; and how fine a bargain those people made, who sacrificed the liberty of the Spanish Netherlands, and that part of the trade of Britain, to the States, under this pretence.[1]

St. John's concern for the 'liberty of the Spanish Netherlands' was not limited to a dislike of the Barrier Treaty, for with the replacement of Cadogan by Orrery early in 1711 he began to receive displeasing reports of Dutch conduct in executing the provisional administration of those lands. Though there had been no love lost between Cadogan and van der Bergh, yet since 1708 the English had been able to get their own way in most matters in which they intervened; but now real discord began once more to appear.

The problem of raising funds for the upkeep of the Imperial and Palatine troops garrisoned in Flanders involved the States-General in a dispute with the Council of State of the Spanish Netherlands, in which St. John found much to criticise in the Dutch attitude. At the beginning of April, moreover, he learnt that the Dutch were willing to make a loan to Charles III in return for the mortgaging to them of the revenues of the posts of the Spanish Netherlands for another ten years. This seemed 'pretty shocking' to St. John. He told Orrery that he must be a 'Screen' to the Spanish Netherlands 'against all Tyranny & Oppression from whatever Quarter it may come' and he added:

We are not ignorant here of the views which the Dutch have in respect to these

[1] Wishart to St. John, 20 March 1711, Hague, S.P. Holl. 237; St. John to Raby, 10 April, 4 and 22 May, 5 and 12 June 1711, Whitehall, S.P. Holl. 241; St. John to Orrery, 12 June 1711 (O.S.), *B.L..*, i, pp. 242–7; *ibid.*, i, pp. 247–51, St. John to Drummond, 12 June 1711 (O.S.); Bourne, *op.cit.*, p. 107; W. T. Morgan, 'Queen Anne's Canadian Expedition of 1711', *Bulletin of the Department of History, etc., in Queen's University, Kingston, Ontario*, May, 1928, p. 16; W. T. Morgan, 'South Sea Company and the Canadian Expedition', *Hispanic American Historical Review*, viii, 2, p. 159.

Provinces, & how by Barrier, by Mortgage, or by Enclosure they contrive to reduce them absolutely to their Obedience.[1]

These instructions were after Orrery's own heart, and he hastened to write to Heinsius urging the use of more 'tenderness' in dealing with this people, whose interest, he declared, was 'inseparable' from that of the queen, 'especially in point of commerce ....'. Meanwhile he had learnt that the Dutch had decided to raise more funds by mortgaging the 'comptoirs' at Ghent, Bruges and Ostend for a further eight years. This he thought quite unreasonable. 'I think the revenues of this Country are too much mortgaged already', he wrote to St. John, 'I think these poor people are unreasonably overcharg'd & I think the States have already made these Countries too much dependent upon 'em ....'; and to justify his 'backwardness' in agreeing to the Dutch proposition he sent home letter after letter emphasising – and condoning – the hostility towards the Dutch that he found on all sides.

He received most sympathetic replies from St. John, who, moreover, declared to Drummond that

These unhappy countries have found the government of those who pretend to be the assertors of public liberty so tyrannical and barbarous, that you know better than I how near they are driven to despair.

Opposition came from an unexpected source, however, with the intervention of Townshend's successor, Raby, who, by his own account, was 'by no means partial' to the Dutch. On May 8th (N.S.) he wrote to Orrery to tell him that he had been convinced of the justice of the Dutch case, and his letter contained a passage which shows that he at least still attached importance to the maintenance of a 'good understanding' with the Dutch:

The necessity of this war makes us obligd to joyn with this State, & that makes me write to yr Ldship so amply that we who are imployd by what they call here the New Ministry may show them we are as sensible as those of the necessity there is of a good understanding between the Queen and the States, & that we will do full as much to contribute to it in all things reasonable, for 'tis my poor opinion we doe a great service to the present Ministry to establish a Confidence between them & this State & by what I find here, it will be easy for us to do it.[2]

---

[1] St. John to Wishart (copy), 20 March 1710/11, Whitehall, F.E.B. Holl. 79; *ibid.*, St. John to Marlborough (copy), 20 March 1710/11, Whitehall; St. John to Orrery (copies), 30 March and 6 April 1711, Whitehall, F.E.B. Flanders 12; St. John to Drummond, 6 April 1711 (O.S.), *B.L.*, i, pp. 140–4.

[2] Orrery to (St. John), 23, 27 and 30 April, and 7 May 1711, Brussels, S.P. Flanders 60; St. John to Orrery (copies), 27 April and 8 May 1711, Whitehall, F.E.B. Flanders 12; St. John to Drummond, 27 April 1711 (O.S.), *B.L.*, i, pp. 168–72; Raby to Orrery (copy), 8 May 1711, Hague, S.P. Holl. 239; Orrery to (Harley), 18 May 1711, Brussels, *H.M.C. XV pt. iv*, pp. 685–6.

Raby's intervention forced Orrery to change his tune, but an alteration in his views was also brought about as the natural result of his increasing experience of the conduct of the Council of State. Though he continued to be reluctant to force the Council to submit to the Dutch scheme, he began to admit, in his reports to St. John, that the blame for the troubles of the Condominium could not be apportioned quite as simply as he had imagined. If the Dutch were guilty of 'too great stiffness', the Council of State certainly displayed 'too great scrupulousness'. 'There are faults I think on both sides', he admitted on June 22nd, though he added that 'these people wou'd be more in the wrong than they are if they were better us'd'. St. John, too, began to substitute complaints about 'the backwardness which the Council of State show towards doing any thing for the service of the Prince & for the Common Interest' for his previous lamentations for their sufferings under the heel of the Dutch. Anxious as they were to press the Republic roundly, Orrery and his masters had none the less found that the policy of unlimited support for the Council of State against the Dutch was not feasible if the Condominium were to continue to function.[1]

5

St. John was no sooner in office than he started to bombard the unfortunate Townshend with complaints about the war effort of the Dutch in Spain and Portugal. Their explanations as to the state of their troops in Spain he found evasive, and he asserted that they had not fulfilled their obligations to Portugal. Despite the assurances he sent Buys that he regarded English and Dutch interests as inseparable, he had taken office, as Sir Charles Petrie has written, 'with the firm conviction that the allies of Britain ..... wished to reap the whole profit of the war while leaving England to do the fighting'.[2]

He was particularly angered by the attitude of the Dutch to the sending of two thousand additional cavalry to Charles III, whose situation, despite the victories of Almenara and Saragossa, was

---

[1] Orrery to (St. John), 21 May, 11 and 22 June 1711, Brussels, S.P. Flanders 60; St. John to Orrery (copy), 26 June 1711, Whitehall, F.E.B. Flanders 12. Two months later Orrery was willing to concede that the 'considerable alteration of Government' in the Spanish Netherlands advocated by the Dutch might be found necessary after all (Orrery to (St. John), 17 Aug. 1711, Brussels, S.P. Flanders 60).

[2] St. John to Townshend (copies), 29 Sept., 27 and 31 Oct. 1710, Whitehall, F.E.B. Holl. 77; St. John to Buys, 13 Oct. 1710, Windsor, *B.L.*, i, pp. 1–3; Petrie, *op. cit.*, p. 137.

rapidly becoming desperate. Their reluctance to provide even a third of the charge of this augmentation, or to transfer any of the troops in their pay from Flanders to Spain, elicited letters from St. John to Townshend and Drummond which were full of ominous echoes of past and present High Tory propaganda. When the Dutch excused themselves by referring to their own difficulties or to the shortcomings of the Emperor, he retorted that the same arguments might be used by the queen, who 'had done so much not only for the Security of their Barrier, but even for the Enlargement of their Dominions', and had even allowed them their open trade with France. In his letters to Drummond, which he knew would be seen by the Dutch leaders, he mingled expressions of friendship and of eagerness to continue the war with suggestions that the Dutch were gaining much and the British nothing by its continuation – a belief reflected in the columns of the *Examiner*. Such contradictions were inherent in his execution of Harley's instructions to 'press roundly'.[1]

As the year drew to a close complaints about the Dutch attitude to the war in the Iberian peninsula continued to reach Marlborough and Townshend from the prolific pen of St. John. Though he evaded with contemptuous politeness a Dutch request for arrears owing since the days of William III, he insisted that the States should pay *their* arrears to Portugal, that they should make up their forces in Spain, and that they should take a satisfactory resolution about their share of the expense of the 2000 horse. In the matter of making up the deficiencies in the Dutch troops in Spain his remonstrances had the desired effect – but the States were given little respite.

When the news arrived that Stanhope had been defeated and captured at Brihuega the queen herself wrote to the States (on December 16th) urging yet more vigorous efforts on behalf of Charles III. St. John explained his government's reaction to the new situation in a letter to Townshend of January 23rd concerning the difficulties being experienced by the Dutch in providing their share of the augmentation of 2000 horse. 'Her Majty', he wrote,

is ready and willing to do all that she can, yet she would not go faster, nor engage farther than the rest of her Allys, who, as her Majty observes, are much forwarder to make Schemes to bring us into new Expences, than to propose or perform anything for themselves.

----

[1] St. John to Townshend (copies), 31 Oct., 3, 7, 17 and 21 Nov. 1710, Whitehall, F.E.B. Holl. 77; *Examiner*, i, 14, 2 Nov. 1710; St. John to Drummond, 14, 17 and 28 Nov. 1710, Whitehall, *B.L.*, i, pp. 19, 22–31; St. John to Marlborough and Townshend (copy), 24 Nov. 1710, Whitehall, F.E.B. Holl. 77.

Four months later the Dutch augmentation had not materialised and St. John told Raby that he regarded the excuses of the Dutch in this matter as nothing more than a 'juggle'.[1]

On April 17th (N.S.) the Emperor Joseph died after a short and sudden illness. His successor to the Habsburg domains and, almost certainly, to the Imperial crown, was none other than the titular king of Spain, Charles III. The news that Joseph had fallen ill had caused great alarm at The Hague, according to Marlborough, who emphasised in letters to St. John, Harley and Shrewsbury that nothing would be more likely to bring the States 'to an entire dependence on her majesty and the ministry, on which our common safety must, in a great measure, depend', than a declaration by both nations of continued support for the pretensions of Charles III to the Spanish Empire. Indeed, neither England nor the United Provinces was yet ready to avow that they no longer considered these valid; to do so would have weakened their hands in any future bargaining with the French. Consequently both Houses of Parliament agreed, on April 20th, to send an address to the queen reaffirming their support for the continuation of the war on this basis. In London, according to L'Hermitage, there was much praise for the similar resolution already taken by the States-General, who, declared the *Observator* of April 25th,

tho the *Examiner* and his Faction have run them down as a Parcel of Mechanicks and Shopkeepers, uncapable of framing Rules for Administration, come nothing short of their Landed Men in Sense and Politicks.

Raby was 'extreemly pleased to see the good countinance these people keep', and Marlborough's pleasure at this evidence of the 'perfect harmony between England and Holland' found an echo in Defoe's *Eleven Opinions about Mr. H—y*.

In fact, the English ministry was far more interested in gaining sole and permanent possession of Gibraltar than in forwarding the chimerical ambitions of the House of Habsburg. Raby was therefore instructed, on May 11th (O.S.), to point out the unsatisfactory condition of the Dutch regiment in garrison at Gibraltar, with the aim of 'bringing the Dutch themselves to desire to have those home which belong to them', it being 'her Majties desire to have no troops but her

[1] St. John to Vrijbergen (copy), 23 Nov. 1710, Whitehall, F.E.B. For. Min. 257; Marlborough and Townshend to St. John, 9, 16 and 26 Dec. 1710, Hague, *Murray*, v, pp. 235–6, 242–3, 246–7; St. John to Marlborough and Townshend (copies), 5, 8 and 22 Dec. 1710, Whitehall, F.E.B. Holl. 77; Anne to States-General (transcript), 26 Dec. 1710, Whitehall, Add. Ms. 17677 EEE; St. John to Townshend (copy), 23 Jan. 1710/11, Whitehall, F.E.B. Holl. 79; St. John to Raby, 8 May 1711, Whitehall, S.P. Holl. 241.

own in that town'. He met with a decidedly cool reception. The Dutch leaders were not deceived and to the chagrin of the ministry they continued to insist that England must either give up Gibraltar *and* Port Mahon when peace came, or else consent to joint Anglo-Dutch garrisons for both places. St. John was indignant, but he decided that the best policy for the time being would be one of dissimulation.[1]

6

Harley had destroyed the Godolphin ministry, but Marlborough remained. Glad as Harley no doubt was to have avoided the crisis that the General's resignation might have precipitated, the problem of what to do with him was still unsolved. Harley was annoyed to find that his hands were not free in this matter. The last thing that he intended when he took office was to drive the States to make a separate peace with France; he was determined that if any nation was to benefit at the expense of its allies it should be Britain, not the Dutch. It was partly for this reason that Drummond was employed to give comfort and reassurance to the uneasy Dutch leaders. At the beginning of November, however, Drummond informed Harley that unless Marlborough remained as British commander the States, already most anxious for peace, would certainly make their own terms with France. As Godolphin intimated to the queen a month later, unless the ministry were prepared to provoke the immediate breakdown of the Alliance it had no choice but to retain Marlborough. Harley set himself to make a virtue of necessity, but he complained bitterly to Drummond of the States' partiality for Marlborough and the Whigs, which, he declared, showed their ignorance of the 'true condition of this country'.

The commander of the allied armies, then, was still the Duke of Marlborough, but the Allies well knew that he no longer possessed the confidence of the English government. Both at The Hague and in the army this knowledge made the Dutch uneasy, according to Raby, especially since the allied forces no longer possessed a superiority in numbers over the French. This uneasiness expressed itself in a

---

[1] Marlborough to St. John, 21 April 1711, Hague, *Murray*, v, pp. 316–17; Marlborough to Harley, 22 April 1711, Hague, *Coxe*, iii, p. 198; L'Hermitage to States-General (transcript), 24 April/5 May 1711, London, Add. Ms. 17677 EEE; *Observator*, x, 33, 25 April 1711; Marlborough to Shrewsbury, 7 May 1711, Warde, *Coxe*, iii, pp. 204–5; St. John to Raby (copy), 11 May 1711, Whitehall, F.E.B. Holl. 79; Same to same, 29 May 1711, Whitehall, S.P. Holl. 241; (Drummond) to (Oxford), 7 and 24 July 1711 (N.S.), *H.M.C. Portland V*, pp. 22–4, 47–9; *C.W.* 42, p. 80; S. Conn, *Gibraltar in British Diplomacy in the Eighteenth Century* (New Haven, 1942), Ch. i, *passim*.

renewed reluctance of the Dutch to 'venture', which came as a godsend to the High Tories in the task of persuading their 'moderate' allies of the futility of prolonging the war, since it could be used to offset the glamour of Marlborough's real though costly successes.[1]

The indignity of the French recapture of Arleux on July 23rd (N.S.), it was said in London, was due to the deputies' refusal to accept Marlborough's advice that it should be deliberately abandoned. What really influenced English opinion, however, and gave the High Tories a most welcome opportunity to score off Marlborough and the Dutch at the same time, was the deputies' censure of Marlborough for not attacking Villars' army after the celebrated passing of the 'Ne Plus Ultra' lines on August 5th. Marlborough himself was much put out that he should be criticised for not attempting what no officer 'that has the least judgment in these matters' could have considered practicable. 'I cannot but think it very hard', he complained to Heinsius, 'when I do my best, to be liable to such censures'; and his temper cannot have been improved by the deputies' reluctance to countenance the siege of Bouchain, in which, wrote the Judge-Advocate Watkins meaningly, the French were not the only foes the English had to deal with. Despite the Duke's indignant self-justification, Buys and his friends, according to Drummond, persisted in criticising his conduct, and the deputies Goslinga and Vegelin (of whom Watkins remarked that he 'really does act on several occasions as if he was fitter for Bedlam than the place he fills') refused to retract.

The High Tories gleefully spread the news of this contretemps. They had little reason to worry whether the popular reaction was in favour of Marlborough or of the Dutch. According to Brigadier Sutton, who had travelled to London with the news of the passing of the Lines, it was the deputies who were generally blamed in London, and rightly so. 'I believe your Valliant Deputys', he wrote to Watkins,

being animated by the force of new pickled herrings, had a mind to show their Brother frogs how thirsty after blood they were, and since they are so much upon their mettle I wish his Grace wou'd make use of them in the marais beween the Scheld and Senset.

The embarrassing position of the Whigs at this moment was somewhat reminiscent of that in which they had found themselves during the campaign of 1705. If they defended one friend, they attacked, by

---

[1] (Drummond) to Harley, 11 Nov. 1710, Amsterdam, *H.M.C. XV pt. iv*, pp. 619–22; *ibid.*, pp. 623–5, (Harley) to Drummond, 7 Nov. 1710 (O.S.); (Godolphin) to ?, 17 Dec. 1710 (O.S.), *Trevelyan*, iii, pp. 328–30; Raby to Orrery, 21 May 1711, Hague, Add. Ms. 37209; Raby to St. John, 16 June 1711, Hague, S.P. Holl. 239.

implication, another. The *Observator* attempted to escape this dilemma by pointing to the public thanksgiving in the Republic for the passing of the Lines, and, later, to the deputies' praise of Marlborough on the capture of Bouchain. 'You may be sure', it asserted, 'that his Grace does nothing but in concert with the *Dutch*, and other confederate Generals, and particularly of (*sic*) the *Dutch* Field-Deputies'.[1]

At the beginning of September Watkins found that a welcome change had come over the conduct of the deputies, and he praised the energy and deference to Marlborough that they showed at the siege of Bouchain. With the fall of that town on September 13th, however, another difficulty arose, for the States-General themselves refused to sanction Marlborough's plan for laying siege to Quesnoy. As Boyer pointed out in his *Annals* in May 1712, the conduct of the Dutch was obviously affected by their 'conjectures' concerning the secret Anglo-French negotiations; at the same time it was of real use to the ministry in preparing the minds of its fellow-countrymen for the revelation of the results of these discussions.[2]

The same fear of what the English ministry was doing made the Dutch unwilling to agree to a cherished project of Marlborough's whereby an unprecedented number of troops would be kept in winter-quarters close to the French frontier, and would thus be able to open the campaign at a very early date. Here, too, the ministry was able to summon up a fine show of righteous indignation. Marlborough himself was genuinely put out; he felt strongly that unless this project were adopted 1712 might well be a disastrous year for the Allies in the Low Countries, and he sent home long complaints of the States' 'extraordinary backwardness', which Cadogan imagined to be an 'ill understood peice a'conomy' on their part. Marlborough was so far beside himself that he wrote to Harley (now Earl of Oxford) in terms which played right into the latter's hands. 'I am perfectly convinced', he declared,

that, besides the draining our nation both of men and money, almost to the last extremity, our allies do, by degrees, so shift the burden of the war upon us, that, at the rate they go on, the whole charge must at last fall upon England.

Oxford hastened to point to the apparent discrepancy between the

1 Marlborough to Heinsius, 13 Aug. 1711, Avesnes-le-Sec, *van 't Hoff*, pp. 558–9; Marlborough to Slingelandt, 13 Aug. 1711, Avesnes-le-Sec, *Murray*, v, p. 444; *ibid.*, v, p. 444, Marlborough to Dayrolle, 13 Aug. 1711, Avesnes-le-Sec; Watkins to Drummond, 20, 24 and 27 Aug. 1711, Camp before Bouchain, *H.M.C. X pt. i*, pp. 141–3; Sutton to Watkins, 14 Aug. 1711, London, Add. Ms. 33273; *Observator*, x, 66 and 74, 18 Aug. and 15 Sept. 1711.

2 Watkins to Drummond, 3 Sept. 1711, Camp before Bouchain, *H.M.C. X pt. i*, pp. 143–4; *Annals*, x, p. 48.

conduct of the Dutch in this matter and their reluctance to accept the English propositions for a peace conference. 'Ours is a very unlucky situation', he wrote to Marlborough on October 19th,

> that everyone is shrinking from the war, and at the same time casting the burden upon Britain, and yet unwilling to let her have the least advantage. I would to God that our allies would resolve either to make a good war or a good peace.

St. John, too, was able to counter Buys' exhortations to continue the war by alluding to the fate of this project.[1]

7

The first real counterblast to Tory criticisms of the conduct of the war and of the abortive peace negotiations appeared about the beginning of January 1711 in the shape of four *Letters to a Tory-Member*, written by Marlborough's chaplain, Francis Hare. Of these, two were devoted to the 'Management of the War' and two to the 'Negotiations for a Treaty of Peace'.

Hare began by considering the argument that a good peace could have been had after Ramillies. If we had made peace then, he asserted, we should have attained neither of our two principal war aims – the restitution of the Spanish Monarchy to the House of Austria, and a good Barrier – even if the latter object was now out of favour amongst those who were 'silly enough to wish against .... the Safety of the *Dutch*'. Neither of these conditions, he went on, was offered after Ramillies:

> There is no need of telling you, what Barrier was offer'd for the *Netherlands*, which the *Dutch* were most concern'd in, who don't use to neglect good offers to come at Peace, if we may believe the Faction, who have for a long time pretended to fear nothing so much, as their quitting the Alliance for their own separate Interest. Tho' now the noble Firmness they have shewn in adhering to it, till Terms may be had to the Satisfaction of all Parties, is by these ill designing Politicians, who can take everything by a wrong Handle, imputed to them for a Crime; a Crime perhaps, that they may not be guilty of much longer; or if they are, 'tis not for want of some Mens taking the most effectual Methods to cure them of a Fault, which I don't remember they were ever before blam'd for.

---

[1] Marlborough to Eugene, 9 Sept. 1711, Camp before Bouchain, *Murray*, v, p. 485; *ibid.*, v, pp. 514–15, Marlborough to Albemarle, 28 Sept. 1711, Camp nr. Bouchain; *ibid.*, v, p. 518, Marlborough to Shrewsbury, 1 Oct. 1711, Camp nr. Bouchain; Marlborough to (Oxford?), 2 Oct. 1711 (N.S.), Lansdowne Ms. 1236; (Drummond) to Heinsius, 25 Sept. 1711, London, Archief Heinsius 1590; Cadogan to ?, 15 Oct. 1711, Bouchain, S.P. Mil. 4; Marlborough to St. John, 26 Oct. 1711, St. Amand, *Murray*, v, pp. 553–4; Marlborough to Oxford, 26 Oct. 1711, Marchiennes, *Coxe*, iii, p. 256; *ibid.*, iii, p. 255, same to same, n.d.; *ibid.*, iii, pp. 253–4, Oxford to Marlborough, 19 Oct. 1711 (O.S.); St. John to Marlborough (copy), 20 Oct. 1711, Whitehall, F.E.B. Holl. 78; St. John to Strafford, 26 Oct. 1711, Whitehall, S.P. Holl. 241.

To complaints about the neglect of the war in Spain he replied that there were too many disadvantages to waging an offensive war in that country, and this he 'proved' by the unwillingness of the Dutch to send their troops there; though when he came to deal with criticisms of Marlborough's conduct of the war in Flanders he displayed considerably less confidence in the wisdom of the Dutch, who, he said, deserved the blame that had been heaped upon Marlborough.

In considering the negotiations of 1709 he emphasised that the Dutch did nothing without the concurrence of their allies, and at the same time praised their firmness and their 'Probity, Plainness, and Honesty'. One of his justifications for Article XXXVII, however, was that if the allies had gone on to fight Philip V after a separate peace with France, England would soon have found herself fighting alone! As for Geertruidenberg, the only criticism that he thought could be made of the Dutch was that they had allowed the negotiations to last as long as they had, and he inveighed against the 'foolish, *Frenchify'd, Anti-Dutch* Politicks of some Men' who would rather lose Spain altogether than suffer any advantage (in the form, that is, of 'cautionary towns' in Flanders) to accrue to the Dutch.

Hare was at the disadvantage of having been forced on to the defensive, but even so his case was really not good enough to be presented as an apology for the late ministry. Attack was more congenial work for the pamphleteer than defence, and the High Tories found much to attack in Hare's work. One of them in particular, after suggesting that the Dutch had only been kept from making peace in 1709 by means of bribes, threw all restraint to the winds when he considered Hare's remarks about the 'Probity, Plainness and Honesty of the *Dutch*'. In a few lines he touched all the chords of High Tory feelings on this subject:

This is certainly his own Thought, he could never borrow it, for in my little Reading, I cannot call to Mind that I ever met with it before, he should have added their *Religion* to complete the Character, and have sent us to *Japan* to enquire about it, if we could find no satisfactory Information nearer. *Pumica* (*sic*) *fides* grew into a Proverb among the *Romans*, and has been in the latter Ages frequently apply'd to that honest Nation, that another great Man speaking of them said, *delenda est Carthago*. There is scarce any corner of the World that has not furnish'd us with Instances of their *Probity, Plainness and Honesty*, witness *Amboyna, Polloroon, Sumatra, Bantam* and many other Places in the *East-Indies*; *Guiana, Surinam* and others in the *West*; their Behaviour towards their Patroness Queen Elizabeth, the Fishery in our own Seas, and infinite other Instances, which I have not leisure nor Inclination to repeat, nor should I take the least notice of them were they not publickly known to all Mankind.[1]

[1] *C.W.* 93, pp. 6–7, 15–16, 19, 30; *C.W.* 94, pp. 1, 6, 15; *C.W.* 95, pp. 7–10, 17, 38–9; *C.W.* 96, pp. 13–14, 29–31, 60; *C.W.* 73, pp. 13, 18.

8

On March 30th St. John wrote to Drummond that 'the want of a peace on all sides is evident', and a week later he followed this up by telling Drummond to let Buys know he was anxious to agree with the States the terms on which peace could be made. Buys' eagerness to take up this offer was thwarted by Heinsius' jealousy of his prominence in the affair, but meanwhile St. John gave the first indication that the new ministry was not willing to stand by the Barrier Treaty. He made known, in general terms, its dissatisfaction with this 'last and great sale of the British interest' in his letters to Raby of April 19th and 20th, and his instructions to the ambassador to pass on these sentiments to the Dutch leaders may well have been prompted by Raby's own report that Sinzendorf now had hopes that the Dutch would 'come to treat with the Emperor on that matter'. St. John made it clear that he was sure of the full support of the overwhelming majority of his fellow-countrymen:

. . . . if the Barrier Treaty comes to be publickly known and considered in parliament, it will be absolutely impossible to keep the ferment down. All ranks, all parties of men, will unite in their protestations against it.[1]

Before he could learn of the reaction of the Dutch to this intimation he made a still greater revelation, for in his letter to Raby of April 27th he announced that 'Proposals' had been received from the French, without, of course, making any mention of the secret negotiations which had led up to them. He warned Raby that the Dutch would no doubt be much alarmed at the clause which stipulated for them a Barrier 'agreeable to England', and he added that

The fear the Dutch will conceive of our obtaining advantageous terms for Britain, will naturally put them on trying underhand for themselves, and endeavouring to make us the dupes of the peace, as we have been of the war.

His next letters to Raby insisted that it was time for Britain to stop ruining herself for the advantage of her allies, pointed to Dutch encroachments on British trade and deficiencies in their quotas, and mocked at their 'pretence of poverty'. On May 26th (N.S.) Raby was able to send home a report of the reactions of the Dutch leaders to St. John's revelations. He was sure that they were very desirous of peace, but thought the propositions 'very dark and general' and wished

---

[1] St. John to Drummond, 30 March and 6 April 1711 (O.S.), *B.L.*, i, pp. 133–8, 140–4; Raby to St. John, 24 April and 8 May 1711, Hague, S.P. Holl. 239; St. John to Raby, 19 and 20 April 1711, Whitehall, *B.L.*, i, pp. 153–8; Raby to Harley, 5 May 1711, Hague, *H.M.C. Portland IX*, pp. 290–2; *Montgomery*, pp. 206–9.

that the French would explain themselves more. On the other hand, wrote Raby,

I find that expression in the propositions of a barrier according to the conveniency of England, with the noyse the Imperials have made about the bariere, workes upon them & if rightly managed they may yet come to make some reasonable explications of that treaty, much more advantageous to England than it has been already.

St. John replied that, as far as the French proposals were concerned, the States must place their trust in the queen. As Mrs. Montgomery has pointed out, the failure of the Dutch to respond to the feelers that it had put out in early April had given the ministry 'an excellent pretext for withholding its confidence from the Dutch', and from now on it did nothing to inform the States of the progress of the negotiations with France. Raby, moreover, was called to London, ostensibly to give his views on the attitude of the Dutch towards the claims of the Duke of Savoy, and also towards the 1709 Barrier Treaty. While still at The Hague, however, he sent St. John a lengthy analysis of the effect that his revelations had had. He perceived that, for all the Dutch leaders' dissimulation, the French propositions were 'by no means agreeable to them', and suspected that they were now intriguing with France for better terms for themselves. He was especially distrustful of Buys, and he pointed out to St. John that yet another good reason for England to be dissatisfied with the Barrier Treaty was that there was not 'one article on our side in that Treaty that makes voy'd our engagement to them in case they make a separate peace with france .....'. It would, in fact, be necessary to take great care if we were not to be the dupes of the peace, as we were of the war (St. John's own phrase repeated), owing to the unaccountable 'confidence and generosity' that we had formerly shown towards 'these people who never had in any one circumstance the least for us'. We could now see the results of our folly in agreeing to

that extraordinary unparalleled clause in the treaty of Barrier, that they shoud have half the advantage of any treaty or agreement we should make with the King of Spain.

They showed no enthusiasm for the war in Spain but they none the less insisted on keeping their garrison at Gibraltar and expressed great uneasiness at our 'Secret Expedition', which they believed was designed for the West Indies (it was actually destined for Quebec), 'as if wt we gained from the Enemy was a loss to them'. He warned St. John, however, that these remarks woud not be proper for the publick, for tho all this is as I have represented it, & worse yet we must for our own sakes go on, hand in hand with these people & the more we seem united & to act in publick in concert with them the more & stronger we shall apear to the French.

There was, too, another reason for caution, as Raby pointed out to St. John on June 20th, namely, 'that they may have no reason to accuse us for taking the least measures towards a peace without them'. The illusion of Anglo-Dutch coöperation was, in Raby's view, needed to manage not only the French court but also the English people.

With Raby's return home it began to be rumoured in London that a peace was once more in agitation at The Hague, and that it was proposed to leave Philip in Spain. Defoe, who had always asserted that the new ministry would never consent to this, derided these reports: 'What gross Thoughts', he asked, 'must we have of Things to conceive such a Peace? – What are the *Dutch* reduc'd to, that they should come in to it?'. In fact, of course, the Dutch were not being consulted, though it is interesting to see how the myth of Anglo-Dutch solidarity was being maintained by Defoe. It was as the representative of the queen alone, and not of the Allies, that Matthew Prior travelled secretly to Paris in July to meet Torcy.[1]

At his interview with Torcy on June 22nd Prior showed how much his masters still valued the eventual concurrence of the Dutch in their plans by insisting upon French assurances concerning a Barrier 'propre à contenter les Hollandois', as Torcy put it; he also assured the Frenchman that there would be no difficulty in obtaining Dutch consent to the retention of Spain by Philip V. At this same interview he saw letters from Petkum which convinced him that the Dutch were trying to regain control of the negotiations, a development which St. John had long foreseen and provided against, and rumours of which Drummond had recently been investigating.[2]

Prior's return to England in mid-August, together with the French agent, Mesnager, was made public knowledge by the intervention of an indiscreet Customs officer. From now on the negotiation was an open secret. St. John, who set little store by the assurances that Drum-

---

[1] St. John to Raby, 27 April 1711, Whitehall, *B.L.*, i, pp. 172–9; Same to same (copy), 4 May 1711, Whitehall, F.E.B. Holl. 79; Same to same, 6 and 22 May 1711 (O.S.), *B.L.*, i, pp. 185–95, 225–7; Raby to St. John, 26 May, 2 and 20 June 1711, Hague, S.P. Holl. 239; St. John to Raby, 1 June 1711, Whitehall, S.P. Holl. 241; *Review*, viii, 36 and 44, 16 June and 5 July 1711; *Weber*, pp. 110–15.

[2] (Drummond) to (Oxford), 7 and 14 July 1711, Amsterdam, *H.M.C. Portland V*, pp. 22–4 and 28–9; *ibid.*, pp. 34–5, 'Prior's Journal', 23 July 1711; L. G. Wickham Legg, *Matthew Prior: A Study of his Public Career and Correspondence* (Cambridge, 1921), pp. 152–3; *E.H.R.*, xxix, pp. 528–9.

mond sent him of Dutch eagerness for peace, and declared that the
only peace that Heinsius desired was one of which he had sole direction,
yet thought it advisable to make some attempt to soothe the 'umbrage'
that was taken in the Republic when Dutch suspicions of the ministry
were thus confirmed. Through Drummond he assured the Dutch
leaders that

Britain will act honourably to the last; no peace without the States is to be had;
or even was thought of here, but a peace must be in concert with them.

In his correspondence with Heinsius Oxford, too, attempted to lull
the suspicions of the Dutch leaders. Again and again he assured the
Pensionary that the discussions with Mesnager were in purely general
terms, and that as soon as any specific proposals were made by the
French the Republic would be informed of them. To add verisimilitude
to his assurances he also advocated an offensive-defensive alliance
between the two nations to operate after a peace, and urged that the
Republic should send a representative to London with powers to
conclude this. Such assurances as these were probably meant to serve
a dual purpose: first, to dissuade the Dutch from continuing the
approaches to France which had been revealed to Prior; and secondly,
to dissuade them from making any attempt to appeal to English
opinion against the behaviour of the ministry. St. John and his
colleagues were playing a dangerous game, which the intervention of
the Dutch at this point might well spoil; indeed, Petkum was confident
that the negotiations would merely discredit the Tories and hasten
the fall of the ministry. Only when it could set forth the prospect of
substantial advantages for its country would it be ready to withstand
the reproaches of the Dutch. It could not yet afford to endanger its
standing in the country by giving apparent confirmation of Hare's
charge of 'Frenchify'd, Anti-Dutch Politicks'. Nothing would have
pleased the Whigs more than a formal disclaimer from the Dutch of
any knowledge of the negotiations.[1] Fortunately for the ministry's
plans, the Republic had had no representative of any rank in London
since the death of Vrijbergen on July 3rd (O.S.).[2]

[1] (Drummond) to (Oxford), 7 and 14 July, 4 and 7 Aug. 1711, Amsterdam, *H.M.C. Portland V*, pp. 22–4, 28–9, 61, 66; Oxford to Heinsius, 6 and 24 July, 7 Aug., 14 and 19 Sept. 1711 (O.S.), *Weber*, pp. 401–9; St. John to Drummond, 14 and 28 Aug. 1711, Whitehall, *B.L.*, i, pp. 313–15, 339–41; Petkum to Rouillé (translation), 5 Sept. 1711 (N.S.), *H.M.C. XIV pt. ix*, p. 356; (St. John) to Drummond, 4 Sept. 1711, Windsor, *H.M.C. X pt. i*, p. 145; Drummond to Heinsius, 18 and 21 Sept. 1711, London, Archief Heinsius 1590. Boyer emphasises the delicacy of the ministry's position: 'The Generality of the Nation ... continued to entertain great Jealousies about the present Negotiation ...', (*Annals*, x, p. 250); and *cf. C.W.* 175, pp. 62–3.

[2] Through Drummond the ministers had been cajoling the Dutch to recall Vrijbergen, who,

Under these circumstances, the news that Buys was coming to London to investigate the rumours about Mesnager's mission must have made the ministers all the more anxious to reach a speedy settlement with the French envoy. Shrewsbury, it is true, was ill at ease about the direction that the discussions were taking, and it may have been as a result of his apprehensions that on September 25th Prior made a last-minute attempt to obtain additional concessions for the Allies. On the same day, however, Dr. Jonathan Swift, now the confidant of Oxford and St. John, recorded that agreement was virtually complete and that Raby, recently created Earl of Strafford, would soon return to The Hague to inform the Dutch of the result of the discussions; 'and then', he added, 'there will be the devil and all to pay; but we'll make them swallow it with a pox'.

On September 27th Mesnager signed two documents. The first was a list of special advantages for England, including the *Asiento*, Gibraltar and Minorca. The second, 'the paper for Holland', as St. John called it, outlined in general terms the basis on which the claims of the rest of the Allies would be dealt with, but omitted the most important provisions of the first. By this Louis acknowledged Anne and the Protestant Succession, and agreed that France and Spain should never have the same ruler, that the Empire should have its 'Barrier', and that Dunkirk should be dismantled in return for an 'equivalent'. As far as the Dutch Barrier was concerned, this paper went no further in specifying what form it would take than had the French proposals of April.

The ministry had completed the first part of its programme. It now had to try to wring approval – however reluctant – of its proceedings from its allies. To Strafford, who had been absent from The Hague since June, was assigned the vital task of gaining the acquiescence of the Dutch. His instructions, signed on October 1st, laid down the methods that he was to use. He was to begin by informing them of the *second* convention signed by Mesnager, to which he would add assurances that Britain had no intention of making peace separately from them. He was next to

insinuate strongly .... how just reason we should have to be offended, & to look on ye proceeding between them & us as very unequal, if they shou'd pretend to have any further uneasiness on this head.

As for the Barrier Treaty, he was to inform them that

nothing can be more odious to the people of these kingdoms than many parts of

they alleged, 'was in so deep with our late Ministry'. They declared themselves ready to welcome Goslinga – Marlborough's arch-critic! – as a replacement (Drummond to Heinsius, 28 Jan., 7 and 17 Feb. 1711, Amsterdam, Archief Heinsius 1590; P. Wentworth to Raby, 23 Jan. 1710/11 , London, *Wentworth Papers*, p. 176).

of this treaty, & that nothing has prevented that National and universal indignation which wou'd have broke out upon this occasion but the greatest care &
industry which has been us'd to calm the minds of those who are acquainted
with the terms of this Guaranty, & to keep the same as secret as possible from
those who are not yet appriz'd of them.

Strafford was next to press the Dutch to choose a place within the
Republic for the holding of a congress to conclude the peace, and to
send passports for the French plenipotentiaries without delay. He was
to hint, too, that the French might have been brought to offer more
had the Allies not displayed such 'jealousy' of Anglo-French transactions, and if the Dutch insisted on continuing the war he was to make
it clear that the queen was no longer willing to bear a burden dispro-
portionate to that shouldered by her allies.[1]

There was, says Mrs. Montgomery, one weak point in all this,
namely, the need that the ministry felt to hold the congress in the
Republic rather than in England. One reason for this, she suggests,
was that it did not yet feel sure enough of its position to risk giving
the Whigs an 'opportunity to stir up popular feeling against the negotiations'. This seems likely enough, but Drummond (now in London)
was nevertheless engaged in holding the threat of a London congress
over Heinsius' head. Many people, he wrote on September 28th,
seemed displeased that the negotiations were likely to be carried on
in the Republic, saying that this had been the scene of so many
fruitless attempts. This ominous assertion was accompanied by others
of a similar nature. Men of all parties, Drummond alleged, were crying
out against the Dutch for attempting to prolong the war because of
the great profit it was bringing them, and not one man in a hundred
would fail to welcome any peace whatever, no matter how bad it
might be.

The possibility of a London peace congress was also dwelt upon by
Defoe in his *Reasons why this Nation ought to put a Speedy End to this
Expensive War* . . ., which appeared at the end of September. This
work deserves some attention, for Defoe had evidently been commissioned to prepare the way for the simultaneous revelation of the second
Mesnager convention and of the expected Dutch acceptance of it,
which St. John was confident that Strafford's 'fair as well as peremp-
tory manner' would obtain. Defoe began by emphasising how necess-

---

[1] Shrewsbury to St. John, 25 and 27 Aug. 1711, Heathrop, *B.L.*, i, pp. 333–7; *Journal to
Stella*, ii, p. 352, 25 Sept. 1711, London; (Shrewsbury) to (Oxford), 27 Sept. 1711 (O.S.),
H.M.C. Bath I, p. 212; Instructions for Strafford, 1 Oct. 1711, Windsor, *B.L.*, i, pp. 398–403;
Legg, *op.cit.*, p. 166.

ary it was to have peace, especially in view of the 'ruinous' campaigns of 1709 and 1710. He next repeated, with approval, the accusations about the attitude of the Dutch deputies at Geertruidenberg that had been made by the French plenipotentiaries, and went on to hint that the death of the Emperor Joseph had made it desirable for the English government to reconsider the question of the 'Spanish Monarchy Entire'. As for those who accused the ministry of planning a separate treaty, he continued, why should not *we* 'be trusted with the Peace, though we have born the Burthen of the War'; and why was not London 'as fit a Place to treat with the *French* in as *Gertruydenberg*'? Why should not the Dutch send their ministers to us, as we had formerly to them? There was no reason to fear that they would be left out of the negotiations, nor, he added, making the most of the fact that the Dutch had made no protest against the ministry's proceedings,

do we find that the *Dutch* themselves are in the least manner jealous or uneasy at our Measures, though the Endeavours of some People to make them so, may not have been wanting; but on the other hand, are no doubt, by mutual Concert with our Court, sending over Two Plenipotentiaries, to be present here at any Conferences that may be held on this occasion.

To suggest that we were not fit to be trusted with making the conditions of our own peace, he declared,

as if *Britain* was under the Tutelage of the *Dutch* .... or that their Politicks were the Standard, by which every Step we took was to be Tryed .... is making such an idol of the *Dutch*, as the *Dutch* themselves do not desire, or can have any reason to expect.

Defoe ended with several arguments in favour of partitioning the Spanish Monarchy, and to these he appended two alternative schemes of partition, both of which, it may be noted, gave the entire Spanish Netherlands to the Dutch.[1]

In the first days of October London was full of rumours about the peace, and to these Defoe, in his *Review*, adopted the same defensive attitude that he had displayed in his pamphlet. He professed himself unable to believe that any treaty could have been entered upon without the consent and concert of the Dutch, for their well-known 'vigilance to their own Safety and Interest' would have led them to complain if they had not been consulted. On the day on which these words appeared in print, October 9/20, Strafford arrived at Helvoetsluys and, finding Buys there awaiting a favourable wind for his

---

[1] (Drummond) to Heinsius, 28 Sept. 1711, London, Archief Heinsius 1590; St. John to Strafford (copy), 9 Oct. 1711, Whitehall, F.E.B. Holl. 79; *C.W.* 52, pp. 25, 33–7; *Montgomery*, p. 128.

journey to England, showed him his instructions – the first official
information concerning the Anglo-French negotiations that the Dutch
had received since May!

Four days later Strafford reported that, although his news had
caused 'much consternation' at first, it now seemed probable that the
Dutch would 'take the ply of aquiescing to what the Queen has
proposed'. Their only serious apprehensions, he added, were about
their barrier; but two days after this he wrote to St. John that the fear
had been 'artificially spread' that 'England was jealous of their strength
and had engaged underhand with the French not to allow them any
barrier'. They would be happy enough, he declared, once they had more
detailed assurances on this subject. Meanwhile he not only threatened
them that the queen would make peace separately if they did not
coöperate with her, but also advised his government to show a similar
'resolution'. Only by such measures could they be prevented from doing
everything possible to break off this negotiation and start one of their
own, so accustomed were they 'to give the law to all their allies, espe-
tially to England'.

Meanwhile the partial revelation to their own countrymen of their
activities had taken place somewhat sooner than the ministers seem to
have intended. They had evidently hoped to be able to publish the
articles to which Mesnager had agreed in the second 'paper' together
with the news that the Dutch had accepted them; this was fairly
obviously what was anticipated in Defoe's writings at this time. On
October 13th, however, the cat slipped out of the bag. The *Daily
Courant* printed the 'paper', which, a few days before, had been
privately communicated to the representatives of the Allies in London
for the information of their governments. Well might the ministry vent
its wrath upon the Imperial envoy Gallas, alleged author of this
leakage, for it had not reckoned upon appealing to public opinion so
soon.[1]

9

The immediate public reaction to the 'Seven Articles' or the 'Seven
Preliminaries', as they were variously called, was far from favourable.
On September 28th Oxford had written to Heinsius that not only 'the

[1] *Review*, viii, 85 and 87, 9 and 13 Oct. 1711; *Daily Courant*, 3121, 13 Oct. 1711; Strafford
to St. John, 24 and 26 Oct. 1711, Hague, S.P. Holl. 240; Strafford to Oxford, 26 Oct. 1711,
Hague, *H.M.C. Portland IX*, pp. 293–4.

necessity of the nation' but also 'the bent of the people' required 'a good peace', but even the High Tories were by no means unanimous in their approval of the terms that had been disclosed, many of them declaring that the 'convention' printed in the *Daily Courant* was obviously spurious. On this point L'Hermitage is in agreement with the annalist Jones, whose words carry conviction:

It is hard to express how strangely the generality of People, of both Parties, and even some of the best Friends of the present M———y, were surpriz'd at the Publication of the *Preliminaries*, who look'd upon them as *Captious, Insidious,* and *Insufficient* to ground a Treaty upon; nay, many of them would not believe them to be genuine.

The ministry acted quickly to stem the tide of these 'murmurings'. Rather than embroil itself further than was necessary with its allies by making any official pronouncement, it chose the government-inspired *Post Boy* as the medium for its counter-move, the publication of the special advantages promised to England in the first Mesnager convention. The ordinary issue of the *Post Boy* for October 13th had already announced, in answer to some conjectures made two days previously in the *Evening Post,* that it had learnt 'from undoubted Hands' that Louis XIV had agreed not only that the fortifications and harbour of Dunkirk were to be ruined, but also that Cadiz would be garrisoned by England and that the English South Sea Company would obtain all the concessions that it desired from Spain. Later in the same day, when the public response to the *Daily Courant's* revelations had become apparent, a special 'Postscript' appeared which detailed the commercial and territorial advantages which had actually been procured. The ministry had been forced to risk the wrath of its allies in an attempt to retain its support at home.[1]

A veritable flood of publications followed upon the revelation of the two sets of 'preliminaries'. So fierce was the pamphlet war, and so apprehensive was the ministry of its consequences, that by October 26th no less than fourteen publishers and printers had already been brought before the Queen's Bench. The onslaught was opened by the *Flying Post,* which indicated the direction that the Whig attack would take by printing together, and without comment, the new 'preliminaries' and those of May 1709, a theme that was speedily developed by Arthur Maynwaring in his *Remarks on the Preliminary Articles.* In

---

[1] Oxford to Heinsius, 28 Sept. 1711 (O.S.), *Weber*, pp. 410–11; *Post-Boy*, 2562, 13 Oct. 1711; L'Hermitage to States-General (transcript), 16/27 Oct. 1711, London, Add. Ms. 17677 EEE; *Jones, 1711*, p. 386; *C.W.* 114, p. 726; *C.W.* 113, vi, p. 696. For the ministry's connection with the *Post Boy* see Hanson, *op.cit.*, p. 98.

general, the Whigs chose to emphasise how ruinous to English interests would be the recognition of Philip V, rather than to expound the objections that the Allies would undoubtedly raise. They no doubt realised that the latter course would have played into the hands of their opponents; indeed, Hare went out of his way to emphasise, in *A Letter to a Member of the October Club*, that once a peace had been made the Dutch would be unwilling to raise a finger to stop Louis XIV from seizing full control of Spain. They did not hesitate, moreover, to find clear indications of Jacobitism in the ministry's activities. If the Tories got their way, declared a Whig ballad, the Pretender would soon be on the throne, and

> The *Dutch* shall be ruin'd, the Whigs shall be damn'd,
> And *Austria's* House be confounded;
> And *Gaul* shall rejoice, while our Allies are shamm'd,
> And our quarrels with *France* are compounded.

Similarly, another Whig pamphlet pointed out that the peace that was envisaged would leave the Dutch barrier just as much at the mercy of France as it had been before, and reminded its readers that

there is a mutual stipulation for our *Protestant Succession*, and for their *Barrier* in the very same Treaty; a Treaty which has lately been much complain'd of, and with good Reason by some People, because it stood in the way of a Treaty of their own.

The same pamphlet (which, it should be added, gave no evidence of any knowledge of the details of the Barrier Treaty) denied the Tories' assertion that in treating with Mesnager they had merely followed the example given more than once by the Dutch. The latter, it asserted, 'never courted in the Cabinet those they had conquer'd in the Field', nor 'in this War sent an Agent to *France*, vested with Authority, to propose a shameful Peace'.[1]

The caution of the Whigs in pressing the objections of the Dutch was met by a corresponding reluctance on the Tory side to goad the Republic too far while its attitude to the negotiations was still in the balance. The *Post Boy* found no reason to doubt that 'that prudent Republic' would be very well satisfied with the stipulations concerning its barrier, and for several weeks it printed items of 'news', ostensibly sent from The Hague, to show that this was the case. Defoe not only defended the 'articles' in the *Review*, but continued to assert that there

---

[1] *Flying-Post*, 3127, 16 Oct. 1711; L'Hermitage to States-General (transcripts), 19/30 Oct. and 26 Oct./6 Nov. 1711, London, Add. Ms. 17677 EEE; *C.W.* 127, *passim*; *C.W.* 92, p. 12; *A Welcome to the Medal* (in C.W. 142, pp. 98–102); *C.W.* 158, pp. 10–11, 33–4.

were no grounds for believing that they had not been concerted in consultation with the Dutch. He also alleged that there was talk in some quarters of privately supplying the Dutch with money to encourage them to carry on the war without England, but he assured those who were planning this that the Dutch had a better understanding of their own interests than to agree to 'so Empty a Project'. He expanded this theme in a pamphlet entitled *The Ballance of Europe,* which was partly a re-hash of his earlier *Reasons Why this Nation should put a Speedy End to this Expensive War*. In this work, too, he went so far as to suggest that the display of enthusiasm for the war by the Dutch and English governments on the death of the Emperor had perhaps been deliberately concerted by them both in order to conceal the Anglo-French negotiations. Even if this were not so, he pointed out, the Dutch had themselves once entertained Mesnager for three months without acquainting us of it. Only one pamphlet, however, made any serious reflections upon the Dutch at this time. This was a reply, perhaps by Swift, to Maynwaring's *Remarks*, which declared in plain words what was merely hinted at in the 'preliminaries', namely that the 'Equivalent' that France demanded for the demolition of Dunkirk could and should be provided out of the prospective Dutch barrier gains.[1]

The ministry, not yet apprised of the Allies' reactions to the 'articles', was plainly on the defensive, and was certainly losing ground at home. Despite all it could do the funds dropped and continued to drop. Here again the evidence of the annalist Jones is valuable, though allowances must certainly be made for a Whig bias. The publication of the first Mesnager convention, he tells us, did not have 'any great Effect upon the Generality of the Nation, who continued to entertain an indifferent Opinion of the present Negotiation ....'. 'The Dislike of the *French* Proposals', he adds, 'increas'd every day', and so too did the 'noise' that this caused, 'so that *Pamphlets* of all sorts flew about like Hail...'. Several High Tory Lords, reported L'Hermitage, were determined to express their dislike of the 'preliminaries' when Parliament met, and meanwhile attempts to address the queen in favour of the steps she had taken were meeting with a conspicuous lack of success. The projected peace, he wrote on November 9th, was still 'peu goûtée' by Whigs and Tories alike. Abroad, too, observers had little confidence in the ability of the ministry to survive this crisis. Petkum's Paris corres-

---

[1] *Post Boy*, 2563, 16 Oct. 1711; *Review*, viii, 89, 92–3, 18, 25 and 27 Oct. 1711; *Annals*, x, p. 262; *C.W.* 39, pp. 12, 30–3; *C.W.* 174, pp. 14, 17.

pondent, who only three weeks before had been confident that the Tories had such overwhelming support that nothing could impede the negotiations, expressed the fear, on November 9th (N.S.), that 'the English may be persuaded by the Dutch and their other Allies to continue the war', while Petkum himself assured Rouillé that 'everyone in England .... is scandalised at the terms of peace'.[1]

The ministry's position was hardly strengthened by the arrival of Buys in London on October 19th, accompanied by the highly accurate rumour that the true purpose of his visit was to thwart the ministry's plans for a peace based on the 'articles'. Oxford hoped that these rumours would not 'render him very agreeable to the bulk of this nation', and warned Heinsius that 'if this affair of peace be at a stand when the Parliament meets, I dread the consequences of it', but the ministry's concern at the direction that events seemed to be taking was apparent from the way in which Strafford, still waiting for the States' acquiescence in the queen's proceeding, mingled more and more brow-beating with his blandishments. This point did not go unnoticed by the observant Jones, who wrote:

.... our Ministry were not a little uneasie at the Difficulties which they met with, both at Home and Abroad, to set a Negotiation on Foot. However, they appear'd fixt in the Resolution to pursue the Scheme they had laid, and in order to that used their utmost Endeavours to engage the States General to come into their Measures; for which purpose the Earl of *Strafford* .... made very pressing Instances with their High Mightinesses.[2]

Strafford was confident that the 'true Lovers of their Country' amongst the Dutch were for joining with the queen, and waxed highly indignant at the difficulties that were being made by those who were unwilling to end a war that had been so profitable to them. He continued to urge his government to be firm, and he himself threatened the Dutch leaders in plain terms that England was prepared, if necessary, to make a separate peace. Drummond, too, acting on instructions, delivered similar menaces to Heinsius, and also repeated St. John's earlier warnings that if the terms of the Barrier Treaty were made known the ministry would be quite unable to restrain the resulting ferment against the Dutch. For all his blustering, however, Strafford was

---

[1] (Paris correspondent) to Petkum (translations), 19 Oct. and 9 Nov. 1711 (N.S.), *H.M.C. XIV pt. ix*, pp. 360, 362; L'Hermitage to tates-General (transcripts) 23 Oct./3 Nov.., 26. Oct./6 Nov., and 9/20 Nov. 1711, London, Add. Ms. 17677 EEE; Petkum to Rouillé (translation), 6 Nov. 1711 (N.S.), *H.M.C. XIV pt. ix*, pp. 356–7; P. Wentworth to Strafford, 2 Nov. 1711, Hampton Court, *Wentworth Papers*, p. 205; Buys to Heinsius, 13 Nov. 1711 (N.S.), cited in *Weber*, p. 130; *Jones, 1711*, pp. 386, 389.

[2] Oxford to Marlborough, 19 Oct. 1711 (O.S.), *Coxe*, iii, pp. 253–4; Oxford to Heinsius, 19 Oct. 1711 (O.S.), *Weber*, pp. 411–13; *Political State*, ii, p. 316; *Jones, 1711*, p. 390.

worried. He considered that one reason for the reluctance of the Dutch to agree to a conference was the refusal of the French to allow it to be held at The Hague. This prohibition, he felt, hit at the Holland merchant oligarchs where they felt it most – their pockets – and he urged Oxford to persuade the French to give way on this. The most important reason for Dutch recalcitrance he still considered to be the equivocal treatment in the 'articles' of their barrier claims and the terms of their trade with France, and he sent home repeated requests for more specific information on this subject. He even gave indications of some personal uneasiness at the continuing evasiveness of his masters on these topics:

The dutch in honour, & Policy, ought to be made easy in the barrier, her Ma: ty shall have, upon mature consideration, & seeing what she could obtain of the French, thought safe & reasonable for them, & I believe they will find her Ma: ty has obtain'd from France the best Tarrif she could for them.

He continued, however, to point out their past misdeeds to the Dutch leaders with the most brutal frankness, and on November 9th (N.S.) he was able to report that the Province of Friesland, despite all that 'those here in the Party of the Whigs' could do, had resolved in favour of sending passports for the French plenipotentiaries. This he regarded as a great point gained; the Dutch, he wrote,

tho formerly they led us by the nose yet seeing we will be their dupes no longer, grow mighty tractable, & we may now do with them what we please.

Only a desire to await the outcome of Buys' mission, he reported, prevented the other Provinces from following suit. This pleasing development, which he characteristically believed to be the result of his own forceful persuasions, brought about no modification in the mixture of threats and reproaches with which he continued to entertain the Dutch leaders. Small wonder that Watkins, himself somewhat uneasy about the news from England, could not perceive at The Hague that Strafford had 'gain'd the friendship or good word of any one person here'.[1]

At home, meanwhile, the ministry had been doing its best to nullify the representations and to thwart the investigations of Buys, to the

[1] *Montgomery*, p. 224 (reference to Drummond to Heinsius, 27 Oct. 1711 (N.S.)); Strafford to (Electress of Hanover) (copy), 28 Oct. 1711, Hague, Stowe Ms. 241; Strafford to Bristol, 30 Oct. 1711, Hague, Ms. Rawl. A. 286; Strafford to Rivers (draft), 31 Oct. 1711, Hague, Add. Ms. 22222; Strafford to Oxford, 3 Nov. 1711, Hague, *H.M.C. Portland IX*, pp. 294-7; Strafford to St. John, 4, 7, 10 and 13 Nov. 1711, Hague, S.P. Holl. 240 (the second of this series is dated 7 Oct. in error); (Strafford) to Argyle (draft), 9 Nov. 1711, Hague, Add. Ms. 22221; (Watkins) to (Drummond) (draft), (10 Nov. ?) 1711, (Hague), Add. Ms. 33273 (dated 10 Oct., but cannot have been written before Strafford's return from England on 20 Oct.); *C.W.* 113, vi, p. 721.

rumours of whose intentions St. John professed to ascribe the continued fall in the funds. 'We want a peace,' he wrote to Strafford on
October 23rd,

and the sense of the nation is for it, whatever noise may be made about London,
by those who find their private account in the universal calamity.

The Dutch envoy was told that the queen would not bind herself to
agree 'preliminaries' with the Republic before any conference with the
French, and that if the Dutch wanted, while treating, to continue
fighting, 'the burden of the war' would have to be 'laid more equally'.
The ministers were reluctant to give written replies to any of Buys'
inquiries, and were indeed highly anxious to be rid of him, for, as the
queen herself declared to Oxford, it would be impossible to open
Parliament until a reply had been received from the Dutch. Watkins,
at The Hague, thought that the States would have sent a better
advocate had they really intended to defy the queen, but St. John grew
more and more exasperated by the desire of the Dutch for some better
safeguard than the 'articles' and some vague expressions of the queen's
good-will. 'So many years together', he complained, 'has this nation
received the law from the influence of their councils, that they are
come to think themselves possessed of a sort of prescriptive right to
govern us for ever'.[1]

Strafford's warnings of the concern of the Dutch about their barrier
and their trade with France had not gone altogether unheeded. Partly,
perhaps, to soothe Shrewsbury's reviving scruples, a memorial was sent
on October 29th to Torcy's agent Gaultier asking that the French
should give more particular explanations of their intentions towards
the Allies. It included the following remarks:

The Dutch aim at nothing but their barrier, and their commerce, and provided
the Queen can, without fear of being disowned, specify, within a small matter,
the barrier which France is willing to yield to them; and that she may assure
them of the tariff of 1664, there is no room to doubt but the States General will
enter, without any difficulty, into the negotiation as it has been concerted.

The 'fear of being disowned', however, did not prevent the commission-
ing of Drummond to offer Heinsius the tariff of 1664 if the Dutch would
agree to a Barrier 'which would not make their friends jealous';

---

[1] St. John to Strafford, 23 and 30 Oct. 1711, Whitehall, *B.L.*, i, pp. 425–7, 454–8; St. John
to Buys (transcript), 26 Oct. 1711, Whitehall, Add. Ms. 17677 YY; Anne to Oxford, 26 Oct.
1711 (O.S.), *H.M.C. Bath I*, p. 214; St. John to Strafford, 26 Oct. and 2 Nov. 1711, Whitehall,
S.P. Holl. 241; Same to same, 30 Oct. 1711, Hampton Court, *B.L.*, i, pp. 445–50; Watkins to
Drummond, 13 Nov. 1711, Hague, *H.M.C. X. pt. i*, p. 144; *C.W.* 18, vi, p. 10 (note by Dartmouth).

instructions which he executed on November 13th (N.S.), long before any reply could have been obtained to the request sent through Gaultier.[1]

IO

Meanwhile Strafford was rapidly losing all patience at the failure of the other provinces to follow the lead of Friesland. By November 15th (N.S.) he was convinced that it was the object of the Dutch to wrest the conduct of the peace from the queen's hands and to obtain the terms they desired for their barrier and commerce while preventing England from gaining the slightest advantage. They were so jealous of us, he complained, that

> they think what ever Brittain shall obtain of an advantage .... is a prejudice to them, tho it no ways interferes with theirs other wayes then that of seeing an increase in their Rival Brittain ....

Worse still, he had

> observed within this six or eight days that these people have a certain air of assurance they had not before, that the Parliament wont approve of the measures the Queen & her Ministers have taken, & I doubt we shall see they will defer their answer till they see the opening of the Parliament.

As it happened, Strafford's calculation was incorrect. The hesitating Heinsius finally gave way, urged on by some particularly outspoken menaces from Strafford himself, and it was largely at the Pensionary's instances that the States of Holland and, on November 21st, the States-General, agreed to supply the much-disputed passports.[2]

The ministry had won the second round in its battle to make the peace, but the month's delay that the Dutch had been able to exact had made this a somewhat barren victory. Despite the continued assurances of the *Post Boy*, there could now be no effective pretence that the concurrence of the Dutch had been anything but submission to coercion. Strafford's warning that the Dutch were now relying on the coming session of Parliament to thwart the queen's measures was just as valid after their ostensible surrender as it had been before. He himself continued to send home highly alarming reports. On November

---

[1] Shrewsbury to (Oxford), 28 Oct. 1711 (O.S.), *H.M.C. Bath I*, p. 214; Memorial to Gaultier, 29 Oct. 1711, Hampton Court, *Cobbett*, vii, appendix, pp. cxix-cxx; *Montgomery*, p. 227 (reference to Drummond to Heinsius, 13 Nov. 1711 (N.S.)).

[2] Strafford to St. John, 15 and 20 Nov. 1711, Hague, S.P. Holl. 240; Strafford to Heinsius, 19 and 21 Nov. 1711 (N.S.), *C.W.* 113, vi, pp. 724–6; Strafford to Bristol, 21 Nov. 1711, Hague, Ms. Rawl. A. 286.

24th, for example, he wrote to the Bishop of Bristol, Dr. Robinson (recently created Lord Privy Seal, and formerly envoy to Sweden) assuring him that

after the even beginning the conferences they will try all artifices to baffle the negotiations backed by the Emperor and our ennemys in England . . . .

Though the ministry had desired the acquiescence of the Dutch partly in order to gain the support of 'moderates' of all kinds for its peace plans, this had been given after such delays and with such obvious reluctance as to be of next to no use for this purpose. The ministers might express their pleasure at the Dutch submission – some, like Shrewsbury, for example, might even show genuine gratitude to the Republic for giving way – and the Whigs their annoyance, but the really important fact was that it would be of little help to the Tories in meeting the parliamentary challenge that now seemed more and more probable.[1]

The rumours that discontented Tory Lords would join with the Whigs to fight the peace were still rife, and the ministers could see for themselves that their propagandists were fighting a losing battle against the Whig onslaught. Throughout November the ministerial writers remained on the defensive, justifying the actions of the ministry but severely limiting their counter-attacks. The egregious Roper, editor of the officially inspired *Post Boy*, was actually placed under arrest for printing a strongly-worded attack on some of the Allies.[2] There were at first very good reasons, quite apart from the ministry's desire to win support on the broadest possible basis, for this policy of caution. The news of the Dutch agreement to the queen's requests did not arrive in London till November 14th, and meanwhile the ministers had no desire to drive the Republic into the arms of the still more recalcitrant Emperor: private bullying by Strafford was a very different thing from public name-calling by a known hireling of the government.

None the less, the defensive propaganda of which Defoe was the foremost exponent was proving insufficient for its task. Not only had

---

[1] Strafford to Bristol, 24 Nov. 1711, Hague, Ms. Rawl. A. 286; Strafford to St. John, 24 and 27 Nov. 1711, Hague, S.P. Holl. 240; Oxford to Heinsius, 16 Nov. 1711 (O.S.), *Weber*, pp. 413–14; Shrewsbury to Oxford, n.d., *H.M.C. Bath I*, pp. 360–1; P. Wentworth to Strafford, 25 Nov. 1711, Hampton Court, *Wentworth Papers*, pp. 211–13.

[2] L'Hermitage to States-General (transcripts), 13/24 and 16/27 Nov. 1711, London, Add. Ms.17677 EEE. Roper's arrest was not necessarily a result of ministerial caution. It may have been rather a sign of Lord Chief Justice Parker's 'great zeal and officiousness to prosecute authors and printers of weekly and other papers writ in defence of the administration', of which Swift complained (*C.W.* 175, p. 38).

Defoe been to some extent personally discredited by his apparently time-serving change of allegiance in 1710, but the Whigs now enjoyed all the advantages of an attacking position that the Tories had experienced in the election of that year. A pamphlet entitled *Armageddon*, probably by Defoe, which appeared about the beginning of November, showed how thin the arguments of the 'Harleyite' propagandists were wearing. The purpose of Buys' visit to London was too well known for there to be much point in continuing to talk of 'the visible Concert there has been all along with the *Dutch*', or to pretend that the reports in the *Post Boy* and elsewhere of 'clandestine' agreements with France were totally unfounded. Such writers as Roper, declared the author of *Armageddon*, in an obvious attempt to appeal to the Whigs and Tory waverers, were the worst enemies of the ministry, in that they tried to embroil it with its allies. In the *Review* Defoe supplemented these pamphlet arguments by trying to show that the Dutch government, as well as the English, was really very concerned about the prospect of Spain and the Indies being in the hands of the Emperor.

The Whig pamphleteers, on the other hand, sensing the dissatisfaction at home and abroad with the ministry's measures, were growing bolder. They were also beginning to turn their attention more and more to the ministry's treatment of the Allies. Even Swift was willing to admit, by implication at least, that this was the most vulnerable aspect of Harley's peace policy; hence, he recorded, its opponents had 'changed their battery, and accused the ministers for betraying the Dutch'. In A *Caveat to the Treaters* William Wagstaffe, replying to several pamphlets by Defoe, not only defended the conduct of the Dutch at Geertruidenberg, but asserted that it very ill became the subjects of the queen to be more eager for peace than their 'brave, couragious and necessary Allies' the Dutch, whose debts, on the authority of the Tory Davenant, were 'far more in proportion to their Ability, than the Debts of *Great Britain* in proportion to ours'. He alleged, moreover, that the suggestion made by Defoe in his schemes of partition that the Dutch should have the entire Spanish Netherlands was merely 'a Copy of his Countenance, and to sew Divisions among the Allies'. Another Whig author devoted himself to replying to Defoe's *Reasons why this Nation should put a Speedy End to this Expensive War*. Defoe's approval of the French complaints about the Dutch management of the 1710 negotiations showed him, he asserted, to be 'an advocate for *France*'. He too made much of the fact that 'their Taxes are .... above twice as heavy as ours'. It is true, he went on, that it is not easy for us to continue the war, but neither was it easy for the Dutch to defy Louis XIV in 1701, when the French army was on their frontiers. The 'article' that stipulated an 'Equivalent' for the demolition of Dunkirk, he added, was nothing more than an indirect attack on the Barrier Treaty and thus on the Protestant Succession.

The most outspoken attack on the 'articles' that concerned the Dutch occurred in *A Vindication of the Present Ministry*, published on November 26th, a pamphlet written in so ironical a vein that it has been attributed to Defoe. On the face of it such an attribution seems unlikely, but the way in which it attacked the 'New Preliminaries' by pretending that they were too bad to be genuine is certainly reminiscent of the author of *The Shortest Way with the Dissenters*. This *Vindication* paid much attention to the 'article' which dealt with the Dutch barrier. To tell the Dutch, as this 'article' did, that they should have 'such places as shall be mention'd', it declared, was in fact to say 'that they shall not have what has been mention'd'. This could mean nothing else but that 'our Good and Great, and most Faithful Allies' were to be 'turn'd out of the Acquisitions, that are the Price of their Blood and Treasure'. 'Tis impossible!' it continued:

If Faith and Justice did not in the strictest manner oblige us to insist on a good Barrier for the *Dutch*, the brave and honourable Part they have Acted in this War, and the great Regard they have had to the Interest of *England*, highly deserves it of us; 'tis the least that in gratitude we can do for them.

No one properly acquainted with their government, or with their dependence on commerce, could seriously think that they wanted to prolong the war from selfish ends; indeed, the *Vindication* went on, nothing had given us more alarm during the war than the fear that the Dutch might make a premature peace. We were mistaken, however, for they had displayed a 'noble firmness' and a strict adherence to England, despite French offers of a barrier and commercial advantages of their own choosing if they would desert us. 'They judged', it declared,

that no terms *France* could give, can be so truly· for their Interest, as to cultivate a perfect good Understanding with *England* .... Behold now their Reward! These brave and faithful Allies are to be sacrific'd, to nobody knows what Interest; their Adherence to us, and Rejection of all private Offers, is made Matter of Reproach .... we desert them, because they would not desert us ....

Even if we had no sense of gratitude or honour, it continued, we should at least have some regard to our safety, since the Dutch were our 'Fence and Barrier' against France, as well as being the guarantees of our Succession. Even more scandalous, it asserted, was the 'article' concerning Dunkirk:

Is this not now a pretty Story? Must not *Holland* like mightily to be told, that they shall be oblig'd to give up a good part of the Barrier, *Lille* and *Tournay* suppose, Places upon which their Security so much depends, to purchase a Security for the *English* Trade?

In any case Louis XIV, having obtained his 'Equivalent', would never carry out the promised demolition. It was evident that the 'articles' as a whole represented a deliberate attempt to 'confound' the Dutch barrier, and that 'no M———y that could be pick'd in all *England,* except profest Jacobites, could ever be so capable to giving their Consent to them'. What we should do, concluded the *Vindication*, was to emulate the 'steddy Conduct' of Heinsius in insisting on the May preliminaries as a basis for negotiation.

A few days after the publication of the *Vindication* there appeared *A Letter from an Exchange Broker to a Country Gentleman*, which maintained the satirical pretence that the 'preliminaries' were not genuine, and gave this as a reason for not selling South Sea Company stock. If, however, they *had* been genuine, it added meaningly, it would have been very wise to sell this stock, for France and Spain together would have ruined our South Sea trade, and we could certainly not have expected any help in this from the Dutch, after betraying them so basely.[1]

While the paper war raged, the opening of Parliament was prorogued from week to week. The first prorogation seems to have been due to a determination to await the results of Strafford's persuasions, but further prorogations followed after the news of the States' submission had reached London. The ministers, it was said, were not yet confident of the temper of their supporters; and, indeed, Strafford's reports from The Hague could leave them in no doubt that their opponents would have the Dutch on their side. On December 8th (N.S.) Strafford declared that now that they had, from Buys, some inkling of the far-reaching objections of the ministry to the Barrier Treaty, all Dutchmen regretted their submission:

Our friends, and those the most for peace repent what they have done, and it is certain those for the continuance of the war triumph over them, and tell them they are my dupes, and are sacrificed to an English Ministry, enemy to their Republic, but I have again assured them they shall find the contrary . . . .

---

[1] *Review*, viii, 99, 10 Nov. 1711; *C.W.* 38, pp. 8–22, 36, 45; *C.W.* 191, pp. 8 *sqq.*, 74–5; *C.W.* 124, pp. 9–10, 16–17, 22, 36–7; *C.W.* 190, pp. 12–20, 40–1; *C.W.* 119, pp. 4, 11; *C.W.* 175, pp. 70–1.

The three plenipotentiaries the Dutch seem to have pitched upon already are those who have been the most for peace; those who will carry their speculations very deep, say they are chose to have them from being in the States General, who must give their directions to their Plenipotentiaries so that by their absence the party for the war will be so much stronger in the Government here, and that they may be the sacrifice if they can bring the people to think the peace is not as advantageous as they might expect.

The situation of the ministry, losing ground at home and with the Allies eager to see its downfall, called for bold, if not desperate, measures. Something was needed to ensure the support of the English people for the ministry whatever the Allies might do or say. It says much for the political sense of Oxford and St. John that they saw this need and fulfilled it. Their decision was indeed a bold one, for it meant that for the future they would have to contend with the unceasing enmity of all their allies. It was, simply, to abandon the caution which their advocates had, for the most part, hitherto employed in favour of an unrestrained campaign of abuse and vilification of their allies, a campaign calculated to appeal not only to the age-old hatred of the foreigner so characteristic of the English but particularly to the more recent special aversion from the Dutch. The chief spokesman for the ministry would no longer be Defoe, who was still celebrating the unanimity of interest of Britain and the United Provinces, but Swift.[1]

II

It was the declared intention of the Tory government from its beginning to save English trading interests from the impending ruin which threatened them, so it was said, owing to the disastrous management of the Godolphin ministry. One of the ways in which the ministry demonstrated this determination was by adopting a high tone in disputes with its Dutch allies over questions of trade and commerce. The High Tory line was that the Whigs, 'being far more zealous for a *neighbouring Nation* than for *their own*', had sacrificed 'several *Branches of our Trade*, to the Interest of that Republick'. It was not merely that the ministry, greedy for the *Asiento*, found Article XV of the Barrier Treaty quite unacceptable; as St. John declared,

our commerce has been neglected, while the French have engrossed the South-

---

[1] *Review*, viii, 105, 24 Nov. 1711; L'Hermitage to States-General (transcript), 27 Nov./8 Dec. 1711, London, Add. Ms. 17677 EEE; Strafford to Oxford, 8 Dec. 1711, Hague, *H.M.C. Portland IX*, pp. 302-7.

Seas trade to themselves, and the Dutch encroach daily upon us, both in the East-Indies, and on the coast of Asia.[1]

The Whigs, of course, held up the concern of the Tory 'landed interest' for the state of trade to ridicule, and strove to show that it was wholly simulated. 'Are not the *Dutch*', asked the *Medley*, the Whig rival to the *Examiner*,

as the *Examiner* and the Tory-Writers represent them, a despicable sorry People, *Herring-Curers*? And why, but because they have a *Trading-Interest* only; no Landed-Interest, no Church-Interest, in which we have a great Advantage over them: Tho *Old Double* (*i.e.* Davenant) says, they have thirty six Millions Sterling ready Cash in the Bank of *Amsterdam*, four times as much as we have in all Britain.[2]

A question that arose early in the year was whether Britain should take advantage of Louis XIV's prohibition of trading with the Dutch to re-open commerce with France. The High Tories were much in favour of such a step. 'Our good Allies the *Dutch*', declared one of their number,

who knew how to consult their Profit as well as any Nation under the Canopy of Heaven, had enrich'd themselves by this Trade to such a Degree, that it was high Time for their Friends and Confederates to step in for a Share with them ...

The *Examiner*, too, abused the old ministry for having allowed the Dutch to trade with 'the Enemy as in times of Peace'. On February 8th the question came before the House of Commons, which straightway appointed a Committee to bring in a Bill to repeal the Act prohibiting trade and commerce with France in so far as it related to the importation of wines.

While the Committee did its work it was to Defoe in the *Review* that the task fell of justifying such a measure. In three successive issues he emphasised the great riches the Dutch had obtained by trading with France during the war. This, he claimed, was the reason why Amsterdam, once so clamorous for peace, was now so averse to it. Much of their gains, he went on, had come from conducting British trade with France – above all the trade in Scottish fish. 'The *Dutch*', he declared,

come and catch the Fish at their doors, and carry them to *France*, the Market which the *Scots* had before, and the Poor Fisher Men in *Scotland* may blow their Fingers instead of curing of Fish.

Why, then, he asked, since the Dutch had enriched themselves by

---

[1] St.John to Raby, 6 May 1711 (O.S.), *B.L.*, i, pp. 185–95; *C.W.* 183, p. 16.
[2] *Medley*, 19 and 30, 5 Febr. 1710/11 and 23 April 1711.

our voluntarily being shut out of trade with France, should we not do likewise now that they also were shut out by the edict of the French king? We should remember, he continued in a later issue, that

the *Dutch*, however our fast Friends and Faithful Allies in our Politick Interests, are none of our best beloved Friends in Trade . . . .

Their activities in the African trade were clear enough evidence of this.

Despite the objections to this measure of various interested groups, above all the Portugal merchants, the bill became law before the session ended. On receipt of this news, the Dutch became 'somewhat uneasy', according to a Tory writer who blamed the Whigs for working up groundless apprehensions amongst them. The States of Holland even went so far as to talk of formally prohibiting trade with France, but of this Dayrolle remarked, on August 4th (N.S.), that

if they could oblige the French Court to use them as before in relations to their Trade, I am afraid their resolution would fall, it going against their own Inclination and only because of the ill usage of the French.[1]

The continuing misdeeds of Dutch men-of-war and privateers were a considerable source of irritation to the Oxford ministry at this time. The clandestine landing of prohibited or dutiable goods upon British shores by Dutch men-of-war had long been a subject of complaint against the Dutch ally. In 1696 a convention had been drawn up to allow the boarding of Dutch men-of-war in English harbours by English revenue officers, with a reciprocal concession to the Dutch, but it had never been ratified. In queen Anne's war this smuggling was resumed on a large scale. On one occasion in 1707 alone, for example, it seems that more than 40,000 gallons of brandy were landed in the Firth of Forth. A peculiarly blatant incident at Tilbury in the same year led to complaints by Godolphin himself and a renewed demand for boarding rights, as well as a protest on an unofficial level by the *Observator*. All these representations were unavailing, and in the following years the Commissioners of Customs continued to receive reports that coconuts, wines, brandy and other articles were being 'run ashore' from Dutch warships.[2]

[1] *Review*, vii, 144–6, 24 and 27 Feb., and 1 March 1710/11; *ibid.*, viii, 10, 17 April 1711; *Examiner*, i, 44, 31 May 1711; Dayrolle to St. John, 4 Aug. 1711, Hague, S.P. Holl. 238; C.W. 143, pp. 87–8.

[2] Commrs. of Customs (Scotland) to Taylor (abstract), 12 Aug. 1707, Edinburgh, *Cal. Tr. Bks.*, xxi, 2, p. 429; Commrs. of Customs to Godolphin (abstract), 26 Sept. 1707 (O.S.), *Cal. Tr. Papers, 1702–7*, p. 537; Same to same (abstract), 26 Jan. 1707/8 (O.S.), *Cal. Tr. Papers, 1708–14*, p. 5; *Observator*, vi, 95, 28 Jan. 1707/8; Lowndes to Commrs. of Customs, 21 Feb. 1707/8 (O.S.), *Cal. Tr. Bks.*, xxii, 2, p. 144; Commrs. of Customs (Scotland) to Lowndes (abstract), 25 April 1708 (O.S.), *Cal. Tr. Papers, 1708–14*, p. 32; *ibid.*, p. 137, Commrs. of Cus-

The smugglers seemed, indeed, to be gaining in confidence. In 1711 force was used against Scottish customs officers at Leith by the crew of the *Helvoetsluys*, and this brought forth another official protest, this time by St. John. Not only, he declared, did this smuggling defraud the queen of the duties that should have been paid, but it also meant that 'de grandes sommes en espèce' were going out of the country.

That St. John's representations were quite as ineffective as those of his predecessors was demonstrated on June 15th, 1712, when a customs officer named James Woolley was killed near Plymouth in a skirmish with members of the crew of the Dutch man-of-war *Skyland*. This incident aroused some public interest, being reported in the *Post Boy* for June 28th, and on August 29th St. John wrote to Strafford of the 'frequent complaints' of the continued smuggling activities of Dutch men-of-war, and particularly of the 'barbarous murther' of Woolley. Accordingly, on September 30th (N.S.) Strafford submitted a memorial on these matters to the States-General. The reply that he received was very far from giving satisfaction to his masters, for all suggestion that the *Skyland* had been engaged in smuggling was denied, and it was instead alleged that the Dutch crew had been maliciously attacked by English customs officers.[1]

St. John was equally determined to obtain satisfaction for all injuries suffered by British ships at the hands of Dutch privateers. The conduct of these privateers, especially those of Zeeland, had long been the despair of English representatives in the Republic, who soon learnt how difficult it was to obtain any kind of redress. As Dayrolle had explained to his government in 1708, the States-General could exercise almost no control over the Zeeland Admiralty, and from this body, to whose consideration all complaints about the Zeeland privateers were referred, 'very little justice' was to be expected. Townshend, too, had discovered that the Dutch were 'very dilatory' in dealing with matters of this sort. In 1711, however, a case arose which St. John was determined to prosecute to a satisfactory conclusion. The *Society* of Cork had, according to its owners, been seized by a

toms to Godolphin (abstract), 13 Sept. 1709 (O.S.); *Cal. Tr. Bks.*, xxiv, 2, p. 586, 5 Sept. 1710; G. N. Clark, 'Anglo-Dutch relations of commercial policy and the nine years war of 1688–1697', *Verslag van de Algemeene Vergadering der Leden van het Historisch Genootschap ... Utrecht ... 30 Maart 1932* (Utrecht, 1932), p. 6.

[1] Commrs. of Customs (Scotland) to Lowndes (abstract), 2 June 1711 (O.S.), *Cal. Tr. Papers, 1708–14*, p. 276; St. John to Vrijbergen (copy), 30 June 1711, Whitehall, F.E.B. For. Min. 257; *Post Boy*, 2673, 28 June 1712; St. John to Strafford (copy), 29 Aug. 1712, Whitehall, F.E.B. Holl. 74; Strafford to States-General (copy), 30 Sept. 1712, Utrecht, Add. Ms. 22266; *C.W.* 113, vii, pp. 233–4.

Flushing privateer, its cargo pillaged and its crew tortured, and repeated applications for redress to the Zeeland Admiralty had had no result. St. John protested vigorously against this 'barbarous and inhumane treatment'. British subjects, he declared in letters to Vrijbergen and Raby, had been treated by their allies in a manner 'more cruel than ever wou'd have been committed by our Enemys'. Undeterred by the curious revelation that the *Society* was in fact a French vessel, the *Union* of Nantes, he continued month after month to press this case in characteristically forceful terms, apparently with no success. In May 1713 Strafford was still representing to the Dutch government how much the queen resented the unending delays in this matter and protesting loudly about the alleged violation of treaty rights. Delays of this kind were far from unusual; on August 12th, 1712 (N.S.), in a memorial to the States-General, Strafford brought to their attention another case which was not finally settled until April 1718.[1]

[1] Dayrolle to (Boyle), 12 June 1708, Hague, S.P. Holl. 231; Same to same, 23 April 1709, Hague, S.P. Holl. 232; Townshend to Boyle, 8 Aug. 1710, Hague, S.P. Holl. 235; St. John to Raby, 24 April 1711, Whitehall, Add. Ms. 22266; St. John to Vrijbergen (transcripts), 24 April and 1 May 1711, Whitehall, Add. Ms. 17677 EEE; Strafford to van der Dussen (draft), 30 May 1713, Utrecht, Add. Ms. 22266; *C.W.* 113, vii, pp. 228 *sqq.*

CHAPTER X

THE CAMPAIGN AGAINST THE ALLIES I
(COERCION AND ABANDONMENT)
⟨1711–12⟩

I

The publication on November 27th, 1711, of *The Conduct of the Allies* marks the beginning of a determined policy on the part of the Tory ministry of publicly reproaching and abusing the Allies. This policy, by its very nature welcome to many High Tories, had in any case been made necessary by the cool or even hostile reception given both at home and abroad to the revelation of the clandestine agreements which had been made with Louis XIV. Its aim was therefore both to overcome the doubts which many Englishmen outside the ranks of the Whigs were feeling, and at the same time to deafen them to the complaints or appeals of the Allies.

There can be no doubt that this was a completely deliberate campaign, planned and executed by the ministry. Many years later St. John was to declare this explicitly:

The league made for protracting the war having opposed the queen to the utmost of their power, and by means of every sort, from the first appearances of a negociation: the general effect of this violent opposition, on her and her ministers was, to make them proceed by slower and more cautious steps: the particular effect of it was, to oblige them to open the eyes of the nation, and to inflame the people with a desire of peace, by shewing, in the most public and solemn manner, how unequally we were burdened, and how unfairly we were treated by our allies.[1]

In this campaign pamphlets, periodicals and news-sheets were to play a vital role. Early in 1712 the fact that these propagandist attacks on the Allies were 'approved and directed by my Lord Oxford' was the talk of the town.[2] The official 'inspiration' of *The Conduct of the Allies* is too well established to need further demonstration here;[3] the idea that this work was a 'counterblast' to the Elector of Hanover's

---

[1] *C.W.* 160, p. 137.

[2] 'Mrs. White' to 'Mr. Watson', (Feb. 1711/12), *Macpherson*, ii, pp. 279–82.

[3] Laprade, *Public Opinion and Politics in Eighteenth Century England*, p. 100; Wyon, *op. cit.*, ii, p. 335.

Memorial [1] is not only mistaken (the Memorial was not presented until November 28th and did not find its way into print until December 6th)[2] but also misleading in suggesting a certain lack of premeditation. Francis Hare did not fail to remark the intentional nature of the change that had come over the attitude of the 'ministerial' propagandists towards the Allies. 'They let go their Hold of the late M——y', he declared,

and began to fasten on Our Allies, for their Malice in blackening the former, wou'd not carry the Point far enough: There must be a quarrel pick'd with the *Dutch*, in particular . . . . [3]

Partisan though he was, Hare's assertion was correct. The quarrel would be 'with the *Dutch*, in particular', and it was to the resentment thus aroused against the Republic that a Whig pamphlet published in mid-1712 attributed the success of the ministry in winning support for its policies.[4] At first sight this may seem somewhat curious. For one thing, the Dutch had already acquiesced in the queen's proceedings, however reluctantly, before the ministry launched its campaign. There was, too, a far better and less debatable case against the Austrians, if the ministers were merely looking for a scapegoat. But there were several good reasons for singling out the Dutch. In the first place, even their worst enemies would hardly have denied that they were Britain's 'chief ally'. As such they were to many of the queen's subjects a symbol not only of the Alliance but of the whole intolerable burden of the war. Their alleged connections with the English Whigs, moreover, meant that any successful attack on them would also represent a political victory at home. There was a negative reason, too, why the Dutch were awarded this dubious honour. Prussia and Savoy were, relatively speaking, in the ministry's good books, while the greed and selfishness of Portuguese and Austrians were already regarded as established facts; thus only against the Dutch would an assault be both desirable and profitable. Finally, there was the consideration of convenience. It was easier to work up deep and bitter feeling against the Dutch than against any other ally. In almost every Englishman there still burned at least the embers of the hatreds engendered by Dutch wars and 'Dutch rule', and it was not difficult for Swift and his fellows to fan them once more into flame.

---

[1] *Churchill*, iv, pp. 488, 506.
[2] L'Hermitage to States-General (transcript), 7/18 Dec. 1711, London, Add. Ms. 17677 EEE.
[3] *C.W.* 91, p. 12.
[4] *C.W.* 100, pp. 220–1.

The launching of the campaign against the Allies represented the victory within the ministry of the extremist views of St. John, with the conversion to the need for stronger measures of the more moderate though no less opportunist Oxford. Hence the reappearance of the virulent, government-sponsored *Examiner* on December 13th, after a lapse in publication of several months. To St. John, certainly, the campaign was not merely a necessary manoeuvre to maintain support at home, but a veritable labour of love. He seems already to have considered the Allies, rather than France, as England's real enemy, and it was doubtless with him in mind that the French pleni-potentiaries at Utrecht were informed, in their instructions, that

les Anglais, flattés du personnage que Sa Majesté veut qu'ils fassent en cette importante occasion, conviendront aisément qu'il est de la dignité d'un grand Roi de se montrer irrité contre l'orgueil et l'injustice d'une République éblouie par la prosperité.[1]

To one person on the fringe of officialdom, however, the new campaign must have been a considerable embarrassment. This was Daniel Defoe, whose activities after the appearance of the *Conduct of The Allies* demonstrate that there had indeed been a change of policy. Ever since his spectacular rise to fame as the author of the *True-Born Englishman* Defoe had been something unique in the political life of the day: a governmental writer who also had some pretensions to a mind of his own. Since 1710, however, things had been becoming increasingly difficult for him. It was not only that he was now hated by Whig and High Tory alike. It was also that he had become the advocate of the middle-of-the-road policy which the pressure of events and of his colleagues never gave Oxford much chance to pursue. As the months went by Defoe was constantly having to explain away the deviations of his master from this *via media*, and at the same time to attempt to maintain some modicum of integrity. He had already printed some restrained but pointed criticisms of the Allies, but his Whig conscience seems temporarily to have got the better of him when Swift launched his onslaught. While defending the activities of the ministers themselves he vigorously attacked their hirelings. Up to a point this situation was no doubt pleasing to Oxford, who habitually kept his right hand in ignorance of what his left was doing, and probably welcomed the existence of ministerial propagandists of opposing views, who between them would appeal to a very large

---

[1] Instructions for Huxelles, Polignac and Mesnager, 30 Dec. 1711, Versailles, Legrelle, *La Diplomatie Française* ..., iv, pp. 634-5.

section of his countrymen. In the period that will be examined in this chapter, however, it was a matter of life and death for the ministry that the campaign against the Allies should succeed at home; and the unfortunate Defoe, in the *Review*, in his correspondence with Oxford, and, finally, in some of the most unconvincing pamphlets he ever wrote, was gradually forced to toe the line that Swift had marked out with such enthusiasm.

2

The Conduct of the Allies, written by Swift at St. John's prompting and published anonymously on November 27th, was probably the most influential single publication of the reign of queen Anne. According to one estimate, it sold 11,000 copies in one month, a figure surpassed only by Sacheverell's notorious sermon.[1] Swift's thesis, in brief, was that

no Nation was ever so long or so scandalously abused by the Folly, the Temerity, the Corruption, the Ambition of its domestick Enemies; or treated with so much Insolence, Injustice and Ingratitude by its foreign Friends.

In search for support for this contention he travelled back much farther than 1702, but most of his examples were, naturally enough, drawn from the War of the Spanish Succession. It is no denigration of Swift's genius to point out that his pamphlet shows signs of having been put together in haste. His arguments, though forcefully expressed, are somewhat ill-assorted, and it is obvious to a present-day reader that he had concerned himself less with the logical and cogent development of his theme than with the amassing of every conceivable accusation against the Allies and the late ministry. This relative formlessness makes it possible to consider Swift's references to the Dutch in isolation without doing much injustice to the pamphlet as a whole.

One of Swift's main contentions was that we had no direct interest in the war, that our participation in it should consequently have been as an 'auxiliary' and that it should have been confined mainly to naval warfare. By ignoring these precepts, he claimed, we had impoverished ourselves in order to gain a 'noble territory' for the Dutch who would thus be enabled to 'undersell us in every Market of the World'. We had in fact neglected the war in the Indies for fear of giving offence

[1] *Lecky*, i, p. 61.

to an ally which had never fully observed its own treaty obligations, and probably had never intended to.

From here Swift went on to reveal, apparently for the first time in print, the main provisions, though not the actual text, of the Barrier Treaty. We gained nothing by this, he contended, since the Dutch were already obliged, as our ally, to come to our aid in case of need. What we had done was merely to give the States a claim to regulate our Succession, and at the same time to make them 'entire masters of the Low *Countries*', where, he suggested, they would be able to set up a woollen manufacture that would be our ruin. On top of all this, after thus voluntarily shutting ourselves out of our trade with Flanders we had agreed that they should be favoured equally with us in all the Spanish dominions, though they had 'hardly contributed any thing at all' to the war in Spain.

Next Swift pointed to a long series of Dutch shortcomings during the war. They had gained the 1703 augmentation by pretending to stop their trade with France but had soon opened it up again; they had indulged in various fraudulent practices so as to be able to default in their military quotas unobserved; and contrary to all agreements they used many of 'the Troops of their Quota' to garrison the towns we had conquered for them. Greed alone had prevented their agreeing to Marlborough's winter-quarters project, and as for the war at sea,

they never once furnished their Quota of Ships or Men; or if some few of their Fleet now and then appeared, it was no more than appearing, for they immediately separated to look to their Merchants and protect their Trade.

In this connection he did not fail to make the most of such recent events as Wishart's abortive mission and Dutch inaction during the invasion scare. They had never augmented nor even 'recruited' the troops that they sent to Portugal, he complained, and their slowness in paying subsidies was well shown by their failure to pay any to Portugal for six whole years.

Reverting now to Dutch gains in the Low Countries, Swift asserted that under their 'sovereignty', and 'in Conjunction with our G———l, the Oppressions of *Flanders* are much greater than ever'. This and their 'whole Chain of Encroachments' had been winked at by the late ministry 'because the General was *made easie* . . .', and because the Dutch had blackmailed it with threats of a separate peace. By these means had they obtained the Barrier Treaty, whereby 'we, instead of labouring to make them *safe*, must beggar ourselves to render them *Formidable*'. What, Swift asked, was the point of continuing the war on such a basis? What advantages had we, for example, from the capture of Bouchain,

but that of spending three or four Millions more to get another Town for the States, which may open them a new Country for *Contributions*, and increase the Perquisites of the G——l?[1]

If, as seems likely, the *Conduct* was to some extent a *ballon d'essai*, designed to test public feeling as well as to influence it, the ministry must have been well pleased by its success. In the feverish atmosphere which reigned in London, where one day it was rumoured that the mob at The Hague had threatened to tear Strafford to pieces, and another that there was nothing left for the Dutch to desire in what the French were offering them, Swift's pamphlet created a furore. Its effect in the country was little less, according to Dr. Stratford, sometime tutor to Oxford's son Edward, who informed his former pupil that 'it will put the country gentlemen in the temper you desire, they are very ready to battle it at home for a peace abroad'. It is too much to say that the *Conduct* alone 'saved Oxford's ministry from overthrow', but it would be difficult to overrate its service to the ministers in turning popular attention away from their peace tactics and towards the war record of the Allies. This was the great achievement of the *Conduct*: not the overnight conversion of the ministry's critics but the stimulation on all sides of an avid and searching scrutiny of this record. This comes clearly out of Swift's own assessment of the effects of his work:

Some discourses had been published in print, about the beginning of the session, boldly complaining of certain articles in the Barrier Treaty .... and showing, in many particulars, the unequal conduct of these powers in our alliance, in furnishing their quotas and supplies .... These loud accusations spreading themselves throughout the kingdom, delivered in facts directly charged, and thought, whether true or not, to be but weakly confuted, had sufficiently prepared the minds of the people; and, by putting arguments into every body's mouth, had filled the town and country with controversies, both in writing and discourse.[2]

It would certainly not be long before every single political writer would find himself obliged either to defend or to attack Swift's arguments. Indeed, the first Whig replies came swiftly. On December 1st the *Flying Post* directed a number of not very penetrating queries to the author of the *Conduct*, who was accused of making 'scandalous

[1] *C.W.* 173, pp. 9, 12, 15, 17–18, 21–2, 25, 29–37, 43–4, 48–50, 56, 67, 71.
[2] L'Hermitage to States-General (transcript), 30 Nov./11 Dec. 1711, London, Add. Ms. 17677 EEE; P. Wentworth to (Strafford), 30 Nov. and 4 Dec. 1711, London, *Wentworth Papers*, pp. 216–18; Dr. Stratford to E. Harley, 4 Dec. 1711, Oxford, *H.M.C. Portland VII*, p. 79; *C.W.* 175, p. 99; Stevens, *op.cit.*, p. 38.

reflections' on the Dutch, and five days later the *Protestant Post-Boy* denied that the States could have 'too Strong a Barrier' and suggested that it was frustrated Jacobitism which prompted the *Conduct*'s complaints about the 'mutual Indulgence between the General and the States of Holland'. For the moment, however, publications continued to appear whose composition had been unaffected by Swift's bombshell. The *Observator* warned its readers that any alteration in the Dutch barrier might rob us of Dutch support for our Succession, and Defoe continued to defend the 'preliminaries' but at the same time to deny that the Allies were really against peace. The hack-poets celebrated the 'preliminaries', too: one Whig writer described the fourth 'article' as follows:

> As the King will maintain the Peace when concluded,
> So for fear that the *Dutch* should think they are deluded,
> Of them on a sudden he's grown very Tender,
> And consents for their Good *that they may Surrender*
> *Whate'er has been taken in* Flanders *this War*,
> *And he'll then yeild them back a very good Barr.*

A Tory rival, on the other hand, alleged that we had been the 'Pack Horse' of the Dutch:

> The late Ministry put out the Nation to Nurse,
> With an old Wooden-leg and a Crutch,
> And to *teach* us to go, ty'd our *Lading-strings* too,
> And gave them to hold to the *Dutch*.[1]

Meanwhile, at The Hague, there was an increasing confidence, which can be seen, for example, in the letters of Petkum to Torcy, that the imminent session of Parliament would thwart the ministry's plans. Strafford believed that this was mainly due to the reports of Buys. St. John's attitude towards the Dutch envoy, whom Swift found 'plaguy politick', grew rapidly hostile under the influence of Strafford's warnings, especially since the English envoy was also of the opinion that Buys' reports of St. John's views on the Barrier Treaty were causing the greatest alarm in the Republic. Moreover, complained the Secretary, Buys was not properly instructed:

My Lord, we are not deceived, we see through this slight veil. They propose two things to themselves, first pumping our secret, and engaging the Queen without disclosing their own, or binding themselves. Secondly, they appear to negociate, and by this amusement gain time, till they see what turn the parliament will take, and what is likely to be the effect of the cabals of their friends the Whigs ..

[1] *Observator*, x, 95, 28 Nov. 1711; *Flying-Post*, 3146, 1 Dec. 1711; *Protestant Post-Boy*, 416, Dec. 1711; *C.W.* 51, pp. 40–1; *C.W.* 80; *C.W.* 139, pp. 3–4.

Drummond was instructed to inform Heinsius of the ministry's confidence of success in Parliament, but St. John's declaration that the queen would act as a 'mediatrice' between the States and France in the question of the barrier was not calculated to allay Dutch apprehension on that head. Strafford still wished to make peace in concert with the Dutch, but his alarm at what he heard at The Hague was increased with the arrival of Eugene on his way to become the highly unwelcome guest of the English government. He did his best to convince the Prince of the right of England, which bore most of the burden of the war, to initiate a peace, but he noted with concern that Eugene was in almost continual consultation with the 'warrior party' at The Hague. Like Watkins, away on a mission to the Imperial court, he suspected the Dutch of intriguing with the Emperor behind the queen's back for the continuation of the war.[1]

3

The day appointed for the opening of Parliament was December 7th. On December 6th there appeared in the *Daily Courant* the Hanover Memorial, which subjected the second Mesnager convention to detailed and unfavourable criticism. The Jacobites saw in this an opportunity for prejudicing less extreme Tories against the Hanover Succession by asserting that

the house of Hannover and the States of Holland are united with the Whigs and discontented party of England, against the Queen, her present ministry, and the church of England.[2]

In her speech at the opening of Parliament the queen announced that definite arrangements for a peace conference had been made, and that

Our allies (especially the States General, whose interest I look upon as inseparable from my own) have, by their ready concurrence, expressed their entire confidence in me . . . .

This patently untrue assertion was later repeated by St. John in the Commons' debate on the address, and it did not pass unchallenged. Sir Peter King told the Secretary that he must take them for school-

---

[1] Strafford to St. John, 8, 11 and 18 Dec. 1711, Hague, S.P. Holl. 240; Strafford to (Poulett) (draft), 8 Dec. 1711, Hague, Add. Ms. 22222; St. John to Strafford, 30 Nov. and 4 Dec. 1711, Whitehall, *B.L.*, ii, pp. 26–34; (Watkins) to (Drummond) (draft), 14 Dec. 1711, Aschaffemburg, Add. Ms. 33273; *Montgomery*, p. 235 (reference to Drummond to Heinsius, 4/15 Dec. 1711); *Journal to Stella*, ii, p. 440, 5 Dec. 1711, London; Strafford to Oxford, 18 Dec. 1711, Hague, *H.M.C. Portland IX*, pp. 307–9; Petkum to Torcy (translations), 22 and 24 Dec. 1711 (N.S.), *H.M.C. XIV pt. ix*, pp. 358–9.

[2] *A Letter to a Friend* (in *Macpherson*, ii, pp. 218–22).

children to make such a declaration, and demanded to know whether it was not solely as a result of coercion that the Dutch had given their consent. St. John retorted by asking whether the queen's word was to be doubted, and their overwhelming majority in the Commons eventually won the day for the ministry.

In the Lords, however, the defection of Nottingham and his followers to the Whig ranks (in return for acceptance by the Junto of an Occasional Conformity Bill) brought about a very different result. Nottingham urged the necessity of maintaining 'the express engagements which Great-Britain had entered into with the allies', and the address which the Lords presented to the queen on December 11th contained a clause to the effect that no peace should be made which gave Spain to a member of the House of Bourbon, as well as a careful repetition of the queen's assurances of her regard for the States-General, a feature that was conspicuously absent from the Commons' address.

The ministry was now in a very dangerous position. Oxford kept cool, and in his letters to Heinsius he made it clear that he had no intention of modifying his policies merely because, as he alleged, some foreign ministers had stirred up 'the faction' in the Lords. Instead he forecast 'some necessary alterations heer of great moment'. His firmness, indeed, was such that Buys – whom he plainly suspected of plotting with Nottingham and the Whigs – was brought to deliver the coveted passports which he had hitherto withheld. St. John's letters to Strafford showed that the ministers attributed much of the blame for the unwelcome development in the Lords to the machinations of the Dutch; nor was St. John's temper much improved by Buys' offer to procure from the States-General a resolution contrary to that voted by the Lords if the ministry would stand by Article XV of the Barrier Treaty – the article which ensured a share for the Dutch in all commercial advantages obtained by Britain from Spain. Strafford, meanwhile, found that the Dutch attitude towards their barrier and commerce was very much stiffened by the news from London. They were now confident, he reported, despite his expostulations concerning the inequality between the burdens borne by the two nations, particularly in Spain, that the ministry was under an obligation to yield them half the *Asiento* or else abandon the negotiations. For his part he was certain that if England were to give up the negotiations the Dutch would resume them, and he blamed Marlborough for encouraging the Dutch to oppose the ministry. They were now, he declared, engaged in the play which they like the best, which is making use of the conjuncture to screw all things to their own particular advantage, and to hinder what they can, the encrease of power of commerce to their rival, as they undoubtedly take Great Britain to be.[1]

The ministry was fighting for survival, but it did not call off its campaign against the Allies, either in Parliament or in the press. Indeed it may well have felt that its survival depended upon the success of this campaign, above all with the queen herself. Thus, although the queen gave Buys a letter full of reassurances to take back to his masters, the Commons, after some preliminary inquiries, resolved on December 20th to address her asking for an account to be placed before them

of the Quotas and Proportions of Her Majesty and Her Allies by Sea and Land, during the present War, including Subsidies, and what Agreements or Conventions had been made for the said Quotas and Proportions, and also how the same had been observ'd.

It was evident that the *Conduct of the Allies* was beginning to bear fruit, though the Lords, who, L'Hermitage reported, were becoming more and more hostile to the 'preliminaries', attempted to counter the Commons' move by themselves addressing the queen asking for instructions to be given to the British plenipotentiaries to the forthcoming conference 'to consult with the Ministers of the Allies in *Holland* before the opening of the Congress' and to preserve a 'strict Union' with them. Strafford was pleased with the news of the Commons' resolution, which would, he hoped, 'bring these people to reason'. 'These people & the Imperialists', he added,

conceive hopes, & abandon them, as they receive intelligence from England, & you have demonstration, that as they think us devided they grow more difficult, & raise in their hopes and demands . . . .
There is a sperit of habitude amongst all our allys, to impose what they can upon us, & when they see they cant to submit.[2]

The instructions for Bristol and Strafford, the two British plenipotentiaries to the impending Congress at Utrecht, which were signed on December 23rd, showed that the ministry, however precarious its situation might be, had no intention of relinquishing its claims to

[1] L'Hermitage to States-General (transcripts), 7/18 and 11/22 Dec. 1711, London, Add. Ms. 17677 EEE; St. John to Strafford, 8, 12 and 15 Dec. 1711, Whitehall, *B.L.*, ii, pp. 48–63, 73–8; Oxford to Heinsius, 15 Dec. 1711 (O.S.), *Weber*, pp. 414–15; Strafford to St. John, 1 and 5 Jan. 1712, Hague, S.P. Holl. 243; Strafford to Oxford, 5 Jan. 1712, Hague, *H.M.C. Portland IX*, pp. 312–19; *Cobbett*, vi, cols. 1035–44; *C.W.* 144, p. 11; *Montgomery*, pp. 236–9.

[2] Anne to States-General (transcript), 23 Dec. 1711, St. James', Add. Ms. 17677 FFF; *ibid.*, L'Hermitage to States-General (transcript), 28 Dec. 1711/8 Jan. 1712, London; Strafford to St. John, 8 Jan. 1712, Hague, S.P. Holl. 243; *Political State*, ii, pp. 449, 463–4.

widespread alterations in the 1709 Barrier Treaty. Though the importance of 'appearing United' with the Dutch was emphasised, the British representatives were plainly ordered not to obtain for the Dutch the barrier and commercial terms that the queen had specified until satisfactory 'explanations' had been received of some of the points arising from that Treaty. It would first be necessary to ensure that there would be no prejudice to our trade with the Spanish Netherlands through any 'omission' in Article XV, and our interests would likewise have to be fully safeguarded before we could consider agreeing to Dutch possession of Nieuport, Dendermonde, or the castle of Ghent, which appeared 'to be rather a Barrier against us than against France'. Moreover, the sweeping powers which had been granted to the States 'in case of apparent attack' would have to be limited to the event of 'apparent attack on the part of France'.[1]

While Bristol prepared to join Strafford in the Republic the Whigs attempted to counter the appeal to public opinion that the ministry had made in the *Conduct of the Allies*. In the month of December there appeared, in addition to the contributions of such periodicals as the *Observator*, three considered refutations of Swift's accusations. The most remarkable of these was *A Defence of the Allies and the Late Ministry*, in which Oxford's henchman Defoe launched a violent attack on Swift while at the same time praising the ministry for the steps that it had actually taken. Of the other two, one, *Remarks on a False Scandalous, and Seditious Libel*, was unimpeachably Whiggish. The third was *The Allies and the Late Ministry Defended* by Francis Hare, which was published in four parts (amounting in all to some 275 pages), two of which had appeared by the end of December.

One weakness of this counterblast, apart from the intrinsic disadvantages of a defensive role, lay in its disunity. Hare's aim was above all to defend Marlborough and Godolphin, the anonymous Whig author's to defend the former Whig ministers, while Defoe was engaged upon the task of denying what all the world knew, that Swift and the *Examiner* spoke for the ministry. The essential weakness of these apologists, however, lay not so much in their pamphlets, which were well argued, but in their readers. This had been Swift's strength; he had preached to the half-converted, to readers who were already impatient with the Allies because they were tired of the war. The importance of the *Conduct* lay in its work in *releasing* feeling against the Allies as well as in creating it. The flood-gates were open, and no

---

[1] Instructions for Bristol and Strafford, 23 Dec. 1711, St. James', *B.L.*, ii, pp. 96–105 n.

amount of reasoning could close them until the torrent had subsided.

In short, these pamphlets were ineffective because they relied – indeed, they were forced to rely – on an appeal to reason rather than feeling. In their different ways they subjected Swift's words to an exhaustive scrutiny, but they possessed certain common characteristics. In the first place they all agreed that, whatever else his book represented, Swift was engaged in 'rendring the *Dutch* odious to us'. All defended the Barrier Treaty on the grounds that our security and that of the Dutch were inseparable, and denied that it would have any of the consequences which Swift had predicted; all suggested, with more or less emphasis, that it was Jacobitism that accounted for the attack on this Treaty; and all urged their readers to remember the undying gratitude with which they should regard the Dutch for their part in the Revolution. Many of Swift's allegations regarding the Republic's shortcomings as an ally they sought to refute, and the remainder they attempted to palliate by pointing to its extraordinary efforts in the war. Hare, for example, declared that

considering how very small a Territory the Seven Provinces together make; that they subsist almost entirely by Trade, and That it is mostly confin'd to one, which is not so big as some Counties in *England*; 'tis truly wonderful to see the mighty Efforts they have made: They have outdone the Expectation even of the Enemy; and I dare say the Faction in *England* are the only People in the World that think they have not done enough. To envy so Brave a People any little Branch of Expense they have sav'd, in order to be able to support the more necessary Parts of the War with Vigour, is as barbarous, as to quarrel with them because they have not done more than they are able, is absurd and unreasonable.[1]

Dr. Hare had indeed good reason to be annoyed with Swift and his brethren, for they were submitting him to some merciless treatment, on the score both of his anonymous pamphlet *Bouchain*, and of the sermon that he had preached before Marlborough on the surrender of that fortress. He was reminded by one writer that the Allies were only human, and might err; 'I am credibly informed', added this commentator, 'that even the *Dutch* are Men'. The 'Tories' New Idol', as Defoe bitterly styled Swift, made great play with the comparison that Hare was alleged to have made in his sermon between Marlborough and Moses:

If the D. of M————— be *Moses*, what *Promised Land* is he bringing us to, unless this Sermon be preach'd only to the *Dutch*? He may have promised them *Land*, and they Him something else, and both been as good as their Words ....

1 *Observator*, x, 98, 8 Dec. 1711; C.W. 41, pp. 3, 5, 7–8, 16–17, 20, 24–6, 32–3, 35–6; C.W. 155, pp. 3, 5, 9, 18–19, 21–4, 26, 32–5, 38; *C.W.* 89, (i) pp. 7–10, 26–36, (ii) pp. 3–21, 43–71, (iii) pp. 31–3, 38–41, 44–52, 56–60, 70–1, (iv) pp. 11–16, 33, 39, 41–4, 56–7, 62–4.

In pamphlets like these and in the revived *Examiner* the Tory campaign against the Allies went on in December 1711, but the chief contribution at this time to the cause of 'rendring the *Dutch* Odious' was Robert Ferguson's *Account of the Obligations the States of Holland have to Great-Britain*. This violent attack on the Republic appeared on December 20th, eight days after the *Observator* had rejoiced that the expression in the queen's speech about the Dutch had frustrated those who 'thought to have created a Division betwixt her Majesty and her Allies'.

In a sense this pamphlet was complementary to the *Conduct*. It supplemented Swift's lucubrations on the defects of the Dutch as an ally by gleefully unearthing all the grisly skeletons which generations of propagandists had rattled whenever the Dutch were in disfavour. It set itself to show from past experience what the results always were of 'Agrandizing that ungrateful Nation', with 'their insatiable thirst after Money'. From the use of our fishery alone, it declared, they had gained untold wealth, yet the return that they made to Elizabeth and James I for this and all their invaluable assistance was one of rank ingratitude. It was to recover our rightful sovereignty over the 'British Sea', asserted Ferguson in a passage full of breathtaking misrepresentation, that Charles II had gone to war with them, 'but Faction starved the War, and forced the best of Princes to clap up an ignoble peace'. They did their best to encourage our divisions and to impoverish us throughout Charles II's reign: hence they showed no consideration for us at the Peace of Nijmegen,

Tho' we drove the *French* from the Gates of *Amsterdam*, and retriev'd their whole Country from certain Ruin, by standing their Friends in that Extremity(!)

After these allegations Ferguson went on to deny that the actions of the Dutch in 1688–9 were due to any desire to preserve our Church and liberties. 'It would be very particular indeed', he remarked, 'that they should have such a tender regard for our Liturgy and Religion, and have so little or none at Home'. From this he was led naturally to Dutch abjuration of Christ in Japan, and thus to consider their record in the Indies; Amboyna was, inevitably, described at length and in the most lurid terms. Finally, after some reflections on the Whigs for espousing Dutch interests, he devoted himself to more recent events, ending with some reflections on the subject of the betrayal of allies:

We don't pretend to abandon our Allies, and lay them open to their Enemies, as some of our Good Friends did at the Treaty of *Nimuegen*. We don't prescribe a day to their final Resolution as at *Reswick*. We have taken no Sums of Money from *France* for a bare promise of promoting and effecting a Peace, and then hinder it underhand as much as possible. We shan't put the Plenipotentiaries of the Confederates into Leading-Strings and let them know nothing but what ours are pleas'd to tell them, as at G————————g .... Let our Adversaries, if they please, Pen an Apology on behalf of their dear Friends for B————g their Allies in such a manner.[1]

4

On December 31st the Duke of Marlborough was dismissed from all his posts, and a day later twelve new peers were created in order to give the ministry command of the upper House. By these bold measures the parliamentary deadlock that had existed since December 7th was at an end, and the ministers could now breathe more freely. Buckingham, Lord President of the Council since June 1711, sending good wishes to Strafford for his success at Utrecht, did not despair

to see the States follow not only the Queen's measures, but her Example also, in getting rid of those directly byassed against our common interest & the Public Good.

It was his heartfelt wish to see Heinsius go the way of Marlborough St. John gloated a little over the 'alteration of our state here' in his letters to Strafford, and instructed him to warn the Dutch that Britain was determined to 'alter her measures of waging wars'; nothing else, he was confident, would 'so much convince the Dutch of the necessity of making peace'.

These were no empty words. Now that the *Conduct* had done its work the ministry was ready to carry the campaign a step further, by staging a full dress parliamentary inquiry into the conduct of the Allies. The unchallengeable sanction that would thus be given to Swift's allegations would effectively stop the mouths of such critics as the *Observator*, which in mid-January was advocating a law to punish 'Libelling the Confederates.' If the ministry needed any encouragement to take such a step it must have derived it from the rise in stocks and shares that greeted the news of Marlborough's fall and the thwarting of the Whig Lords. Even the City now began to think that a Tory peace was a good risk. Drummond was able to tell Buys, on January 25th, that a great alteration of affairs in favour of the queen and the ministry had taken place, and warned him that there was more and more support for the Tory arguments against continuing the war.[2]

---

[1] *Observator*, x, 99, 12 Dec. 1711; *Examiner*, ii, 1, 13 Dec. 1711; *C.W.* 86, p. 27; *C.W.* 176, pp. 9–10; *C.W.* 78, *passim*.

[2] Buckingam to (Strafford), 1 Jan. 1711/12 (O.S.), Add. Ms. 22221; St. John to Strafford,

The parliamentary campaign against the Allies had already been opened by the Commons' resolution of December 20th. Since that time the *Examiner* had made much of allied 'impositions', countenanced, so it alleged, by the fallen Marlborough. Another blow was struck when on January 25th the Commons resolved to address the queen asking her to lay the 1709 Barrier Treaty before them. Here, too, the *Conduct of the Allies* had borne fruit. Three days later 'states of war' from 1701–11 were laid before the Commons, and the day after this the Barrier Treaty was submitted to them. Finally, on February 2nd (pursuant to an address of January 31st) they were presented with all the agreements with the Allies from 1703 onwards. With the compilation of this mass of data, the stage was set for the grand inquest.

Accordingly, on February 4th, the Committee of the Whole House compared the details of allied promises with those of allied fulfilment. Their conclusions they embodied in eleven resolutions, all of them damning. The Dutch were resolved to have furnished no more than 12,200 men for Spain, and none since 1708, to have had no troops in Portugal since 1706, to have fallen short of their quota obligations in Flanders by 20, 837 men, and to have failed to observe the proportion of 3 : 2 which had been agreed upon at the outset for the war in Flanders. Moreover, it was resolved, they had not observed the condition on which the augmentation of 1703 had been granted, nor had they paid subsidies in equal proportion to the queen. The first, and certainly the most damaging resolution, was that the States had been deficient in the number of ships that they had supplied each year for the sea-service by as much as two-thirds, and generally by more than half. These resolutions, approved on February 5th by 235 votes to 90, were, as L'Hermitage remarked, almost indistinguishable from the allegations of the *Conduct*, but they contained much substantiating documentation which Swift had not used. The figures given to illustrate the shortcomings of the Allies, particularly those dealing with Dutch naval deficiencies, were highly impressive on paper, and they speedily appeared in print in an 'unofficial' pamphlet with the self-explanatory title of *An Explanation of the Eleven Resolves of the 5th February last, 1711. In which the Nation may see, at one View, the mighty Loss to E——nd ; and the great Advantages and Savings, both in Men and Money, that the A——s and the D——h have made* . . . . In this pamphlet it was estimated

1 Jan. 1711/12, Whitehall, *B.L.*, ii, pp. 129–33; P. Wentworth to Strafford, 4 Jan. 1711/12, London, *Wentworth Papers*, pp. 237–42; St. John to Strafford (draft), 12 Jan. 1711/12, Whitehall, S.P. Holl. 245; *Observator*, xi, 6, 19 Jan. 1711/12; Drummond to (Buys), 25 Jan. 1711/12, London, Add. Ms. 20985; Wyon, *op.cit.*, ii, pp. 353–4.

by a remarkable feat of accountancy that the Dutch had made a clear gain from the war of £ 12,235,847.5.5d. A broadside which appeared at this time also came to its private resolution

that no Nation, no, not a petty Conquer'd Province, was ever treated with more Contempt, or more infamously Bubbl'd and Amus'd, than *Great-Britain* has been by its Al——s, especially the *D——h*.[1]

L'Hermitage was not far wrong in calling the Resolutions 'un préparatif à faire approuver par le parlement les conditions de la paix'. This was certainly a fair description of the use to which the ministry was to put them. Meanwhile they aroused widespread interest. 'Foreign Knavery is the Subject of everybody's Discourse', wrote Defoe on February 12th, who three days before, though emphasising how essential was the maintenance of a good understanding between Britain and the States, had added meaningly that 'just Dealings with each other' and 'a maintaining an Equality in Property and Proportion' were the only means 'to preserve the good Understanding between us ....'. The *Examiner* revelled in the discomfiture of the critics of the *Conduct of the Allies*, and one of the exiled Earl of Middleton's Jacobite correspondents reported that the votes of the Commons had greatly discouraged the Whigs, and hoped that the results of the forthcoming examination of the Barrier Treaty would deal them an even greater blow. The *Protestant Post-Boy*, however, took advantage of the fact that the Resolutions had not been officially published to defend the Allies against some 'papers' that it claimed to have received, which it did by reviving the arguments already used by the critics of the *Conduct of the Allies*. St. John told Strafford frankly, in a letter of February 6th, that the real cause of these Resolutions had been the unsatisfactory attitude of the Dutch towards the peace; had they not, he declared, through their 'perverseness',

suffered themselves to be flattered by the faction, that those who had been dupes, should continue such to the end of the chapter, we might have avoided showing the enemy our nakedness.[2]

---

[1] *Examiner*, ii, 8 and 9, 24 and 31 Jan. 1711/12; L'Hermitage to States-General (transcripts), 29 Jan./9 Feb., 1/12 and 5/16 Feb. 1711/12, London, Add. Ms. 17677 FFF; *Political State*, iii, pp. 44 *sqq.* and 95 *sqq; C.W.* 75; *C.W.* 159.
[2] L'Hermitage to Fagel (transcript), 5/16 Feb. 1711/12, London, Add. Ms. 17677 YYY; St. John to Strafford, 5 Feb. 1711/12, Whitehall, *B.L.*, ii, pp. 175–7; *Review*, viii, 138–9, 9 and 12 Feb. 1711/12; 'Mrs. White' to 'Mr. Watson', (12 Feb. 1711/12) (O.S.), *Macpherson*, ii, pp. 269–71; *Examiner*, ii, 11, 14 Feb. 1711/12; *Protestant Post-Boy*, 72, 16 Feb. 1711/12.

5

With the dismissal of Marlborough the Tory campaign in press and Parliament against the fallen hero was redoubled in fury. In Parliament it was suggested that he had enriched himself by his two and a half *per cent.* perquisite from the supply of bread, to which he replied that the queen's armies had had as much, and as good, bread as those of the States and at the same prices. 'Therefore', he added, in his written vindication, 'I may safely conclude, that if the *English* have had their Bread as Cheap as the *Dutch,* they have had it as Cheap as was possible'. Outside Parliament the accusations against the Duke went much further than this, and dwelt particularly upon his alleged eagerness to enrich the Dutch at Britain's expense. This was the burden of many issues of the *Examiner,* and also of the work of an unusually bellicose Tory versifier who thus greeted the appointment of Ormonde as Marlborough's successor:

> Oh may he still Faithful, still Generous and True,
> His Mistresses En'mies and Britain's subdue,
> May he always press forward in search of a Peace,
> (For a Town in a Year will not make the War cease);
> And instead of a Siege for the *Hollanders'* Profit,
> (For they only make their Advantages of it),
> To the gates of fam'd Paris the following Campaign,
> Advance and demand the Delivery of *Spain.*

The Duke did not lack defenders, however. Thomas Burnet, perhaps not very wisely, praised him for winning

a noble Barrier to our brave Allies, the Dutch .... on whose safety alone depends that of England, nay, and of all *Europe.*

Hare was somewhat more astute in attributing any failure to seize advantages on Marlborough's part during the war to the influence of the Dutch deputies:

one may be sure, that the *Deputies* are something like *Socrates* his Genius, which never put him in Mind of doing any Thing; its whole Business was to check him, when he seemed to be too forward.[1]

Not even the fall of Marlborough could banish the forthcoming congress at Utrecht as a topic for public speculation in the first weeks of January 1711/12. 'Wee are here in a longing expectation of hearing good news from the congresse' wrote the old Duke of Leeds to Straf-

[1] *C.W.* 25, p. 9; *C.W.* 150; *C. W.* 21, pp. 18, 30; *C.W.* 90, pp. 81–2, 324–5.

ford. Defoe was especially active in producing reflections on this subject. While denying that the Dutch had been 'menac'd' into agreeing to negotiate, he defined a good peace as one that put power into the hands of the English and the Dutch, and he re-emphasised the need, both during and after the congress, for a 'strict Union and Confederacy with the *Dutch*'; but he made it clear that he did not think that it was necessary on this account to give the Dutch too extensive a Barrier nor to deny ourselves commercial advantages. The Whig propagandists, on the other hand, found it safer to use a more roundabout way to animadvert on the queen's proceedings. Consequently there began to appear such pointed historical relations as *The History of the Peace with France and War with Holland in the Year 1672 & Seq ....*, and *A Letter from Sir Thomas Bodley, sometime Queen Elizabeth's Agent in Holland, To a great Privy Councillor; Concerning England & ye States General, their entring upon a Treaty of Peace with Philip King of Spain. Published as a seasonable Caution at this Juncture, now a Treaty is in hand with France.*[1]

'Bien des Tories', reported L'Hermitage on January 11th, 'continuent à s'expliquer qu'ils ne croyent pas de paix sûre, si elle ne se fait de concert avec des alliés ....'. It is, indeed, clear that opinion at this time was by no means ripe for a separate peace. That Oxford himself recognised this is apparent from this account of his views given on January 27th by the French agent Gaultier:

Nous donnons en prennant ce parti (*i.e.* in negotiating a separate peace) la prise contre nous à nos mal intentionés Whigs, qui ne manqueraient pas de nous reprocher que nous aurions fait meilleure paix, si tous les alliés étaient demeurés unis ensemble et si nous aurions pris les mesures pour les empêcher de se désunir.

Such caution, however, did not restrain the ministry's hireling, Abel Roper, in his reflections on the Allies in the *Post Boy*. Buys' departure with Bristol, on December 27th, he took as occasion to enlarge upon the intrigues that the Dutch envoy had allegedly carried on during his stay, and on January 12th he announced with a great show of indignation in the written 'Supplement' to the *Post-Boy* that the Dutch plenipotentiaries had been instructed to resolve upon nothing, except in concert with *all* the allies. This showed clearly, he asserted, that the States were trifling with us, but

infallibly, the good Bishop of Bristol, and the brave Earl of Strafford (whose Title seems to have put a new Spirit into Him) will tell their Hoogan-Moogans another story.

1 *Review*, viii, 123-5, 5, 8 and 10 Jan. 1711/12; Leeds to Strafford, 18 Jan. 1711/12, London, *Danby*, ii, pp. 233-4; *C.W.* 101; *C.W.* 123.

This news seems to have given Defoe some concern, for on January 19th we find him hinting that attempts to stir up jealousies against England amongst the Allies had met with some success.[1]

While the ministry anxiously awaited the news of the opening of the congress – 'we are afraid of those scoundrels the Dutch, lest they should play us tricks', commented Swift – there appeared a pamphlet which put forward an unusual point of view on the subject of the Dutch barrier. Its title was *A Project for establishing the General peace of Europe* and its tone was clearly 'ministerial' – the main point of the 'project' was the secret plan of giving Spain to the Duke of Savoy – but it contained one proposal which was far from reflecting the views of St. John, namely, that the whole Spanish Netherlands should be given to the Dutch, provided certain safeguards were observed. 'This', it explained,

will give the *Dutch* a sufficient Territory to maintain themselves, that they may be no more Burthensome to their Neighbours; Nor pretend to keep a Barrier in the other Provinces after such a Manner, as these must be a perpetual seat of War, Which Measure, it seems, they and the House of *Austria* are agreed upon. But this we must think no less Dangerous for us, than to have the Fire frequently in our Neighbours House And Consider, as of no other Use for us, but to keep this Nation in perpetual War, for the Defence of these Provinces....[2]

It would probably be unfair to dismiss this suggestion, reminiscent of Defoe's schemes of partition in his *Reasons Why this Nation ought to put a Speedy End to this Expensive War*, as mere mischievous hypocrisy. It may well be an indication that St. John's views on the Dutch Barrier had not yet gained an unchallenged ascendancy in ministerial circles.

On January 26th (N.S.) the British, Dutch and French plenipotentiaries met at Utrecht. The attitude of the Dutch at this conference did not give much pleasure to Strafford nor to his masters when, some eleven days later, they received his and Bristol's reports. They were, according to Strafford, being 'very stiff' about the Barrier Treaty, the disposition of Spain, the *Asiento*, and even the appointment of a Secretary for the Congress. All this, he considered, was a 'game .... to gain time', and he added that it was clear that their intention was 'having surprised us in the barrier treaty .... to keep us to it'. St. John's

---

[1] *Post Boy*, 2600, 10 Jan. 1711/12; L'Hermitage to States-General (transcript), 11/22 Jan. 1711/12, London, Add. Ms. 17677 FFF; *Flying-Post*, 3168, 19 Jan. 1711/12; *Review*, viii, 129, 19 Jan. 1711/12; Gaultier to (Torcy), 27 Jan. 1712 (N.S.?), cited in F. Salomon, *Geschichte des letzten Ministeriums Königin Annas von England (1710–1714) und der englischen Thronfolgefrage* (Gotha, 1894), p. 157. Jones' comment on Roper's remarks was that Buys, "tis very certain, had no Averseness to a Peace, and yet such Antipathy some People had now conceived against the *Dutch* that he could not escape the Lash of the *Post Boy* in Print ...' (*Jones, 1711*, p. 387).

[2] *Journal to Stella*, ii, p. 478, 26 Jan. 1711/12; *C.W.* 149, pp. 11–12.

reaction to this news was vigorous. He complained to Bristol and Strafford of the 'spirit of Chicane' of the Dutch plenipotentiaries, above all in the matter of the Barrier. He added that the Commons had asked for the 1709 Treaty to be laid before them, and declared:

whenever that House takes it into consideration I am afraid Our Friends in Holland will find the national sense expressed in harder Terms upon this subject than ever the sense of the Queen, or of her Ministers was. It is not many years since that ferment, which used at all times more or less to appear in Britain against the Dutch on account of our Rivalship in Trade, has subsided; and nothing can be more impolitick in them, than the taking of such measures, as must infallibly renew these jealousyes.

The annoyance of the ministry at this first news from Utrecht was reflected in *Peace, or Poverty*, a pamphlet, perhaps by Defoe, published on January 29th. This protested strongly against the Dutch stipulation that no peace should be concluded without the consent of all the Allies. 'Methinks it is a little hard', wrote its author,

that because we have been greatly Impoverish'd, and they exceedingly Enrich'd by the War, it should be continued meerly to fill their Pockets, and empty our own.

The full congress opened on January 29th (N.S.), and by February 12th it was evident to the British representatives that the Dutch had no intention of giving way in their demand for an 'equivalent' for the *Asiento*, a demand in which, in fact, they had been secretly encouraged by the unscrupulous Oxford, through the medium of Drummond. Bristol and Strafford suspected that the States were intriguing underhand with the French with the object of obtaining 'an absolute Equality in the Spanish Trade'. At the same time that they reported this they sent home the news of the 'Specifick Explanation' of their offers which the French had made on February 11th. This explanation included the announcement that Louis XIV intended to keep Aire, St. Venant, Béthune, Douai, Tournai, and Lille, and to exclude six kinds of goods from the tariff of 1664, making the Dutch pay on these as prescribed in the tariff of 1667. The resulting ferment in the Republic was almost inexpressible, according to Boyer, writing a few months later. Even those of the Dutch, he wrote, who were the most eager for peace 'resolv'd to spend their last Penny, to carry on a vigorous war' (and, he added, 'all true Britons' were of the same mind). Strafford was concerned lest these feelings might actually lead to a *rapprochement* of the Dutch and the French, who, he reported, did 'not stick to throw all the blame of the shortnes of their propositions on others'. He, too, testified to the 'general dislike' that the 'Explanation' had evoked.[1]

---

[1] Strafford to Oxford (2 letters), 26 Jan. 1712, Utrecht, *H.M.C. Portland IX*, pp. 322–4

The French 'Explanation' was not welcomed in England, even in ministerial circles. Jones declares that

the Generality of the People entertain'd the *French* Proposals or Demands with the utmost Indignation, and even those who had the most Inclination to a Peace, upon any Terms, seem'd to be asham'd of it . . . . ;

and once more there is confirmation of this annalist's reliability. When the news of the 'Explanation' arrived on February 9th Swift was more concerned by the plenipotentiaries' suspicions that 'the Dutch are playing us Tricks, and tampering with the French', and told his Stella that they were 'dogs'. The under-Secretary Tilson, however, found that

the offers of France give but too much handle to those perverse wits, who can spoil a peace, much sooner than make one . . . .

Echoing this, Lord Berkeley of Stratton, another lesser light of the ministry, told Strafford that he would 'have been mighty glad the clamour had been prevented by some better offers'. 'If they doe not rise in their offers', he added, 'I doe not know what will become of it'.

The Lords expressed the universal displeasure by resolving on February 15th to address the queen urging her not to treat until she was recognised by France, and then only in conjunction with the Allies. The Whig periodicals, too, made the most of this opportunity by pouring scorn on the French offers, and a pamphlet entitled *The Offers of France Explain'd* enlarged on the 'impudence' of Louis' demands. It declared that it was now clear that the French were determined that the Dutch should not have a secure Barrier, but where, it asked, did we stand in all this? 'The Interest of *England*, it seems', it added,

is chang'd . . . . The *French* are innocent, harmless Creatures . . . . the only formidable Enemy to *England* are the *Dutch*. The Neighbourhood of a *Protestant* Ally, who combin'd with the rest of *Europe* are not a match for *France*, is greatly to be fear'd: but the confessedly *exorbitant Power* of a *Popish* prince . . . . is to be courted, establish'd, aggrandiz'd at the Expence of all our Allies; Particularly the surest Ally we have, the *States* . . . .[1]

(the second letter is dated 1712/13 in error); Drummond to (Buys), 25 Jan. 1711/12, London, Add. Ms. 20985; St. John to Bristol and Strafford (draft), 27 Jan. 1711/12 (O.S.), S.P. Holl. 245; Bristol and Strafford to St. John, 12 and 16 Feb. 1712, Utrecht, S.P. Holl. 244; *ibid.*, Strafford to St. John, 16 Feb. 1712, Utrecht; *C.W.* 48, p. 15; *Political State*, iii, pp. 132-3; *Montgomery*, p. 252.

[1] *Journal to Stella*, ii, p. 487, 9 Feb. 1711/12, London; Tilson to Bristol, 13 Feb. 1711/12, Whitehall, Ms. Rawl. A. 286; L'Hermitage to States-General (transcript), 15/26 Feb. 1711/12, London, Add. Ms. 17677 FFF; Berkeley of Stratton to Strafford, 15 Feb. 1711/12 (O.S.), *Wentworth Papers*, pp. 264–5; *Observator*, xi, 14, 16 Feb. 1711/12; *Protestant Post-Boy*, 76, 26 Feb. 1711/12; *Medley*, (ii), 4, 14 March 1711/12; *Jones, 1712*, p. 102; *Political State*, iii, p.133; *C.W.* 136, pp. 1, 5, 11, 13–15.

6

The dissatisfaction of the ministry's followers with the French 'Explanation' does not seem to have resulted in any real falling off of support for the ministers' peace policy. However uneasy 'moderate' Tories might become about what was going on at Utrecht and even about the conduct of the ministry, they realised that things had gone too far now for retreat to be possible. This point of view is clearly expressed in a letter written by Richard Hill, sometime envoy to Savoy, on February 12th. 'We are quite in the dark', he wrote,

as to what is done at Utrecht. The Queen, the Ministry and the majority in each (House) seem as fond of peace as I am, and therefore it will go on. My fondness is grounded on this, that now you have cashiered your General, affronted your allies and are throwing more of the burden of the war on them, I expect it will be an ill war, which is worse than an ill peace; the Ministers have more good reasons.

Any setback that the ministry may have received from the 'Explanation' and the subsequent resolution of the Lords was more than offset by the concurrent activities of the Lower House. These were of almost incalculable assistance to it in its attempt (in the words of Somerville) 'to turn the current of popular odium against the Dutch'. On February 13th, in accordance with an address of February 11th, the instructions and orders to Townshend and Marlborough, and other paper dealing with the negotiations which preceded the conclusion of the Barrier Treaty, were laid before the House. On the following day there began the long-awaited consideration of this Treaty by the Committee of the whole House. The debate which ensued lasted two days and was marked by 'many warm speeches'. It was St. John who took the lead in putting the case against the Treaty. After letters between Townshend and Boyle concerning the former's exceeding his instructions had been read the Secretary told the House 'of what dangerous consequence this treaty was to England'. It was a Barrier, he continued, not only against France but against the Emperor, and, more serious still, it would be of great damage to our trade, above all owing to Dutch possession of Dendermonde, the castle of Ghent and Nieuport. Even king William, he pointed out, had declined to support a former Dutch claim to Nieuport. A Whig member retorted that this danger was imagined, since the Dutch were not to have civil control of these towns, but St. John did not hesitate to reply that, though this was true in time of peace, it would no longer be so if we were to go to war with the Republic. Severe reflections were also made on Article XV of the Treaty, and the alleged injury that was thereby done to British commerce.

The other principal speaker for the ministry was Arthur Moore, St. John's henchman and one of the Commissioners of Trade, who criticised at length that part of the Treaty relating to the Succession. He enlarged on the shame of asking a republic to guarantee our Succession, and the danger of giving it the right to send over a king of its own choice on the smallest pretext. He alleged that the Dutch had been 'backward' in helping us during the 1708 invasion attempt, and declared that the security of the Protestant Succession was merely a pretext for giving up 'to our great rivals in trade what must inivitable put us out of a power of ever resenting any injury they wou'd or shou'd offer us that way'. The ministry was taunted by the Whigs with infringing the royal prerogative, but none the less it was with majorities of more than 150 that three resolutions condemning the Treaty were passed. The first declared that 'there are several Articles destructive to the Trade and Interest of Great-Britain, and therefore highly dishonour-able to her Majesty', the second that Townshend had had neither orders nor authority to conclude several of the articles, and the third that Townshend and all who had advised the ratification of the Treaty were enemies of the queen and of the kingdom. These resolutions were approved by the House on February 16th, and two days later there was similarly approved a resolution that a representation should be made to the queen concerning the Commons' findings in the matters of the allied quotas and the Barrier Treaty and urging that Britain should not furnish more than her just proportion for the future.[1]

The States-General, however, had anticipated the verdict of the Commons, and on February 19th (N.S.) had sent a letter to the queen affirming their right to enjoy all the provisions of the Treaty but at the same time expressing willingness to rectify anything in it that might be prejudicial to British trade. This letter, which appeared in print soon after the Commons' debate, 'did wonderfully reconcile the States General to the generality of the People', according to Boyer. Doubtless he was exaggerating; the delight of Strafford's father-in-law that Townshend had had 'justice' done him must have been typical of

[1] (Hill) to Trumbull, 12 Feb. 1711/12 (O.S.), *H.M.C. Downshire I pt. ii*, p. 900 (dated 1712/13, but references to current events, *e.g.* the death of Ranelagh, show this to be an error); L'Hermitage to States-General (transcripts), 15/26 Feb. and 19 Feb./1 March 1711/12, London, Add. Ms. 17677 FFF; P. Wentworth to Strafford, 15 and 19 Feb. 1711/12, London, *Wentworth Papers*, pp. 266–7; *Political State*, iii, pp. 103–110; *C.W.* 144, p. 40; Somerville, *op.cit.*, p. 500.

very many Englishmen who remained quite unreconciled. None the less, there were indications that in view of the States-General's letter something more was needed to bring public opinion fully behind the attack on the Barrier Treaty. That the *Observator* ascribed the ministry's attitude solely to concealed Jacobitism was only to be expected, but it is perhaps significant that Defoe, who reacted quickly to changes in 'moderate' opinion, complained that there was a growing tendency to single out the Dutch for criticism which could be more justly levelled at other allies, and suggested that this 'Run upon the *Dutch*' was inspired by Jacobite motives.[1]

The ministry was quite undeterred from pressing home its attack. In the last years of Anne's reign the press was being used as never before to mould the opinions of members of Parliament, and those to whose votes or influence they owed their seats, on matters of foreign policy. For some time Swift had been preparing a companion volume to his *Conduct* that would deal solely with the Barrier Treaty. This appeared on February 22nd as *Some Remarks on the Barrier Treaty*, and ably complemented the work already done by the Commons.

A Chinese unacquainted with our internal politics, Swift began, might well imagine, from the history and nature of the Treaty, that we were some minor tributary of the Dutch. Only two of the twenty-one articles had any relation to us, and they only obtained for us what, to all intents and purposes, was already guaranteed by the Grand Alliance. The latter, according to Swift, had meant no more by stipulating a barrier for the Dutch than that Flanders should be in the hands of Spain rather than those of France. Moreover, the provision in the Barrier Treaty that the king of Spain should not take possession until after a peace made the Dutch anxious to continue the war; and, in any case, what with the revenue the king would have to give them, and the fact that so many of the sources of revenue were pawned to them already, the States would, in effect, be 'absolute Sovereigns of all Flanders' in time of peace too, and rich enough to maintain a mighty army.

Many of the barrier towns specified, he pointed out, were a barrier against English trade rather than against France, and, of the clause which obliged us, at the peace, to procure them 'whatever shall be thought necessary besides', he remarked that 'where their *Necessity* will terminate, it is not very easy to foresee'. We were worse off now

---

[1] Sir H. Johnson to (Strafford), 19 Feb. 1711/12, London, Add. Ms. 34144; *Observator*, xi, 15, 20 Feb. 1711/12; *Review*, viii, 143–5, 21, 23 and 26 Feb. 1711/12; *Political State*, iii, p. 107.

in our trade to Flanders than we were under Charles II of Spain, especially with regard to the 'double duties' on our goods going to the 'New Conquests',[1] and yet Article XV of this treaty gave the Dutch a share in all our advantages:

This is *Dutch* Partnership, to share in all our beneficial Bargains, and exclude us wholly from theirs, even from those we have got for them.

The power in our affairs given to them by the Succession clauses the Dutch would no doubt use to ruin us, he went on. Moreover, their striking out of the English 'Counter-Project' the demand that the entire Spanish Monarchy should be yielded as a preliminary to any peace showed very clearly why 'they never sent any Forces to *Spain*': 'They fought only in *Flanders*, because there they only fought for themselves'. Swift concluded his *Remarks* with a comparison of the miserable state of England with that of the Republic:

Let us look upon the reverse of the Medal, we shall see our Neighbours, who in their utmost distress, called for our Assistance, become by this Treaty, even in time of Peace, Masters of a more considerable Country than their Own; in a

---

[1] Swift's revelations concerning these 'double duties' were the first fruit of systematic enquiries, instituted by St. John at the beginning of December, 1711, into the conditions under which British merchants were trading with the Spanish Netherlands. These enquiries were carried out both by the Board of Trade and also by British representatives on the spot (such as Laws, Secretary at Brussels, and Loggan, Consul at Ostend). The Board, in its report of 22 December, in addition to exposing the 'ill & fatal Consequences to this Kingdom' likely to result from the enjoyment by the Dutch of the position in the Spanish Netherlands assigned them by the Barrier Treaty, paid particular attention to the position of the 'New Conquests' (the territories captured since the signing of that Treaty). It found that goods coming from Holland were free of all duties payable on entry into those territories, and that it thus cost Dutch manufacturers at least eight *per cent.* less to export their products thither than it did ours (Board of Trade to St. John (copy), 22 Dec. 1711, Whitehall, C.O. 389/22; based on an undated memorial to the Board from Dorpere, *ibid.*). The reports of Laws and Loggan not only informed St. John of fresh grievances, but also filled in the details concerning the 'New Conquests'. According to Laws all English goods imported into the Spanish Netherlands by way of Ostend, and sold to merchants of that country for resale in the 'New Conquests', had to bear both a duty of entry at Ostend and a duty of entry into the 'New Conquest' for which they were intended. They were, in fact, subject to 'double duties'. If, on the other hand, English merchants sent their goods to the 'New Conquests' without first selling them they had to pay, in addition, a transit duty of two and a half *per cent.* Dutch merchants, however, were exempt from the duties of entry into the 'New Conquests', and the transit duty to which they were liable was a reduced one (Laws to St. John, 25 Jan. 1712, Brussels, S.P. Flanders 61; see also *ibid.*, Loggan to St. John, 30 Dec. 1711, Ostend; *ibid.*, Laws to St. John, 15 Feb. 1712, Brussels; Bindon to ?, 26 March 1712, Bruges, Add. Ms. 22266). These 'double duties' soon became a favourite topic of Tory propagandists, and were specifically complained of in the Commons' 'Representation' (see below p. 306). In their answer to this the States offered to set right all genuine grievances and asserted that it had never been their intention that British trade with the Spanish Netherlands should be at a disadvantage – a declaration that was mercilessly satirised by John Arbuthnot (*C.W.* 6, pt. 3, p. 41). The States' professions would indeed have been more convincing had they been accompanied by any steps to implement them. As it was, the actual and potential grievances of British merchants in the Spanish Netherlands remained both a useful reproach to hurl at the Dutch and a source of genuine concern to the merchants themselves (see Laurence Galdby's memorial to the Board of Trade (copy), 3 April 1712, London, C.O. 389/22).

condition to strike Terror into Us, with fifty thousand *Veterans* ready to invade us, from that Country which we have conquered for them; and to commit insolent Hostilities upon us; in all other Parts, as they have lately done in the *East Indies*.

The remainder of his work included the text of the Barrier Treaty (which the Commons ordered to be printed four days after this pamphlet appeared!), the articles of the Counter-Project that were struck out or amended by the Dutch, and a representation from the English merchants at Bruges concerning the burdens on our trade to the Spanish Netherlands.[1]

The importance of this pamphlet cannot easily be exaggerated. Though we have no such spectacular figures for its sale as for the *Conduct*, yet the Earl of Middleton's correspondent assured him that it had put the finishing touch to the work begun by that publication. 'All the counties of England', he asserted, were

so exasperated .... against the late Ministry and our allies, that they are in some counties ready to address the Queen to punish those that acted in all their vile practices ....

The ministry's opponents, too, gave unimpeachable testimony of the importance of the *Remarks* by producing no less than five detailed 'answers'. Of these, four defended the Treaty in its entirety; the fifth, *The Dutch Barrier Ours*, by far the most convincing of the five, admitted that the commercial clauses needed alteration but pointed to the willingness of the States to agree to this as expressed in their letter of February 19th. It also took up some of Ferguson's accusations, and pointed out that the Dutch had equal cause for complaint against us. Its conclusion was that 'all those who are enemies to *Holland*, are *Enemies* to *England*; and that whatever we do for their Safety, we do for our own'.[2]

The remaining 'answers' were *The Treaty between her Majesty and the States-General .... Consider'd* and the first half of *A Full Answer to the Conduct of the Allies* (both by Hare), *Remarks upon Remarks*, and *The Barrier-Treaty Vindicated*, which is attributed to Stephen Poyntz. Fortunately it is unnecessary to describe the contents of each of these pamphlets in detail, for the 200 pages of *The Barrier-Treaty Vindicated* (which appeared several months after the others, but is dealt with here for convenience) contained every argument used by each of its fellows (with the exception of the views, already noted,

[1] *C.W.* 179, *passim*.
[2] 'Mrs. White' to 'Mr. Watson', (Feb. 1711/12), *Macpherson*, ii, pp. 279–82; *C.W.* 65, pp. 5, 7–8, 15–20.

of *The Dutch Barrier Ours* on the commercial provisions). Poyntz divided his consideration of the Treaty into three main sections, in which he dealt with the questions of the Succession, the Barrier, and commerce. In view of the inveterate opposition to it of France, he began, and the fact that our constitution would not allow a standing army, the Protestant Succession could be secured only by a foreign alliance, and from every point of view, (including the fact that our trade as producers and theirs as carriers were virtually complementary, and involved no real rivalship) the Dutch were our most useful ally. The argument that they would think it necessary to defend our Succession without being bound to do so by a treaty was sheer Jacobite hypocrisy.

As for the barrier itself, Poyntz continued, it was our own true interest 'that there should be a good and sufficient Barrier against France on the Side of the *Netherlands*', for if the French were to conquer the United Provinces they would turn the Dutch navy against us and thus ruin our sea-power and our trade. Moreover, no barrier could be sufficient that was not *at least* equal to that agreed in the Treaty. A single chain of towns, like that laid down in the 1709 preliminaries, was insufficient, and it was noteworthy that the Treaty itself left to the French several places that they had not had under the Treaty of the Pyrenees, which yet had not proved sufficient to stop the inroads of Louis XIV. Experience had taught us that neither treaties with France, nor the forces of the House of Habsburg, even if foreign troops were lent to them, could protect the barrier; therefore, since we were no more willing to keep a standing army abroad than at home, it was to the States that the defence of the barrier had to be committed. To conduct this defence efficiently they would need a secure communication with the barrier fortresses – hence the need for Ghent and Dendermonde. It was reasonable, too, that 'the Country of the Barrier should contribute to the maintenance of it', which it would do whoever was occupying the barrier. In any case, England had already recognised the right of the Dutch 'to a sufficient Barrier, and to have themselves the Defence of it' before the Townshend Treaty; in the proposals made to d'Avaux in 1701, for example, and again in Article VIII of the Grand Alliance and in the 1709 preliminaries.

Such a barrier as was proposed, Poyntz went on, would be far from exposing us to any danger. The restriction of their power in the barrier towns to one of military command, and the provisions of Article XV, made it impossible for the Dutch to encroach on our trade to the Spanish Netherlands without an open rupture with us, and with the

Emperor too, an event which their prudence would certainly make them avoid. As for the complaints about 'double duties', if they were true, why had we heard nothing of them before? It would in fact become all the more their interest to maintain our friendship once they were in possession of this barrier, for in case of a war with us, the barrier 'would be so far from contributing to make them more Rich or Formidable, that it would rather Exhaust and Weaken them with respect to *England*'. The whole revenue of the Spanish Netherlands had not been enough to keep the barrier fortresses 'in a tolerable Posture of Defence' since the Treaty of the Pyrenees, so that the portion of it to be given to the States would be much less sufficient, and they would be weakened – relatively to us – by having to provide a considerable sum out of their own revenue.

Finally, Poyntz dealt with the objections that had been raised to Article XV. He stated categorically that

The Trade of *England* and *Holland* to the Spanish Dominions, had always, by virtue of their respective Treaties with the Crown of Spain, stood upon an equal Foot.

Moreover, it had *in practice* stood on an equal footing, and there was 'no Custom or Prescription to the contrary' in Flanders or anywhere else. In any case, the queen was laid under no obligation by Article XV that she was not already under by Article VIII of the Treaty of Grand Alliance.[1]

While the Whig apologists made what Middleton's correspondent called their 'evading, railing' replies, the Tory propagandists pushed home their undoubted advantage. In a collection of satirical portraits probably published about this time was found the following description:

A Politician Signing the B——— T——y, and two Butter Merchants presenting him with Bags of Money for his Reward.

> The Politician, in his own Conceit,
> Is very wise; but yet he is a Cheat.
> By him his Country is for Gold Betray'd,
> And he by Two *D——h* Boors a Cully made:
> To him they freely do their Money tender,
> He signs their Deeds, and does his Trust Surrender.

In *A Vindication of Oliver Cromwell and the Whiggs of Forty One*, another Tory writer developed the ingenious argument that the

[1] *C.W.* 146, *passimC.W.* 97,; *passim*; *C.W.* 91, pp. 1–40; *C.W.* 157, *passim*.

Barrier Treaty might actually help the Pretender. By making 'our most formidable Rivals the D——h' so overwhelmingly strong at the expense of our own blood and treasure, he declared , we had put it into their power to complete our ruin by joining with France and 'James III' and destroying our trade, nor had we any reason to suppose that gratitude on their part for everything we had done for them would prevent their doing this. Our only safeguard against the Dutch hitherto had been their fear of France, which made them dependent on us; but now we had relieved them of that fear, as part of the Whig scheme for ruining us abroad so as to be able to enslave us at home. The *Examiner*, too, reported a 'Vision' in which 'A Man of Gold' (Marlborough) sold lands and towns to 'the next *Ally*' as quickly as he conquered them, 'whence a *Petty State*, in a short time, grew more *Potent* than the Empire' (*i.e.* Britain).

It was probably at this time that there was published *Natural Reflections Upon the Present Debates about Peace and War*, a pamphlet which gives the impression of having been prepared in December and subsequently brought up to date in view of the developments concerning the Barrier Treaty. This suggested that if the war were to continue we might well ask the Allies for cautionary towns as a guarantee that they would perform their obligations. As for the criticisms of the ministry's way of carrying on the peace, it added, what of the Dutch 'at *Gertruydenberg* in 1709' (*sic*), or for that matter at Ryswick. It also attacked Heinsius for his veiled opposition to the peace now under way, and for his alliance with the Whigs, which was never seen more clearly than in the Memorial presented after Sunderland's dismissal. After reflecting on the conduct of the Dutch at the Peace of Nijmegen (a topic soon to be taken up by the *Examiner*) it went on to attack the Barrier Treaty. The Dutch and their advocates, it asserted, had found a way of extending the barrier endlessly by claiming that the barrier proper needed *its* barrier, which in turn needed *its* barrier, and so on *ad infinitum*. Their attitude towards the revision of this Treaty, moreover, as expressed in their letter to the queen, was far from satisfactory, for they offered only a statement of their good intentions, with no other security than 'their known Justice and Integrity'. 'They say', it continued,

it was ever their Intention that the Subjects of Great Britain should be upon an Equal Foot with their own Subjects as to Trade in the *Spanish* Netherlands. And no doubt it was the same as to *Amboina* and other Places in the *East Indies*.

The Dutch least of all the Allies, it ended, should advocate the continuation of the war, since every gain on the French frontier became their property; in any case we knew that we could expect little of them except in Flanders.[1]

7

The parliamentary campaign against the Allies reached its climax when, on March 4th, the Commons presented to the queen the 'Representation' drawn up by a committee under the chairmanship of Sir Thomas Hanmer. This document, which read like a combination of the *Conduct* and the *Remarks*, consisted largely of a rehash of the 'Eleven Resolutions'. After these, however, came some rather more detailed remarks about the Barrier Treaty than those previously approved by the Commons. The potential danger to our trade from the unnecessary 'communication' towns, and the existing danger from the 'double duties', were both enlarged upon, as well as the need to limit Dutch powers of taking possession of all the Spanish Netherlands to the event of an apparent attack by France, lest we repented of this provision.

if it should at any time happen (which Your Commoners are very unwilling to suppose) that they should quarrel with Your Majesty.

It was asserted, moreover, that Article XV gave the Dutch equal commercial advantages in the Spanish dominions, which *in practice* they had not enjoyed before. Finally, the hope was expressed that all these points could be explained and amended,

so as that they may consist with the Interest of *Great Britain*, and with a rea and lasting Friendship between Your Majesty and the States-General.

When this document was discussed in the Commons on March 1st, the Whigs attempted to refer the 'Representation' back to the committee on the grounds that the question of 'double duties' had not previously been mentioned in the Commons' resolutions concerning the states of war and the Barrier Treaty, but this motion was defeated by 217 votes to 42. Two days after its presentation the 'Representation' – written, as Hampden had said, 'not to inform but to inflame the Nation' – was published together with the queen's answer, which promised that the necessary orders would be given to implement the Commons' recommendations.[2]

---

[1] *Examiner*, ii, 13, 28 Feb. 1711/12; *C.W.* 24, p. 2; *C.W.* 189, pp. 6–10, 15; *C.W.* 116, pp. 6–11, 34–7, 55–6, 58–60, 70–6.

[2] L'Hermitage to States-General (transcript), 4/15 March 1711/12, London, Add. Ms.

The publication of the 'Representation' set the seal on the Tory victory in the campaign against the Allies. Even as late as March 6th Lord Berkeley of Stratton had been positively alarmed by the 'angry humour reigning at present' with regard to the peace; the French offers, he thought, were still having a bad effect, and people were

not wanting to give every thing the worst turn, and to let nothing fall that is likely to give an ill look to those they would expose ....

The ministry, however, had now called in Parliament itself to spike the critics' guns, and, as Swift wrote later,

many persons, who were before inclined to believe that the allies and the late ministry had been too much loaded by the malice, misrepresentations, or ignorance of writers, were now fully convinced of their mistake by so great an authority.

Indeed, even it the Whigs had been able to refute the assertions that had been made, it would have been dangerous for them openly to have challenged the authority of the Commons, and, indirectly, of the queen herself. They were therefore thrown back on their old technique of satirising their opponents, together with the now only too familiar imputations of Jacobitism. In *March and October*, for example, the attitude of the the Tory squires towards Allies was thus burlesqued – perhaps not unfairly:

Confederates – I wish we had never heard the name of them. We have been beating our Brains out against Stone Walls, to take Towns and Countries for them. I wish we had kept to our floating Castles, our Walls of Oak. We might have defy'd all the World. The *Dutch* grow rich by the war, and would have no end of it. They'l be too many for us, if we don't look about us – They hate us, because we are for Monarchy and Episcopacy; 'sbud, *Amboyna* always runs in my Mind – and *Chatham* too, and the *Fishery* – Confederates, quotha, I wish we do not rue the Day we had anything to do with them.

Thomas Burnet, in his *Letter to the People*, attributed the anger of the Tories towards the Dutch to the anxiety of the latter to protect Britain from 'Popery and Slavery', and the same point was made in *The Humble Confession and Petition of a Whig with his Eyes Open*:

.... how comes the only supporter of a *Popish* Pretender to gain so fast the good liking of our High-flying Churchmen, whilst the *Dutch* are become the object of their Scorn, the only Protestant Nation of any force with our selves to stop a *Popish* Inundation ....?

Such were the arguments, too, that were used by the Whig periodicals – the newly-revived *Medley*, the *Protestant Post-Boy*, and the *Ob-*

17677 FFF; Berkeley of Stratton to Strafford, 5 March 1711/12 (O.S.), *Wentworth Papers*, pp. 275–6; *Political State*, iii, pp. 178–93; *C.W.* 106.

servator – all of which found it wiser to criticise the pronouncements of their Tory rivals than to make any explicit reflections on the 'Representation' itself.[1]

The revelations of the 'Representation', on the other hand, were seized on eagerly by the Tory propagandists. Such pamphlets as *The Miserable Case of Poor Old England Fairly Stated* and *The Second Representation of the Loyal Subjects of Albinia*, with an obvious intention of working up public feeling to fever pitch, raged at the Whigs for daring to say even a word in extenuation of the notorious crimes of the Allies. More telling, however, and readable even today, was an urbanely witty allegory, usually attributed to John Arbuthnot, the first part of which, entitled *Law is a Bottomless Pit*, appeared on the same day that the 'Representation' was published. This told how John Bull (England) and Nicholas Frog (the Dutch) pursued a lawsuit against Lewis Baboon (Louis XIV) and the Lord Strutt (Philip V), and how John Bull dismissed his steward Hocus (Marlborough) when he discovered that the latter had been in league with Frog to throw the burden of the suit upon his shoulders. The character of Frog, who, it was pointed out, did not neglect his 'ordinary Business' during the suit, was depicted thus:

Nic. Frog was a cunning sly Whoreson, quite the reverse of *John* in many Particulars; Covetous, Frugal; minded Domestick Affairs; would pine his Belly to save his Pocket, never lost a farthing by careless Servants, or bad Debtors: He did not care much for any sort of Diversions, except Tricks of High German Artists, and *Leger de main*; no Man exceeded *Nic.* in these, yet it must be own'd, That *Nic.* was a fair Dealer, and in that way had acquir'd immense Riches.

The second part of this allegory, *John Bull in his Senses*, followed soon afterwards. In this was included an account of a conference between Don Diego Dismallo (Nottingham) and Mrs. Bull (the Ministry). In reply to Dismallo's praises of Frog's honesty, Mrs. Bull produced a copy of an agreement between Frog and John Bull, to obtain which, she said, '*Hocus* and those Rogues' had kept her husband drunk for five years together. This 'agreement' was, in fact, a burlesque of the Barrier Treaty. The first article, for example, stated that Frog agreed to keep the peace in Bull's family, and, as his executor, had the power to prevent the alteration of his will by Bull or any one else, and also to enter his house at any hour and to 'break open Bars, Bolts, and Doors,

---

[1] Berkeley of Stratton to Strafford, 26 Feb. and 5 March 1711/12 (O.S.), *Wentworth Papers*, pp. 271, 275–6; *Medley*, (ii), 1 and 3, 3 and 10 March 1711/12; *Observator*, xi, 21 and 28, 12 March 1711/12 and 5 April 1712; *Protestant Post-Boy*, 90, 29 March 1712; *C.W.* 126, pp. 27–9; *C.W.* 20, pp. 10–13; *C.W.* 108, pp. 26–9; *C.W.* 175, p. 118.

Chests of Drawers and Strong Boxes'. The other articles were in the same vein; but Diego replied that this was all reasonable, and that Frog was always religiously true to his bargain. To this Mrs. Bull replied by reading a letter from Frog to Baboon which offered to 'make all things easie', if Baboon would give him what he had promised Bull. This, of course, was a reference to the attempts of the Dutch in 1711 to gain control of the negotiations for peace.

While Englishmen became familiar for the first time with the generous, gluttonous, kindly and choleric figure of John Bull, the *Examiner* was developing a new line of attack. On March 13th it asked why the Whigs complained of what the Tories said of the Allies, and suggested that

the chief reason of their complaint, seems to be the Hardships we thereby put upon our *good* Allies, the *Dutch*, who they think would never be guilty of the like Proceedings.

But, it asked, even if we left entirely on one side the several attempts of the States to enter into 'Separate Measures' with France, and also Buys' offer to renounce the recovery of Spain and the Indies if we let them into the *Asiento*, should we not at least learn from their conduct at Nijmegen, where they coerced their allies into a peace? We should do well to emulate this example, which was only what was 'agreeable to the Conduct of a wise People, Frugal, and careful of the good of their Country'. The Whigs were both angered and embarrassed by this ingenious if irrelevant argument. The *Protestant Post-Boy* complained of the *Examiner's* insinuations, but confined its criticisms to the passing reference to the Dutch desire to share in our advantages; it expressed surprise that, after their great outcry about the Barrier Treaty, the Tories were willing to admit that we had obtained any advantages at all. The less cautious *Observator*, however, took up the *Examiner's* main point about Nijmegen. At that time, it argued, the Dutch were reduced to very low circumstances, and we had played them false. To such an inadequate answer the *Examiner* felt no need to reply; instead, in its next issue, it pointed out that the revelations of the 'Representation' fully demonstrated why the Allies, in 1710, had gone so far to try to stop the queen changing her ministry, which, as we could now see,

bore such a generous Friendship to the *States*, that they thought all our Wealth too little to be employed in extending their Dominions: But those who are now in Power among us, are so unreasonable as to think their High-Mightinesses have already too much.[1]

[1] *Examiner*, ii, 15–16, 13 and 20 March 1711/12; *Protestant Post-Boy*, 84, 15 March 1711/12; *Observator*, xi, 22–4, 15, 19 and 22 March 1711/12; C.W. 129, pp. 3–4; C.W. 193, p. 9; C.W. 6, pt. 1, pp. 10, 13–14, 20, and pt. 2, pp. 9–14, 20.

While the Tory propagandists thus drove home the lesson of the 'Representation', Oxford, in a remarkable letter written on March 8th, assured the Pensionary that this was only a foretaste of what would come unless the Republic showed more eagerness to coöperate with the queen. He himself, he declared, had managed to stave off discussion of the Barrier Treaty and Dutch deficiencies in 1711, but, he added,

.... if foreigners will mistake a faction for the people, and a small party for the whole, if the ministers of the Allys think that it is serving their masters by combining together against the Queen and her servants, who have the whole nation on their side, for there are not ten in a hundred against the peace, I say when this happens it makes it extream difficult for the best intention'd and most resolute, to act as they desire, and all that has been possible is to hinder matters going further, and should there be a new Parliament chosen, they would go higher than this has done.[1]

8

While the ministry triumphed at home both in Parliament and in the press, little progress was being made at Utrecht – a fact of which the Tory propagandists were able to make good use. On February 19th Strafford reported that Buys, with the complete backing of Amsterdam, continued to be obdurate on the question of the *Asiento*. Both he and Bristol were convinced, by the beginning of March, that the Dutch were carrying on underhand intrigues not only with the French but also with the Imperialists. Swift commented thus on these reports:

Our Peace goes on but slowly: The Dutch are playing Tricks, and we do not push it as strongly as we ought.

Strafford's suspicions of the 'trickery' of the States with the Emperor were greatly increased when he learnt that the States-General had resolved that Van den Bergh should invite the Austrian minister Heems to coöperate with him in obtaining from the Council of State of the Spanish Netherlands the means to provide bread and forage for the Imperial troops in Flanders. Instead of the queen and States 'being the joynt sovereigns', declared Strafford, "tis become the Emperor and States', and he suggested to St. John that this move might well be an indication that the States and the Emperor had privately concerted the barrier without consulting the queen. Consequently he sent two letters to the Greffier Fagel, on February 26th and March 4th, reminding him that the queen's consent was essential before any step such as that envisaged could be taken. St. John's reaction was unexpected, and

---

[1] Oxford to Heinsius, 8 March 1711/12 (O.S.), *Weber*, pp. 416–18.

probably indicative of his growing confidence of the strength of the British position; while agreeing with Strafford's analysis of the situation, he informed him that the queen

does not see, that it is at all her interest to hinder it. Her name and her authority have been hitherto made use of to assist the Dutch in engrossing to themselves the Dominion of these Provinces, and to give a sanction to a great many arbitrary proceedings. The Queen will therefore be very easy at Monsr Heems' journey, and not take umbrage at his assuming any power, or any influence in those parts.[1]

The Dutch, meanwhile, were trying one expedient after another in their efforts to obtain an 'equivalent' for their share in the *Asiento*. On March 8th Strafford and Bristol found them 'a good deal more compliant than formerly' on this question, for they agreed to receive a copy of the amendments to Article XV that the queen desired, and Drummond, on a visit to Utrecht, found that the British plenipotentiaries were hopeful that the Dutch would soon show more 'complaisance' generally. They were soon disillusioned, however. Strafford was told by Buys that the States would sooner leave Dunkirk undemolished than give up Lille as an equivalent for the demolition, as Louis XIV had demanded. He found, too, that the news of the deaths in the French royal family had greatly encouraged those who desired the prolongation of the war, and he learnt that the States' minister in Berlin was actually doing his best to set the king of Prussia against the queen's measures.

There seem to have been high hopes amongst the Tories that the 'Representation' would bring the Dutch to heel. Although at the end of February it had been the talk of London that "twas dangerous for an Englishman to walk about the streets of Holland', Berkeley of Stratton confidently expected, on March 14th (O.S.), that the Dutch would now 'cringe'; and Oxford was emboldened to write to Buys disabusing him of the notion which he himself had previously encouraged, that the English ministry was willing to obtain an 'equivalent' for the *Asiento* for the States. Strafford found, however, that though the Dutch leaders were 'vext to the heart' at the news, they would not reveal their intentions until they saw what answer the French made to the 'Specific demands' of the Allies, which had been presented on March 5th. They were determined, he reported, not to omit Article XV from the Barrier Treaty, and, moreover,

[1] Strafford to Oxford, 19 Feb. 1712, Utrecht, *H.M.C. Portland IX*, p. 324; Strafford to St. John, 23 Feb. 1712, Utrecht, S.P. Holl. 243; Strafford to Fagel (transcript), 26 Feb. 1712, Utrecht, Add. Ms. 17677 FFF; Bristol and Strafford to St. John, 1 March 1712, Utrecht, S.P. Holl. 244; *Journal to Stella*, ii, p. 496, 23 Feb. 1711/12, London; St. John to Strafford (draft), 10 March 1711/12, Whitehall, S.P. Holl. 245; *C.W.* 113, vii, pp. 97 *sqq.*

the warrior party please themselves they shall bring us into the feild, and then as their expression is we are at sea again.[1]

Deadlock ensued when the French transmitted their reply, however, owing to the refusal of all the Allies save England to receive a verbal answer and the equally determined refusal of the French to put this in writing. The acrimonious wrangles that went on at Utrecht concerning this dispute (which Strafford characterised as a Dutch attempt 'to have brought things into a disorder here and a dependancy upon them') were reproduced in London in the columns of the *Post Boy* and the *Observator*, which respectively attacked and defended the Dutch standpoint. The latter argued with some ingenuity that

the *Dutch* are very much in the right to insist, that the *French* Monsieurs shou'd Treat *wid de Pen*, since the Treaty of *Nimeguen*, which *Abel's* Masters upbraid them with, was enough to convince them, that there's no laying hold on what the *French* say by *Word de Mout*. *Lewis* XIV is an old Dog at Swearing and Forswearing, *Waerichtigh say de Mynheers, Daerom*, we will Trust him no more, but under Hand and Seal.

On April 8th Buys and three of his colleagues informed Bristol and Strafford that they were prepared to cede the towns that Louis XIV had demanded in his 'Explanation' except for Lille, Tournai, and Valenciennes. Despite their firmness in refusing these places, Strafford now thought that they showed 'a great desire to concert sincerely measures with us'. Four days later the British plenipotentiaries reported that some of the Dutch delegates seemed less adamant on the question of the *Asiento* 'equivalent' than hitherto, and that if in all other respects trade to Spain and the Indies remained in the same condition as under Charles II, it seemed that 'the difficulties about their Barrier & Tariffe' would not be insuperable. In fact, however, the States-General had taken a secret resolution on April 9th which insisted on the discussion of the question of an 'equivalent', and the conference that took place on April 14th between the English and Dutch plenipotentiaries was worse than useless. To the Dutch request for details of the terms of the *Asiento* agreement the English replied evasively, concealing the vital concession of the right to send one ship a year to trade in South America, and when the Dutch asked if they might keep Ghent and Dender-

---

[1] Bristol and Strafford to St. John, 8 March 1712, Utrecht, S.P. Holl. 244; P. Wentworth to Strafford, 29 Feb. 1711/12, London, *Wentworth Papers*, pp. 272–3; (Drummond) to (Oxford), 15 March 1712, Amsterdam, *H.M.C. Portland V*, pp. 147–9; Strafford to St. John, 16 and 22 March 1712, Utrecht, S.P. Holl. 243; Oxford to Buys, 8 March 1711/12 (O.S.), Add. Ms. 20985; Strafford to Bristol, 23 March 1712, Hague, Ms. Rawl. A. 286; Strafford to St. John, 25 March 1712, Hague, S.P. Holl. 243; Berkeley of Stratton to Strafford, 14 March 1711/12, London, *Wentworth Papers*, pp. 278–9.

monde the English, acting upon the instructions brought from London by Oxford's kinsman Thomas Harley, took them completely aback by agreeing on condition that the queen might likewise keep Ostend and Nieuport.[1]

St. John hoped that the States' resolution suggesting an 'equivalent' for the *Asiento* was merely the 'last convulsive pang of an expiring faction'. This was not the opinion of Thomas Harley, who found at Amsterdam a jealousy of the possession of the *Asiento* by England that made 'those craving envious people averse to any peace on such terms', nor yet of Drummond, who reported that both the people and the merchant-oligarchs of Amsterdam were 'animated to an incredible degree', partly owing to the 'haughty behaviour' and 'remote proposals' of the French. When, however, the news arrived at The Hague on April 17th that the French had prevented the Dutch armies from stationing themselves along the Sensée, Strafford observed that the Dutch were 'frightened out of their wits' and that it was generally believed that the English had 'betrayed their secret to the French'.

Now reasonably certain of unshakable support at home, the Oxford ministry was beginning to put yet stronger pressure on the States to bring them into line. Already Thomas Harley had brought instructions which contained the plain threat of separate measures by Britain unless the States gave a satisfactory 'explanation' of the Barrier Treaty and went 'hand in hand' with the British at Utrecht. On April 18th Strafford turned the screw a little tighter. He presented to the Deputies of the States-General a letter to them from the queen written in accordance with the recommendations of the celebrated 'Representation'. The really important part of his communication, however, was that which he delivered verbally. The queen, he declared, would not furnish one man more in Flanders than she was bound to in proportion to what the States *actually* provided, and, moreover, if the States did not replace their troops in Portugal and pay the agreed subsidies to that country she would withdraw her troops and not pay her subsidies either. She would accede to Eugene's request that she should pay a third of a sum of four million crowns for the war in Spain, but only when the States provided *their* third. It was evidently the intention of the ministry that the Dutch should be brought to confess their past omissions and to admit that the war could not be carried on if they

[1] Strafford to St. John, 30 March and 8 April 1712, Utrecht, S.P. Holl. 243; *Observator*, xi, 25–6, 25 and 29 March 1712; Bristol and Strafford to St. John, 12 April 1712, Utrecht, *Montgomery*, pp. 266–7.

were to cease to impose upon the queen, but this was far from being the reaction that Strafford observed amongst the Dutch representatives at this conference, nor was it that which was to appear in the reply of the States-General to the 'Representation' itself.[1]

The departure of Eugene from England, lionised but empty-handed, on March 17th, was celebrated without inhibition by the Tory pamphleteers. One pamphlet, for example, gave a description of the banquet that the City of London had planned to give in the 'Popish General' 's honour. The first course was to have been

Four dishes of smother'd Conies, dress'd after the *Dutch* Fashion, and set upon Stands, an Inch higher than the ordinary, to the more com-at-able,

and the second,

Four Cods-Heads roasted, larded with Pickl'd-Herring, caught by the *Dutch* in the *English* Seas, and brought hither to Market.

The Tories had scarcely finished congratulating themselves on the departure of Eugene, however, when a new threat to their position appeared. On April 7th and 8th the intrepid *Daily Courant* published the text of the States' Memorial in reply to the 'Representation', which had been presented to the ministry on April 3rd by the new Dutch envoy van Borssele. The Tories were extremely angry that this document had appeared in print. Although they tried to represent it as a 'long, verbose, empty, and insignificant Reply', it was in fact an able and sincere defence of Dutch conduct throughout the war, and as such it inevitably constituted a powerful indictment of the ministry's policy of coercion; indeed, had public prejudice been less violent, it might well have brought about a revulsion of feeling against the ministry. In fact the Tories were safe, though the conduct of the Commons showed that they were both furious and uneasy. On April 8th they availed themselves of the convenient fiction that the Memorial was not genuine in order to condemn it as a false, scandalous and malicious libel, after which the unfortunate printer and publisher of the *Daily Courant* were taken into custody. Four days later the Commons, their anger still not appeased, took some resolutions regarding the regulation of the press; and though these were never implemented, the new Tory periodical *The Plain Dealer* continued to clamour for some restraint.

[1] Instructions for T. Harley, (19 Feb. 1711/12) (O.S.), *B.L.*, ii, pp. 181–3, 185–90; (T. Harley) to (Oxford), 15 April 1712, Hague, *H.M.C. Portland V*, pp. 155–6; *ibid.*, pp. 158–60, (Drummond) to (Oxford), 15 April 1712, Amsterdam; St. John to Bristol and Strafford (draft), 5 April 1712, Whitehall, S.P. Holl. 245; Strafford to Bristol, 17 April 1712, Hague, Ms. Rawl. A. 286; Strafford to St. John, 19 April 1712, Hague, S.P. Holl. 243; *C.W.* 113, vii, pp. 115 *sqq.*

The publication of the Memorial had in fact had just the reverse of the effect that had been intended, and Oxford and St. John were able to warn the Dutch leaders (through Thomas Harley, and Bristol and Strafford, respectively) that the 'unreasonable humour' of the Dutch was making both Lords and Commons 'uneasy' and 'could have no effect to their advantage'. When St. John replied to the Memorial a month after its publication he completely rejected its implied suggestion that to do 'all in one's power' was to fulfil one's obligations. The queen required that the States should furnish their due proportion, he told Borssele, and to that end she would now see to it that her own war effort did not exceed what was proportionable to theirs.[1]

If the Tories were, for the moment, uneasy about the effect which the new Memorial might have, they felt few qualms of doubt themselves about the conduct of the ministry. St. John and Swift had done their work too well for that. Lord Berkeley of Stratton, for example, recalled that 'it hath been all along their excuse that they did what they could', and he quoted with approval the reply that had once been made to Vrijbergen when he once used the same argument, 'saying they were undone and beggars':

he was told that tho' one would give what could be spar'd, one would not suffer one self to be cheated by beggars.

Moreover, although the Whigs (like Thomas Burnet, for example) were delighted when the Memorial appeared in the *Daily Courant*, the subsequent vote of the Commons cut the ground from under the feet of their propagandists. The Tory *Plain Dealer* could pour scorn on the 'pretended Memorial', call it a satire upon the Dutch, and mock at its talk of 'the Great and Uncommon Efforts' of the Dutch and of their poverty, but the Whig *Medley*, forced to submit to the pretence that the Memorial was not genuine, could only hint darkly that the Dutch no doubt had a satisfactory reply to give to the 'Representation', but that 'the iniquity of the present, had thought to over bear them with Noise and Clamour'. The *Medley* also took up the allegory of John Bull, and denied the suggestions that the 'Frogs' had evil designs on his property. It printed an 'affadavit' signed by Bull which declared

that my Friend *Esq. South* (Charles III) and Mr. *Frog* have all along bore their

---

[1] P. Wentworth to Strafford, 8 April 1712 (O.S.), *Wentworth Papers*, pp. 283–4; L'Hermitage to States-General (transcript), 8/19 April 1712, London, Add. Ms. 17677 FFF; St. John to Bristol and Strafford (draft), 8 April 1712, Whitehall, S.P. Holl. 245; (Oxford) to (T. Harley), 12 April 1712 (O.S.), Add. Ms. 40621; *Plain Dealer*, 2, 19 April 1712; St. John to Borssele (transcript), 8 May 1712, Whitehall, Add. Ms. 17677 FFF; *C.W.* 199, pp. 5–6; *Political State*, iii, pp. 320, 343–82; *C.W.* 144, p. 82; *C.W.* 114, p. 732.

proportions in the Law-Suit, according to their respective Abilities, notwithstanding those Scandalous Aspersions that have been of late cast upon them.

Two days after these words appeared in print there was published the
third part of the John Bull allegory, *John Bull Still in his Senses*, which
dealt with the Memorial in a devastating manner by satirising it as
'Nic. Frog's Letter to John Bull'. In this guise the States' reply was
represented as a masterpiece of self-interested hypocrisy, designed
either to put the control of the peace into Dutch hands, or, better still,
to prolong the war. The moral was the same as that found on the title
page of the *Complete Key to the Three Parts of Law is a Bottomless-Pit*,
also published about this time:

> *War* is a Trade, a Gain, or what else
> Makes Cunning *Nick* in Love with Battels?
> He thrives apace, *John*, Bankrupt, breaks;
> For tho' *Bull* wins, *Frog* sweeps the Stakes.

Allegory was also the weapon used by the author of *The Fable of The
Cods-Heads: or, a Reply to the Dutch-Men's Answer to the Resolutions of
the House of Commons*, at the end of which, however, it was declared in
plain unallegorical terms that

> Each one of the Allies should share
> A just proportion of the War,
> And Stipulated Charges bear,
> Till things for Peace are Riper.
> Or B——ain thou art not to blame,
> If thou the Dance of War disclaim,
> And cease to make all *Europe* Game,
> By paying Europe's Piper.[1]

9

By the end of April the tragi-comedy of Anglo-Dutch 'coöperation' at
Utrecht was drawing to a close. On April 16th St. John expressed the
hope in a letter to Ormonde that their reported distrust of Eugene
might make the States less eager to continue the war, and a day earlier

---

[1] 'T. Fletcher' (T. Burnet) to G. Duckett, 8 April 1712 (O.S.), *T. Burnet's Letters*, pp. 3–6;
Medley, (ii), 12–14, 11, 14 and 18 April 1712; Berkeley of Stratton to Strafford, 15 April 1712
(O.S.), *Wentworth Papers*, pp. 285–7; *Plain Dealer*, 5, 10 May 1712; *C.W.* 6, pt. 3, pp. 40–3;
C.W. 192, title-page; *C.W.* 76.

Drummond was of the opinion that the new British taxes on paper, linen, and silks would cool the ardour of the Amsterdam merchants; but the reports of Thomas Harley and Strafford emphasised strongly that the 'warrior party' had the upper hand, and that any concessions on the part of the English ministry would strengthen rather than weaken their position. The book-dealer Alexander Cunningham bore all this out when he wrote to Oxford from The Hague that he had never seen 'the people here more jealous of us than at present'. St. John was not altogether displeased by these reports. Though he wrote to Drummond expressing his regrets 'that they will continue the bubbles of a faction here', and warning him that if they did not change their tune the queen would no longer count herself under any obligation to them, he told the plenipotentiaries frankly (in a letter of April 29th) that France and Britain might make peace alone

with a much better grace, if, after repeated incitations to open their minds, the Ministers of Holland should continue still silent, than it could be if they freely declared their sentiments, and enterd into formal concert with your Lordships.[1]

When the Dutch plenipotentiaries returned to The Hague for fresh instructions Strafford entertained some hopes that the queen's 'firmness' had at last had the desired effect, and that there was a good chance that five of the provinces would instruct their deputies at the States-General to abandon their objections to the queen's views on their barrier (above all, to the omission of Ghent and Dendermonde) and to give way on the question of the *Asiento*. 'The warrior party', he wrote to Thomas Harley, 'begin to draw in their horns'; and when St. John received these forecasts he wrote to Harley of his pleasure 'that the Dutch are att last in a way of recovery from that phrenzy wch their whig friends communicated to them'. These hopes were disappointed, however; although the deceptive replies that had been given to their enquiries had led Amsterdam to decide to drop the demand for an 'equivalent' for the *Asiento*, the Dutch plenipotentiaries returned from The Hague with instructions that made no concession to British demands, still without powers to conclude, and refusing to discuss anything except the barrier.[2]

[1] (T. Harley) to (St. John?) (draft), 24 April 1712, Hague, Add. Ms. 40621; (Drummond) to (Oxford), 26 April 1712, Amsterdam, *H.M.C. Portland V*, pp. 164–5; St. John to Ormonde, 16 April 1712, Whitehall, *B.L.*, ii, pp. 267–8; Strafford to Bristol, 29 April 1712, Hague, Ms. Rawl. A. 286; Strafford to St. John, 30 April 1712, Hague, S.P. Holl. 243; Same to same, 8 May 1712, Utrecht, S.P. Holl. 244; St. John to Strafford, 29 April 1712 (O.S.), *B.L.*, ii, pp. 294–302; (A. Cunningham) to Oxford, 10 May 1712, Hague, *H.M.C. Portland V*, p. 169; St. John to Drummond, 2 May 1712, Whitehall, *B.L.*, ii, pp. 306–8.
[2] Strafford to Oxford, 10 May 1712, Utrecht, *H.M.C. Portland IX*, pp. 328–9; Strafford

This was the moment for which St. John had been waiting. For weeks past public feeling in England had been both sounded and prepared by rumours of a separate peace which would, as St. John told Strafford, 'render the terms of the Treaty more solidly advantageous to Britain'. The moment was now ready to apply the ultimate pressure, short of armed attack, upon the Dutch. St. John was now sure that he had the nation behind him, so sure that he could tell Thomas Harley that he began to wish

that the Dutch may continue still dully obstinate, rather than submit to the Queen's measures, since we do not want them either to make or support the peace, and since it will be better settled for England without their concurrence than with it.

Accordingly, he wrote to Bristol and Strafford that 'it is now their business to come towards the Queen, since her Majty has gone far enough towards them'; and, to make a *rapprochement* more difficult, Strafford was recalled to London, while Bristol was told not merely that he should end his efforts to procure the 1664 tariff for the Republic, but also that the queen no longer considered herself under any obligations to the Dutch, and that he was absolutely to

decline treating with the Ministers of the States either on the subject of the amendments to the Barrier Treaty, or of the general policy of the peace, or of any other subject whatever.

Drastic as these instructions were, they were as nothing to those that were sent by St. John to Ormonde on May 10th. These – the notorious 'Restraining Orders' – enjoined the English commander to avoid both siege and battle until further notice. They were of course secret, but not for long, since on May 28th (N.S.) Ormonde, challenged by Eugene, was forced to reveal them. Four days later Bristol announced his instructions to the Deputies of the States-General. The Dutch were as astonished as they were angry. Their reaction to these revelations disgusted Thomas Harley – 'I wish you would have let me gone out of this country before I take a perfect aversion to it', he wrote to St. John – but Drummond noted the failure of a visit made by Hop to Amsterdam to raise an extraordinary loan for carrying on the war in Spain, and added that 'this town is resolved to see what sort of a peace is to come from England e'er they engage in a new war'. It did not have to wait for long.[1]

to T. Harley, 10 May 1712, Utrecht, Add. Ms. 40621; *ibid.*, St. John to T. Harley, 3 May 1712, Whitehall; St. John to Bristol and Strafford (draft), 3 May 1712 (O.S.), S.P. Holl. 245; Bristol and Strafford to St. John, 17 May 1712, Utrecht, S.P. Holl. 244; *Montgomery*, pp. 270–1.

[1] St. John to Strafford, 3 May 1712, Whitehall, *B.L.*, ii, pp. 308–11; *ibid.*, ii, pp. 323–4,

St. John's instructions to Ormonde were, of course, the outcome of secret negotiations with France, which had gone so far that when Gaultier asked the Secretary what Villars should do if Eugene and the Dutch took the offensive, he answered 'that there would be nothing to be done but to fall upon him and cut him to pieces, him and his army'. They were also the logical culmination of a 'whispering campaign' in favour of a separate peace that had been going on in the Tory press for several weeks. It seems to have been the aim of some of the Tory writers – particularly Roper – to build up such an expectation of an immediate peace as to ensure that the slightest rumour that the Allies were unwilling to countenance this would cause great exasperation in England. To this end, as L'Hermitage noticed, the Tory newspapers contradicted themselves cheerfully. They would at one time assure their readers that the peace was almost concluded on the basis of a renunciation by Philip V of his claim to the French Crown, and that the Allies were satisfied with this; at another they would announce that the Allies were raising fresh objections and were not (as a report 'from the Hague' in the *Post Boy* said) 'too earnestly inclin'd to make Peace upon the Foot of the present Negotiations'. This would be the cue for the Tory commentators to launch yet more furious attacks on the Allies for thus attempting to prolong the war for their own profit. The *Plain Dealer* professed to be unable to believe that even the Dutch could be so ungrateful as not to come into the queen's measures, since they owed everything to her; but it removed its tongue from its cheek when it animadverted on a report that the Dutch were fitting out a fleet to come and chastise Britain if she 'persisted to disoblige them'. The *Examiner*, accusing the Whigs of wishing to prolong the war in the interest of the Dutch,

the increase of whose Dominion and Trade so evidently depends upon our prosecuting this lingering war, tho' to the Destruction of our own Lands and Commerce,

suggested to its readers that the Dutch were thinking of allowing Villars to gain a victory in Flanders in the hope that this would lead to the recall of Marlborough by the queen. Charles Leslie, in his pamphlet *Salt for the Leach*, declared that the design of 'some' at the Utrecht congress was

St. John to T. Harley, 10 May 1712, Whitehall; *ibid.*, ii, pp. 319–21, St. John to Ormonde, 10 May 1712, Whitehall; St. John to Bristol and Strafford (draft), 10 May 1712, Whitehall, S.P. Holl. 245; *ibid.*, St. John to Bristol (draft), 16 May 1712, Whitehall; Bristol to St. John, 3 June 1712, Utrecht, S.P. Holl. 244; (T. Harley) to (St. John) (draft), 3 June 1712, Utrecht, Add. Ms. 40621; (Drummond) to ?, 7 June 1712, Amsterdam, *H.M.C. Portland V*, pp. 178–9; *Political State*, iii, pp. 318–19.

only how to obstruct it, by starting New Invented Methods and Delays .... But why should they make too much Haste, while the Burden of the War lies chiefly upon us, and the whole Advantage is to be Theirs?

Defoe, still intermittently preaching moderation, admitted that when the Tories argued for a peace they made no scruple to 'insult the *Dutch* as Treacherous Confederates'.[1]

Nor were such insults confined to print. The *Protestant Post-Boy* complained that some people

rail at the *Dutch*, and even threaten them with their Anger already, as I have heard in *Coffee Houses*, and other *Publick Places*.

This it attributed to the 'Old Spirit of Animosity against the *Dutch*' amongst 'the *Papists*, and all that *Faction*', 'out of Envy to their Industry and Liberty ....'. The *Observator*, while continuing to complain that the Allies were being libelled, noted on several occasions the apparent inconsistencies in what the Tory news-sheets wrote about the peace. On May 21st, for example, it remarked:

'Tis not long since they inveigh'd bitterly against the *Dutch* Barrier, and cry'd out, That it would be ruinous to the Trade, and dangerous to the Safety of *England*; and at this moment are publishing their virulent Reflections upon it; yet now *Abel* tells us 'tis adjusted to the satisfaction of the *Dutch*. So that these Schismatical and Antimonarchical Republicans, of late the Abhorrence of the Party, are now, if we may believe *Abel*, become their *Darlings* ....

Not all the *Observator's* scorn, however, could repair the injury that 'Abel''s deliberate raising and disappointing of hopes was doing to what goodwill towards the Dutch remained in England.

One of the most discussed of all the 'virulent Reflections' on the Barrier Treaty was *Some remarks on the Letters between the L—d T——nd, and Mr. Se—tary B—le*, published on May 1st. This claimed that the letters in question gave the best possible indication of the true motives behind the conclusion of the Barrier Treaty. The object of the Whigs, it continued, had been to 'keep the *Dutch* steady to the carrying on the War', so as to preserve their own power at home; the pretence of concern for the Succession was mere hypocrisy. They were content to make this bargain at the price of the 'sacrificing both of our Honour and Trade to them'; and the Dutch,

as adverse as they pretend to be to Peace at present .... would be glad to make One to Morrow, if the Present Ministry would buy it of them at *half the Price*.

[1] *Review*, viii, 163, 8 April 1712; L'Hermitage to States-General (transcripts), 11/22 April and 27 May/7 June 1712, London, Add. Ms. 17677 FFF; *Post Boy*, 2648, 1 May 1712; *Plain Dealer*, 4–5, 3 and 10 May 1712; Gaultier to Torcy (translation), 21 May 1712 (N.S.), *Churchill*, iv, p. 542; *Examiner*, ii, 24–5, 15 and 22 May 1712; *C.W.* 117, pp. 2–8.

In its detailed consideration of the letters it made much of Boyle's complaint of Heinsius' 'menacing insinuations', inviting every 'true Briton' to

consider the QUEEN of *Great Br——n* not only brought to consent, but to Beg and Truckle to the Menaces of a *P——y* of *Holland*, to obtain such a Treaty.

In a similar vein it examined all the 'vile Condescensions' that had been made by the ministry during the course of the negotiations, in return for which we had obtained 'worse than nothing', namely, the right of the Dutch to come here with a foreign army whenever the Whigs thought fit. It continued, in a passage that convinced L'Hermitage that the author was not 'dans les intérêts de la révolution et de la succession protestante', by asserting that even in 'the late *happy Revolution*' the Dutch Guards had caused matters to go 'somewhat farther' than had been intended, and it praised the Commons for sending them home in 1697.[1]

IO

After the presentation of the 'Representation', it had been in the pamphlets, news-sheets and periodicals that the campaign against the Allies had mainly been carried on. The role of Parliament in this campaign had become a secondary one, though the Commons had done its duty in condemning the States' Memorial, and the Commissioners for the examination of Public Accounts had been at work to find further evidence of Dutch wickedness, a search which ended in the revelation that the States owed Britain £ 11,514.10.2 for naval supplies. When, however, the news of the 'Restraining Orders' and of Bristol's declaration to the States-General became known in London on the morning of May 26th, it became evident that Parliament would soon loom large once more in the conduct of the peace. Boyer found that the news 'occasioned a general unexpressible Surprize', but Strafford, who had been in London since May 15th, pointed out, in a letter to the Electress of Hanover, that the Commons were 'in great uneasiness . . . . to have a peace', and had expected that the queen would have declared herself on this matter on that very day (May 26th). When she did not do so, he continued, there were 'some warme speeches' made, it being said

---

[1] *Observator*, xi, 31, 35, 39, 41–2, 16 and 30 April, 14, 21 and 24 May 1712; L'Hermitage to States-General (transcript), 9/20 May 1712, London, Add. Ms. 17677 FFF; *Protestant Post-Boy*, 109–10, 13 and 15 May 1712; *C.W.* 168, *passim*.

'that if the Queen met with any difficulty from her Allies, if she would lay it before the Parliament they would ease her . . . .'. 'This uneasiness', he declared, 'shows that any peace almost woud be agreable to the nation, & yet I am persuaded we shall have a good one . . . .'. This last was the kind of assurance, according to L'Hermitage, that was being given in private by the close adherents of the ministry to doubting members of Parliament, who had succumbed to the universal astonishment at the latest developments. They were being assured, he wrote to his masters, that all the assumptions and conclusions that were being made as a result of the news were incorrect.

No sooner was the news of the 'Restraining Orders' published in a 'postscript' to the *Flying Post* than the Whigs were in full cry. Defoe was highly alarmed; the news, he wrote to Oxford, had raised 'a mighty popular clamour' and done 'much mischief through the nation', and he begged him for a commission to write something to 'take off all the edge of the popular surprise some people think they have raised in the nation'.[1] The Whigs, however, had no intention of waiting for Defoe to vindicate the ministry. They acted quickly, and on May 28th attacked the ministry in both houses on the question of Ormonde's instructions. Their main hopes were pinned on the proceedings in the Lords where, despite the creation of Tory peers, the ministry was still far less sure of unfailing support than in the Commons.

It was Halifax who opened the attack in the Lords by reflecting on the orders that Ormonde was reported to have displayed, and proposing that an address be made to the queen asking that her general be ordered to take the offensive in concert with the Allies. He was supported by Godolphin and Marlborough, and with the intervention of the latter the debate became more concerned with his past conduct than with the present behaviour of the ministry. This turned the discussion decidedly in favour of the ministry, especially since Oxford refused to confirm that the report in the *Flying Post* was true, and forcefully denied that a separate peace had ever been intended. 'Such a peace', he declared,

would be so foolish, villanous, and knavish, that every servant of the queen must answer for it with his head to the nation. The allies are acquainted with our proceedings, and satisfied with the terms.

This assurance seemed to knock the bottom out of the Whig case, and

---

[1] L'Hermitage to States-General (transcripts), 6/17 May and 27 May/7 June 1712, London, Add. Ms. 17677 FFF; Strafford to Electress of Hanover, 26 May 1712, London, Stowe Ms. 224; (Defoe) to (Oxford), 27 May 1712 (O.S.), *H.M.C. Portland V*, pp. 177–8; *Political State*, iii, p. 415.

Halifax attempted to withdraw his motion; Strafford, however, forced it to a division, in which it was defeated by 68 votes to 40. Strafford did not leave matters there; he now put into effect a plan that had been concerted at a meeting at Lord Orrery's house the previous day, and proposed that an address be made to the queen requesting her to lay before the House details of the 1709 and 1710 peace negotiations. In support of this motion, which received the backing of Marlborough and Townshend and was passed without a division, he declared that he had learnt from one of the two employed by the Dutch in these negotiations (it was generally assumed that he referred to Buys) that the Pensionary had communicated no more to the ministers of the Allies concerning the conferences than he had judged proper to let them know, and that the States had then agreed to give up Naples and Sicily, which, he added, 'showed even at that time, that the recovery of the whole monarchy of Spain was looked upon as unpracticable'. The ministry, Strafford remarked, in a letter to Bristol, had 'come off triumphantly' in the Lords, and he was now confident that the Dutch would

be very humble, for they will see let the Queen make what peace she will, it will be accepted by her Parliament, & have their sanction.

Although it was true that Oxford had thought fit to ensure the support of the Lords by stating a deliberate falsehood, the overwhelming victory gained by the ministry in the Commons, where a similar motion put forward by Pulteney was defeated by 203 votes to 73, showed that Strafford's confidence was, for once, fully justified. The Commons rounded off the day of victory by resolving on an address expressing entire confidence in the queen's assurance that she would submit the peace to them for their consideration before concluding it. There could no longer be the slightest doubt that the campaign against the Allies had succeeded. The ministers gained new confidence; Strafford, for example, told the visiting Austrian minister Hohendorff that the Dutch were now declaring their readiness to make a new Barrier Treaty, but that the ministers (in Hohendorff's words) 'ne vouloient plus auqu'un Engagement, avec des Gens irraisonables et qui n'avoient ny honnêteté, ny sincérité, dans leurs manières d'agir'.[1]

All Britain waited anxiously for the declaration about the peace that Oxford had promised within a few days. The Whigs, meanwhile,

[1] Strafford to Bristol, 8 June 1708, (N.S.), London, Ms. Rawl. A. 286; L'Hermitage to States-General (transcript), 30 May/10 June 1712, London, Add. Ms. 17677 FFF; Hohendorff's report of 11 June (N.S.), *Weber*, p. 468; *Coxe*, iii, pp. 304–9; *Cobbett*, vi, cols. 1138–9.

vanquished in Parliament, carried the fight into the country by means of their periodicals. Their rather half-hearted attacks on the ministry's policy betrayed their consciousness that for the moment there was nothing they could say which would bring about any lessening of the solid support that the ministry enjoyed. The *Observator* and the pseudo-*Medley*, for example, contented themselves with pointed but threadbare historical dissertations on Anglo-Dutch relations under queen Elizabeth and Charles II.

The Tory writers were, for the moment, still retaining some shred of restraint. The pretence had to be kept up, for a little longer, that the Dutch were going hand in hand with the queen. Thus, jubilant though they must have been at the outcome of the debates of May 28th, they did not yet openly attack the Dutch leaders. The *Examiner*, for example, restricted itself to reprinting and commenting on a long extract from the *Amsterdam Gazette* concerning the English clergy, in which, so it alleged, an attempt was made to equate High Churchmen with Non-Jurors. It remarked that it was to be hoped that Dutch notions would 'never be a Pattern for ours, either in Religion or Government', and asked:

Is there a Mongrel Sect in *Christendom*, which does not Croak, and Spawn, and Flourish, in their *Sooterkin* Bogs?

Defoe, evidently working at high speed, completed two pamphlets and sent them to Oxford for approval. They were written, so he said, against 'the tyranny of our neighbours' and 'in answer to the Dutch memorials'. The writer of the *Defence of the Allies* had come to terms with the needs of the ministry and the wishes of his countrymen, but his letter to Oxford of June 5th has a somewhat conscience-stricken air:

I am far from exciting the people against the Dutch, and believe it is not the Government's view to injure or to break with the Dutch; but it seems necessary and I believe it is your aim to have the Dutch friends and not masters, confederates not governors; and to keep us free from a Dutch as well as a French management.

Defoe may also have been the author of a pamphlet that appeared at this time entitled *The Present Negotiations of Peace Vindicated from the Imputation of Trifling*, though it is more likely to have been written by Secretary St. John himself. This vigorously defended the ministry against Whig charges of being too 'forward' to make peace, though it seems to have been written before the revelation of the 'Restraining Orders'. It asserted categorically that it had been the French who made the first move in the negotiations, and that since then the Dutch had gone hand in hand with us. If it was true that the Dutch had been 'backward' in agreeing with us, it went on, this was but a very weak argument against our proceedings:

for, if the *D——ch* are, as they have been Cordially Represented a-late, a Covetous, Rapacious, Selfish People, it's no wonder they were for playing their Old Game at *G————burgh*, Grasping at all in the Dark, and not standing to the Decision of an Open Congress: Besides they wanted their Old *W——sh English G——l* and Plenipo, who acquiesc'd to everything they demanded for the Good of their State, connived at their Fraudulent Practices in the Field, and gave them a Barrier so pernicious to the Trade of *G—— B————*, and so encroaching upon *F——*, that they could not easily be wrought to change Hands; but supposing they were brought to consent to a Congress upon the Earnest Sollicitation of our *M————y*, they have long since Cancell'd the Obligation, by telling us in their Letter, concerning the *Barrier Treaty*, what Pains they took, and how Meritorious their Industry was in furthering our Scheme of Peace.[1]

I I

The ferment in the Republic continued while England waited for the queen's promised declaration. Bristol was somewhat embarrassed by the reproaches that were being hurled at the ministry, as can be seen in a passage from his despatch to St. John on June 10th (N.S.), in which he 'humbly supposed' that 'nothing we can participate in, will be thought too much for the Dutch & that so far we shall continue to support their pretensions, because they are our own'. The 'uneasiness' of the Dutch, he reported, was above all due to their not knowing 'what is to be their lott'. Drummond, however, found little indication of any reduction in the Barrier and tariff demands of Amsterdam, where, he added, 'great pains' had been taken 'to foment the common people', and they grew 'very ill-natured'. From the army an English officer wrote home that the Dutch were 'stark mad' at the conduct of the English: 'and', commented the recipient of his letter, 'I'm sure We have always been soe to be guided by them'.

On June 3rd Strafford wrote to Bristol that 'the great discovery' was appointed for June 5th, and that he hoped that it would be as good for the Dutch and the Imperialists as if they had made it themselves. On both counts he was mistaken. It was on June 6th that the

---

[1] *Medley*, (ii) (Baldwin), 27, 2 June 1712; *Observator*, xi, 45, 4 June 1712; *Examiner*, ii, 27, 5 June 1712; (Defoe) to (Oxford), 5 June 1712 (O.S.), *H.M.C. Portland V*, p. 180; *C.W.* 162, pp. 9, 13–16, 28–30. A word of explanation of the term 'pseudo-*Medley*' may be thought necessary here. The first 20 issues of the second series of the *Medley* proper were published by Mrs. A. Baldwin; the issues from no. 21 (12 May) onwards by J. Baker. Mrs. Baldwin, however, continued to publish a pseudo-*Medley* on the same days and in the same guise as the true *Medley*.

queen made her speech to both Houses, and the terms were such as to dismay the Dutch and to make Imperial acceptance out of the question. They represented a failure for the diplomacy of the ministry, since Philip V had unexpectedly preferred to renounce his claims to France and remain on the Spanish throne rather than to take immediate possession of Savoy, with a good chance of eventual succession to the French throne, as a reward for giving up Spain to the Duke of Savoy. This alone made it impossible that the Emperor would come into the Ministry's measures. The Dutch were offered terms which showed no improvement on those brought to them by Thomas Harley: the tariff of 1664 except certain species, and the Barrier of 1709 'except two or three towns'. The chief bait for England was that, once an armistice was concluded, English forces would occupy Dunkirk.

There can be no doubt that the queen's declaration disappointed the high hopes that had been entertained by her subjects. The funds, which had risen before her speech, dropped back again, and there were few scenes of rejoicing in London on the night of June 6th. Nevertheless, so well had the ministry and its propagandists prepared the ground in anticipation of this moment that the Whigs were powerless to prevent Parliament approving these terms. In the Commons, indeed, they did not even dare to divide against the address of thanks to the queen for fear lest the Tories might then word it yet more strongly. In the Lords, however, on June 7th, it was proposed that a clause be added to the address of thanks asking the queen to take such measures as would bring the Allies to join with her in a mutual guarantee. Strafford figured prominently in this debate, declaring amongst other things that the States profited so much, and had gained so much power, by the war, that they would willingly continue it for another hundred years, and therefore would infallibly make use of the suggested guarantee to prolong the war indefinitely. When Marlborough rose to say that the ministry was guilty of breaking its engagements with the Allies, Strafford insinuated that it was the 'secret correspondence' of Marlborough and the Whigs with the Dutch that encouraged the latter to be backward in the peace. To this Cowper made a sharp rejoinder which included the reminder that

according to our Laws, it could never be suggested as a Crime, in the Meanest Subject, much less in any Member of that August Assembly, to hold Correspondence with our Allies: Such Allies especially, whose Interest Her Majesty had declared to be Inseparable from Her Own, in Her Speech at the Opening of this Session......

This rebuke failed to deflate the self-important Strafford, for he intervened once more when Wharton enquired about a letter from the States-General to the queen of June 5th (N.S.), which he had seen in the newly arrived *Gazette de Hollande*. This was a letter protesting against the 'Restraining Orders' and Bristol's instructions, and giving a detailed account of them. Oxford admitted that it was genuine, but said that it was so completely founded on misunderstandings as to be totally lacking in authority, and Strafford, supporting this, declared that he had received a letter from Bristol denying that he had made the declaration which this letter attributed to him. The Whig motion was finally defeated by the very great margin of 81 to 36, no less than twelve acknowledged Whigs voting with the ministry. Twenty-four lords, however, put their names to a formal protest, which declared that the ministry had broken Article VIII of the Treaty of Grand Alliance, and that the proposed barrier was 'wholly insufficient'. This was printed and widely distributed, but on June 13th the Lords voted to expunge both this and a previous protest (dealing with the 'Restraining Orders') from the records of the House, and on June 24th an Order in Council was made to discover the printer and publisher.[1]

Another publication to which Parliamentary exception was taken was the States-General's letter to the queen, which appeared in English on June 9th under the title of *A Letter from the States General to the Queen of Great Britain, about the Duke of Ormond's Orders not to Fight, and the Bishop of Bristol's Declaration, That the Queen thought Herself disengaged from all Obligations to the Dutch*. In the Commons on June 10th a resolution was taken to address the queen expressing indignation that this had appeared in print, and asking that she would answer no more communications that were thus made public knowledge. On this occasion Lechmere accused the ministers of imputing the blame for the publication of their letter to the States in order to avoid answering it. In fact, however, the queen had already answered it on June 9th, in a reply which complained of the printing of the letter as equally contrary to good policy and to decency, since it represented an appeal to the people rather than an address to the sovereign. She assured the

---

[1] Bristol to St. John, 10 and 17 June 1712, Utrecht, S.P. Holl. 244; Strafford to Bristol, 14 June 1712 (N.S.), London, Ms. Rawl. A. 286; (Drummond) to (Oxford), 16 June 1712, Amsterdam, *H.M.C. Portland V*, pp. 180–2; Sir T. Cave to Lord Fermanagh, 9 June 1712 (O.S.), *Verney Letters*, i, p. 272; L'Hermitage to States-General (transcripts), 10/21 and 13/24 June 1712, London, Add. Ms. 17677 FFF; *Political State*, iii, pp. 332–46; *C.W.* 107; *Montgomery*, pp. 276–7. The Austrian Hohendorff, on a special mission to London, reported that 'Le Public parôit très mal content de l'harangue de la Reine' (*Weber*, p. 472) – but he was probably moving in Whig circles.

States of her good intentions towards them provided that they would take measures in concert with her, and informed them that Strafford would soon be returning with orders to do everything in his power, together with Bristol, to renew an entire confidence between the two nations.

The parliamentary rout of the Whigs was completed in the Commons when, on June 17th, a motion by Hampden suggesting that all the Allies be made guarantees of the Protestant Succession was defeated by 133 votes to 38, and in its place a resolution was approved to address the queen expressing complete confidence in her care of such matters. This overwhelming success in Parliament emboldened the more extreme Tories; on June 10th L'Hermitage reported that

on dit qu'on accordera une bonne barrière à Vos Hautes Puissances si elles veulent acquiescer au reste, et en même tems on entend dire à quelques uns de ceux qui témoignent un si grand désir pour la paix qu'on recommencera bientôt la guerre et que ce sera contre V.H.P.

Such sentiments were for the moment mainly confined to talk, since the Tory propagandists were still awaiting news of the Dutch reception of the queen's plan. Nevertheless, there was a stronger note of menace used when the Dutch were spoken of in many of the pamphlets and periodicals published immediately after the queen's speech than had been present before. The *Plain Dealer* declared that the queen would never 'Bend to their Designs' if the Dutch continued 'obstinate', and that their 'Prevaricating Memorial' contained 'downright Insolence' under 'a show of Compliment and Respect'. The *Examiner* greeted the queen's speech by pointing to her 'peculiar care' for the States' interests, which had led her to stipulate that they should have almost entire the barrier and commercial terms that they had demanded in 1709; but a week later it directed the attention of its readers to 'the stubborn and crafty opposition of some Allies abroad' who had done their best to prevent the queen's efforts for peace from succeeding. Easily the most violently anti-Dutch piece of Tory propaganda which appeared at this time was *The Dutch won't Let us have Dunkirk*, a pamphlet probably designed as a counterblast to the States' letter of June 5th. This characterised the Dutch as 'the *Crab-Lice* of Europe', who intended to stick to us until they had drained us dry. Their letter to the queen, it declared, showed that they were unwilling to let us have Dunkirk, which, indeed, was not surprising, for

If *Great Britain* gain, or is but in the least likely to gain any Advantage whatever, they clamour against it . . . . . . but if we any ways interfere with their Trade, *Amboyna*'s the word, nothing but a Massacre can attone for it.

After digressing on such well worn subjects as Amboyna, the British fishery, English help to the Republic in its early years and the returns that it made, and the Dutch wars, the author asserted that the Dutch wanted to continue the war so that they might be enriched and we undone; indeed, they would rather massacre us again than let us hold Dunkirk. The malice of the 'Undermining, You-tricking Dutch' towards Britain, he went on, was almost unbelievable:

There is not a D—chman in that Antimonarchical C-m-nW—lth but has more Venome in his Heart, and between his Teeth, against Majesty and Monarchy, than ther is Venome under the Teeth of a Snake or Serpent.[1]

Compared to this Defoe's new-found animosity towards the Dutch was mildness itself. In the *Review* he expressed his confidence that the Dutch would agree to the queen's measures once they realised that she was in earnest, but also declared that our attitude towards the pretensions of Philip V had been made more favourable by the resentment that we 'Entertain'd at the Conduct of the Dutch', and suggested that 'the blame of that lie at their Door who deserve it'. Moreover, in two pamphlets published on June 7th (only eleven days after he had suggested to Oxford that he might write something to 'take off all the edge of the popular surprise'!) Defoe spiritedly defended the conduct of the ministry. Of these, *A Farther Search into the Conduct of the Allies* was precisely what its name implies – a rehash of the *Conduct*, brought up to date. In it Defoe made much of the charge that the Whigs had sacrificed our national interests and security to the Dutch, not only by signing the Barrier Treaty and conniving at their deficiencies, but also by spreading the notion 'that those who are for a Peace, do it with a Design, by the Assistance of *France* to introduce the Pretender'. We had humbled ourselves before the Dutch both in the Barrier Treaty and at Geertruidenberg, and now their attitude towards the peace seemed to be to force us to continue the war without even making up their own deficiencies. As indications of this attitude he quoted their alleged offer in October 1711 to lend England four million pounds to carry on the war, their coming to Utrecht without full powers to conclude, their attempt to revive the 1709 preliminaries as a basis for negotiation, their failure to give a satisfactory 'explanation' of several points in the Barrier Treaty, and, lastly, their ineffectual attempt to

---

[1] *Plain Dealer*, 9–10, 7 and 14 June 1712; Anne to States-General (transcript), 9 June 1712, Kensington, Add. Ms. 17677 FFF; *ibid.*, L'Hermitage to States-General (transcripts), 10/21, 13/24 and 17/28 June 1712, London; *Examiner*, ii, 28–9, 12 and 19 June 1712; *Political State*, iii, pp. 351–9, 361–2; *C.W.* 171; *C.W.* 70, pp. 3–8.

gainsay the 'Representation'. The other pamphlet, *Reasons against Fighting*, dealt specifically with the 'Restraining Orders'; whoever complained about these, Defoe declared, it was to be hoped that it was not the Dutch, in view of the use that they had made of field deputies throughout the war so as to have, in effect, command of British armies and generals. This practice, of course, had been encouraged by those amongst us who 'were come into a State of Pupillage to the States', and it might well be asked

whether it is more wonderful that any People should thus Sacrifice their Countries Interest to a Selfish Neighbour, and with a profound and implicit Submission should give themselves over to the Management of a Foreign Nation? or that the same People should now complain that Her Majesty assumes a little Her right of judging when it is Right or Safe to hazard Battle, or not, as well as the *Dutch*.

It was necessary that a battle should be prohibited since the machinations of the Whigs had destroyed all confidence between us and our allies; it was even possible that the allied leaders and the Whigs had agreed to allow our armies to suffer a setback in the hope that this would ruin our present ministry. In any case, we wanted peace, and our proceedings had been fully justified by the 'Insolence' of our allies, not only on the present occasion, and the 'dangerous Correspondence' between 'some People abroad' and a 'Party at home', which was now complaining of our harsh treatment of the Dutch because they wanted us to remain the 'Tools and Engines to the *Dutch* Avarice and *Imperial* Ambition'.

The Whigs were far less vocal in attacking the peace by defending the Allies at this juncture than were the Tories in defending it by attacking them. Indeed, the only pamphlet published at this time which attempted to vindicate the Dutch was *A Dialogue Between a New Courtier and a Country Gentleman*, in which the courtier's violently anti-Dutch advocacy of the peace proposals was contrasted with the declarations of friendship for the States that the queen had made throughout the war. It was perhaps at this time, too, that there appeared a ballad to the tune of 'Lillibulero' attacking the 'Treaty on foot', of which the second verse and chorus ran thus:

A Bargain our Queen made with her good Friends,
The *States*, to uphold the Protestant Line;
If a Bad Peace is made, that Bargain then ends,
And spoils her good Majesty's gallant Design.

Over, over, *Hanover*, over,
Haste and assist our Queen as our State;
Hast over, *Hanover*, fast as you can over;
Put in your Claim, before 'tis too late.[1]

12

When the news of the queen's speech arrived at The Hague the Dutch, so Bristol reported, were thrown into the greatest alarm, nor was this diminished when on June 25th (N.S.) Ormonde declared that he was instructed to carry out a 'suspension of arms' of two months duration that had been arranged by his government and that of France, and, when fighting had been suspended, to occupy Dunkirk. Three days later Bristol informed the Deputies of the States-General of the terms on which the Dutch could come into the 'Suspension'. They were those which the queen had specified in her speech. The Dutch, wrote Thomas Harley to Oxford, now showed 'the greatest malice imaginable toward the administration in England'. They were doing their best to make the Duke of Savoy uneasy at the terms proposed for him by the queen, and were hoping to keep all their actual powers in Flanders rather than submit to the proposed barrier. The party for the war, he continued, 'have so heated the Common people that those who are for peace have not ventured to declare their opinion openly'.[2]

St. John was not greatly surprised at this news. He had predicted to Bristol that the news of the 'cessation' would alarm the Dutch, but hoped that the proceedings of Parliament, and the imminent surrender of Dunkirk, would 'effectually undeceive the States, and humble their pride', and when he learnt from Bristol and Harley of their 'Clamour' and 'rage' he assured the former that he had reason to think that

tho' they kick and flounce like wild beasts caught in a toil, yet the cords are too strong for them to break. They will soon tire with struggling, and when they are tired grow tame . . . .

On the same day on which these words were written, June 20th, Strafford was presented with instructions to take back to The Hague. He and Bristol, these ran, were to make it clear to the Dutch that it was *their* conduct that had forced the ministry to adopt its present

[1] *Review*, viii, 189–90, 7 and 10 June 1712; *C.W.* 44, *passim*; *C.W.* 49, *passim*; *C.W.* 62, pp. 14–20; *C.W.* 133.
[2] Bristol to St. John, 24 and 28 June 1712, Utrecht, S.P. Holl. 244; (T. Harley) to (St. John) (draft), 24 June 1712, Utrecht, Add. Ms. 40621; *ibid.*, (T. Harley) to (Oxford) (draft), 28 June 1712, Utrecht; *Political State*, iv, pp. 1 *sqq.*

measures, and that they must accept the exclusion of 'four species' of goods from the tariff of 1664 and the surrender of Lille as an 'equivalent' for Dunkirk. The Dutch would have less reason to complain of this latter concession in view of the burdens that they had been heaping on our trade with Lille. On June 20th, too, St. John performed a no doubt welcome duty. Calling together the ministers of all those powers with troops in the queen's pay he told them that Ormonde had found the commanders of these 'auxiliaries' unwilling to join in a proposed retirement from the allied army, and he warned them of the danger of the queen's resentment. The point at issue now, he said, was not whether there would be peace or war, but whether the control of the negotiations would remain in the queen's hands or be seized by the States. He added that nothing would illustrate this more clearly than if the Dutch now pretended to continue to fight, since every one knew that they would be in no condition to do so once the troops in British pay had retired.

St. John's words had little immediate effect either on the auxiliaries or on the Dutch themselves. On July 1st Thomas Harley, still at Utrecht, was hopeful that the Deputies from Amsterdam would sway the States of Holland in favour of agreeing to the queen's measures. The 'warrior party' was very active, he wrote, but was dependent on Amsterdam for funds for the continuation of the war, and he believed that that town would 'sooner open their sluices for their defence than open their Bank to the lovers of war in England & Holland'. Bristol, too, thought that the Dutch seemed 'to have dropped a good deal of their ill humour'. The return of Strafford on July 6th (N.S.), however, did much to blight these hopes. On his arrival, when celebrations of the fall of Quesnoy on July 3rd were still going on, he declared (so it was reported) that 'they made a great noise for a Paltry town'; and when he communicated his instructions two days later the worst fears of the Dutch were confirmed. Strafford did nothing to soften the blow, for, as he complacently wrote to St. John, 'Sharp handling dose better with these people than the best words'.[1]

On July 9th the States of Holland resolved that the 'cessation' should not be accepted on the terms proposed. Strafford thereupon left The

[1] St. John to Bristol, 14 June 1712, Whitehall, *B.L.*, ii, pp. 377–9; Same to same (draft), 20 June 1712 (O.S.), S.P. Holl. 245; *ibid.*, Instructions for Bristol and Strafford (draft), 20 June 1712, Kensington; L'Hermitage to States-General (transcript), 20 June/1 July 1712, London, Add. Ms. 17677 FFF; (T. Harley) to (Auditor Harley) (draft), 1 July 1712, Utrecht, Add. Ms. 40621; *ibid.*, (T. Harley) to (Oxford) (draft), 1 July 1712, Utrecht; Bristol to St. John (copy), 1 July 1712, Utrecht, Add. Ms. 31137; Strafford to St. John, 9 July 1712, Hague, S.P. Holl. 243; *Political State*, iv, p. 13.

Hague for the army, refusing to confer further until the States had instructed the field deputies to suspend hostilities, and Bristol returned to Utrecht. Drummond still hoped, as late as July 12th, that Amsterdam might rebel against the continuation of the war, though he added that

one is hardly safe here from the people at present who is not of their opinion, or wise enough to keep his tongue in public company, or to stay altogether out of it.

On the following day the States-General submitted to the Provinces a list of points to be agreed before an armistice. These stipulated that Strasbourg should be ceded to the Empire, that Maximilian Emmanuel should withdraw from the Spanish Netherlands as soon as peace was concluded, and that the States themselves should have Lille, Tournai and Condé, and the entire tariff of 1664. The unanimous agreement of the Provinces to this resolution involved the virtual rejection of the queen's offer.

Meanwhile Strafford, who arrived at the allied camp on July 12th, was discovering that in the army as at The Hague the Dutch were, as an English officer wrote home, 'very angry with us'. His 'sharp handling' had no effect upon the field deputies, and he found that the auxiliaries stood firmly beside 'the reigning faction in Holland', who, he went on, were

pushing things to an extremity, to wrest this negotiation out of the Queen's hands and continue the war, tho there is more appearance of misfortunes & confusions then of success.

Ormonde and Strafford were powerless to enforce the cessation of arms upon their allies. On July 16th the allied armies under Eugene drew off from the British camp, a development for which Strafford held the field deputies – 'the hottest and most violent of their whole country' – very largely to blame. The breach between the British and their allies was now complete. 'This is an od situation but it will justify the insincerity of the Dutch', commented Strafford, with one eye on opinion at home; for himself, he found nothing incongruous in now referring to the Allies as the 'new enemy'.[1]

At home, meanwhile, the tone that the Tories adopted towards the Dutch, both in public and in private, grew less and less restrained as it

---

[1] (Drummond) to (Oxford), 12 July 1712, Amsterdam, *H.M.C. Portland V*, pp. 195–7; Lord Fermanagh to R. Verney, (12 July 1712?), *Verney Letters*, i, p. 272 (dated 12 June (O.S.), but its contents indicate that it must be later); Strafford to St. John, 15 and 16 July 1712, Château Cambrésis, S.P. Holl. 243; Strafford to Bristol, 16 July 1712, Château Cambrésis, Ms. Rawl. A. 286; *Political State*, iv, pp. 24–5; *Montgomery*, pp. 281–3.

became apparent that the States would not submit to the queen's measures and, moreover, that the auxiliaries were following their lead. St. John became more and more menacing when writing to Bristol about the Dutch; on June 24th he hinted that the queen might turn the tables on the Dutch leaders by appealing to their people and pointing out that all the present difficulties were due to the 'want of concert' on their part. A day later he wrote to Thomas Harley that if she were to do so 'those who are in the Regency would pass their time but ill'. On July 3rd he repeated this hint, writing that they were so 'distracted by ye intrigues of those who play them off, by vain hopes and groundless fears', that they would have to have 'their own Work done by other hands'.

London was full of contradictory rumours about the intentions of the Dutch, and of what would happen if they did not come into the queen's measures. The *Post Boy* reported that the confederates were planning to give some affront to the British troops, and Swift heard that the Dutch were willing to go to any lengths to prevent Ormonde from taking possession of Dunkirk. On July 1st, according to L'Hermitage, it was still widely believed that the Dutch would submit, but three days later, when this seemed less likely, it was being said that Britain would not merely make a separate peace, but would then unite with France against the recalcitrant Allies. L'Hermitage found this last difficult to believe, since what the English people wanted was peace, and not a fresh war.[1]

Whatever the truth of such rumours as this, or of the stories that a plot engineered by the Dutch and the Whigs against the queen's life had lately been discovered, and that Marlborough and others had been arrested 'as endeavouring to make their Escape to Holland', there was no doubt who was responsible for spreading them. As Swift, the head of the ministerial propagandists, wrote on July 1st, 'We rayl now all against the Dutch, who indeed have acted like Knaves Fools and Madmen'. The *Examiner* and the *Plain Dealer* surpassed themselves in their efforts 'to render the Allies the more odious to the People', as Boyer put it. The *Examiner* devoted an issue to exposing the alleged Dutch-Whig intrigue to wreck the peace, an attempt, it asserted, prompted entirely by Dutch jealousy of Britain and their desire to retain that 'ignominious

---

[1] St. John to Bristol (draft), 24 June 1712, Whitehall, S.P. Holl. 245; St. John to T. Harley, 25 June 1712, Whitehall, *H.M.C. Portland V*, pp. 193–4; Swift to Archbishop King, 26 June 1712, Kensington, *Swift Corres.*, i, pp. 329–32; L'Hermitage to States-General (transcripts), 1/12 and 4/15 July 1712, London, Add. Ms. 17677 FFF; St. John to Bristol (copy), 3 July 1712, Whitehall, Add. Ms. 31137; *Political State*, iv, pp. 18–20.

Bargain', Article XV of the Barrier Treaty. In another issue it ironi-cally thanked Marlborough for having encouraged the Dutch to take such measures as would enable the queen, if she so desired, to desert them with a clear conscience. The *Plain Dealer* continued with redoub-led vigour its attacks on both the States' Memorial in answer to the 'Representation' and their more recent letter, and did not hesitate to draw a parallel, at which Defoe had already hinted in *Reasons Against Fighting*, between the 'Restraining Orders' and the conduct of the Dutch deputies in 1705. It also gave currency to a rumour that the Dutch were fitting out a fleet to besiege Portsmouth.[1]

Defoe, meanwhile, in the *Review*, was evolving a thesis that he was soon to propound in pamphlet form. On June 28th he was of opinion that the Dutch would not join with the Emperor in continuing the war, though he admitted that this was not 'the Judgment of the Town'. The news of the fall of Quesnoy, however, together with the apparent reluctance of the States to come into the cessation, began to make him think differently. If these allied successes continued, he wrote, we might have to intervene to prevent the aggrandizement of the Empire. He continued to denounce rumours such as that of a Dutch squadron being fitted out to intercept our going to Dunkirk as 'forged Stories', and thanked God that 'things are not come to that yet'. But, he added, what if they did? And was it not possible that they would if the Allies, egged on by the Whigs, continued the fight against France? Such action on their part could have but three possible consequences: they might be unsuccessful, in which case 'the Dutch must be *Ruin'd*'; they might be victorious, and then 'we must be Ruin'd'; or else we might think it necessary to guard against the latter event by joining France and making war against the Dutch. Thus, with calm and unemotional deliberation, Defoe prepared his readers for a possible war with the Dutch, though he still hoped it could be avoided:

Let the wisest Man alive propose a Medium for this, if he can, except a Peace can be made to quiet and satisfie all Parties, and this I cannot but yet hope for, from the Wisdom and Prudence of the *Dutch*.

The Whig periodicals could do little but raise their hands in horror at the allegations and insinuations of the Tories, but their appeals to reason and to history could have little effect in the almost hysterical atmosphere of London in the summer of 1712, where, as St. John

[1] *Examiner*, ii, 30–1, 26 June and 3 July 1712; *Plain Dealer*, 12–13, 28 June and 5 July 1712; *Journal to Stella*, ii, pp. 544–5, 1 July 1712, Kensington; *Observator*, xi, 54, 5 July 1712; *C.W.* 82; *Political State*, iv, p. 19.

recalled years later, 'the clamour could not have been greater, if the queen had signed her peace separately'. The *Medley* devoted itself to drawing an elaborate implied parallel between the English betrayal of the Dutch in 1672 and the current situation. The *Observator* spoke out more, praising the Dutch for supplying the auxiliaries with bread, which we had denied them unless they would come into the cessation, and criticising various Tory 'libels' by name as attempts to undermine the Protestant Succession. On July 2nd it printed a 'letter' which deplored the 'disgust' which, it admitted, was apparent throughout the country because the Dutch were continuing the war. They had a right to their own opinion, this asserted, had shown their firmness to us in 1710, and were 'our best Neighbours, and a standing Bulwark against Popery and Slavery'. There was, moreover, little real trade rivalry between us, since they competed with us only as carriers – unlike France. Their interest as traders lay entirely in the repose of Europe – unlike that of France. We gained a great deal from our trade with them – but not from that with France. On these and all other grounds, it concluded,

'tis not our Interest so unthinkingly to fall upon the Dutch .... for I dare be bold to say, though it may be their Misfortune to fall first, our Ruin will not be long after ....

Such arguments, however reasonable, lacked appeal for a nation which had drunk deep of the heady wine of xenophobia. In fact, there was no effective answer that the Whigs could make to such publications as the *Post Boy* which, taking up the *Observator* on an incautious appeal to British honour, asked

Where is the Honour of the British Nation, whilst a Sett of Factious (I had like to have said Rebellious) Subjects are magnifying the Power, the Strength of Holland, in Opposition to their own Country, and impudently tell us, That the Dutch will not suffer our Queen to make a Peace.[1]

---

[1] *Review*, viii, 198–201, 28 June, 1, 3 and 5 July 1712; *Observator*, xi, 52–4, 28 June, 2 and 5 July 1712; *Medley*, (ii) (Baker), 35, 30 June 1712; *Post Boy*, 2675, 3 July 1712; *C.W.* 160, p. 140.

CHAPTER XI

THE CAMPAIGN AGAINST THE ALLIES II

(THE TORY PEACE)
⟨1712–13⟩

I

The separation of the British troops from the allied armies marked the opening of the supreme test of British feeling towards the peace policies of Oxford and Bolingbroke. This test was of short duration, being ended only eight days later by the disaster of Denain, which virtually assured the eventual submission of the Republic to the queen's will, but not for one moment was there any question of its outcome. Even the Junto chief Halifax felt compelled to admit that the campaign against the Allies achieved triumphant success in July 1712. In a note to Burnet's *History* he wrote that

the nation in general, at that time, ran warmly into the peace, from a persuasion artfully worked up and propagated, that we had been the dupes of our allies.

The ministry had done its work well, and knew that it could now rely on support at home for the suspension of arms, and even for a separate peace, should the Allies prove obstinate. What gave it cause for alarm was no longer the state of opinion at home but the state of affairs abroad, and the possibility that the Allies might succeed against France without British aid and thus wreck all its plans. There is even evidence in pamphlets and periodicals published at this time that, rather than admit such a development, the ministry was prepared to use armed force to defend France against the Dutch and Austrians. In the days before Denain suggestions of this kind were freely made by one of the foremost 'ministerial' propagandists. Even after the allied defeat this campaign, for such it undoubtedly was, went on. It would no doubt be fruitless to speculate whether, had Eugene been the victor at Denain, British opinion would have been behind the ministry had it then gone to the aid of France; but there is some evidence to show that, after Denain, the suggestions that a war with the Dutch might be necessary aroused no great enthusiasm.

This 'Dutch War' campaign did not end until the Republic virtually capitulated to the British government at the end of September. From that time until the signing of the Peace on April 11th, 1713 (N.S.), there was little change in the British attitude towards the Dutch. That this was so was at least partly due to the success of the ministerial propagandists – above all, perhaps, of Swift. Whatever verdict we may wish to pass on the Oxford ministry's conduct of the peace, we must recognise as one of its outstanding features the extremely successful and unprecedentedly systematic use of the press in order to obtain support at home. Swift himself, writing after the peace, was ready to point the moral:

.... had not some active pens fallen in to improve the good disposition of the people, upon the late change, and continued since to overthrow the falsehood, plentifully, and sometimes not unplausibly, scattered by the adversaries, I am very much in doubt, whether those at the helm would now have reason to be pleased with their success.[1]

2

On July 7th (O.S.) London was full of contradictory rumours, all of them spread by the Tory propagandists. The *Medley* asserted that it was 'the Humour of the Age to be delighted with Nonsense', since the Tories were capable of asserting at one and the same time that British troops were in Dunkirk and that the Dutch were preventing our occupying that town; or, again, that the Dutch were about to come into the queen's measures, that they would have a good barrier, and, on the other hand, that they were determined to continue the war and that it was not a 'Farthing matter what became of such ungrateful Allies'. On this day, too, one of the first of a long series of addresses from all over the country complaining of the 'Artifices of pretended Friends abroad' was presented to the queen. None the less, so great had been the confidence of many Englishmen that the Dutch would submit to the queen's terms that even when the news arrived of Ormonde's defection from the allied army it was still thought by some (according to Peter Wentworth) that they would not hold out for long. On the following day, however, Wentworth found that such hopes were fading, and he wrote to his brother that

At St. James's Coffe house they expect the Dutch will hold & stand fast by the Emperor & conquer France this summer by themselves.[2]

Such a prospect was far from welcome to the ministry and its sup-

[1] *C.W.* 18, vi, p. 132 (note by Halifax); *C.W.* 175, pp. 124–5.
[2] *Medley*, (ii) (Baker), 37, 7 July 1712; P. Wentworth to (Strafford), 7 July 1712, London, Add. Ms. 34144; Same to same, 8 July 1712, London, *Wentworth Papers*, pp. 290–1; *Post Boy*, 2678, 10 July 1712 (address of Mayor and Corporation of Cardigan).

porters. St. John, now Viscount Bolingbroke, showed his alarm by making vain attempts to persuade the King of Prussia, whose obstinacy, he declared, was doing much to 'sooth the opiniâtreté, of the the Dutch, to accept the suspension of arms. It was rapidly becoming clear that the Dutch were determined to stand by the Emperor in trying the fortunes of another campaign in the hope of breaking the measures of the ministry. The correspondents of the court of St. Germains noted with glee that this development gave pleasure to none except the Junto and their followers, who were 'losing ground every day'. Even in the City, they reported, the King of France began to be mentioned 'as a very honest man, and a fair dealer'. From Naples the dying Shaftesbury might write of 'the most sad shame and reproach of our nation, wch I never thought to have liv'd to see', but Speaker Bromley, travelling through the Home Counties, found an unprecedented 'inquisitiveness' upon the road, and

an impatience to hear the peace proceeded well, and that Dunkirk was in the possession of the Queen; even in Buckinghamshire great satisfaction was expressed on these expectations, and I was told the middle and trading sort of people were asking one another whether they might not now drink the French King's health.[1]

The ministry, haunted by the prospect of the victorious Republic making a peace highly prejudicial to British interests with a humbled French King, did nothing to discourage the hostility towards the Dutch engendered by their rejection of the suspension of arms. On the contrary it encouraged the conditional advocacy of a war with the Dutch which had already been undertaken by Defoe. It was still Defoe who took the lead in this 'campaign'. In the *Review* he declared his confidence that the Dutch knew their own interest better than to carry on the war, but at the same time he hinted that if they did they would certainly have the joint forces of France and England to contend with. He indignantly denied that to point this out was to call for a Dutch war; if such a disaster came about, he argued, it would be the fault of the Whigs, who were giving the Dutch underhand encouragement to persist in their desperate measures. The Whig periodicals did not let such statements pass unheeded. The two *Medley's* made much of the apostasy of the Whig Defoe, and the pseudo-*Medley* further

[1] Bolingbroke to Breton (copy), 8 July 1712, Whitehall, F.E.B. Prussia 52; Shaftesbury to Furly, 19 July 1712, Naples, *Forster*, pp. 269–72; S. Johnson to ?, 8 July 1712 (O.S.), *Macpherson*, ii, pp. 333–4; *ibid.*, ii, pp. 335–6, (Plunket) to (Middleton), 21 July 1712, Utrecht; Bolingbroke to Bristol (draft), 10 July 1712, Whitehall, S.P. Holl. 245; Bromley to (Oxford), 12 July 1712, Baginton, *H.M.C. Portland V*, pp. 202–3.

declared that our chances of success in a war with the Dutch were very small. The *Observator* listed five arguments against a Dutch war, one of which stated that

......if we may guess at Things to come, by Things past, the people of *Great-Britain* will scarce contribute with the same Cheerfulness to a War against our Allies, so many of whom are Protestants, as against *France* and *Spain* ....

The suggestion that a Dutch war would be 'against the General Inclination of the People' was also made in a pamphlet published at this time entitled *An Enquiry Into the Danger and Consequences of a War with the Dutch.* This argued that, even if we were not immediately ruined by losing the war, we would be so eventually by the 'inexpressible hardships' that such a contest would put upon our trade and even more so by the advantages that it would present to France and the Pretender. The aversion of the 'common people' to a Dutch war could also be safely prophesied:

They have been long our Friends and Confederates, have often Assisted, Relieved, Deliver'd Us in our Embroiled Circumstances, and we cannot without Reluctance, desire to fight against a People whom we have so often acted in Conjunction with: We have look'd upon them as our Friends, as our Brethren, in the late War, and it must be with Regret, that our People should rejoyce in contrary Extremes, and sheath their Swords in the Bowels of those, who they shook Hands with before.

Though Defoe was the only ministerial writer actually to talk of a Dutch war, the *Examiner* and several pamphleteers did their best to make such a suggestion acceptable by doing all they could to blacken the Republic. Now that the Dutch were openly 'defying' the queen they abandoned what shreds of restraint they had retained. In addition to its old cry that the Dutch, in alliance with the Whigs, were now fighting – at our expense – for dominion rather than safety, the *Examiner* proclaimed that the policy of the Dutch leaders, some of whom it attacked by name, was so contrary to the true interest of the Republic that they would be in great danger of being 'De-Witted' were it not that

the Common People in *Holland* have always professed a Hatred to the *English* Nation, whether from the Brutalities of their Natures, or their looking upon us as Rivals in their Trade....

The *Examiner*, moreover, quoted at length from the notorious 'Delenda est Carthago' speech of the first Earl of Shaftesbury, and in so approving a fashion that the *Observator* remarked that it was evidently the design of 'the *French* and their Faction .... to exterminate the *Dutch* abroad, and the *Whiggs* and Dissenters at home'. The *Medley* further commented that Marlborough's unforgivable fault was that he had been an 'implacable Foe to our best Friends the *F——h*, and a Friend to our worst Enemies the *D——h*'. The *Post-Boy*, meanwhile, surpassed itself in the tendentiousness of its presentation of 'news' from The Hague. On July 14th, for example, this paragraph appeared in its 'Postscript':

Hague, July 22, N.S. After all the late Assertions, That this Republick exerted herself even beyond her Strength, during the Course of this War, it should now seem, That rather than suffer the English to enjoy any Advantages in Trade, she will try whether she is not capable of carrying on the War at least without them.[1]

At this time, too, there appeared two of those 'historical' surveys of the misdeeds of the Dutch Republic which are a familiar feature of English pamphlet literature in the years 1711–13. They ran true to type in making much of Dutch ingratitude, trickery, perjury, cruelty, greed, faithlessness and brutality, all of these traits being illustrated by episodes taken from the history of the Republic. One of them, *A History of the Dutch Usurpations*, suggested that the Dutch had recently done their best, by means of the 1709 Barrier Treaty, to exclude us from the Flanders trade as completely and as unfairly as they had done from that of the East Indies. It went on in true High Tory style to point once more the contrast between the alleged lethargy of the Dutch in conducting the war and their refusal to accept peace. The other pamphlet, *A Search After Dutch Honesty*, perhaps by Defoe, was similar to this but was able to add one more complaint to the long list, for by the time it was written the news had arrived of Ormonde's march north and the refusal of Dutch commanders to admit his army into the towns under their control.

The event which aroused most interest in Britain between the suspension of arms and Denain was the occupation of Dunkirk by British troops under Hill on July 19th (N.S.). The Tory writers made the most of this concrete evidence of the ministry's success. Swift celebrated the event in a poem which began:

> Spight of *Dutch* Friends and *English* Foes,
> Poor *Britain* shall have Peace at last;
> *Holland* got Towns, and we got Blows,
> But *Dunkirk's* ours, we'll hold it fast.

[1] *Medley*, (ii) (Baldwin), 37 and 39, 7 and 14 July 1712; *Review*, viii, 202–6, 8, 10, 12, 15 and 17 July 1712; *Observator*, xi, 55–6, 9 and 12 July 1712; *Examiner*, ii, 32–3, 10 and 17 July 1712; *Medley*, (ii) (Baker), 38–9, 11 and 14 July 1712; *Postscript to Post Boy*, 2679, 14 July 1712; *C.W.* 71, *passim*.

Another Tory versifier rejoiced in the chagrin of the Allies – 'Our *Whigs* are mad, the *Dutch* repine' – and yet another in the thwarting of 'republican' schemes

> To the Joy of all those that wish well to our *Nation*,
> And to her Whigg Foes eternal Vexation,
> Whose good will to *Britain, in plain Terms*, is such
> They'd rather that *Dunkirk* was giv'n to the Dutch.

To this spate of verse there was a Whig contribution. There appeared a pamphlet entitled *Occasional Poems on the Late Dutch War, and the Sale of Dunkirk*, which consisted mainly of reprints of anti-Court, pro-Dutch poems written during the second anglo-Dutch war. The main interest of this work, however, is in the one new poem which it contained. Entitled 'A Satyr against the Dutch', this was in fact a satire on the various High Tory arguments against the Dutch, who it was complained, were not willing to leave us alone to become slaves to Popery:

> These are *They*, who maugre Old Kindnesses,
> Dare now oppose (Oh D—gs) our *Glorious Peace*.
> Nor with'r new Way of Treating will agree,
> But brand it with th'opprobrious Name of *Treachery*.
> 'Tis hard, you'll say, we can't do what we please,
> Without such meddling *Sooterkins* as these ....
> Yet These wou'd *Guarantees* be after all
> Of our *Succession*; Ay, when they're hang'd they shall ....
> No, rather lets be Wretched in their Spight,
> And *Frogland* sink, tho' *Britain* suffer by't. [1]

3

On July 14th the news reached London that Ormonde, marching northwards, had changed direction and was making for Ghent. Though the exiled Earl of Ailesbury believed that this would 'open the eyes' of the States-General, L'Hermitage thought that it was not much liked in London where, he added, the Tories were meeting with little success with their 'Dutch war' campaign. Even the subsequent

[1] *C.W.* 99, *passim*; *C.W.* 54, *passim*; *C.W.* 178; *C.W.* 60; *C.W.* 81; *C.W.* 135, pp. 22–4.

seizure of Ghent and Bruges by Ormonde, he reported, evoked from many people the comment that all this must have been previously concerted with the French; though the refusal of the Dutch commandants in some places to allow any of the British forces to enter their towns, 'which insolent proceeding', remarked the English *chargé d'affaires* at Brussels' 'tis hoped will be resented as it deserves', did in fact occasion 'bitter Reflections against the Dutch'. [1]

A more reliable test of the current attitude towards the Dutch was provided when, on July 17th, the news of the allied disaster at Denain reached London. Swift's reaction at Kensington to this news – 'this perhaps may cool their Courage, & make them think of a Peace' – was very similar to that of Watkins with the British army. It seems true, as Wyon has pointed out, that most people learnt of Denain without displeasure, and

hoped that the Dutch and Imperialists would be convinced by their disasters that, without the aid of England, it was useless for them to pursue the war.

It should be noted, however, that political writers of all shades seemed slow to realise the magnitude of the change that had now come over the international situation. In particular, the 'Dutch War' argument went on, though Defoe's contention that we could not afford to risk a Dutch victory over the French had now lost its validity. It is unlikely that this was due to any underestimation in governmental circles of the importance of Denain; indeed, Bolingbroke now turned down a suggestion from Torcy for joint action against the Allies on the grounds that the queen could now hope that 'at last they will see their errour and concur with her Majty'. Nevertheless, the ministerial propagandists went on whipping up feeling against the Dutch, and even in favour of a Dutch war.

The news of Denain, according to L'Hermitage, was received 'selon la disposition des esprits', a formula sometimes employed in his letters to gloss over the fact that public reactions in some matter had not been favourable to the Dutch. He went on to emphasise (as, too, did the *Observator*) that only the 'partisans de France' were pleased at the turn of events. Three days later, however, he himself virtually denied this by admitting that

Le peuple .... par des écrits qui se publient journellement pour l'animer, est dans un si grand préjugé, que tout ce qui peut forcer à la paix de quelle manière que ce puisse estre, est bien reçu par la plus part ....

[1] Ailesbury to (Watkins), 25 July 1712, Brussels, *Thibaudeau*, 2nd ser., i, p. 23; Laws to Tilson, 25 July 1712, Brussels, S.P. Flanders 61; L'Hermitage to States-General (transcripts), 15/26 and 18/29 July 1712, London, Add. Ms. 17677 FFF; *Political State*, iv, p. 85.

A typical reaction seems to have been that of Lord Berkeley of Stratton:

I could not but be sorry for the success the French have lately had, but am not at all soe for the Dutch being humbled who seem'd for some years to have lost the tramontane, and to forget what they and their neighbours were.

The Tories did not, indeed, spare many tears for the misfortunes of the Allies. Even in print they could hardly forbear to sneer, whether it was in a contemptuous account of the battle of 'Bicoque' (Denain) itself, or in the fourth part of the John Bull allegory, in which Bull, standing on the battlements of 'Ecclesdoun', sees Frog and asks him:

How comest thou to go with thy arm ty'd up? Has old *Lewis* given thee a rap over the Finger-ends? Thy Weapon was a good one when I weilded it, but the Butt-end remains in my Hands.

In Dublin, where it was already rumoured that Ormonde was remaining in Flanders 'with a design to compel the Dutch to a peace in case they obstinately stand out', and that Britain would ally herself with France and Sweden, Dr. (later Bishop) Berkeley heard 'from a gentleman of my acquaintance just come from London' that

the account of my Lord Albemarle's defeat was publicly cried about the streets by the title of good and joyful news.

'God grant', he added, 'that we have not a war with the Dutch' [1].

To most observers, however, it was evident that Denain had made it unnecessary to consider the possibility of a Dutch war. Hopes ran high that the Dutch would submit at once to the queen. So great was the desire for peace that a groundless rumour that the Dutch plenipotentiaries at Utrecht had proposed by new plan for a general peace gained widespread belief at the beginning of August. An address to the queen from the borough of Montrose expressed the hope that Denain had taught the Allies a lesson and would overcome their obstinacy, and one of Hearne's correspondents, who professed to have 'no Kindness for the dutch nation', was anxious that all things should now 'tend to a Generall peace in Europe'. On August 3rd (N.S.) Watkins still supposed that 'their courage is now pretty well cool'd', and when he heard next day that the French had invested Douai he expected a cessation of arms.[2]

[1] Watkins to Harrison, 27 July 1712, Drongen, Add. Ms. 22201; *Journal to Stella*, ii, p. 551, 17 July 1712, Kensington; Bolingbroke to Ormonde (draft), 19 July 1712, Whitehall, S.P. Holl. 245; L'Hermitage to States-General (transcripts), 22 July/2 Aug. and 25 July/5 Aug. 1712, London, Add. Ms. 17677 FFF; *Observator*, xi, 59, 23 July 1712; Berkeley of Stratton to Strafford, 12 Aug. 1712 (O.S.), *Wentworth Papers*, pp. 297–8; Berkeley to Percival, 18 Aug. 1712, Trinity College Dublin, *Berkeley*, pp. 102–4; *C.W.* 148, pp. 46–8; *C.W.* 6, pt. 4, pp. 36–7; Wyon, *op.cit.*, ii, p. 407.

[2] Watkins to Harrison, 3 Aug. 1712, Drongen, Add. Ms. 22201; Watkins to Tilson, 4 Aug.

The Whigs did their best to decry these hopes of Dutch submission. The pseudo-*Medley*, for example, pointed to the past 'firmness' of the Dutch in times of peril, and suggested that this disaster would probably 'more and more animate the Confederates against the Perjury and Tyranny of *France*'. Defoe, on the other hand, though denying a rumour that the Dutch had already agreed to the queen's terms, declared himself certain that they would do so eventually. He did not think Denain was an occasion for rejoicing, but it would have been no more so if the Dutch had beaten the French. Perhaps, he added, God's hand could be seen in the outcome of the battle; but on August 5th he pointed out in the *Review* that we must no more allow France to overrun the Dutch than we would have allowed the Dutch to overrun France. Those Englishmen who actually wanted to see France take away the Dutch Barrier, he continued, were mad, since this would eventually involve us in another war with France. The Tory *Plain Dealer* also detected in the outcome of Denain evidence of divine intervention on behalf of 'Her Majesty's Endeavours in procuring Peace'; but, unlike Defoe, it took advantage of the reported submission of the Dutch to revile them as though they were a beaten enemy.[1]

High though the hopes might be that Denain had produced, attacks on the Allies in pamphlets and periodicals did not grow less intense. On the contrary, it was nine days after the news of Denain had been received that the propaganda campaign in favour of a war with the Dutch reached its climax, though not its end. On July 26th there appeared Defoe's *Justice and Necessity of a War with Holland, in Case the Dutch Do not come into Her Majesty's Measures, Stated and Examined*. Most of this was written before anything was known in England of the allied defeat, but it is interesting that it was thought appropriate to publish it at this time. This and all the rest of the anti-Dutch pamphlets, which continued to appear in as great numbers as ever, pose a problem to which there seems to be no really satisfactory answer: what was their real object, in so far as they were officially inspired? There was no longer any obvious reason for the ministry to inflame public feeling to the degree to which its hacks evidently

---

1712, Drongen, S.P. Flanders 61; G. Hearne to Hearne, 3 Aug. 1712 (O.S.), *Hearne*, iii, pp. 422–3 n.; *Post Boy*, 2710, 23 Sept. 1712 (address from borough of Montrose); *Political State*, iv, p. 108.

[1] *Review*, viii, 208–9, 22 and 24 July 1712; *Medley*, (ii) (Baldwin), 42, 25 July 1712; *Plain Dealer*, 17, 2 Aug. 1712; *Review*, (ix), 2 and 4, 5 and 12 Aug. 1712 (the ninth volume of the *Review* appeared as 'volume I').

aspired. It had already triumphed at home, and Denain had virtually ensured its triumph abroad. The advocacy of a 'Dutch war', as the annalist Jones pointed out, had always been

Curious politicks .... in the Mouth of those, who alledged but just before, that we were under a Necessity of making a Peace with *France*, because we could not carry on the War any longer.[1]

Why then continue this advocacy and all the rest of the anti-Dutch propaganda? The ministers (unlike Dr. Berkeley) seem to have appreciated the significance of Denain, but they may well have valued the prolongation of the campaign both as a safeguard against a popular reaction in favour of the Allies and as a means of maintaining pressure on the wavering Dutch leaders. At the same time, it seems likely that we have here the case of a campaign which, originally contrived and controlled with an eye to specific aims, meets with such success and gathers such momentum that its creators are carried along with it, possibly unconsciously, beyond the end which they had in view.

Defoe's pamphlet was not one of his happiest. After a long preliminary survey of the gradual deterioration of Anglo-Dutch relations (entirely ascribed, of course, to the misdeeds of the Dutch), he proceeded to demonstrate the justice of a war with the Republic. This he did by asserting that if the queen were forced to go to war with the Dutch in order to save France, it would really be the Dutch who had gone to war with her, since she would merely be performing her duty in maintaining the balance of power! What might make such a war *necessary*, he went on, was the continuance of the existing correspondence between the Allies and the factious opposition in England, who believed that if they could continue the war they could force the queen to change hands again. A postscript dealt with the situation as it appeared after Denain. It was to be hoped, wrote Defoe in a tone of polite blackmail, that the Dutch would now realise that, just as if they had pursued the war with success they would have had to fight us,

so if failing of that Success, they should prove so unhappy as to want Her Majesties Assistance for Defence of their own Countrey, they would have small Reason, Her Majesties Goodness alone excepted, to expect Help from a Princess who they have treated in such a Manner as they have done her Majesty.

While Defoe supplemented these arguments in the *Review*, and the *Plain Dealer* reinforced them by suggesting that the Dutch leaders were aiming at 'Universal Empire', the Whig periodicals devoted

---

[1] *Jones, 1712*, p. 315.

much space to their refutation. The two *Medleys* and the *Observator* mingled indignation and irony in their attacks on their Tory rivals. The pseudo-*Medley* of July 28th, for example, printed a systematic criticism of the advocacy of a Dutch war. The only reason the *Review* had ever given for this, it declared, was

that we must not suffer the Confederates to beat the *French*, lest they shou'd afterwards beat us. I hope his Fears of that are now pretty well over, and if he be true to his own argument, he must own that we have more Reason to hinder the *French* from beating the *Dutch* any further, lest they shou'd beat us next.

If the *Review* liked the prospect of a Dutch war as little as it said it did, the pseudo-*Medley* went on, it should write against it and not for it. As for such other arguments as that put forward by the *Plain Dealer*, these were 'so very weak that they serve only to express the Rancour and betray the Judgment of those who make use of them', who, to conceal the inadequacy of their case, were now publishing pamphlets containing all the scandal that had been thrown at the Dutch in the reign of Charles II.[1]

Pamphlets of the kind mentioned by this critic were indeed continuing to appear. On July 19th was published *Dutch Alliances*, a detailed account of the Amboyna 'massacre', the preface to which contained the following passage:

May the Divine Providence inspire all Christian Kingdoms and States with sincere Dispositions to Peace; but if it must be our Fate to continue this, or enter into a new War, I hope it will be with Antagonists that have as little Christianity as those in the present Narrative, which .... is now published to show those of our Country their Folly, who would ruin their own Nation, to advance the Interest of the *Dutch*, out of a vain Opinion they have of the love they bear to their Faction: But by the following Relation they may find, that the Question was not, Whether they were Tories or Whiggs? but whether they could get anything by our Destruction? which, to accomplish, they made Use of the utmost Barbarity.

The preface to another account of Amboyna published about this time explained that its purpose was to refute those who 'would very freely consent to betray their own Native Country into the hands of a cruel and blood thirsty People ...'. Such sentiments formed a particularly outspoken variation on the theme of Dutch ingratitude, which was now becoming the burden of many Tory writings. Week after week the *Examiner* took up this subject, bemoaning the fact that the corrupting influence of 'Dutch Politicks' had hitherto blinded us

---

[1] *Medley*, (ii) (Baldwin), 40–1 and 43, 18, 21 and 28 July 1712; *Plain Dealer*, 15, 19 July 1712; *Observator*, xi, 58 and 60–1, 19, 26 and 30 July 1712; *Medley*, (ii) (Baker), 41, 21 July 1712; *Review*, viii, 210–11, 26 and 29 July 1712; *C.W.* 45, *passim.*

to it. *Lewis Baboon turned Honest,* the fourth and last part of the John Bull allegory, which satirised Dutch conduct since the opening of the Utrecht conference, contained a long soliloquy by John Bull on this very topic, part of which read thus:

After I have beggar'd myself with his troublesome Law-Suit, with a Pox to him, he (Frog) takes it in mighty Dudgeon because I have brought him here to end Matters amicably, and because I won't let him make me over, by Deed and Indenture, as his lawful Cully; which, to my certain Knowledge, he had attempted several times .... he is a tradesman, a self-seeking Wretch, but how camest thou to bear all this, John? The Reason is plain; Thou conferrest the Benefits, and he receives them; the first produce Love, and the last Ingratitude: Ah! *Nic. Nic.* thou art a damn'd dog, that's certain; thou knowest too well that I will take care of thee, else thou would'st not use me thus: I won't give thee up, it is true; but as true as it is, thou shalt not sell me according to thy laudable Custom.

Dutch ingratitude, too, was the subject of several addresses to the queen. From Wexford, for example, an address was made on August 7th which animadverted at length on the 'many indignities' offered to the queen, even by 'those of your Allies, from whom your Majesty has best deserv'd ... who has so truly made them *Mighty*' despite the fact that they

declin'd that reasonable Share and Burthen of the War, which became those chearfully to take, who were immediately to gain or lose by event of it.

Shaftesbury's 'Delenda est Carthago' speech was once more revived, this time under the title of *Dutch Ingratitude Exemplified*.[1]

The Whig pamphleteers, on the other hand, no longer hesitated to range themselves unequivocally on the side of the Dutch. Braving such taunts as Ward's

> Whate'er the *Dutch* propose shall be allow'd
> To tend to Europe's universal good.
> What *Britain* does, beneath the Royal Care,
> So wisely manage, must be thought unfair,

they sought to refute all 'the Reproaches that are very lavishly cast upon the *Dutch* by several Invidious Pens', in the words of a pamphlet entitled *Dutch Generosity, and English Gratitude*. The main theme of this work was the shameful way in which Charles II had repaid his debt of gratitude to the Republic. This was a topic also taken up in the pulpit by the minister of Covent Garden, who referred in his sermon

[1] *Examiner*, ii, 35, 36 and 38, 31 July, 7 and 21 Aug. 1712; *Post Boy*, 2762, 22 Jan. 1712/13 (address from county of Wexford; for similar addresses see *ibid.*, 2687, 2689, 2696, and 2705, 31 July, 5 and 21 Aug., and 11 Sept. 1712); *C.W.* 64, *passim*; *C.W.* 6, pt. 4, pp. 3–4; *C.W.* 68; *C.W.* 87, preface.

of August 3rd to the violent but not fatal epidemic fever that was sweeping London, and reminded his hearers (in L'Hermitage's words)

que le roy Charles II lorsqu'il étoit en Hollande, étoit si contant de la bonne réception qu'on luy avoit fait, qu'il avoit assuré les États Généraux de sa sincère amitié mais que dès qu'il fut rétablie il l'eut bientôt oublié et qu'après son manquement de foy, les maladies contagieuses suivirent, et qui furent précedées par une pareille à celle cy, et qu'aujourd' huy on avoit le même malheur à craindre.

The Whigs were out to show that the record of Anglo-Dutch relations was not as favourable to England as the Tories pretended, and this attempt was carried a step further when there was printed, under the title of *The British Constitution Consider'd*, a letter written by Denzil Lord Holles to van Beuningen in 1676. The argument that this letter contained was full of meaning when related to the situation in 1712. Although the Court was entirely in the French interest, it declared, 'the parliament and People of *England* have a mighty Affection to your State'; the States should therefore make a public appeal to the English against the policy of their rulers.

Others Whig writers devoted themselves to the problems of the present rather than of the past. In contrast to the Tories, their theme was one of *English* ingratitude, their picture one of

> Alliances broke,
> Our best Friends ill treated,
> False to the Treaties we've made with the *Dutch* ....

In *A Justification of the Dutch From several late Scandalous Reflections* and *A Letter from a Tory Freeholder* these sentiments were expounded at length. Both brought forward every possible argument to show that it was we who had broken faith with the Dutch and not they with us, that only they could judge what barrier would be adequate for them, that we had no authority to impose conditions upon them, and that they were very far from thinking a wilful prolongation of the war to be in their interest. The former pamphlet, too, styled the propaganda campaign against the Allies a 'Jacobite trick' to make easier 'the Reverse of the Established State of these Kingdoms'; the latter, in the guise of a Tory, replied to talk of Dutch schemes for ruining our trade by remarking that

'twas an odd way of Reasoning in our Party to insist upon the Danger of our being over-power'd or out-rival'd by the *Dutch* in Trade. while the *French* run away not only with all the Trade of *Spain* and the *West-Indies*, but the whole *Spanish* Monarchy ....

The menace from the Dutch to our trade, to our livelihood even, had indeed a prominent place in the armoury of the ministry's protagonists. The *Examiner*, for example, after declaring that between sovereign powers there could be no ties of friendship, but only of interest, accused the Whigs and the late ministry of ignoring this principle by aggrandizing the Dutch on the pretext of 'natural friendship' and confederacy. 'Ask any Merchant in *London*', it went on,

or Clothier in the Country, whether *France* or *Holland* be the more formidable rival to *Britain* in point of Trade? If it be the latter, is it for our Advantage to be perpetually increasing their Riches, Strength and Greatness? A Substantial Barrier against *France* they will certainly have by our Procurement; and it is for our advantage that they should: But it is not for our Advantage that they should have all the Netherlands ....

This suggestion – that the Dutch were more dangerous rivals to our trade than the French – was combated by the Whig *Flying Post*, which suggested not only that the French had ousted us from the Spanish trade, but also that trade with France would involve us in an annual loss of some £ 700,000, while that with Holland gained us £ 1,400,000 every year. It was, however, given weighty support in Davenant's reports to the Commissioners of Public Accounts, published in 1712. The first report was largely concerned with the conditions of trade with France, which it found to be on the whole advantageous. The second dealt with our trade to the Dutch Republic, and was largely devoted to giving the lie to the 'vulgar notion' that the large 'overbalance' in our favour in this meant that it was highly profitable to us. Davenant explained that much of this overbalance could be accounted for by goods which the Dutch bought not for consumption, but for re-export, and if anyone doubted that it was they and not we who reaped the benefit from their eventual sale, he added, they should note that, far from receiving bullion from the Republic, we had exported thither in the past fifteen years more than to all other countries in Europe. We had also to consider that they reaped much of the benefit from our East India trade, owing to our prohibition of the sale of East India silks and other materials; that our exports thither had undergone an abnormal increase owing to the needs of the war; and that the great amounts that they had in our funds meant that we were constantly paying them large sums in interest and annuities. Moreover, the war had 'brought a vast Increase of Wealth to the Body of their People', and had increased their foreign trade; the bank of Amsterdam now contained more gold and silver specie than were current over all the rest of Europe. All this, due largely to our carrying on the war by the wrong methods – 'by Land-Armies we enrich other Countries' – meant that the Dutch would now be a most dangerous trade rival. While not seeking to end our friendship with them, it was our duty to protect our national interest, to which end we must maintain a strong navy, emulate many of the virtues of the Dutch themselves, but, above all,

First of all upon the Settlements of a Peace, in all future Treaties of Commerce we shall make with other Countries, we are to fence particularly against the Arts and Incroachments of the Dutch, who, beyond all Disputes, are our most dangerous Rivals in Trade; we must bear a watchful Eye near all their Proceedings, and never yield to 'em in any point wherein National Interest and Profit is concern'd .... so that if they will not be contented to Live and let Live, and bear themselves towards us hereafter in a Friendly Manner, and cease to undermine us in every part of the Commercial World .... we must in good Earnest undertake the Herring-Fishery, which will give full Imployment as well to the Rich as to the Poor.[1]

4

The hopes of the speedy submission of the Dutch to the queen's will which had been entertained in England after Denain were doomed to disappointment. Though the successes of Villars' army were almost uninterrupted throughout the summer, the Dutch did not withdraw from the struggle. The best that the ministry could obtain to satisfy its countrymen's desires for peace was a Treaty prolonging the suspension of arms with France for a further four months, which was concluded in Paris by Bolingbroke on August 19th (N.S.).

The unexpected recalcitrance of the Dutch gave a new impetus to the campaign against the Allies. In issue after issue the *Examiner* exclaimed against the Dutch. If there *were* such a phenomenon as 'natural friendship' between nations, it declared, it was easy to see from the recent conduct of the Dutch whether we ought to prefer theirs to that of France. It was they who had deserted us by refusing the suspension of arms, and thus brought upon themselves Denain, where 'the Lives of so many thousand Men have been so wantonly thrown away'. A 'generous enemy' would not have used us as ill as the Dutch had done, yet their gazettes were now full of lies about us, and our Whigs were loud in their praises. To accuse us, as they did, of making a separate peace was absurd; a separate peace occurred only when

one of the Allies, without consulting or acquainting the rest, and *before the End*

---

[1] L'Hermitage to States-General (transcript), 8/19 Aug. 1712, London, Add. Ms. 17677 FFF; *Examiner*, ii, 37, 14 Aug. 1712; *Flying-Post*, 3528, 16 Aug. 1712; *C.W.* 196, pt. II, p. 4; *C.W.* 67, *passim*; *C.W.* 104, p. 15; *New Song in Two Parts* (in *C.W.* 142, pp. 76–81); *C.W.* 112, *passim*; *C.W.* 121, pp. 12–15, 18–19; *C.W.* 31, ii, *passim*.

for which the Warr commenced is obtained, treats *Clandestinely*, and *concludes a Peace* with the Common Enemy.

Not one of these conditions, it continued, obtained in the current situation.

A similar spirit pervaded a pamphlet entitled *The Speech of a Noble Peer*, published on August 23rd. According to this we had been rescued from an attempt by English 'Dutchmen' to enslave us, by means of perpetual war, 'under an Olygarchy of Tyrants, if not a *Dutch* Democracy'. Denain it described as 'the seasonable Chastisement the *Dutch* lately met with for their unfriendly Obstinacy', and the Dutch as

our only Rivals in Trade, Enemies to our Church and Government, and never our fast Friends but for their own Security; a People who have slighted a Queen who hath been their Nursing-Mother, encourag'd a faction to be Proud and Contumelious, and have too evidently aim'd at the ruin of a Country, whose Prince and whose Subjects have, in all times of danger, been their only Deliverers.

Another pamphlet, *An Exhortation to the Love of our Country*, inveighed similarly against the Whigs for espousing the interests of 'our beloved *Amboyna* Conf——tes', 'the only Enemies we have to struggle with, to obtain for our selves a *reasonable* share in the Advantages of a Peace', and

our most formidable Rivals, who, however at present in L—gue with us, have been ever (when their least Interest prompted 'em), most notoriously Treacherous and Ungrateful to us.

'Should not', it continued,

the Blood of a Britain boil at the ungrateful Insolence of that People so often, so constantly, upon all Occasions, (when not deter'd by their Interest) repeated to us? Would one think there could be after this such a Miscreant as a *Britain* to favour them?

The 'miscreant' Whigs were not to be suppressed, however, not even by the new Stamp Tax, which sounded the knell of several periodicals on both sides. The *Flying Post* now became the chief Whig organ, devoting less and less space to 'news' and more and more to comment. It asserted repeatedly that all the Tory attacks on the Dutch were in reality attempts to undermine the Protestant Succession:

What else can be the reason for such bitter Exclamations by our Jacks against the Dutch, who so kindly, a few Years ago, deliver'd us from the Consternation and Fears we were in of Popish Bondage and Slavery? Why, truly, they are Guarantees for our Succession, and therefore they are a set of Naughty People that should presume to bring us another Protestant King; Therefore, the Barrier, that by Treaty was given to them, must, if our Jacks can prevail, be given to the French, to enable them to support the Imposter.

This too was a principal theme of *A Certain Information of a Certain Discourse*, a satire on the ministry's peace policy which was so spirited that it eventually led to the prosecution of its author, Thomas Burnet. Burnet devoted much attention to mocking and refuting the various arguments for a war with the Dutch, and

the Steps, by which the *Tories* have been brought to hear of a War with *Holland*, not only with Patience, but Applause, when the thought of it, wou'd have shock'd the Hottest of them two Years ago.

'I shall always count Talking a Step towards Acting', he declared,

and I am sure the Party now uppermost talk very confidently of such a War; and a Book was lately Printed to prove it reasonable, which Book was written, as I am inform'd, by the Direction of very Great Men.

In the Whig stronghold of Lynn, 'the capital of the territory of King Walpole', Defoe found that it was widely believed to be the ministry's intention to make the Dutch give up their barrier, and to declare war on them as soon as peace with France was proclaimed. But the Whigs were still not entirely without hope that the Dutch might continue the war, and we find from a letter of the pamphleteer Maynwaring to the Duchess of Marlborough that this vain hope was increased by the news of the solitary allied success after Denain, the capture of Fort Knoque. It was now said that the Dutch were 'resolved to make another campaign, and perish by the enemy rather than submit to this destructive peace'.[1]

What is of most interest at this time is the reaction not of High Tories or Whigs, but of the more moderate Tories, to the 'unfriendly obstinacy' of the Dutch. Defoe's *Review* gives some useful hints of this. On August 16th it contained a satirical survey of the state of opinion in England about peace and war. The friends of the Dutch, it pointed out, rejoiced at their carrying on the war, though this would end by making us quarrel with them. The friends of the Pretender, on the other hand, were for French victories over the Dutch, though these would embroil us with the French. Although he continued from time to time to warn the Whigs that by advising the Dutch to continue the struggle they were seeking to ruin them, in the very next issue of the *Review* Defoe showed that he realised that the important question was no longer the

---

[1] *Flying-Post*, 3260, 3276 and 3280, 21 Aug., 27 Sept. and 7 Oct. 1712; *Examiner*, ii, 39–40, 42–4, 28 Aug., 4, 18 and 25 Sept. and 2 Oct. 1712; (Defoe) to (Oxford), 20 Sept. 1712, Lincoln, *H.M.C. Portland V*, pp. 223–5; Maynwaring to Sarah, 24 Sept. 1712 (O.S.), *P.C.D.M.*, ii, pp. 81–3; (Defoe) to (Oxford), 3 Oct. 1712, Newcastle, *H.M.C. Portland V*, pp. 229–30; *C.W.* 169, pp. 5, 14–15, 18–23; *C.W.* 74, pp. 5–8, 21–6; *C.W.* 19, pp. 4–36; *Political State*, v, pp. 38–9.

justice and necessity of a war with the Dutch, but what should be done if the French grew 'superiour to the Confederates', and the latter asked for help. He told those who said 'Damn the Dutch' that every blow given to the Dutch was a wound for Britain, and that

every Town taken from them, beyond the just Barrier necessary for their Safety you must take back again for them; and if the *French* refuses to hearken to Reason, or stand to what is determined for him to stand to, you must act against *France* again with all your might.

That Defoe was not speaking merely for himself in voicing his concern at the continuing success of the French in the field can be seen from letters written by two 'moderate' men, Richard Hill and Peter Wentworth. Commenting on August 27th on the new Treaty for the suspension of arms, Hill explained that the incomplete state of the suspension was the reason that there had been no 'noisy expressions of joy' in England, and of the peace he wrote:

How we are to come at that peace is still a secret; but ye sence of ye nation begins to be jealous of ye rapid superiority wch ye French are getting over ye allies; tho it is not yet fashionable to think so. Peace is now everybody's desire, as well to save ye Dutch, as to save ourselves .... but as ye conditions of ye peace are kept more private than could well have been hoped, there is room still for lyes & railings.

Peter Wentworth's letter of October 7th to his brother Strafford shows the same uneasiness about the turn affairs had been taking since Denain. After describing the various arguments about the peace that were currently to be found in 'papers of both sides', he went on to say that, for himself, he thought that those who could bring the Dutch into the queen's measures without a war deserved 'all imaginable praise'; "tis peace England wants', he continued,

and not to change wars. But the difficulty that lies upon her Majesty's ministers, 'tis fear'd will come from another quarter, that the French won't be persuaded to grant all that for our allies we have stipulated, and we are now so broak among ourselves that it will not be in our power to force them to keep their words, and then where will be our good peace.

It would seem that some at least of the ministry's supporters had remained impervious, or had ceased to respond, to the 'Dutch war' propaganda and generally to the more extreme aspects of the pamphlet campaign against the Allies. Perhaps fortunately for the ministry, it was not forced to put the feelings of its followers on these matters to the test, for four days after Peter Wentworth had written this letter his brother arrived in England with the virtual capitulation of the Dutch.[1]

---

[1] Review, (ix), 5–6, 11 and 20, 16 and 19 Aug., 6 Sept. and 7 Oct. 1712; Hill to Hanmer,

5

It was not entirely the obstinacy of the Dutch that had held up the renewal of negotiations after Denain. Various difficulties in the continuing Anglo-French negotiations made it highly desirable from the British point of view that the Dutch should have no chance to make their peace with France until these were resolved. As Mrs. Montgomery puts it, 'the sole difficulty was to prevent the return of the Dutch to negotiations until Anglo-French affairs were adequately settled'. On August 9th Strafford had high hopes that the Dutch 'in a very little time' would 'throw themselves entirely into the Queens measures'. The peace party was in the ascendant, he reported, and needed only Tournai and Condé to save its face. All parties were so alarmed at the violence of the Imperialists that they were actually glad that the British held Ghent and Bruges, and Amsterdam was resolved to declare for peace. Ormonde and Watkins, with the British army, were confident that their ill success in the field would speedily bring the Dutch into the queen's measures, and on August 12th Strafford wrote to the Electress of Hanover assuring her that they were now ready for this.[1]

The over-sanguine Strafford was somewhat disappointed when he travelled from Utrecht to The Hague, for there he discovered that the Dutch had not yet abandoned the 1709 Barrier Treaty and that Sinzendorf was 'turning' them as he pleased. Back again at Utrecht, however, he found the Dutch plenipotentiaries as submissive as he could wish. As he wrote to the Electress on August 27th, the Dutch and the Imperialists now seemed to be vying with each other to see which would come first into the queen's measures. The Dutch, he wrote to Thomas Harley (now at Hanover), 'were become the most humble fawning fearfull creatures imaginable' and only asked to know what they should have before concluding. All this, however, was a great deal too fast for the British ministry; as Strafford's chaplain Ayerst commented, the Dutch and Imperialists perhaps made 'more haste than is desired till our affairs are settled'. The French victory at Denain had made Louis XIV raise his terms, and on August 2nd

---

27 Aug. 1712, Richmond, *Hanmer Corres.*, pp. 134–7; P. Wentworth to Strafford, 7 Oct. 1712, Windsor, *Wentworth Papers*, pp. 301–2; *Political State*, iv, p. 253.

[1] Strafford to Bolingbroke, 9 Aug. 1712, Utrecht, S.P. Holl. 243; Strafford to Oxford, 9 Aug. 1712, Utrecht, *H.M.C. Portland IX*, pp. 335–8; Ormonde to Strafford, 10 Aug. 1712, Drongen, *H.M.C. XV pt. ii*, pp. 213–14; Strafford to Electress of Hanover, 12 Aug. 1712, Utrecht, Stowe Ms. 241; Watkins to Strafford, 21 Aug. 1712, Ghent, Add. Ms. 22201.

(O.S.) Bolingbroke and Prior had left London for Paris in an attempt, as Swift put it, 'to hasten the Peace before the Dutch are too much mauld: and to hinder France from carrying the Jest of beating them, too far'.[1]

While these and subsequent Anglo-French discussions were going on it was the task of Bristol and Strafford to see to it that the Dutch did not steal a march on Britain. A fight between some servants of the Dutch plenipotentiary Rechteren and those of Mesnager proved a godsend to them in this connection. Their manipulation and magnification of this incident led to the breaking off of all conferences between French and Dutch. Their line, apparently concerted with Torcy, was to blame 'cet yvrogne Rechteren', as Bolingbroke styled him, for the entire incident, and this was seized on by Englishmen hostile to the Dutch as yet another subject for reproach. Lord Berkeley of Stratton wrote of the 'heat of Count Rechteren', and Watkins, whose political views had undergone a marked change since the days when he was one of Marlborough's 'family', of his 'insolent and brutish behaviour'. This, too, was the version made current in England by Defoe in his *Enquiry into the Real Interest of Princes in the Persons of their Ambassadors*, in which it was hinted, though not affirmed, that the whole incident was part of an allied plan to 'destroy the Treaty, rather than conclude a Peace'. Even Boyer, in the volume of the *Political State* published some months later, though sympathetic to Rechteren, thought that the Dutch had tried to prolong the dispute so as to put off the making of a bad peace.[2]

The use made by Britain and France of the Rechteren-Mesnager dispute made the obtaining of peace by the Dutch completely dependent on the mediation of Britain, and thus achieved a long-standing aim of the Oxford ministry. Even now, however, the ministry, with its own negotiations with France not yet completed, was in no hurry to complicate matters by treating with the Dutch. Instead it watched with complacency as the Dutch tried first one way, and then another, to overcome French intransigency in the Rechteren-Mesnager affair. In his letters Strafford could barely conceal his amusement at the

---

[1] Strafford to Bristol, 15 Aug. 1712, Hague, Ms. Rawl. A. 286; Strafford to Bolingbroke, 17 Aug. 1712, Hague, S.P. Holl. 244; *Journal to Stella*, ii, p. 554, 7 Aug. 1712, London; Ayerst to Watkins, 22 Aug. 1712, Utrecht, Add. Ms. 38852; Strafford to Electress of Hanover, 27 Aug. 1712, Utrecht, Stowe Ms. 224; Strafford to T. Harley, 27 Aug. 1712, Utrecht, Add. Ms. 40621.

[2] Berkeley of Stratton to Strafford, 5 Aug. 1712 (O.S.), *Wentworth Papers*, p. 295; Watkins to Harrison, 24 Aug. 1712, Ghent, Add. Ms. 22201; Bolingbroke to Torcy, 27 Aug. 1712 (N.S.?), *Thibaudeau*, 2nd ser., i, p. 313; *C.W.* 43, p. 22; *Political State*, iv, p. 189.

way in which 'Frog' blew now hot, now cold, though Bristol feared that the 'warrior party' might carry the matter further than had been intended by using it to break up the Congress completely. On the whole, however, Strafford found 'these people mightily sunk with their misfortunes' and more inclined to submit to the queen than ever. All they asked for was to know what barrier they would have, and he urged Oxford strongly on September 13th (N.S.) that Tournai should be included in it, as essential to Dutch security. The most important cause of their amenableness, he added, was the advantage that Britain now had over them in being able to trade with France under the Treaty for the suspension of arms; an advantage which Prior had already characterised as 'the most effectual means to oblige our Maritime Neighbours to enter the Queen's measures', and which Drummond thought at the beginning of October would do more than anything else to 'make us long for peace'.[1]

Bolingbroke himself would have been glad to see France keep Tournai, but, as he wrote to Prior on September 29th, he realised that he could not count on the support of English opinion in this matter; 'if it comes once to be known', he wrote,

and it is not possible the secret should be kept, that Holland would have concluded their peace at the same time as the Queen, provided they might have had Tournay, we shall not dare to leave them behind us; and I must tell you, on this occasion, that some of our best friends among the Tories would, in such a case, join to condemn us.

He confided similar fears to Gaultier, admitting that if the Dutch were now to submit to the queen, she would be obliged to help and support them to the utmost in order 'to close the mouths of the Whigs'. Bolingbroke was not unaware that there was a section of moderate Tory opinion which was becoming somewhat uneasy about the cleavage among the Allies. Perhaps it was this realization which, on September 17th, prompted him to include in a letter to Strafford, along with a whole series of complaints and reproaches against the Dutch, a hint that 'the Queen's compassion and the National pity' could now be moved by 'a wise and plain answer' to her proposals from the States. This more coöperative attitude may well have been strengthened by reports that the ministry received soon afterwards from Paris and

[1] Prior to Dartmouth, 9 Sept. 1712, Fontainebleau, S.P. France 154; Strafford to Watkins, 9 Sept. 1712, Utrecht, Add. Ms. 34077; Strafford to Bristol, 11 Sept. 1712, Hague, Ms. Rawl. A. 286; Strafford to Bolingbroke, 13 Sept. 1712 (N.S.), S.P. Holl. 244; Strafford to Oxford, 13 and 16 Sept. 1712, Hague, H.M.C. Portland IX, pp. 340–6; Strafford to Bolingbroke, 16 Sept. 1712, Hague, S.P. Holl. 243; Bristol to T. Harley, 21 Sept. 1712, Utrecht, Add. Ms. 40621; (Drummond) to (Oxford), 4 Oct. 1712, Amsterdam, H.M.C. Portland V, p. 227.

The Hague. From Paris Prior wrote that the Dutch, unable to negotiate directly with the French, had approached the Elector of Bavaria with the proposition that he should have the Spanish Netherlands provided that they kept 'full and eternal possession' of the towns that they now possessed. It was obviously necessary for the ministry, which was refusing to give up Ghent and Bruges until British trade with the Spanish Netherlands had been safeguarded, to nip such an arrangement in the bud. Moreover, from The Hague came the news of the rising temper of the populace, and of insults offered to Strafford and to the representatives of France and Savoy. At first Drummond believed that these were the work of French refugees, but by the beginning of October (N.S.) he was convinced that the people had become thoroughly incensed against Britain and a British peace, and in this Strafford agreed with him. It is not impossible that the ministry thought it desirable to close with the Dutch leaders before the mood of the Dutch people forced them to become less amenable.[1]

The Dutch acted swiftly when they realised that Britain might now help them to gain Tournai. On October 5th they made proposals to Bristol and Strafford which in effect constituted an offer to agree to the queen's terms on condition that they were given Tournai and Condé and that the Spanish Netherlands went to the Emperor and not Maximilian Emmanuel. When Bolingbroke received this news, and saw the letter that Heinsius had written at the same time to Oxford, he realised that the prospect of a separate peace had finally disappeared. He straightway warned the French, through Prior, that public opinion in Britain would not sanction the abandonment of the Dutch if they were now, as seemed likely, to come into the queen's measures. 'The aim of these people seems to be', he wrote,

either to restore their union with the Queen, and by her means to make their peace with France and Spain, or else, by publishing how far in consideration of her, they have receded from their first demands, and by submitting in terms of the greatest humility, to move the compassion of mankind towards them, and some degree of indignation towards us, as if we were too partial in favour of France.

He therefore instructed Prior to let Torcy know that 'if the Dutch

---

[1] Drummond to Oxford, (rec'd 17 Sept. 1712), Amsterdam, *H.M.C. Portland V*, pp. 221-2; Bolingbroke to Strafford (draft), 17 Sept. 1712, Whitehall, S.P. Holl. 245; Same to same, 17 Sept. 1712, Whitehall, *B.L.*, iii, pp. 75-6; *ibid.*, iii, pp. 94-9, Prior to Bolingbroke, 28 Sept. 1712, Versailles; (Drummond) to (Oxford), 1 Oct. 1712, Hague, *H.M.C. Portland V*, pp. 225-6; Gaultier to Torcy, 22 Sept. 1712 (O.S.), *Weber*, p. 339; Strafford to Bolingbroke, 4 Oct. 1712, Utrecht, S.P. Holl. 243; Bolingbroke to Prior, 29 Sept. 1712, Windsor, *B.L.*, iii, pp. 111-25; *Lecky*, i, p. 123; *C.W.* 113, vii, p. 249.

do submit, we must not continue in this strangeness towards them', and to Torcy himself he wrote demanding Tournai for the Republic.

Although Strafford had expressed his confidence on October 4th that the Dutch would sign a peace to the queen's liking as soon as they were assured of Tournai, he seems at first to have doubted the sincerity of their approach of October 5th. He wrote to Watkins on October 6th in terms which well illustrate the amused contempt with which he viewed the Dutch leaders:

Nick Frog continues his old courses, one minute he dispairs, leaves you master intirely of his fate, owns without you he is undone, & must accept of wt you'l please to procure him, & the next minute flyes off, grows whimsical, bold, & saucy, & talks of doing the Devil & all, with Squire South . . . .

On October 9th, however, he and Bristol were formally presented with the Dutch proposals, and shortly afterwards he was summoned to England to receive fresh instructions. The ministers had realised that, whatever their own inclinations, opinion in England would not favour a cold reception of the Dutch offer; 'The queen must save them', commented Oxford, 'in spite of their own opiniâtreté'.[1]

In London it was public knowledge in the first week of October that the Dutch had made overtures to the British plenipotentiaries, and it was even said that the rumoured disagreements within the ministry were over the question of whether they should be accepted or not. The story that the ministers were divided and Bolingbroke in disgrace was mocked at in a pamphlet entitled *Beware of the Pretender* which accused those 'Dutchify'd Mongrels', the Whigs, of being so desperate that they would 'snap at the least Crust of Hopes the *Dutch* condescend to cast among them . . . .', and this theme of 'The Whigs turn'd Dutchmen' was further pursued by Edward Ward in a poem, published on October 14th, which consisted of a venomous attack on Whigs and Dutch alike.

On October 10th, according to L'Hermitage, no one felt sure what attitude the ministry would take to the new Dutch move. The secret of its intentions was well kept – even Swift seems not to have been informed at first – and while it awaited Strafford's arrival the *Examiner* reflected with unabated vehemence on the many ways in which the late ministry had given up the honour of Britain in order to further the

---

[1] Strafford to Prior (translation), 4 Oct. 1712 (N.S.), *C.W.* 113, vii, p. 249; Strafford to Watkins, 6 Oct. 1712, Utrecht, Add. Ms. 34077; Bolingbroke to Prior, 29 Sept. 1712, Windsor, *B.L.*, iii, pp. 111–25; *ibid.*, iii, pp. 130–4, Bolingbroke to Strafford, 30 Sept. 1712 (O.S.); Oxford to Bristol, 30 Sept. 1712 (O.S.), Ms. Rawl. A. 286; *Political State*, iv, pp. 252–3; *Montgomery*, pp. 287–8.

interests of the Dutch. When Strafford arrived in London, on October 13th, it was widely assumed that he had come to receive new instructions concerning the Dutch overtures, and eight days later the attitude of the ministry seems no longer to have been a secret, since we find Swift writing to Archbishop King to tell him of the Dutch submission, and of the queen's decision to obtain Tournai for them. A few days later it was once more strongly rumoured in London that peace would soon be concluded, and it was even said that the Dutch had privately concerted their new overtures with the ministry before making them formally. Swift adjudged them to be 'fully humbled'.[1]

The pleasure aroused by these developments was not universal. Defoe criticised the Whigs for being 'angry' that the Dutch were 'suppos'd to be coming into the Peace', and, indeed, Archbishop King wrote to Swift that nothing had given him greater mortification for years than the news of the terms to which the Dutch had submitted. The Whig propagandists now emphasised that the renunciation which Philip V was to make was quite insufficient to ensure the separation of the thrones of France and Spain, and on November 5th there appeared an English version of *Les Soupirs de L'Europe*, originally published in Holland, which made this point and many more against the plan which the queen had outlined in her speech of June 6th. The *Examiner* admitted that it was true that there might not be as many guarantees as could be wished for the renunciation, but it declared that all such mischiefs should

be upon the Heads of those who envy *Her Majesty* the Glory of finishing this great work, and are as backward in their *Quota's* of Councel and Wisdom, as they were in those of Men and Money.

For the rest, the *Post Boy* speedily countered the translation of *Les Soupirs de l'Europe* by itself publishing, in 'serial' form, a translation of the French reply to that work. This reply was also published soon afterwards in pamphlet form, under the title of *The Queen, The Present Ministry, Lewis XIV and Philip V Unanswerably Vindicated*, with the addition of a preface which consisted of a vitriolic attack on the Whig attitude to the peace. The Whigs, this asserted, were

Men who *delight in War*, and, therefore, are for him who will carry that on *Longest*; as appears from their present Usage of the *Dutch*, whom they begin to load with opprobrious Names, for leaving his Imperial Majesty in the Lurch.

---

[1] *Examiner*, ii, 45, 9 Oct. 1712; *Journal to Stella*, ii, pp. 563, 566, 9 and 28 Oct. 1712, London; L'Hermitage to States-General (transcripts), 10/21 and 14/25 Oct. and 24 Oct./4 Nov. 1712, London, Add. Ms. 17677 FFF; Swift to Archbishop King, 21 Oct. 1712, London, *Swift Corres.*, i, pp. 346–7; *C.W.* 14, pp. 2, 4–5; *C.W.* 196, pt. III, pp. 3–23.

For all this, however, the Tory writers did not themselves cease to load the Dutch with 'opprobrious names'. On November 6th the *Examiner* recalled to its readers the dangers to British trade from the 1709 Barrier Treaty. This reminder may well have been intended to prepare readers for the revelation of the British reply to the Dutch, and the publication of Poyntz's *Barrier Treaty Vindicated* at this time may also have been in anticipation of this, though its intentions were very different from those of the *Examiner*. The imminent departure of Marlborough into voluntary exile also encouraged the *Examiner* to reflect on the Dutch, in expressing the hope that he would take the opportunity to convince Heinsius 'that his once hopeful Cullies are irrevocably Relapsed into their Senses'. The same theme inspired another Tory writer to put these words into Marlborough's mouth:

> Sometimes a Journey too I'll take,
> To visit my *Dutch* Friends at th'Hague,
> They must caress me, or they're Clowns,
> I made 'em Pennyworths of Towns;
> 'Gainst which I knock'd out Britain's Brains,
> And spent its Coin in long Campaigns .... [1]

Agreement between Britain and the States was not in fact quite as near as many Englishmen – including the commander-in-chief, Ormonde – imagined. Four days after Strafford's arrival in London Bolingbroke wrote to Bristol that the queen was not 'entirely satisfyed as to the manner of that Republick's coming into her measures'. While in the Republic all 'reasonable' men, according to Drummond, were eager to settle the Rechteren affair and unwilling to prolong the war, the Cabinet took its time in preparing an answer which would give details of its dissatisfaction with the Dutch submission. There was some dissension even about giving Tournai to the States, and Strafford wrote to Bristol on November 4th:

Frog I hope will get the cheife town we have stuck upon for him, but nothing more, & yet very great opposition was even made against that.

By November 7th the Cabinet had concluded what was in fact their ultimatum to the Republic, in reply to the Dutch proposals of October

---

[1] *Review*, (ix), 27, 1 Nov. 1712; Archbishop King to Swift, 4 Nov. 1712, Dublin, *Swift Corres.*, i, pp. 348–9; *Examiner*, iii, 2, 3 and 5, 6, 13 and 27 Nov. 1712; *Post Boy*, 2731–3, 2735–6, 11, 13, 15, 20 and 22 Nov. 1712; L'Hermitage to States-General (transcript), 11/22 Nov. 1712, London, Add. Ms. 17677 FFF; *C.W.* 151, p. (8); *C.W.* 186, p. 5.

5th (N.S.). As stated in the instructions to Bristol and Strafford, dated November 11th, its most important condition was that the States should 'agree entirely to lay aside the whole barrier-treaty', and instead agree to the project of a new Treaty drawn up by the British ministry.

As Mrs. Montgomery has pointed out, the object of this new project, very unlike that of the Townshend Treaty, was to reduce the power of the Dutch in the Spanish Netherlands. No longer were the States to have the Upper Quarter of Guelders, nor the 'communication' fortresses, including Dendermonde. Many frontier fortresses promised under the 1709 Treaty or since conquered were no longer to form part of the barrier, and British trade with the Spanish Netherlands was safeguarded and further restrictions placed upon Dutch use of their revenues. Article XV was entirely omitted, because (in Bolingbroke's words)

it has been the most resented of any Art in that Treaty, and is the greatest instance of imposition that perhaps one nation ever presumed to put on another.[1]

In a letter to Torcy Bolingbroke made it plain that these were the queen's final offers. The ministry, he wrote, were confident that the Dutch would acquiesce, but

si contre notre attente, les États-Généraux prenoient le parti de vouloir, après la cession de Tournay, former les demandes ultérieures, et embarrasser la négociation de nouveau, la Reine se contentera d'avoir fait pour eux tout ce qu'elle a pu, et dans ce cas, Monsieur, les Plénipotentiaires de sa Majesté signeront avec ceux des alliés qui voudront y entrer, le traité particulier avec la France et l'Espagne.

The ministry was in no hurry to present its ultimatum to the States. Confident of Dutch concurrence whenever it did so, it wanted more time to negotiate undisturbed with France on the difficult problem of the fishing rights off the coast of Newfoundland. It was therefore not till November 20th that Strafford set out again for the Republic. One day later Bristol reported to Bolingbroke that some of the Dutch leaders were 'in the utmost pain' that Strafford had not yet returned with the ministry's answer, and said that 'those that are for peace' were 'very much exposed'. Bolingbroke's reply to this well illustrates the mood in which the ministry had sent Strafford on his fateful journey:

[1] Ormonde to (Bolingbroke), 15 Oct. 1712, Ghent, S.P. Mil. 7; Bolingbroke to Bristol (draft), 17 Oct. 1712, Whitehall, S.P. Holl. 245; Strafford to Bristol, 4 and 7 Nov. 1712, St. James', Ms. Rawl. A. 286; *ibid.*, Drummond to Bristol, 16 Nov. 1712, Amsterdam; Bolingbroke to Strafford, 11 Nov. 1712, Whitehall, *B.L.*, iii, pp. 171–3; Instructions for Bristol and Strafford (draft), 11 Nov. 1712 (O.S.), S.P. Holl. 245; Project of Treaty of Succession and Barrier (draft, in Latin, with marginal notes, by Bolingbroke, in English), S.P. Holl. 245; *Montgomery*, p. 298.

The Gentlemen who make this Complaint would do very well to remember, how long their concurrence with the Queen has been retarded, what dangerous uncertaintys our affairs have been left in by their delay, and to what hazards we have been exposed by their obstinacy for so many months past.[1]

6

On December 8th (N.S.) Strafford submitted his government's proposals to the States-General, making it clear that the offer would not hold good unless all conditions were quickly accepted. The States acted speedily to refer the matter to the Provinces, and at The Hague on December 9th Drummond found 'a good deal of resignation to the Queen's pleasure', and universal unwillingness to 'hazard the carrying on the war'. Two days later Strafford wrote to the Electress of Hanover that 'they seem very well sattisfyed with this new Barrier here', and that

they now seem sensible that I have been their friend, & they see that without me they would not have obtaind Tournay. They find their Credit sunck & that they cant depend upon the promises of the court of Vienna, & think themselves happy that the Queen still offers them her friendship, & to unite with them.

Reports of the British ultimatum and the first Dutch reactions to it arrived in London on December 1st (O.S.). Bolingbroke immediately wrote to the plenipotentiaries of the queen's 'satisfaction' that the Dutch were 'at last sincerely employed to finish a good work, which they have so long delayed'. L'Hermitage, not an entirely reliable witness in an affair about which he himself had strong feelings, reported that, even though nothing much had been hoped for from the proposals that Strafford had taken over, 'bien des gens ne s'attendoient pas qu'elles fussent si extraordinaires'. Everyone, he wrote on December 5th, was anxious to know what resolution the States would take, but some of the Tories has received the news of the proposals with a silence that betokened astonishment rather than acquiescence, and other were asserting that the reports were false. Such, however, were not the reactions of Peter Wentworth, who was glad to learn that his brother was 'like to succeed so well for ye Publick', and added:

I am but a Poor Politian yet I was always of opinion 'twou'd do well to have the Dutch with us, tho I have heard some say they were not worth the seeking after.[2]

[1] Bolingbroke to Torcy, Nov. 1712, Whitehall, B.L., iii, pp. 176-80; Bristol to Bolingbroke, 2 Dec. 1712, Utrecht, S.P. Holl. 244; Bolingbroke to Bristol and Strafford (draft), 28 Nov. 1712, Whitehall, S.P. Holl. 245.

[2] (Drummond) to (Oxford), 9 Dec. 1712, Hague, H.M.C. Portland V, pp. 248-50; Strafford to Electress of Hanover, 11 Dec. 1712, Hague, Stowe Ms. 224; Bolingbroke to Bristol and

Some, indeed, were even now saying that the Dutch were 'not worth the seeking after'. The *Flying-Post* reported that a health had recently been drunk at Trowbridge 'to the prosperity of the French King and his Friends, and to the Destruction of the Dutch'; and Defoe, once more using the *Review* in the cause of 'Moderation', described how Whigs and Tories were still at loggerheads about their respective attitudes to the Dutch. That unwearying scourge of the Dutch, the *Examiner*, devoted much of its space in December to attacking the *Barrier Treaty Vindicated*, thus acknowledging the seriousness of the challenge that that pamphlet had made to the ministry's new Project. It developed at length the argument that the guarantee of our Succession had been unnecessary, since it was in any case the interest of the Dutch to defend it, and went on to argue that it exposed our liberties and religion to great dangers from foreign interference. It asserted, too, that the queen's new barrier proposals were as far-reaching as the terms of the Pyrenean treaty, and that the Dutch demand for 'communication' towns was prompted by designs on our commerce. In connection with this last point it added:

We do say, that the *Dutch* are our Rivals, and the only formidable Rivals of *Britain* in Trade; We do say, that they have never miss'd any Opportunity, either by secret Fraud or open Violence, to destroy our Factories and ruin our Commerce: We appeal for the Truth of this to former Times, to what they have done, even during this War, when we were laying out our all for their Support and Aggrandizement; and to their Conduct not only in the *East Indies*, but even in the *Netherlands*, within sight of our People, as if it was not enough to do us Mischief, without insulting us at the same time.

After making many assertions concerning the danger and prejudice to our trade and liberty from several provisions of the Treaty, the *Examiner* went on to point out that, despite the great advantages accruing to them from it, the Dutch had already broken the Treaty. This they had done by the imposition of 'double duties' in the Spanish Netherlands, where our trade was already ruined as a result. So much, it continued, for the cant about a perpetual union of interest between us and the Dutch; as soon as we claimed anything for ourselves the Dutch dropped this pretence, which was indeed merely a means for deluding us into making ourselves

a province to a crazy, sickly State (so Sir *William Temple* describes it in its Constitution) which we generously rais'd from the Dirt and Mire, which we Nurs'd, Foster'd, and Brought up, and who once actually offered to put themselves under our Protection and Government.

Strafford (draft), 2 Dec. 1712, Whitehall, S.P. Holl. 245; L'Hermitage to States-General (transcripts), 5/16 and 8/19 Dec. 1712, London, Add. Ms. 17677 FFF; P. Wentworth to (Strafford), 8 Dec. 1712, Windsor, Add. Ms. 34144; *Montgomery, p.* 293.

While the Provinces debated the queen's proposals encouraging reports continued to reach the ministry from the Republic. In Rotterdam Orrery concluded from both the discourse and behaviour of the 'generality of these people' that they would agree. Under these circumstances he could not approve of Strafford's threat that the queen would make peace before Parliament met whether the Dutch joined her in this or not. On the other hand he found that 'the bus'ness of the Upper Quarter of Guelder goes down very uneasily with 'em'. Strafford, on a private visit to Amsterdam, discovered not only

the Magistrates resolved to come into the Queens measures, hoping thereby to obtain the four Species & the upper quarter of Guelderland; but the common people speaking with more reverence of ye Queen than formerly & much pleas'd with the hopes of a speedy peace.

Despite Dutch concern about the question of the four species, however, Bolingbroke was determined to make no move yet to settle Franco-Dutch commercial differences. He explained in a letter to the plenipotentiaries that once these were 'determined either in favour of the French or the Dutch there would then remain no dispute between them', whereas

her Majty has herself some points relating to Commerce & N. America which are of very great consequence to the Interest of her subjects and the honour of this Treaty still to settle.[1]

By December 13th Swift, busy obtaining information from Gaultier which he could use to demonstrate 'the Roguery of the Dutch', was confident that peace would be made 'very soon', since 'the Dutch are almost entirely agreed, & if they stop we shall make it without them; that has been long resolved'. Six days later he heard from Bolingbroke that four of the Provinces had complied with the queen's demands, and that the rest were expected to do so immediately. This news, which Berkeley of Stratton found to be 'very agreeable here', shattered the last hopes of the Whigs. In the *Flying-Post* appeared 'A letter from a Dr. of Physick in *Mijnheer-Borough*' which suggested in veiled and regretful terms that an inclination towards a 'bad' peace was gaining ground in the Republic, and, as December drew to a close, a Whig ballad-writer produced a gloomy prognostic for 1713:

---

[1] Orrery to (Bolingbroke), 16 Dec. 1712, Rotterdam, S.P. Flanders 61; *Flying-Post*, 3306, 6 Dec. 1712; Bristol and Strafford to Bolingbroke, 20 Dec. 1712, Utrecht, S.P. Holl. 244; Bolingbroke to Bristol and Strafford (draft), 9 Dec. 1712, Whitehall, S.P. Holl. 245; *Review*, (ix), 36, 9 Dec. 1712; *Examiner*, iii, 7–8, 11 and 18 Dec. 1712.

> Now, now comes on the Tories Year,
> *Frenchmen* have Hopes and Britons Fear;
> *Perkin* intends to govern here,
> And be our Faith's Defender.
> For *France* is become our good Ally,
> Th'Emperor too and the *Dutch* must fly,
> Unless they will bow to our M————y,
> And *Flanders* and *Spain* surrender.

On December 30th (N.S.) the States-General agreed to the queen's plan with certain reservations, which they embodied in a letter to the queen. Four days later the Dutch plenipotentiaries at Utrecht told Strafford that they had powers to agree to the new Barrier Treaty, though they had orders not to sign till the outcome of the States' letter to the queen was known. An English observer at Utrecht reported the reaction of the Dutch to these developments: 'an universal joy and gladness', he wrote,

has overspread their whole Country; & one may justly say, their zeal & inclinations for peace outgo their former obstinacy a bar & half's length. You'l pardon the familiar simile.

While Bristol and Strafford waited for the queen's reply to the States' letter they staved off the re-opening of conferences between French and Dutch by making further use of the Rechteren-Mesnager dispute, in connection with which the *Flying Post* had recently published a letter, purporting to be written by 'Count Mesnager's Footman', which heartily thanked the *Examiner* and the *Post Boy* for insulting the Dutch on his behalf. They were put out, however, to find that private meetings between French and Dutch representatives were going on in order to agree upon a solution to the quarrel, and embarrassed by the eagerness of the Dutch to put an end to it on any terms.[1]

7

The States-General's letter to the queen was delivered by van Borssele on December 30th (O.S.). It contained a request for modifications of

---

[1] *Flying-Post*, 3308 and 3313, 11 and 23 Dec. 1712; *Journal to Stella*, ii, pp. 581 and 585, 12 and 18 Dec. 1712, London; R. Smith to Ellis, 3 Jan. 1713, Utrecht, Add. Ms. 28916; Berkeley of Stratton to Strafford, 26 Dec. 1712 (O.S.), *Wentworth Papers*, pp. 310–11; Bristol and Strafford to Bolingbroke, 8 and 10 Jan. 1713, Utrecht, S.P. Holl. 246; *A New Ballad* (in *C.W.* 142, pp. 143–4).

the queen's proposals, which, in his letter of January 7th to Bristol
and Strafford, Bolingbroke completely rejected, not without expressing
some annoyance that the Dutch had seen fit to raise these difficulties.
The following remarks are typical of the tone which he used:

Upon the demand of putting a Dutch Garrison into Fort *St. Mary* in case the
point of Dendermonde is not yielded, yr Lps may take notice how insincere the
States are in their pretences, and how much more they aim at blocking up the
great Towns, and interrupting the Trade of the Netherlands, than barely at
keeping a Communication with their Barrier . . . Fort St. Mary which lyes below
Antwerp cannot be very usefull for that purpose, but seems rather intended to
be a bridle to that City, and to strengthen their command over the Commerce of
the Schelde.

His temper was not improved by the fact that the States' letter had
been printed in the *Flying-Post* at the same time that it had been
presented to the queen. He instructed the plenipotentiaries to remonstrate in 'the severest terms' about this 'affront and indignity',
adding that if such proceedings were to continue we should 'break
off all Correspondence with the Dutch', and that

we have good reason to believe that the States are running once more into that
dangerous Error, which has cost them already so dear, of depending upon Efforts
to be made on our side of the water to disturb the Queen's affairs, and that in
this View they will keep us in suspense as much as in them lyes, in expectation of
what may be done in Parliament to strengthen them by perplexing the Treaty.

To Shrewsbury, newly arrived in Paris to represent the queen there,
he wrote in a similar vein. If his reply to the States seemed harsh, he
explained, it should be attributed to

the knowledge we have that the Dutch change only in appearance, and that even
these submissive measures are taken in concert with our Whigs here.

The queen's formal reply, which was also sent on January 7th, was
in a somewhat different tone, rejoicing in the willingness of the States
to come into her measures, and likening her care of their interests to
that of Elizabeth. For all its 'harshness', the ministry recognised that
the Dutch objections were requests, not conditions.

Bolingbroke's conviction that the States would still do everything
in their power to trick the queen was fully shared by Swift, who sent
to Archbishop King on January 3rd a long description of the underhand intrigues of the Dutch with France throughout the war 'until
these few months'. Although his uncomfortably contrary correspondent
was far from convinced by all this, Swift found confirmation of his
belief in the States' letter, and thought that the ministry was showing
weakness in proroguing Parliament for three weeks more to give the

Dutch more time to agree. 'Those Puppyes the Dutch will not yet come in', he fumed,

tho' they pretend to submit to the Qu—— in every thing: but they would fain try first how our Session begins, in hopes to embroyl us in the House of Lds. & if my advice had been taken, the Session should have begun, & we would have trusted the Parlmt to approve the Steps already made towards the Peace, & had an Address perhaps from them to conclude without the Dutch, if they would not agree. Others are of my mind; but it is not reckoned so safe, it seems.

One can only wonder whether the popular reaction to the States' letter had been such as to disincline the ministry from taking the strong line advocated by Swift.[1]

In the political writings that appeared at this time we can see the chagrin of the Tories that the Dutch had succeeded in delaying the peace, if only for a few weeks, and the last vain hopes of the Whigs, born of desperation, that the States' letter indicated a resolve not to submit to the queen. The *Examiner*, of course, voiced the feelings of the Tories. 'The *Menacing Pensionary* has scruples', it jeered, 'he desires time to look out for something else to demand', and it told the Dutch that they must either fall in with the queen's measures or else declare plainly that they recognised no government in Britain save 'Whigarchy'. The *Flying-Post* retorted that all the ministry's proceedings were a breach of the Grand Alliance, and that what they were actually offering was that 'the Dutch are to have the Barrier which they ask, except those Places which are indeed the Barrier which they ask'. The *Britain*, a new periodical, also commented that the *Examiner* was providing

but a very Melancholy Prospect of what we are to expect from Peace, if he has any Influence . . . . . We shall hear of nothing but *Amboyna* and the Fishery.

The Tories were roused, however; the *Examiner* began once more to mention Shaftesbury and 'Delenda est Carthago', and on January 20th a pamphlet appeared which, amidst a farrago of accusations hurled at the Whigs, included details of their continual and, indeed, current plotting with the Dutch to aggrandize the States at our expense in return for Dutch help in raising insurrection at home.

The Whigs, on the other hand, made all possible capital from the States' letter. The *Flying-Post* was emboldened to assert, on January

---

[1] Swift to Archbishop King, 3 Jan. 1712/13, London, *Swift Corres.*, ii, pp. 1–4; *Journal to Stella*, ii, pp. 600–3, 4 Jan. 1712/13, London; Bolingbroke to Bristol and Strafford (draft), 7 Jan. 1712/13, Whitehall, S.P. Holl. 248; Bolingbroke to Shrewsbury, 7 Jan. 1712/13, Whitehall, *B.L.*, iii, pp. 281–5; Anne to States-General (transcript), 7 Jan. 1712/13, St. James', Add. Ms. 17677 YYY; Archbishop King to Swift, 22 Jan. 1712/13, Dublin, *Swift Corres.*, ii, pp. 6–10; *Montgomery*, p. 296.

20th, that there was 'not one of our A——s' that was contented with the projected peace. The issue in which this statement appeared was devoted to an examination of a 'half sheet', which had just appeared, entitled *A View of the Taxes, Funds, & Publick Revenues of England*. This consisted of various tables, from which it was calculated that the true average annual expense of the war to Britain had been just under five million pounds. An explanatory sheet which accompanied these tables pointed out that, on the authority of the *Conduct of the Allies* itself, the expenses of the Dutch had been almost as much as this, although no one could claim that their resources were anywhere near as great as ours. In fact, concluded this sheet, it was evident that they had exerted themselves almost *twice* as strenuously in the war as had Britain.[1]

It was above all to the question of the Barrier Treaty that the minds and pens of political writers were turned by the States' letter. Only in February and March 1712 had there been more written on this topic than now. Two pamphlets appeared in answer to *The Barrier-Treaty Vindicated*, both of them consisting mainly of arguments already employed by Swift and others in the previous year. One of these, *Remarks on the Barrier Treaty Vindicated*, contained the veiled suggestion that it was our true interest to play France and the Dutch off against each other in the Low Countries rather than to allow either of them to become dominant. Was it not, it asked, in any case better to keep the Dutch dependent on us for further improvements to their Barrier so as to ensure their support for our Succession? Could we really think they would 'assist us purely to save that which perhaps they'll think or pretend to think in no Danger, and to get dry Blows?' Like the second pamphlet – *A Letter to the Examiner, Concerning the Barrier-Treaty Vindicated* – this had much to say and more still to hint about the dangers of a foreign guarantee of our Succession. This second pamphlet also asked what necessity there was that the Dutch should have sole control of the Barrier. Why, it asked, could not the current joint administration be continued? 'This', it declared,

would keep the Barrier equally secure against France, and more safe against any Encroachments may be made upon our *Flemish* trade.

It poured scorn on Poyntz' assertion that the Dutch would not be our rivals in trade, which, it commented,

is a pretty bold Stroak indeed .... Indeed, his Modesty will not suffer him to

[1] *Examiner*, iii, 16 and 19, 16 and 26 Jan. 1712/13; *Flying-Post*, 3325–6, 20 and 22 Jan. 1712/13; *Britain*, 6, 24 Jan. 1712/13; *C.W.* 194, *passim*; *C.W.* 188.

say, they *have not* been so . . . . and I think we may as well form our Judgments of what *will be*, from what *has been*, as take his Word for it.

On the Whig side there appeared Maynwaring's posthumously published *Short Account and Defence of the Barrier-Treaty*, and a pamphlet, most of which was originally published in the *Flying-Post*, entitled *An Answer to the Examiner's Cavils against the Barrier-Treaty of 1709*. Both had much in common with the many previous Whig apologies. Maynwaring made much of the rights of the States by treaty to a Barrier not less than that of 1709, and engaged in a lengthy defence of Townshend's action in agreeing to Article XV. The Dutch would never have desired this clause had they not been alarmed by the 'discovery' of the Treaty of Commerce with Charles III, he wrote, and Townshend would certainly never have agreed to it had he

thought there was any Hopes of her Majesty's preserving the good Effects of those Treaties to Her own Subjects exclusive of all others, after such a Step taken, by one of the King of *Spain's* Ministers.

This made him think it not wrong to consent to the article

at that Critical Juncture, when the States were, by all possible Management, to be kept firm to the Recovery of the whole *Spanish* Monarchy . . . .

The *Answer to the Examiner's Cavils* dealt painstakingly but spiritedly with the attacks that the *Examiner* had launched at *The Barrier-Treaty Vindicated*. It represented the *Examiner* as a '*Hotspur*, saying with a great deal of Frankness',

> ——I'll give thrice so much Land
> To any well deserving *Bourbon* Friend;
> But with the *Dutch*, those Ras——ls, mark ye me,
> I'll cavil for the Ninth Part of a Hair.

His attitude, it continued, seemed to be: 'Why can't these unreasonable People be contented with as sorry a *Barrier* now, as it has been their Fortune to meet with so often before?' All his arguments, it asserted, were intended merely to conceal the fact that Britain ran

More Hazard of being made a *Province to France*, that has lately invaded it, than of being conquered by a People who at most seem only to aspire to *British Pilchards and Herrings*! [1]

That the Dutch wanted no more of Britain than her pilchards and herrings was a proposition to which the Tories in their current mood were hardly likely to agree; indeed, one of the articles of a satirical

---

[1] *C.W.* 153, *passim; C.W.* 125, *passim; C.W.* 128, *passim; C.W.* 3, *passim*.

'Whig-creed' published at this time by the *Examiner* was that 'The *Dutch* never design to take any Advantages in the way of Trade, to the Prejudice of their *good Allies*'. Defoe, however, whose return to 'the middle of the road' was probably representative of the swing of 'moderate' Tories away from the policies of the High-Fliers, at least denied that the Dutch, or any other trading nation, had or could have enriched themselves from the war.

The most discussed comment at this time on our commercial relations with the Dutch occurred in one of the most discussed pamphlets published in the year 1713, the *Observations upon the State of the Nation, in January 1712/13*. The author of this work (published on January 23rd) was at the time universally believed to be Nottingham, but this has never been satisfactorily established. Its object was, in any case, clear – to make one last attempt to turn public opinion against the forthcoming peace. Its main theme was the danger to the European balance of power of the actual, if not theoretical, union of France and Spain at which we were conniving. It did not deny that the Dutch barrier was 'well secured', but it asserted that, since we had shown so much eagerness to tear up the first Barrier Treaty, the Dutch were hardly likely to have much confidence in our goodwill to the Protestant Succession and their own assistance to it would thus be understandably weak. We were also in great danger of overlooking the serious threat to our trade from France while we 'bellowed' at the Dutch:

I cannot without Concern and Indignation observe how very Modish it is to lay load upon the *Dutch*, and how tamely Men submit to see them abused in our *News-Letters* and *Prints* in so vile a manner. That the *Dutch* may have over-reached us in Trade may for ought I know be true: Tho' they have cleared themselves of so many Things which have been lay'd to their Charge, that perhaps it will be most advisable to suspend our judgments till those Matters are put in a clearer Light. But be it so: In Trade they are our Rivals, and we trust in our Governors that they will take care of the Interests of the Nation in that particular, as well as in others, and we are easy upon that Head. But let the Dutch have been what they will towards us in point of Trade . . . . it is certain, that the *States-General* are at this time next to us the greatest Support of the *Protestant Interest* in *Europe*. And I shall not be afraid to assert, that the Preservation of the *Protestant Religion* has been under God owing to that Commonwealth.[1]

Questions of trade rivalry were also exercising the mind of Strafford, who, on January 24th (N.S.), was still awaiting, not without some impatience, the queen's answer to the States' letter. Commenting

---

[1] *Examiner*, iii, 13, 5 Jan. 1712/13; *Review*, (ix), 50, 24 Jan. 1712/13; *C.W.* 79, pp. 13, 18–19, 32.

on the project – now advocated by the Imperialists – of assigning the Spanish Netherlands to the Elector of Bavaria, he remarked that 'such a weak Prince' must of necessity fall tributary to one of his neighbours, and that it 'might be as fatal to England to have the Spanish Low Countries entire under the Dutch as under the French'. He enlarged on this theme when urging that Upper Guelders should be in Prussian rather than Dutch hands, since, he wrote,

closing them (the Dutch) on that side, and making them entirely secure against all neighbours whatsoever may one day or other be fatal to us, and I am persuaded we can't help quarrels about commerce, for since I have been here, I can't get justice done in many subjects of complaints from our merchants.

Four days later, on January 28th, the queen's answer was communicated to the Dutch, and on January 30th, after obtaining agreement to an alteration in the wording of the Preamble, the States finally submitted and the second Barrier Treaty was signed – yet another proof, remarked Strafford in a letter to Oxford, that the best way to obtain the concurrence of the Dutch was to present them with an ultimatum.

The high Tories were jubilant when the news of this surrender reached them. A pamphlet which probably appeared at this time gives a good indication of their feelings:

....with much a–do, thro' the great Fatigue of our Plenipotentiaries, after a long and tedious Conference, we have drawn in the *Hollanders* to our Alliance, like a forc'd put; for they being enriched by our Poverty, would still have prosecuted the War, had they met with Success or Encouragement; Their own private Ends made them forget their Duty and Respect for our Alliance, which was once reckon'd a Shield and Safeguard to their Poor Distressed States.

The *Examiner* celebrated the queen's success in at last bringing the States 'to believe, That only *She* can make them happy .... after permitting their Jealousies and Cunning to try all other *Resorts*'. The Whigs, according to Bolingbroke, did their best to extract some advantage from this crushing disappointment to their hopes by pretending that the new Treaty was 'in effect the same with that which my Lord Townshend made'; though their authors continued to accuse the Tories of libelling the Dutch and of favouring the French. [1]

8

On January 31st the French plenipotentiaries at Utrecht declared themselves content with the satisfaction offered by the Dutch and the

[1] Strafford to Oxford, 24 and 29 Jan. 1713, Utrecht, *H.M.C. Portland IX*, pp. 357–63; *Flying Post*, 3331, 3 Feb. 1712/13; *Britain*, 9, 4 Feb. 1712/13; *Examiner*, iii, 22, 6 Feb. 1712/13; *C.W.* 198, p. 3; *Montgomery*, pp. 297–8.

Rechteren-Mesnager dispute at last was over. Not all the difficulties in the way of a peace to the Oxford ministry's liking had yet been overcome, however. It found the French, for example, still inclined to withdraw from some of the concessions to the Dutch to which they had previously agreed. Bristol and Strafford were concerned to find that they were talking of making exceptions to the assurances about Franco-Dutch commerce that they had already given, but still more serious was the French attempt to make additions to the territories around Tournai and Ypres which, Bolingbroke had agreed, might be retained by France. This latter difficulty was complicated by the fact that Bolingbroke had omitted to inform the Dutch of this agreement, but he nevertheless insisted that France should abandon these additional claims. On February 17th he sent to the French, through Shrewsbury, an ultimatum from the queen stating her final terms both for her own peace with France and for those of the Allies. In urging acceptance of this, Shrewsbury was to point out how far the queen had made the Dutch recede from their original demands, emphasising particularly that she was now supporting France in refusing Condé for the barrier, in demanding that the question of the 'four Species' exempted from the tariff of 1664 should be referred to Commissioners, and in claiming the retention by France of two at least of the dependencies of Ypres and Tournai. The need for some sort of ultimatum to France was widely recognised in London; as Peter Wentworth wrote to Strafford on February 17th,

Tis for some time we have known'd that the Dutch & the rest of the Allies are ready to come into the Queen's measures, but now it begins to be thought, by some people that it was not thought so (by) before, that the French will be upon the chican, & not so ready to leave everything too the Queen, as has been formerly boasted.[1]

The rival Dutch and Prussian claims to Upper Guelders presented another problem for the ministry. The pro-Prussian Strafford explained to his masters that Dutch insistence on this point was connected with the renewed favour that the project of a 'Barrière en arrière' had now won in the Republic. This idea – of a barrier along the Dutch rather than the French frontier of the Spanish Netherlands – he regarded as a pernicious one. The Dutch had taken it up again, he suggested, because

[1] Bristol and Strafford to Bolingbroke, 3 Feb. 1713, Utrecht, S.P. Holl. 246; (Bolingbroke) to Bristol and Strafford (draft), 13 Feb. 1712/13, Whitehall, S.P. Holl. 248; Bolingbroke to Shrewsbury, 17 Feb. 1712/13, Whitehall, *Hardwicke S.P.*, ii, pp. 510–20; P. Wentworth to Strafford, 17 Feb. 1712/13, London, Add. Ms. 34144; *Montgomery*, pp. 299–300.

though they have signed the new treaty of Barrier (they) are vexed at bottom to see they could not carry matters their own way, and those of the contrary party to peace, think they have no way left to wound what is done, but crying out that the barrier now allotted them is not sufficient, and that the expense of keeping the troops in the barrier will be too great a charge on the State.

The aim of the scheme was thus, he continued, to discredit the ministry, make the Republic less dependent on British friendship, and enable Eugene (who was expected to become Governor-General of the Spanish Netherlands) do discriminate against British commerce. On January 28th (O.S.) Bolingbroke wrote to the plenipotentiaries that neither the Dutch nor the Prussians deserved much help from the queen, but in a letter of March 3rd he gave some deceptive encouragement to the Republic, thanks to

the signing of the Treaty of Succession and Barrier, and the other instances of respect and submission, which the Dutch have since shown.

Like Strafford, Orrery felt no sympathy with Dutch complaints about the expense of the barrier and Dutch attempts to increase the revenues they were already receiving from the Spanish Netherlands. His attitude in this matter was in line with his policy of gaining commercial concessions from the Emperor by playing on his jealousy of the Dutch position in the Spanish Netherlands. This policy reached its climax when Orrery suggested that the queen should make a separate treaty with the Emperor concerning trade with the Spanish Netherlands. The suggestion was made in a letter to Bolingbroke of February 6th (N.S.), and it may not have been altogether by coincidence that a fortnight later there appeared in the *Examiner* some vague but meaning references to the conduct of the Dutch in connection with the commerce of the 'New Conquests'. This scheme, however, was nipped in the bud by the withdrawal of the Imperialists from the Congress, and meanwhile Orrery found much to occupy him in the conduct of the Condominium. Now that British trade with the Spanish Netherlands was safeguarded by the Second Barrier-Treaty Orrery was even more anxious than the Dutch to insist upon the subordination to the 'Conference' of the Maritime Powers of the Council of State, whose 'Protector' he had previously declared himself. Only two months before he had complained of 'the ungracious manner of the Deputy of the States' at Brussels towards the people there, but now he was impatient at the States' delay in authorizing their Deputy to 'punish'em in conjunction with me for their disobedience wch they have not yet done'. The 'punishment', which was inflicted in March, consisted in the turning out of every member but one of the Council of State.[1]

At home, according to Bolingbroke, the Whigs continued to 'pretend to deplore the hard fate of the Dutch, and to insinuate their dissatisfaction', and it was partly in order to answer these cries that Strafford procured a letter to the queen from the States which gave 'the clearest testimonies of submission to, and confidence in, her Majesty'. Though the 'battle for the peace' was all but won, the Tory propagandists were still unrestrained in their comments concerning the Dutch. The *Examiner*, for example, denouncing the effects of a 'foreign education', complained that it might turn an Englishman into a 'clumsie *Dutchman*'. The *Britain* retorted by comparing the virtues that might be learnt in the Dutch Republic to the vices that would result from a French education. This drew from the *Examiner* a furious attack on the way in which 'Whig Republicans' eulogised 'the *Dutch* Model'. After claiming that it had no desire to 'raise Envy or Emulation' between Britain and the Dutch, it went on to consider the constitution and history of the Republic. It was in no sense 'popular', it remarked, and owed its origin neither to a dislike of monarchy nor to a longing for Calvinism but simply to a defence of privilege. But the Dutch in fact had none of those liberties which were so cherished in Britain, being merely an 'absolute oligarchy'. Their much vaunted 'toleration' was at discretion, not by law, and their lack of any durable constitution led to 'continual Turns and Revolutions'. It was true that 'in all their Management' there was 'some regard paid to the Inclinations and Temper of the People', but the same might be said even of absolute tyrannies.

The Tory writers were also much concerned to refute the arguments against the peace that had been put forward in the *Observations upon the State of the Nation*. Defoe led the attack in *Not——am Politicks Examin'd*, in which he had little to say of that pamphlet's remarks concerning the Dutch except to admit, in passing, that it might 'in some measure be true' that 'the popular method of railing at the *Dutch*' was meant to prepare the way for the Pretender. In another 'answer' George Sewell had more to say on this subject. He saw no reason to take the squabbles of English and Dutch journalists so seriously:

---

[1] Orrery to ?, 9 Dec. 1712, Hague, S.P. Holl. 575; Orrery to (Bolingbroke), 23 Jan., 6 and 9 Feb. 1713, Brussels, S.P. Flanders 62; Bolingbroke to Bristol and Strafford (drafts), 28 Jan. and 3 March 1712/13 (O.S.), S.P. Holl. 248; *Examiner*, iii, 23, 9 Feb. 1712/13; Strafford to Oxford, 22 Feb. 1713, Utrecht, *H.M.C. Portland IX*, pp. 367–71; *Montgomery*, pp. 299–305.

The *Dutch* seem to have a great Share in our Author's Affection; and it is agreed, between all thinking men, that our *News Papers* use them a little too hardly, as on the other Hand, theirs do ours. They I believe cannot give so good a Reason for that Treatment as we: That they have over reach'd us in *Trade*, is own'd by him; and we may add, *insulted* us in our *Politics*; and, in other Cases equally provoking to generous Spirits. But what does a little piquering between *Abel*, and the *Amsterdam Courant* signify?

What was important was that there was no longer any breach between us; the Barrier Treaty was signed, and there was

no difference between us and the *Dutch*, but who shall reap the greatest Benefit in the ensuing *Peace*: and we can hardly say, That there is so much as that at present.

In the *Review* Defoe supplemented his previous comments by pointing to such contradictions in the *Observations* as that 'The *Dutch* are our Rivals in Trade, and have Cheated us, and therefore must not be rail'd against'. The *Examiner*, too, made much of the admission that the Dutch had imposed upon us in matters of Trade. 'My great Quarrel to them has been on that Head', it declared, and went on to accuse the author of the *Observations* of trying to make the Dutch suspect us, and of insulting his own country by describing the Dutch as the head of the Protestant interest. The *Britain* swiftly took up this last assertion: did the *Examiner* mean, it asked, that we had been the head of the Protestant interest between 1660 and 1688? [1]

In the political writing of March 1712/13, there can be seen a growing preoccupation with the question of the Protestant Succession, which may also have been inspired in part by the fears on this subject expressed in the *Observations*. Defoe, for all his apostasy, was no crypto-Jacobite, and at the beginning of March there appeared a pamphlet in his best ironic vein, in defence of the Hanoverian Succession, under the title of *Reasons against the Succession of the House of Hanover*. Towards the end of this work he abandoned irony, and asserted that one reason why some people had an aversion to the Electoral House was 'because as they are taught to say, they are *Dutchmen*', and

they can by no means think of another Dutch Succession without Abhorrence; nay, the Aversion is so much greater than their Aversions to Popery, that they can with much more Satisfaction entertain the Notion of a Popish *French* Pretender than of the best Protestant in the World, if he hath any thing belonging to him that sounds like a *Dutchman*. And this is some Peoples Reason against the *Hanover* Succession; a Reason which has produced various Effects in the World since the Death of that Prince (William III) even to creating National Anti-

---

[1] *Examiner*, iii, 24, 27–8, 13, 23 and 27 Feb. 1712/13; Bolingbroke to Strafford, 20 Feb. 1712/13, Whitehall, *B.L.*, iii, pp. 452–4; *Britain*, 14 and 16, 21 and 28 Feb. 1712/13; *Review* (ix), 63, 26 Feb. 1712/13; *C.W.* 47, pp. 22–3; *C.W.* 164, pp. 22–4, 27.

pathies in some People to the whole People of *Holland*, and to wish us involved in a War with the *Dutch*, without any foundation of a Quarrel with them or any Reason for those Aversions.

The *Britain*, too, laid down that 'He who is an enemy to the *Dutch* . . . . is certainly a Friend to the Pretender', but the *Examiner* mocked at the way in which the Whigs posed as defenders of Protestantism while lauding the Dutch Republic, whose toleration of the 'Romish Church' was well known, and where 'the Superstitions of *Rome*' were gaining more and more 'in the Sentiments and Affections of that People'. Another pamphlet observed that, though we accused the Dutch of planning to aggrandize themselves and ruin us,

they show'd how much they hated us, by engaging to secure the Protestant Succession in the House of *Hanover*, against any Foreign Force or Home Seditions.

When the *Examiner* challenged the Whigs to produce a formula which would provide infallible security against Popery, the *Britain* suggested 'Wholesome Severities' against those that insulted the Revolution or railed 'with unparallel'd Insolence against the *Dutch*'. Under the influence of the *Examiner* and his fellows, it continued, even foot-soldiers could now be heard saying that 'the *Dutch* were never Friends to *England*', and the like. While the *Britain* thus attacked the *Examiner* for its 'Flings at the *Dutch*' a pamphlet appeared to show that the Dutch *were* in fact, in the words of its title, 'better Friends than the French, to the Monarchy, Church, and Trade of England . . . .'. Its author, John Withers, set himself to refute all the arguments that were used to show that they were 'never Friends to *England*'. His pamphlet deserves some attention here, since it shows in a very complete fashion what answers those well disposed to the Dutch were making to the allegations of Swift and his fellows.

Withers began by considering the reflections on the 'Antimonarchical' principles of the Dutch and their intrigues with the Whigs to subvert our constitution. Their form of government, he replied, was a matter of necessity rather than of choice, they had been better friends to our kings than the monarchy of France (for example, in the treatment of the exiled Charles II), and if we did not like them because of the form of their government then we would have to quarrel with the whole world. As for their being enemies to the Church of England, they had always shown toleration of the Anglican faith – unlike the French! Their open trade with France during the war was the next criticism with which he dealt. Not only were they more in need of French wines than

we, he explained, having no liquor of their own (and 'I might add, that
their foggy Air and ill Diet renders 'em the more excusable'), but in
any case we too had traded with the enemy – with Spain at the beginning of the war (even before the setting up of 'Charles III') and with
France, *via* Ireland, throughout it. The fourth allegation that Withers
considered was that 'they have rook'd us of our Money, but done little
or nothing to promote the Common Cause'. To this he replied that we
had been as much concerned to enter the war as they, but they had
none the less maintained many thousand more troops than we had,
that their taxes were incomparably heavier than ours, and that of the
coin we had sent over to them, much had been used to pay our own
troops, and the rest had been made up for by Dutch purchases of our
exports. Nor was it true that 'their Success in *Flanders* has render'd
'em too potent and imperious'. Their power to do us mischief was still
incomparably less than that of France, a strong barrier in their hands
was necessary for our safety, 'The Constitution of their Government'
was 'not fitted for making of large conquests', and there was no one in
Holland who pretended a title to the British crown. As for the trade
rivalry of which we heard so much, he went on, it was in fact the French
who were our rivals in the vital branches of our trade, especially in wool.
Finally, he dealt with the insinuation of 'our Modern *Libellers*' that
because of Amboyna 'the *Hollanders* are a parcel of barbarous Villains
and deserve no quarter from us'. We should remember, he wrote, that
there was no very certain account of the guilt or innocence of the vic-
tims, and that in any case English 'Bucaniers', especially Morgan, had
committed far greater barbarities.[1]

9

When seven weeks had passed since the signing of the Barrier Treaty
and peace had not yet been concluded, it began to be said in London
that the Dutch were responsible for the delay. 'We say here', wrote
Peter Wentworth on March 10th, 'that the Dutch & Lord T (*i.e.* Oxford)
are trying who shall have the better'. It was said that the Dutch were
still hoping that the much-prorogued Parliament, when it met, might
obstruct the peace, but that Oxford was determined that they should
sign the peace before the session opened. Impatience with the alleged
delay of the Dutch increased when it became known that they were

---

[1] *Britain*, 18, 24–5, 7 March 1712/13, 28 March and 1 April 1713; *Examiner*, iii, 31, 9
March 1712/13; *C.W.* 50, pp. 31–2; *C.W.* 154, pp. 28–9; *C.W.* 200, *passim*.

objecting to signing a peace in which the Emperor was not included, and then, when this objection had been overcome, that they wished to sign their peace four days after Britain had signed hers. In the *Review* of March 26th Defoe demonstrated how unreasonable it was for the Dutch to oppose signing because the Emperor did so, since his was the only power in Europe which grudged them their barrier. The *Examiner* suggested on the following day that the 'two *Sister Factions* in *Britain* and *Holland*' were responsible for urging these policies on the Dutch, with the aim of sowing dissension between their countries. On the next day Swift, in a letter promising Archbishop King some startling revelations about the conduct of the Dutch in 'these two last intriguing years', was able to announce that peace was imminent; but on March 31st Wentworth reported as the talk of London

that the Dutch will not sign with us, may be three or four days after, & they seem to be very confident that they have gain so much time as to work that with the French court that they cou'd not obtain from our Ministry, that they in all places are to have the same advantages of trade with us.[1]

These rumours were exploded when on April 3rd the news arrived that on April 11th (N.S.) both Britain and the Republic had signed their respective peaces with France. It was with 'a great deal of joy', according to Wentworth, that it was learnt that the Dutch had signed with the British, for this had not been generally expected; 'several pocket questions', as he put it, had been lost as a result, 'and many a fine speech spoilt on this occasion'. At court the next day, he wrote to his brother,

everybody was mightily pleased, and a world of members of the house of Commons wish't me joy of the glory you had in bringing this great affair about; even some that used to say 'damn the Dutch, no matter if they sign or not', express their satisfaction and own it worth the while staying so long for them......

Strafford was delighted that the action of Bristol and himself in 'delaying so long signing for the dutch' was now extremely approved of by his countrymen, even though they had been 'so angry' before. The course adopted by the plenipotentiaries in this matter had in fact been dictated by elementary prudence. They had strict instructions to sign as soon as possible, but, as Swift afterwards remarked, 'as it would certainly be more popular to their country, so they conceived it would be more safe for themselves' to wait for the Dutch to come in. Two

[1] P. Wentworth to (Strafford), 10 March 1712/13, and 31 March 1713, London, Add. Ms. 34144; *Review*, (ix), 75, 26 March 1713; *Examiner*, iii, 36, 27 March 1713; Swift to Archbishop King, 28 March 1713, London, *Swift Corres.*, ii ,pp. 14–17.

years later they had cause to congratulate themselves on their foresight, without which they would probably have found themselves in exile with Bolingbroke and Ormonde, or with Oxford in the Tower.

The first rejoicing at the news that peace had been concluded was not prompted by its terms, for the final details of these were as yet unknown except in official circles. What mattered to most people was that after eleven years of war, three, four, six, or even all of which they believed to have been unnecessary, peace had at last been granted to them. The only Englishmen whose minds were much exercised at this moment by the question of what *sort* of peace it was were Whigs like Thomas Burnet, who wrote to a friend: 'Shall I congratulate or condole you upon the Peace? I'll do neither by Letter, nor can I yet, for nobody knows what the Peace is'.

The last word on the peace should in all justice be given to the ministerial propagandists who, above all in their campaign against the Allies, had done a great deal to foster a climate of opinion in which the mere fact of peace, regardless of what its terms might be, was received with enthusiasm. In the *Review* Defoe celebrated the signing of the peace by suggesting that the fact that the Dutch had not had the honour and advantages of ending the war was a judgment of God upon them for refusing the French offers of 1709, 'even against their Inclination and Judgment'. It is undoubtedly to the *Examiner*, however, that the final word belongs. Triumphantly it mocked at the Whig propagandists on April 10th:

How boldly did they affirm, in behalf of the *States*, That they would carry on the War without us .... Have they not basely bely'd the *Dutch*, and, after this, who can depend upon their Veracity .... Here they cannot blame me, since their Confutation comes from the *Hague*: *The* Dutch *have spoke Truth, and shamed the* Whigs! [1]

Note to Chapters X and XI

Since this book went to press there has appeared Mr Michael Foot's *The Pen and The Sword*, a vivid study of the genesis and results of *The Conduct of the Allies*. Its only real defect is that by taking the dismissal of Marlborough and the creation of the twelve peers as its climax it unwittingly does less than justice to the power of the 'ministerial' pens, which so successfully prepared men's minds not only for these crucial measures but also for the whole process of the coercion and abandonment of the allies.

[1] P. Wentworth to Strafford, 6 April 1713, London, *Wentworth Papers*, pp. 327–8; *Review*, (ix), 80, 7 April 1713; *Examiner*, iii, 40, 10 April 1713; T. Burnet to G. Duckett, 11 April 1713 (O.S.), *T. Burnet's Letters*, pp. 34–6; Strafford to Orrery, 24 April 1713, Utrecht, Add. Ms. 37209; *C.W.* 175, p. 186.

CONCLUSION

When Anne came to the throne there was general delight at the end of 'foreign' rule and a feeling that England was now, for the first time since the Revolution, the mistress of her own fortunes. At any other time such emotions might have welled up in an almost universal expression of hostility towards the Dutch, at last displaced from the controlling position which, many Englishmen thought, they had long enjoyed in the government of England. The popular conception of the Dutch as dangerous, unscrupulous commercial rivals might once more have gained the upper hand as it had in the time of the Dutch wars. That it did not was due perhaps partly to the new confidence that England was beginning to feel in her standing as a Great Power – no longer was the urge for aggressive self-assertion so great – and partly to the fact that, with the removal of William III from the scene, one of the greatest obstacles to a less hostile attitude towards the Dutch had disappeared.

Primarily, however, the absence of such a reaction was due to the fact that the queen, her chief ministers, and most of her politically conscious subjects had accepted the necessity of a war with France; a war in which an alliance with the Dutch was, for better or worse, essential. The need for the successful prosecution of that war was placed above all other considerations, and the Dutch were consequently regarded above all as allies, and judged as such. At first sight this may seem a self-evident proposition, hardly worthy of remark, but it would be a mistake to look upon it in this light. In the Nine Years War there had been no such general agreement on the standpoint from which the Dutch should be viewed. In addition to those extreme Whigs or Jacobites whose attitude to the Dutch was governed by their role in the Revolution, some judged them on their performance as allies, some as merchants and traders, some mainly for the past record of their relations with England, and many for the part – real or imagined – that they were then playing in English affairs. A similar diversity of outlook is revealed by a close study of the British attitude towards the Dutch

in the last year of Anne's reign, after the conclusion of peace. There
were then two main issues which governed opinion about the Dutch.
For the non-Jacobite ministers and those of their followers who were
unwilling to look the problem of the Succession in the eye, there were
the alleged dangers from Dutch 'encroachments' in the Low Countries.
Here then we see the Dutch viewed primarily as commercial rivals;
but for the Whigs, for some 'moderates', and (as always) for the Jacobites there was the position of the Dutch *vis-à-vis* the Protestant Succession.

In the War of the Spanish Succession it would have been perfectly
possible for a similar variety of outlook to have existed. There was no
decline either in Jacobitism or in Whig glorification of the Revolution,
there were still fruitful sources of commercial dispute – above all,
perhaps, the question of the Scottish fisheries – and it was widely
believed that the Dutch, hand in glove with the Whigs, were still
angling for the control of English affairs. The conduct of the war,
however, and later of the peace, overrode all these considerations, and
the Republic was judged accordingly. When its conduct seemed to be
in keeping with what was required from a good ally it came into favour;
when it did not it speedily fell out of it. The favour of a Tory might
mean merely absence of criticism, and the disfavour of a Whig somewhat less enthusiastic praise, but the principle still holds good. Allowing
for the prejudices and prepossessions of the individual concerned it was
the conduct of the Dutch *as an ally* which was the determining factor
in the shaping of the British attitude towards them during the War of
the Spanish Succession.

This was the universal touchstone of opinion, the basis on which
the British attitude rested. In fact, of course, this basis was never
firm; the popular conception of the function of a good ally was constantly changing. At one time it would be to participate wholeheartedly in a
war waged primarily at sea; at another to fight great land-battles. A
good ally might be expected to eschew all talk of peace; or, again, to
agree to whatever was put forward in that sacred name. At any given
time there might well be much division of opinion within the nation as
to the duties of a good ally. Despite all this uncertainty and variability,
however, there remained the fundamental assumption that the Dutch
were allies first, and everything else – commercial rivals, 'Dissenters',
republicans, ex-enemies – second. They were to be judged primarily by
the relation between their conduct and what was considered as the
best means of furthering or finishing the war. Neither before the war

nor after its close did Englishmen find any such common standpoint from which to view their Dutch neighbours. It is this far from meaningless abstraction which provides the present study with its true unity.

The main point of interest, then, in this study has been the way in which the British attitude towards the Dutch varied, not only as a result of the conduct of the Republic, but also on account of the changes of view in Britain as to the proper method of carrying on the war. Behind these fluctuations, it is true, was the still very real feeling of commercial jealousy. We may find it displayed in the dispute about trade and correspondence with the enemy, in the struggle over the Barrier Treaty, and, throughout the reign, in the question of the British fishery. It had not disappeared, and when the war was over it once more dictated the attitude of many Englishmen towards the Dutch. Even during the war it played its part in turning popular feeling against the Dutch and against the war. But it did not dominate the feelings of most men towards the Republic. It seems probable, for example, that, at least up to the end of 1711, the mass of merchants and traders gave their support to the war policies of the Whigs. In 1705, again, the High Tories failed miserably to turn the trade and correspondence dispute to account, despite the disappointments of the campaign of that year. Even when the Oxford ministry was doing everything in its power to work up feeling against the Dutch it was, significantly enough, the conduct of the Republic *as an ally* on which it made its heaviest onslaught. Their shortcomings in the field, their naval and military deficiencies, their 'league' with the Whigs, their alleged responsibility for the failures to obtain peace in 1706, 1709, and 1710, their 'insults' to the queen and their alleged desire for the indefinite prolongation of the war – these were the main points of attack, though the familiar libels of bygone days also appeared.

To the historian of opinion the final years of the War of Spanish Succession are of peculiar interest. The change of ministry in 1710 was followed by the growth of closer ties between 'public' and 'official' opinion, and in the ensuing years, above all from the end of 1711 onwards, can be seen the first large-scale attempt by an English government to influence public opinion on questions of foreign policy. That this was considered necessary is an eloquent tribute to the fact that the Crown and its ministers no longer had a free hand even in this traditional sphere for the exercise of the prerogative. This attempt consisted largely in a campaign designed to arouse hostility towards the Dutch. Throughout the war the British attitude towards the Dutch had been largely an aspect of the British attitude towards the war; with the launching of this campaign against the Allies it became a vital factor in the struggle for peace.

It is in this final period of the War that is revealed most clearly the problem underlying this, (and indeed any study of public opinion.) This is the problem of defining the interplay between opinion and policy. In the present context, though its detailed workings may remain obscure, the general nature of this process appears with unusual clarity. It is not to be doubted that opinion about the Dutch was of very great influence in determining political developments within Britain. If the campaign against the Dutch had not succeeded the Oxford ministry might well have been wrecked on the question of the peace, so critical was its position immediately after the revelation of the 'seven preliminaries'. Even at this time, however, when public opinion was playing so great a part in the internal affairs of Britain, it cannot be pretended that the Oxford ministry was kept in power, its policy of coercion and abandonment vindicated, and the Peace of Utrecht made possible by the spontaneous expression of a sovereign popular will. The overwhelming popular support that the Oxford ministry acquired for its peace policies was largely due to the shrewd and unscrupulous action of the ministers themselves in initiating an intensive propaganda campaign designed to play upon the growing war-weariness of their countrymen and their traditional and deep-rooted hostility towards the Dutch. For the politicians of queen Anne's reign public opinion was not a voice to be ignored, save at their peril, but neither was it a command to be obeyed; it was an instrument to be adapted to their own purposes. The triumph of the Oxford ministry at home and abroad in the last phase of the war showed as never before in English history how powerful an instrument it could be in the hands of men who recognised its potentialities and understood its control. This was perhaps the supreme political heritage of Oxford and Bolingbroke, more important by far for the future than the parliamentary manoeuvres of the one or even than the constitutional precepts of the other. 'Diplomacy resting upon an appeal to public opinion' (is a technique usually associated with nineteenth-century statesmen and twentieth-century demagogues, but it had been unmistakably) foreshadowed in the campaign against the Allies.

BIBLIOGRAPHY

Note: The contemporary works cited or referred to have been listed in full, as have the documentary materials used, both published and unpublished. The list of secondary works, however, is a highly select one, being restricted to those books which have proved of substantial value. Bibliographical details of other secondary works will be found in the footnotes.

Entries in square brackets indicate the abbreviation by which the work concerned is referred to in the footnotes. In the case of single contemporary works, such reference is by means of the number allotted to each work in the bibliography. Thus Addison's *Present State of the War* is cited in the footnotes as *C.W.* 1, and so on.

The following abbreviations are used throughout the footnotes and the bibliography:

E.H.R	*English Historical Review*
Ec. H.R.	*Economic History Review*
Hunt. Lib. Bull.	*Huntington Library Bulletin*
Hunt. Lib. Quart.	*Huntington Library Quarterly*

A. *Contemporary Works*

Note: After most entries there appear

(*a*) A reference to the collection in which the work was consulted (except in the case of reprints and established works of reference). Mention of a collection does not necessarily mean that the work concerned is not to be found in one or more of the other collections used. In this connection the following abbreviations have been made use of:

B.M.	British Museum
L.T.	University College London, Lansdowne Tracts.
Bart.	Bodleian Library, Bartholomew Collection.
God.	Bodleian Library, Godwyn Collection.

(*b*) The number(s), if any, under which the work is listed in the following:

W.T. and C. S. Morgan, *A Bibliography of British History (1700–1715)* (Bloomington, Indiana, 1934–42). [*M*]

G. Davies, *Bibliography of British History* .... 1603–1714 (Oxford, 1928). [*D*]

C. L. Grose, *A Select Bibliography of British History, 1660–1760* (Chicago, 1939). [*G*]

(i) *Single Works*

1. (ADDISON, JOSEPH), *The Present State of the War, and the Necessity of an Augmentation, Consider'd.* London, 1708 (1st. edn. 1707). *B.M.* E. 1981(1). *M.* J11

2. *The Answer to Mr. B------- Speech.* (1705). In Boyer's *Annals*, iii, appendix, pp. 77–91.
3. *An Answer to the Examiner's Cavils against the Barrier-Treaty of 1709.* London, 1713. *God.* 1892(9). *M.* P47.
4. *Answer to the Lord Haversham's Speech .... on Wednesday the 19th of November, 1707.* (1707). *B.M.* 9502.g.6(4).
5. *An Appeal from the City to the Country ....* London, 1710. *B.M.* T.1761(6). *M.* M 20.
6. (ARBUTHNOT, JOHN?) *Law is a Bottomless Pit ....* Four parts. London, 1712. *B.M.* E.1984(2, 3, 5) and T.1107(22). *M.* 047.
7. (ATTERBURY, FRANCIS), *To the Wh--s Nineteen Queries, a Fair and Full Answer, by an Honest Torie ....* London, 1710. *L.T.* 198(7). *M.* M45.
8. *An Auction of State Pictures.* London, 1710. *God.* 2748(1).
9. B----, B., *The Exorbitant Grants of William the III Examin'd and Question'd ....* London, 1703. *L.T.* 139(1). *M.* F22
10. B----, J., *The Interest of Great Britain Consider'd; in an Essay upon Wool, Tin and Leather ....* London, 1707. *B.M.* 712.c.8. *M.* J45.
11. ——, *A Memorial Briefly pointing at some advantages of the Union of the Two Kingdoms ....* London, 1702. *B.M.* 103.i.65. *M.* E46.
12. (BARON, WILLIAM), *An Historical Account of Comprehension and Toleration ... Part I ....* London, 1705. *B.M.* T.749(6). *M.* H38.
13. (——), *Separation and Sedition Inseparable ....* London, 1703. *B.M.* 4133.a.53. *M.* F27.
14. *Beware of the Pretender ....* 1712. *B.M.* 816.m.3(147). *M.* 0368.
15. BREWSTER, Sir FRANCIS, *New Essays on Trade ....* London, 1702. *B.M.* 288.b.27. *M.* E75.
16. *A Brief Account of the Tack, in a Letter to a Friend.* 1705. *B.M.* T.1754(3). *M.* H276.
17. BURNET, GILBERT, *A Compleat History of the Glorious Life and Actions of ... William the Third ....* London, 1702. *God.* 399(4). *M.* E91.
18. ——, *History of My Own Time.* Vols. v and vi. Oxford, 1833 (2nd.edn.).
19. (BURNET, THOMAS), *A Certain Information of a Certain Discourse ....* London, 1712. *B.M.* 104.b.8. *M.* 0114.
20. (——), *A Letter to the People, to be left for them at the Booksellers ....* London, 1712. *B.M.* 1474.b.8. *M.* 0401.
21. (——), *Our Ancestors as Wise as we ....* London, 1712. *B.M.* 8132.aaa.1 (7). *M.* 0116.
22. 'A Catalogue of Books to be sold by Auction at ye D. of Malb. Lodgins in St. Jams. on Sunday ye 25th July An: 1704' (Ms). *B.M.* Add.Ms.34729 (West Papers).
23. *The Changes: or, Faction Vanquish'd. A Poem ....* London, 1711. *B.M.* 1481.f.19(8). *M.* N105.
24. *The Cheating Age Found Out, When Knaves was most in Fashion ....* London, (c.1712). *B.M.* 12350.bb.22. *M.* H84.
25. (CHURCHILL, JOHN, Duke of Marlborough), *The Case of His Grace the D--- of M----------* .... 1712. *B.M.* E.2187(9). *M.* 0424.
26. CHURCHILL, SARAH, Duchess of Marlborough, *An Account of the Conduct of the Dowager Duchess of Marlborough ....* London, 1742.
27. *A Collection of the Parliamentary Debates ....* Vols. iii, v and vi. 1739–1741.
28. (COWPER, WILLIAM, Earl), *A Letter to Isaac Bickerstaff, Esq: Occasion'd by the Letter to the Examiner.* London, 1710. *B.M.* T.1761(24). *M.* M151.
29. (DAVENANT, CHARLES), *Essays upon Peace at Home and War Abroad ...*

Part I. London, 1704 (actually published in 1703). *B.M.* 502.e.11. *M.* F100.

30. (———), *New Dialogues upon the Present posture of Affairs ... Vol. II ....* London, 1710. *L.T.* 170(4). *M.* M164.

31. ———, *A Report to the Honourable the Commissioners for ... Taking, Examining, and Stating the Public Accounts ....* Part II. London, 1712. *L.T.* 170(5). *M.* O164.

32. (———), *Sir Thomas Double at Court, and in High Preferments ....* London, 1710. *L.T.* 170(3). *M.* M166.

33. (———), *Tom Double Return'd out of the Country: or, the True Picture of a Modern Whig ....* London, 1702. *L.T.* 170(2). *M.* E137.

34. *A Debate between Three Ministers of State on the present Affairs of England ....* London, 1702. *B.M.* T.1990 (4). *M.* E142.

35. (DEFOE, DANIEL), *The Advantages of Scotland by an Incorporate Union with England. Compar'd with those of a Coalition with the Dutch, or League with France.* 1707. *B.M.* 1103.f.53. *M.* J45.

36. (———), *Advice to all Parties.* London, 1705. *B.M.* 1389.g.48. *M.* H120.

37. (———), *Advice to the Electors of Great Britain, occasioned by the intended Invasion from France.* London, 1708. *B.M.* 8133.c.58(7). *M.* K120.

38. (———), *Armageddon: or, the Necessity of Carrying on the War ....* London, (1711). *B.M.* 1103.a.2(2). *M.* M175.

39. (———), *The Ballance of Europe ....* London, 1711. *B.M.* E.1994(2). *M.* N140.

40. (———), *The Consolidator, or, Memoirs of Sundry Transactions from the World in the Moon ....* London, 1705. *B.M.* G.13507. *M.* H124.

41. (———) (?), *A Defence of the Allies and the Late Ministry ....* London, 1712. *B.M.* 8132.aaa.1(6). *M.* N142.

42. (———), *Eleven Opinions about Mr. H----y, with Observations.* London, 1711. *L.T.* 179(3). *M.* N143.

43. (———), *An Enquiry into the Real Interest of Princes ....* London, 1712. *God.* 1132(9). *M.* O171.

44. (———) (?), *A Further Search into the Conduct of the Allies and the Late Ministry ....* London, 1712. *L.T.* 200(6). *M.* O172.

45. (———), *The Justice and Necessity of a War with Holland ....* London, 1712. *B.M.* 1093.d.4. *M.* O177.

46. (———), *A Modest Vindication of the Present Ministry ....* London, 1707. *Bart.* 272(7). *M.* J153.

47. (———), *Not-----am Politicks Examin'd ....* London, 1713. *B.M.* T.1583(4). *M.* P186.

48. (———), *Peace, or Poverty ....* London, 1712. *Bart.* 302(28). *M.* O180.

49. (———), *Reasons against Fighting ....* 1712. *B.M.* 8029.c.87. *M.* O185.

50. (———), *Reasons against the Succession of the House of Hanover ....* London, 1713. *L.T.* 192(3). *M.* P189.

51. (———), *Reasons why a Party among us, and also among the Confederates, are obstinately bent against a Treaty of Peace with the French at this time ....* London, 1711. *B.M.* E.2191(7). *M.* N153.

52. (———), *Reasons why this Nation ought to put a Speedy End to this Expensive War ....* London, 1711. *L.T.* 199(9). *M.* N154.

53. (———), *A Reply to a Pamphlet Entituled, The L--d H--------'s Vindication of his Speech &c.* London, 1706. *L.T.* 141(19). *M.* I117.

54. (———) (?), *A Search after Dutch Honesty; Or, the Old Use and Custom of that Nation to their Friends and Allies ....* 1712. *B.M.* 1093.d.5. *M.* O186.

55. (———), *A Spectator's Address to the Whigs.* 1711. *Bart.* 283(12). *M.* N187.

56. (——) (?), *A Speech without Doors*. London, 1710. B.M. 698.h.13.
    M. M190.
57. (——) (?), *A Supplement to the Faults on Both Sides* .... London, 1710.
    B.M. E.1988(5). *M*. M191.
58. DENNIS, JOHN, *Britannia Triumphans: or the Empire Sav'd, and Europe
    Deliver'd* .... London, 1704. *B.M*. 161.1.33. *M*. G162.
59. ——, *A Proposal for putting a Speedy End to the War* .... London, 1703.
    B.M. 101.c.26. *M*. F125.
60. *The Description of Dunkirk* .... 1712. *B.M*. 11602.i.12(4). *M*. O211.
61. (DES MAIZEAUX, PIERRE) (?), *A Letter from a Gentleman at the Court of
    St. Germains, To one of his friends in England* .... London, 1710. *B.M*.
    E.1981(9). *M*. M195.
62. *A Dialogue Between a New Courtier and a Country Gentleman*. 1712.
    B.M. E. 1997(3). *M*. O196.
63. (DRAKE, JAMES), *The History of the Last Parliament, Begun at Westminster,
    the Tenth Day of February ... An. Dom.1700* .... London, 1702.
    B.M. 809.d.24. *M*. E165. *D*. 427. *G*. 3032.
64. *Dutch Alliances; or, Plain Proof of Their Observance of Treaties* ....
    London, 1712. *B.M*. E.1994(4). *M*. O61.
65. *The Dutch Barrier Our's* .... London, 1712. *B.M*. E.1999(12). *M*. O651.
66. *The D---- Deputies. A Satyr*. London, 1705. *B.M*. 1O77.k.24(2). *M*. H148.
67. *Dutch Generosity, and English Gratitude, Exemplified in their Treatment of
    each other in Peace and War* .... London, 1712. *B.M*. 101.d.41. *M*. O214.
68. *Dutch Ingratitude Exemplified, Being the Lord Chancellor's Speech
    in a Late Reign*. London, 1712. Bart. 305(52). *M*. O215.
69. *The D---h Politicks Examin'd: or, the Danger of a Defensive War
    to the Confederates* .... London, 1705. *B.M*. 101.c.33. *M*. H149.
70. *The Dutch won't Let us have Dunkirk* .... 1712. *B.M*. 1474.b.3. *M*. O216.
71. *An Enquiry into the Danger and Consequences of a War with the Dutch*.
    London, 1712. *B.M*. 1093.d.7. *M*. O170.
72. *An Essay Towards the History of the Last Ministry and Parliament* ...
    London, 1710. *B.M*. E. 1981(4). *M*. M222.
73. *An Examination of the Third and Fourth Letters to a Tory Member* ...
    London, 1711. *B.M*. 101.d.17. *M*. N266.
74. *An Exhortation to the Love of our Country* .... London, 1712.
    B.M. 8132.aaa.1(8). *M*. O234.
75. *An Explanation of the Eleven Resolves* .... London, 1712. *B.M*.
    8122.f.23. *M*. O235.
76. *The Fable of the Cods-Heads: or, A Reply to the Dutchmen's Answer to the Reso-
    lutions of the House of Commons*. (1712). *B.M*. 11602.i.12(7*). *M*. O237.
77. FAGEL, Baron F. N., *The Baron de Fagel's Account of the Campagne in
    Portugal of 1705* .... London, 1708. *B.M*. 1197.f.14. *M*. K163.
78. (FERGUSON, ROBERT), *An Account of the Obligations the States of Holland
    have to Great Britain, and the Returns they have made both in Europe and
    the Indies* .... London, 1711. *L.T*. 199(12). *M*. N214.
79. (FINCH, DANIEL, Earl of Nottingham) (?), *Observations upon the State
    of the Nation, in January 1712/3*. London, 1713. *L.T*. 171 (11). *M*. P 447.
80. *The French Preliminaries. A New Ballad* .... Amsterdam, 1712.
    B.M. 112.f.44(37).
81. *French Sincerity Exemplified by the Surrender of Dunkirk* ....
    (1712). *B.M*. 1871.e.9(163). *M*. O262.
82. *A Full and True Account of a most horrid and cruel Plot* .... London,
    1712. *B.M*. 816.m.3(150). *M*. O35.

83. *The Game at Picquet; or, a Memorial to the Great Britains.* 1707. B.M. 8223.e.1(152). *M.* J204.

84. (GILDON, CHARLES), *The Golden Spy; or, a Political Journal of the Brtiish Nights Entertainment of War and Peace, and Love and Politics* .... London, 1709. *B.M.* 12614.cc.21. *M.* L144.

85. *Great Britain's Union, and the Security of the Hanover Succession, Consider'd. In a Letter from Windsor of the 30th of December 1704, to a Member of Parliament in London.* London, 1705. *B.M.* T.1754(5). *M.* H186.

86. H., W., *A Modest Attempt to prove Dr. H --- not the Author of the Bouchain Dialogue.* London, 1712. *L.T.* 199(6). *M.* O289.

87. HALL, R., *The History of the Barbarous Cruelties and Massacres, Committed by the Dutch in the East-Indies.* London, 1712. *B.M.* 1295.b.22.

88. (Hanover, Electress of), *A Letter from Her Royal Highness, the Princess Sophia* ... *With another from Hannover, Written by Sir Rowland Gwynne to the* ... *Earl of Stamford.* London, 1706. *B.M.* T.1666(12). *M.* I238.

89. (HARE, FRANCIS), *The Allies and the Late Ministry Defended against France and the Present Friends of France* .... Four parts. London, 1711–12. *L. T.* 186(1–4). *M.* N261.

90. (———), *The Conduct of the Duke of Marlborough* .... London, 1712. *B.M.* 1202.e.2. *M.* O306. *D.*1135. *G.*3358.

91. (———), *A Full Answer to the Conduct of the Allies* .... London, 1712. *B.M.* 101.d.33. *M.* O309.

92. (———), *A Letter to a Member of the October-Club* .... London, 1711. *B.M.* E.1994(3). *M.* N269.

93. (———), *The Management of the War, in a Letter to a Tory-Member.* London, 1711. *L.T.* 185(2). *M.* N270.

94. (———), *The Management of the War, in a Second Letter to a Tory-Member.* London, 1711. *L.T.* 185(3). *M.* N271.

95. (———), *The Negotiations for a Treaty of Peace, in 1709, Consider'd, in a Third Letter to a Tory-Member. Part the First.* London, 1711. *L.T.* 185(4). *M.* N273.

96. (———), *The Negotiations for a Treaty of Peace, from the Breaking Off of the Conference at the Hague, to the End of those at Gertruydenberg, Consider'd, in a Fourth Letter to a Tory-Member. Part II.* London, 1711. *L.T.* 185(5). *M.* N272.

97. (———), *The Treaty between her Majesty, and the States-General* ... *Consider'd.* London, 1712. *L.T.* 200(8). *M.* O310.

97. (HARLEY, ROBERT), *Faults on Both Sides: or, an Essay upon the Original Cause, Progress and Mischievous Consequences of the Factions in this Nation* .... London, 1710. *B.M.* E.1988(3). *M.* M284.

99. *A History of the Dutch Usurpations* .... London, 1712. *B.M.* 8079.bbb.2. *M.* O329.

100. *A History of the Peace, from the Arrival of M. Mesnager* .... (1712). In *Somers Tracts,* xiii (2nd edn., 1815). *M.* O332.

101. *The History of the Peace with France and War with Holland in the Year 1672. & Seq.* .... London, 1712. *B.M.* E.1997(9). *M.* O333.

102. *The History of the Republick of Holland* .... Two vols. London, 1705. *B.M.* G.15273–4.

103. (HOADLY, BENJAMIN), *The Voice of the Addressers* .... London, 1710. *B.M.* T.1767(16). *M.* M231.

104. (HOLLES, DENZIL Lord) (?), *The British Constitution Consider'd, with a Character of the Court and Parliament in the Year 1676. In a Letter from*

Denzil Lord Hollis, to Monsieur van Beuningen, sometime Ambassador in the Courts of England and France, from the States-General. London, 1712. *B.M.* T.1990(17). *M.* O101.

105. (HORNBY, CHARLES), *A Caveat against the Whiggs, in a Short Historical View of their Transactions* .... Four parts. London, 1710–12. *L.T.* 200 (1–4). *M.* M324.

106. (House of Commons), *The Humble Representation of the House of Commons to the Queen, with Her Majesty's Most Gracious Answer Thereunto.* London, 1712. *L.T.* 171(6). *M.* O341.

107. (House of Lords), *The Protest of the L---s, upon A--------- Her M------ for her Sp----* .... (1712). *B.M.* T.1990(19). *M.* O346.

108. *The Humble Confession and Petition of a Whig with his Eyes open* ... London, 1712. *Bart.* 300(5). *M.* O356.

109. *An Inquiry into the Causes of our Naval Miscarriages ... The Second Edition* .... London, 1707. *B.M.* Harl.Ms.6287, ff. 75–93. *M.* H225.

110. J(USTICE), A(LEXANDER), *A General Discourse of Commerce* .... 1707. *B.M.* 8227. pp. 3(2). *M.* J264. *D.* 1880.

111. ——, *A General Treatise of the Dominion and Laws of the Sea* .... London, 1705. *B.M.* 21.a.12. *M.* H232. *D.* 1302. *G.* 595.

112. *A Justification of the Dutch from several late Scandalous Reflections.* London, 1712. *B.M.* 1093.d.6. *M.* O369.

113. LAMBERTY, G. DE, *Mémoires pour servir a l'histoire du XVIII Siècle* .... Vols. ii–vii. Amsterdam, 1735–6.

114. (LEDIARD, THOMAS), (Continuation of) *The History of England ... by M. Rapin de Thoyras* .... Vol. iii. London, 1737.

115. ——, *The Life of John, Duke of Marlborough.* Vols. i–ii. London, 1736.

116. (LESLIE, CHARLES) (?), *Natural Reflections Upon the Present Debates* .... London, 1712. *B.M.* E.1995(2). *M.* O392.

117. (——) (?), *Salt for the Leach* .... London, 1712. *B.M.* E.1997(6). *M.* M376.

118. *A Letter from a Foreign Minister in England to Monsieur Pettecum* ... London, 1710. *L.T.* 187(1). *M.* M742.

119. *A Letter from an Exchange Broker to a Country Gentleman* .... London, 1711. *B.M.* 101.d.2. *M.* N354.

120. *A Letter from an Hollander to one of his Friends in Paris* .... (1706). *Bart.* 311(22). *M.* I236.

121. *A Letter from a Tory Freeholder* .... London, 1712. *B.M.* T.1075(21). *M.* O397.

122. *A Letter from Monsieur Pett--m to Monsieur B --s.* (1710). In Boyer's *Annals,* ix, appendix, pp. 46–52. *M.* M383.

123. 'A Letter from Sir Thomas Bodley, sometime Queen Elizabeth's Agent in Holland .... Published as a seasonable Caution at this Juncture ...' (Ms.). *B.M.* Lansdowne Ms. 814.

124. *A Letter to a High-Churchman* .... London, 1711. *B.M.* 8122.b.71. *M.* N360.

125. *A Letter to the Examiner, Concerning the Barrier-Treaty Vindicated.* London, 1713. *B.M.* 8132.aa.13(5). *M.* P280.

126. *March and October, A Dialogue.* London, 1712. *L.T.* 191(4). *M.* O423.

127. (MAYNWARING, ARTHUR), *Remarks on the Preliminary Articles Offer'd by the French King* .... London, 1711. *B.M.* 8122.aa.2(1). *M.* N416.

128. (——), *A Short Account and Defence of the Barrier Treaty.* London, 1713. *God.* 1145(99). *M.* P403.

129. *The Miserable Case of Poor Old England Fairly Stated, in a letter to a Member of the Honourable House of Commons* .... 1712. *L.T.* 171(9). *M.* O477.

130. *The Miseries of England, from the Growing Power of her Domestick Enemies. A Poem.* London, 1702. *B.M.* 11645.e.56. *M.* E341.

131. (MONTAGU, CHARLES, Earl of Halifax), *Seasonable Queries concerning a New Parliament.* (1710). In Boyer's *Annals*, ix, appendix, pp. 144–7. *M.* M276.

132. *A New description of Holland, and the rest of the United Provinces in General* .... London, 1701. *B.M.* 794.d.1.

133. *A New Song. Being a Second Part to the same Tune of Lillibulero, &c.* (1712). *B.M.* 112.f.44(24).

134. *The Occasional Letter: No I, concerning several particulars in the New Association* .... London, 1704. *L.T.* 140(21). *M.* G354.

135. *Occasional Poems on the Late Dutch War* .... London, 1712. *B.M.* 164.m.66. *M.* O503.

136. *The Offers of France Explain'd.* London, 1712. *B.M.* E.2187(8). *M.* O507.

137. (OLDMIXON, JOHN), *The History of Addresses. With Remarks Serious and Comical* ... *Part II* .... London, 1711. *B.M.* G.13514. *M.* L309.

138. PAXTON, PETER, *A Discourse Concerning the Nature, Advantage, and Improvement of Trade.* London, 1704. Goldsmiths Library (Univ. of London) XVIII.OO.3. *M.* G370. *G.* 757.

139. *The Peace-Haters: or, a New Song, For the Illumination of those that won't See* .... London, 1711. *B.M.* 164.m.54. *M.* N473.

140. *The Picture of a Low Flyer.* (1704?). *B.M.* 8122.g.11. *M.* G375.

141. *The Picture of the first Occasional Conformist (Job 1.6.) Drawn in Little.* (1705?). *B.M.* 1871.e.9(145). *M.* H349.

142. *A Pill to Purge State Melancholy* .... London, 1715. *B.M.* 1078.i.18.

143. P(ITTIS), W(ILLIAM), *The History of the Present Parliament and Convocation* .... London, 1711. *B.M.* 8132.d.67(1). *M.* N482. *G.* 3035.

144. ——, *The History of the Proceedings of the Second Session of this Parliament* .... London, (1712). *B.M.* 8132.d.67(2). *M.* O540.

145. *Poems on Affairs of State.* Vols. ii and iv. London, 1703 and 1707 (5th.edn.) *B.M.* 1077.1.17 and 19. *D.* 2467. *G.* 1748.

146. (POYNTZ, STEPHEN), *The Barrier-Treaty Vindicated.* London, 1712. *L.T.* 184(3). *M.* O548.

147. (PRICE, ROBERT), *Gloria Cambriae: Or, The Speech of a Bold Britain in Parliament, against a Dutch Prince of Wales.* (1702). In *Somers Tracts*, iii (1748). *M.* E214.

148. *Prince Eugene Not the Man You took him for: or, A Merry Tale of a Modern Heroe.* London, 1712. *B.M.* G. 14755. *M.* O227.

149. *A Project for establishing the General Peace of Europe* .... London, 1712. *B.M.* E.1955(7). *M.* O558.

150. *The Queen's and the Duke of Ormond's New Toast.* (1712?). *B.M.* 11602.i.12(6). *M.* O40.

151. *The Queen, The Present Ministry, Lewis XIV. and Philip V. Unanswerably Vindicated* .... London, 1712. *Bart.* 304(17). *M.* O41.

152. R., B., *The Principles and Designs of the High Church Party* .... London, 1710. *B.M.* T.1761(29). *M.* M535.

153. R., T., *Remarks on the Barrier–Treaty Vindicated* .... London, 1713. Bodleian Library 12.0.781. *M.* O574.

154. *Reflections upon the humour of the British Nations in Religion and Politicks.* London, 1713. *B.M.* 101.d.66. *M.* P190.

155. *Remarks on a False, Scandalous and Seditious Libel* .... London, 1711. *B.M.* 101.d.19. *M.* N582.

156. *Remarks on the Letter to the Author of the State-Memorial.* London, 1706. *B.M.* 8132.b.15. *M.* I116.

157. *Remarks upon Remarks*: *or the Barrier-Treaty and Protestant Succession Vindicated* .... London, 1711. *B.M.* 101.d.11. *M.* N583.

158. *Remarks upon the Present Negotiations of Peace Begun between Britain and France,* London, 1711. *B.M.* 1103.a.2(4). *M.* N516.

159. *Resolutions Without Doors. Upon the Resolutions Within Doors* .... (1712). *B.M.* 1876.f.19(96).

160. ST. JOHN, HENRY, *Bolingbroke's Defence of the Treaty of Utrecht, being Letters VI–VIII of 'The Study and Use of History'.* Cambridge, 1932.

161. (——), *A Letter to the Examiner.* 1710. *L.T.* 196(20). *M.* M82.

162. (——), *The Present Negotiations of Peace Vindicated from the Imputation of Trifling.* London, 1712. *B.M.* 1475.a.33. *M.* O183.

163. *Seldom comes a Better*: *or, a Tale of a Lady and her Servants.* London, 1710. *B.M.* T.1810(15). *M.* M630.

164. (SEWELL, GEORGE), *Remarks upon a Pamphlet Intitul'd 'Observations upon the State of the Nation in January 1712/3'.* London, 1713. *L.T.* 175(4). *M.* P534.

165. SHAW, JOSEPH, *Letters to a Nobleman From a Gentleman travelling thro' Holland, Flanders and France* .... London, 1709. *B.M.* 303.d.21. *M.* L373.

166. (SHIPPEN, WILLIAM) (?), *Faction Display'd. A Poem.* London, 1709 (1st.edn.1704). *B.M.* 11603.d.15(5). *M.* G433.

167. *A Short Defence of the Last Parliament, Answer'd Article by Article.* London, 1702. *B.M.* E.1977(12). *M.* E457.

168. *Some Remarks on the Letters between the L--d T------nd, and Mr. Se----ary B--le* .... London, 1712. *God.* 1891(7). *M.* O666.

169. *The Speech of a Noble Peer.* London, 1712. *Bart.* 305(15). *M.* O627.

170. *A Speech without Doors, concerning the most effectual way of providing Forty Thousand Landsmen, as England's Quota in the Present Grand Confederacy.* London, 1702. *L.T.* 138(17). *M.* E471.

171. (States General), *A Letter from the States General to the Queen of Great Britain* .... 1712. *B.M.* 1876.f.19 (27). *M.* P428.

172. (STEPHENS, WILLIAM), *A Letter to the Author of the Memorial of the State of England.* London, 1705. *B.M.* 698.i.4(8). *M.* H369.

173. (SWIFT, JONATHAN), *The Conduct of the Allies, and of the late ministry in beginning and carrying on the present war.* Ed. C.B. Wheeler, Oxford, 1916 (1st.edn. 1711). *M.* N569. *D.* 607. *G.* 3036.

174. (——) (?), *Cursory, but Curious Observations of Mr. Ab-l R--er* .... London, 1711. *B.M.* E.1944(1). *M.* N570.

175. ——, *History of the Four Last Years of the Queen.* In Swift's *Prose Works* (ed. Temple Scott), x, London, 1902 (1st. edn. 1758).

176. (——), *A Learned Comment on Dr. Hare's Excellent Sermon* .... London, 1711. *B.M.* 698.h.13(10). *M.* N576.

177. ——, *Memoirs relating to that Change which happened in the Queen's Ministry in the Year 1710.* In Swift's *Political Tracts, 1713–1719* (ed. H. Davis and I. Ehrenpreis), Oxford, 1953.

178. (——) (?), *Peace and Dunkirk; being an Excellent New Song upon the Surrender of Dunkirk to General Hill* .... London, 1712. *B.M.* 1850.c. 10(13). *M.* O659.

179. (——), *Some Remarks on the Barrier Treaty, Between Her Majesty and the States-General* .... *L.T.* 184(2). *M.* N584. *G.* 3037.

180. (THOMPSON, JOHN, Lord HAVERSHAM), *The Lord Haversham's Vindication of his Speech in Parliament. November 15, 1705.* London, 1705. *L.T.* 141(18). *M.* H202.

181. ——, *Memoirs of the late Right Honourable John Lord Haversham, from the Year 1640 to 1710* .... London, 1711. *L.T.* 196(12). *M.* N287.
182. TINDAL, N., *Continuation of Mr. Rapin de Thoyras's History of England* ... Vol.i. London, 1751.
183. (TRAPP, JOSEPH), *The Character and Principles of the Present Set of Whigs.* London, 1711. *B.M.* E.1987(5). *M.* N615.
184. (——), *A Letter out of the Country, To the Author of the Managers Pro and Con.* London, 1710. *B.M.* T.1761(4). *M.* M712.
185. (——), *Most Faults on one Side* .... London, 1710. *B.M.* E.1988(7). *M.* M713.
186. *A Trip to Germany: or, the D--- of M----------'s Farewel to England* .... (1712?). *B.M.* 11602.i.12(32*).
187. *True English Advice to the Kentish Freeholders.* (1710). *B.M.* 1850.c. 5(63).
188. *A View of the Taxes, Funds, & Publick Revenues of England* .... (1712?). *B.M.* Harl. Ms. 4226, ff. 37–9. *M.* O704.
189. *A Vindication of Oliver Cromwell and the Whiggs of Forty One* .... London, 1712. *B.M.* 101.d.43. *M.* O703.
190. *A Vindication of the Present Ministry* .... London, 1711. *B.M.* 1103.a.2(3). *M.* N163.
191. (WAGSTAFFE, WILLIAM), *A Caveat to the Treaters: or, the Modern Schemes of Partition Examin'd* .... London, 1711. *L.T.* 198(11). *M.* N635.
192. (——), *A Complete Key to the Three Parts of Law is a Bottomless-Pit* .... 1712. *B.M.* E.1984(6). *M.* O711.
193. (——), *The Second Representation of the Loyal Subjects of Albinia.* London, 1712. *B.M.* E.1999(2). *M.* O713.
194. (——), *The Testimonies of several Citizens of Fickleborough* .... London, 1713. *Bart.* 303(8). *M.* P42.
195. (WALPOLE, ROBERT), *Four Letters to a Friend in North Britain* .... London, 1710. *B.M.* 4106.b.84. *M.* M471.
196. (WARD, EDWARD), *The Poetical Entertainer: or, Tales, Satyrs, Dialogues, &c* .... Nos. II and III. London, 1712. *B.M.* 1078.h.6. *M.* O721 and O719.
197. (——), *Vulgus Britannicus; or, the British Hudibras.* London, 1710. *B.M.* 11631.d.28. *M.* M476.
198. *We are bravely serv'd at Last, by the Q---n and P-----m--t.* (1712). *Bart.* 305(54).
199. *The Whigs Feast: or, the Protestant Entertainment Design'd by the City for a Popish General.* London, 1712. *B.M.* 15396(1). *M.* O230.
200. (WITHERS, JOHN), *The Dutch better Friends than the French, to the Monarchy. Church, and Trade of England* .... London, 1713 (2nd.edn.). *L.T.* 192(7). *M.* P675.

(ii) *Periodicals*

(ADDISON, JOSEPH), *The Whig-Examiner.* London, 1710, weekly. Reprinted with *Medleys for the Year 1711*, London, 1712. *B.M.* 522.d.4. *M.* V337.
BOYER, ABEL, *The History of the Reign of Queen Anne, Digested into Annals.* Vols. i–vi and viii–x. London, 1703–13, annually. *B.M.* 9512.aaa.27. *M.* V128. *D.* 70. *G.* 3020. [*Annals*]
——, *The Political State of Great Britain* .... Vols. i–iv. London, 1711–13, twice a year. *B.M.* P.P. 3400. *M.* V252. *D.* 75. *G.* 78. [*Political State*]
The Britain. London, 1713, twice weekly. *B.M.* Burney Coll. *M.* V25.
CHAMBERLAYNE, E. and J., *Angliae Notitiae.* 19th, 20th, and 21st edns. London, 1700, 1702, 1704. *B.M.* P.P. 3360. *M.* V5. *D.* 2191. *G.* 112.

Daily Courant. London, 1702–14, usu. daily. *B.M.* Burney Coll. *M*. V47. *D*. 2515. *G*. 71.

(DEFOE, DANIEL), *The Review*. London, 1704–13, weekly, twice weekly and thrice weekly. The most complete collection is in the facsimile edition ed. A. W. Secord (New York, 1938). *M*. V334. *D*. 2517. *G*. 75.

The Examiner. London, 1710–14, weekly and twice weekly. *B.M*. 627.m. 20. *M*. V81. *D*. 2524. *G*. 77.

Flying-Post or the Post-Master. London, 1702–14. Thrice weekly. *B.M*. Burney Coll. *M*. V88. *D*. 2512. *G*. 74.

(JONES, DAVID), *A Compleat History of Europe* .... London, 1705–20, annually. *B.M*. P.P.3405. *M*. V40. *G*. 3009. [*Jones*]

(LESLIE, CHARLES), *The Rehearsal*. London, 1704–9, weekly and twice weekly. *B.M*. Burney Coll. *M*. V271. *D*. 2518. *G*. 76.

The London Gazette. London, twice and thrice weekly. *B.M*. O.G.E. 70. *M*. V146. *D*. 2502. *G*. 68.

The Medley (1st. series). London, 1710–11, weekly. Reprinted as *Medleys for the Year 1711*, London, 1712. *B.M*. 522.d.4. *M*. V168. *D*. 2525.

The Medley (2nd. series). London, 1712, twice weekly (see p. 325, n.). *B.M*. Burney Coll. *M*. V168. *D*. 2525.

The Moderator. London, 1710, twice weekly. *B.M*. P.P. 3611.1ca. *M*. V180.

The Plain Dealer. London, 1712, weekly. *B.M*. Burney Coll. *M*. V246.

The Post Man. London, 1702–14, thrice weekly. B.M. Burney Coll. *M*. V259. *D*. 2510. *G*. 73.

The Protestant Post-Boy. London, 1711–12, thrice weekly. *B.M*. Burney Coll. *M*. V266.

The Reviewer Review'd .... London, 1705, three issues. *B.M*. Burney Coll. *M*. V279.

(ROPER, ABEL, and others), *The Post Boy*. London, 1702–14, thrice weekly. *B.M*. Burney Coll. *M*. V255. *D*. 2511. *G*. 72.

Scots Observator. London, 1708, twice weekly. *B.M*. Burney Coll. *M*. V288.

(STEELE, RICHARD, and others), *The Tatler*. London, 1709–11, thrice weekly. Reprinted in 4 vols., ed. G. A. Aitken (London, 1898–9). *M*. V301. *D*. 2526. *G*. 99.

(TUTCHIN, JOHN, and others), *The Observator*. London, 1702–12, weekly and twice weekly. *B.M*. Burney Coll. *M*. V224. *D*. 2516. *G*. 69.

B. *Documents*

(i) Unpublished

Algemeen Rijksarchief (The Hague)
Archief Heinsius [A. H.] 1590. Letters from Drummond, 1711.

Bodleian Library
Ms. Rawl. A. 286. Robinson Papers.

British Museum

Additional Manuscripts [Add. Ms.]:
  4041.   Sloane Correspondence.
  4291.   Correspondence of H. Davenant.
  7058–9, 7063–4, 7068–9, 7075, 7077.
              Stepney Papers.

17677 YY, ZZ, AAA, BBB, CCC, DDD, EEE, FFF, GGG, WWW, YYY.
Copies of correspondence relating to England; transcribed at the expense of the English Government, from the archives of the United Provinces at The Hague.

20985. 'Verbaal van de Negotiaten van Vrede t'Utrecht, 1712–13', vol. III.

21551. Original Letters, mainly to Stepney.

22196, 22198, 22201, 22221–2, 22265–6, 31131, 31137, 34143–4.
Strafford Papers.

28055–7. Godolphin Correspondence.

28910–4, 28916, 28918.
Ellis Correspondence.

29588–9. Nottingham Papers.

33273, 38852.
Letters to Watkins.

34077(II). Miscellaneous Original Letters.

34514, 34518.
Mackintosh Collection (transcripts).

37155. Diplomatic Correspondence of Stepney.

37209. Orrery Papers.

38500. Townshend Papers.

40621(2). Correspondence of Thomas Harley.

40776. Vernon Papers.

41178(K). Letters from Marlborough to Townshend, 1709–10.

41683. Stanhope Papers.

Duke of Portland Mss.: Lord Godolphin.

Lansdowne Manuscripts:
849.   Miscellaneous State Papers.
1236.   Royal Letters.

Stowe Manuscripts:
222–6.   Hanover State Papers.
241–2.   State Papers and Correspondence collected by Astle.
244–5.   Letter Books of A. Stanhope.

Public Record Office
Colonial Office Papers:
ser. 388, vol. 9: Board of Trade [C.O. 388/9].
ser. 389, vol. 18: Commercial Entry-Book, 1702–5. [C.O. 389/18].
ser. 389, vol. 22: Commercial Entry-Book, 1711–12. [C.O. 389/22].

State Papers Foreign:
Flanders, vols. 57, 59–62. [S. P. Flanders].
France, vol. 154 [S. P. France].
Holland, vols. 224–248, 574–5. [S. P. Holl.].
State Papers Foreign, Foreign Entry Books:
Denmark, vol. 4. [F.E.B. Denmark].
Flanders, vols. 12–13. [F.E.B. Flanders].
Empire, vols. 39–40. [F.E.B. Emp.].

Prussia, vols. 51–2. [F.E.B. Prussia].
Holland, vols. 69, 71–9. [F.E.B. Holl.].
Portugal, vol. 108. [F.E.B. Port.].
Sweden, vol. 154. [F.E.B. Sweden].
Miscellaneous, vols. 203–4. [F.E.B. Misc.].
Foreign Ministers (in England), vol. 257. [F.E.B. For. Min.].
State Papers Military:
vols. 2, 4 and 7. [S.P. Mil.].

(ii) Published

BALL, F. ELRINGTON, *ed.*, *The Correspondence of Jonathan Swift, D.D.* ....
Two vols. London, 1910. [*Swift Corres.*].

BLACKLEY, W., *ed.*, *Diplomatic correspondence of the Rt. Hon. Richard Hill.*
Two vols. London, 1845. [*Hill Corres.*].

BROWNING, A., *Thomas Osborne Earl of Danby.* Vol. ii (letters). Glasgow, 1944.
[*Danby*].

BUCK, C. and DAVIES, G., *edd.*, 'Letters on Godolphin's Dismissal in 1710'.
Hunt. Lib. Quart., iii (1939–40).

BUNBURY, Sir H., *ed.*, *The Correspondence of Sir Thomas Hanmer, Bart* ....
with a Memoir of his Life .... London, 1838. [*Hanmer Corres*].

CARTWRIGHT, J. J., *ed.*, *Wentworth Papers, 1705–39.* London, 1883.

(CHURCHILL, SARAH, Duchess of Marlborough), *Private Correspondence of Sarah
Churchill, Duchess of Marlborough* .... London, 1838. [*P.C.D.M.*].

COLE, C., *Historical and Political Memoirs* .... *1697–1708.* London, 1735.
[*Cole*].

COXE, W., *Memoirs of the Duke of Marlborough.* Three vols. London, 1847
(Bohn edn.). On occasion reference is made to the fuller first edition (1819).
[*Coxe*].

——, *Memoirs of the Life and Administration of Sir Robert Walpole* .... Vols.
i and ii. London, 1798. [*Coxe: Walpole*].

CRA'STER, H. H. E., *ed.*, 'Letters of the First Lord Orkney during Marlborough's
Campaigns'. *E.H.R.*, xix (1904).

CRICHTON, A., *ed.*, *The Life and Diary of Lieut. Col. J. Blackader.* Edinburgh,
1824. [*Blackader*].

DAVIES, G., *ed.*, 'The Seamy Side of Marlborough's War'. *Hunt. Lib. Quart.*,
xv (1951–2).

DAVIES, G. and TINLING, M., *edd.*, 'Letters of Henry St. John to James Brydges',
Hunt. Lib. Bull., viii (1935).

——, 'Letters from James Brydges ... to Henry St. John ...'. *Hunt. Lib.
Bull.*, ix (1936).

DOBLE, C. E. and RANNIE, D. W., *edd.*, *Remarks and Collections of Thomas
Hearne, 1705–24.* Vols. i–iii. Oxford, 1884–8. [*Hearne*].

FIRTH, C. H., *ed.*, *Naval Songs and Ballads.* 1908. (*Navy Record Society Publications*, vol. xxxiii). [*Firth*].

FORSTER, T., *ed.*, *Original Letters of Locke; Algernon Sidney; and Anthony
Lord Shaftesbury.* London, 1830. [*Forster*].

FOXCROFT, H. C., *ed.*, *A Supplement to Burnet's History of My Own Time.*
Oxford, 1902. [*Foxcroft*].

GRAHAM, J. M., *ed.*, *Annals and Correspondence of the Viscount and the First
and Second Earls of Stair.* Vol. i. Edinburgh, 1875. [*Stair Annals*].

GRAHAM, W., *ed.*, *Letters of Joseph Addison.* Oxford, 1941. [*Addison's Letters*].

HAWTREY, E. C., ed., *The Private Diary of William, First Earl Cowper, Lord Chancellor of England*. Eton, 1833. [*Cowper*].

HEYWOOD, T., ed., *The Norris Papers*. Manchester, 1846. (Chetham Society: Remains historical and literary ... Vol. ix).

Historical Manuscripts Commission [*H.M.C.*].

——, *Report VIII, Appendix pt.i* (Duke of Marlborough Mss.).

——, *Ibid., App. pt. ii* (Duke of Manchester Mss.).

——, *Rep. IX, App. pt. ii* (Alfred Morrison Mss.).

——, *Rep. X, App. pt. i* (Stirling Home-Drummond-Moray Mss.).

——, *Rep. XII, App. pt. iii* (Coke Mss., Vol. III).

——, *Ibid., App. pt. v* (Rutland Mss.).

——, *Rep. XIII, App. pt. ii* (Portland Mss., Vol. II).

——, *Rep. XIV, App. pt. iv* (Kenyon Mss.)

——, *Ibid., App. pt. ix* (Hare and Round Mss.).

——, *Rep. XV, App. pt. ii* (Hodgkin Mss.)

——, *Ibid., App. pt. iv* (Portland Mss., Vol. IV).

——, *Bath Mss.*, Vols. I and II.

——, *Buccleuch Mss.*, Vol. II pt. ii.

——, *Downshire Mss.*, Vol. I pt. ii.

——, *Egmont Mss.*, Vol. II.

——, *Mar and Kellie Mss.*

——, *Ormonde Mss.*, n.s., Vol. VIII.

——, *Portland Mss.*, Vols. V and VII–IX.

HOFF, B. VAN 'T, ed., *The Correspondence of John Churchill and Anthonie Heinsius, 1701–11*. The Hague, 1951. [*van 't Hoff*].

(House of Commons), *Journals of the House of Commons*. Vol. xvii. [*C.J.*].

(House of Lords), *Journals of the House of Lords*. Vol. xvii. [*L.J.*].

——, *The Manuscripts of the House of Lords*. Vols. v–viii. London, 1910–23. [*H. of L. Mss.*].

(Houses of Parliament), *Statutes at Large*. Vol. iv. London, 1799.

LEGG, L. F. WICKHAM, ed., *British Diplomatic Instructions, 1689–1789*. Vol. ii: *France: 1689–1721*. London, 1925. [*B.D.I. France*].

——, 'Torcy's Account of Matthew Prior's Negotiations at Fontainebleau in July 1711'. *E.H.R.*, xxix (1914).

LOCKHART, G., ed., *The Lockhart Papers*. Vol. i. London, 1817.

LUTTRELL, NARCISSUS, *A Brief Historical Relation of State Affairs ....* Vols. v–vi. Oxford, 1857. [*Luttrell*].

MACPHERSON, JAMES, ed., *Original Papers: Containing the Secret History of Great Britain, from the Restoration to the Accession of the House of Hanover ....* Vol. ii. London, 1775. [*Macpherson*].

MURRAY, G., ed., *Letters and Dispatches of John Churchill, First Duke of Marlborough, 1702–12*. Five vols. London, 1845. [*Murray*].

PARKE, G., ed., *Letters and Correspondence of the Rt. Hon. Henry St. John, Lord Viscount Bolingbroke*. Four vols. London, 1798. [*B.L.*].

Public Record Office

(HEADLAM, C., ed.), *Calendar of State Papers, Colonial Series, America and West Indies*. Vols. for Jan.–Dec. 1, 1702; Dec. 1, 1702–1703; 1704–1705; 1706–June 1708; 1710–June 1711. London, 1912–24. [*C.S.P. Col.*].

(MAHAFFY, R. P., ed.), *Calendar of State Papers, Domestic, Anne*. Vols. i–ii. London, 1916. [*C.S.P. Dom. Anne*].

(SHAW, W. A., ed.), *Calendar of Treasury Books*. Vols. xix, xxii pt. 2 and xxiv pt. 2. London, 1938(47) and 1940(50). [*Cal. Tr. Bks.*].

(REDINGTON, J., *ed.*), *Calendar of Treasury Papers*. Vols. for 1702–7 and 1708–14. London, 1874 and 1879. [*Cal. Tr. Papers*].
Journal of the Commissioners for Trade and Plantations. Vols. for 1704–8/9 and 1708/9–1714/15. London, 1920 and 1925. [*Journal of C. of T.*].

RAND, B., *ed.*, *Berkeley and Percival . . . The Correspondence of George Berkeley . . . and Sir John Percival*. Cambridge, 1914. [*Berkeley*].

——, *Life, Unpublished Letters . . . of Anthony, Earl of Shaftesbury . . . .* London, 1900. [*Rand*].

SMITH, D. N., *ed.*, *Letters of Thomas Burnet to George Duckett, 1712–22*. Oxford, 1914. [*T. Burnet's Letters*].

(THIBAUDEAU, A. W., *ed*), *The Collection of Autograph Letters and Historical Documents formed by Alfred Morrison. First series*, vols. i–v. *Second series*, vols. i–ii. 1883–91 and 1893–6. [*Thibaudeau*].

VERNEY, Lady M. M., *ed.*, *Verney Letters of the Eighteenth Century from the Mss. at Claydon House*. Vol. i. London, 1930. [*Verney Letters*].

VREEDE, G. W., *ed.*, *Correspondance Diplomatique et Militaire du Duc de Marlborough, du Grand-Pensionnaire Heinsius et du Trésorier-Général des Provinces-Unies, Jacques Hop*. Amsterdam, 1850. [*Vreede*].

WILLIAMS, H., *ed.*, *Journal to Stella* (by Jonathan Swift). Vol. ii. Oxford, 1948.

(YORKE, PHILIP, Earl of HARDWICKE, *ed.*), *Miscellaneous State Papers . . . .* Vol. ii. London, 1778. [*Hardwicke S.P.*].

C. *Select List of Secondary Works*

ALPHEN, G. VAN, *De Stemming van de Engelschen tegen de Hollanders in Engeland . . . 1688–1702*. Assen, 1938. [*van Alphen*].

CHURCHILL, W. S., *Marlborough, His Life and Times*. Vols. ii–iv. London, 1933–8. [*Churchill*].

COBBETT, WILLIAM, *The Parliamentary History of England*. Vols. vi–vii. London, 1810. [*Cobbett*].

GEIKIE, R., and MONTGOMERY, I., *The Dutch Barrier, 1705–1719*. Cambridge, 1930. [*Geikie*] and [*Montgomery*].

GEYL, P., 'Moderne Historische Apologetiek in Engeland', and 'Nederland's Staatkunde in de Spaanse Successie-Oorlog'. In *Kernproblemen van Onze Geschiedenis*. Utrecht, 1937. [*Kernproblemen*].

LECKY, W. E. H., *History of England in the Eighteenth Century*. Vol. i. London, 1878. [*Lecky*].

NOORDEN, C. VON, *Europäische Geschichte im Achtzehnten Jahrhundert*. Three vols. Düsseldorf, 1870–82. [*von Noorden*].

TREVELYAN, G. M., *England Under Queen Anne*. Three vols. London, 1930–4. [*Trevelyan*].

VEENENDAAL, A. J., *Het Engels Nederlands Condominium in de Zuidelijke Nederlanden . . . 1706–1716*. Part 1. Utrecht, 1945. [*Veenendaal*].

WEBER, O., *Der Friede von Utrecht*. Gotha, 1891. [*Weber*].

INDEX

Addison, Joseph 14, 176 n., 184–5, 232.
Admiralties, Dutch 35–6, 54, 56, 59, 91, 241.
Admiralty, English 36, 91, 119, 172–3.
Ailesbury, Thomas Bruce, 2nd Earl of 34–5, 342.
Albemarle, Arnold Joost van Keppel, 1st Earl of 29, 201, 344.
Alègre, Yves, Marquis d' 130–1, 143.
Almanza, Battle of, *1707* 159, 162–3, 167.
Almenara, Battle of, *1710* 245.
Almonde, Philips van 37.
Amboyna, 'Massacre' of, *1623* 86, 101, 112, 289, 305, 307, 328–9, 347, 352, 368, 378.
Amsterdam 34, 38–9, 41, 43, 46, 52, 132, 157, 160, 162, 166, 177, 179, 199, 216, 273, 310, 313, 317–8, 325, 332–3, 355, 365.
Anne, queen of England *passim.*
Antwerp 178, 184, 367.
Arbuthnot, John 301 n., 308–9, 316.
Army in Low Countries, augmentations of, 44–7, 70, 89, 118, 124, 167–8, 181–2, 189–90, 242, 281; command of, 27, 31. See also Low Countries.
Ashby v. White 84, 100.
Ashley, Dr. Maurice 182.
Asiento 234, 257, 272, 285, 295–6, 309–13, 317.
Ath, Siege of, *1706* 139.
Athlone, Godard van Reede, 1st Earl of 34.
Atterbury, Francis 225.
Augustus II, king of Poland 159.
Ayerst, William 355.

Badajoz, Siege of, *1705* 103–4.
Barcelona, Siege of, *1705* 125.
Baron, William 30, 100.
Barre (French agent) 24.
Barrier, Dutch 17–8, 128, 133–4, 138, 142, 150, 152, 172, 177, 189–90, 192, 195–6, 199–200, 207, 246, 255, 257, 260, 262, 265–7, 270–1, 283–5, 287, 293–7, 312,
317, 320, 323, 325, 327–8, 331, 338, 345, 349–50, 353–4, 357, 371, 373–4, 378. See also Treaties.
Bergh, Johan van den 193, 202, 243, 310.
Berkeley, George 344, 346.
Berwick, James Fitzjames Duke of 182–3.
Blackader, John 21, 105–6, 109.
Blathwayt, William 32.
Blenheim, Battle of, *1704* 21, 41, 77–8; effect of on English attitude to Dutch, 89–90, 110, 127, 159.
Bolingbroke, Viscount See St. John.
Bonn, Siege of, *1703* 62.
Borssele, Philips Jacob van 314–5, 366.
Bouchain, Siege of, *1711* 249–50, 282, 288.
Boufflers, Louis-François, Duc de 31, 33, 184.
Boyer, Abel 42, 116–7, 122, 137, 178, 227, 250, 256 n,. 296, 299, 321, 334, 356.
Boyle, Henry 176, 196, 200, 203, 207–8, 210, 215–7, 222–3, 241, 298, 320–1.
Brabant 31.
Brewster, Sir Francis 8.
Brihuega, Battle of, *1710* 246.
Bristol, Bishop of See Robinson.
Britain 368, 375–7.
Britain, Great *passim.*
Bromley, William 90–1, 339.
Bruges 178, 181, 183–4, 244, 302, 343, 355, 358.
Brussels, Relief of, *1708* 184.
Brydges, James 209, 224.
Buckingham, John Sheffield, 1st Duke of 290.
Burgundy, Duke of 182.
Burnet, Gilbert 22, 45, 48, 197, 337.
Burnet, Thomas 293, 307, 315, 353, 380.
Butler, Thomas 193, 201.
Buys, Willem 112, 115, 126, 129, 131, 141, 146–7, 150, 162, 167–8, 179–80, 190, 192–3, 195, 217–8, 222, 227, 245, 249, 251, 253–4, 257, 259, 264–6, 269, 271, 283, 285–6, 290, 294, 309–12, 323.

Fagel, François 310.
Fagel, François Nicolaas, Baron 79, 102–4
Ferguson, Robert 289–90, 302.
Field-Deputies, Dutch   See Dutch.
Fishery, British 10–11, 98–9, 170–1, 273, 289, 329, 383.
Flanders 27–8, 30.
Flying Post 261, 282, 322, 350, 352, 364–70.
France *passim*; see also 'Explanation', Peace, 'Proposals'.
Frederick I, king of Prussia 191, 210, 215, 311, 339.
Frederick IV, king of Denmark 71.
Friesland 265, 267.
Furly, Benjamin 28, 156, 200.

Gallas, Johann Wenzel, Count of 222, 260.
Galway, Henri Massué de Ruvigny, Earl of 79, 102–4, 131.
Gaultier, François, Abbé 266–7, 294, 319, 357, 365.
Geertruidenberg   See Peace.
Geikie, Roderick 134–5, 141, 200, 205, 210.
Gelderland 175.
Geldermalsen, Adriaen van Borssele, Baron van 31.
Generals, Dutch   See Dutch.
George, Prince, of Denmark 30, 32, 182.
George Augustus, Electoral Prince of Hanover 118, 226.
George Louis, Elector of Hanover 192, 277, 284.
Geyl, Dr. Pieter 199, 235.
Ghent 177–8, 181, 183–4, 244, 287, 298, 303, 312–3, 342–3, 355, 358.
Gibraltar, capture of, *1704*, 80–1; siege of, *1704–5*, 102; joint occupation of, 131, 247–8, 254.
Gildon, Charles 194–5.
Godolphin, Sidney, 1st Earl of 24, 27–8, 32–4, 36, 50–1, 57–8, 61, 63, 65, 67–8, 74, 77, 80, 86–96, 101–7, 111–2, 114–5, 119, 122–3, 125–7, 129, 131–7, 139–44, 146–51, 156, 158, 160, 162, 163 n., 164–9, 173–4, 176–80, 182, 184, 189–91, 196–7, 200–1, 204–6, 209, 213–4, 218–24, 227–8, 230–1, 248, 272, 274, 287, 322.
Goslinga, Sicco van 163 n., 249.
'Great design', Marlborough's, *1703* 62.
Grumbkow, Joachim Ernest von 215.
Guelders, Upper quarter of 210, 215, 362, 365, 372–3.
Guiscard, Antoine de 235.

Hague, The *passim*.
Halifax, Charles Montagu, Earl of 95, 143–5, 149, 151–3, 155, 165, 192, 223, 225, 322–3, 337.
Hampden, Richard 306, 328.

Hanmer, Sir Thomas 306.
Harcourt, Sir Simon 181.
Hare, Francis 106, 109, 133, 199, 222, 251, 256, 262, 278, 287–8, 293, 302.
Harley, Robert, 1st Earl of 24, 28, 32, 77–80, 82–4, 87–9, 92–6, 103, 106–8, 110–5, 117, 119, 122, 126–7, 130–1, 142, 146, 149, 152, 154–7, 160, 164, 167, 173–7, 181, 190, 204, 209, 214, 221–3, 227–31, 233–6, 238–9, 246–8, 250–1, 256–7, 260, 264–6, 269, 272, 274, 277, 279, 282, 285, 287, 294, 296, 310–3, 315, 317, 322–4, 327, 329, 331, 337–8, 356–9, 372–3, 378, 380, 384.
Harley, Thomas 313, 315, 317–8, 326, 331–2, 334, 355.
Haversham, John Thompson, 1st Baron 93, 98, 117–8, 120–2, 143, 171–2, 175.
Hearne, Thomas 111, 170, 344.
Heathcote, Sir Gilbert 72.
Hedges, Sir Charles 33, 38, 42, 45–6, 48, 53, 56–60, 69, 80, 82, 152.
Heems, Arnold von 310–1.
Heinsius, Antonie 19, 32, 42–5, 57, 59–63, 65–8, 70, 79, 82–3, 95, 103, 107, 110, 112, 135–6, 138–41, 144–7, 153–4, 163 n., 166–8, 174, 178, 180, 183, 192–3, 195–6, 199–202, 206–8, 210–1, 216–7, 222–3, 239, 244, 249, 253, 256, 258, 260, 264, 266–7, 271, 284–5, 290, 305, 310, 321, 323, 358, 361.
Helvétius, Adriaan 148, 164.
Hennequin, Gualtherus 140.
Hervey, John, Baron Hervey of Ickworth 4.
Hill, John 341.
Hill, Richard 53–5, 57–8, 60–1, 66–8, 70–1, 76, 78, 80, 298, 354.
Hoadly, Benjamin 226.
Hohendorff (Austrian minister) 323.
Holland *passim*; States of, 42–4, 46, 82–4, 95, 267, 274, 332.
Holstein-Gottorp, Administrator of 130.
Hompesch, Reynout Vincent, Baron 107.
Hop, Jacob, Baron 135–8, 202, 318.
Hornby, Charles 237.
Huy, Siege of, *1703* 65–6.

Ingoldsby, Richard 107, 139.
Invasion, attempted, *1708* 175–6
Ireland 73.
Italy, French armies in 42.

Jamaica 40, 72–3, 172.
James II, king of England 17, 29.
James Edward, Prince (the Old Pretender) 18, 64, 175–6, 192, 232, 242, 262, 305, 329, 340, 353, 376.
Jones, David 63, 71, 107, 112, 115, 122, 179 n., 261, 263–4, 297, 346.